MARKETING STRATEGY & COMPETITIVE POSITIONING

At Pearson, we have a simple mission: to help people make more of their lives through learning.

We combine innovative learning technology with trusted content and educational expertise to provide engaging and effective learning experiences that serve people wherever and whenever they are learning.

From classroom to boardroom, our curriculum materials, digital learning tools and testing programmes help to educate millions of people worldwide – more than any other private enterprise.

Every day our work helps learning flourish, and wherever learning flourishes, so do people.

To learn more, please visit us at **www.pearson.com/uk**

Sixth edition

MARKETING STRATEGY & COMPETITIVE POSITIONING

Graham Hooley • Nigel F. Piercy •
Brigitte Nicoulaud • John M. Rudd

Pearson

Harlow, England • London • New York • Boston • San Francisco • Toronto • Sydney • Dubai • Singapore • Hong Kong
Tokyo • Seoul • Taipei • New Delhi • Cape Town • São Paulo • Mexico City • Madrid • Amsterdam • Munich • Paris • Milan

Pearson Education Limited
Edinburgh Gate
Harlow CM20 2JE
United Kingdom
Tel: +44 (0)1279 623623
Web: www.pearson.com/uk

First published in 1993 as Competitive Positioning: The key to market success (print)
Second edition published 1998 by Prentice Hall Europe (print)
Third edition 2004 (print)
Fourth edition 2008 (print)
Fifth edition 2012 (print)
Sixth edition published 2017 (print and electronic)

ISBN: 978-1-292-01731-0 (print)
      978-1-292-01734-1 (PDF)
      978-1-292-17145-6 (ePub)

British Library Cataloguing-in-Publication Data
A catalogue record for the print edition is available from the British Library

Library of Congress Cataloging-in-Publication Data
A catalog record for the print edition is available from the Library of Congress

10 9 8 7 6 5 4 3
20 19 18 17

Print edition typeset in 10/12pt Sabon MT Pro by SPi Global
Print edition printed and bound by CPI UK

NOTE THAT ANY PAGE CROSS REFERENCES REFER TO THE PRINT EDITION

BRIEF CONTENTS

CONTENTS

PART 1
MARKETING STRATEGY

PART 2
COMPETITIVE MARKET ANALYSIS

PREFACE

Since the fifth edition of this book, published in 2011, developed economies around the world have continued to feel the aftershocks of the deepest recession since the Great Depression of the 1930s that started with the well-publicised "credit crunch". Despite some continuing academic debate about the causes and extent, there is now little doubt that climate change and global warming is beginning to have a significant impact on our physical environment. Technology and the ever-growing acceptance and use of social media are having a profound effect on customer expectations and experience.

Whilst appearing to move out of recession and beginning to enjoy some degree of economic growth, governments of major national economies are still left with unprecedented levels of national debt and austerity programmes introduced in 2010 are continuing in an attempt to rebalance the books for example in the European Union. These have caused severe hardship to citizens of countries such as Greece and Spain where unemployment reached a high of around 24% in 2015.

Despite these on-going economic difficulties climate change has not been ignored. Caused by a combination of factors including build up of CO_2 in the atmosphere due to emissions from the burning of fossil fuels such as coal and oil, deforestation and animal agriculture, and feedback loops created through the shrinking of the polar ice caps and glaciers that reflect solar radiation, a number of implications are becoming apparent. As ice melts so sea levels rise, and weather patterns become less predictable. Extreme weather events come more frequent, water and food security become greater concerns, and subtropical deserts expand. Climate change poses significant challenges for businesses. Sustainable energy technologies such as wind, solar, wave and thermal biomass are now being pursued more vigorously and attempts to reduce energy consumption (of cars, buildings and airplanes) are creating new business opportunities. Increasingly companies, public sector organisations, individuals and nations are signing up to measures such as sourcing more raw materials locally to reduce 'carbon miles' and limiting the use of high-emission travel options to reduce their carbon footprint as in the Paris Agreement of December 2015 where 195 countries adopted the first ever legally binding climate deal.

In parallel the technology revolution is in full swing: driverless cars are a reality, members of the Y generation communicate and share their feedback via social media, customers are looking for consistent experiences across all shopping channels even the traditional taxi business model has been disrupted by an app.

Within this context, throughout this sixth edition we have attempted to identify new approaches to doing business that will promote sustainability, both for the organisations adopting them and for the environment (economic, social and natural) in which they operate.

Marketing Strategy and Competitive Positioning 6e deals with the process of developing and implementing a marketing strategy. The book focuses on competitive positioning at the heart of marketing strategy and includes in-depth discussion of the processes used in marketing to achieve competitive advantage within the context introduced above.

The book is primarily about creating and sustaining superior performance in the marketplace. It focuses on the two central issues in marketing strategy formulation – the identification of target markets and the creation of a differential advantage. In doing that, it recognises the emergence of new potential target markets born of the recession, increased concern for climate change and disruption from on-going technological advances. It examines ways in which firms can differentiate their offerings through the recognition of environmental and social concerns and innovation.

Topics examined include service quality and relationship marketing, networks and alliances, innovation, internal marketing and corporate social responsibility. Emphasis is placed on the development of dynamic marketing capabilities, together with the need to reassess the role of marketing in the organisation as a critical process and not simply as a conventional functional specialisation.

The book structure

Part 1 is concerned with the fundamental changes that are taking place in how marketing operates in organisations and the increasing focus on marketing as a process rather than as a functional specialisation. The central questions of the market orientation of organisations and the need to find better ways of responding to the volatile and hard to predict market environments lead us to emphasise the market-led approach to strategic management and the framework for developing marketing strategy which provides the structure for the rest of the book. Our framework for strategic marketing planning provides the groundwork for two critical issues on which we focus throughout this volume: the choice of market targets and the building of strong competitive positions. Central to this approach is the resource-based view of marketing and the need to develop, nurture and deploy dynamic marketing capabilities.

Part 2 deals with the competitive environment in which the company operates and draws specifically on recent changes brought about by recession and concerns for sustainability. Different types of strategic environment are first considered, together with the critical success factors for dealing with each type. Discussion then focuses on the 'strategic triangle' of customers, competitors and company in the context of the environment (social, economic and natural) that the firm operates in. Ways of analysing each in turn are explored to help identify the options open to the company. The emphasis is on matching corporate resources, assets and capabilities to market opportunities.

Part 3 examines in more detail the techniques available for identifying market segments (or potential targets) and current (and potential) positions. Alternative bases for segmenting consumer and business markets are explored, as are the data collection and analysis techniques available. Selection of market targets through consideration of the market attractiveness and business strength is addressed.

Part 4 returns to strategy formulation. The section opens with discussion of how to create a sustainable position in the marketplace. Three chapters are concerned with specific aspects of strategy formulation and execution. The new chapter on competing through the marketing mix has been retained from the fifth edition and expanded to reflect increasing use of new media to promote, distribute and create market offerings. The roles of customer service in relationship-building and innovation to create competitive advantage are considered in depth.

Part 5 examines implementation issues in more detail. The section includes chapters on strategic customer management and corporate social responsibility as well as updated chapters on strategic alliances and networks and internal marketing.

Part 6 provides our perspective on competition for the second decade of the 21st century. The various themes from the earlier parts of the book are draws together in order to identify the major changes taking place in markets, the necessary organisational responses to those changes and the competitive positioning strategies that could form the cornerstones of effective future marketing.

New to this edition:

- Updated content to reflect the on-going global economic crisis and its impact on business and marketing.
- New coverage including the impact of emerging markets on innovation, the perverse customer as a market force, the new realities in competing through services and market analysis and segmentation.
- Updated chapters on strategic customer management and strategic alliances.
- Increased emphasis on competing through innovation including new business models such as Uber, Netflix and new types of retailing.
- Updates vignettes at the beginning of chapters focusing on companies such as Amadeus, Mastercard and Samsung Pay and including discussion questions.
- New cases throughout the book including Ryanair, Amazon and Lego.
- Up-dated online resources include an Instructor's Manual and PowerPoint slides for instructors, along with additional case studies for students.

The book is ideal for undergraduate and postgraduate students taking modules in Marketing Strategy, Marketing Management and Strategic Marketing Management.

ACKNOWLEDGEMENTS

We wish to acknowledge the support of many friends, colleagues, students and managers who have helped shape our ideas over the years.

Our first and biggest thanks must go to Professor John Saunders, our friend, colleague and co-author of the first three editions of this book. John is an outstanding marketing scholar who has made a very significant contribution to both marketing thought and practice over the years. Much of his contribution to the early editions remains in the current edition and we thank him for his generosity in allowing it to continue to be included.

We would also like to acknowledge the contributions of a number of outstanding management and marketing scholars with whom we have been fortunate to work and learn from over recent years: Professor Gary Armstrong, George Avionitis, Amanda Beatson, Suzanne Beckmann, Jozsef Beracs, Pierre Berthon, Günther Botschen, Amanda Broderick, Rod Brodie, Peter Buckley, John Cadogan, Frank Cespedes, David Cook, David Cravens, Adamantios Diamantorpoulos, Susan Douglas, Colin Egan, Heiner Evanschitztky, John Fahy, Krzysztof Fonfara, Gordon Foxall, Mark Gabbott, Brandan Gray, Gordon Greenley, Salah Hassan, J. Mac Hulbert, Nick Lee, Peter Leeflang, Ian Lings, David Jobber, Hans Kasper, Costas Katsikeas, Philip Kotler, Giles Laurent, Gary Lilien, Jim Lynch, Malcolm MacDonald, Felix Mavando, Sheelagh Mattear, Hafiz Mizra, Kristian Müller, Neil Morgan, Hans Muhlbacher, Niall Piercy, Leyland Pitt, Bodo Schlegelmilch, David Shipley, Stan Slater, Anne Souchon, Jan-Benedict Steenkamp, Vasilis Theohorakis, Rajan Varadarajan, Michel Wedel, David Wilson, Berend Wirenga, Robin Wensley, Michael West, Veronica Wong and Oliver Yau.

We would like to pay particular tribute to the role of our friend and colleague, the late Peter Doyle. We have learned an enormous amount from Peter over the years and owe him and incalculable debt for helping us shape and sharpen our ideas.

Graham Hooley
Nigel F. Piercy
Brigitte Nicoulaud
John M. Rudd
December 2016

PUBLISHER'S ACKNOWLEDGEMENTS

We are grateful to the following for permission to reproduce copyright material:

Figures

Figure 3.2 from *The Economist Newspaper Limited, London* 09/09/2008; Figure 3.5 adapted from "Supplier Relationships: A Strategic Initiative," by Jagdish N. Sheth, Emory University and Arun Sharma, University of Miami. Figure 2, Shift in Organizational Purchasing Strategy, page 18. This paper extends research published by the authors in Industrial Marketing Management (March 1997). Please address correspondence to Arun Sharma, asharma@bus.miami.edu, Department of Marketing, University of Miami, P.O. Box 248147, Coral Gables FL 33124, Telephone: (305) 284 1770, FAX: (305) 284 5326; Figure 3.6 from *COMPETITIVE ADVANTAGE: Creating and Sustaining Superior Performance,* Simon & Schuster, Inc. (Porter, M.E. 1998) Copyright © 1985 by Michael E. Porter. Reprinted with the permission of Free Press, a Division of Simon & Schuster, Inc. All rights reserved; Figure 3.9 from iPodlounge.com, Data are for every two months from November 2001 to May, 2004. Thus 11 is November 2001, 1.02 is January 2002 etc.; Figure 3.12 adapted from *Competitive Marketing: A Strategic Approach,* 3rd ed, Cengage (O'Shaughnessy, J. 1995) Reprint rights ISBN: 978-0-415-09317-0, Table 9.1, Porter's evolutionary stages vs traditional PLC approach, page 315. Reproduced by permission of Cengage Learning EMEA Ltd; Figure 6.9 adapted from *Competing for the Future,* Harvard Business School Press (Hamel, G. and Prahalad, C.K. 1994) used by permission; Figure 9.1 adapted from *Market-Led Strategic Change: Transforming the Process of Going to Market,* Taylor & Francis Books (Piercy, N.F. 1997) (ISBN 9781856175043), p. 298; Figure 10.4 adapted from *COMPETITIVE ADVANTAGE: Creating and Sustaining Superior Performance* (Porter, M.E. 1985) Copyright © 1985 by Michael E. Porter. Reprinted with the permission of Free Press, a Division of Simon & Schuster, Inc. All rights reserved; Figures 11.5 and 11.6 from *New Scientist,* 2004, October 16. www.newscientist.com. Reed Business Information Ltd; Figure 12.2 and Figure 16.4 adapted from *Market-Led Strategic Change: Transforming the Process of Going to Market,* 4th ed (Piercy, N. 2009) Copyright Butterworth-Heinemann (2008); Elsevier Ltd, Global Rights Department c/o Butterworth-Heinemann; Figure 13.4 from *Relationship Marketing for Competitive Advantage,* Butterworth-Heinemann (Payne, A., Christopher, M., Clark, M. and Peck, H. 1995). Elsevier Science Ltd (UK); Figures 13.6 and 13.11 adapted from Parasuraman, A., Zeithaml, V.A. and Berry, L.L. (1985), 'A conceptual model of service quality and the implications for further research', *Journal of Marketing,* Fall, 41–50. American Marketing Association; Figure 17.4 from 'The link between competitive advantage and corporate social responsibility' by Michael E. Porter and Mark R. Kramer, December 2006. Copyright © 2006 by the Harvard Business School Publishing. Used by permission; Figure 17.5 adapted from 'Walmart's European adventure', in *Market-Led Strategic Change: Transforming the Process of Going to Market* Taylor & Francis (Piercy, N.F.) p. 39 (ISBN 9781856175043), reproduced by permission of Taylor & Francis Books UK.

Tables

Table on page 9 from *Market Driven Management,* John Wiley & Sons (Webster, F.E. 1994), Reproduced with permission of Blackwell Scientific in the format Republish in a book via Copyright Clearance Center; Table 6.1 from The Global Top Ten Brands, Interbrand's 2001, 2009, 2010, 2013 Best Global Brands Report, www.interbrand.com; Table 7.1 from *Occupation Groupings: A Job Dictionary,* 6th ed, 2006. https://www.mrs.org.uk/pdf/occgroups6.pdf. The Market Research Society.

Text

Case Study on page 4 from Puma gives the boot to cardboard shoeboxes, *Financial Times,* 14/04/2010 (Wilson, J. and Milne, R.), © The Financial Times Limited. All Rights Reserved; Case Study on page 25 from Lego enters a new dimension with its digital strategy, *Financial Times,* 27/09/2015 (Milne, R.), © The Financial Times Limited. All Rights Reserved; Case Study on page 28 from Asos founder turns to online homeware, *Financial Times,* 28/06/2010 (Kuchler, H.), © The Financial Times Limited. All Rights Reserved; Quote on page 44 from Gov.uk website, https://www.gov.uk/government/organisations/uk-export-finance/about, accessed 2014, September, Gov.UK. OGL, licensed under the Open Government Licence v.3.0; Case Study on page 50 from Amazon eyes online sales boost through "Fire" smartphone, *Financial Times,* 19/06/2014 (Mishkin, S.), © The Financial Times Limited. All Rights Reserved; Case Study on page 54 from Recession-hit Aga trials green energy, *Financial Times,* 12/03/2010 (Jones, A.), © The Financial Times Limited. All Rights Reserved; Case Study on page 86 from Food group shifts strategy to volume growth, *Financial Times,* 10/01/2010 (Daneshkhu, S. and Wiggins, J.), © The Financial Times Limited. All Rights Reserved; Case Study on page 88 from Amadeus set to soar on airline bookings, *Financial Times,* 26/02/2015 (Hale, T.), © The Financial Times Limited. All Rights Reserved; Case Study on page 105 from Balderton plugs into teenagers' attention spans, *Financial Times,* 18/06/2010 (Bradshaw, T.), © The Financial Times Limited. All Rights Reserved; Case Study on page 106 from

Gatwick seeks greater competition with BAA, *Financial Times,* 21/06/2010 (Sherwood, B.), © The Financial Times Limited. All Rights Reserved; Case Study on page 128 from Adidas struggles to catch up with Nike's runaway success, *Financial Times,* 07/08/2015 (Whipp, L and Shotter, J.), © The Financial Times Limited. All Rights Reserved; Case Study on page 130 from Waterstone's links up with Paperchase, *Financial Times,* 06/05/2010 (Felsted, A.), © The Financial Times Limited. All Rights Reserved; Case Study on page 154 from Miele focuses on old-fashioned quality, *Financial Times,* 13/11/2003 (Marsh, P.); Case Study on page 158 from Jaeger targets younger shoppers, *Financial Times,* 15/04/2010 (Felsted, A.), © The Financial Times Limited. All Rights Reserved; Case Study on page 186 from Nestlé refines its arsenal in the luxury coffee war, *Financial Times,* 28/04/2010 (Betts, P.), © The Financial Times Limited. All Rights Reserved; Case Study on page 188 from E-reader market cuts prices again, *Financial Times,* 02/07/2010 (Gelles, D.), © The Financial Times Limited. All Rights Reserved; Case Study on page 212 adapted from A passion that became a brand, *Financial Times,* 24/02/2010 (Simonian, H.), © The Financial Times Limited. All Rights Reserved; Case Study on page 214 from The public image: Kodak, *Financial Times,* 10/05/2010 (Bradshaw, T.), © The Financial Times Limited. All Rights Reserved; Case Study on page 234 from No-frills Ryanair faces test with Business Plus, *Financial Times,* 27/08/2014 (Boland, V. and Wild, J), © The Financial Times Limited. All Rights Reserved; Case Study on page 238 from Samsung to launch new mobile payment service in the US, *Financial Times,* 25/09/2015 (Jung-a, S.), © The Financial Times Limited. All Rights Reserved; Case Study on page 267 from Volvo's heart will "remain in Sweden", *Financial Times,* 29/03/2010 (Reed, J.), © The Financial Times Limited. All Rights Reserved; Case Study on page 268 from Black Friday breaks records at John Lewis, *Financial Times,* 02/12/2014 (Barrett, C.), © The Financial Times Limited. All Rights Reserved; Case Study on page 296 from Sensory ploys and the scent of marketing, *Financial Times,* 03/06/2013 (Budden, R), © The Financial Times Limited. All Rights Reserved; Case Study on page 298 from Dyson to double numbers in UK engineering team, *Financial Times,* 26/04/2010 (Kavanagh, D.), © The Financial Times Limited. All Rights Reserved; Case Study on page 330 from Apple moves into fashion business with Watch launch, *Financial Times,* 10/09/2014 (Bradshaw, T. and Waters, R), © The Financial Times Limited. All Rights Reserved; Epigraph on page 332 from Awkward customers, *Financial Times,* 12/02/2003, p. 12 (Skapinker, M.); Case Study on page 332 from The customer is more right than you know *Financial Times,* 19/05/2010 (Moules, J.), © The Financial Times Limited. All Rights Reserved; Case Study on page 358 from Property portals hand control to homeowners *Financial Times,* 22/08/2014 (Allen, K.), © The Financial Times Limited. All Rights Reserved; Epigraph on page 365 from Stewart, T.A. (2006), 'The top line', *Harvard Business Review,* July–August, 10; Case Study on page 365 from Letting go can cut both ways, *Financial Times,* 29/06/2009 (Southon, M.); Case Study on page 398 from Power of the mummies key to Nestlé's strategy in DR Congo, *Financial Times,* 01/10/2014 (Manson, K.), © The Financial Times Limited. All Rights Reserved; Case Study on page 400 from MasterCard cashes in on smart transit, *Financial Times,* 02/07/2015 (Edgecliffe-Johnson, A.), © The Financial Times Limited. All Rights Reserved; Case Study on page 426 from UPS and FedEx turn focus to consumer behaviour, *Financial Times,* 12/08/2014 (Wright, R.), © The Financial Times Limited. All Rights Reserved; Case Study on page 429 from GM backs away from drive to end use of 'Chevy' *Financial Times,* 10/06/2010 (Simonin, B.), © The Financial Times Limited. All Rights Reserved; Case Study on page 458 from EasyJet blazes trail on customer service, *Financial Times,* 23/12/2013 (Wild, J.), © The Financial Times Limited. All Rights Reserved; Epigraph on page 460 from Porter, M.E. and Kramer, M.R. (2011), 'Creating shared value', *Harvard Business Review,* January–February, 62–77; Case Study on page 460 from Eco-friendly fabrics, *Financial Times,* 16/04/2010 (Sims, J), © The Financial Times Limited. All Rights Reserved; Case Study on page 496 from How Skanska aims to become the world's greenest construction ...Innovation begins at home: Group puts its slant on sustainable housing. http://www.ft.com/cms/s/0/73a1bea4-a61a-11e3-8a2a-00144feab7de.html\#axzz4IHkjdYlh, © The Financial Times Limited. All Rights Reserved; Case Study on page 500 from Hanwang sets its e-reader sights high, *Financial Times,* 26/04/2010 (Hille, K.), © The Financial Times Limited. All Rights Reserved; Case Study on page 519 from Twitter builds on its character *Financial Times,* 15/04/2010 (Gelles, D.), © The Financial Times Limited. All Rights Reserved.

Photos

Alamy Images: ACORN 1 296, Terry Allen 460, Greg Balfour Evans 88, British Retail Photography 130, Matthew Chattle 268, James Copeland 330, Ian G Dagnall 234, epa european pressphoto agency b.v. 426, 494, Roger Harvey 54, Jim Holden 86, IanDagnall Computing 458, David Lee 94, Ian Leonard 106, Oleksiy Maksymenko Photography 267, MBI 105, Niall McDiarmid 253, REUTERS 238, sjscreens 358, Kumar Sriskandan 398, Torontonian 128, uk retail Alan King 225, vario images GmbH & Co.KG 73; Centre Parcs Ltd 169; Corbis: © EVERETT KENNEDY BROWN / epa 275; Dyson 115, 298; Getty Images: AFP 71, 154, Bloomberg / Duncan Chard 186, Bloomberg / Chip Chipman 519, Bloomberg / Patrick T. Fallon 25, Bloomberg / Andrew Harrer 188, Bloomberg / Gary Malerba 429, Bloomberg / Maurice Tsai 500, BEN STANSALL / AFP 158, Justin Sullivan 50; Mondelez UK Ltd 99; Phil Jesson (A-Z logo reproduced by permission of Geographers' A-Z Map Company Ltd) 365; PhotoDisc: Jacobs Stock Photography 214; Press Association Images: Philip Toscano / PA Archive 400; Puma United Kingdom Ltd. 4; SuperJam 332; Zai AG: Zai Rider Simon.

PART 1
MARKETING STRATEGY

The first part of this book is concerned with the role of marketing in strategy development and lays the groundwork for analysing the two central issues of competitive positioning and market choices.

Chapter 1 discusses marketing as a process of value creation and delivery to customers that transcends traditional departmental boundaries. We examine the issue of market orientation as a way of doing business that places the customer at the centre of operations, and aligns people, information and structures around the value-creation process. We also recognise the role of organisational resources in creating sustainable competitive advantage. The chapter concludes with a set of fundamental marketing principles to guide the actions of organisations operating in competitive markets, and by identifying the role of marketing in leading and shaping strategic management.

Chapter 2 presents a framework for developing a marketing strategy that is then adopted throughout the rest of the text. A three-stage process is proposed. First, the establishment of the core strategy. This involves defining the business purpose, assessing the alternatives open to the organisation through an analysis of customers, competition and the resources of the organisation, and deciding on the strategic focus that will be adopted. Second is the creation of the competitive positioning for the company. This boils down to the selection of the target market(s) (which dictates *where* the organisation will compete) and the establishment of a competitive advantage (which spells out *how* it will compete). Third, implementation issues are discussed, such as the achievement of positioning through the use of the marketing mix, organisation and control of the marketing effort.

The ideas and frameworks presented in Part 1 are used to structure the remainder of the text, leading into a more detailed discussion of market analysis in Part 2, segmentation and positioning analysis in Part 3, the development of competitive positioning strategies in Part 4, and strategy implementation issues in Part 5.

CHAPTER 1
MARKET-LED STRATEGIC MANAGEMENT

> The purpose of marketing is to contribute to maximising shareholder value and marketing strategies must be evaluated in terms of how much value they create for investors.
>
> Peter Doyle (2008)

Puma gives the boot to cardboard shoeboxes

Puma is to eliminate the humble cardboard shoebox and plans to produce half of its sportswear from sustainable sources as part of a push to use ethical credentials to steal a march on rivals.

Jochen Zeitz, former chief executive, said Puma wanted to become the 'most sustainable' sportswear company, but offered collaboration with other companies on its packaging technology, which includes the use of a corn starch-based product to replace plastic in wrapping clothing and in carrier bags in the group's stores.

The initiatives by the world's third-largest sporting goods maker – which vies for consumer spending with Adidas, its German neighbour and rival, and Nike of the US – shows how environmental concerns are prompting consumer goods companies to alter production and marketing methods.

Mr Zeitz said Puma had decided to pre-empt any potential legislation that would enforce more environmentally sustainable practices. 'Puma must face the reality that neither its business nor the retail industry are currently sustainable in a way that does not affect future generations,' the company said.

Source: www.puma.com

Puma has unveiled a reusable bag to replace boxes for shipping shoes from factories to consumers from late next year. The company also said at least half its footwear, clothing and accessories would in time be produced from recycled or organic products.

Puma, owned by PPR, the French luxury goods group, said its new packaging and production methods would initially increase costs. 'If you buy recycled material or organic it costs more . . . we hope there will be more [cheap] supplies in the future,' Mr Zeitz said.

2014 marked a turning point in Puma's footwear packaging concept. Their customers and retail partners repeatedly reported issues regarding difficulties in the handling of the Clever Little Bag in the retail environment, which led to the development of a new, more conventional footwear packaging. To uphold high environmental standards, the new PUMA shoebox is made from over 95% recycled and fully FSC® certified material.

Source: from 'Puma gives the boot to cardboard shoeboxes', *Financial Times*, 14/04/2010 (Wilson, J. and Milne, R.).

Discussion questions

1 What issues are Puma trying to address?

2 How are Puma's plans in line with the marketing concept?

Introduction

Peter Doyle (2008) points out that the primary overarching goal for chief executives of commercial companies is to maximise shareholder value. Is this at odds with increasing awareness and attention to environmental and social responsibility? Surely firms seeking to maximise shareholder value will pay scant regard to the natural and social environment in which they operate, taking what they can irrespective of the consequences, to make a quick buck? Isn't this the essence of market-based capitalism – red in tooth and claw?

Wrong! The essence of the shareholder value approach is the long-term sustainability of the organisation through the creation of *lasting* value. Indeed, Doyle also argues that shareholder value is often confused with maximising profits. Maximising profitability is generally considered to be a short-term approach (and may result in eroding long-term competitiveness through actions such as cost cutting and shedding assets to produce quick improvements in earnings). Maximising shareholder value, on the other hand, requires long-term thinking, the identification of changing opportunities and investment in the building of competitive advantage.

The role of marketing in the modern organisation poses something of a paradox. As Doyle (2008) again points out, few chief executives come from a marketing background, and many leading organisations do not even have marketing directors on their boards. Indeed, in many firms, the marketing *function* or *department* has had little or no strategic role; being relegated to public relations (PR), advertising or sales roles. However, there has been a change over the last decade or so, regarding the importance of the *marketing concept* in setting the strategic direction and influencing the culture of firms. Greyser (1997), for example, notes that marketing has successfully 'migrated' from being a functional discipline to being a concept of how businesses should be run. Similarly, marketing is talked of as a key discipline in organisations other than conventional commercial enterprises, for example in not-for-profit enterprises such as charities and the arts, in political parties, and even in public sector organisations, such as universities and the police service.

Managers increasingly recognise that the route to achieving their commercial or social objectives lies in successfully meeting the needs and expectations of their customers (be they purchasers or users of services). The concept of the customer has always been strong in commercial businesses, and as supply has outstripped demand in so many industries so customer choice has increased. Add to that the vast increase in information available to customers through media sources such as the Internet, and the power in the supply chain has shifted dramatically from manufacturer, to retailer/supplier, to end customer. In such a world, organisations that don't have customer satisfaction at the core of their strategic decision making will find it increasingly hard to survive.

In the not-for-profit world the concept of the 'customer' is taking more time to get established but is no less central. Public sector organisations talk in terms of 'clients', 'patients', 'students', 'passengers', and the like. In reality all are customers, in that they 'receive' benefits from an exchange with an identifiable entity or service provider. Where customers can make choices between service providers (within the public sector or outside it) they will choose providers who best serve their needs. Increasingly private sector providers are identifying areas where customers are not well served by the public sector, and providing new choices (in healthcare, education, security services and transport, for example).

While organisational structures, operational methods and formal trappings of marketing can and should change to reflect new developments and market opportunities, the philosophy and concept of marketing, as described in this chapter, are even more relevant in the business environment faced today than ever before.

This first chapter sets the scene by examining the marketing concept and market orientation as the foundations of strategic marketing, the role of marketing in addressing various stakeholders in the organisation, and the developing resource-based marketing strategy approach.

1.1   The marketing concept and market orientation

1.1.1 Evolving definitions of marketing

One of the earliest pieces of codification and definition in the development of the marketing discipline was concerned with the marketing concept. Over 50 years ago Felton (1959) proposed that the marketing concept is:

> A corporate state of mind that exists on the integration and coordination of all the marketing functions which, in turn, are melded with all other corporate functions, for the basic objective of producing long-range profits.

Kotler *et al.* (1996) suggested that the defining characteristic is that:

> The marketing concept holds that achieving organisational goals depends on determining the needs and wants of target markets and delivering the desired satisfactions more effectively and efficiently than competitors do.

At its simplest, it is generally understood that the marketing concept holds that, in increasingly dynamic and competitive markets, the companies or organisations which are most likely to succeed are those that take notice of customer expectations, wants and needs and gear themselves to satisfying them better than their competitors. It recognises that there is no reason why customers should buy one organisation's offerings unless they are in some way better at serving their wants and needs than those offered by competing organisations.

In fact, the meaning and domain of marketing remains controversial. In 1985 the American Marketing Association (AMA) reviewed more than 25 marketing definitions before arriving at their own (see Ferrell and Lucas, 1987):

> Marketing is the process of planning and executing the conception, pricing, planning and distribution of ideas, goods and services to create exchanges that satisfy individual and organisational objectives.

This has since evolved further, but very much embraces the broad ideas expressed in this initial definition. The AMA's most recent (July 2013) definition of marketing is:

> Marketing is the activity, set of institutions, and processes for creating, communicating, delivering, and exchanging offerings that have value for customers, clients, partners, and society at large.

Taken together, these definitions position marketing as being embedded within an organisation, and as something that has extensive impact outside the organisation. They

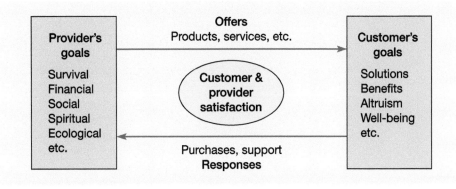

Figure 1.1
Mutually beneficial
exchanges

also reinforce the notion of the centrality of the marketing concept, value, process, mutually beneficial exchange and customer relationships. These issues may or may not be managed by a marketing department or function. These definitions lead to a model of 'mutually beneficial exchanges' as an overview of the role of marketing, as shown in Figure 1.1.

Definitions of marketing are, of course, extremely useful, however the reality of what marketing means operationally, and in reality, is a much more difficult topic. Webster (1997) points out that, of all the management functions, marketing has the most difficulty in defining its position in the organisation, because it is simultaneously culture, strategy and tactics. He argues that marketing involves the following:

- **Culture:** marketing may be expressed as the 'marketing concept' i.e. a set of values and beliefs embedded in employees that drives organisational decision making through a fundamental commitment to serving customers' needs, as the path to sustained profitability.
Strategy: as strategy, marketing seeks to develop effective responses to changing market environments by defining market segments, and developing and positioning product offerings for those target markets.
- **Tactics:** marketing as tactics is concerned with the day-to-day activities of product management, pricing, distribution and marketing communications such as advertising, personal selling, publicity and sales promotion.

The challenge of simultaneously building a customer orientation in an organisation (**culture**), developing value propositions and competitive positioning (**strategy**) and developing detailed marketing action plans (**tactics**) is complex. It is perhaps unsurprising that the organisational reality of marketing often falls short of the demands suggested above.

1.1.2 Market orientation

Marketing Science Institute studies during the 1990s attempted to identify the specific activities that translate the philosophy of marketing into reality, i.e. to achieve market orientation. In one of the most widely quoted research streams in modern marketing, Kohli and Jaworski (1990) defined market orientation in the following terms:

a market orientation entails (1) one or more departments engaging in activities geared towards developing an understanding of customers' current and future needs and the factors affecting them, (2) sharing of this understanding across departments, and (3) the various departments engaging in activities designed to meet select customer needs. In other words, a market orientation refers to the organisation-wide generation, dissemination, and responsiveness to market intelligence.

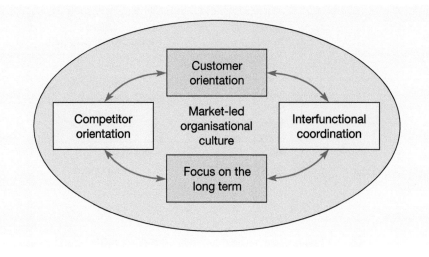

Figure 1.2
Components and
context of market
orientation

This view of market orientation is concerned primarily with the development of what may be called market understanding throughout an organisation, and poses a substantial management challenge.

In another seminal contribution to this discussion, Narver and Slater (1990) defined market orientation as:

> The organisational culture . . . that most effectively and efficiently creates the necessary behaviours for the creation of superior value for buyers and, thus, continuous superior performance for the business.

From this work a number of components, and the context of marketing, are proposed (see Figure 1.2):

- **customer orientation:** understanding customers well enough continuously to create superior value for them;
- **competitor orientation:** awareness of the short- and long-term capabilities of competitors;
- **interfunctional coordination:** using all company resources to create value for target customers;
- **organisational culture:** linking employee and managerial behaviour to customer satisfaction;
- **long-term creation of shareholder value:** as the overriding business objective.

Although research findings are somewhat mixed regarding the impact and efficacy of market orientation, there is a significant and compelling amount of support for the view that market orientation is associated with superior organisational performance, i.e. financial performance and non-financial performance such as employee commitment, and *esprit de corps* (Jaworski and Kohli, 1993; Slater and Narver, 1994; Cano *et al.*, 2004; Kumar *et al.*, 2011).

However, it has also been suggested that there may be substantial barriers to achieving market orientation (Harris, 1996, 1998; Piercy *et al.*, 2002). The reality may be that executives face the problem of creating and driving marketing strategy in situations where the company is simply not market oriented. This is probably at the heart of many strategy implementation problems in marketing (see Chapter 16).

An interesting attempt to 'reinvent' the marketing concept for a new era of different organisational structures, complex relationships and globalisation, which may be relevant to overcoming the barriers to market orientation, is made by Webster (1994).

Table 1.1 The fabric of the new marketing concept

1	Create customer focus throughout the business
2	Listen to the customer
3	Define and nurture the organisation's distinct competencies
4	Define marketing as market intelligence
5	Target customers precisely
6	Manage for profitability, not sales volume
7	Make customer value the guiding star
8	Let the customer define loyalty
9	Measure and manage customer expectations
10	Build customer relationships and loyalty
11	Define the business as a service business
12	Commit to continuous improvement and innovation
13	Manage culture along with strategy and structure
14	Grow with partners and alliances
15	Destroy marketing bureaucracy

Source: Webster (1994).

He presents 'the new marketing concept as a set of guidelines for creating a customer-focused, market-driven organisation', and develops 15 ideas that weave the 'fabric of the new marketing concept' (Table 1.1).

Webster's conceptualisation/ 'checklist' represents a useful and helpful attempt to develop a pragmatic operationalisation of the marketing concept.

We can summarise the signs of market orientation in the following terms, and underline the links between them and our approach here to marketing strategy and competitive positioning:

- Reaching marketing's true potential may rely mostly on success in moving past marketing activities (tactics), to marketing as a company-wide issue of real customer focus (culture) and competitive positioning (strategy). The evidence supports suggestions that marketing has generally been highly effective in tactics, but only marginally effective in changing culture, and largely ineffective in the area of strategy (Day, 1992; Varadarajan, 1992; Webster, 1997; Varadarajan, 2012).
- One key is achieving understanding of the market and the customer throughout the company and building the capability for responsiveness to market changes. The real customer focus and responsiveness of the company is the context in which marketing strategy is built and implemented. Our approach to competitive market analysis in Part 2 provides many of the tools that can be used to enhance and share an understanding of the customer marketplace throughout the company.
- Another issue is that the marketing process should be seen as interfunctional and cross-disciplinary, and not simply the responsibility of the marketing department. This is the

real value of adopting the process perspective on marketing, which is becoming more widely adopted by large organisations (Hulbert *et al.*, 2003). We shall see in Part 4 on competitive positioning strategies that superior service and value, and innovation to build defensible competitive positions, rely on the coordinated efforts of many functions and people within the organisation. Cross-functional relationships are also an important emphasis in Part 5.

- It is also clear that a deep understanding of the competition in the market from the customer's perspective is critical. Viewing the product or service from the customer's viewpoint is often difficult, but without that perspective a marketing strategy is highly vulnerable to attack from unsuspected sources of competition. We shall confront this issue in Part 3, where we are concerned with competitive positioning.

- Finally, it follows that the issue is long-term performance, not simply short-term results, and this perspective is implicit in all that we consider in building and implementing marketing strategy.

A framework for executives to evaluate market orientation in their own organisations is shown in Box 1.1. However, it is also important to make the point at this early stage that marketing as organisational culture (the marketing concept and market orientation) must also be placed in the context of other drivers of the values and approaches of the organisation. A culture that emphasises customers as key stakeholders in the organisation is not inconsistent with one that also recognises the needs and concerns of shareholders, employees, managers and the wider social and environmental context in which the organisation operates.

Box 1.1	Market orientation assessment

1 Customer orientation

	Strongly agree	Agree	Neither	Disagree	Strongly disagree	Don't know
Information about customer needs and requirements is collected regularly	5	4	3	2	1	0
Our corporate objective and policies are aimed directly at creating satisfied customers	5	4	3	2	1	0
Levels of customer satisfaction are regularly assessed and action is taken to improve matters where necessary	5	4	3	2	1	0
We put major effort into building stronger relationships with key customers and customer groups	5	4	3	2	1	0
We recognise the existence of distinct groups or segments in our markets with different needs and we adapt our offerings accordingly	5	4	3	2	1	0

Total score for customer orientation (out of 25)

2 Competitor orientation

	Strongly agree	Agree	Neither	Disagree	Strongly disagree	Don't know
Information about competitor activities is collected regularly	5	4	3	2	1	0
We conduct regular benchmarking against major competitor offerings	5	4	3	2	1	0
There is rapid response to major competitor actions	5	4	3	2	1	0
We put major emphasis on differentiating ourselves from the competition on factors important to customers	5	4	3	2	1	0

Total score for competitor orientation (out of 20)

3 Long-term perspectives

	Strongly agree	Agree	Neither	Disagree	Strongly disagree	Don't know
We place greater priority on long-term market share gain than short-run profits	5	4	3	2	1	0
We put greater emphasis on improving our market performance than on improving internal efficiencies	5	4	3	2	1	0
Decisions are guided by long-term considerations rather than short-run expediency	5	4	3	2	1	0

Total score for long-term perspectives (out of 15)

4 Interfunctional coordination

	Strongly agree	Agree	Neither	Disagree	Strongly disagree	Don't know
Information about customers is widely circulated and communicated throughout the organisation	5	4	3	2	1	0
The different departments in the organisation work effectively together to serve customer needs	5	4	3	2	1	0
Tensions and rivalries between departments are not allowed to get in the way of serving customers effectively	5	4	3	2	1	0
Our organisation is flexible to enable opportunities to be seized effectively rather than hierarchically constrained	5	4	3	2	1	0

Total score for interfunctional coordination (out of 20)

5 Organisational culture

	Strongly agree	Agree	Neither	Disagree	Strongly disagree	Don't know
All employees recognise their role in helping to create satisfied end customers	5	4	3	2	1	0
Reward structures are closely related to external market performance and customer satisfaction	5	4	3	2	1	0
Senior management in all functional areas give top priority to creating satisfied customers	5	4	3	2	1	0
Senior management meetings give high priority to discussing issues that affect customer satisfaction	5	4	3	2	1	0

Total score for organisational culture (out of 20)

Summary

From the totals obtained above:
Customer orientation (out of 25)
Competitor orientation (out of 20)
Long-term perspectives (out of 15)
Interfunctional coordination (out of 20)
Organisational culture (out of 20)
Total score (out of 100)

Interpretation

- 80–100. This indicates a high level of market orientation. Scores below 100 can still, however, be improved!
- 60–80. This indicates moderate market orientation. Identify the areas where most improvement is needed.
- 40–60. This shows that there is a long way to go in developing a market orientation. Identify the main gaps and set priorities for action to close them.
- 20–40. This indicates a mountain ahead of you! Start at the top and work your way through. Some factors will be more within your control than others. Tackle those first.

Note: If you scored '0' on many of the scales you need to find out more about your own company!

1.2	**The resource-based view of marketing**

While academic researchers and managers in marketing have been struggling with understanding what being 'market oriented' means (what it is, how to measure it and how to build it), a revolution has been taking place in the field of strategic management.

The dominant view of strategy in the 1980s and early 1990s had been that proposed by, among others, Michael Porter of the Harvard Business School (Porter, 1980, 1985). While there has been much academic discussion and debate on this perspective, it is an approach that is still a fundamental piece of strategic management theory. Under this view the key to strategy was deemed to lie in industry dynamics and characteristics. Porter suggested that

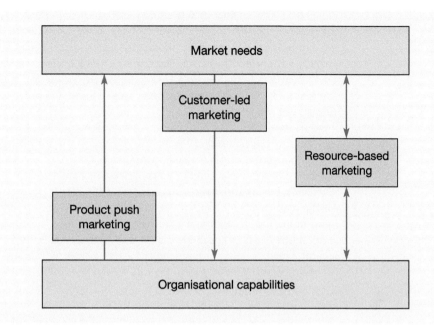

Figure 1.3
Marketing
approaches

some industries were inherently more attractive than others, and that the factors driving industry competition were the key determinants of profitability. Under the new approach, however, the focus for explaining performance differences shifted from outside the firm (the industries in which it operated) to within the firm itself (its resources and capabilities).

Termed the resource-based view of the firm (Wernerfelt, 1984) with a focus on 'core competencies' (Prahalad and Hamel, 1990) this new approach suggested that performance was essentially driven by the resource profile of the organisation, and that the source of superior performance lay in the possession and deployment of distinctive, hard to imitate or protected resources.

Our view on strategy and marketing is that these two approaches can be combined to the benefit of both. They do, however, throw into stark relief the different approaches to strategy in general, and marketing in particular, still evident in many organisations today. Three main alternative approaches are apparent (see Figure 1.3):

- **Product push marketing.** Under this approach firms focus their activities on their existing products and services and look for ways to encourage, or even persuade, customers to buy. This is a myopic interpretation of the resource-based view, i.e. we have a resource (our product or service) that we are good at producing and that is different from what competitors offer. The key thing is to make customers want what we are good at. Day (1999) identified this approach in the IBM statement of goals in 1983. Under that statement the firm set out objectives to grow the industry, to exhibit product leadership across the entire product line, to be most efficient in all activities undertaken, and to sustain profitability. What is remarkable about these goals is that customers are not mentioned once. The entire focus was on what IBM did then (1983) and how it could be done more efficiently. Interestingly, IBM's performance in the 1980s was poor, and they have since completely revised their business model to be much more relationship focused and market-led – performing much better as a result.
- **Customer-led marketing.** The other extreme is customer-led marketing (Slater, 1998). Under this approach organisations chase their customers at all costs. The goal is to find what customers want and, whatever it is, give it to them. This can also lead to problems. In the 1980s Procter & Gamble was being hit by increasingly aggressive competitors and squeezed by increasingly powerful retailers. It reacted by giving customers more choice, heavy promotions and deals to stimulate purchases, and aggressive salesforce targets.

The result was product proliferation on a grand scale (there were at one time 35 variants of the Bounce fabric conditioner!). Customers were confused by the over-complex promotions (deals, coupons, offers, etc.) and retailers became angry at having to stock a wide variety of choices on their shelves; in addition this approach does not allow manufacturers to maximise scale economies in production and product line extensions can cause chaos and logistical nightmares. Being excessively customer led can lead to a short-term orientation resulting in trivial incremental product development efforts and myopic research and development (R&D) (Frosch, 1996). Christensen and Bower (1996) go further, suggesting that 'firms lose their position of industry leadership . . . because they listen too carefully to their customers'.

- **Resource-based marketing.** In this text we advocate a middle ground between these two extremes. In this approach firms base their marketing strategies on equal consideration of the requirements of the market and their abilities to serve it. Under this approach a long-term view of customer requirements is taken in the context of other market considerations (such as competitor offerings and strategies, and the realities of the supply chain), together with mapping out the assets, competencies and skills of the organisation to ensure they are leveraged to the full. By the late 1980s IBM had recast its approach in its market-driven quality campaign along the lines: 'if we can be the best at satisfying the needs and wants of customers in those markets we choose to serve, everything important will follow.' The newer approach recognised the centrality of the customer, but also the need to be selective in which markets to serve, ensuring they were markets where IBM's resources (its assets and capabilities) gave it the chance of leadership.

Resource-based marketing essentially seeks a long-term fit between the requirements of the market and the abilities of the organisation to compete in it. This does not mean that the resources of the organisation are seen as fixed and static – far from it. Market requirements evolve over time and the resource profile of the organisation must be continuously developed to enable it to continue to compete, and indeed to enable it to take advantage of new opportunities. The essential factor, however, is that opportunities are seized where the organisation has an existing or potential advantage through its resource base, rather than just pursued *ad hoc*. These points will be returned to when we discuss the assessment of company marketing resources (Chapter 6) and the criteria for selecting those markets in which to operate (Chapter 9).

First, however, we need to explore how market orientation and marketing resources impact on organisational performance. To do this we introduce the idea of organisational stakeholders.

1.3   Organisational stakeholders

Why do organisations exist? The simple answer for commercial organisations may be to earn returns on their investments for shareholders and owners of those organisations. For non-commercial organisations, such as charities, faith-based organisations, public services and so on, the answer may lie in the desire to serve specific communities. But organisations, both commercial and non-profit, are rarely driven by such simple goals. Often there are many demands, sometimes complementary, sometimes competing, that drive decisions. For example, James Dyson's decision to move production of his household appliances out of the United Kingdom to Asia in early 2002 for cost reasons (responsibility to shareholders to operate efficiently) resulted in a considerable backlash from the local community over the impact on jobs and livelihoods in the region (responsibility to employees and the local community).

All organisations serve multiple stakeholders (Harrison and St John, 1994; Mitchell *et al.,* 1997). Some, however, will be given higher priority than others in the way decisions are made and resources allocated (Rowley, 1997; Ogden and Watson, 1999). Research into the

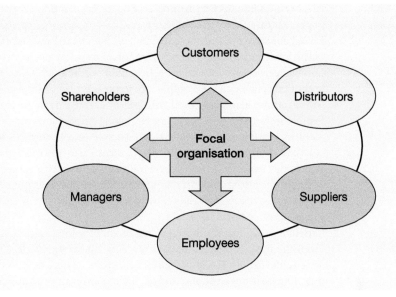

Figure 1.4
Organisational
stakeholders

transition economies of central and Eastern Europe, for example, found that in many state-owned enterprises (SOEs) the major stakeholders were the employees, and organisational objectives centred on providing continuity of employment (Hooley *et al.*, 2000). This orientation persists in many former SOEs following privatisation and sell-off to the commercial sector; although this is now changing. For many of the commercial firms surveyed the prime objectives centred on profitability and short-term return on investment.

The long-term implications of climate change and global warming have led many organisations to begin to recognise the importance of the physical/natural environment in their planning and actions. Indeed, the natural environment could be seen as a further 'stakeholder'.

In the context of commercial organisations a number of primary stakeholders can be identified (see Figure 1.4) (Greenley and Foxall, 1996, 1997). These include shareholders and owners, managers, employees, customers, suppliers and the society in which they operate. While the market-oriented culture discussed above serves to place customers high in the priority ranking, the reality for most organisations will be a complex blend of considerations of all relevant stakeholders.

Doyle (2008) discusses the motivations and expectations of the various stakeholder groups as follows:

- **Shareholders** may be of two main types. First, there may be individuals with emotional and long-term personal ties to the business. Increasingly, however, shareholders nowadays are financial investors, both individual and institutional, that are seeking to maximise the long-term value of their investments. Paradoxically, this desire for long-term shareholder value may drive many firms to make short-term decisions, to maximise share price or dividends.
- **Employees** may also have long-term commitment to the firm. Their priorities are generally some combination of compensation (through wages and salaries), job satisfaction and security (of employment). These may be at odds with the value of the firm to shareholders. Few employees would agree that their personal job loss through 'downsizing' is a price worth paying for increasing shareholder value! Some firms, however, put a great deal of effort into understanding employee motivations. Skandia, the Swedish insurance company, for example, regularly surveys employees with a view to aligning their personal and corporate goals (*Fortune*, 11 March 2002). The John Lewis Partnership have 91,000 permanent staff 'Partners', who own 42 John Lewis shops across the UK (31 department stores and an online business) and 325 Waitrose supermarkets.

The business has annual gross sales of over £10bn and the Partners share in the benefits and profits of the successful businesses. They also involve their employees in decision making through meetings between management and elected staff representatives. Seen as a result of this environment, staff turnover at John Lewis Partnership is very low. In the recent economic recession it was noticeable how many companies negotiated reduced working hours and/or pay cuts with their employees to preserve jobs rather than make people redundant.

- **Managers** are also concerned with personal rewards in the form of salaries and prestige. Professional managers may have less long-term commitment to the firm and see their roles as temporary staging posts on their longer-term career journeys. Managerial 'success' is often measured by short-term gains (in sales, for example, or efficiency), which may not necessarily equate to longer-term performance improvement for the firm. Much of the initial cause of the recent credit crunch was put down to the excessive bonus culture in investment banks that encouraged short-term risk-taking at the expense of longer-term performance.

- **Customers** are the ultimate source of shareholder value. As Doyle (2008) points out, 'even the most focused financial manager understands that the source of a company's long-term cash flow is its satisfied customers'. There is, however, an inherent danger of pursuing customer satisfaction at the expense of all other considerations. Customers might be 'delighted' by lower prices or higher quality offerings than competitors, but if the underlying costs exceed the prices that customers are prepared to pay the firm will not remain in business very long. In this respect the blind pursuit of customer satisfaction may be at odds with longer-term shareholder value creation.

- **Suppliers and distributors** also have a stake in the business. Suppliers rely on the firms they serve to ensure the achievement of their own goals. Again, suppliers may be looking for security, predictability and satisfactory margins. When the UK retailer Marks & Spencer (M&S) hit financial problems in 1999–2000 many of the long-term relationships they had with their suppliers such as Courtaulds became casualties. M&S began to source materials wider afield to cut costs and the trust and relationships built over a long period of time with their suppliers were quickly eroded, ending in legal action in some instances. Distributors too are stakeholders in the business. In the automobile industry, car distributors are normally closely allied to individual car makers through franchise agreements. The success or otherwise of the manufacturer in developing and marketing the right cars for the market will impact directly on the distributor. Again, the distributor may be seeking predictability and continuity at satisfactory margins.

To these stakeholders identified by Doyle (2008) we would add the following:

- **Society and the community** in which a firm exists can be significantly affected by its actions. Plant closures are an obvious example. When the UK coal industry shrank significantly in the 1970s and 80s the effects on local communities was vast. Mining towns in Yorkshire and the Midlands experienced high rates of unemployment as new job creation lagged behind pit closures. Positive community relations can engender high degrees of loyalty to businesses, as was evident during the takeover by Kraft of Cadbury in early 2010. Local residents and workers alike campaigned for Cadbury to remain a 'UK firm', largely due to concerns regarding future large-scale reductions in the workforce, and also the possibility of manufacturing moving to another part of the world. At time of writing, however, it appears that these concerns were largely unfounded. The business case for being socially responsible can be compelling (see Carroll and Shabana (2010) including reducing risks and costs; strengthening reputation and legitimacy; and building competitive advantage).

- **The natural or physical environment** has not traditionally been seen as a stakeholder in the conventional use of the term. It is, however, a proxy for future society: what we do to the environment and the natural resources available today, will affect future generations who will have to deal with the consequences tomorrow. It has been argued that while previous generations may not have completely understood the environmental impact of their actions (in particular the burning of fossil fuels), the implications today are quite clear.

Action at national and supranational levels has been, until very recently, fairly elusive (i.e. the failure of the climate change talks in Copenhagen in December 2009 to result in significant commitment to limit carbon emissions). However, the European Union is now leading the way and following the Paris Climate Conference (COP21), held in December 2015, a total of 195 countries have agreed to adopt the first ever, universal, legally-binding global climate deal. Individual organisations in both the private and public sectors are increasingly taking action to reduce emissions and energy consumption, and mitigate their effects on the environment. This makes good commercial sense too, as energy bills for many organisations are the second-highest controllable expense after staff.

For non-profit organisations the identification of stakeholders and their requirements may be even more complex:

- **Owners** of the organisation may be hard to identify and their interests difficult to define. For example, who 'owns' the Catholic Church, or Greenpeace, or the Labour Party? Many might argue that the owners are those who support such organisations, the church-goers, the activists and the members. Or are employees (such as the Pope and the clergy) the owners? In the case of organisations such as the National Health Service (NHS), or the police service, or education, are the owners society in general, the taxpayers, or the government of the day that sets priorities and performance targets?
- **Customers** may be defined as those the organisation seeks to serve. The customers of the Catholic Church may be those who attend mass on Sundays. They may also, however, extend to others the Church wishes to appeal to and whose behaviour and beliefs it seeks to influence. Who are the customers of the NHS – the patients? Or those who avoid the service through heeding health warnings? Who are the customers of higher education? The students? Their parents who fund them? Or the employers who seek their skills on graduation? Who are the customers for the police service? Society in general that needs protection from criminals? The criminals themselves? Or the taxpayers who fund them? Different definitions of customers may result in different interpretations of what they are looking for, what their expectations and requirements are. Failure to identify and meet the needs of different customers destroys market position. For example, while doctors and police officers struggle with the idea that they exist to provide customer value, their position is being eroded by the growth of alternative medicine, medical tourism (improving choice) and private security services and systems.
- **Employees,** we might conclude, are relatively easy to identify. Their motivations, however, may be far more complex than in the commercial sector. What motivates nurses to work such long, hard hours for relatively little financial reward? Why do people volunteer to staff charity shops for no payment? Why do activists risk their lives to prevent the dumping of oil platforms or nuclear waste at sea? In the non-profit sector employees may or may not receive financial rewards. Often their prime motivators are not financial, but centre far more on satisfaction derived from contributing to a cause they cherish or value.
- **Society and community** have perhaps always been high on the list of priorities for many non-profit organisations. Charities exist to serve the society in which they operate (but would they necessarily call them 'customers'?).

While the considerations of many of the above stakeholders may be complementary they may also be in conflict at times (Clarkson, 1995). For example, the desire of shareholders for long-term value creation may be at odds with the demands of suppliers and distributors for continuity, security and satisfactory margins. The demands placed on a firm through being customer led may have significant impacts on the roles and activities of managers and employees, not all of them welcome. This confusion may be compounded when individual stakeholders assume more than one role. For example, managers and employees may also be shareholders in commercial organisations. They could also, from time to time, be their own customers!

In any organisation there will be a blend of orientations towards the various stakeholders. We would argue, however, that a strong orientation towards the market, as discussed at the outset of this chapter, can be a unifying force that helps achieve other stakeholder goals.

1.3.1 The contribution of marketing to stakeholder objectives

There is increasing evidence that firms which do well in the marketplace also do well financially, adding to the value of the firm for shareholders. Homburg and Pflesser (2000), for example, have shown that firms adopting a market-oriented culture perform better financially than those that do not. Many other studies have also shown direct links between market orientation, customer satisfaction and firm financial performance (see Lafferty and Hult, 2001, for a summary).

Figure 1.5 shows the effects of market-oriented culture on firm activities and performance. The degree of market orientation, as discussed above, is a deeply embedded cultural aspect of any firm (Deshpandé *et al.*, 1993). Where market orientation is high all organisational functions are focused on their role in, and contribution to, creating superior customer value. This in turn affects the way those functions are managed, and the priorities they pursue. For example, human resource management and training is often directed towards customer awareness and service, and reward structures are designed to encourage customer satisfaction generation. Where market orientation is high, employee job satisfaction and commitment have also been demonstrated to be high (see Siguaw *et al.*, 1994; Selnes *et al.*, 1996; Piercy *et al.*, 2002) creating a motivated workforce focused on the needs of customers (see Heskett *et al.*, 2003). Sir Charlie Mayfield, Chairman of the John Lewis Partnership, puts it this way: 'The John Lewis Partnership faces similar challenges to other major retailers but in one respect our response is very different. That's the energy and passion of our Partners who, as co-owners of our business, drive our work to operate an evermore sustainable and responsible business' (John Lewis Partnership website **http://www.johnlewispartnership.co.uk/csr/our-employees.html**, September 2014).

High levels of market orientation also lead to an emphasis on developing marketing assets such as company and brand reputation (Aaker, 1991), market innovation capabilities (Slater and Narver, 1995; Han *et al.*, 1998) and the development of customer relationship management (CRM) skills (Gummesson, 1999).

Well-developed marketing resources (assets and capabilities), when deployed in the marketplace, can lead to superior market performance. Satisfied and well-motivated staff (a prime marketing asset), for example, can make a significant contribution to creating satisfied and loyal customers (Heskett *et al.*, 2003) and subsequently increased sales volume

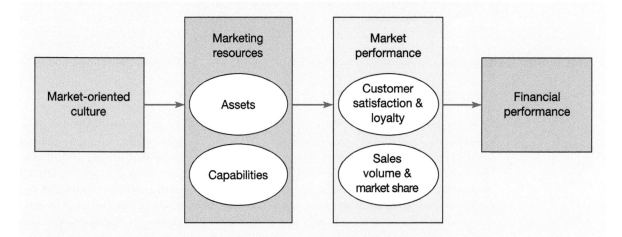

Figure 1.5 Marketing and performance outcomes

and market share. Reputational assets, such as well-known and respected brands, together with well-developed marketing capabilities such as CRM and market innovation skills, also affect market performance directly.

The link between market performance and financial performance is also well established. Customer satisfaction and loyalty leads to greater sales volume and market share (Anderson and Sullivan, 1993; Rust and Zahorik, 1993; Wells, 1994/5), which in turn leads to financial performance. One suggested route is through the impact of economies and advantages of scale.

A second route, explained in detail by Doyle (2008), suggests that shareholder value is determined by anticipated future cash flows, adjusted for the cost of capital. In this view the crucial task of management is to maximise the sum of future cash flows, and hence maximise shareholder value. Marketing's contribution will be to develop strategies that deliver enhanced cash flows through, for example, successful new product launches, or the creation of strong brands which can command high margins and market shares. Under this view the focus of marketing is on developing and protecting assets (such as brands or market share) that have the potential to deliver enhanced cash flows in the future. Doyle sees the role of marketing as driving value creation through the optimum choice of markets and target segments in which to operate, the creation of a differential, or competitive advantage in serving those targets, and the development of an appropriate marketing mix for delivery.

In summary, marketing can contribute to satisfying the needs of employee and manager stakeholders through providing for security, compensation and job satisfaction. Where the firm is better at serving its customers, more adept at winning orders in the face of competition, it is more likely to survive into the future. There is also evidence that where firms are more market oriented their employees get more satisfaction out of their jobs (Slater and Narver, 1995). This in turn can lead to a virtuous circle of improvement, as happy, motivated staff, generate increasingly satisfied customers, so that organisational performance improves, and staff become more satisfied; and so on. Similarly, the most effective route to achieving the profit and performance desires of supply chain partners is through market success. Heightened success through partnerships and alliances can serve to bond organisations together, creating more stability and predictability in the supply and distribution chain. Nonetheless, concerns of customers and employees for the environment, for social justice, for fair employment, and other social priorities have led to renewed emphasis on corporate social responsibility and good corporate citizenship. However, importantly, as we shall see in Part 5, thinking has changed from altruistic behaviour to meet moral obligations to pursuing social initiatives as part of the value proposition and a source of competitive advantage (see Chapter 17).

1.4	**Marketing fundamentals**

Following from the underlying marketing concept outlined above, the considerations of alternative stakeholders, and the logic of resource-based marketing, we can distil a set of basic and very pragmatic marketing principles that serve to guide marketing thought and action. The principles follow the logic of value-based processes described by Webster (1997). Each of these principles seems so obvious as not to require stating. However, recognition of these principles and their application can revolutionise how organisations respond to, and interact with, their customers.

Principle 1: focus on the customer

A first principle of marketing that emerges from our comments throughout goes back to the marketing concept itself. This recognises that the long-term objectives of the organisation, be they financial or social, are best served by achieving a high degree of customer focus – but not a blind focus! From that recognition flows the need for a close investigation of customer wants and needs, followed by a clear definition of if and how the company can best serve them.

It also follows that the only arbiters of how well the organisation satisfies its customers are the customers themselves. The quality of the goods or services offered to the market will be judged by the customers on the basis of how well their requirements are satisfied. A quality product or service, from the customers' perspective, is one that satisfies or is 'fit for purpose' rather than one that provides unrequired bells, whistles or luxury.

As Levitt (1986) demonstrates, adopting a market-led approach poses some very basic questions. The most important include:

- What business are we in?
- What business could we be in?
- What business do we want to be in?
- What must we do to get into or consolidate in that business?

The answers to these fundamental questions can often change a company's whole outlook and perspective. In Chapter 2 we discuss more fully business definition and show how it is fundamental to setting strategic direction for the organisation.

Principle 2: only compete in markets where you can establish a competitive advantage

Market selection is one of the key tasks for any organisation – choosing where to compete and where to commit its resources. Many factors will come into the choice of market, including how attractive the market appears to the firm. Especially important, however, in competitive markets will be the question: do we have the skills and competencies to compete here? The corporate graveyard is littered with firms that were seduced into markets which looked attractive, but when competition got tough they found they had no real basis on which to compete. Many of the dot.com failures of the early 2000s were firms that saw an opportunity but did not really have the skills and competencies to establish an advantage over other dot.coms or 'bricks and mortar' firms.

Principle 3: customers do not buy products

The third basic marketing principle is that customers do not buy products, they buy what the product can do for them, or to put it another way, the problem it solves. In other words customers are less interested in the technical features of a product or service than in what benefits they get from buying, using or consuming the product or service.

For example, the do-it-yourself (DIY) enthusiast putting up bookshelves will assemble the tools for the job. One of these could be a drill bit to make the holes in which to screw the shelf supports, on which to place the shelf. However, the DIY enthusiast does not want a quarter-inch drill bit, but a quarter-inch hole. The drill bit is merely a way of delivering that benefit (the hole) and will only be the solution to the basic need until a better method or solution is invented. We can go further – what is really wanted is storage for books (or indeed alternative ways of storing knowledge and information in electronic media). Competition will not come just from other manufacturers of drill bits, but from laser techniques for making holes in the wall; wall designs that incorporate shelving studs in their design; adhesives that will support shelves; or alternative ways of storing and accessing books such as the Amazon Kindle e-reader. This is the difference between an industry (firms with similar technology and products) and a market (customers with a problem to solve or a need to meet). In this sense, white goods manufacturers may see themselves as an industry, i.e. they all produce white boxes with electric motors, but the markets they serve are the laundry market, the food storage market, and so on. Similarly, gardeners don't really want a lawnmower. What they want is grass that is 1 inch high. Hence a new strain of grass seed, which is hard-wearing and only grows to 1 inch in height, could provide very substantial competition to lawnmower manufacturers, as could artificial grass substitutes or fashions for grass-free garden designs.

This is far from mere academic theorising. One trend in retail marketing in the grocery business is category management. Retailers are defining categories around customer needs, not manufacturers' brands. For example, one common category is 'ready-meal replacement' – the challenge to manufacturers is to prove to the retailer what their products and brands add to the value of the category. Putting category definition at its simplest:

The manufacturer makes	*potato crisps.*
The retailer merchandises	*salty snacks.*
The customer buys	*lunch!*

Looking at a market from the customer's perspective may suggest a very different view of market opportunities and the threats to our competitive position.

It is critical that marketers view products and services as 'bundles of benefits', or a combination of attractions that all give something of value to the customer.

One mission for the marketing executive is to ensure that the organisation gears itself to solving customers' problems, rather than exclusively promoting its own current (and often transitory) solutions.

Principle 4: marketing is too important to leave to the marketing department (if there is one)

It is increasingly the case that marketing is everyone's job in the organisation, and taking the cultural stance we examined earlier this is indeed understandable, hence the actions of all can have an impact on the satisfaction the customer derives.

In an early work, King (1985) highlights a number of misconceptions as to what marketing is. One of the most insidious misconceptions he terms 'marketing department marketing', where an organisation employs marketing professionals who may be very good at analysing marketing data and calculating market shares to three decimal points, but who have very little real impact on the products and services the organisation offers to its customers. The marketing department is seen as the only department where 'marketing is done', so that the other departments can get on with their own agenda and pursue their own goals.

As organisations become flatter, reducing layers of bureaucracy, and continue to break down the spurious functional barriers between departments, so it becomes increasingly obvious that marketing is the job of everyone. It is equally obvious that marketing is so central to both survival and prosperity that it is far too important to leave only to the marketing department.

However, it is clear that we must avoid simply stating that marketing is 'everyone's job' and leaving it at that. If marketing is everyone's job it may become 'no one's job'. Greyser (1997) points to the need for simultaneous upgrading of market orientation and downsizing of the formal marketing function as two sides of the same issue:

> While the marketing function ('doing marketing') belongs to the marketing department, becoming and being marketing-minded is everybody's job. What happens when (almost) everybody is doing that job? As companies have become more marketing-minded, there have been substantial reductions in the formal 'marketing departments' which do marketing. In short, a corollary of the trend to better organisational thinking about marketing is the dispersion of the activity of marketing, e.g. via task forces.

Principle 5: markets are heterogeneous

It is becoming increasingly clear that most markets are not homogeneous, but are made up of different individual customers, sub-markets or segments. While some customers, for example, may buy a car for cheap transport from A to B, others may buy for comfortable travel, or safe travel, or energy efficient travel, and still others may buy for status reasons or to satisfy and project their self-image. Products and services that attempt to satisfy a segmented market through a standardised product almost invariably fall between two or more stools and become vulnerable to more clearly targeted competitors.

Picking up on Principle 2, it is evident that a basic way of segmenting markets is on the basis of the benefits customers get in buying or consuming the product or service. Benefit segmentation (see Chapter 7) has proved to be one of the most useful ways of segmenting markets for the simple reason that it relates the segmentation back to the real reasons for the existence of the segments in the first place – different benefit requirements.

Market heterogeneity has another effect. Concentration in the customer base – facilitated by mergers and acquisitions and attrition rates – has become a daily reality for companies in business-to-business marketplaces. The emergence of powerful, dominant customers underlines the importance of strategic sales capabilities and strategic account management approaches to give specialised attention to customers who can leverage the seller's dependence on them. It is difficult to consider marketing strategy in business-to-business markets without recognising the deep-seated implications of this factor. We devote Chapter 14 to this topic.

Principle 6: markets and customers are constantly changing

It is a truism to say that the only constant is change. Markets are dynamic and virtually all products have a limited life that expires when a new or better way of satisfying the underlying want or need is found; in other words, until another solution or benefit provider comes along.

The fate of the slide rule, and before that logarithmic tables, at the hands of the pocket calculator is a classic example where the problem (the need for rapid and easy calculation) was better solved through a newer technology. The benefits offered by calculators far outstripped the slide rule in speed and ease of use. But pocket calculators themselves are now superseded by applications (apps) on mobile telephones that provide all the functionality of the high specification technical calculators of a few years ago.

This recognition that products are not omnipotent, that they follow a product life cycle pattern of introduction, growth, maturity and decline, has led companies to look and plan more long term; to ensure that by the time the current breadwinners die there are new products in the company's portfolio to take their place.

Also evident is the need for constant product and service improvement. As customer expectations change, usually becoming more demanding in the benefits they expect from a given product or service, so organisations need to upgrade their offerings continuously to retain, let alone improve, position.

There are two main processes of improvement. The first is through innovation, where a relatively large step is taken at one point in time. The advent of the pocket calculator was a significant innovation that virtually wiped out the slide rule industry overnight. Other step changes in technology such as the advent of digital television and radio, and the MP3 player, have served to change whole industries in a similarly short period of time.

The second approach to improvement is a more continuous process whereby smaller changes are made but on an insistent basis. This approach has been identified by a number of writers (e.g. Imai, 1986) as a major contributor to the success of Japanese businesses in world markets during the 1960s, 70s and 80s. The Japanese call continuous improvement 'kaizen' and see it as an integral part of business life. Increasingly, organisations are attempting to marry the benefits of step change innovation with continuous (kaizen) improvement. Figure 1.6 illustrates this process diagramatically.

The impact of technological change has been felt most, perhaps, in the computer industry. It is sometimes hard to remember that computers were invented *after* the Second World War because they are now such a pervasive part of both business and home life. Toffler (1981) noted in *Computer World* magazine:

> If the auto industry had done what the computer industry has done over the last thirty years, a Rolls Royce would cost $2.50, get around 2,000,000 miles to the gallon and six of them would fit on the head of a pin!

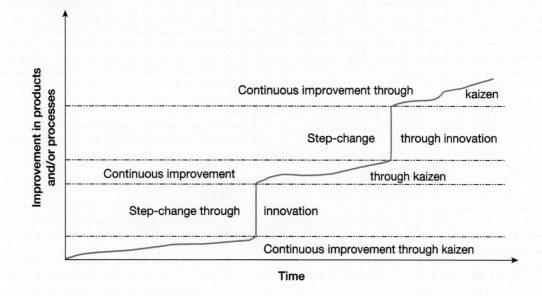

Figure 1.6 Product and process improvement

If that was true 35 years ago just think what the analogy would be today!

The challenges raised by the economic recession have also hastened change in some markets. Increasingly price-sensitive customers are now shopping around more (using the greater amount of information available online) and becoming more deal-conscious. Conversely firms with strong relationships with their customers have been more able to weather the economic storm.

Global warming and climate change are creating markets for new products too. New versions of old products (such as wind turbines and hybrid and electric cars) are being developed and marketed, concerns about extreme weather events are affecting where homes are built (less on the floodplains along river banks) and concerns about rising sea levels are affecting how new homes are built (on the north-west coast of the Netherlands increasingly homes are being built on rafts that can rise or fall with changes in sea level).

1.5 The role of marketing in leading strategic management

In order for strategic management to cope with the changing marketing environment there is a need for it to become increasingly market led. In taking a leading role in the development and the implementation of strategy the role of marketing can be defined in the way shown in Figure 1.7. That role is threefold.

1.5.1 Identification of customer requirements

The first critical task of marketing is to identify the requirements of customers and to communicate them effectively throughout the organisation. This involves conducting or commissioning relevant customer research to uncover, first, who the customers are and, second, what will give them satisfaction.

Who the customers are is not always obvious. In some circumstances buyers may be different from users or consumers; specifiers and influencers may also be different. Where services are funded, for example, by central government the suppliers may be forgiven for the (mistaken) view that government is their customer.

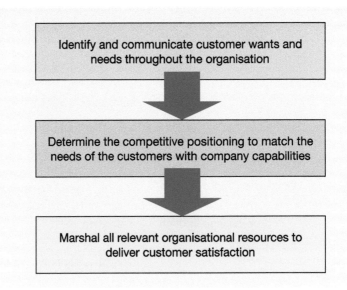

Figure 1.7
The role of
marketing in the
organisation

Customers *expect* a degree of benefit from purchasing or using a product or service. However, they may actually *want* something more, but believe they have to settle for second best because of budget or other constraints. The organisation that can give customers something closer to what they want than what they expect has an opportunity to go beyond customer satisfaction and create 'customer delight'.

Customer expectations, wants and needs must all be understood and clearly communicated to those responsible for designing the product or service, those responsible for creating or producing it, and those responsible for delivering it. Identifying what customers require is discussed in Chapter 4.

1.5.2 Deciding on the competitive positioning to be adopted

Recognising that markets are heterogeneous and typically made up of various market segments each having different requirements from essentially similar offerings leads to the need to decide clearly which target market or markets the organisation will seek to serve.

That decision is made on the basis of two main sets of factors: first, how attractive the alternative potential targets are; and second, how well the company can hope to serve each potential target relative to the competition. In other words, the relative strengths or competencies it can bring into play in serving the market. These two related issues are discussed at length in Part 4.

1.5.3 Implementing the marketing strategy

The third, and arguably the most difficult key task of marketing, is to marshal all the relevant organisational resources to plan and execute the delivery of customer satisfaction. This involves ensuring that all members of the organisation are aware of what is expected of them and are coordinated in their efforts to satisfy customers, and that no actual or potential gaps exist between offer design, production and delivery.

Chapters 14, 15 and 16 address implementation and coordination issues more fully.

Summary

This chapter has sought to review the marketing concept and demonstrate its importance in providing a guiding approach to doing business in the face of increasingly competitive and less predictable marketing environments. This approach we term market-led strategic management. A number of marketing principles were discussed, together with the role of marketing in strategic management. The remainder of Part 1 presents a framework for developing a market-led approach.

Case study   Lego builds new dimension with digital vision

Danish group launches toys-to-life game giving children the opportunity to put physical playthings into virtual worlds

Imagine Homer Simpson driving the Batmobile down the Yellow Brick Road. Or Superman steering a DeLorean Time Machine through Middle-earth.

What was once fantasy will become reality this week when Lego and Warner Bros launch their big-budget game Lego Dimensions.

It marks a crucial step in the Danish toymaker's digital strategy. The game – whose starter pack will be priced at a hefty $100 – pushes it into a new segment: the toys-to-life category, worth $700m a year in the US alone.

'Lego is the archetypal toys to life experience. We are just pushing those digital borders continually so we remain present and relevant in all the environments where children want to play,' says John Goodwin, the finance director.

Toymakers have been hit hard by the emergence of smartphones and tablets, as children spend increasing amounts of time in digital play on such devices. Lego has managed to buck that trend, largely thanks to the strength of its physical products as it became the world's biggest toymaker by sales in the first half of this year.

But, while it has developed a successful line in video games through Warner's TT Games, the privately owned Danish company has struggled in other digital ventures with a number of flops.

'I don't think they have conquered the digital world. It's hard to point to something digital that they have done that is successful. But what you are seeing now is the first attempts for Lego to create some kind of hybrid physical-digital experience,' says

David Robertson, co-author of *Brick by Brick: How Lego Rewrote the Rules of Innovation and Conquered the Global Toy Industry*.

That increases the pressure all the more on Lego Dimensions, a sprawling game that cost the same as a blockbuster film to develop and featuring different brands including Doctor Who, Back to the Future and Ghostbusters.

For their $100, players will get a game for Sony's PlayStation, Microsoft's Xbox or Nintendo's Wii, alongside almost 300 Lego pieces used to create a controller, as well as three characters: Batman, Gandalf from *Lord of the Rings* and Wyldstyle from *The Lego Movie*. Additional kits featuring other characters – from the Wicked Witch in *The Wizard of Oz,* through to Scooby Doo and Wonder Woman to Krusty the Clown – will cost $15–$30 and unlock new games levels and include vehicles for game play.

The game works by recognising which characters and vehicles are placed on a controller and making them part of the action, which takes place over 14 levels – one for each brand involved. Typical Lego

▶

flourishes are included, such as an ability to rebuild each vehicle in three different ways.

'I wanted to make a game like this eight years ago. With my own kids, I could see how they would play with Lego: Batman and Gandalf together. When I saw toys to life, I knew this was the mechanism,' says Jon Burton, the founder of British developer TT Games.

The game, which took 160 people three years to develop, is launching in a crowded marketplace. Activision Blizzard's Skylanders game has dominated the toys-to-life category since it launched in 2011, but has been joined by Disney's Infinity – which will feature Star Wars' figures this Christmas – and Nintendo's Amiibo lines.

Liam Callahan, an analyst at market research group NPD, says the toys-to-life sector was worth $710m in the US in the year to the end of August, up 6 per cent on the previous year. He argues that, even though the price is high and there is plenty of competition, Lego Dimensions should be a success thanks to the toymaker's brand and the huge number of other brands and characters involved in the game. 'Our research shows that the main market for these types of games are young males; but with the range of toys for Lego Dimensions, there may be a wider age and gender for main consumer as well as a cross-generational appeal for families,' he adds.

Mr Burton says that the broad pitch is deliberate as he pushed to include levels from Portal, a puzzle video game, and Back to the Future to appeal to adults as well as children. 'There is a bigger market for this toys to life than just six to 12-year-olds,' he adds.

Mr Goodwin is eager to underline that Lego is not betting the company on Dimensions. But he is keenly aware of the importance of the toymaker making a success of its digital offering.

'What is obvious is the digital and physical is something of a distinction we make but children don't . . . From a Lego brand point of view, we continue to be anchored in the physical brick experience. But we are going to explore more ways that you can build strong linkages between the physical and digital worlds,' he says.

Lego took the decision to concentrate on the physical brick when it neared financial collapse in 2004. As part of its recovery under chief executive Jørgen Vig Knudstorp, over-diversification was diagnosed as one of its ills and its video games development arm was sold off.

Mr Burton, who was also an executive producer of *The Lego Movie,* says each company decided to

focus on what they were best at: 'They handle bricks, we handle the digital side.'

Another recent collaboration is Lego Worlds, a game still only in limited beta release that many see as the toymaker's answer to Minecraft. Players can build worlds, buildings and figures using Lego bricks with nearly all the freedom of the physical world, while new ideas are being incorporated according to what Lego's online community suggests.

Mr Goodwin and Mr Burton say there is more to come, especially around making the digital experience more 'real'. The toys-to-life category works by the controller reading a chip in a character's base, meaning that if Batman is placed on Superman's base the machine will still think it is Superman. Similarly, only the exact model or vehicle will be imported into the game, not whatever the player imagines. Mr Goodwin hopes that will change one day.

Mr Robertson says that Lego's great success has been building a range of products and experiences around the physical brick – so that children cannot just play with the products but also watch a television show, go to an event or see a display in a toy shop. Its digital push should be seen in that light, he argues, although he also says Lego could gradually develop into more of a digital company. 'Maybe you and I might be talking in 2020 about what is the core of Lego: is it physical or digital?'

Mr Goodwin dismisses such talk, arguing that if you 'put bricks in front of kids they just love to build'.

Losing strategies: Award-winning games but not sales winners

Success is far from guaranteed for Lego Dimensions as some of the toymaker's previous digital efforts show. Lego Universe, an ambitious and costly attempt to replicate the experience of playing with bricks in a game, developed by dozens of workers, was killed off within months of its launch in 2010.

At about the same time, a single Swedish computer enthusiast working part-time developed Minecraft, which became one of the biggest-selling games of all time and is in Jon Burton's words 'a digital version of Lego'.

John Goodwin says that failure led to Lego realising it needed to be more agile when dealing with digital products than physical ones: 'Other companies put their games out in beta [an early development stage] and constantly reiterate it. That's not part of our DNA. We have a tendency to want to have perfection by the time it gets into consumer hands.'

More recently, Lego Fusion won a string of awards in the US but it was unsuccessful in grabbing children's attention and that too was discontinued. It allowed players to create two-dimensional models with physical bricks that they then imported into the game using a smartphone or tablet camera. 'One product was unusable, one was not fun,' summarises David Robertson, a professor at the Wharton School in Pennsylvania.

Mr Goodwin adds, somewhat ruefully: 'It's not about winning awards, it's about delighting consumers constantly and we weren't able to do that.'

Source: from 'Lego enters a new dimension with its digital strategy', *Financial Times*, 27/09/2015 (Milne, R.).

Discussion questions

1 Evaluate and comment on Lego's market orientation using the market orientation assessment form (see Box 1.1) to support your analysis.

2 Which of the three approaches to marketing presented in this chapter do you think best describes Lego's approach? Why?

3 What marketing principles are in evidence in this case?

CHAPTER 2

STRATEGIC MARKETING PLANNING

> Strategy is the matching of the activities of an organisation to the environment in which it operates and to its own resource capabilities.
>
> **Johnson, Scholes and Whittington (2008)**
>
> Planning is an unnatural process; it is much more fun to do something. The nicest thing about not planning is that failure comes as a complete surprise, rather than being preceded by a period of worry and depression.
>
> **Sir John Harvey Jones, Chairman of Imperial Chemical Industries (ICI) 1982–1987**

Asos founder turns to online homeware

One of the founders of Asos, the fast-growing online fashion retailer, has launched a website focusing on the competitive homewares market.

Quentin Griffiths, who left Asos as it turned its first profit in 2005, started Achica this year along with co-founder Will Cooper and it now has 20,000 members, they say.

The site holds 48-hour sales of sought after homeware brands, including Royal Crown Derby china and Yves Delorme bed linen, at up to 70 per cent off. The UK market for homeware is about £10.7bn ($16.1bn), according to research by Verdict. Mr Griffiths expects that Achica could take up to 5 per cent in the next five years.

He said homeware was lagging behind fashion because initially people had been cautious about making high-ticket purchases on the Internet. Online homeware is already a competitive market with stores such as John Lewis and Marks and Spencer seeing strong sales. Fashion retailers H&M and Zara have also launched homeware businesses online.

Mr Griffiths says an advantage to selling homeware brands online is that the company avoids paying storage costs as it only stores products for the brief period before they are sent to a consumer. Achica would not hold stock that has not already been sold.

Unlike many sites that focus on one-off sales, the retailer does not just sell last season's stock.

Retailers anticipate pressure on disposable income from the government's harsh austerity measures may help discount sale sites. In western Europe, Forrester Research expects 11 per cent growth rate for online retail sales during the next five years, going from $93bn in 2009 to $156bn (£62bn to £104bn) in 2014.

Source: from 'Asos founder turns to online homeware', *Financial Times*, 28/06/2010 (Kuchler, H.).

Discussion questions

1 Why did Quentin Griffiths enter the competitive homewares market?

2 How is he trying to compete?

Introduction

The essence of developing a marketing strategy for any organisation is to ensure that its capabilities are matched to the market environment in which it operates, not just for today but into the foreseeable future. For a commercial organisation this means ensuring that its resources and capabilities match the needs and requirements of the competitive markets in which it operates. For a not-for-profit organisation, such as a charity or a public utility, it means achieving a fit between its abilities to serve and the requirements of the publics or causes it is seeking to serve. At the heart of strategy lies a need to assess critically both the organisation's resource profile (often referred to as its strengths and weaknesses) and the environment it faces (its opportunities and threats).

Strategic planning attempts to answer three basic questions:

1 What is the business doing now?
2 What is happening in the environment?
3 What should the business be doing?

Strategy is concerned primarily with effectiveness (doing the right things) rather than efficiency (doing what you do well). The vast bulk of management time is, of necessity, concerned with day-to-day operations management. A time audit for even senior management will often reveal a disproportionate amount of time spent on routine daily tasks, with the more difficult and demanding task of planning further into the future relegated to a weekend or week-long conference or 'retreat' once a year. In many successful companies however, thinking strategically, or sitting back from the present concerns of improving what you do now and questioning what it is you are doing, is a constant process.

Fundamental to strategic thinking is the concept of 'strategic fit', as exemplified in the quote at the start of this chapter from Johnson, Scholes and Whittington (2008) and shown diagrammatically in Figure 2.1. For any strategy to be effective it needs to be well tuned both to the needs and requirements of customers (the market conditions in which it is implemented) and to the resources and capabilities of the organisation seeking to implement it. No matter how wonderfully crafted and articulated the strategy, if it is not focused on meeting the needs of customers, it is doomed to failure. Similarly, if the organisational resources necessary for its implementation are not available, or cannot be acquired, success will be illusive.

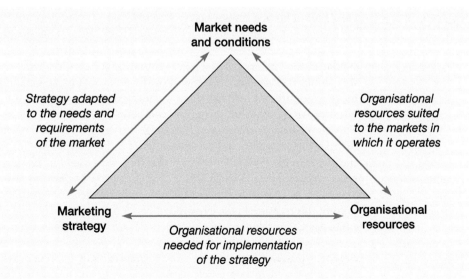

Figure 2.1
Strategic fit

As with the adoption of a marketing philosophy throughout the organisation, the adoption of strategic thinking goes beyond the brief of marketing management alone. All senior executives in the company or organisation have a responsibility for developing the strategic profile of the company and giving it a strategic focus. Strategic planning and strategic marketing planning share many activities, although strategic planning has more breadth and covers all business activities. A market orientation must permeate the whole of an organisation, but the strategic marketing plan is just one of several functional plans that feed into the overall strategic plan of a company. Marketing management however, with its specific responsibility for managing the interface between the organisation and its environment (both customers and competitors), has an increasingly important role to play in overall strategy development.

Marketing strategy should be set in the context of overall corporate strategy. Once the over-all direction of the organisation has been decided, with appropriate input from all relevant stakeholders, the marketing strategy will need to be aligned to ensure that direction is achieved.

2.1 Defining the business purpose or mission

For many organisations a useful starting point in strategy formulation is to define its mission or purpose. Tim Smit, founder and chief executive of the Eden Project in Cornwall, set out to build the biggest global eco-brand and to change the way people think about themselves and their relationship with the planet on which they live. The mission was stated as: 'to promote the understanding and responsible management of the vital relationship between plants, people and resources leading to a sustainable future for all'. That guiding principle helped secure £40 million of UK lottery funding, together with £43 million of private investment to create a complex of greenhouse domes spanning 37 acres in a disused clay pit at St Austell. As importantly, it gave the people working on the project a worthwhile set of objectives to strive for and be committed to. Visitor numbers have been huge (exceeding 1 million in the first four months), despite the relatively inconvenient location, and the Eden brand is now set to expand into other parts of the world (*The Guardian,* 18 March 2002).

Defining the business purpose or mission requires the company to ask the fundamental questions first posed by Levitt over half a century ago (see Levitt, 1960):

- What business are we in?
- What business do we want to be in?

Many years ago, so marketing folklore has it, a new managing director took over at Parker Pens. One of his first actions was to assemble the board of directors, stand before them holding the top of the range Parker of the day and ask, 'Who is our greatest competitor?'

The first answer to emerge from the board was Shaeffer. Shaeffer produced a pen very similar to the Parker. It had a good reputation for quality, had a similar stylish finish and was similarly priced at the top end of the market. The new managing director was not, however, impressed with this answer. 'We certainly compete to some extent with Shaeffer, but they are by no means our major competitor.'

A newer member of the board then suggested that the major competitor might be Biro-Swan, the manufacturers and marketers of a range of ballpoint pens. While these retailed considerably cheaper than the Parker he reasoned that they were used for the same purpose (writing) and hence competed directly with Parker. The business definition was now changing from 'quality fountain pens' to 'writing implements' and under this definition pencils could also be considered as competitors, as could the more recent developments in the market of fibre tip pens and rollerball pens. 'Your thinking is getting better,' said the MD, 'but you're still not there.'

Another board member then suggested that perhaps the major competitor was the telephone, which had been gaining more widespread use in recent years. Under this view of the market they were in 'communications' and competing with other forms of communication including the written word (perhaps competing here with typewriters and more recently word processors) and other (verbal) means of communication. 'More creative thinking,' said the MD, 'but you still haven't identified the main competitor.'

Eventually the MD gave his view of the major competitor. To an astonished board he announced, 'Our major competitor is the Ronson cigarette lighter!' When asked to explain his reasoning he defined the market that the company was in as the 'quality gift market'. Analysis of sales of Parker pens showed that the majority of purchases were made by individuals buying them as gifts for other people. When they considered what to buy, often a major alternative was a quality cigarette lighter and hence the definition of the market (example courtesy of Graham Kenwright).

This definition has widespread implications for the marketing of the product. Packaging assumes a more important role, as does the development and maintenance of a superior quality image. Price is perhaps less important than might have been thought under alternative market definitions. Distribution (through the outlets where potential customers buy gifts) also becomes more important.

This example serves to illustrate how asking a basic question such as 'Who is our major competitor?' or 'What market are we in?' can affect the whole of the strategic direction of the company.

2.1.1 Mission formulation and statement

Formulating the mission into a brief and concise statement that can be communicated across the organisation can help engender a sense of common purpose and also provide guidelines for how decisions will be made and resource allocations prioritised in the future. Poorly constructed statements, however, especially those offering nothing more than 'motherhood and apple pie', can cause more damage than good by creating derision among employees, managers and even customers.

Hooley *et al.* (1992) discuss the elements that go to make up an effective statement of mission. These are shown in Figure 2.2. An effective mission statement needs to spell out the following:

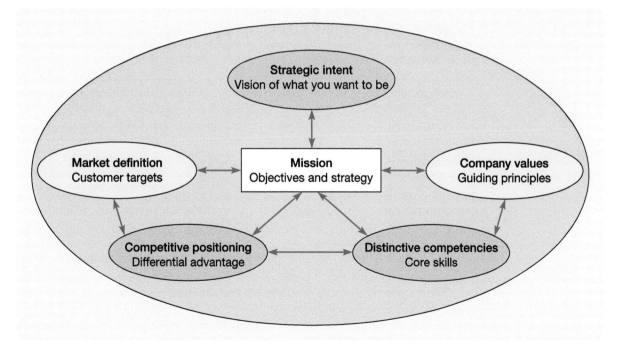

Figure 2.2 Components of mission

1 The **strategic intent** (see Hamel and Prahalad, 1989), or vision of where the organisation wants to be in the foreseeable future. Hamel and Prahalad cite examples of strategic intent for Komatsu (earthmoving equipment manufacturers) as being to 'encircle Caterpillar' and for the American Apollo space programme as 'landing a man on the moon ahead of the Soviets'. Vision need not be as competitive as these examples. The vision of an organisation such as a university might be enshrined in the achievement of a set of worthy social goals. For a charity the vision may be to improve the quality of life for particular groups of people or animals.

2 The **values of the organisation** should be spelt out to set the ethical and moral tone to guide operations. Mars (confectionery) articulates five 'principles' that guide the actions and decision making of their employees. These are:

Quality. The consumer is our boss, quality is our work and value for money is our goal.
Responsibility. As individuals, we demand total responsibility from ourselves; as
   Associates, we support the responsibilities of others.
Mutuality. A mutual benefit is a shared benefit; a shared benefit will endure.
Efficiency. We use resources to the full, waste nothing and do only what we can do best.
Freedom. We need freedom to shape our future; we need profit to remain free.

Source: Mars website, **http://www.mars.com/global/about-mars/the-five-principles-of-mars.aspx,** accessed September 2014.

Clearly, once value statements or, as in the example above, statements of organisational principles are articulated, it is important that they are adhered to. If not, then there is little point in spending time and effort in producing them. Additionally, certain stakeholders may become cynical about the underlying business ethos driving an organisation that might do this.

Similarly, assertions about concern for the environment in mission statements can sound hollow if not followed with deeds and actions.

3 The **distinctive competencies of the organisation** should be articulated clearly, stating what differentiates the organisation from others of its kind – what its distinctive essence is. This is a difficult but necessary thing for many organisations to articulate. It seeks to spell out the individuality of the organisation, in essence why it exists as a separate entity and what is special about it.

4 **Market definition,** in terms of major customer targets that the organisation seeks to serve and the functions or needs of those customers that will be served. The insurance company Sheila's Wheels has clearly focused on the needs of a well-defined market target, as reflected in its brand name and its business purpose: 'a car insurance company designed for the female driver' (**www.sheilaswheels.com**). Many successful entrepreneurs such as Richard Branson of Virgin have built their businesses around a clear definition of customer targets and their needs, seeking to serve them across many different product fields.

5 Finally, the mission should spell out where the organisation is, or intends to be, **positioned** in the marketplace. Its uniqueness and distinctiveness. This is the result of bringing together market definition and distinctive skills and competencies.

Business definitions that are too narrow in scope are dangerous – they should include definition of both target market and function served. The key to definition by function is not to be blinded by the company's perception of the function but to allow the customer view to come through.

In a classic paper from over half a century ago that has stood the test of time, Ted Levitt (1960) provided many examples of companies adopting a myopic view in defining their businesses. The railroads believed they were in the railway business, not transportation, and failed to take note of alternative means of transport. The oil industry believed they were in the business of producing oil, not in the business of producing and marketing energy. In defining the business it is necessary to understand the total product or service customers are buying and what benefits it delivers, and avoid the trap of concentrating too much on the physical features offered.

The second question posed at the start of this section – What business do we want to be in? – is often more difficult to answer. It requires a thorough analysis of the options open to the organisation and an understanding of how the world in general, and the company's markets in particular, are changing.

2.2   The marketing strategy process

Once the purpose of the organisation has been defined the marketing strategy can be crafted to help achieve that purpose. We can view the development of marketing strategy at three main levels: the establishment of a core strategy, the creation of the company's competitive positioning, and the implementation of the strategy (see Figure 2.3).

The establishment of an effective marketing strategy starts with a detailed, and creative, assessment both of the company's capabilities – its strengths and weaknesses relative to the competition – and the opportunities and threats posed by the environment. On the basis of this analysis the core strategy of the company will be selected, identifying marketing objectives and the broad focus for achieving them.

At the next level, market targets (both customers and competitors) are selected and/ or identified. At the same time the company's differential advantage, or competitive edge, in serving the customer targets better than the competition is defined. Taken together the identification of targets and the definition of differential advantage constitute the creation of the competitive positioning of the organisation and its offerings.

At the implementation level a marketing organisation capable of putting the strategy into practice must be created. The design of the marketing organisation can be crucial to the success of the strategy. Implementation is also concerned with establishing a mix of products, price, promotion and distribution that can convey both the positioning and the

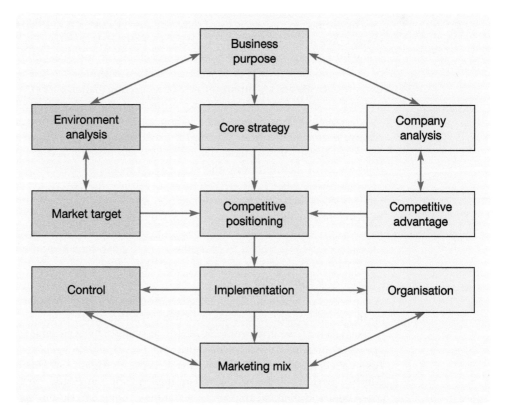

Figure 2.3
The marketing
strategy process

products and services themselves to the target market. Finally, methods of control must be designed to ensure that the strategy implementation is successful. Control concerns both the efficiency with which the strategy is put into operation and the ultimate effectiveness of that strategy. Each of the three main levels of strategy is now considered in more detail.

2.3   Establishing the core strategy

The core strategy is both a statement of the company's objectives and the broad strategies it will use to achieve them. To establish the core strategy requires a detailed analysis of the resources available and the market in which the organisation will operate, both within the context of achieving the overall business purpose or mission.

2.3.1 Analysis of organisational resources

Any organisation could create a long list of the resources it has at its disposal. Not all of those resources, however, will be equally useful in crafting or implementing a marketing strategy. Similarly, if it is sufficiently self-critical, any organisation could list many weaknesses, but not all of those will be fatal. In defining the core strategy, organisations attempt to define the distinctive resources (assets and capabilities) that serve to define the organisation. This helps to set the bounds on what options are open to the organisation and to identify where its strengths can be utilised to the full, while minimising vulnerability to its weaknesses. Core competencies or core skills may result from any aspect of the operation. They may stem from the skills of the workforce in assembling the product effectively or efficiently, from the skills of management in marketing or financial planning, or from the skills of the R&D department in initiating new product ideas or creating new products on the basis of customer research. What is important from a marketing strategy perspective, however, is whether they can be utilised in the marketplace to provide superior customer value.

The distinctive competencies of the company may lie in its marketing assets of image and market presence or its distribution network or after-sales service. The crucial issue in identifying distinctive competence is that it be something exploitable in the marketplace. Distinctive technological skills in producing a product are of little value if there is no demand for that product. Hence an important role of marketing management is to assess the potential distinctive competencies of the organisation in the light of exploitability in the market.

The counterbalance to distinctive competencies or exploitable strengths, are weaknesses relative to the competition. Where, for example, competitors have a more favourable or protected supply of raw materials, or a stronger customer loyalty, the company must be fully aware of its limitations and generate strategies to overcome, or circumvent, them. Structural weaknesses, those inherent in the firm's operations, brought about by its very mode of doing business, may be difficult or even impossible to eliminate. Strategies should be developed to shift competition away from these factors, to make them less important to competitive success. Other weaknesses may be more easily avoided once they have been identified, or even changed to strengths by exploiting them in a different way.

The product portfolio

A key aspect of understanding an organisation's resources is to undertake a portfolio analysis of the various offerings it has available on the market.

Being 'one or two in all we do' is the driving philosophy of General Electric (GE), an American conglomerate whose activities range from power stations to electric light bulbs. The businesses of GE are amazingly diverse. One of its most successful subsidiaries is market leader in America for electric light bulbs, a mature, high-volume, low-priced commodity. Other divisions make domestic electrical appliances of all types, another makes medical equipment including body scanners, and one of the most successful parts of the company is market leader in the military and commercial aero engine markets. It is clear that the different businesses within the company are operating in different markets, with different opportunities and threats, and utilising different corporate skills and resources. It is therefore important to ensure that appropriate objectives and strategies are formulated for each business unit and that these objectives and strategies support each other. The process of balancing the activities across this variety of business units involves portfolio planning, which is the subject of this chapter.

Consider, for example, the challenge for Virgin of managing a group of businesses spanning airlines and rail travel, music and cinemas, financial services, drinks, clothing and cosmetics, and a variety of smaller enterprises. We shall see that this is an example of growth by collaboration and of portfolio management, with both successes and failures. The sale, for example, of Virgin Megastores provided the capital for most of the subsequent investments in new areas to exploit the Virgin brand.

Portfolio analysis is the foundation for making important choices – for investment and for strategic direction. These examples underline the importance of portfolio issues and the central role of marketing variables, as opposed to purely financial criteria, in making portfolio choices.

More than four decades ago Drucker (1973) identified seven types of businesses which still have resonance today:

1 **Today's breadwinners** – the products and services that are earning healthy profits and contributing positively to both cash flow and profits.
2 **Tomorrow's breadwinners** – investments in the company's future. Products and services that may not yet be making a strong financial contribution to the company, but that are in growth or otherwise attractive markets and are expected to take over the breadwinning role in the future, when today's breadwinners eventually fade.
3 **Yesterday's breadwinners** – the products and services that have supported the company in the past, but are not now contributing significantly to cash flow or to profits. Many companies have a predominance of businesses of this type, indicating that they have been slow to invest in future developments.
4 **Developments** – the products and services recently developed that may have some future, but where greater investment is needed to achieve that future.
5 **Sleepers** – the products and services that have been around for some time, but have so far failed to establish themselves in their markets or, indeed, their expected markets have failed to materialise. These are allowed to remain in the portfolio in the hope that one day they will take off.
6 **Investments in managerial ego** – the products and services that have strong product champions among influential managers, but for which there is little proven demand in the marketplace. The company, because of the involvement of powerful managers, continues to put resources into these products in the hope of their eventually coming good.
7 **Failures** – the products and services that have failed to play a significant role in the company's portfolio and have no realistic chance of doing so. These are kept on the company's books largely through inertia. It is easier to do so than admit defeat and withdraw or divest them.

The product life cycle (or death cycle) provides a link between the businesses identified by Drucker (see Figure 2.4). As they stand, developments, sleepers or ego trips contribute little to the company, but it is hoped that they may one day do so. The markets they are in may be highly attractive but, because of underinvestment, the company has little ability to serve them. If left alone as they are, with no extra investment being made in them, the businesses will follow the death cycle and become failures.

Strategically, a company faces a dilemma with these businesses. If left alone they are unlikely to succeed, so a choice has to be made between investing in them, or getting out. In even the largest companies it is impossible to pursue all attractive markets, so the first portfolio decision is one of double or quits. If the choice is to invest, then the aim is to build the

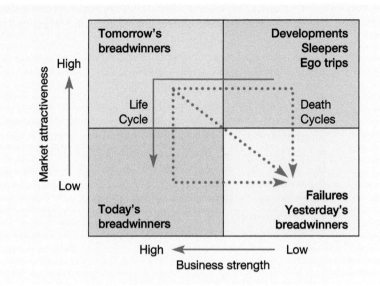

Figure 2.4
Product types in
the portfolio

business until it is strong enough to become one of tomorrow's breadwinners. This usually means achieving some degree of market dominance in a growth sector. If successfully managed, the product will mature to become one of today's breadwinners and, as it ages, one of yesterday's. As with all things, the difficulty in the portfolio is not starting ventures, but knowing when to kill them and when to concentrate resources where success can be achieved.

Portfolio planning

Any diversified organisation needs to find methods for assessing the balance of businesses in its portfolio and to help guide resource allocation between them. A number of portfolio planning models have been developed over the past 40 years to facilitate this process. The earliest and most basic model was the Growth-Share Matrix, developed by the Boston Consulting Group. More sophisticated models have been developed by consultants Arthur D. Little and McKinsey, as well as by commercial companies such as Shell and General Electric. All, however, share a number of key objectives (Grant, 1995):

1 Development of business strategies and allocation of resources (both financial and managerial). By assessing the position of a business in its industry, together with the prospects for that industry over the medium to long term, investment priorities can be set for individual businesses. Those businesses that are strong in attractive markets are likely to be self-sustaining financially. They will, however, require attentive management to ensure they continue to achieve their potential. Hold or build strategies will typically be indicated. Weak businesses in attractive markets may require further investment to build a position for the future. Products in declining sectors may be less deserving of resource allocation unless turnaround strategies are likely to reverse market trends. In declining markets, products are often managed for cash flow to enable resources to be reallocated to areas of the portfolio with more potential.

2 Analysing portfolio balance. In addition to suggesting strategies for individual businesses, portfolio analysis assists assessment of the overall portfolio balance in terms of cash flow, future prospects and risk (see Figure 2.5). Cash flow balance is achieved where investments in businesses with potential are met through surpluses from current or past breadwinners. The extent to which the cash flow is out of balance suggests opportunities for expansion or acquisition (in the mid-1990s Microsoft was said to be sitting on a cash mountain of around $7 billion and looking for profitable new, synergistic businesses in which to invest) or the need to raise capital from external investors (see Figures 2.6 and 2.7). A crucial element of portfolio planning is to help assess the future prospects

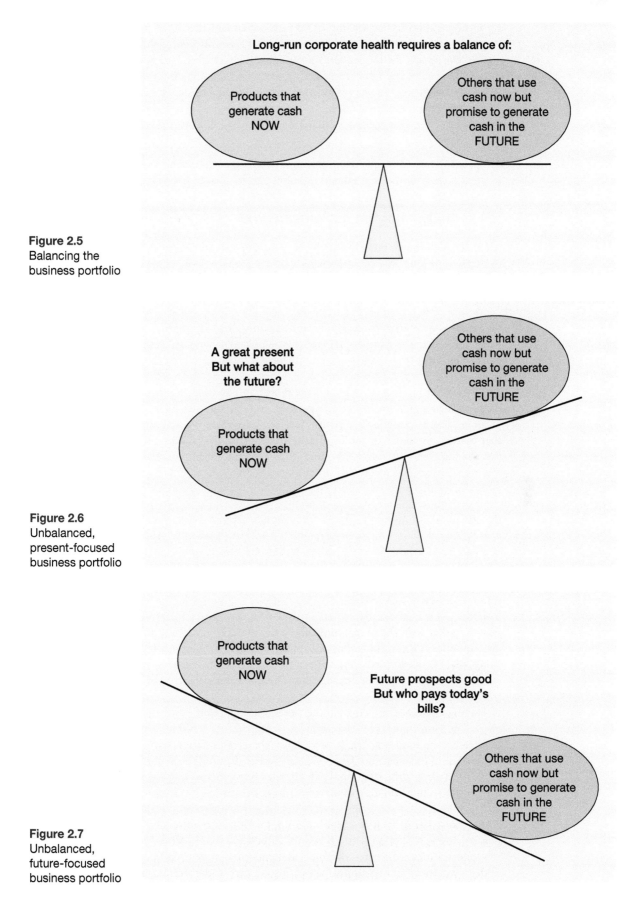

Figure 2.5
Balancing the
business portfolio

Figure 2.6
Unbalanced,
present-focused
business portfolio

Figure 2.7
Unbalanced,
future-focused
business portfolio

of the organisation as a whole. Too heavy a dependence in the portfolio on yesterday's products may indicate a healthy current cash flow, but unless that is invested in tomorrow's products the longer-term future may be in doubt. Too many future investments without a solid enough current cash generation may suggest an overstretched portfolio. Finally, assessing the risks associated with individual businesses enables a firm to spread its overall risk, ensuring not all its ventures are high risk but allowing some more risky ventures to be balanced by perhaps less rewarding but more predictable activities.

Strengths and weaknesses can only be determined effectively through a systematic and comprehensive audit of the firm's resources and their utilisation relative to the competition. Chapter 6 describes in more detail how this can be accomplished.

2.3.2 Analysis of the markets served

An analysis of the markets in which the company operates, or wishes to operate, can serve to throw into focus the opportunities and threats facing the company. Those opportunities and threats stem from two main areas: the customers (both current and potential) and competitors (again both current and potential).

Most markets are segmented in one way or another. They consist of heterogeneous customers, or customers with varying needs and wants. Asking 'How is the market segmented?' can provide valuable insights into customer requirements and help in focusing on specific market targets.

In computers, for example, there are several ways in which the total market could be segmented. A simple, product-based segmentation is between mainframe, minicomputers and PCs. IBM has long dominated the mainframe market. Recognising the difficulties in tackling such a giant head-on, competitors sensibly focused their efforts on the minicomputer market, for smaller users with different requirements, and established dominance of that market. Similarly in the PC market Apple was very successful in leading the market prior to the dominance of 'IBM-compatible' machines using successive generations of Intel microprocessors and Microsoft operating systems.

Canon is also in the computer market but has taken a different tack. It recognised that computer users do not just need computers. They also need peripheral devices to enable them to use the computer to the best advantage. Canon carved a strong niche in the market as suppliers of inkjet colour printers while Hewlett-Packard focuses on laser printers.

Even within these broad product-based definitions of the market, however, further segmentation exists. Toshiba and Compaq (now HP) have focused on portable, laptop computers, while Sony has started the trend of 'living room entertainment computers' and smart TVs (**www.sony.co.uk**).

In the 1990s Sega, Nintendo and Sony were hugely successful in developing the computer games market with cheap machines and addictive software. Late entrant Sony became the leader with its PlayStations. For some time the market had been forecast to decline as the games and PC markets converge due to the increased power, availability and lower cost of Pentium-powered PCs. The market has remained remarkably resilient, however, and has continued to grow.

Having examined the current and potential segmentation of the market, the next step in assessing alternatives is to search for untapped, or under-tapped, opportunities in the market. In the food market, for example, changes in eating habits are currently taking place. Two of the most significant are the increased emphasis on convenience foods and the trend towards healthier eating. Both changes have opened up new opportunities to those companies willing and able to take advantage of them.

Van den Bergh, for example, was quick to spot the potential for margarine spreads that do not cause harmful cholesterol build-up. Its Flora pro-activ, and similar products from Benecol, are spreads that actually reduce cholesterol, while others add to it.

Opportunities are created through fundamental changes taking place (as with increased health awareness and its impact on eating habits) in the market or through competitor inability to serve existing needs. Apple's initial success in the microcomputer market was in part due to the fact that IBM originally chose not to enter the market, while Compaq and Dell's success rested on IBM's neglect of changing distribution channels. Market gaps can exist because companies cannot fill them (they do not have the skills and competencies to do so) or they choose not to fill them for one reason or another.

Nearly 40 years ago Abell (1978) discussed the importance of timing in recognising and capitalising on opportunities. His concept of 'strategic windows' is as relevant today as it was then. It focuses attention on the fact that there are only limited periods during which the fit between the requirements of the market and the capabilities of the firm is at an optimum. Investment should be timed to coincide with periods when such strategic windows are open, and conversely disinvestment should be considered once a good fit has been eroded. A good deal of the success of Japanese companies in world markets during the last two decades of the twentieth century was attributed to an ability to time their entry such that their competencies and the market requirements were closely in tune.

In addition to considering the opportunities open to the organisation it is important to examine the threats facing it. These stem from two main sources – a changing marketplace that the firm is not aware of or capable of keeping up with, or competitive activity designed to change the balance of power within the market.

A changing world requires constant intelligence-gathering on the part of the organisation to ensure that it can keep abreast of customer requirements. Keeping up with technological developments can be particularly important in many markets. The pocket calculator destroyed the slide rule market in the early 1970s and the digital watch caused severe (if temporary) problems for Swiss watch manufacturers in the mid-1970s; now music downloads and MP3 players are leading to the demise of the compact disc. Changes also occur in customer tastes. Fashions come and go (many of them encouraged by marketers), but in markets where fashion is important keeping up is crucial. Chapter 4 deals in more detail with customer analysis.

The second major type of threat an organisation may face is from its competition. Increasing competition, both from domestic and international sources, is the name of the game in most markets. As competitors become more sophisticated in seeking out market opportunities and designing marketing programmes to exploit them, so the company itself needs to improve its marketing activities. In the United Kingdom many industries have failed or have been unable to respond adequately to increased international competition and have suffered the consequences. It is telling, for example, that in the highly competitive laptop computer market the first sub-three-pound lightweight computers – demanded by business users weary of carrying heavier machines around the world – did not come from existing PC manufacturers, but from Sony leveraging their core competence of making things smaller. In the more sophisticated marketing companies rigorous competitor analysis commands almost as much time as customer and self-evaluation. Substantial effort is geared to identifying competitors' strengths and weaknesses and their likely strategies (see Chapter 5).

2.3.3 SWOT analysis

The above analysis of organisational strengths and weaknesses (essentially an internal focus) can be brought together with the analysis of the market (an external focus) to create a SWOT (strengths, weaknesses, opportunities and threats) analysis (see Figure 2.8).

The purpose of SWOT is twofold. First, it seeks to identify the most significant factors, both internal and external, affecting the organisation and its markets. It provides a quick, executive summary of the key issues. Second, however, by looking at where strengths and weaknesses align with opportunities and threats it can help strategy formulation (see Figure 2.9). The organisation can begin to see where its strengths might be best deployed, both offensively and defensively, as well as where its weaknesses leave it vulnerable to market change or competitor action.

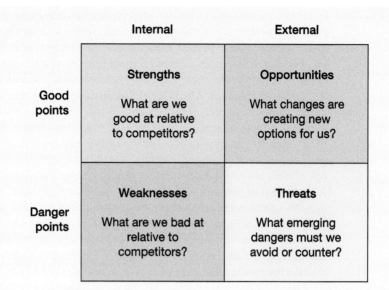

Figure 2.8
SWOT analysis

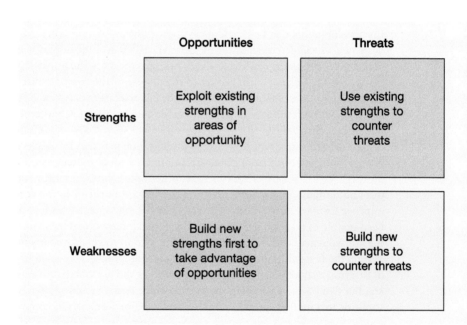

Figure 2.9
SWOT strategic
implications

2.3.4 Core strategy

On the basis of the above analysis the company seeks to define the key factors for success (KFS, sometimes termed 'critical success factors') in its particular markets. Key factors for success in the industry are those factors that are crucial to doing business. The KFS are identified through examining the differences between winners and losers, or leaders and also-rans in the industry. They often represent the factors where the greatest leverage can be exerted, i.e. where the most effect can be obtained for a given amount of effort.

In the grocery industry, for example, the KFS can centre on the relationships built up between the manufacturer and the retailer. The power of the major multiples (less than half a dozen major food retail chains now account for around 80 per cent of food sales in the United Kingdom) is such that if a new food product does not obtain distribution through the major outlets a substantial sector of the potential market is denied.

In commodity markets the KFS often lie in production process efficiency, enabling costs to be kept down, where pricing is considered the only real means of product differentiation.

A further consideration when setting the core strategy for a multi-product or multi-divisional company is how the various corporate activities add up, i.e. the role in the company's overall business portfolio (see Chapter 6) of each activity.

Having identified corporate capabilities, market opportunities and threats, the key factors for success in the industry in which the firm operates and the role of the particular product or business in the company's overall portfolio, the company sets its marketing objectives. The objectives should be both long and short term. Long-term objectives indicate the future overall destination of the company: its long-term goals. To achieve those long-term goals, however, it is usually necessary to translate them into shorter-term objectives, a series of which will add up to the longer-term goals. Long-term objectives are often set in terms of profit or market domination for a firm operating in the commercial sector. Non-profit-making organisations, too, set long- and short-term goals. The long-term goal of Greenpeace, for example, is to save the world's environment. Shorter-term goals in the mid-2000s centred on single, high-profile campaigns, such as making Apple computers greener, to global issues, such as stopping world climate change.

Often short-term and long-term goals can become confused, and there is always the danger that setting them in isolation can result in a situation where the attainment of the short-term goals does nothing to further the long-term objectives and may, in some instances, hinder them. For example, a commercial company setting long-term market domination goals will often find short-term profit maximisation at odds with this. Many of the managers, however, will be judged on yearly, not long-term, performance, and hence will be more likely to follow short-term profit objectives at the expense of building a stronger market position (see the discussion in Chapter 1 on stakeholder motivations).

The core strategy of the organisation is a statement of how it intends to achieve its objectives. If, for example, the long-term objective is to be market leader in market X, with a share of market at least twice that of the nearest competitors, the core strategy may centre on using superior technology to achieve this, or it may centre on lower prices, or better service or quality. The core strategy will take advantage of the firm's core competencies and bring them to bear wherever possible on the KFS to achieve the corporate objectives of the company.

The core strategy to be pursued may vary at different stages of the product or service's life cycle. Figure 2.10 shows alternative ways in which a company may go about improving the performance of its products or services.

A basic choice is made between attempting to increase sales or improve the level of profitability achieved from existing sales (or even reduced sales in a declining market). When the objectives are to increase sales, again two fundamental approaches may be taken: to expand the total market (most easily, though not exclusively, achieved during the early growth stages of the life cycle) or to increase share of the existing market (most often pursued during the late growth/maturity phases).

Expand the market

Market expansion can be achieved through attraction of new users to the product or service, identifying new uses for the product or developing new products and services to stimulate the market. New users can be found through geographical expansion of the company's operations (both domestically and internationally). Asda (now owned by Walmart), for example, pursued new customers for its grocery products in its move south from the Yorkshire home base while Sainsbury's attacked new markets in its march north from the south-east. Also, Aldi and Lidl have been very successful in moving into the UK from their European base. Alternatively, new segments with an existing or latent need for the product may be identifiable. Repositioning Lucozade as a high-energy drink found a new segment for a product once sold exclusively to parents of sick children.

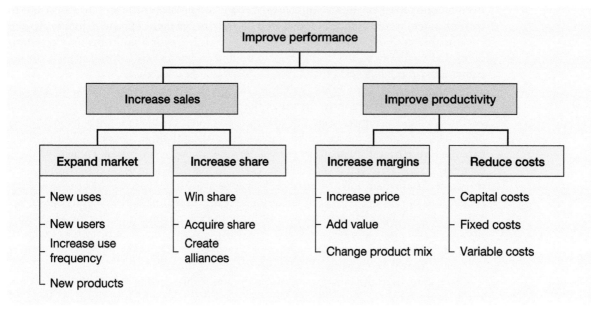

Figure 2.10 Strategic focus

The spectacular growth of the 'no-frills' airlines, easyJet and Ryanair, is founded not simply on taking market share but on growing the market – i.e. 'more people fly more often'. Ryanair, in particular, with its carefully chosen routes where it is the only flyer, has on occasion experienced fourfold traffic growth.

Land Rover, the hugely successful manufacturer of the Freelander, Discovery and Range Rover brands, aimed to increase the demand for 4 × 4 vehicles by encouraging drivers of other types of car to switch. It first identified car drivers who were keen on adventure through leaflets and direct mail, and this was followed up by a campaign of telemarketing, direct mail and dealer contact, offering extended test drives without the dealer present. In 12 months the campaign added 80,000 high-quality prospects to the database, and generated 10,000 test drives of which 28 per cent were converted into sales. The company estimates that its investment of just under £1 million has resulted in £100 million worth of extra sales.

For some products it may be possible to identify new uses. An example is the use of the condom (largely abandoned as a means of contraceptive for the more popular pill and IUD in the 1960s and 1970s) as a defence against contracting HIV-AIDS. In household cleaners Flash was originally marketed as a product for cleaning floors, but now is also promoted as an all-purpose product for cleaning baths and basins.

Increase share

Increasing market share, especially in mature markets, usually comes at the expense of existing competition. The main routes to increasing share include: winning competitors' customers; merging with (or acquiring) the competitors; or entering into strategic alliances with competitors, suppliers and/or distributors. Winning competitors' customers requires that the company serves them better than the competition. This may come about through identification of competitor weaknesses, or through better exploitation of the company's own strengths and competencies. Each of the elements of the marketing mix – products, price, promotion and distribution – could be used to offer the customer added value, or something extra, to induce switching.

Increasing usage rate may be a viable approach to expanding the market for some products. For example, breakfast cereals are now being promoted as healthy, any time of day snacks or, even, slimming aids (such as Kellogg's Special K). Also, a significant trend during the recent global economic crisis was for organisations to offer loyalty schemes for customers in order to increase purchase frequency, share of 'purse' and customer retention.

Improving profitability

With existing levels, or even reduced levels, of sales, profitability can be improved through improving margins. This is usually achieved through increasing price, reducing costs, or both. In the multi-product firm it may also be possible through weeding of the product line, removing poorly performing products and concentrating effort on the more financially viable. The longer-term positioning implications of this weeding should, however, be carefully considered prior to wielding the axe. It may be, for example, that maintenance of seemingly unprofitable lines is essential to allow the company to continue to operate in the market as a whole or its own specifically chosen niches of that market. They may be viewed as the ground stakes in the strategic game essential to reserve a seat at the competitive table.

2.4   Creation of the competitive positioning

The competitive positioning of the company is a statement of market targets, i.e. where the company will compete, and differential advantage, or how the company will compete. The positioning is developed to achieve the objectives laid down under the core strategy. For a company whose objective is to gain market share and the broad approach to that is to win competitors' customers, for example, the competitive positioning will be a statement of exactly how and where in the market that will be achieved.

2.4.1 Market targets

While the discussion of core strategy required an analysis of customers and competitors to identify potential opportunities and threats, competitive positioning selects those targets most suited to utilising the company's strengths and minimising vulnerability due to weaknesses.

A number of factors should be considered in choosing a market target. Broadly, they fall into two categories: assessing market attractiveness and evaluating the company's current or potential strengths in serving that market (see Porter, 1987).

Market attractiveness is made up of many, often conflicting, factors, and it is important that a sensible, rounded and structured review is undertaken. Other things being equal, however, a market will generally be more attractive if the following hold:

It is large.
It is growing.
Contribution margins are high.
Competitive intensity and rivalry are low (and the current incumbents do not provide high levels of satisfaction)
There are high entry and low exit barriers.
The market is not vulnerable to uncontrollable events.

Markets that possess all these features do not exist for long, if at all. They are, almost by definition, bound to attract high levels of competition and hence become less attractive to other entrants over time. For small- or medium-sized companies small and/or static markets, which do not attract more powerful competitors, may be more appealing. In a market where high entry barriers (such as proprietary technology, high switching costs, etc.) can be erected the company will be better able to defend its position against competitive attack (see Chapter 10).

All markets are vulnerable to some extent to external, uncontrollable factors such as general economic conditions, government legislation or political change. Some markets, however, are more vulnerable than others. This is especially true when selecting among international market alternatives. In the international context one way UK companies assess vulnerability to external political events is through the Department for Business, Innovation and Skills' Export Credit Guarantee Department. They state their responsibilities as follows:

> We work closely with exporters, banks, buyers and project sponsors and have 90 years' experience of supporting exports to, and investments in, markets across the world. We do this principally by providing loans to buyers of UK goods and services and guarantees, insurance and reinsurance against loss, taking into account the government's international policies. We:
>
> - insure UK exporters against non-payment by their overseas buyers
> - help overseas buyers to purchase goods and services from UK exporters by guaranteeing or funding bank loans to finance the purchases
> - share credit risks with banks to help exporters raise tender and contract bonds, in accessing pre- and post-shipment working capital finance and in securing confirmations of letters of credit
> - insure UK investors in overseas markets against political risks.
>
> *Source*: Gov.uk website, **https://www.gov.uk/government/organisations/uk-export-finance/about**, accessed 2014, September.

Under the scheme advice about the risks involved in entering a particular market is freely available and insurance against default in payments is accessible.

Domestically, the company must weigh the power of various pressure groups in determining market vulnerability. The company's strengths and potential strengths in serving a particular market must be considered relative to customer requirements and to competitor strengths. Other things being equal, the company's existing strength in a market will be greater where (relative to the competition) the following hold:

It commands a high market share.
It is growing faster than the market.
It has unique and valued products or services.
It has superior quality products.
It has better margins.
It has exploitable marketing assets.
It can achieve production and marketing efficiencies.
It has protected technological leadership.

As with assessing market attractiveness, it is unlikely that in any market a particular company will enjoy all the above favourable characteristics. In any situation the management will have to assess the relative importance of each aspect of strength in evaluating overall strength in serving that market (target market selection is covered in more detail in Chapter 9).

Having selected the market target or targets on the basis of market attractiveness and current, or potential, business strength in serving the market, the company creates its differential advantage, or competitive edge, in serving the market.

2.4.2 Differential advantage

A differential advantage can be created out of any of the company's strengths, or distinctive competencies relative to the competition. The essential factors in choosing how to create the advantage are that it must be on a basis of value to the customer (e.g. lower prices, superior quality and better service) and should be using a skill of the company that competitors will find hard to copy.

Porter (1980) argues that competitive advantage can be created in two main (though not exclusive) ways: through cost leadership or differentiation (see Figure 2.11).

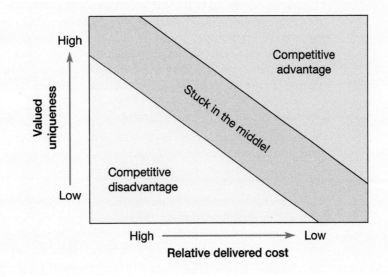

Figure 2.11
Routes to
competitive
advantage

Cost leadership

The first type of advantage involves pursuing a cost leadership position in the industry. Under this strategy the company seeks to obtain a cost structure, significantly below that of competitors while retaining products on the market that are in close proximity to competitors' offerings. With a low cost structure above-average returns are possible despite heavy competition.

Cost leadership is attained through aggressive construction of efficient scale economies, the pursuit of cost reductions through experience effects, tight cost and overhead control, and cost minimisation in R&D, services, salesforce, advertising, etc. The cost leadership route is that followed aggressively by Ryanair in the budget airline market.

Cost leaders typically need high market shares to achieve the above economies, and favourable access to raw materials. If, for example, efficient production processes, or superior production technology enabling cheaper production, were identified as company strengths or distinctive competencies, they could be effectively translated into a competitive advantage through cost leadership. Similarly, if backward integration (merger with, or acquisition of, suppliers) has secured the relatively cheaper supply of raw materials, that asset could also be converted into a competitive advantage.

This strategy is particularly suitable in commodity markets where there is little or no differentiation between the physical products offered. Where products are highly differentiated, however, the strategy has the major disadvantage in that it does not create a reason why the customer should buy the company's offering. Low costs could be translated into lower price, but this would effectively be a differentiation strategy (using price as the basis on which to differentiate).

Differentiation

The second approach to creating a competitive advantage is differentiation, i.e. creating something that is seen as unique in the market. Under this strategy company strengths and skills are used to differentiate the company's offerings from those of its competitors along some criteria that are valued by consumers.

Differentiation can be achieved on a variety of bases, for example by design, style, product or service features, price, image, etc. The major advantage of a differentiation strategy, as opposed to a cost leadership strategy, is that it creates, or emphasises, a reason why the customer should buy from the company rather than from its competitors. While cost leadership creates an essentially financially based advantage for the company, differentiation creates a market-based advantage (see Figure 10.3).

Products or services that are differentiated in a valued way can command higher prices and margins and thus avoid competing on price alone. An example of this is Fairtrade goods (bananas, coffee, tea etc.). These are differentiated by the way in which the suppliers are rewarded for their efforts. Generally the prices charged are higher than for non-Fairtrade products, but a growing segment of consumers are prepared to pay higher prices to be assured that producers in developing economies are not being unduly exploited.

Differentiation and cost leadership

The two strategies are not mutually exclusive, and could both be pursued simultaneously. Indeed, differentiation, especially through superior quality, can often result in lower unit costs through achieved gains in market share and attendant economies of scale and/or experience effects.

Each of the two basic approaches to creating a differential advantage has its attendant risks. Cost leadership may be impossible to sustain due to competitor imitation (using, for example, similar technology and processes), technological change occurring that may make it cheaper for newer entrants to produce the products or services, or alternatively competitors finding and exploiting alternative bases for cost leadership (see the discussion of cost drivers in Chapter 10). Cost leadership is also a risky strategy where there is a high degree of differentiation between competitive offerings. Differentiation creates reasons for purchase, which cost leadership does not. In addition, cost leadership typically requires minimal spending on R&D, product improvements and image creation, all of which can leave the product vulnerable to competitively superior products.

Differentiation as a strategy is also open to a variety of risks. If differentiation is not based on distinctive marketing assets it is possible that it will be imitated by competitors. A low price positioning, for example, might seem attractive in harsh economic times, but unless costs are also low compared with competitors it could spark costly price wars that seriously erode or eliminate margins. This risk can be minimised by building the differentiation on the basis of competencies or marketing assets that the company alone possesses and which cannot be copied by competitors. In addition, the basis for differentiation may become less important to customers or new bases become more important. These latter points should be guarded against by constant customer and competitor monitoring. A further danger of the differentiation strategy is that the costs of differentiating may outweigh the value placed on it by customers.

For both the cost leadership and differentiation approaches that seek to appeal industry-wide there is the added risk that focusers or nichers in the market (those competitors that focus their activities on a selected segment) may achieve lower costs or more valued differentiation in specific segments. Thus, in markets where segmentation is pronounced, both the basic approaches carry high risks. Chapter 10 explores further these approaches to creating a defensible position in the marketplace.

2.5 Implementation

Once the core strategy and the competitive positioning have been selected the task of marketing management is to implement those decisions through marketing effort. The three basic elements of implementation – marketing mix, organisation and control – are discussed next.

2.5.1 Marketing mix

The marketing mix of products, price, promotion and distribution is the means by which the company translates its strategy from a statement of intent to effort in the marketplace. Each of the elements of the mix should be designed to add up to the positioning required.

Viewed in this light it is evident that decisions on elements of the mix, such as pricing or advertising campaigns, cannot be considered in isolation from the strategy being pursued. A premium positioning, for example, differentiating the company's offerings from the competition in terms of high product quality, could be destroyed through charging too low a price. Similarly, for such a positioning to be achieved the product itself will have to deliver the quality claimed and the promotions used communicate its quality. The distribution channels selected, and the physical distribution systems used or created, must ensure that the products or services get to the target customers.

Where elements of the mix do not pull in the same direction but contradict each other, the positioning achieved will be confused and confusing to customers.

2.5.2 Organisation

How the marketing effort and the marketing department are organised will have an effect on how well the strategy can be carried through.

At a very basic level it is essential for the required manpower, as well as financial resources, to be made available. Given the resources, however, their organisation can also affect their ability to implement the strategy effectively. The traditional organisational forms found in marketing are functional and product (brand) management.

Under a **functional organisation** the marketing department consists of specialists in the various marketing activities reporting to a marketing coordinator (manager or director). Typical functions include sales management, advertising and promotions management, market research and new product development. An extension of the functional design is geographic organisation where, within the functions (such as sales management), managers have responsibility for specific geographic markets. Functional designs offer simplicity of structure and foster a high level of expertise in each function. They are often the first step in a company adopting a higher profile for the marketing function as a whole. They are most applicable where the number and complexity of products or services the company has on the market are limited.

Product (or brand) management, pioneered in 1927 by the US multi-national Procter & Gamble for its ailing Camay soap brand, vests responsibility for all the marketing activities of a particular product in one product manager. In diversified companies with many different products the system has the major advantage of coordinating under one individual the entire mix of marketing activities, and hence making it more likely that they will all pull in the same direction. In the larger companies product managers are able to call on the talents of functional specialists as and when necessary.

Dramatic changes in the marketing environment have caused many companies to rethink the role of the product manager. Today's consumers face an ever-growing set of brands and are now more deal-prone than brand-prone. As a result consumer marketing companies are shifting away from national advertising in favour of pricing and other point-of-sale promotions. Brand managers have traditionally focused on long-term, brand-building strategies targeting a mass audience, but today's marketplace realities demand shorter-term, sales-building strategies designed for local markets.

A second significant force affecting brand management is the growing power of retailers. Larger, more powerful, and better informed retailers are now demanding and getting more trade promotions in exchange for their scarce shelf space. The increase in trade promotion spending leaves less money for national advertising, the brand manager's primary marketing tool.

To cope with this change Campbell Soups created **brand sales managers.** These combine product manager and sales roles charged with handling brands in the field, working with the trade and designing more localised brand strategies. The managers spend more time in the field working with salespeople, learning what is happening in stores and getting closer to the customer.

Other companies, including Colgate-Palmolive, Procter & Gamble, Kraft and Lever Brothers, have adopted **category management** (see Spethman, 1992). Under this system brand managers report to a category manager, who has total responsibility for an entire product line. For example, at Procter & Gamble the brand manager for Dawn liquid dishwasher detergent reports to a manager who is responsible for Dawn, Ivory, Joy and all other light-duty liquid detergents. The light-duty liquids manager, in turn, reports to a manager who is responsible for all of Procter & Gamble's packaged soaps and detergents, including dishwasher detergents, and liquid and dry laundry detergents. This offers many advantages. First, the category managers have broader planning perspectives than brand managers do. Rather than focusing on specific brands they shape the company's entire category offering. Second, it better matches the buying processes of retailers. Recently retailers have begun making their individual buyers responsible for working with all suppliers of a specific product category. A category management system links up better with this new retailer 'category buying' system.

Some companies, including Nabisco, have started combining category management with another idea: **brand teams** or **category teams.** Instead of having several brand managers Nabisco has three teams covering biscuits: one each for adult rich, nutritional and children's biscuits. Headed by a category manager, each category team includes several marketing people/brand managers, a sales planning manager and a marketing information specialist handling brand strategy, advertising and sales promotion. Each team also includes specialists from other company departments: a finance manager, an R&D specialist, and representatives from manufacturing, engineering and distribution. Thus category managers act as a small business, with complete responsibility for the performance of the category and with a full complement of people to help them plan and implement category marketing strategies.

For companies that sell one product line to many different types of market that have different needs and preferences, a **market management organisation** might be most effective. Many companies are organised along market lines. A market management organisation is similar to the product management organisation. Market managers are responsible for developing long-range and annual plans for the sales and profits in their markets. This system's main advantage is that the company is organised around the needs of specific customer segments.

During the 1990s Elida-Gibbs, Unilever's personal care products division, scrapped both brand manager and sales development roles. They had many strong brands, including Pears, Fabergé Brut, Signal and Timotei, but sought to improve their service to retailers and pay more attention to developing the brands. To do this they created two new roles: brand development managers and customer development managers. **Customer development managers** worked closely with customers and also took over many of the old responsibilities of brand management. This provided an opportunity for better coordination of sales, operations and marketing campaigns. The change left **brand development managers** with much more time to spend on the strategic development of brands and innovation. Additionally, they were given the authority to pull together technical and managerial resources to see projects through to completion.

This reorganisation clearly went beyond sales and marketing. Cross-functional teamwork is central to the approach and also extends to the 'shop floor'. The company benefited greatly from the changes and customer development managers increased the number of correctly completed orders from 72 per cent to 90 per cent in a very short time. Further, brand development managers developed Aquatonic (an aerosol deodorant) in six months, less than half the usual time.

Increased attention is also being given to organisational approaches based on key processes of value creation and delivery rather than traditional structures and mechanisms. Traditional organisational approaches are often seen as too slow, unresponsive and cumbersome to deal with rapidly changing markets, new Internet-based competition, and strategies depending on alliances and partnering. For example, **venture marketing organisation** is one such approach (Aufreiter *et al.*, 2000). It was this approach that allowed Starbucks to take its Frappucino from a line manager's idea to a full national launch in less than a year. In its first year Frappucino contributed 11 per cent of Starbucks' US sales. More generally, the pressure is towards more effective integration of company resources around value creation, sometimes regardless of traditional organisational structures (Hulbert *et al.*, 2003).

Whichever structure or organisation is adopted by the company, individuals with the skills necessary to carry out the various marketing tasks are needed. Two sources of personnel emerge: internal to the company or brought in from outside. When entering new markets bringing in external expertise can be a shortcut to creating in-house the knowledge needed. Skills can be improved and extended through training programmes held within the company or through outside training agencies.

2.5.3 Control

As the marketing strategy is being executed an important role of the marketing department is to monitor and control the effort. Marketing managers, after all, have a vested and significant interest in being able to justify and quantify the outcomes of their actions and expenditure (Hanssens and Dekimpe, 2012).

Performance can be monitored in two main ways: on the basis of market performance and on financial performance. Market performance measures such things as sales, market share, customer attitudes and loyalty, and the changes in them over time can be related back to the original objectives of the strategy being pursued. Performance measures should, however, include factors other than those used to set objectives to ensure that pursuit of those objectives has not lost sight of the wider implications.

Financial performance is measured through a monitoring of product contribution relative to the resources employed to achieve it. Often a basic conflict between marketing and financial performance may arise. Where the marketing objectives are long-term market domination, short-term financial performance may suffer. Where managers are rewarded (i.e. promoted or paid more) on the basis of short-term financial performance it is likely that long-term marketing objectives may be sacrificed to short-term profit. In comparing the strategies pursued in a number of UK markets by Japanese firms and their UK competitors, Doyle *et al.* (1986) found that the Japanese were more prepared to take a longer view of market performance, compared with the short-term profit orientation pursued by many of the UK firms.

Much attention has focused on the development of 'marketing metrics' as a better way of linking marketing activities and financial returns to the business (Ambler, 2000; Moorman and Lehman, 2004). Ambler reports the most important marketing metrics used by companies are:

- relative perceived quality;
- loyalty/retention;
- total number of customers;
- customer satisfaction;
- relative price (market share/volume);
- market share (volume or value);
- perceived quality/esteem;
- complaints (level of dissatisfaction);
- awareness;
- distribution/availability.

Ambler argues that linking marketing to business performance requires that such metrics be reported to top management regularly, compared with forecasts and compared with competitors, with the drivers of buyer behaviour clarified and monitored.

A final important element in implementation is contingency planning, i.e. answering the question: 'What will we do if?' Contingency planning requires a degree of forecasting competitive reaction to the plans developed should they be implemented and then estimation of the likely competitive moves. Forecasting a range of likely futures and making plans to deal with whichever occur is termed scenario planning.

Summary

Strategic marketing planning involves deciding on the core strategy, creating the competitive positioning of both the company and its offerings, and implementing that strategy.

The above is as true of the one-product firm as it is of the large multi-national containing many different businesses. For the conglomerate, however, there is an added dimension to planning. That extra dimension consists of portfolio planning, ensuring that the mix of businesses within the total corporation is suitable for achieving overall corporate objectives.

Case study   Amazon eyes online sales boost through 'Fire' smartphone

Amazon has a decent shot at shaking up a smartphone market controlled by Samsung and Apple as well as selling more of everything to its customers with its new Fire smartphone, unveiled on Wednesday in Seattle.

But first, it has to find a way to convince consumers to buy the phone.

'Is it a good product and a neat idea? Yup. Will it be a success? Question mark,' says Mohan Sawhney, a management professor at Northwestern University who has studied Amazon.

Another question is just what constitutes success: muscle in on the smartphone market or driving more sales of the multitude of products sold via Amazon?

The phone is likely to funnel users towards buying more from Amazon, says Michael Graham, an internet analyst at Canaccord Genuity. Getting users of its hardware to buy more goods from its online store is how Amazon profited from the Kindle line of tablet and e-readers, in spite of selling many of those at or below cost.

The phone also comes with a free year of Amazon Prime membership, worth $99, allowing unlimited free shipping and a catalogue of digital music, movies and television shows. Users can store in Amazon's cloud an unlimited number of photos that they take with the device.

Prime users are more lucrative for Amazon than regular customers, says Mr Graham, and Firefly could encourage phone owners to use Amazon, rather than use search engine Google, as their main place to search for purchases.

But the challenge, says James McQuivey, an analyst with Forrester, is that entry into the phone market is tough to crack. Buying a phone typically means locking into a two-year contract, or paying more for a faster upgrade. The difficulty convincing consumers to wager

on whether they will like a new device in two years had stymied many purchases – some early phones from Microsoft sold fewer than 20,000, he says.

Bringing more users into Prime and trying to sell more Amazon goods 'are shrewd and calculated moves, and the phone in theory could be a tremendous extension of that strategy, but you've got to get people to want one', he says. 'I'm not sure [the Fire] will impress consumers to the tune of millions of them running out to buy it.'

The Fire starts with a 32GB model that sells for $199 on a two-year contract through AT&T, the only US carrier offering the device. Without a contract, it costs $649.

That places the Fire on par with Apple's iPhone and Samsung's high-end Galaxy line of devices – a part of the market that is increasingly competitive as sales slow and users are reluctant to switch from familiar brands and operating systems. Many other would-be contenders, including HTC, Motorola and Nokia have struggled to gain market share.

To help Amazon succeed where others failed, Jeff Bezos, Amazon's chief executive, brought to the launch in a Seattle warehouse a device that mixes content, customer services and hardware.

Best known for its online shopping mall, Amazon also controls a global network of warehouses, one of the world's largest commercial cloud storage operations, and has access to a growing catalogue of digital music, movies and films – expanded weekly with the launch of a Spotify-like music streaming service.

The Fire sports a 3D display that uses four infrared cameras to track users' head motion and pivot games or maps in line with how the viewer is looking at them. It also has a visual search tool named Firefly.

With Firefly, a user can point the phone's camera at anything from a book to a shaker of salt or a poster and either extract and save information – such as an email address – or navigate directly to a product page on Amazon to buy it.

'What we saw was an opportunity to prove some new capabilities that really hadn't been done before in premium smartphones,' says Ian Freed, Amazon's vice-president for the Fire phone. 'We've seen innovation stagnate a bit over the past two to three years.'

Analysts with Jefferies, the brokerage, estimate that Foxconn, the phone's manufacturer, will produce roughly 200,000 phones a month in the coming months.

Amazon decline to comment on plans to launch the phone in Europe, but people familiar with the company say it is holding discussions with Vodafone and O2 in the UK about possibly launching there.

By December or January – after the big back to school and holiday sales – it should be clear how well the phone is doing in the US, says Mr McQuivey. If Amazon reduces the price or adds more benefits, such as an additional year of Prime membership, it would be a sign that the initial launch underwhelmed the market and a rethink was needed.

'There are levers that Amazon could still pull if it needs to,' he says.

Source: from 'Amazon eyes online sales boost through "Fire" smartphone', *Financial Times*, 19/06/2014 (Mishkin, S.).

Discussion questions

1 What is driving Amazon's entry into the smartphone market? Is it an ego trip?

2 How does it fit in Amazon's vision 'to be earth's most customer centric company; to build a place where people can come to find and discover anything they might want to buy online'?

3 What strategic focus does the move signify? What alternatives are open to Amazon and how could Amazon pursue them?

PART 2
COMPETITIVE MARKET ANALYSIS

Part 2 examines the analysis of competitive markets in finer detail through the four chapters described below.

Chapter 3 commences with a discussion of the changing market and competitive environment facing many firms and organisations in the 2010s. Frameworks such as PEST analysis for analysing change in the broader macro-environment are introduced and strategies for operating in changing markets discussed. The chapter then focuses on the competitive, or industry environment. This begins with a discussion of the Five Forces Model of industry competition and an introduction of the product life cycle, followed by a review of strategic groups and industry evolution. Environmental stability is assessed, together with SPACE analysis. Finally, the Advantage Matrix is reviewed as a means of assessing the key characteristics of an industry when forming strategy.

Chapter 4 considers customer analysis. Information requirements are first discussed, followed by sources of customer information. The variety of marketing research techniques available to aid customer analysis is examined. The discussion then turns to the processes by which customer data are collected and how those data can be turned into information to aid marketing decision making.

Chapter 5 addresses competitor analysis. Following a discussion of competitive benchmarking the dimensions of competitor analysis are discussed, together with techniques for identifying competitor response profiles. The chapter concludes with a review of sources of competitor information.

Chapter 6 is concerned with the internal analysis of an organisation's resources, assets and capabilities that can be leveraged in its target markets. Starting from a broad, resource-based view of the firm and the identification of its core competencies, the chapter moves to the more detailed issues of auditing resources and itemising specific marketing assets, such as brands, reputation, supply chain strengths and partnerships. The chapter concludes with a framework to build a profile of a company's marketing capabilities.

CHAPTER 3
THE CHANGING MARKET ENVIRONMENT

'The road goes on and on, down from the door where it began. Now far ahead the road has gone, and I must follow if I can. Pursuing it with weary feet, until it joins some larger way, where many paths and errands meet. And whither then? I cannot say.'

Frodo Baggins, in *The Fellowship of the Ring*, by JRR Tolkien

Recession-hit Aga trials green energy

Aga Rangemaster said it was taking part in a pilot scheme in which one of its ovens is being run on biogas derived from food waste.

Details of the experiment emerged on Friday as Aga Rangemaster – which also makes stoves and refrigerators, as well as owning the Fired Earth tile store chain – reported a 97 per cent drop in annual profits as the recession hit sales.

Aga Rangemaster 2009 results

Sales	Pre-tax profit	Earnings per share	Dividend
£245m	£0.5m	2.5p	0
↓12%	↓97%	↓83%	NA

Source: Alamy Images: Roger Harvey.

The centrepiece of many country kitchens, Aga ovens have been criticised by some for wasting energy by pumping out heat when it is not needed.

Aga Rangemaster has been trying to address this issue by making its ovens programmable.

It has also been experimenting with alternative energy sources, through moves such as a collaboration with BiogenGreenfinch, a specialist in recycling food waste into energy.

In a pilot scheme set up recently in Ludlow, Shropshire, a regular gas-fuelled Aga has been modified so that it can run on biogas produced from food waste by anaerobic digestion, a natural biological process.

William McGrath, the chief executive of Aga Rangemaster, said that the pilot scheme had shown that Aga ovens would run 'quite comfortably' on biogas as the alternative fuel became more mainstream.

The group said that the sharp falls in demand experienced in the first half of 2009 had levelled out in the second half, adding that demand had strengthened in some areas.

Mr McGrath said: 'Certainly, we would be disappointed if we weren't seeing revenues picking up in 2010.' He also said that exports of its UK-made cooker to continental Europe would benefit from the pound's weakness against the euro.

Source: Adam Jones, 'Recession-hit Aga trials green energy', **www.ft.com**, 12 March 2010.

Discussion questions

1 What do you think are the key marketing issues faced by Aga?

2 How can they address these issues?

Introduction

Of central importance in developing and implementing a robust marketing strategy is awareness of how the environment in which marketing takes place is changing. At its simplest, the marketing environment can be divided into the competitive environment (including the company, its immediate competitors and customers) and the macro-environment (the wider social, political and economic setting in which organisations operate). Competition between firms to serve customers is the very essence of modern, market-led economies. Since the middle of the twentieth century competition has been intensifying as firms seek to create competitive advantage in ever-more crowded markets and with increasingly demanding customers. This chapter provides a number of tools for understanding the competitive environments in which firms operate and recognising the opportunities and threats they present. It can provide no simple rules for achieving competitive success, but can explain the forms of industry environment that exist, the competition within them, and when and why certain strategies succeed.

It should be borne in mind, however, that **industries** and **markets** are not the same thing – industries are collections of organisations with technologies and products in common, whereas markets are customers linked by similar needs. For example, white goods firms comprise an industry – companies that make refrigerators, washing machines and so on. On the other hand, laundry products constitute a market – the products and services customers use to clean their clothes. This distinction is important for two reasons. First, if we only think about the conventional industry we may ignore the potential for competition for our customers from companies with different products and technologies that meet the same need. For example, conventional financial services companies were wrong-footed by Virgin's entry into the market with simplified products and direct marketing techniques, and seemed unable to respond to the entry of diverse firms such as supermarkets and airlines into financial services.

Second, there are signs that many companies are having to abandon traditional industry definitions under pressure from distributors and retailers. For example, **category management** in grocery retailing is fundamental, the retailers being concerned with managing a category of products that meet a particular need such as laundry, meal replacement or lunch, not with individual products or brands. The effects of category management can be bizarre – Walmart discovered, for example, a relationship between the purchase of disposable nappies and beer on Friday evenings. The explanation was that young fathers were being told by their partners to stock up on nappies on the way home from work. They reasoned this was a good opportunity (or reason?) to stock up on beer as well. These products are now merchandised together on Fridays. The point is that we should temper any conclusions we draw about the industry by recognising that markets may change in ways that invalidate conventional industry definitions.

Systematic analysis of the business environment typically commences at the macro level, highlighting aspects of the broader environment that may impinge on the specific markets the firm operates in. At a more specific industry level, however, the identification of the forces driving competition within industries can be a useful starting point. We then go on to discuss strategic groups, which provide a useful basis for understanding opportunities and threats facing individual firms. It is within those strategic groups that firms compete to grow, survive or decline.

3.1 A framework for macro-environmental analysis

Here we deal with the nature of change in the macro-environment and examine its impact on organisational marketing strategies.

The importance of understanding the macro-environment is twofold. First, we should recognise the marketing impact of change in the business environment and be in a position to respond. But, second, we should also be alert to the fact that the nature of the change facing organisations is itself changing. For example, Haeckel (1997) noted that of all the pressures driving companies to revitalise their marketing processes:

> the leading candidate is a change in the nature of change: from continuous (but incremental) to discontinuous [because] when discontinuous change makes customer requests unpredictable, strategic leverage shifts from efficiency to flexibility and responsiveness – and to investments that enable a firm to sense unanticipated change earlier and co-ordinate an unprecedented response to it faster.

Many important changes are taking place in the environment in which marketing operates, and some important examples are summarised briefly below (see also Drucker, 1997). However, this can never be a comprehensive list for the reasons Haeckel identified above. For our purposes, change is discussed under three main headings. Taken together these are often referred to as PEST analysis (see Figure 3.1) – political and economic, social (including legal and cultural) and technological environments. We discuss the political and economic environments together as the interplay between the two often makes it difficult to disentangle their individual impacts. A political change here can create an economic effect there, and changes in the economy may well precipitate political action or change.

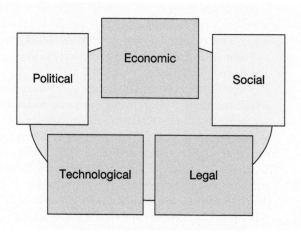

Figure 3.1
PEST analysis of the macro-environment

> ### 3.2   The economic and political environment

The global economic recession of 2008–10 was the deepest since the Great Depression of the 1930s. Triggered by a financial crisis brought about through unsustainable lending practices by banks, the credit crunch rapidly spread to the 'real' economy as firms of all sizes in developed economies found it increasingly difficult to raise operating funds. Similarly, consumer credit dried up significantly reducing spending power of consumers. In the UK the *Financial Times* index of 100 leading shares (the FTSE 100) plunged from a high of 6,500 before the recession to a low of 3,500 in March 2009. As businesses struggled to survive and unemployment rose, government tax takings fell significantly and governments around the world found that they had to increase their borrowing to record levels to keep services operating.

In attempts to bolster their economies governments adopted massive fiscal stimulus packages and reduced interest rates to record low levels. In November 2008 China had pumped $586bn into a stimulus package and in April 2009 Japan followed suit with a $153bn package. In 2009 the USA passed the American Recovery and Reinvestment Act committing £787bn to boosting the US economy.

The impact of these economic shocks was to be felt for many years to come. While the private sector recession may have been declared officially over by January 2010 in most developed countries, the public sector recession was just starting. In attempts to rebalance the books and reduce national debt levels, governments began to raise taxes, cut public sector spending, or combinations of these actions. Where the public sector is a significant employer (especially in Western Europe) the public sector recession in mid-2015 still has the potential to knock back into the private sector, raising fears of a 'double-dip recession'.

Interestingly, there are some markets that are counter-cyclical to economic activity. One such is education. At times of economic downturn the demand for higher education can actually increase, in part because jobs are scarcer, in part because individuals feel the need to further differentiate themselves through education to stand out from others in the labour market. Figure 3.2 shows the relationship between demand for MBA programme places and economic growth.

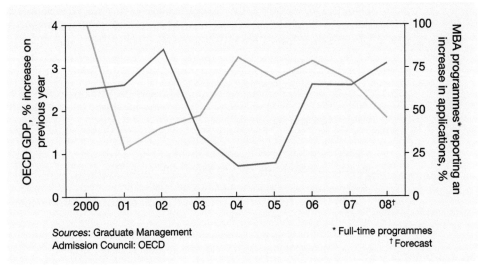

Figure 3.2 Demand for MBA programmes and economic cycles

Source: The Economist (2008).

Sources: Graduate Management Admission Council: OECD

* Full-time programmes
† Forecast

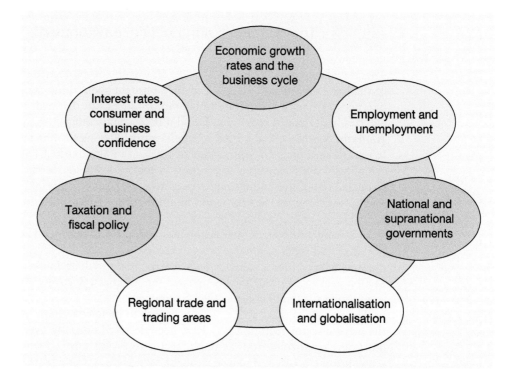

Figure 3.3
The economic
and political
environment

Even before the credit crunch, however, many of the developed economies were experiencing a slowing of economic growth. While economic growth is undoubtedly cyclical, the indications are that the developed economies are unlikely to see again the rates of growth experienced in the first few decades after the Second World War. Many organisations will have to learn to live with low growth in their once-buoyant markets. Where growth objectives once dominated management thinking other criteria, such as profitability, are now becoming more important. Figure 3.3 shows a number of key considerations of which firms need to be aware when assessing the political and economic environments in which they operate.

The European Single Market and its enlargement

January 1992 saw the realisation of the dream of many Europeans with the creation of the European Single Market. The Single Market of over 320 million consumers was created to allow the free flow of products and services, people and capital between the member states. As such it was intended to improve economic performance by lowering costs of trading across national borders within the European Union (EU), and to encourage economies of scale of operation rivalling the US internal market. By January 2002 a single European currency, the euro, had been introduced into the euro-zone (all but a handful of the EU member states), further facilitating trade and exchange across the old political borders.

However, it also had its problems. With economies in the zone operating at different speeds, and facing different levels of public sector debt but without the freedom to set separate exchange or interest rates, difficulties began to emerge. In early 2010 the Greek economy (within the euro-zone) caused particular concern, followed by Spain and Portugal, as debt levels rose and the countries' credit rating were lowered, casting a doubt on the survival of the euro-zone.

In October 2002 a referendum in the Irish Republic paved the way for the enlargement of the European Union through the accession of ten new states, the three Baltic states – Latvia, Lithuania and Estonia, Hungary, Poland, the Czech Republic, Slovakia, Cyprus, Malta and Slovenia, in May 2004. That enlargement had significant implications for many organisations, both commercial and non-commercial, as Europe expands. The population of the European Union rose by around 20 per cent while GDP rose by only 5 per cent (Fishburn and Green, 2002). Significant differences in labour costs, for example, are likely to raise questions of location for many firms. Hourly labour costs ranged from €3.7 to €40.1 across the EU 28 Member States in 2013.

Internationalisation and globalisation

While Western, developed economies have struggled to maintain momentum during the recession, the inexorable rise of China and India as the economic super powers of the future has continued. By 2050 it is estimated that the population of India will overtake China at around 1.6 billion in each, compared with 700 million in Europe and 400 million in the United States of America. While Western economies stagnated or declined during the recession the Chinese economy continued to grow, albeit at a slower rate than previously. Growth in 2015 was estimated at 3.3 per cent compared with 13 per cent in 2007 (and an average for the previous 30 years of over 10 per cent). Early in 2016 China's economic growth was reported to be at its slowest in 25 years (growing at 6.9 per cent in 2015 compared to 7.3 per cent a year earlier), contributing to a reduced growth rate in other world economies.

The last decade of the 1900s saw dramatic changes in East–West relationships. The dismantling of the Berlin Wall, the liberalisation of the economies of central Europe (Poland, Hungary, the Czech Republic, Slovakia) and the break-up of the Soviet Union signalled many potential changes in trading patterns.

While the political barriers have been coming down in Europe, there is some concern that the emergence of regional trading blocs ('free trade areas') will have a dramatic impact on the future of free world trade. The European Single Market post-1993, closer economic relations in the Asia Pacific region (Australia, Singapore, Thailand, South Korea, the Trans-Pacific Partnership signed in January 2016.) and the North American Free Trade Alliance zone (the United States, Canada and Mexico) are emerging as massive internal markets where domestic-based, 'international' trade will become freer.

At the same time, trade between trading blocs or nations outside them may become more restricted. Major trading partners such as the United States and Japan are increasingly entering into bilateral trade deals (e.g. the US–Japan deal on semiconductors). While most politicians espouse the goals of free international trade (see, for example, Brittan (1990), then EC Competition Commissioner, speaking at the EC/Japan Journalists' Conference), the realities of the 1990s were a concentration of trade within blocs and reduced trade between them.

3.3   The social and cultural environment

Coupled with the changing economic environment has been a continuous change in social attitudes and values (at least in the developed West) that are likely to have important implications for marketing management (see Figure 3.4). Examples include the following.

Demographic change

The Western 'demographic time bomb' has started to have an impact on diverse businesses. With generally better standards of living, life expectancy has increased across the world (according to the Global Health Observatory by 2013 average life expectancy had risen by six years since 1990).

The grey market

In the developed West the over-60s age group currently makes up around 23 per cent of the population, and is predicted to rise to nearer one-third by 2050 (and projected to grow by 56 per cent between 2015 and 2030 worldwide). These 'grey' consumers are relatively rich.

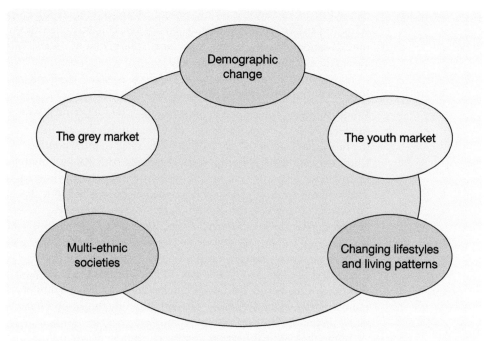

Figure 3.4 The social and cultural environment

The over-50s own around three-quarters of the world's financial assets and control half of the discretionary budget. Perhaps surprisingly, however, around 90 per cent of consumer advertising is aimed at the under-50s. Marketers are increasingly coming to recognise the potential value of this market and target more offerings and promotions towards them (Fishburn and Green, 2002).

Barratt Developments in the United Kingdom, for example, has been particularly quick to capitalise on this change in the demographic profile and has specialised in providing retirement homes for the elderly. Demographic changes of this type vary significantly between countries and regions throughout the world, and warrant serious study as a fundamental influence on demand for different products and services. In Japan, for example, it is predicted that by 2030 around 37 per cent of the population will be older than 65 compared with 5 per cent in 1950 and 19 per cent in 2000.

There are also significant financial implications of the greying of Western society. Increased longevity, coupled with economic slowdown, has led to significant challenges to pension funds. Many defined benefit (final salary pension, or career average) schemes have been underfunded and forced to change terms and conditions for members. This could have significant implications for the purchasing power of tomorrow's pensioners.

The youth market

At the other end of the spectrum the youth market has also become more affluent and poses new opportunities for marketers. Fashion and music industries have been quick to recognise this new-found affluence. Much of the success of Virgin Records (sold to Thorn EMI for over £500 million in early 1992) was based on understanding and catering for this market. Clothes stores too, such as Now and Next, built their early successes on catering to the teenage market.

Related to this youth market has been the emergence of the enigmatic 'Generation X' consumer – the cynical, world-weary '20-somethings' – who are hostile to business values and traditional advertising and branding, and reject many conventional product offers. The pay-off in understanding the values and preferences of this type of consumer has been substantial for companies such as Nike in clothing and footwear and Boss in fragrances and clothing – these consumers react positively to pictures of athletes vomiting on their sports shoes at the end of the race, and Nike's advertising copy: 'We don't sell dreams. We sell shoes . . . Don't insult our intelligence. Tell us what it is. Tell us what it does. And don't play the national anthem while you do it.' Marketers are also now targeting generation Y and anticipating how generation Z will consume. Generation Y is entering the workforce in the mid-2010s and is the one that mostly populates social media channels and as such possesses substantial influence. These consumers also react differently to advertising appeals than their parents, the baby boomers (Loroz and Helgeson, 2013).

Multi-ethnic societies

Many Western societies are becoming increasingly multi-ethnic. In the United Kingdom, for example, by 2011 ethnic minorities represented 12.1 per cent of the population and forecasts predict the number will reach 20 per cent by 2051. This group spends some £10 billion a year, and includes many socially mobile and affluent groups. As well as being a target for specialised products and services, ethnic minorities are increasingly vocal about what they object to in conventional marketing and advertising. For example, some brands have been labelled as 'ethnically insensitive', such as Persil's TV advertisement showing a Dalmatian dog shaking off its black spots, or McDonald's TV advertisement showing a stereotypical young black man listening to very loud music while driving. On the other hand, some marketers have earned praise for being 'ethnically sensitive': for example BT's radio advertisements in Hindi to promote long-distance phone calls, and W.H. Smith for stocking ethnic greetings cards (Dwek, 1997).

Changing living patterns and lifestyles

There has also been an increase in single-person households, predicted by Euromonitor to be the fastest-growing household profile worldwide, not just in the West, between 2014 and 2030. This is leading to the development of smaller goods or services targeted at singles, such as Daewoo's mini washing machine and Cerca Travel's two-day 'solo wedding' packages for single women.

A further development has been the significant growth in the number of women in employment, be it full- or part-time. This has led to changes in household eating patterns, with an emphasis on convenience foods and cooking. It has, in turn, led to increased markets for products to make cooking and meal preparation easier and quicker, such as the Kitchenaid or Kenwood multifunction food processors that can do everything from food preparation to cooking, or recipe boxes that can be bought in the supermarket or delivered to people's homes.

Coupled with greater concern for the environment is greater concern for personal health. There has been a dramatic movement in the grocery industry, for example, towards healthier food products, such as wholemeal bread, bran-based cereals, and 'superfoods'. This movement, originally dismissed by many food manufacturers as a passing fad among a minority of the population, has accelerated with the marketing of organically produced products and low-sugar, salt-free products, free from additives, colourings and preservatives (the British government imposed a tax on sugar in March 2016). Fitness products in general, from sportswear and exercise machines to the membership of gyms and leisure clubs, have enjoyed very buoyant markets. By 2014 over 22 per cent of household expenditure in the United Kingdom was spent on leisure activities and products.

Also of relevance to the overall economic conditions in which organisations operate is the political environment. In the US a Democrat, Barack Obama, was returned to the White House in 2008, and in the UK the May 2010 election resulted in the first coalition government (between the Conservative and Liberal Democrat parties) in over 60 years. Political leaders and their parties set the economic agenda – more or less taxation, more or less public spending, more or less investment, more or less public ownership. This in turn creates opportunities and challenges for all sectors of the economy.

3.3.1 Social, cultural and environmental pressures on organisations

Customers are becoming increasingly demanding of the products and services they buy. Customers demand, and expect, reliable and durable products with quick, efficient service at reasonable prices. What is more there is little long-term stability in customer demand. Competitive positions are achieved through offering superior customer value, yet without constant improvement 'value migration' will occur – buyers will migrate to an alternative value offering (Slywotzky, 1996).

J. Sainsbury plc, for example, is a family-dominated business which operates the super-market chain that has changed the food and wine British consumers buy in fundamental ways. For a generation Sainsbury's was the market leader in the grocery business and was the watchword for quality, choice and innovation in food and wine – by the 1990s the company had become a British 'institution'. Tesco Stores, by contrast, was the second player, which had grown from a downmarket discount retailer, originally associated with its founder's slogan of 'pile it high, sell it cheap', into a supermarket operator. In 1995 Sainsbury's lost market leadership to Tesco. This was accompanied by a massive slump in Sainsbury's share value, and continued losses of market share to Tesco. Sainsbury's continued its strategy of the 1980s into the 1990s. Tesco, meanwhile, developed a repositioning strategy based on product and store quality, backed by a massive investment in information technology to dramatically improve operational efficiency and value to customers. Sainsbury's strategy became outdated but, worse, the company showed few signs of being able to develop a coherent response to the new situation (Piercy, 1997). More recently, 'discounters' Aldi and Lidl saw their share of the market increase year on year, reaching a joint 10 per cent by December 2015, their appeal having widened to the middle classes.

A second major trend, exacerbated by the recession and looking set to continue, is that customers are less prepared to pay a substantial premium for products or services that do not offer demonstrably greater value. While it is undeniable that well-developed and managed brands can command higher prices than unbranded products in many markets, the differentials commanded are now much less than they were and customers are increasingly questioning the extra value they get for the extra expense. The sophisticated customer is less likely to be attracted to cheap products with low quality, but is also unlikely to be won by purely image-based advertising. The implications are clear – differentiation needs to be based on providing demonstrably superior value to customers.

Increased questioning of the industrial profit motive as the prime objective for commercial enterprises has grown. Some are going further in explicitly measuring their performance through the 'Triple Bottom Line' (TBL) of People, Planet and Profit. The phrase originated in the early 1990s (Elkington, 1994) and recognises that business has responsibilities not only to shareholders but also to other stakeholders affected directly or indirectly by the business. 'People' relates to the human capital in the company – both the people working in the organisation and the community in which a company conducts its business. Fairtrade practices, for example, seek to ensure farmers and producers of foodstuffs receive fair recompense for their labours. 'Planet' relates to the natural capital the organisation uses and its attempts to minimise environmental impact. Organisations practising a TBL approach endeavour to minimise their ecological footprint through controlling use of energy, switching to renewable energy sources where possible and reducing manufacturing waste. 'Profit' is the net economic value created by the organisation and goes beyond the internal profit created by a firm to encompass the economic impact the organisation has on its wider economic environment and society. In short, the triple bottom line approach aims at creating sustainable businesses in a more sustainable environment.

A further social/cultural change has been in attitudes to, and concern for, the physical or natural environment. Environmental pressure groups impact on businesses, so much so that major oil multinationals and others spend large amounts on corporate advertising each year to demonstrate their concern and care for the environment. The activities of groups such as Greenpeace have begun to have a major impact on public opinion and now affect policy making at the national and international levels. It is to be expected that concern for the environment will increase and hence will be a major factor in managing that prime marketing asset – company reputation. The significance of the impact on business is underlined by the three year Save The Arctic campaign of Greenpeace and others against Shell's drilling there. In September 2015 Shell announced they were withdrawing their plan.

Cars such as the Ford Ka, the Renault Twingo and the Mercedes Smart car are examples of compact, fuel-economical, low-emission vehicles, designed and produced for city use, as an answer to environmental pressure and stricter legislation on pollution levels in cities. Many car manufacturers are also now offering hybrid or totally electric cars. The entry of BMW in 2014 in the electric car market gives it a more 'mainstream' status.

3.4   The technological environment

The latter part of the twentieth century saw technological change and development impact on virtually every industry sector. A number of significant developments are discussed below.

A shortening of commercialisation times of new inventions. Photography, for example, took over 100 years from initial invention to commercial viability. The telephone took 56 years, radio 35 years, television 12 years and the transistor only 3 years. Looked at another way, the telephone took 40 years to reach 10 million users worldwide, the television 18, the personal computer 15 and the World Wide Web only 5.

This shortening of commercialisation times has, in turn, led to a shortening of product life cycles, with products becoming obsolete much more quickly than previously. In the Japanese electronics industry, for example, the time between perception of a need or demand for a new product and shipment of large quantities of that product can be under five months (e.g. Matsushita colour TVs). Computer integration of manufacturing and design is helping to shorten product development times. It has been estimated that in automobiles this has been in the order of 25 per cent.

Through technological changes whole industries or applications have been changed dramatically almost overnight. In 1977–78 cross-ply tyre manufacturers in the United States lost 50 per cent of the tyre market to radials in just 18 months (Foster, 1986b).

Newer technology has a major impact on particular aspects of marketing. The advent of the microcomputer and its wide availability to management initially led to increased interest in sophisticated market modelling and decision support systems. Increased amounts of information can now be stored, analysed and retrieved very much more quickly than in the past. Now, the impact of the Internet Revolution can be felt in customer experience and relationship management and all elements of the marketing mix. For example, virtual products take over from their physical equivalent: in March 2016 the British newspaper *The Independent* ceased to exist in paper form, and social media have transformed how companies communicate with their audiences. Audi has opened virtual showrooms in major world cities and customers are looking for a seamless omni-channel experience when they shop online instead of in a physical store.

Innovative marketing research companies have been quick to seize on the possibilities afforded by the new technology for getting information to their clients more quickly than competitors. Suppliers of retail audits (see Chapter 6) can now present their clients with online results of the audits completed only 24 hours previously. In a rapidly changing marketplace the ability to respond quickly, afforded by almost instantaneous information, can mean the difference between success and failure.

The 'data warehouses' created by the capture of customer data are increasingly a major marketing resource for companies, which has the potential for achieving stronger and more enduring relationships than competitors – examples include the data collected by retailers such as Tesco and Sainsbury's through their loyalty card schemes; the customer information held by airlines to monitor the purchase behaviour of their frequent flyer customers; and the customer data gained through the direct marketing of products such as financial services.

Even the small business (if it invests in the modest costs of establishing a website) can access markets throughout the world at almost no cost. This changes fundamentally the costs of market entry and the competitive structures of the markets affected.

3.4.1 Technological pressures on organisations

Technology continues to develop at a bewildering pace, affecting not just the high-tech industries such as telecommunications and personal computers but also other industries that make use of the new technologies. Bill Gates, writing in *The World in 2003* (Fishburn and Green, 2002), goes so far as to predict that computers per se will soon disappear. Increasingly they will be integrated into other products. It has been estimated that people in the United States already interact with 150 embedded 'computer' systems every day (in products such as mobile phones, petrol pumps and retail point-of-sale systems), utilising 90 per cent of the microprocessors currently in use. Similarly, the Semiconductor Industry Association (again reported in Fishburn and Green, 2002) estimates that in 2001 alone the microchip industry produced around 60 million transistors for every man, woman and child on earth, increasing to well over 1 billion in 2010.

Changes in the way in which computer chips are made are likely to further boost computer power and lower costs. The newer laser-assisted direct impact technique allows minute features to be stamped on to molten silicon. As of 2015 the highest number of transistors per chip is over 5.5 billion, to be found in Intel's 18-core Xeon Haswell-EP. Moore's law (i.e. the doubling of transistor counts every two years) is still valid 50 years on.

Time and distance are shrinking rapidly as firms use the Internet to market their offerings to truly global markets. One result is that cross-national segments are now emerging for products and services from fast foods, through books and toys, to computers and automobiles.

3.5 Changes in marketing infrastructure and practices

In addition to the changes noted above there are several important changes taking place in the general marketing environment and in marketing practices.

In many markets increased levels of competition, both domestic and international, are reaching unprecedented levels. In the three years following the start of the global recovery in 2010, Britain's exports increased by 14.7 per cent in terms of value, and volumes rose by 7.2 per cent. Exports increased to a record £304.3 billion in 2013, up from £300.5 billion in 2012, according to the Office for National Statistics. HSBC forecasts UK exports will increase by 5 per cent between 2016 and 2020 and then decrease to 4 per cent between 2020 and 2030.

3.5.1 Globalisation of markets

Some writers (e.g. Farley, 1997) have argued that many markets are becoming increasingly global in nature and no business, however big or small, is exempt from global competition. The reasoning centres on the impact of technology on people throughout the world. Technology has made products more available and potential consumers more aware of them. Farley believes we are currently experiencing a move towards gigantic, world-scale markets where economies of scale in production, marketing and distribution can be vigorously pursued. The result will be significantly lower costs, creating major problems for competitors that do not operate on a global scale. Many of these cost advantages are being realised as companies operating within the EU's Single Market rationalise their production and distribution facilities.

The counter-argument to the globalisation thesis is that markets are becoming more fragmented, with consumers more concerned to express their individuality (King, 1985) than to buy mass-produced, mass-marketed products. In addition, there is little evidence of the existence of widespread preference for the cheapest products available. The demand for low prices, relative to other product benefits and extras, is not proven in many markets. Each market should be examined individually and the factors likely to affect it explored.

Whether one subscribes to the globalisation argument or not, one factor is clear: organisations ignore international competition at their peril. The UK motorcycle industry is a textbook example of a once supreme industry now virtually non-existent because of its failure to recognise and respond to the threat posed by cheap, good quality, Japanese motorbikes.

At the same time as markets are becoming more global, so the existence of distinct market segments is becoming clearer. The most successful firms are those that have recognised this increasing importance of segmentation and positioned their companies so as to take best advantage of it. Van den Bergh is a prime example in the UK yellow fats market. They have clearly identified several main segments of the market and positioned individual brands to meet the needs of those segments (see Chapter 9). The company now commands in excess of 60 per cent of the margarine market through a policy of domination of each distinct market segment.

Founded in 1953 by Bernard and Laura Ashley, the Laura Ashley company was based on a quintessentially British design concept, characterised by the long flowing skirts and romantic floral designs that were the foundation of the company's success in the 1960s and 1970s. With its Victorian and Edwardian-style designs, Laura Ashley wallcoverings were favoured in locations such as the British Embassy in Washington and at Highgrove, home of the Prince of Wales, and its floral smocks and chintzes were favoured by the young Princess Diana. From its early designs for women's clothes the company expanded rapidly into fabrics, wallcoverings and paints, linked by the central design concept. Manufacturing plants were established in Wales, and by 1997 the company operated more than 400 retail stores worldwide covering dozens of countries, including more than 150 in the United States. By 1997 the company had sales of £320 million, but was issuing repeated profit warnings, and its shares had lost three-quarters of their value in 12 months. The loss-making manufacturing units started to declare redundancies. The death of the founder in 1985 had marked a turning point. The loss of vision for the company at that point was accompanied by losses in most of the following 12 years. Ann Iverson (then chief executive) faced the problem of turning the company around and reclaiming its position with the affluent 35–50-year-old female fashion buyer. City commentators pointed to the strength of new competitors such as Ralph Lauren in this core market and concluded that 'Its management must decide what to be, preferably before the money runs out' (*Daily Telegraph,* 1997; Olins, 1997a). Unfortunately, the company incurred heavy losses in 1998 and was bought the same year by MUI Asia Ltd, but initially the company still had no focus. Over the years until 2015, fashion's share of the overall business decreased to 17 per cent. Despite a commitment to increasing brand awareness, ensuring global relevance of the products and growth, the company reported a four-year low profit (March 2016) of £19.4m and sales down to £289.5m. This was attributed to the franchise business, with the UK business remaining strong. Laura Ashley's chairman said: 'We remain optimistic for the future and are confident that the strength of the brand and the enduring appeal of our product ranges mean we are well positioned for continued growth' (*Financial Times,* 2016, March 23).

3.5.2 The role of marketing

The role of marketing in the modern corporation has been subject to far-reaching reappraisal. It is possible to argue that the marketing function has a major role to play in keeping the company up to date with changes in its broader environment and the competitive environment.

However, the way that role is fulfilled is likely to reflect major forces of change, such as increasingly sophisticated customers; the move from an emphasis on single sales transactions to long-term customer relationships; the role of information technology (IT) in changing how markets and organisations work; and the development of the network organisation consisting of a group of companies collaborating to exploit their core competencies linked together by a mix of strategic alliances, vertical integration and looser partnerships (Webster, 1994). The implications for how marketing will operate are profound (see Chapter 15).

3.6 New strategies for changing macro-environments

In reaction to the above a number of critical issues are emerging for marketing management and theory.

First, and central to developing a sustainable competitive advantage in rapidly and often unpredictably changing circumstances, is the ability to learn fast and adapt quickly (Dickson, 1992). A major challenge for any organisation is to create the combination of culture and climate to maximise learning (Slater and Narver, 1995).

Slow to change has been the high-street retailer W.H. Smith. Almost every UK high street and rail station has a W.H. Smith retail outlet, selling magazines and newspapers, books, stationery, cassettes/compact discs and videos. Its bookstalls first appeared in 1792, and W.H. Smith had a market value of £1.1 billion in 1997 with 10 million customers a week buying in its stores. However, during the 1980s and 1990s, W.H. Smith's traditional core market was attacked by strong competitors. On the one side there was a growth in specialist retailers such as Dillons, and on the other was a dramatic expansion by the main supermarket groups in selling books, newspapers and music/videos. W.H. Smith had bought its own specialists, such as Dillons and Our Price, but the commercial position of the core retail chain continued to decline. Many of the peripheral businesses were sold by Bill Cockburn, the chief executive who spent the mid-1990s trying to position the company as a 'world-class retailer' before resigning in 1996. Management at the problematic retail chain claim that W.H. Smith is a middle-of-the-market variety chain, serving consumers who are not Dillons customers or Tesco customers. The retail business is struggling to find a role and has been left behind by market change. Analysts suggest that the underlying retail concept and trading format has had its day, leaving the business with no credible growth strategy in its core business (Olins, 1997b; Weyer, 1997). The chain is now divided into two businesses: travel and retail. Whilst the travel business has been steadily growing over the past few years the retail side has continued to shrink. This is explained by the move from paper to digital. The company is also criticised for pursuing a defensive strategy and poor shopping experience, putting in doubt its sustainability (Lynn, 2015).

In increasingly demanding, crowded and competitive markets there is no substitute for being market oriented. This does not, however, imply oversophisticated marketing operations and elaborate marketing departments. Staying close to the customer, understanding their needs and requirements and marshalling the firm's resources, assets and capabilities to deliver superior value is what counts. Here the resource-based view of the firm (see Hamel and Prahalad, 1994) can add important new insights into achieving the necessary fit between firm and market (Day, 1994a).

The shift from transactions-based marketing to relationship marketing has intensified in many markets as firms seek to establish closer bonds with their customers (see Payne, 1995). They will need to realise, however, that for any relationship to last requires benefits on both sides. Too many early attempts at 'relationship building' have been simply mechanisms to buy temporary loyalty. Relationship building will need to become far more sophisticated.

Firms are also increasingly practising 'multi-mode marketing' – pursuing intense relationship-building strategies with some customers, less intense strategies with others and arm's length strategies with yet others, depending on the long-term value of the customer and their requirements.

3.6.1 Marketing strategies

However, to suggest that firms need to develop new strategies as times change may not go far enough. The problem may not just be that we need to develop new strategies, but that we have to develop wholly new approaches to strategy. For example, at the 1997 Academy of Marketing Science conference two leading marketing thinkers (Jag Sheth and David Cravens) spoke of the trends in strategic development that they believe have to be confronted.

Sheth challenged conventional marketing thinking along the following lines:

- **Global positioning:** Sheth urges strategists to think about globalisation and focus on core competencies, instead of thinking about the domestic market and a portfolio of business and brands. He suggests the need for a different approach to delivering shareholder value (see Figure 3.5).
- **The master brand:** Sheth argues that strength comes from a brand identity that links all parts of the business – this is the fundamental strength of Toyota and Honda compared with the dozens of brands operated by General Motors.
- **The integrated enterprise and end-user focus:** the challenge of managing people, processes and infrastructure to deliver value to an end user.
- **Best-in-class processes:** customers do not, for example, compare an airline's service just with that of other airlines; the new standards for the airline to meet come from service excellence at companies such as Federal Express and Marriott Hotels – the challenge is to meet world-class standards from wherever they come.
- **Mass customisation:** the imperative is to achieve scale economies but at the same time to produce a product or service tailored to the individual customer's requirements.
- **Breakthrough technology:** new technology will underpin every aspect of the marketing process, even the product itself, in ways that may seem outlandish. For example, a new product in Japan is the 'smart toilet'. Avoiding technical details, basically the person just sits there and the machine does the rest. However, the machine also produces a diagnosis

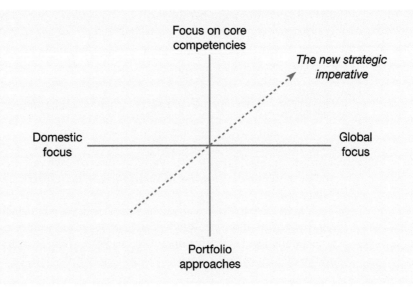

Figure 3.5
The shift in strategy for delivering shareholder value

Source: Adapted from Sheth (1994).

of waste output, as well as measuring the user's temperature and blood pressure. Useless technology? Not in situations where there is an ageing population with potential medical problems and insufficient hospital places. For around $600 the home has a first line of medical diagnosis, which may save many lives.

Cravens underlined the message that traditional views of strategy may quickly become obsolete. He argued that the strategy paradigms of the last 20 years are increasingly inadequate as we enter a new era of 'market-based strategy'. His predictions took the following forms:

- **Markets shape business strategy:** Cravens suggests that the market will be seen as the dominant force shaping how business operates – this is the factor that links industrial economics, total quality management (TQM), financial investment appraisal and business process re-engineering.
- **Networks of interlinked product markets:** he notes that traditional boundaries based on conventional product markets will blur and become irrelevant, and this blurring will become the norm. Look, for example, at the move of grocery supermarkets such as Sainsbury's and Tesco into banking and financial services. How else do we make sense of Virgin's moving from music to retailing to airlines to rail transport to financial services to cosmetics to drinks to clothes, all under the single Virgin brand?
- **The move from functions to processes:** he also suggests that the new era of market-based strategy is one where we will increasingly focus on the process of going to market, not on the interests of traditional departments and specialists.
- **Strategic alliances:** for many companies the future will be one of collaboration and partnership (to allow them to focus on core competencies), not one of traditional competition.
- **The balanced scorecard:** keeping score involves evaluating the benefits we deliver to all the stakeholders in the organisation.

These predictions imply the need to create new types of strategies, not just more of the same. They also underline the critical importance of building market-sensing and organisational learning capabilities, to allow organisations to understand what is happening and to act accordingly.

The above factors all combine to make strategic planning in general, and marketing planning in particular, more difficult now than they have ever been before. They also make them more vital activities than they have ever been before. Strategic marketing planning today attempts to build flexibility into the organisation to enable it to cope with this increased level of complexity and uncertainty and to take full advantage of the changing environment. At the heart of that planning process is the creation of a strong competitive position and a robust marketing strategy, the subject of the remainder of this text.

3.7 The Five Forces model of industry competition

Porter (1980) suggested that five main forces shape competition at the level of strategic business units and that a systematic analysis of each in turn can help managers identify the keys to competitiveness in their particular industry. The five forces are shown in Figure 3.6.

The Five Forces Model is not merely of use to commercial organisations. It can also be used by organisations in the public and not-for-profit sectors to better understand their customers, suppliers and other organisations with whom they may be competing for support (financial or otherwise). Each of the five forces is discussed in turn below.

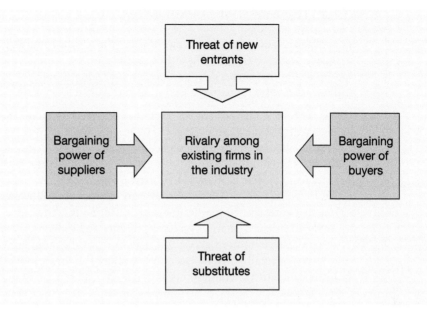

Figure 3.6
Five forces driving
competition

3.7.1 Rivalry among existing companies

A prime source of competition in any industry is among the existing incumbents. This rivalry is likely to be most intense where a number of conditions prevail:

- **Where the competitors in the industry are roughly evenly balanced** in terms of size and/or market share. The UK chocolate market is a case in point where three rivals, Cadbury, Nestlé and Mars, all command roughly equal market shares. Competition between them for an extra percentage point of the market is intense, leading to high levels of advertising spend, strong price competition and continuous launch of new products.

- **During periods of low market growth,** especially during the mature and decline stages of the product life cycle (see below). Under such conditions individual company growth is achieved only at the expense of competitors, and hence rivalry intensifies. The mobile telephone market is a case in point, where growth slowed in the early 2000s and existing firms such as Ericsson and Nokia found themselves with excess production capacity and entered into increased price competition to secure sales.

- **Where exit barriers are high.** If firms find it difficult to exit a market once they have entered, they are more likely to compete hard for success. High initial investments may create psychological (or egotistical) barriers to exit, high costs of redundancy (monetary or social) may deter exit, or e-market presence may be necessary to enable the firm to compete in more lucrative segments (for many state-owned mail services the cost of remaining in business is to continue to deliver mail to expensive to reach, out of the way places).

- **Where product differentiation is low.** In markets where customers see little variation across products, where intrinsic quality and external value are perceived to be similar, competition for sales tends to be more intense. The prime reason is that customer switching costs are low – the cost (financial, inconvenience, etc.) to a customer of changing from one supplier to another.

- **Where fixed costs are relatively high.** High fixed costs relative to variable costs require greater sales volume to cover them. Until that volume is achieved rivalry can be intense. In power supply industries the fixed costs of power generation are substantial compared with the variable costs of supplying power, leading to intense rivalry among generators.

3.7.2 The threat of market entry

In addition to considering existing rivals, organisations should also consider the potential for new entrants to emerge. The airline industry, for example, has seen a number of low-cost 'no-frills' entrants such as easyJet and Ryanair enter the market. A number of conditions make market entry more likely. Entry barriers can be low where the following hold:

- **Costs of entry are low.** The Internet, for example, has meant that many industries which once required substantial capital and investment for market entry are now more vulnerable to entry by lower-resourced competitors. Amazon.com, for example, entered into book retailing online with modest capital but without the need to invest in substantial bricks and mortar in the way that existing book retailers had.
- **Existing or new distribution channels are open to use.** Johnson and Scholes (1988) point out that entering the market for beer in Germany, the United Kingdom and France is hindered by the system of financing of bars and pubs by the large brewers. This 'tied system' has guaranteed access to the market for the large brewers but restricted access to new and small brewers, essentially acting as a barrier to market entry.
- **Little competitive retaliation is anticipated.** The expectation of retaliation by existing incumbents can be one of the most significant deterrents to market entry. For example, IBM signalled their determination to defend their mainframe computer market in the 1980s against entrants to such an extent that others entered different sectors of the market rather than compete head on with 'Big Blue'. Conversely, where incumbents are considered weak, or lacking in resolve to defend their markets, the likelihood of new entrance is greater. The financial state of the large airline carriers in the late 1980s and 1990s meant that they were not in a strong position to see off the low-cost entrants that undercut their fares significantly. They had little leeway to retaliate, and the new entrants knew it.
- **Differentiation is low.** When differentiation between the offerings of existing incumbents is low there is likely to be more scope for new entrants to offer something unique and valued in the market.
- **There are gaps in the market.** In markets where the existing incumbents are not adequately serving the wants and needs of customers there is more opportunity for entrants to establish themselves in underserved, or neglected, segments of the market. Highly segmented markets, in particular, where existing firms are slow to recognise diversity in customer requirements, provide tempting opportunities for new entrants.

3.7.3 The threat of substitutes

New entrants may use the existing technology of the industry, or they may attempt to revolutionise the market through leapfrogging. Indeed, technological substitution may come from new entrants or from existing firms doing things in new ways. Substitution can increase competitiveness of an industry for a number of reasons:

- **By making existing technologies redundant.** Classic examples include the decimation of the slide rule industry by the advent of pocket calculators; apps; the overtaking of mechanical timepieces by electronic technologies and, now, wearable technologies; and the advent of digital television replacing analogue. Where technologies are changing rapidly, competition between firms to stay ahead also tends to be intense.
- **By incremental product improvement.** Even where industries are not revolutionised overnight by step-changes in technology, existing market offerings may become quickly dated. Technological development in the computer industry, for example, proceeds apace, with personal computers becoming out of date almost as soon as they have

been shipped! The advent of e-mail as a means of communication has not made the letter obsolete, but it has had a significant impact on postal services. E-mail is simply a letter posted down the telephone wires rather than in a letterbox. More recently Facebook, Instagram and Snapchat have replaced SMS and e-mail as a communication medium favoured by young people.

3.7.4 Bargaining power of suppliers

The balance of power between the members of an industry, its suppliers and its customers can significantly affect the level of competitiveness experienced by all. Where suppliers and/ or customers have greater power than the members of the industry competition within the industry for scarce suppliers or scarce customers tends to be more intense. Suppliers tend to have more bargaining power where the following hold:

- **Suppliers are more concentrated than buyers.** Where there are few organisations capable and willing to supply, their power over their buyers tends to be greater. Similarly, where buyers are more fragmented, and purchase in relatively small quantities, their power relative to their suppliers is likely to be low.
- **Costs of switching suppliers are high.** If the supplier provides a key ingredient for the purchaser that is difficult or costly to source elsewhere, their bargaining power is likely to be greater. Where the supplier provides commodity products that can be easily purchased elsewhere, they will have less bargaining power. Welsh sheep farmers, for example, have found that their individual bargaining power with the supermarkets and butchers' chains that sell their meat is low, but when they band together in collectives their power increases.
- **Suppliers' offerings are highly differentiated.** Where suppliers' products are distinct and different, either through tangible differences in standards, features or design, or through less tangible effects such as branding and reputation, they are likely to hold more bargaining power. The power of Intel, for example, as a supplier of computer chips (which are increasingly commodity products) is enhanced through the reputation and branding of Intel among the ultimate customers for computers. This pull-through effect enhances the power of Intel in supplying to computer manufacturers and assemblers.

Source: Getty Images: AFP.

3.7.5 Bargaining power of buyers

The buyers or customers of the output from an industry also exert pressures that can affect the degree of competition within it. Buyers tend to be more powerful in the supply chain where the following is true:

- **They are more concentrated than sellers.** Fewer buyers than sellers, especially where individual buyers account for large volumes of purchases and/or the sellers produce relatively small amounts each, means greater bargaining power for the customer. In grocery retailing, for example, a handful of major multiples command such a large percentage of total sales that they can practically dictate terms to their suppliers.
- **There are readily available alternative sources of supply.** Especially in the supply of commodity products or services, it may be relatively easy for buyers to buy elsewhere.
- **Buyer switching costs are low.** Where the inconvenience or cost of switching suppliers is low, greater power resides with the buyer who can 'shop around' more to get better deals.

3.7.6 Competitiveness drivers

Taken together, these five forces offer a useful framework for assessing the factors likely to drive competition. They also suggest ways in which the players in the industry – current incumbents, suppliers and buyers – might seek to alter the balance of power and improve their own competitive position. We can summarise as follows. Where the following industry characteristics are present, expect greater levels of competition:

There is little differentiation between market offers
Industry growth rates are low
High fixed costs need to be recovered
High supplier switching costs
Low buyer switching costs
Low entry barriers
High exit barriers

As we shall see later (Chapter 10), one of the most successful ways of countering a highly competitive environment is to differentiate your offering from that of competitors, in a way that is of value to customers. That creates buyer switching costs, higher entry barriers, and helps create a defensible position in the market irrespective of industry growth rates or costs of supply.

3.8	**The product life cycle**

The product life cycle (PLC) is an insightful tool into an industry's competitive environment (Cravens and Piercy, 2009) and market dynamics. Its premises are that:

- All products have a limited lifespan until a better solution to the customer's problems comes along.
- Life cycles of products follow more or less predictable patterns or phases (see Figure 3.7).
- Market conditions, opportunities and challenges vary over the life cycle.
- Strategies need to adapt over the life cycle.

Chapter 11 will address this last point, while each of the four key stages (introduction, growth, maturity and decline) will be introduced here.

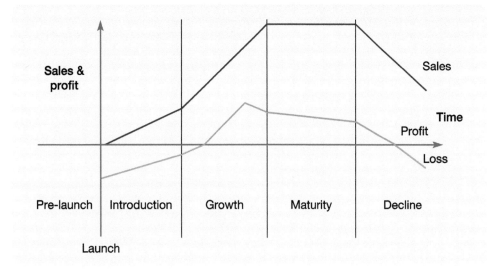

Figure 3.7
The product
life cycle

Introduction stage

The product is launched into the market and generally sales are slow to pick up because customers and distribution have to be found and convinced. If the product is new to the world (e.g. the first iPad) it will face little or no competition and the company will have a pioneer advantage and appeal to innovators. If it is an addition (e.g. the Samsung Edge in the smartphone market) it will be targeted at a new segment and fit the 'ideal' of that segment better than alternative solutions. The key question here has to do with how quickly competitors will launch a variant. This is normally the stage for build strategies (see Chapter 10).

Investment costs are likely to be very high prior to launch. The Airbus A380 is a good case in point (see Figure 3.8):

Figure 3.8
Airbus A380's
development costs
were €11bn!

Source: Alamy Images:
vario images
GmbH&Co.KG.

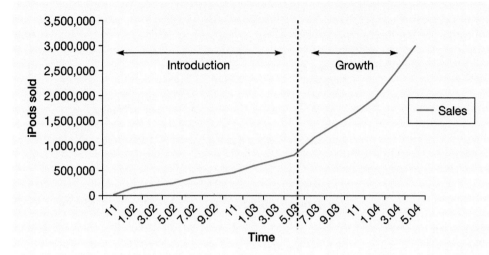

Figure 3.9
Sales of iPods

Source: iPodlounge.com. Data are for every two months from November 2001 to May 2004. Thus 11 is November 2001, 1.02 is January 2002 etc.

Growth stage

The growth stage is characterised by a rapid increase in sales as the product starts to attract different types of customers and repeat purchases may start (see Figure 3.9). Critically, it is at this stage that competitors assess the product's market and profit potential and decide on their competitive moves. They may decide to modify or improve their current offerings or enter the market with their own new products (e.g. Microsoft Zunes as the 'iPod killer'). If not, they may use the other elements of the mix to detract attention from the product, i.e. an advertising campaign or a price promotion. It is possible that defensive attacks may be required to prevent the curve from flattening.

Maturity stage

At this stage the rate of growth slows down significantly. This stage tends to last longer than the previous ones and is, probably, the most challenging one: it is a fact of life for most marketers that the markets they have to deal with are mature! This is a stage of severe competition, market fragmentation and declining profits, due to over-capacity in the industry. Indeed, competitors will try to uncover untapped niches and/or enter price wars. This leads to a clear-out and the weaker competitors will exit, possibly becoming suppliers to the stronger ones or being bought by them (as we are currently seeing in the car industry). The survivors will be either companies supplying the bulk of the market, competing on a high volume–low margin basis, or market nichers. Many firms will try to buck the trend and revamp their PLCs (not always successfully as both KitKat and Barbie experienced after unsuccessfully launching new variants of their products) or expand the market by creating a new segment, and hence extra demand overall, as Swatch did.

Mature markets are also likely to see a degree of product substitution, where one product form gives way to another. One example is the US car market where increasing gasoline prices, coupled with increasing concern over emissions, has led to a decline in the sports utility vehicle (SUV) market but a rapid increase in sales of hybrid cars (see Figure 3.10).

Decline stage

This stage is marked by a slow or rapid decline of the sales of the product. Decline may be due to better solutions (e.g. new technology such as the USB flashdrive replacing floppy and zip disks) supplanting weaker ones, a change in consumer tastes or an increase in competition, be it domestic or international.

Road to salvation
The dramatic decline in SUV sales in the US over the last three years is mirrored by a steep rise in sales of hybrid cars

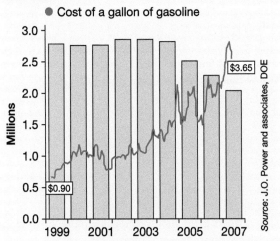

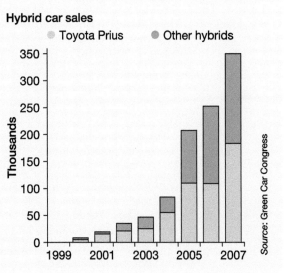

Figure 3.10 US car sales

3.9   Strategic groups

Within industries a useful basis for analysis can be the strategic group. A strategic group is composed of firms within an industry following similar strategies aimed at similar customers or customer groups. Coca-Cola and Pepsi, for example, form a strategic group in the soft drinks market (Kay, 1993). The identification of strategic groups is fundamental to industry analysis because just as industries can rise or fall despite the state of the overall business environment, so strategic groups with the distinctive competencies of their members can defy the general fluctuations within an industry.

Indeed, understanding the dynamics of existing strategic groups can be productive to understanding their vulnerability to competitive attack. For example, pursuing the Coca-Cola and Pepsi illustration, these firms compete on the basis of massive advertising spend on image and packaging to position against each other. They will respond to each other's advertising and promotion with anything except one thing – price. Coca-Cola and Pepsi have experienced price wars and they do not like them. This made the big brands highly vulnerable to attack by cheaper substitutes. Since 2014 Sainsbury's own labels outsell brands and Waitrose recently delisted most of its Tropicana and Copella lines to replace them with own label juices.

The separation of strategic groups within a market depends on the barriers to mobility within the industry. For instance, all the companies within the UK shipbuilding industry tend to compete with each other for high value added defence contracts, but their lack of cheap labour and resources means that they are not in the same strategic group as the Korean or Japanese suppliers or bulk carriers. Other barriers may be the degree of vertical integration of companies, as in the case of British Gypsum and its source of raw materials for making plaster-board within the United Kingdom, or Boots Pharmaceuticals with its access to the market via Boots retailing chain. At a global level, geopolitical boundaries can also cause differences. For instance, the fragmented buying of the European military and the small production runs that result tend to position European defence contractors in a different strategic group from their US counterparts. Similarly, the differences in technology, reliability and safety standards form barriers between Russian and Western aerospace manufacturers.

As well as the barriers surrounding them, strategic groups also share competitive pressures. Within the US defence industry firms share similar bargaining power with the Pentagon and influence through the political lobbying system. This can help protect them from non-US suppliers, but does not give them an advantage within their home market. The threat from substitutes or new entrants may also provide a unifying theme for strategic groups. Within the computer industry suppliers of low-cost products such as Compaq are facing intense competition from inexpensively manufactured alternatives including desktop, laptop and even palmtop machines. Companies within the higher value added mainframe businesses are under less threat from low-cost mainframe manufacturers, but are being squeezed by increasingly sophisticated and networked PCs. Finally, strategic groups often share common competitors because they are often competing to fulfil similar market needs using similar technologies.

The map of strategic groups within the US car market shows their dynamics (Figure 3.11). The presentation is simplified into two dimensions for ease of discussion but in reality a full analysis may use more. In this case the strategic groups show their clear geographical and historic origins. The Big Three – GM, Ford and Chrysler – though badly affected by the recent recession, remain dominant in supplying a broad range of cars with high local content. In this they retain some technological and styling expertise in the supply of regular and luxury sedans, but until recently had the common basic defence of promoting import restrictions.

Another group is the Faded Champions, which were once the major importers into the US market. Both are European companies whose US ventures have either seen better days,

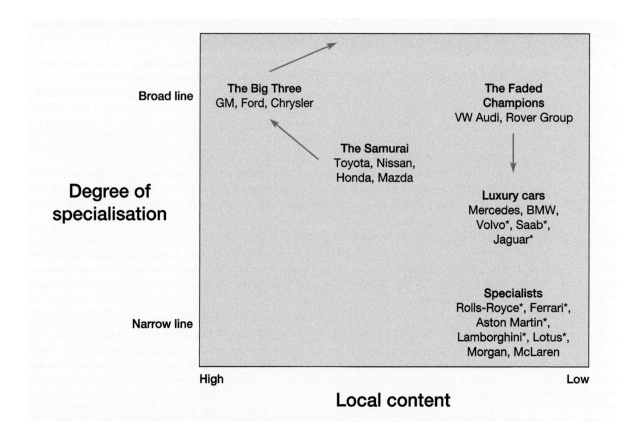

Figure 3.11 Map of strategic groups in the US automobile market

Note: * Brands now owned by large-scale American or European manufacturers.

in the case of Volkswagen/Audi, or much better days, in the case of the Rover Group. Once suppliers of a relatively broad range of vehicles, both these companies retreated towards the luxury car sector where they appeared to have little competitive edge. When Rover was acquired (and then rapidly sold off again) by the German luxury car manufacturer BMW it reconfirmed its positioning at the cheaper end of the market, complementary to, rather than in direct competition with, the BMW range. The demise of the Faded Champions in the United States is not due to the Big Three, but to the entry of the Samurai into the US market. Initially the quality and low cost of the Japanese strategic group gave them an advantage over the European broad-range suppliers, but now the Japanese are gaining even more power by becoming local manufacturers and therefore overcoming the local content barriers.

High European labour costs have meant that they operate in strategic groups selling high added-value luxury cars or specialist cars, the luxury cars being supplied by relatively large-scale manufacturers with moderately wide product ranges (e.g. the German firm Mercedes-Benz), or specialist manufacturers producing the very expensive, small-volume products (e.g. the British Morgan cars).

The strength of the barriers surrounding the industry is reflected by recent shifts that have taken place. Although the Samurai have never successfully attacked the hard core of the Big Three, they have continued to nibble away at the weaker imports: first the Faded Champions with cheap, reliable family cars and more recently the luxury car makers with the advent of the Lexus and other luxury offerings. Even though they are very large, the Big Three have found it difficult to defend their position by developing their own luxury cars and so have been seeking to defend their flanks against the Samurai by purchasing European manufacturers such as Jaguar, Volvo, Saab, Lamborghini, Aston Martin and Lotus. After years of the Big Three and the Samurai avoiding direct competition, the luxury car market has become the point where the two meet. Although the Samurai have not found it appropriate to purchase European companies in order to overcome entry barriers to those sectors (with the exception of Toyota, which has bought, and sold, Lotus), so distinct are the luxury car markets that both Honda and Toyota launched totally new ranges with new brand names and distribution systems to attack the market (the Acura and the Lexus).

With the luxury car market already being fought over, the next stand-up battle between the Big Three and the Samurai is in the specialist market where the Americans have again been purchasing European brands and the Japanese have been aggressively developing 'Ferrari bashers'. Although the one-time distinct strategic groups are becoming blurred as the main protagonists enter new markets, it is to be noted that in all cases the strategy involves establishing distinct business units with the skills appropriate for the strategic groups being fought over. Examination of the US automobile market shows that even when markets are mature there can be areas of rapid growth and competition, such as the luxury car and specialist markets. And the different expertise and situation of the strategic groups means that the protagonists from the different groups may well compete in different ways.

The inability of companies to understand the differences in strategic groups is one that causes the frequent failures of companies entering new markets by acquisition. Although the broad business definition, products being sold and customers may be similar within the acquired and the acquiring company, where the two are in different strategic groups there can be major misunderstandings. Although having great expertise in the domestic market, many UK retailers have found international expansion very difficult because of the competition they face in the new markets and their failure to understand the strategic groups they are entering. Examples include Boots' acquisition in Canada and Dixons' in the United States where, although their international diversification was into the same industries as those with which they were familiar in the United Kingdom, those skills that allowed them to beat competition within their strategic groups at home did not transfer easily internationally. Were the companies facing the same competition within the European markets it is likely that their ventures would have been more successful. In a sense that is what the Japanese have been doing, as their industries have rolled from country to country across the world, where their major competitors are their own compatriots whom they have faced in many markets in the past.

3.10   Industry evolution and forecasting

The critical issues to be addressed within an industry depend on its evolutionary stage. Porter (1980) discusses the evolution of industries through three main stages: emergence, transformation to maturity and decline (see Figure 3.12). These stages follow in much the same way as products are represented as following more or less identifiable life cycle stages (see O'Shaughnessy, 1995, for a comparison of the product life cycle and Porter's Industry Evolution Model). However, industry evolution is to the product what the product life cycle is to the brand. For example, whereas in the music industry the product life cycle may relate to vinyl records or CDs, industry evolution embraces the transition from cylinders to 78s, 45s, vinyl albums, 8-track cartridges, cassettes, compact discs, digital audio tape and subsequent digital technologies.

Uncertainty is the salient feature within emerging industries. Recent developments in broadcasting show this most clearly. There is no technological uncertainty about the basic technologies involved in achieving the direct broadcasting of television programmes by cable or satellite, but there are vast uncertainties about the combination of technologies to be used and how they should be paid for. In the early 1980s the discussion was about cable and the terrific opportunities offered for industrial redevelopment by cabling declining UK cities such as Liverpool. In the United States many cable channels emerged, but with no particular standard and with numerous channels that had a short life. In only a few years the vast infrastructure requirements of cable have been replaced by the equally capital-intensive but more elegant solution of satellite television. Even there, however, there has been uncertainty about whether to use high-, low- or medium-powered satellites and the means of getting revenue from customers. In the United Kingdom to that brawl has been added uncertainty concerning British regulations, those of the European Union and the activities of the broadcasting channels, which were once the oligopolistic supplier. It is not surprising that with this uncertainty consumers have shown reluctance in adopting the new viewing opportunities open to them. However, with the recent advent of the connected home via Smart TVs or new technologies such as Amazon Fire Stick, Google Chromecast and Apple TV as well as fast broadband, consumers are quickly switching to SVOD (Subscription Video On Demand) and catch-up TV services.

The high losses that can be associated with the emergent stage of an industry are shown by the losses incurred by the pioneers of the competing technologies in the video industry.

Stage	*Issues*	*Strategies*
Emergence	Technological uncertainty Commercial uncertainty Customer uncertainty Channel uncertainty	Locate innovators and early adopters Establish standard Reduce switching cost risk Encourage trial
Transition to maturity	Slow growth, falling profits Excess capacity, intense competition Increased customer power Extended product line	Marketing mix marketing Customer retention, segmentation Efficiency focus Coordination
Decline	Substitution by newer technologies Demographic change	Focus or divest

Figure 3.12 Industry evolution

Source: Adapted from O'Shaughnessy (1995).

Out of three competing video disc and video cassette recording technologies in the mid-1980s only one, VHS, survived into the twenty-first century (to then be replaced by DVD and Blu-Ray). Two of the losers in that earlier round (Philips with the laser disc and V2000 VCRs, and Sony with the BetaMax format) managed the emergence of laser-based reproduction in the late 1980s and 1990s more carefully. The two industry leaders collaborated in the development of a compact disc (CD) standard and licensed the technology widely in order to accelerate its diffusion and reduce customer uncertainty. With the establishment of a single technology the compact disc was less prone to the software shortages that made video discs so unattractive to customers. Customers still faced potentially high switching costs if they traded in their existing album collection for CDs, but the impact of this was reduced by focusing on segments that were very conscious of hi-fi quality and heavy users. The CD was also capable of being integrated into existing hi-fi systems and quickly became an established part of budget rack systems.

In the transition to maturity, uncertainty declines but competition intensifies. Typically the rapid growth, high margins, little competition and apparent size of industries within the late stage of emergence attract many competitors. Those who sought to avoid the uncertainty in the early stages now feel the time is right for them to enter the market. This decision usually coincides with a transition to maturity within a marketplace where competition increases, profits fall, growth slows and capacity is excessive as more producers come on stream. Also, by now a dominant design has typically emerged, and hence competitors are forced to compete on a basis of price or the extended/augmented product. In technological terms, there is a switch to process technology; in marketing terms, a switch from entrepreneurship to the management of the marketing mix; that is, towards efficiency, coupled with the careful identification of market segments with a marketing mix to address them.

Not unexpectedly, companies that fail to notice this transition from entrepreneurial to more bureaucratic management find things difficult. Take, for instance, Sinclair, which was still seeking to differentiate the market in the mid-1980s with the QL microcomputer after the emergence of the IBM PC had established industry standards. Equally, examine the increasing difficulties that Amstrad faced once its entrepreneurial, cost-cutting and channel strategies had been followed by industry leaders such as IBM and Olivetti.

An industry's decline is usually caused by the emergence of a substitute or a demographic shift. Two main strategies are usually appropriate: either divest or focus on the efficient supply of a robust segment. Although the basic options are few, industries often find this decision a difficult one because of the vested interests within the sector declining. It is extraordinary that at this last stage there seem to be more organisational choices about how to implement the basic strategies than at any other stage in an industry's evolution. At a clinical level there can be the decision to divest or milk a company within a declining sector. There is the option of carefully nurturing a long-lasting, lingering target market; or for the entrepreneurial zest of an opportunist who can take advantage of the shifting needs. There is certainly much money to be made in the remnants of industries as AEM, a subsidiary of RTZ, has found. It specialises in aviation engineering and maintenance of products that are no longer the main focus of the leading airframe and aero engine manufacturers.

Industry evolution shows the violent shifts that occur within an industry as it progresses from stage to stage. Not only do the major issues change, but the management tasks and styles appropriate are equally shifting. Industry evolution also shows that their very success can lead to failure for some firms that do not adapt their approaches and styles to changing conditions. Firms that have been highly successful in entrepreneurial mode during emergence may find it difficult to make the transition to a more bureaucratic way of operating. Similarly, those that have learned to live with stability and maturity may find difficulty managing the business during industry decline where a highly focused, cost-restrained way of operating is appropriate. Understanding the stage of industry evolution is essential if a company is to avoid managing in an environment with which it is unfamiliar, with an inappropriate management style.

3.11   Environmental stability

A limitation of Porter's Industry Evolution Model is the rigid association of technological and marketing uncertainty with only the emerging stage of an industry. This may not be so. For instance, the UK grocery trade has certainly been mature for generations, but the growth of supermarkets and hypermarkets, the removal of retail price maintenance and the move towards out of town and online shopping have meant the market has faced great turbulence, despite its maturity. Ansoff's (1984) theory is that environmental turbulence is fundamental to understanding industries, but it should not be seen as relating only to the early stages of industry life cycle.

A distinction is drawn between marketing and innovation turbulence (Table 3.1). The reason for this is apparent when one considers many industries, such as the automobile industry, where competition has been rapidly changing but for which the competing technologies have changed little. The determinants of environmental turbulence parallel industry evolution in relating uncertainty to the stage of the product life cycle for both marketing and innovation turbulence. However, along with the emerging stage, decline and the transition from stage to stage can spell danger for the unwary company. And in some markets the antecedents of marketing and innovation turbulence are quite different.

Figure 3.13 provides a mechanism for combining two dimensions of turbulence and shows how two strategic groups in the same industry can be facing different environments. Within the UK food retailing trade the environment for the leading grocers, such as Sainsbury's and Tesco, is *developing* in terms of both marketing and innovation. The shift out of town is continuing for larger outlets (though there are signs that concerns for the environmental impact of out of town shopping may lead to a slowdown of this trend), as is the move towards larger establishments; but the pattern is well understood, as is the position of the main protagonists within the industry. Similarly, major changes with electronic point-of-sale (EPOS) and stock control technologies have been absorbed by this sector and are now a well-established part of their activities. The same applies to the move online and click-and-collect services. The intersection of the developing market turbulence and developing innovation turbulence not surprisingly indicates that the overall environmental turbulence is appropriately classified as developing.

Table 3.1 Determinants of environmental turbulence

Association of high marketing turbulence	Association of high innovative turbulence
High % of sales spent on marketing	High % of sales spent on R&D
Novel market entrant	Frequent new products in the industry
Very aggressive leading competitor	Short product life cycles (PLCs)
Threatening pressure by customers	Novel technologies emerging
Demand outstripping industry capacity	Many competing technologies
Emergence, decline or shifting stage of PLC	Emergence, decline or shifting stage of PLC
Low profitability	Low profitability
High product differentiation	Creativity is a critical success factor
Identification of latent needs a critical success factor	

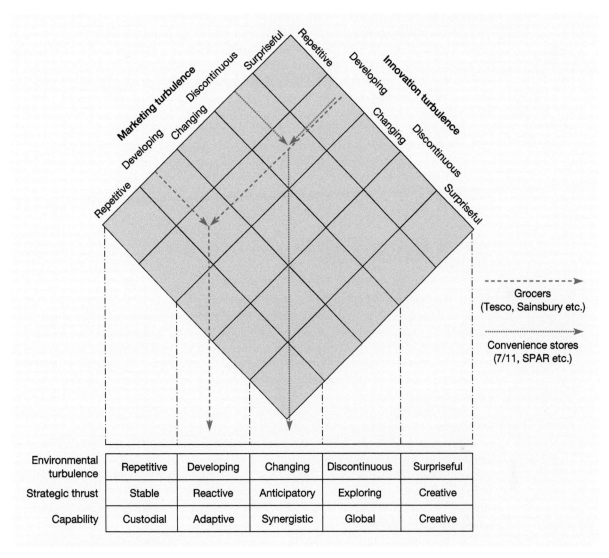

Figure 3.13 Environmental turbulence

Source: Based on Ansoff (1984) Figure 3.4.5, p. 222.

Environmental turbulence	Repetitive	Developing	Changing	Discontinuous	Surpriseful
Strategic thrust	Stable	Reactive	Anticipatory	Exploring	Creative
Capability	Custodial	Adaptive	Synergistic	Global	Creative

The situation of the leading grocers contrasts with the convenience stores, which form another strategic group within the same industry. Although their innovation turbulence is similar to leading grocers, they face *discontinuous marketing* turbulence. This is due to their not yet having faced the shift from in-town to out of town shopping, and their existence within the emergent phase of an industry in which many new entrants are appearing. Although in the same industry as the leading grocers the convenience stores, therefore, face *changing environmental* turbulence.

Ansoff draws broad strategic and managerial conclusions from the differences in environmental turbulences that companies face. Whereas, he suggests, the leading retailers see the need to be *reactive* in terms of their strategic thrust and have the ability to adapt, he would suggest that the convenience stores need a more dynamic management style, where they *anticipate* shifts in the environment and look for synergistic opportunities. Within that context the convenience stores have concentrated on a series of goods for which their position is critical, such as alcoholic beverages, milk and soft drinks, which constitutes a very large proportion of their sales.

From a marketing point of view there is great importance in correctly assessing environmental turbulence. A firm must try to match its capability to appropriate environments or develop capabilities that fit new ones. The Trustee Savings Bank (TSB) and many other retailing banks in the United Kingdom have shown the dangers of believing their resources can enable them to operate in unfamiliar style. TSB in particular almost epitomised custodial management, where it provided an efficient service in a standard way to a very stable market for a long time. Even more than other banks it meant the company was built around closed systems and operations where there was little need for entrepreneurship. The privatisation of TSB gave it a dangerous combination of a large amount of money and wider opportunities, together with a massively changed banking environment. Two almost inevitable developments have occurred: (a) the bank has shown its inability to manage businesses with a more dynamic environment; and (b) it has found itself unable to work out what to do with its cash mountain. A solution was eventually found in the merger with Lloyds Bank, which could provide the necessary capabilities. However, in 2009 the European Commission ruled that the British government's 43.4 per cent stake in the Group represented state aid and it was split up in 2015.

3.12   SPACE analysis

SPACE (strategic position and action evaluation) (Rowe *et al.*, 1989) analysis extends environmental analysis beyond the consideration of turbulence to look at industry strength and relates this to the competitive advantage and financial strength of a company. Like Shell's Directional Policy Matrix and other multidimensional portfolio planning devices it is a method of summarising a large number of strategic issues on a few dimensions. One of the dimensions is of environmental stability (Table 3.2), which includes many of the facets of environmental turbulence. However, with SPACE analysis environmental instability is seen as being counterbalanced by financial strength, a company with high liquidity or access to other reserves being able to withstand environmental volatility.

Industry strength is the second environmental dimension considered. This focuses on attractiveness of the industry in terms of growth potential, profitability and the ability to use its resources efficiently. For a company within the industry these strengths are no virtue unless a company has a competitive advantage. SPACE analysis, therefore, opposes industry strength by competitive advantage (Figure 3.14) to provide a gauge of a company's position relative to the industry.

Rating a company and the industry on each of the four dimensions gives the competitive profile abAB in Figure 3.14. The example clearly shows a company in a weak position: moderately high environmental instability is not balanced by financial strength, and the competitive advantage of the company is not great compared with the overall industry strength.

The relative size of the opposing dimension gives a guide to the appropriate strategic posture of a firm. For example, from Figure 3.14, A + a and B + b show the overall weight of the SPACE analysis to be towards the bottom right-hand quadrant. This indicates a **competitive posture,** which is typical of a company with a competitive advantage in an attractive industry. However, the company's financial strength is insufficient to balance the environmental instability it faces. Such firms clearly need more financial resources to maintain their competitive position. In the long term this may be achieved by greater efficiency and productivity, but likely is the need to raise capital or merge with a cash-rich company.

Firms that find their strategic posture within the **aggressive quadrant** are enjoying significant advantages yet are likely to face threats from new competition. The chief danger is complacency, which prevents them gaining further market dominance by developing products with a definite competitive edge. The excessive financial strength of these companies may also make it attractive for them to seek acquisition candidates in their own or related industries.

A **conservative posture** is typical of companies in mature markets where the lack of need for investment has generated financial surpluses. The lack of investment can mean that these companies compete at a disadvantage and lack of opportunities within their existing markets makes them vulnerable in the long term. They must, therefore, defend their existing products to ensure a continued cash flow while they seek new market opportunities.

Table 3.2 SPACE analysis – components

Company dimensions	Industry dimensions
Financial strengths	*Environmental stability*
Return on investment	Technological changes
Leverage	Rate of inflation
Liquidity	Demand variability
Capital required/available	Price range of competing products
Cash flow	Entry barriers
Exit barriers	Competitive pressures
Risk	Price elasticity of demand
Competitive advantage	*Industry strength*
Market share	Growth potential
Product quality	Profit potential
Product life cycle	Financial stability
Product replacement cycle	Technological know-how
Customer loyalty	Resource utilisation
Competition's capacity utilisation	Capital intensity
Technological know-how	Market entry ability
Vertical integration	Productivity

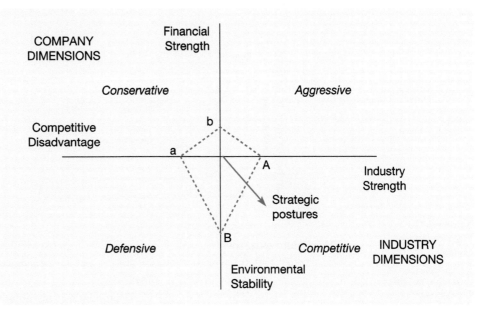

Figure 3.14
SPACE analysis
map

Source: Based on
Rowe *et al.* (1989)
Exhibit 6.10, p. 145.

Companies with a **defensive posture** are clearly vulnerable. Having little residual strength to combat competition, they need to foster resources by operating efficiently and be prepared to retreat from competitive markets in order to concentrate on ones they have a chance of defending. For these it just appears to be a matter of time before either competition or the environment gets the better of them.

3.13   The Advantage Matrix

Once strategic groups within a market have been identified, it becomes apparent that the groups have differing levels of profitability. For instance, in the machine tool industry conventional lathes are almost a commodity and frequently produced at low cost in the emerging economies. But in another part of the industry, say flexible manufacturing systems, profits can be quite high for those companies with special skills. Recognition of this pattern led the Boston Consulting Group (1979) to develop the Advantage Matrix, which helps to classify the competitive environments that can co-exist within an industry. The framework identifies two dimensions: the number of approaches to achieving advantage within a market and the potential size advantage. In Figure 3.15 the quadrants of the Advantage Matrix show how relationships between relative size and return on assets for companies can differ.

The **stalemate** quadrant represents markets with few ways of achieving advantage and where the potential size advantage is small. Companies in such a strategic group would therefore find trading akin to a commodity market. These can be relatively complex products, as in the case of desktop computers, where the technologies are well known, product designs are convergent despite constant technological improvement, and similar sources of supply are used by everyone. Both large and small manufacturers are using overseas suppliers, and consumers are well able to compare product with product. Attempts to differentiate the market, as tried by IBM with its PS/2, have failed. Therefore competitors are forced to compete mainly on the basis of efficient manufacturing and distribution.

The **volume** quadrant represents markets where the opportunities for differentiation remain few yet where potential size advantages remain great. This has occurred within some of the

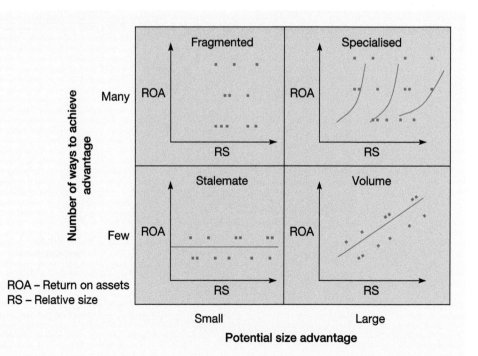

Figure 3.15
The Advantage
Matrix

Source: Based on
unpublished material from
the Boston Consulting
Group.

peripheral markets that support desktop computers. In particular, the printer industry has come to be dominated by Canon, Hewlett-Packard and IBM. The reason for this is the convergence in needs of users of printers and the mass production of the intrinsically mechanical printer units. Unlike microcomputers, where the manufacturing process is one of assembly of basically standard components in a very fixed fashion, as any user of printers will know there are numerous ways of solving the printing and paper-feed problems. This results in an industry where large economies of scale can be achieved by a few dominant suppliers. Where there are markets of this form, battles to achieve volume and economies of scale are paramount. Dominant companies are likely to remain dominant for some time once their cost advantage is achieved, although there is always a threat from a new technology emerging that will destroy the cost advantage they have fought to obtain. In this way Hewlett-Packard joined the band of leaders within the printer market by becoming the industry standard in the newly emerged market for laser printers.

Specialised markets occur when companies within the same market have differing returns on scale. This occurs most conspicuously among suppliers of software for microcomputers. Within the overall market for software there are clear sub-sectors with dominant leaders. It is also apparent that the market leaders, because of their familiarity and proven reliability, are able to charge a price premium. Microsoft Office, for example, is fast establishing leadership of the integrated office software sector at prices ahead of its major competitors. Within the games sector Atari is less able to command premium prices, although its dominance does mean it is reaping size advantages within its own segments. The result in these specialised markets is therefore a series of experience curves being followed by different companies. Within these specialised markets the most successful companies will be those that dominate one or two segments. Within the market for microcomputer software this has often meant that they will be the companies creating a new generic class of product, as Microsoft achieved with its Windows products – making the IBM PC as user friendly as its Apple Mac rival.

Fragmented markets occur when the market's requirements are less well defined than the stalemate, volume or specialised cases. Several parts of the computer peripheral market conform to this pattern. In contrast to the demand for printers, the specialised users of plotters have a wide variety of requirements and the opportunities for colour and high resolution mean that an unlimited variety of differentiated products can be made. Similarly, in the provision of accounting software, alternative specifications are numerous and therefore many different prices and products co-exist in the same market. Where this fragmentation has occurred, success depends on finding niches where particular product specifications are needed. Each niche provides little opportunity for growth; therefore, a company hoping to expand depends on finding a multiplicity of niches where, hopefully, some degree of commonality will allow economies to be achieved.

Summary

Several broad conclusions can now be drawn and their implications for marketing management identified.

First, in many industries the days of rapid domestic growth are gone forever. In those where high rates of growth are still possible competition is likely to be increasingly fierce and of an international nature. It is no longer sufficient for companies to become marketing oriented. That is taken for granted. The keys to success will be the effective implementation of the marketing concept through clearly defined positioning strategies.

Second, change creates opportunities for innovative organisations and threats for those who attempt to hold it back. It is probable that there will be a redefinition of 'work' and 'leisure', which will provide significant new opportunities to those companies ready and able to seize them. The changing demographic profile, particularly in terms of age, marital status and income distribution, also poses many opportunities for marketing management.

Third, the speed of change in the environment is accelerating, leading to greater complexity and added 'turbulence', or discontinuity. Technological developments are combining to shorten product life cycles and speed up commercialisation times. The increasing turbulence in the market makes it particularly difficult to predict. As a result, planning horizons have been shortened. Where long-range plans in relatively predictable markets could span 10–15 years, very few companies today are able to plan beyond the next few years in any but the most general terms.

Fourth, successful strategies erode over time. What has been successful at one point in time, in one market, cannot guarantee success in the future in the same or other markets.

A systematic analysis of the competitive or industry environment in which an organisation operates consists of four main components: (1) an analysis of the five forces driving industry competition (rivalry among existing incumbents, the threat of entry and substitution, the bargaining power of buyers and suppliers); (2) the recognition of the strategic groups within a market that can allow a company to address its efforts towards specific rather than general competitors; (3) the recognition of the different competitive environments and scale economies that can exist within the sub-markets in which the strategic clusters operate; and (4) the degree of turbulence within markets. Through understanding these, a company can identify the sort of competition that is likely to exist within chosen segments and the types of strategy that are likely to lead to success. From the study of turbulence they can also find a guide to necessary orientation of the company and the blend of custodial management and entrepreneurial flair that will be needed to manage the venture. Just as segmentation allows a company to direct its resources towards fulfilling a particular set of customer needs, the industry analysis helps a company to build its defences towards a specific group of competitors, and build its strengths in accordance with the type of market it faces.

At the outset we noted, however, that studying the industry alone is not enough – it may blind us to changes in the sources and types of competition we will face in the future and fundamental changes in the structure of markets. To our analysis of industry we must add our understanding of customers and competitors, as well as our real capabilities as an organisation. These are the topics of the chapters that follow.

Case study   Food group shifts strategy to volume growth

Franck Riboud is famously impatient with the stock market's short-termism. So when the executive chairman of Danone in November disappointed analysts by downgrading growth forecasts, he reacted in typical style.

'The crisis is not our main concern; our main concern is to construct the next 15 years for this group,' he said.

With that in mind, Mr Riboud has shifted strategy to volume growth rather than sales growth. His view appears to be that setting a high sales target in the current economic environment would put undue pressure on managers, risking mistakes and shortcuts to achieve the growth. Much better to cut prices and increase volumes than to shut factories, he has said.

Instead the group prefers to reinvest cost savings as it expands and deepen sales in new markets rather than pledge to boost continually profit margins.

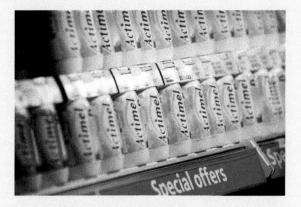

The company sells its products – including Activia yoghurt and Actimel yoghurt drink, as well as Evian, Badoit and baby food, including Milupa, to 700m people worldwide. It aims to achieve its mission to 'bring health through food to the largest number of people' by selling to 1bn people by the end of 2011. Although its international sales are expanding, it still relies on Western Europe for 48 per cent of its sales.

After 12 years at the helm of Europe's third-largest food group after Nestlé and Unilever, Mr Riboud has transformed Danone from a conglomerate into a streamlined business that his father, Antoine Riboud, whom he replaced, would not have been able to recognise. Now focused on three main sectors – yoghurt, spring water, and baby food along with a small clinical nutrition business – he jettisoned beer, biscuits, cheese and other 'unhealthy' food and drink on the way.

Selling low-growth businesses helped Danone achieve one of the best organic growth rates in the sector, making it a stock market darling – its compound annual growth rate was 8.9 per cent between 2001 and 2007.

While there is no argument about the company's ability to drive sales growth, its commitment to shareholder value is more debatable, according to Alex Molloy, analyst at Credit Suisse, citing Danone's c12.3bn takeover of Numico, the Dutch baby food business in 2007 and this past year's c3bn rights issue: 'Strategically the Numico acquisition was great but they paid so much for it that it has not created shareholder value.'

In November Danone cut its sales target over the medium-term to 'at least 5 per cent' from 8–10 per cent previously, citing changes in consumer behaviour. It also abandoned guidance on profit margins and earnings per share growth but said that annual free cash flow would reach €2bn by 2012.

Analysts were disappointed. 'Without a premium growth rate against its peers, we do not see how the stock can return to a premium valuation,' wrote analysts at Royal Bank of Scotland.

Mr Molloy said: 'The debate now is whether this crisis has washed out the trend for the great sales growth there was between 1997–2007. Only time will tell but we are positive because people like healthy and convenient food.'

For Danone, the shift towards volume rather than sales growth means targeting and expanding sales in emerging markets. But because people in these countries are less wealthy than in more prosperous countries, the company cannot expect to generate the same profit margins. Its cheapest yoghurt is sold in Bangladesh at 6 euro cents in an 80g cup. In France, plain Activia yoghurt sells for 26 euro cents for 125g.

Danone is experimenting with selling its Activia yoghurt in powdered form, which would allow it to bypass expensive cold storage costs.

Source: from 'Food group shifts strategy to volume growth', *Financial Times*, 10/01/10 (Daneshkhu, S. and Wiggins, J.).

Discussion questions

1 What environmental factors is Danone responding to by shifting strategy to volume growth rather than sales growth?

2 Explain why Danone is focusing on only three main sectors. Why these sectors?

3 What rationale can you give for the fact that Danone has retained its water brands (such as Evian, Volvic and Badoit) in view of recent criticisms of bottled water? Use the Advantage Matrix to help you build your argument.

CHAPTER 4
CUSTOMER ANALYSIS

When the future becomes less visible, when the fog descends, the forecasting horizon that you can trust comes closer and closer to your nose. In those circumstances being receptive to new directions becomes important.
You need to take account of opportunities and threats and enhance an organisation's responsiveness.

Igor Ansoff, quoted by Hill (1979)

Amadeus set to soar on airline data sales

Amadeus, the Spanish company that provides the technology behind airline flight bookings, is set to report results in stark contrast to the airlines it serves, as it benefits from a 40 per cent share of a growing air travel market.

On Friday, the group's full-year results are expected to show the effect of its expansion from flights into hotel reservations and the growth of its IT solutions business. Its share price has been charting a sustained upwards trajectory for much of the last five years, hitting an all-time high on Monday this week, for a market capitalisation of more €16bn.

Amadeus makes most of its money through its global flight distribution system, which manages transactions between customers and about 120 of the world's airlines, many of which take place on online price comparison websites. Its growth is therefore linked directly to an increase in global air traffic.

But despite Amadeus being recognised by Bloomberg as the 11th largest software company in the world, and second in Europe, Luis Maroto, group chief executive, struck a cautious tone when asked about his company's future prospects.

'It's nothing new,' he said. 'Travel is very much linked to economy . . . This is coming more from Asia due to the size of the populations there,' he adds.

However, analysts suggest that much of Amadeus' value lies in what it can glean from the billions of transactions it processes: a perspective on the purchasing habits of consumers.

Improved personalisation – from the interrogation of 'big data' – enables airlines to tailor their products and services to the personal whims of individual consumers.

Amadeus has already begun to sell aggregated user information to airlines, revealing customers' search habits. It provides a growing revenue stream for the company. Mr Maroto has said this will form part of the business model in future.

The company, however, faces certain challenges. It competes mainly with other global distribution services, including US group Sabre and UK-based Travelport, both of which listed last year. 'Sabre and Travelport are trying to gain market share,' noted Gonzalo Sanz, an analyst at Mirabaud Securities.

Airline companies have also attempted to provide their own IT infrastructure, which threatens to cut Amadeus out of the loop and reduce the number of transactions flowing through its system.

On this front, though, analysts have suggested the tide may be turning in Amadeus' favour. Last summer, Ryanair, which had previously refused to place itself on global distribution platforms, relented and announced a partnership with the company.

Source: from 'Amadeus set to soar on airline bookings', *Financial Times*, 26/02/2015 (Hale, T.).

Discussion questions

1 Where does most of Amadeus' value lie?

2 What information do companies need to have about their customers?

Introduction

Information is the raw material of decision making. Effective marketing decisions are based on sound information; the decisions themselves can be no better than the information on which they are based. Marketing research is concerned with the provision of information that can be used to reduce the level of uncertainty in decision making. Uncertainty can never be eliminated completely in marketing decisions, but by the careful application of tried and tested research techniques it can be reduced.

The first section of this chapter looks at the information needed about customers to make effective marketing decisions. This is followed by a brief discussion of the various research techniques available for collecting data from the marketing environment. The use of these techniques in a typical marketing research study aimed at creatively segmenting a market and identifying current and potential product/service positions is then discussed. The chapter concludes with a discussion of how marketing-related information can be arranged within an organisation and the development of marketing decision support systems (MDSS).

4.1   What we need to know about customers

Information needed about customers can be broadly grouped into current and future information. The critical issues concerning current customers are: (1) Who are the prime market targets? (2) What gives them value? (3) How can they be brought closer? and (4) How can they be better served?

For the future, however, we also need to know: (1) How will customers and their needs and requirements change? (2) Which new customers should we pursue? and (3) How should we pursue them?

4.1.1 Information on current customers

The starting point is to define who the current customers are. The answer is not always obvious as there may be many actors in the purchase and use of a particular product or service. Customers are not necessarily the same as consumers. A useful way to approach customer definition is to recognise five main roles that exist in many purchasing situations.

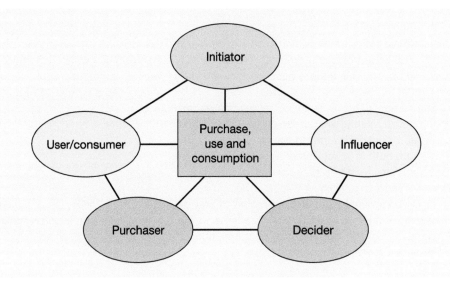

Figure 4.1
Who is the
customer?

Often several, or even all, of these roles may be conducted by the same individuals, but recognising each role separately can be a useful step in more accurately targeting marketing activity (see Figure 4.1).

The roles are as follows:

1 **The initiator.** This is the individual (or individuals) who initiates the search for a solution to the customer's problem. In the case of the purchase of a chocolate bar it could be a hungry child who recognises her own need for sustenance (or pleasure!). In the case of a supermarket the reordering of a particular line of produce nearing sell-out may be initiated by a stock controller, or by an automatic order processing system.

2 **The influencer.** Influencers are all those individuals who may have some influence on the purchase decision. A child may have initiated the search for a chocolate bar, but the parents may have a strong influence (through holding the purse strings) on which product is actually bought. In the supermarket the ultimate customers will have a strong influence on the brands ordered – the brands they buy or request the store to stock will be most likely to be ordered.

3 **The decider.** Taking into account the views of initiators and influencers some individual will actually make the decision as to which product or service to purchase. This may be back to the initiator or the influencer in the case of the chocolate bar. In the supermarket the decider may be a merchandiser whose task it is to specify which brands to stock, what quantity to order and so on.

4 **The purchaser.** The purchaser is the individual who actually buys the product or service. They are, in effect, the individual that hands over the cash in exchange for the benefits. This may be the child or parent for the chocolate bar. In industrial purchasing it is often a professional buyer who, after taking account of the various influences on the decision, ultimately places the order attempting to get the best value for money possible.

5 **The user.** Finally comes the end user of the product or service, the individual who consumes the offer. For the chocolate bar it will be the child. For the goods in the supermarket it will be the supermarket's customers.

What is important in any buying situation is to have a clear idea of the various actors likely to have an impact on the purchase and consumption decision. Where the various roles are undertaken by different individuals it may be necessary to adopt a different marketing approach to each. Each may be looking for different benefits in the purchase and consumption process. Where different roles are undertaken by the same individuals different approaches may be suitable depending on what stage of the buy/consume process the individual is in at the time (see Figure 4.2).

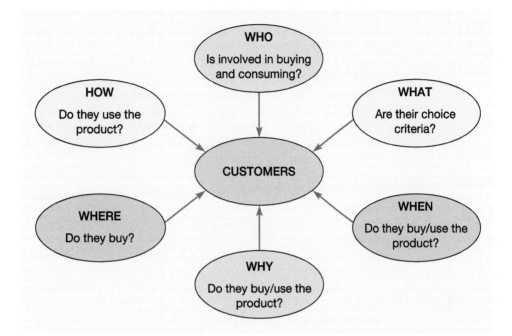

Figure 4.2
Understanding
customers – the
key questions

A central theme of this text is that most markets are segmented; in other words different identifiable groups of customers require different benefits when buying or using essentially similar products or services. Identifying who the various customers are and what role they play then leads to the question of what gives them value. For each of the above members of a decision-making unit (DMU), different aspects of the purchase and use may give value.

For example, in the child's purchase of a chocolate bar a number of benefits may emerge. The child/initiator/decider/user gets a pleasant sensory experience and a filled stomach. The parent/influencer gets a feeling of having steered the child in the direction of a product that is nutritious and good value for money. In a business purchase, such as a tractor, the users (drivers) may be looking for comfort and ease of operation, the deciders (top management) may be looking for economical performance, while the purchaser (purchasing officer) may be looking for a bulk purchase deal to demonstrate their buying efficiency. Clearly the importance of each actor in the decision needs to be assessed and the benefits each gets from the process understood.

Having identified the motivators for each actor attention then shifts to how they can be brought closer to the supplier. Ways of offering increased benefits (better sensory experiences, enhanced nutritional value, better value for money) can be examined. This may involve extending the product service offering through the 'augmented' product (see Levitt, 1986).

For business purchases a major route to bringing customers closer is to develop mutually beneficial alliances that enhance value for both customer and supplier. A characteristic of Japanese businesses is the closeness developed with suppliers so as to ensure continuity of appropriate quality supply of semi-finished material 'just in time' for production purposes.

Better service is at the heart of improving customer relations and making it difficult for customers to go elsewhere. Surveys in the United States have shown that, of lost business, less than 20 per cent is down to poor products and only 20 per cent down to (relatively) high prices. The major reason for losing business is predominantly poor service – more than 40 per cent of cases.

4.1.2 Information on future customers

The above issues have been concerned with today's customers. Of importance for the future, however, is how those customers will change. There are two main types of change essential to customer analysis.

The first is changes in existing customers: their wants, needs and expectations. As competition intensifies so the range of offerings open to customers increases. In addition, their experiences with various offers can lead to increased expectations and requirements. A major way of dealing with this type of change is continuous improvement (or the kaizen approach of the Japanese).

In the hi-fi market continuous product improvements, coupled with some significant innovations such as the MP3 player, have served to increase customer expectations of both the quality of sound reproduction and the portability of equipment. A manufacturer still offering the products of the 1980s or even 1990s in the 2010s would soon find its customers deserting in favour of competitors' offerings.

The second type of change comes from new customers emerging as potentially more attractive targets. Segments that may be less attractive at one point in time might become more attractive in the future. As social, cultural and economic change has affected living standards so has it affected the demand for goods and services. There is now, for example, increased demand for healthy or organically grown foods, green energy generation equipment and services such that markets which might have been less attractive in the 1990s or even the beginning of the 2000s are now booming or starting to grow.

The main ways in which organisations go about analysing their customers is through marketing research (to collect relevant data on them) and market modelling (to make sense of that data). Each is discussed below.

4.2 Marketing research

The use of marketing research services by a variety of organisations, from commercial firms to political parties, has increased dramatically in recent years. The sector is worth more than £3 billion annually in the United Kingdom alone according to the Market Research Society (**www.mrs.org.uk**). Not only large companies and organisations benefit from marketing research. It is possible, through creative design of research studies, for organisations with smaller budgets to benefit from marketing research studies. Commercial research organisations will conduct studies for clients costing as little as £2,000, depending on the research being undertaken. See **http://www.marketresearchworld.net/index.php** for a summary of the types of research available and the methodologies used.

The advent of the Internet and the ubiquitous e-mail has opened the way for new marketing research methods and approaches. These are discussed in Chapter 11.

Figure 4.3 shows the range of marketing research activities engaged in by research agencies. In the United Kingdom there are currently over 400 agencies providing research services. Some companies, such as BMRB (**http://www.bmrb.co.uk/**), offer a wide variety of services. Others specialise in particular types of research (such as qualitative research). For a comprehensive listing of companies in the United Kingdom providing marketing research services, and where appropriate their specialisations, see **http://www.rbg.org.uk/**. Each type of research is discussed below.

4.2.1 Company records

An obvious, but often under-utilised, starting point for gathering marketing data is through the effective use of the company's own records. Often large amounts of data that can be used to aid marketing decisions (both strategic and tactical) are held in unlikely places within the company (e.g. in the accounts department). Data on factors such as who purchases and how much they purchase may be obtained from invoice records. Similarly, purchase records may show customer loyalty patterns, identify gaps in customer purchasing and highlight the most valuable customers.

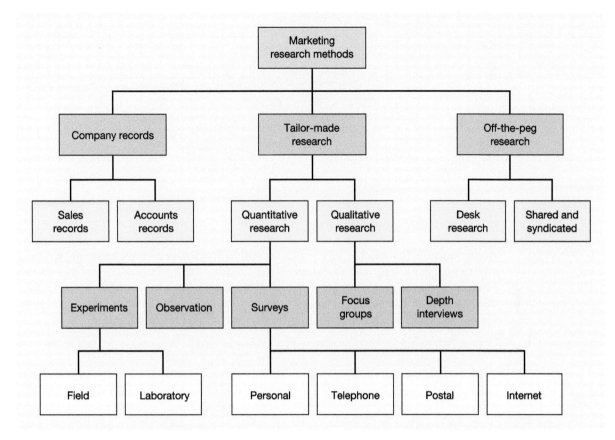

Figure 4.3 Marketing research methods

The value of internally collected data is dependent, however, on how it is collected in the first place. Unfortunately sales data are often not collected or maintained in a form that facilitates use for marketing decision making. As a general rule it is desirable to collect routine data on as detailed a basis as possible to allow for unforeseen data analysis requirements. For example, sales records should be kept by customer, customer type, product, product line, sales territory, salesperson and detailed time period. Data of this type would allow the isolation of profitable and unprofitable customers, territories and product lines, and identify trends in the marketplace.

In direct marketing it is said that the best customer prospects are often existing customers. Adequate sales records should reveal frequencies of purchase, latent and lapsed customers, and may suggest alternative products that could be of interest. In the mail order business, catalogue companies keep records of the types of product customers have bought from them. This enables additional catalogues, more specialist in nature, to be targeted at the most likely prospects.

The British supermarket Tesco is successfully using its loyalty card – Clubcard – to build profiles of its customers so that it can 'generate a map of how an individual thinks, works and, more importantly, shops. The map classifies consumers across 10 categories: wealth, promotions, travel, charities, green, time poor, credit, living style, creature of habit and adventurous' (*The Guardian,* 20 September 2005). Also in the UK, Asda does not have a loyalty card but still manages to hold a lot of information on how their customers spend their money. For example, the retailer discovered that the purchase of champagne is likely to be accompanied by that of a gift bag: the result is that gift bags are now located next to the champagne in the stores (*The Sunday Times,* 19 December 2004).

Tesco Clubcard

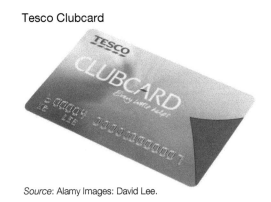

Source: Alamy Images: David Lee.

4.2.2 Off-the-peg research

As the name implies, off-the-peg research consists of tapping into existing research services, often locating and using data that are already in existence but held externally to the company. Much basic information, such as market sizes and growth rates, broad social and economic trends, customer firms and competitor firms, is already available in some form or another. Crouch and Housden (2003) classify three main types of off-the-peg research:

1 Research using the very large body of already published data, usually termed secondary or desk research.
2 Research using data available from regular market surveys of syndicated research. Both the costs of the research and the data collected are shared by the syndicate of research buyers.
3 Research in which the method of data collection is shared, but the data are not. Off-the-peg research instruments, such as omnibus surveys, are employed to collect client-specific data.

Secondary desk research

Secondary desk research uses data that have already been published by someone else. The researcher is a 'secondary' user of the research. Secondary data have the advantages of being relatively cheap and quick to obtain (when you know where to look!), and can also be reliable and accurate. Unfortunately secondary data are often out of date and not specific enough to answer the majority of marketing questions. Secondary data will, for example, often tell you how many customers buy each competitor's offering but won't tell you why.

In the United Kingdom there are very many sources of secondary data; the major problem facing the inexperienced researcher is finding them. The government publishes a great deal of statistical information about industry, trade, commerce and social trends. Most of these data are free, or charged for at the cost of publishing only. The starting point for identifying relevant government statistics is **http://www.statistics.gov.uk/hub/index.html**. Increasingly it is possible to use commercial online information services such as Harvest (**http://harvest.sourceforge.net/**) to search through alternative sources and to scan quickly what data are already available.

Secondary data vary dramatically in quality, both from country to country and from supplier to supplier within a particular country. In assessing the accuracy of secondary data the following questions should be borne in mind:

1 Who collected the data and why? (Are they likely to be biased in their reporting?)
2 How did they collect the data? (Sample or census? Sampling method used? Research instruments?)
3 What level of accuracy do they claim? (Does the methodology support the claim?)
4 What use did they put the data to? (Is its use limited?)

Primary research

Primary, or field, research is undertaken where the secondary sources cannot provide the detail of information required to solve a particular problem or to sufficiently aid the decision making. Primary research involves the collection of new data, often directly from customers, or from distribution intermediaries (such as retailers or wholesalers).

Syndicated research

Syndicated research occurs where a group of research buyers share the costs and the findings of research among themselves. The majority of such syndicated research services are conducted by the larger marketing research agencies and the results are sold to whoever will buy.

In the United Kingdom syndicated research is carried out in a wide variety of markets, though primarily in consumer markets. Typical examples include the Target Group Index (TGI) of Kantar Media (**http://www.tgisurveys.com/**) and the various media research services, including the National Readership Survey (**http://www.nrs. co.uk/index.html**) and the television viewing survey, BARB (**http://www.barb.co.uk/ index/index**).

There are a great many sources of syndicated research covering a wide variety of markets. They have the major advantages that the methodology is usually tried and tested, the samples are often bigger than individual companies could afford to survey on their own and they are considerably cheaper than conducting the research for one company alone.

The disadvantages are that the data are limited in their usefulness to monitoring sales over time, identifying trends in markets and competitors and tracking advertising and other promotional activity. They do not allow further probing of motivations for purchase, nor indeed any additional, company-specific questioning.

Shared research

The final type of research to be classified as off-the-peg is research where some of the costs and fieldwork are shared by a number of companies but the results are not. Omnibus surveys are regular research surveys that are being undertaken using a predetermined (off-the-peg) sampling frame and methodology. Individual clients then 'buy a seat' on the omnibus by adding their own questions. These are asked, along with the questions of other clients, and the results tabulated against such factors as social class, ACORN (A Classification of Residential Neighbourhood) category, age, etc.

BMRB Omnibus, for example, have a range of omnibus surveys including weekly face-to-face interviews with 2,000 adults (age 15+), interviews with 1,000 young people (age 7–19) monthly, mobile phone based surveys of 500 adults (aged 16–49) and 1,000 Internet users (aged 16–64) surveyed online (**http://www.bmrb-omnibus.co.uk/**). Omnibus research has the major advantages of low cost (as the fieldwork costs are shared by all participating companies) and added flexibility, in that each client can ask his or her own questions of a typically large sample of respondents. The number of questions that can be added to an omnibus is, however, generally limited to between 6 and 10 and, because the respondent will be asked questions about a variety of product fields in the same interview, questions are best kept short and factual to avoid respondent fatigue.

In summary, there is a wide variety of off-the-peg sources from which the company or organisation wishing to conduct market or social research can choose. They have the advantages over conducting primary research in that they have established methodologies and are relatively quick and cheap to tap into. The disadvantages lie in the scope and number of questions that can be asked. Before undertaking costly primary research, however, marketing managers are well advised to examine the possibilities that off-the-peg research offers.

4.2.3 Tailor-made research

Tailor-made research, in contrast to off-the-peg, provides the organisation undertaking the research the flexibility to design the research to exactly match the needs of the client company. Depending on those needs there is a variety of techniques available (see Figure 4.3). The techniques are broadly categorised as qualitative and quantitative.

In qualitative research emphasis is placed on gaining understanding and depth in data that often cannot be quantified. It is concerned with meaning rather than numbers, usually involving small samples of respondents but probing them in depth for their opinions, motivations and attitudes. Quantitative research, on the other hand, involves larger samples, more structured research instruments (questionnaires and so on) and produces quantifiable outputs. In major studies both types of technique may be used together. Qualitative research is often used in the early, exploratory stages of research (see Figure 4.4), and quantitative research then used to provide quantification of the broad qualitative findings.

Qualitative techniques

Qualitative techniques are essentially unstructured or semi-structured interviewing methods designed to encourage respondents to reply freely and express their real feelings, opinions and motivations. There are two main techniques used in qualitative research: the group discussion (variously termed focus group or group depth interview) and the individual depth interview.

Group discussions usually take the form of a relaxed, informal discussion among 7–9 respondents with a group leader or moderator ensuring that the discussion covers areas relevant to the research brief. The discussions are typically held in the moderator's home (in the case of consumer studies) or in a hotel room (for industrial groups). The advantage of the group set-up is that it encourages interaction among the participants, which can generate broader discussion than a one-to-one interview-and-answer session. Its value as a research technique rests with the quality of the group moderator (usually a trained psychologist) and their ability to encourage wide-ranging but relevant discussion of the topics of interest. Products can be introduced into the group for trial and comment in an informal setting conducive to evaluation.

Figure 4.4
Uses of qualitative research

Group discussions were used effectively in the development of the advertising message 'naughty but nice' for fresh cream cakes (see Bradley, 1987). A series of group discussions discovered feelings of guilt associated with eating fresh cream cakes and that the advertising could capitalise on this by emphasising the sheer pleasure of cream cakes and the slightly naughty aspects of eating them. Feelings and emotions of this sort could not have been obtained from quantitative research. The relaxed, informal settings of the group discussion were essential to obtaining the clues that led to the advertising copy development.

The depth interview takes place between one interviewer (again often a trained psychologist) and one respondent. It is used extensively for deeper probing of motivations, especially in areas of a confidential nature, or on delicate subjects where it is necessary that rapport and trust is built up between the interviewer and the respondent. Many of the techniques used in depth interviews have been developed from clinical psychology, including the use of projective techniques such as word associations and Kelly Repertory Grids (see Chapter 8, page 208).

Qualitative research is often used as preliminary research prior to a more quantitative investigation. In this context it can help in the wording of questions on a further questionnaire, indicate what questions to ask and elicit important product and brand features and image dimensions. Qualitative research is also used on its own in motivation studies, for the development and pretesting of advertising messages, for package design evaluation, for concept testing and new product testing. The major limitation of qualitative research is that its cost and its nature make it impossible to employ large samples and hence it can be dangerous applying the findings to large populations on the basis of the small sample involved.

Quantitative techniques

Quantitative research techniques include surveys, observation methods and experimentation of one type or another.

Surveys are a vast subject in themselves. There are four main types of survey, depending on how the interviews are conducted: personal interviews are where the interviewer and the respondent come face-to-face for a question-and-answer session; telephone interviews, an increasingly used research technique, are conducted over the telephone; postal surveys use the mail services to send self-completion questionnaires to respondents; and surveys on the Web. Figure 4.5 shows the main uses to which surveys are put.

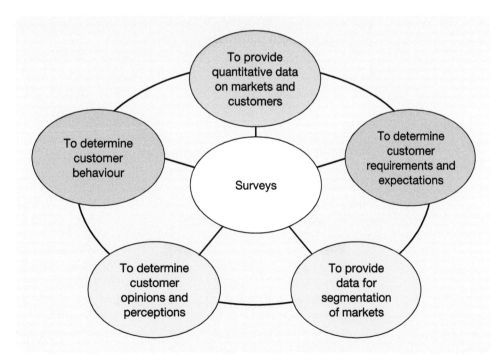

Figure 4.5
Uses of surveys

Each technique has its advantages and drawbacks. Personal interviews are the most expensive to conduct, but offer the greatest flexibility. They are particularly useful where respondents are asked to react to attitudinal statements and more complex questions that may require some clarification by the interviewer.

Telephone interviews are particularly useful when data are required quickly. They do not entail the costs of physically sending interviewers into the field, can be closely controlled and the data collected entered directly on to a computer for analysis. The majority of opinion polls are now conducted in this manner, facilitating next-day reporting in the sponsoring newspapers. The drawbacks of telephone interviews are that more and more people screen their calls so that respondents are harder to reach and that the interview is less personal than a face-to-face encounter, requiring it to be kept relatively short. It is not possible to show prompts and other stimuli during a telephone conversation.

Postal surveys are the cheapest method of all. They are useful in locating geographically dispersed samples and for situations where the questionnaire is long and detailed. Response rates, however, can be low and there is little control over who responds. The lack of personal contact requires a very clearly laid out questionnaire, well pretested to ensure clarity.

Web-based surveys, either mobile or online, are fast growing. Mobile surveys via apps are particularly apt in reaching people who may not normally participate in research.

Observation techniques can be particularly useful where respondents are unlikely to be able or willing to give the types of information required. Crouch and Housden (1996) cite the example of research into what items a shopper has taken from a supermarket shelf, considered for purchase but not bought. Direct questioning after the shopping trip is unlikely to produce accurate data as the respondent simply will not remember. Observation of shopping behaviour in the store can provide such data.

Observation can be conducted by individuals, as in the case of the supermarket behaviour noted above, or observation of traffic density on particular roads, or by instruments designed to monitor behaviour. The prime example of the latter is the 'PeopleMeter' recording device used in television viewing research. A black box is attached to the television sets of a sample of viewers and records when the set was turned on and what channel it was tuned to. Each individual in the household has a code key that is activated when they are in the room. Data are transmitted from the home to the research company via the telephone network overnight, enabling rapid analysis of viewing data. In recent years PeopleMeters have been widely adopted throughout the developed and developing world as methods of monitoring TV viewing and audiences.

The final type of quantitative research of interest here is experimentation. Experiments are either carried out in the field or in-house (laboratory). Field experiments take place in the real world and the subjects of the experiments typically do not know that they are part of an experiment. The prime example is test marketing, where a new product will be marketed in a limited geographic region prior to a decision on whether to launch the brand nationally or internationally. In-house experiments are conducted in a more controlled but less realistic setting where the respondents know they are taking part. Figure 4.6 shows the main uses for experiments in marketing.

Broadbent (1983) describes the use of regional experiments in the development and testing of advertising copy for Cadbury's Flake. Cadbury's Flake competes in the confectionery countline market. The brand sales had grown steadily until the total countline market went into decline. Flake sales, however, declined at twice the market rate. An attitudinal study was undertaken that showed a high proportion of lapsed users found the product too messy/crumbly. As this represented the major reason for purchase by the heavy users of the brand it was not considered desirable to change the product design.

An alternative advertising message was developed emphasising 'every little piece of flake is sheer enjoyment' and making an art out of eating Flake. There were various techniques shown for getting the last crumbs – tipping back the chair, using a paper plate and sucking the last crumbs through a straw.

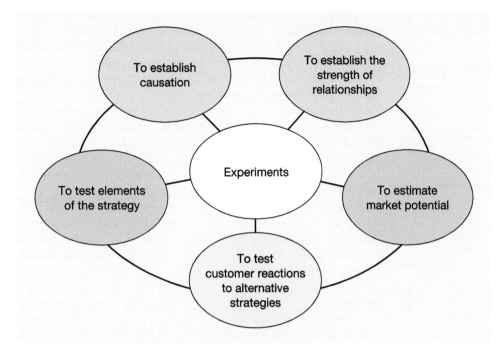

Figure 4.6
Uses of
experimentation

Cadbury's Flake

Source: Courtesy of Mondelez UK Ltd.

The new advertisements were tested in the Lancashire and Yorkshire television regions and sales closely monitored compared with the rest of the country. Using syndicated sources and specially commissioned surveys it was estimated that in the 18 months of the test unit sales had increased by 16 per cent over and above what would have been expected. Both initial purchase and repeat purchase rates were shown to have increased. The campaign was judged to have turned the negative (mess) into a positive (delicious morsels of Flake) through the humour of the ads and was extended on a limited basis to other areas.

There have been several recent innovations in test marketing. Full-scale testing, as described above, suffers from a number of problems. It is costly, time-consuming and alerts the competition to changes in marketing strategy or new products about to be launched. As a result there has been an increase in other, smaller-scale testing methods.

Simulated supermarket tests make grocery products available in a simulated environment. They can be helpful in estimating trial rates, testing purchase intents created by exposure to test advertisements and testing individual elements of the marketing mix such as packaging, pricing and branding. Supermarket panels, recruited within the shoppers of a particular chain, have their purchases recorded through laser scanning and related to purchase card numbers. These panels can be particularly useful in the limited market testing of new brands.

As with off-the-peg research, the variety of tailor-made research available is very wide. There are a great many market research agencies with varying expertise and skills. While it is still true to say that the majority of expenditure on marketing research comes from the larger, fast-moving consumer goods companies, it is possible for smaller companies to take advantage of the research services and sources available (especially off-the-peg research).

Market research techniques are also increasingly being used to investigate non-commercial problems. Research was used heavily, for example, to investigate drug abuse by young people prior to an advertising campaign designed to tackle the problem. The Oxfam charity has used survey research to help it understand the motivations behind charity donations and to help identify 'prime donor segments'. During the run-up to the 2015 General Election in the United Kingdom both major political parties spent heavily on market and opinion research to gauge the mood of potential voters. Opinion poll results (sponsored by the media and political parties) were published almost daily in the three-week run-up to the election. In the event the polls got the results wrong, prompting an investigation that concluded that there was an under-representation of certain groups in the surveys.

In the context of competitive positioning, market research provides the raw data with which it is possible to segment the market creatively and it can help to identify current and potential product positionings. For example, Customer Care Research (**http://www. customer-care-research.com/**), which draws on the techniques mentioned above but follows the story of a purchase (a case study), is helping marketers refine their positions in 'job-to-be-done' segments. One such marketer discovered that his milkshakes were not just competing with other milkshakes but also with doughnuts, bagels, bananas and, more importantly, boredom, and was then able to improve his product to do the job better (see Christensen *et al.*, 2007; also Berstell and Nitterhouse, 2005).

4.3 The marketing research process

A typical segmentation and positioning research project might combine the use of several of the techniques described above to investigate a particular market. Figure 4.7 shows the various stages.

Problem definition

The first step is to define clearly the problem to be tackled. Typically, a series of discussions between marketing research personnel (internal or external to the company) and marketing decision makers are necessary to ensure that the research project is tackling the correct issues.

Exploratory research

As part of problem definition, and a starting point in the research process itself, exploratory research will be used to identify information gaps and specify the need for further research.

Initially, secondary sources can be utilised. Company records can be employed, alongside off-the-peg desk research, to quantify the market and draw its preliminary boundaries.

Qualitative research might then be used to explore with customers and/or potential customers why and how the particular product was used. At this stage, group discussions may be relevant in many consumer markets. In industrial markets, while group discussions are successfully employed, a preferred route is often personal, depth interviews with key customers.

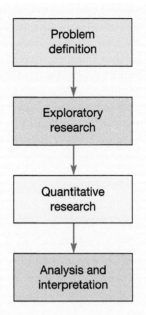

Figure 4.7
Stages in a
comprehensive
marketing research
project

In a segmentation and positioning study the focus of this qualitative research will be to identify the prime motivators to purchase (i.e. the major benefits being sought) and any demotivators. The research should also seek to identify relevant competitors and explore their strengths and weaknesses in serving the market. Finally, hypotheses about how the market could be segmented should be developed: these can be researched further during the later stages of the research project.

Quantitative research

While qualitative research will help in formulating hypotheses about how the market is segmented and what factors influence purchase, because of the small and normally non-representative samples involved it is unlikely to be adequate in itself for segmentation purposes. Typically it will be followed by a quantitative study (a personal survey most often) utilising a sufficiently large and random sample to enable market segment sizes to be estimated and strength of opinions to be gauged.

Such a quantitative study might ask respondents to evaluate competing products on a series of attributes that have been identified as important during the qualitative research. Further, respondents could be asked to rate how important to them personally each attribute is and to express what characteristics their 'ideal' product would have. Background customer characteristics could also be collected to enable any market segments uncovered to be described in ways helpful to further marketing activity (see Chapter 7).

Experimentation might also be used in the quantitative phase of a segmentation and positioning study. Product samples might be placed with existing and potential customers to gauge reaction to new or improved products. Conjoint analysis experiments might be used to estimate reaction to hypothetical product combinations.

Analysis and interpretation

Following data collection, statistical techniques and models can be employed to turn the data generated into meaningful information to help with the segmentation. Factor analysis might be used to reduce a large number of attitudinal statements to their underlying dimensions, or underlying factors. Cluster analysis could be used to group respondents on the basis of several characteristics (attitudes, likes, dislikes or background demographics) into meaningful segments. Perceptual mapping techniques could be employed to draw models of customer perceptions on two, three or more relevant dimensions. These techniques are discussed in more detail in Chapter 8.

Finally, the results will be presented to and discussed with the senior marketing decision makers to aid their interpretation of the market in which they are operating.

The essence of a successful research project is to use the data-gathering and analysis techniques that are relevant both to the product type being investigated and the stage in the research project where they are being employed. By utilising innovative techniques and looking at markets afresh it is often possible to gain new insights into market structure and hence aid the sharpening of target market definition.

The final section in this chapter looks at how information is organised within the firm.

4.4   Organising customer information

Information is organised within the company through the marketing information system (MIS). This system may be formally structured, physically consisting of several personnel and a variety of computer hardware and software, or it may be a very informal collection of reports and statistics piled on an executive's desk or even contained in their head!

Conceptually, however, the system can be represented as in Figure 4.8 (developed from Little, 1979). The information system has five basic components: a market research interface concerned with collecting and gathering raw data from the marketing environment; the raw data collected through the market research interface; statistical techniques that can be used to analyse, synthesise and collate the raw data, to turn it into information; market models that utilise both the raw data and statistical techniques to describe the marketplace, to simulate it or to predict it; and finally a managerial interface that allows the decision maker access to the information and models to aid their decision making.

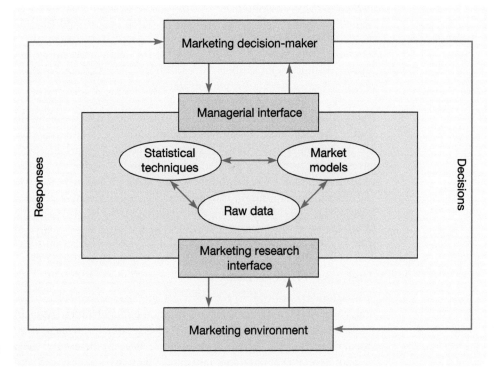

Figure 4.8
Marketing decision
support systems

Raw data

As discussed above, data come into the system from a variety of sources, from internal and external, secondary and primary sources. The data are stored in various forms (e.g. on paper, in people's heads, on computer). Increasingly data are being stored on machine-readable media or the Cloud. The increased availability of computer hardware and software has made it increasingly possible to store large amounts of data in a form that is readily accessible and easily analysed.

Statistical techniques

The processes available to synthesise and summarise the raw data are called statistics. A wide variety of statistics is available but often the most important are the simple ones that allow data to be summarised (such as averages, means, standard deviations, ranges, etc.) so that many small, often diverse observations can be condensed into a few important numbers (for a comprehensive review of statistical techniques available to analyse marketing data, see Green *et al.*, 1993; Diamantopoulos and Schlegelmilch, 1997; Hair *et al., 1998).

Market models

A model is a representation of the real world. Most managers have an implicit model of the markets in which they operate in their own minds. For example, they can give an expectation of the effect of changing price on sales of the product based on their experiences. This is essentially their internal model of the price/sales relationship. In examining data through the use of statistical techniques the analyst may wish to test out the model of the market he or she already has. Alternatively, the objective may be to build a new model of the market to help managerial understanding of the forces that affect demand and overall company performance. There are models covering all parts of marketing activity. Lilien *et al.* (1992) undertook a comprehensive review of these attempts 'to bring order to the chaos of collected facts'.

Managerial interface

If the information system is to be of value to the marketing decision maker, they must have access to that system in such a way as to facilitate and encourage easy use. The interface between the manager and the MIS can consist of an individual (a marketing information officer), a report or set of reports produced on a regular or intermittent basis, or, increasingly commonly, a computer terminal or a microcomputer. With the relevant software to facilitate use of the MIS direct, 'hands-on' access for the decision maker can encourage wider use of the system and experimentation with the various models developed.

Marketing decision support systems

In the 1990s there was a change in emphasis in marketing from information systems (MIS) to marketing decision support systems (MDSS). The distinction may seem merely one of semantics but is, in fact, fundamental. While MIS placed emphasis on provision of information, primarily in the form of facts and figures, MDSS changes the emphasis to aiding decision making through the provision of question-and-answer facilities. In other words MDSS allows analysis rather than merely retrieval of information.

Decision support systems can have several types of output. These have been grouped into two types: data oriented and model oriented.

1 **Data-oriented decision support systems** focus on data retrieval and simple analysis using statistical techniques. This can include, for example, straightforward data retrieval of such items as stock levels. Systems of this type are effectively information systems rather than decision support systems as defined above.

2 **Model-oriented decision support systems,** on the other hand, focus on simulation and representation of aspects of the real world. Accounting models, for example, calculate the consequences of planned actions on the financial performance of the company. Representational models estimate the consequences of action of one type or another. An advertising model may estimate the effects of running a particular advertising campaign. Optimisation models provide guidelines for action by generating the optimal solutions consistent with a series of constraints. For example, given an advertising budget, a target audience and a required average viewing frequency an optimisation model could be used to select the most effective combination of media and insertions.

Implementation of MDSS in marketing has, however, been slower than predicted, but with the advent of PCs and user-friendly programs, and increased storage and programming capabilities, allowing for almost instant management information, the use of decision support systems in marketing is now well established. Several characteristics of MDSS are worth noting:

1 MDSS support decisions! They are not merely data retrieval systems, but are actively designed to help managers make better decisions. In addition they support, rather than replace, managerial decision making.
2 MDSS are essentially interactive. They allow the manager to ask questions, receive inputs and experiment with decisions to estimate the likely outcomes. As such they are more effective where a manager has the scope to use the system directly.
3 MDSS should be flexible and easy to use. Ease of use is a major characteristic essential to gaining widespread use of an innovation such as MDSS poses in many organisations. Flexibility is desirable to allow the system to respond to a variety of information and decision support needs.

Expert systems for marketing decision support

Developments in computer hardware and software offer exciting opportunities for marketing management. The developments in expert systems and artificial intelligence that enable not only the modelling of marketing phenomena but also the decision-making processes of 'experts' in the field promise to revolutionise the whole field of decision support.

The directions in which these developments will move are still evolving at present (Wierenga, 2010). What is certain, however, is that marketing decisions will become more data-based (there is already a data explosion in marketing) and there will be an increased need to organise those data in meaningful ways to enable them to be used quickly and effectively. In particular, increased computing and modelling power will enable decisions to be tested in simulated environments prior to implementation in the real world.

Summary

Understanding customers is central to developing a coherent positioning strategy. This chapter has examined first, the types of information about customers that can be useful in determining competitive position and second, the marketing research methods available for collecting that information. The process typically undertaken to identify potential market segments and their needs was then discussed. Finally, developments in organising and presenting data were examined.

Case study   Balderton plugs into teenagers' attention spans

Balderton Capital, one of Europe's largest venture capital firms, has recruited a group of teenagers to advise it on the latest technology trends.

Balderton, based in London, has invested in Bebo, Betfair and Codemasters. It manages $1.9bn (£1.3bn) in committed funds.

Last month, the venture firm invited 11 15-year-olds to an hour-long private trip on the London Eye for an inaugural meeting.

The teenagers named themselves 'Prestige 11', after the top accolade in a video game, and were given iTunes vouchers as a thank-you. They plan to meet every two or three months and continue to chat and swap ideas on a Facebook group.

Balderton hopes to understand how the teenagers of today will spend their time and money as the adults of tomorrow.

'We think very long term,' said Roberto Bonanzinga, the Balderton partner leading the scheme, who argues few VCs use the services in which they invest.

Mr Bonanzinga has two objectives: discovering new services before they hit the media or investor radar; and testing new ideas pitched by entrepreneurs.

Information gleaned could be particularly useful in Balderton's early stage investments, he says. 'Understanding how consumer behaviour is evolving is super important.'

For now, YouTube and Facebook remain by far the most popular websites among the group. Facebook has completely replaced other email and instant-messaging services.

Immediacy is critical. 'Three hours not replying to a text message would be really rude,' said Tomas Albert, of west London, one of the Prestige 11.

Few pay for music, with many using filesharing networks, believing that artists and labels 'make enough money'. Movies are usually rented from a DVD outlet rather than from the Internet, but only because downloading takes too long.

'They don't collect things,' said Mr Bonanzinga. 'They don't have the need of owning, they have the need of using.'

Source: Alamy Images: MBI.

As a result, teenagers' bedrooms are more likely to be stacked with boxes of video games than the records that adorned their parents' or even older siblings' rooms.

A majority use the Internet on their mobile phones, with several using smartphones such as the iPhone and BlackBerry.

Many are prepared to spend up to £10 ($15) to buy an application for mobiles or an iPod touch, particularly for games, but the lifespan of an app is short.

'We don't stick to anything much longer than a couple of weeks,' said Tomas.

Source: from 'Balderton plugs into teenagers' attention spans', *Financial Times,* 18/06/10 (Bradshaw, T.).

Discussion questions

1 What type of customer information is Balderton trying to uncover?

2 What other methods could Balderton use to gather this type of information?

3 What stages should Balderton use in conducting marketing research?

CHAPTER 5
COMPETITOR ANALYSIS

Two brief notes for consideration on the *nature of competition*:

In the final of the men's 100 metres at the World Athletics Championship in 2009, Tyson Gay clocked a time of 9.71 seconds for the 100 metres. This was his personal best at that moment, and faster than any man, in any other round of the tournament. However, running in the same race was a man by the name of Usain Bolt (you may have heard of him), who ran a 9.58, won the gold medal and set a new world and tournament record time.

Two walkers were out backpacking together in the woods. Around a bend in the trail they came face to face with a bear. One walker drops to his knee, fetches his running shoes from his backpack and begins removing his hiking boots. The other walker just stares and says, 'There is no way you can run faster than that bear.' The kneeling stranger stands up and replies, 'I don't have to be faster than the bear, I only have to be faster than you.'

The takeaway from the above notes is that *performance is always evaluated relative to the competition* (see Sabnis and Grewal, 2012).

Gatwick seeks greater competition with BAA

Gatwick Airport signalled the first moves to increase competition among London's airports on Monday with the launch of a new brand identity and advertising campaign.

The marketing drive, part of a £1bn scheme to improve London's second airport, is an attempt to create a 'challenger brand' to BAA, the operator that owns Heathrow and was recently forced to sell Gatwick as part of a shake-up ordered by competition authorities.

On the first day of its busy summer season, Global Infrastructure Partners, which bought Gatwick last December, unveiled a new signature-style logo and a campaign aimed at giving Gatwick a friendlier image. It will start

Source: Alamy Images: Ian Leonard.

running an advertising campaign on Wednesday with the slogan: 'Your London airport'.

The push to win passengers from Heathrow and Stansted is just the kind of move the Competition Commission hoped to stimulate when it ordered BAA, the dominant airport operator, to sell Gatwick and Stansted airports, as well as either Glasgow or Edinburgh.

The plan to differentiate Gatwick from BAA airports heralds the roll-out of a £1bn investment programme to overhaul the airport's facilities. While Heathrow's image was dented by the so-called 'Heathrow hassle' factor of delays and outdated facilities, Gatwick has also suffered from similar complaints.

Stewart Wingate, Gatwick's chief executive, said the new owner had accelerated the delivery of new facilities and introduced plans for faster check-in facilities and new security lanes.

A new inter-terminal transit will open in July and an extension to the airport's north terminal will create a plaza for passengers. There will also be a new check-in system, allowing passengers to tag their bags themselves and drop them more quickly, and a 'fast-track' system aimed at reducing the queues for security screening.

Gatwick said the programme would mean improvements to almost every part of the airport including 'the South Terminal departure lounge, entrance forecourts, immigration hall, baggage systems and the North Terminal Interchange'.

The airport hopes to increase passenger figures from 33m to more than 40m by 2018.

Mr Wingate said the new brand was important not just to attract new passengers but also to 'galvanise our staff internally now that we are competing with BAA'.

He said: 'This is an important milestone as we compete to make Gatwick London's airport of choice for passengers and airlines. We want it to be something fresher, a lot more innovative and creative.'

While the sell-off of Gatwick prompted speculation that a new owner might attempt to win permission for a second runway at Gatwick, the coalition government has expressly ruled out new runways at London airports. Mr Wingate said that although an area of land for a possible second runway had been safeguarded, Gatwick's focus at the moment was solely on the one existing runway and two terminals.

Source: from 'Gatwick seeks greater competition with BAA', *Financial Times*, 21/06/2010 (Sherwood, B.).

Discussion questions

1 What are the issues that Gatwick is trying to address?
2 How is Gatwick addressing these issues?

Introduction

Sun Tzu (see Clavell, 1981, for a very accessible translation), the great fourth-century BC Chinese general, encapsulated the importance of competitor analysis:

> If you know your enemy as you know yourself, you need not fear the result of a hundred battles. If you know yourself but not the enemy, for every victory you gain you will suffer a defeat. If you know neither the enemy nor yourself, you will succumb in every battle.

Some of the ideas expressed in Sun Zhu's writing are equally valid and applicable in modern business markets. However, one of the main issues facing business strategists today is the degree of complexity faced in some competitive markets, and it is now possible that in a modern business, the main competitor, customer and collaborator are the same company! For example, in the construction industry many large capital projects now require firms previously used to competing aggressively with each other to collaborate for mutual benefit. The complexity, and hence ambiguity faced by executives in many modern markets, underline yet further the imperative of identifying and understanding competitors.

Without knowledge of competitors' strengths and their likely actions it is impossible to formulate the central component of marketing strategy, i.e. a group of customers where an organisation possesses competitive advantage over the competition. Similarly, since competitive advantage is a relative concept, a company that has poor understanding of its competitors can have no real understanding of itself.

Several studies demonstrate a positive link between a clear understanding of competitor strategies and actions, and corporate performance (see, for example, Kapelianis *et al.*, 2005).

Japan's leading companies retain Sun Tzu's obsession with enemy (competitor) analysis. Although successful Eastern and Western companies are alike in many ways (Doyle *et al.*, 1986), the commitment of Japanese companies to gathering information has been identified as a major distinguishing feature of their business strategies. As one example, Lehmann and Winer (1991) report that one Mitsubishi intelligence unit in the United States filled two entire floors of an office building in New York. Indeed, as long ago as the early 1980s *Business Week* described how Japanese companies had established surveillance posts throughout the heartland of the US computer industry in California's Silicon Valley, monitoring US technology development by hiring American software experts. This is not now, of course, limited to Japanese companies, and most successful organisations invest a significant amount of resources annually in order to gather, analyse, interpret and act on market-based data.

This chapter provides a framework for the essential activities of gathering, disseminating and acting on competitor intelligence. It covers four areas:

1 benchmarking against rivals;
2 the dimensions of competitor analysis;
3 the choice of 'good' competitors;
4 the origin, sources and dissemination of competitive information.

5.1 Competitive benchmarking

Competitive benchmarking is the process of measuring your company's strategies and operations against 'best-in-class' companies, both inside and outside your own industry (Swain, 1993). The purpose is to identify certain practices and methodologies that can then be adopted or adapted to improve your own performance. Benchmarking usually involves four main steps.

5.1.1 Identifying who to benchmark against

Industry leaders are obvious firms to compare your own activities against. Central to such an analysis will be identifying the keys to their success in the market. What is it they do differently from others? What makes the difference to their operations? Why are they winners?

In non-profit organisations, such as hospitals and universities, benchmarking also takes place. For hospitals the 'best in class' might be considered those with the lowest mortality rates during operations, or the highest patient throughput. For universities 'best in class' might be those with the best research reputations, highest employability rates for graduates, highest students' satisfaction scores or those most able to attract students to their courses.

Benchmarking may also, however, be undertaken against lesser players in the overall market. New entrants or smaller, more focused firms may have particular strengths from which the firm can learn. These strengths may be in a particular aspect of their operations rather than their operations in total. One firm may be a leader, for example, in terms of customer service, while another may be the best in the industry at cost control. In universities benchmarking against the best providers of distance learning education, or the best researchers in a particular field, might be appropriate.

Organisations also benchmark specific activities (such as procurement and purchasing) against other organisations outside their immediate sector where lessons can be transferred. When Xerox wanted to improve their order processing and warehousing they benchmarked themselves against L.L. Bean, the mail order company, which was believed to be far more 'cutting edge' than Xerox's main competitors (Swain, 1993). Many companies now look to organisations like Amazon and UPS as exemplars for order processing and warehouse management.

5.1.2 Identifying what aspects of business to benchmark

All aspects of business across the complete value chain (see below) are candidates for benchmarking. Scarce resources and time constraints generally dictate the selection of a few key central processes for detailed benchmarking. These will initially centre on the key factors for success in the industry. Initial focus will also typically be on processes that account for significant costs, make a significant impact on customer satisfaction and show greatest room for improvement. Subsequently analyses may be further broadened in attempts to create fresh competitive advantages in new areas of operation.

5.1.3 Collecting relevant data to enable processes and operations to be compared

Data on one's own operations may be relatively easily available, but where competitors are benchmarked commercial secrecy may make access to relevant data difficult. Swain (1993) suggests three main sources of competitor information for benchmarking: published sources; data sharing; and interviews.

- **Published sources** include company reports, technical (trade) reports, industry studies and surveys commissioned by governments or industry associations. For example, in consumer goods markets *Which?* provides comprehensive and useful published reports that compare product performance from a consumer perspective. Obviously websites and web forums are also excellent sources of data, however the quality and usefulness of these sources can vary, depending on the specific sector or industry.
- **Data sharing** may take place in industry forums such as conferences, through direct, formal contacts or more informal contacts. In most industries employees and managers of competing firms meet from time to time and swap information with each other, either consciously or subconsciously.
- **Direct interviews** with customers, distributors, industry experts, former employees of competitors, regulators, government officials, etc. may also be useful in collecting data on competitor operations for benchmarking purposes. Customers that may have defected from you to a close competitor can also be a great source of comparative data. Indeed, competitors' customers in particular are a rich source of information on competitor processes. Questioning customers on the levels of service they received, for example, or the manner in which complaints were handled, can help to identify the processes used behind the scenes to deliver that service.

5.1.4 Comparison with own processes

The final stage in the benchmarking process is to compare and contrast the processes of the identified 'best in class' organisations with the firm's own processes, to identify actions that need to be taken as a consequence, and the setting-up of processes to measure and monitor improvement.

Once the comparisons have been made and the areas for direct attention identified a number of options may be apparent. First, the firm may conclude that its own operations are close to best practice and will continue with them, striving to improve where possible. Second, the firm may conclude that its processes are inadequate or suboptimal and need to be overhauled. This may involve setting up new processes that mirror those of the best practices identified. Alternatively, it may involve adopting best practice processes from other industries that will enable the firm to leapfrog the competition and gain competitive advantage from process innovation. One consideration here is, of course, the resources available to the organisations considering change (can we do this?), and also the underlying strategy of what they are trying to achieve (should we do this?). Any changes, based on benchmarking data, must still 'fit' with the strategy of the organisation.

Where new processes are proposed, or existing processes reinforced, measurable targets should be set that will enable the firm to assess its progress towards achieving better practices. These targets should be specific (e.g. 'answer 95 per cent of telephone calls by the third ring') and achievable within specified timeframes. Hence consideration should be given to the ability of those tasked with achieving the new targets, i.e. have they ever performed at this level previously? Do they, or will they, require training and/or incentives in order to perform at this level? Etc.

Beyond the benchmarking value of competitor analysis a clearer picture of competitor strategies, strengths and weaknesses also helps firms to develop more effective competitive strategies. We now discuss the main processes involved in competitor analysis for the purposes of strategy formulation.

5.2   The dimensions of competitor analysis

In the medium term the focus of competitor analysis must be firms within the same strategic group as the company concerned. In the longer term, however, there is a danger in the analysis being so constrained. The industry as a whole must be scanned for indirect competitors that may have the resources or the need to overcome the entry barriers to the incumbent's strategic group. Although entry barriers may be high, if the incumbent's strategic group shows high profits or growth potential beyond the rest of the market it is likely to attract new entrants.

The UK financial services sector is an example of where conventional competitors have lost business to the entry of new-style competitors. These include a) direct marketing operations such as Direct Line, based on telemarketing, b) the entry to banking by major supermarkets such as Sainsbury's, Tesco and Marks and Spencer, exploiting their customer base and existing retail locations, and c) the piecemeal entry of diverse firms such as British Gas, British Airways and the oil companies that have cherry-picked financial product offerings. It follows, then, that a second source of threat could be potential entrants into an industry, or substitutes. Part of the failing of EMI in the body scanner market was their neglect of entrants that their own success attracted. Rather than build defences or foster coalitions against an almost inevitable onslaught, the company chose to continue to exploit the market as if it was the sole supplier. Perhaps the greatest failing was its falling behind in product quality and its inability to develop a support network for its product (Kay, 1993).

In the longer term, substitutes are the major threat to an industry. These not only bring with them new processes and products with advantages that can totally undermine the incumbents' capabilities (as the scanner did for certain forms of X-ray machine): they are also likely to bring with them new and hungry competitors that are willing to question conventional industry practices. Once IBM entered the PC market it was quite successful relative to its target competitors (Apple and Hewlett-Packard) but had great difficulty in handling the new competition (Toshiba and Dell), which its standardised PC attracted. A more recent example is that of downloads that have revolutionised the music industry, and largely precipitated the demise of pre-recorded CDs, with Apple (originally a computer company) becoming the key player.

Competitor analysis, therefore, involves evaluating a series of concentric circles of adversaries: innermost are the direct competitors within the strategic group, next come companies within the industry that are driven to overcome the entry barriers to the strategic group, and then the outermost potential entrants and substitutes (Figure 5.1).

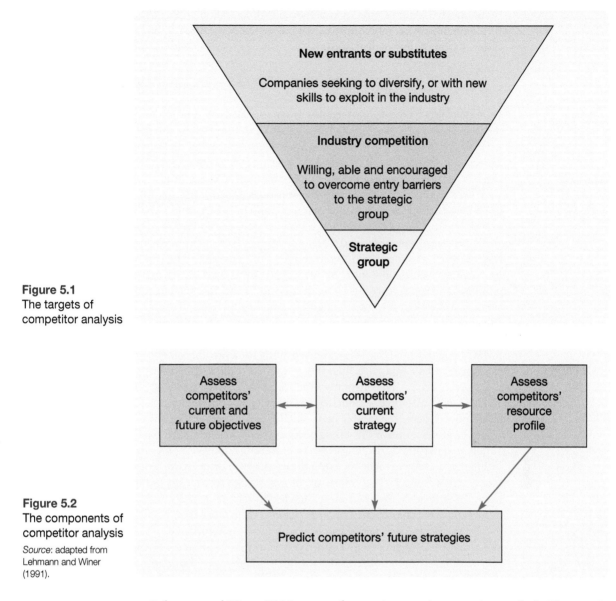

Figure 5.1
The targets of
competitor analysis

Figure 5.2
The components of
competitor analysis

Source: adapted from
Lehmann and Winer
(1991).

Lehmann and Winer (1991) suggest four main stages in competitor analysis (Figure 5.2):

1 **Assessing competitors' current and future objectives**: understanding what the competitor is setting out to achieve can give clues as to the direction it will take and the aggressiveness with which it will pursue that direction.
2 **Assessing the competitors' current strategies**: by understanding the strategies used by competitors in pursuit of their goals and objectives the firm can identify opportunities and threats arising from competitor actions.
3 **Assessing competitors' resources**: the asset and capability profile of competitors shows what they are currently able to do. Those resources may not be fully deployed at present but can give further clues as to how the competitor will move in the future, or how the competitor will react to threats.
4 **Predicting competitors' future strategies**: by combining the above analyses the firm can begin to answer perhaps the most fundamental question in competitor analysis: what is the firm likely to do in the future?

Each of the above is now discussed in detail. In particular, potential sources of information are suggested, together with ways in which the analyses might be conducted. The aim of the analysis is not just to describe the competitor, but to be able to gauge the competitor's future intentions or, more importantly, what the competitor is likely to do in response to the evaluating firm's own actions.

5.2.1 Assessing competitors' current and future objectives

Understanding the goals or objectives of competitors can give guidance to strategy development on three levels (see Figure 5.3). Goals can indicate where the company is intending to develop and in which markets, either by industry or internationally, major initiatives can be expected. The areas of expansion could indicate markets that are to be particularly competitive but may simultaneously signify companies not so committed.

Where the intention is profitable co-existence it is often better to compete in areas that are deemed of secondary interest to major companies rather than to compete directly. Such was the opportunity created when both General Motors and Ford once declared that the small car markets in the United States and Europe were intrinsically unprofitable and therefore of little interest to them. Interestingly, both are now actively pursuing this market as its potential has become more apparent. Pressures on the environment from automobile pollution and road crowding are leading governments to implement measures to encourage smaller cars with more efficient engines, including lower road taxes for cars emitting lower CO_2 emissions. Competitive responses to this pressure from governments have led to massive investment in the hybrid and electric cars we now see on our roads, e.g. Nissan Leaf and BMW's i3 and i8; and this is just the beginning for a revolutionary phase of development in car design and manufacture. This illustrates that goals change as circumstances change and competitors need to be constantly monitored for shifts in strategic direction.

Goals may also give a guide to the intensity of competitor activity and rivalry. When the likes of Procter & Gamble or General Electric declare that they are only interested in being the number one or the strong number two in markets in which they operate it is to be anticipated that they will compete very hard for every new market they enter.

Finally, a company's goals can indicate the type of trade-off it is likely to make when faced with adversity. The obsession of many US overseas subsidiaries with the need to report back steady and slowly increasing profits has meant that they have often been willing to relinquish market share in order to achieve their short-term profit goals.

The goals can have implications across the broad portfolio of a company's activities. When competing against a diversified company ambitious goals in one sector may indicate that commitment to another is diminishing. Equally, very large and diversified companies may often not be able to take advantage of their huge financial strengths because of their unwillingness to make strategic shifts in their resources. There is also a chance that financially driven companies may be unwilling to take the risks of new ventures, preferring instead to pick the bones of those that were damaged in initially taking the risk.

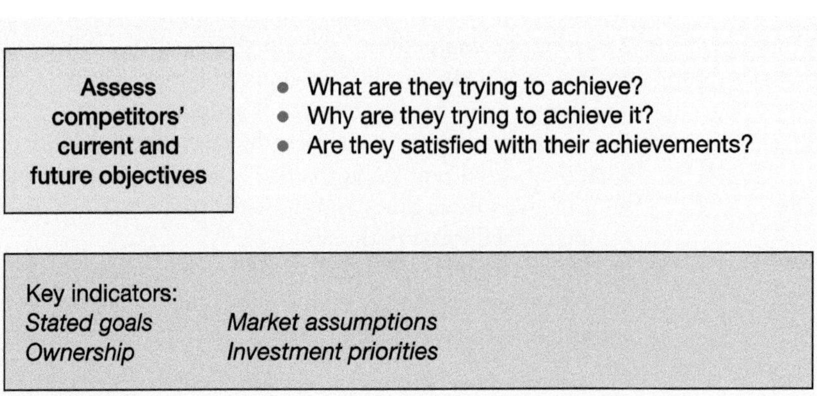

Figure 5.3
Competitor
objectives

Competitor goals and objectives can best be inferred from observation of the strategies they are pursuing, together with pronouncements they make through company reports, press releases, etc. For example, decisions to build additional production facilities are a clear signal of growth objectives. The recruitment of staff with particular skills (identified through observation of recruitment advertisements) can indicate new directions in which the competitor may go.

Reward structures for staff can also indicate objectives. Where sales staff, for example, are rewarded on a percentage of sales commission the practice suggests that sales volume (rather than profitability) is a key objective (Lehmann and Winer, 1991).

Also indicative of future goals can be the ownership structure of the competitor. Competitors owned by employees and/or managers may give a higher priority to providing continuity of employment than those owned by conventional shareholders. Likewise, competitors run through the public sector may set higher priorities on social goals rather than profitability. Competitors owned as part of diversified conglomerates may be managed for short-term cash rather than long-term market position objectives.

Underlying assumptions

Assumptions that a firm has about itself and the market affect the goals and objectives it sets and can be a source of opportunity or threat. Examples of flawed assumptions being made by companies and their dire consequences are many. In the 1960s, Cunard assumed that as the cost of transatlantic travel was so high people would want a leisurely crossing rather than spending a large amount of money in flying the Atlantic in a few hours. The result of this faulty logic by Cunard and other operators of passenger liners was a massive increase in the tonnage of liners being constructed in their last few years of useful life. Similarly, Dunlop's assumption that it was pre-eminent in tyre rubber technology meant that it neglected Michelin's development of steel-braced radials. The result was a catastrophic decline in its own market share, accompanied by a decline in the total market size that occurred because of the longer life of Michelin's new development. Having assumed pre-eminence in an established market, Dunlop's position was made intractable by its inability to develop new products.

Dunlop and Cunard were not atypical in their inability to see changing market conditions. Indeed, there is a tendency for incumbent companies to be dismissive of new entrants and new technologies as being of little significance, or maybe catering for some faddish segment of the market. Such was the case of the Swiss watch industry when first faced with competition from Japanese digital alternatives. Thus the evaluation of assumptions of competitors and those made by a firm itself can be of major strategic significance to a company. Having said this, there is a clear gap between the need and the ability of firms to question their own assumptions.

Analyses of how major firms often react to technological threats show they are rarely able to change their historic orientation. O'Shaughnessy (1995) explains how incumbents often avoid the problems rather than taking evasive action. He suggests that there is a tendency for firms to force the evidence to fit preconceptions; become deaf to any evidence at odds with their beliefs; predict the most feared competitive action as a defence in case there is any future post-mortem after such action occurs and predict that competitive action will be that to which the manager's favourite strategy is an effective counter-strategy as a way of getting support for that strategy.

5.2.2 Assessing competitors' current strategies and activities

Assessing the current strategy involves asking the basic question: 'What exactly is the competitor doing at the moment?' (see Figure 5.4). This requires making as full as possible a statement of what each competitor is trying to do and how they are trying to achieve it. It is an essentially complex activity to which the components of marketing strategy outlined in Chapter 2 can give some structure.

Three main sets of issues need to be addressed with regard to understanding current competitor strategies. First, identification of the market or markets they have chosen to operate in: their selection of target markets. Second, identification of the way in which they have chosen to operate in those markets: the strategic focus they are adopting with regard to the type of competitive advantage they are trying to convey. Third, the supporting marketing mix that is being adopted to enable the positioning aimed for to be achieved. Beyond these three core elements of strategy it can also be helpful to assess the organisation of the marketing effort – the structures adopted – to facilitate implementation of the strategy.

Competitors' target markets

The broad markets and more specific market segments competitors choose to compete in can often be inferred from an analysis of the products and services they are offering, together with the ways in which they are pricing, promoting and distributing them. These elements of the marketing mix are generally highly visible aspects of a firm's activities and available for competitors to analyse.

The features built into products and the type and extent of service offered will be good indicators of the types of customer the competitor is seeking to serve. In the automobile industry, for example, the products made by Jaguar Land Rover, a subsidiary of Tata Group, indicate clearly the types of customers being pursued. Skoda, now owned by Volkswagen, on the other hand, offers very different cars to the market, suggesting a completely different target market. Prices charged will also often be an indicator of the target market aimed for. In grocery retailing, for example, Aldi and Lidl have consistently pursued a minimum-range, low-price strategy in attempts to attract price-sensitive, bulk grocery purchasers rather than compete directly with industry leaders such as Tesco and Sainsbury's on quality and service; although this is changing. Aldi in particular have been extremely successful at eroding market share from the larger and more embedded players in the UK grocery retailing market.

Advertisements and other promotional materials can also give clues as to the target markets aimed for. The wording of advertisements indicates the values the advertiser is attempting to convey and imbue in the product/service offered. Again in automobiles traditional Volvo advertising has clearly focused on safety, appealing to safety-conscious, middle-class families. BMW advertising concentrates on technical quality and the pleasures of driving, suggesting a younger target market. The media in which the advertisements appear, or the scheduling adopted, will also give indications of the target market aimed for. Similarly, the distribution channels the competitor chooses to use to link customers physically with offerings may give clues as to the markets aimed for.

Competitors' strategic focus

Most successful companies attempt to build their strategies on the differential advantage they have over others in the market. This is an important consideration in two ways. It is clearly necessary to base the differential advantage on customer targets and it is important to avoid basing one's competitive strategy on trying to build strengths where one is always

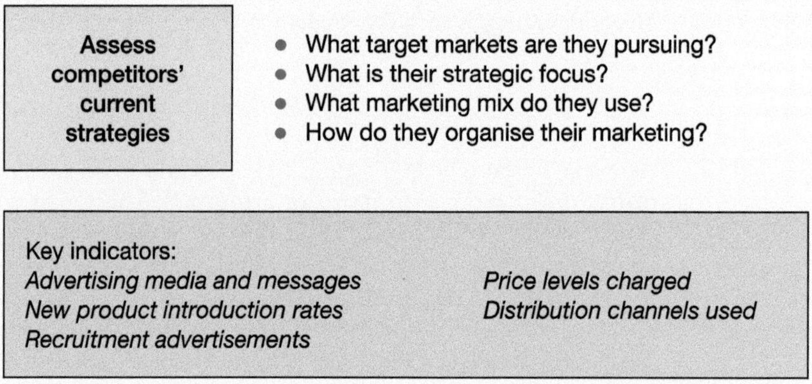

Figure 5.4
Competitor
strategies

going to be weak relative to competitors. For instance, in the jewellery trade it is possible to compete through design or distribution, but absolutely impossible to try to compete with De Beers through securing one's own supply of uncut diamonds.

There are two main routes to creating a competitive advantage. The first is through low costs relative to competitors. The second is through providing valued uniqueness, differentiated products and services that customers will be willing to pay for.

Signals of competitors adopting a low-cost focus include their attention to overheads in the balance sheet, the vigour with which they pursue low-cost factor inputs and the tight financial controls they exert on all functions and activities. The cost leadership route is a tough one for any firm to follow successfully and requires close, relentless attention to all cost drivers. As noted above, in the UK grocery market Aldi and Lidl have adopted this rigorous approach, restricting product lines and providing a largely 'no-frills' service.

Providing something different, but of value to customers, is a route to creating competitive advantage all players in a market can adopt. The creative aspect of this strategy is to identify those differentiating features on which the firm has, or can build, a defensible edge. Signals of differentiation will be as varied as the means of differentiation. Greater emphasis on customer service, added features to the product, special deals for volume or continued custom and loyalty schemes are all means of differentiation. All are highly visible to competitors and show the ground on which a given supplier has chosen to compete.

Competitors' supporting marketing mix

As discussed above, analysis of the marketing mix adopted by competitors can give useful clues as to the target markets at which they are aiming and the competitive advantage they are seeking to build with those targets. Analysis of the mix can also show areas where the competitor is vulnerable to attack.

The Dyson Small Ball Vaccuum Cleaner

Source: Courtesy of Dyson.

Detailed analysis of competitors' products and services, particularly through the eyes of customers, can be used to highlight competitor weaknesses. It is after examining how vacuum cleaners typically lost their suction as their bags filled that James Dyson developed the bagless vacuum cleaner.

Analysis of competitor pricing strategies may identify gaps in the market. For example, a firm marketing vodka in the United States noted that the leader offered products at a number of relatively high price points but had left others vacant. This enabled the firm to position its own offerings in a different market sector.

Both the message and the media being used by competitors warrant close analysis. Some competitors may be better than others at exploiting new media such as satellite or cable. Others may be adept at their use of public relations. Again, analysis will show where competitors are strong and where they are vulnerable.

Finally, understanding the distribution strengths and weaknesses of competitors can also identify opportunities. Dell, for example, decided to market its PCs direct to businesses rather than distribute through office retail stores where its established competitors were already strong.

Competitors' marketing organisation

Consideration of organisation is important because of the way that it can dictate strategy. For a long time Procter & Gamble's brand management structure was held up as a marketing ideal. This was probably the case when the US market was dominant and lessons learned there were relatively easily transferred downstream to less developed parts of the world. However, with the United States' relative economic decline compared with the rest of the world, Unilever's more flexible structure allowed them to transfer ideas across boundaries more easily and be more flexible to emerging local needs. Indeed, Procter & Gamble itself has now moved away from its product management structure.

Understanding the competitors' organisational structure can give clues as to how quickly, and in what manner, the competitor is likely to respond to environmental change or competitive actions. Competitors where responsibility for products is clearly identified are often able to respond more quickly than firms where responsibility is vague or confused. Firms organised around markets, rather than products, are most likely to spot market changes early and be in a position to lead change rather than simply react to it.

The position of marketing within the organisational structure can also provide clues to current and future strategy. In many traditional companies marketing is considered merely part of sales, responsible simply for advertising and other promotional activities. In such cases the voice of marketing may not be easily heard at the strategic decision-making level. In still other firms marketing may be seen as a guiding philosophy that will ensure a much more market-responsive set of actions. Clues to the position of marketing may lie in the background of the CEO, the visibility within the firm of senior marketing executives and, indeed, their previous career tracks. The appointment of a new marketing director from fast-moving consumer goods at Madame Tussaud's, the waxworks, signalled a far more customer-responsive and aggressive approach to the marketing of the attraction.

A useful tool for analysing current activities of competitors is the value chain.

Value-chain analysis

Porter (1985) identifies five primary activities that add value to the final output of a company (Figure 5.5). Areas where value is also destroyed, or eroded, can also be identified through this technique.

1 **Inbound logistics** involves managing the flow of products into the company. Recent attention to just-in-time manufacturing has shown how important this can be to the efficient operation of a company and how by management of its suppliers and their quality a company can add to the quality of its final products.

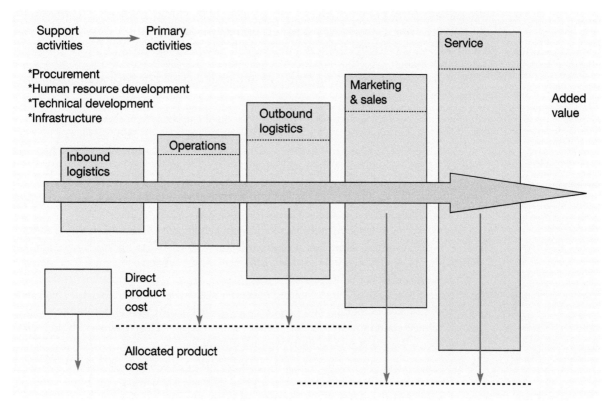

Figure 5.5 The value chain and direct product costing

2 **Operations** have long been seen as the central activity of businesses. These comprise the processes whereby the inbound items are changed in form, packaged and tested for suitability for sale. Traditionally this has been seen as the area where value is added to a company's products. At this stage value can be added beyond the normal capital and manpower inputs by the maintenance of high quality, flexibility and design.

3 **Outbound logistics** carry the product from the point of manufacture to the buyer. They therefore include storage, distribution, etc. At this stage value can be added through quick and timely delivery, low damage rates and the formulation of delivery mechanisms that fit the operations of the user. Within the fertiliser industry, the now bought-out ICI once added tremendous value to its products by offering blends that fitted the specific needs of farmers at certain times of the year, and delivery modularisation which fitted the farmers' own systems. Then, taking it a stage further, deliveries were taken to the field rather than to the farm or indeed spreading could be also be undertaken by the supplier.

4 **Marketing and sales** activities inform buyers about products and services, and provide buyers with a reason to purchase. This can concern feedback, which allows the user company to fit their operation's outbound logistics to user requirements or by helping customers understand the economic value of products that are available. Taking the ICI example again, part of the original marketing activity involved showing how some of its products could be used to equalise the workload on a farm throughout the year, and therefore use the overall labour force more efficiently. The embedded and integrated approach certainly added value and competitive clout for ICI at the time.

5 **Service** includes all the activities required to keep the product or service working effectively for the buyer, after it is sold and delivered. This can involve training, return of goods policies, a consultation hotline and other facilities. Since customer satisfaction is central to achieving repeat sales and word-of-mouth communication from satisfied customers, after-sales service is clearly a major part of added value.

In support of the primary activities of the value chain, Porter (1985) also identified support activities. These are procurement, human resource development, technological development and infrastructure. Each, of course, feeds into the stages of the primary activities of the value chain.

There are several ways in which analysis of the value chain can provide an insight into competitors.

- It can reveal cost advantages that competitors may have because of their efficient manufacture, inbound or outbound logistics. It may also reveal why, with better marketing, sales and service, a company making intrinsically similar products may be achieving higher added value through their operations.
- Many conventionally oriented companies perceive operations as their primary source of added value and therefore leave opportunities for competitors that take a more extended view of the value they can add in the customer's eyes.
- Where the value added is costed effectively it can help locate economical ways of adding value to the customer. There are often numerous ways of achieving this, such as in the efficient management of single sourcing and just-in-time inbound logistics; total quality being incorporated in the operations, thus reducing the service requirements and maybe adding to the appeal of the marketing and sales activity by offering extended warranties; well-targeted marketing and sales activities which assure that maximum perceived added value is communicated to the customer while incurring lower marketing and sales activity than if blanket sales activity was attempted.

A company's assumptions about how its costs are allocated across products and elements of the value chain can provide clear competitive guidelines. For instance, many companies add most of their overheads to manufacturing operations where inputs can usually be measured. This occurs despite products having vastly different inbound logistics, outbound logistics, marketing, sales and service expenditures. The result can be that the final price of the products in the marketplace has little bearing on the overall inputs and the value chain.

Similarly, where the overheads are allocated equally across products, direct product pricing can show where some products are being forced to carry an excessive burden of overheads, so allowing a competitor to enter the market and compete effectively on price. When a company is competing in many different markets it is very likely that its allocated product costs are completely out of line with some of the markets in which it is competing. This can act as an overall constraint upon its intention to support those products or give it little commitment to them. IBM encountered this problem in its PC marketing, where the margins were incapable of carrying the allocated overheads that were borrowed from its mainframe and mini-PC business. This became particularly true in IBM's venture into the home computer market with the 'Peanut', which was launched with a totally inappropriate and uneconomical performance to price ratio.

5.2.3 Assessing competitors' capability profiles

The above discussion has highlighted what the competitor is seeking to achieve and what it is doing now. Also critical, of course, are the degrees of freedom open to the competitor. What might it do in future?

The assessment of a competitor's resources involves looking at their strengths and weaknesses. Whereas a competitor's goals, assumptions and current strategy would influence the likelihood, time, nature and intensity of a competitor's reactions, its resources, assets and capabilities will determine its ability to initiate and sustain moves in response to environmental or competitive changes (see Figure 5.6).

Competitor resource profiles (see Section 5.1 above on benchmarking) can be built in much the same way as a firm conducts an analysis of its own assets and capabilities. A useful starting point is to profile competitors against the key factors for success in the particular industry. Among these could be operational areas (such as research and engineering or

Assess competitors' resource profile	• Marketing culture? • Marketing assets and capabilities? • Production and operation capabilities? • Financial resources?

Key indicators:
Customer relationship strength   *Product availability*
New product success rates   *Promotional expenditure*
Quality of the people

Figure 5.6
Competitor
resources

financial strength) or generic skills (such as the company's ability to grow, quick response capability, ability to adapt to change, staying power or innovativeness).

Lehmann and Winer (1991) suggest concentrating the analysis under five key competitor abilities.

1 **Ability to conceive and design.** Assessing the ability of a competitor to innovate will help the firm to predict the likelihood of new products being brought to market, or of new technologies being employed to leapfrog existing products. Indications of this type of ability come from assessing technical resources (such as patents and copyrights held), human resources (the calibre of the creative and technical staff employed) and funding (both the total funds available and the proportion devoted to research and development, relative to industry average).

2 **Ability to produce.** In manufacturing industries this will include production capacity and utilisation, while in service industries capacity to deliver the service will be critical. Firms with slack capacity clearly have more opportunities to respond to increased demand. Similarly, service firms that can manage their resources flexibly by, for example, calling on temporary but sufficiently skilled and motivated staff may enjoy more flexibility than those with a fixed staff with rigid skills. Ability to produce is signalled by physical resources (such as plant and equipment) together with human resources (including the skills and flexibility of the staff employed).

3 **Ability to market.** Despite strong innovation and production abilities a competitor may be relatively weak at marketing its products or services to customers. Assessing marketing capability is best accomplished through examining the elements of the marketing mix. Central to this analysis, however, will be the assessment of the skills of the people involved in sales, marketing, advertising, distribution, and so on. Also important will be the funds available and devoted to marketing activities. How well does the competitor understand the market? The answer to this question may lie in the extent and type of marketing research being undertaken.

4 **Ability to finance.** Financial resources act as a constraint in any organisation. Due to the recent economic crisis, access to finance has been a major issue for small- to medium-sized enterprises, in particular in the UK and Europe. A rise in the number of web-based crowd funding platforms has allowed firms that would not be able to access finance through traditional routes, e.g. banks, to raise funds for investment in products and services and also start-up proposals. Examination of published accounts can reveal liquidity and cash flow characteristics of competitors where available Again, however, such hard data should be supplemented with assessments of the qualities and skills of the human resources available within finance.

5 **Ability to manage.** The characteristics of key managers can send clear messages on strategic intentions. Indicators include the previous career paths and actions of powerful managers, the reward systems in place, the degree of autonomy allowed to individual managers and the recruitment and promotions policies of the firm.

Figure 5.7 shows a summary sheet a company has used to assess the relative capability of 'self' against three competitors: A, B and C. In this, six dimensions have been determined as critical and a company has rated itself and three competitors on each key factor using a scale ranging from −2 (very poor) to +2 (very good). The result are profiles that suggest the companies are quite similar in their overall capabilities and average scores, which clearly identify the company on a par with competitors A and B overall. However, the total score should not be allowed to cloud the differences of the main protagonists in the market, because their relative strengths clearly show that they may move in different directions given similar opportunities. For instance, Company A could build on its European strength in marketing applied technology, whereas Company B may be forced to depend on differentiation achieved through technological breadth and strength in R&D to maintain its market position. However, if the technology or market shifts in a direction that requires major expenditures, Company B may be weaker compared with A or 'self'. An inspection of the competitive capabilities also suggests that, although Company C looks weak overall, it could be a good acquisition by 'self'. Although weak in the financial and technological areas it has a strong European marketing presence and therefore may be capable of providing 'self' with rapid access to the European markets.

5.2.4 Predicting competitors' future strategies

The ultimate aim of competitor analysis is to determine competitors' response profiles – that is, a guide to how a competitor might behave when faced with various environmental and competitive changes. This covers such questions as the following:

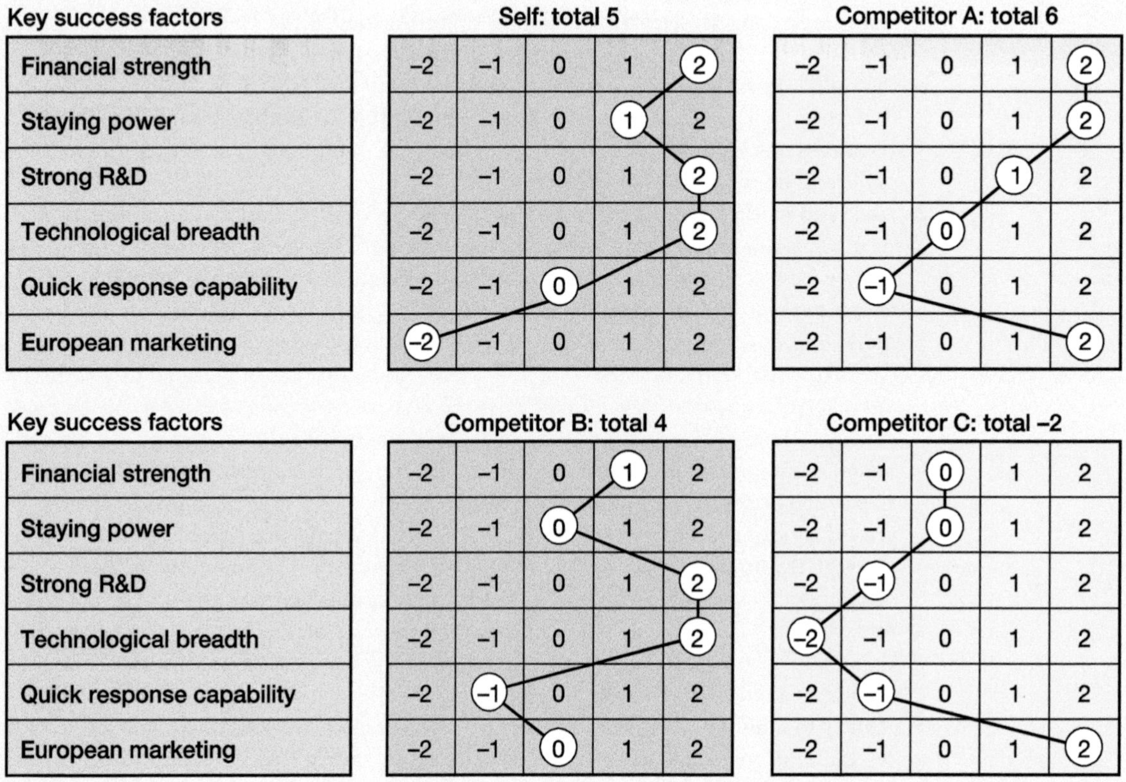

Figure 5.7 Competitor capabilities

- **Is the competitor satisfied with the current position?** One that is satisfied may allow indirect competitors to exploit new markets without being perturbed. Alternatively, one that is trying to improve its current position may be quick in chasing market changes or be obsessed by improving its own short-term profits performance. Knowledge of a company's future goals will clearly play an important part in answering this question.
- **What likely moves or strategy shifts will the competitor make?** History can provide some guide as to the way that companies behave. Goals, assumptions and capabilities will also give some guidance as to how the company can respond effectively to market changes. After looking at these a company may be able to judge which of its own alternative strategies is likely to result in the most favourable reaction on the part of the competitors.
- **Where is the competitor vulnerable?** It takes no great insight to realise that it would be foolish for a company to take on a market leader in the areas where it is strongest. Much better to compete against large and relatively successful competitors in niche markets where large scale is a disadvantage, e.g. in rapidly changing markets where bureaucracy may lead to inflexibility in responding to niche competition. Complacency of leaders in markets can provide major opportunities for the well-informed and targeted niche competitor. The leader's feeling of invulnerability may be its weakness, and one that could lead to its downfall. In truth, businesses, like armies, cannot defend themselves on all flanks, from all positions, at all times. No company is ever all-powerful at all places. In the past, the Virgin brand has been particularly skilful, and relatively successful in the short term, at identifying opportunities in markets where existing competitors had key vulnerabilities. For example, attacking financial services suppliers through branding, high value and product simplicity in its direct marketing strategy. Also choosing to take on Coca-Cola and Pepsi brands with a low price 'Virgin Cola'.
- **What will provoke the greatest and most effective retaliation by the competitor?** Whereas market leaders may accept some peripheral activity, because of the low margins they perceive, anti-trust laws or the scale involved, other actions are likely to provoke intense retaliation. History gives us examples: this is what Rolls-Royce learned to expect whenever it approached the US market for aero engines, what Laker airways found when they openly challenged the major airline carriers on the transatlantic route, and what the small Yorkshire-based company Dalepak found when its chopped meat burgers started making inroads into Unilever's market share. There is little sense, even for the most powerful businesses, antagonising strong competitors when there are less sensitive routes to success available.

Besides providing a general guideline, a competitor's response profile depends on obtaining a view of how a competitor is likely to respond, given various stimuli (see Figure 5.8). Porter (1980) suggests examining the way a competitor may respond to the feasible strategic moves by a firm and feasible environmental changes. This first involves assessing

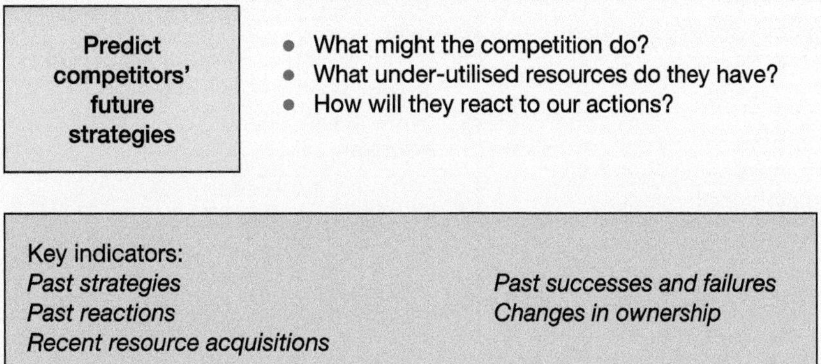

Figure 5.8
Future competitor strategies

the vulnerability of a competitor to the event, the degree to which the event will provoke retaliation by the competitor and, finally, the effectiveness of the competitor's retaliation to the event.

The aim is to force a company to look beyond its own moves and towards those of its competitors and, like a great player of chess, think several moves ahead. It involves a firm thinking of its moves in a broad, strategic framework rather than the incremental manner in which strategies often emerge. Or, by following a series of seemingly small incremental shifts in pricing and promotion, a firm may be perceived to be making a major play in the marketplace and incur the wrath of major players. It is clearly better for A to consider the alternative moves carefully rather than make a series of moves, each one of which makes local sense, without regard to B's counter-moves and the long-term consequences of incremental action.

5.3 Choosing good competitors

When a company chooses to enter a market it also chooses its competitors. In the selection of new opportunities, therefore, it is important to realise that not all competitors are equally attractive. Just as markets can be attractive and a company's strengths can fit those markets, so competitors can be attractive or unattractive. Porter (1985) lists the characteristics that make a good competitor. In Figure 5.9 these features are organised to show how certain features of competitors can make them attractive.

The competitively mature company understands the market it is operating in and enhances, rather than destabilises, the environment of the strategic group. The good competitor can help promote the industry's stability by understanding the rules governing the market and by holding realistic assumptions about the industry and its own relative position. In this way it is unlikely to embark on strategies that are unprofitable and which result in zero-sum competition; such as precipitating price wars or unprofitable practices.

A good competitor can support industry structure if it invests in developing its own product and enhancing quality differentiation and market development rather than confrontational price-cutting or promotional strategies. In that way barriers to entering the industry are enhanced because the market becomes relatively fragmented and the impact of one company or new entrant is diminished. The global pharmaceutical industry tends to have this structure, where legislation and the differentiation of drugs allow a large number of medium-sized companies to survive in many leading markets.

	Balance	**Strength**	**Weakness**
Competitive maturity	• Understand the rules • Realistic assumptions • Support industry structure	• Credible/viable • Know the industry costs	• Clear weaknesses • Limited strategic concept
Reconcilable goals	• Moderate strategic stake • Accept current profitability • Desire cash generation	• Comparable ROI targets	• Short time horizons • Risk averse

Figure 5.9
Good competitors

A further advantage of a competitively mature company is that it can provide a steady pressure towards the efficient operations of those with which it is competing. It can provide respectability and standards, and ensure that the market does not become too 'comfortable' for the incumbents. The danger, then, as many state monopoly industries have shown, is that once the protection is removed, or competition is allowed, they find themselves too weak, or rigid to change. Pressure increases when the leading competitor has a thorough understanding of industry costs and therefore sets standards for cost-efficient services.

Finally, the existence of the credible and viable large company within the strategic group can act as a deterrent to other entrants. A good competitor, therefore, can provide both pressure to keep its competitors lean and an umbrella under which the industry can develop steadily.

A good competitor is a company that has a clear understanding of its own weaknesses and therefore leaves opportunities for others in the market. Within the UK banking market after the 'Big Bang' there was clearly a shortage of good competitors when, once the market was deregulated, many clearing banks acquired diverse activities and offered excessive salaries in areas they did not understand. The result was over-capacity, collapsing profits and a weakening of the UK banking industry generally. A wiser competitor would have been more aware of its strengths and weaknesses and would have avoided ventures that would not only weaken its profitability but also damage the market generally. In that sense a company with a limited strategic concept or a clear idea of the business it is in is a better competitor than one with more vague statements about its intent. (Note that the 'Big Bang' referred to above was a deregulation of the financial industry in the UK, championed by the then Prime Minister Margaret Thatcher. In essence it was a series of measures designed to remove restrictive practices from financial markets (such as fixed minimum commissions), and increase transparency, efficiency and levels of competition in this sector.)

A good competitor will have reconcilable goals that make it comfortable within the market it operates, less likely to make massive strategic shifts and tolerant of moderate intrusion. Where its strategic stake is moderate a good competitor may not see market dominance or the maintenance of its own market position as a principal objective. If under pressure it may be willing to retreat from the market or, when faced with greater opportunities, may choose to grow elsewhere.

Moderation in desired profitability is also an advantageous characteristic of a competitor. If driven by the need to increase the returns it is obtaining, the industry's ability is likely to be disturbed by major investments in new products, promotional activity or price cutting. A company that accepts its current profitability will be a seeker of stability rather than of new opportunities.

The desire of a competitor to maintain its cash flow can have a further impact on promoting an industry's stability. Most ventures that involve destabilising an industry depend on investing in research and development, marketing and/or construction of new cost-cutting plant. A company with strict cash requirements is therefore less likely to embark on such costly ventures.

The reconcilable goals of a good competitor can also provide a beneficial, steady pressure on the other companies within the industry. If a competitor has comparable return on investment targets to its stakeholders, it will face similar competitive pressures to the rest of the industry. In contrast, a state-owned competitor, which does not face the same profitability requirements, or one that is funded from markets with different expectations from one's own, can be unhealthy. Within the European Union, the British Steel Corporation (now part of Tata Steel, following a succession of takeovers and mergers) faced a regulated market against European competitors, heavily subsidised by state governments. Rather than competing with these however, it chose to concentrate on speciality steels where the competitors were often in the private sector and therefore faced similar expectations. In a global context, many firms have found it very difficult competing with the Japanese, who have a lower cost of money from their home stock market, which is also less volatile and responsive to short-term changes than its Western counterparts.

A feature of many Western companies that made them good competitors for the Japanese has been their short time-horizon. This means that when faced with adversity the Western companies the Japanese face have often cut back investment to maintain short-term profitability or have taken a fast route to corporate success rather than investing for internal growth. Risk aversion can also lead to a competitor's being more attractive. Where there is a fear of making errors there are likely to be followers within an industry, which gives more agile companies a chance to gain an advantage when the technology or market changes.

Clearly, finding a market in which the competitors are good on all fronts is unlikely, just as it is impossible to find a market that is completely attractive and consistent with a company's own strengths. But by examining competitors and looking for markets where they tend to be good rather than wayward a company is likely to face a more stable environment and one in which opportunities are there to be taken.

The diversity of competition makes it difficult to draw generic classes of companies that are likely to be good competitors. Some groups can be identified as likely to be the good or bad competitors but, in all these cases, there are likely to be many exceptions to the rule. Porter (1985) identifies smaller divisions of diversified firms as one likely group of good competitors. These may not be viewed as essential to the long-term corporate strategy and they often face tough profitability targets. In a global sense, this is still particularly true of US multinationals, which have shown a remarkable willingness to retreat home when faced with adversity. They are also often given particularly tough profitability objectives with little support or understanding in the overseas market. Part of this stems from the belief that what is good enough for the home market is good enough for the overseas subsidiaries, and that all the major lessons can be learned at home (Wright *et al.*, 1990).

Another group of potentially good competitors can be old established companies with a dynastic interest in the industry. This can be because the companies are strong and set high standards but are careful (as in the case of Sainsbury's in the UK) or because they are moderate in their expectations (as many UK manufacturing companies have been).

Among groups that are more difficult to compete with, and hence not 'good competitors' for the incumbent firm, could be new entrants from other industries that break the mould of established competition in the markets. They could also be new entrants in a market that have made major investments and therefore have a large stake in terms of ego and money in making a venture a success. By not fully understanding the market, they may destabilise competition and also be willing to accept zero, or low, profits for a long time.

Of course, the issue here is not good or bad from an ethical point of view. They are just bad competitors to compete with, although the new standards they bring to an industry and the services they provide to the consumer can do great good to the consumers and the economies concerned. Moreover they *are* good at competing, just not good to be competing against. Marc Andreessen, founder of Netscape (the Internet's first commercial browser) is reported to have said: 'Everyone should be in a business once in their lives that competes with Microsoft, just for the experience.' He added that once was enough though (*The Economist,* 9 March 2002).

| 5.4 | Obtaining and disseminating competitive information |

It has been said that the inability of commanders to obtain and use military intelligence is one of the major reasons for displays of military incompetence (Dixon, 1976). The same is true of competitive intelligence. Also, given the competitive nature of both war and commerce, it is not surprising that the means of gathering information on an enemy or the competition are similar in both method and ethics. And, in both cases, the legality of methods has not been a barrier to their use. The final section of this chapter draws together the alternative means of gathering competitive information (see Figure 5.10). In doing so it

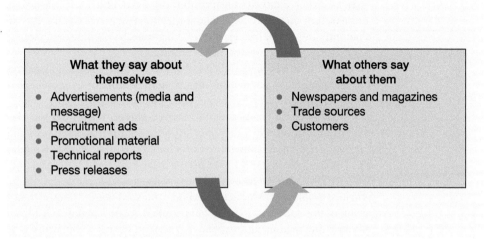

Figure 5.10
Sources of
competitor
information

follows a sequence of declining morality, but seeks to make no judgement about the ethics of many approaches mentioned.

At the most basic level a company can collect **published statistical information** on competitors and markets. Many companies will have such information on their records from market studies or from published sources on public companies. A problem with many of these sources is their disaggregation and the frequent inconsistency between various government statistics and those provided by a range of market research companies. Increasingly, use of the Internet can provide much background information. Search engines allow investigators to search very wide sources rapidly to obtain up-to-date information on competitors and markets.

A company's own **publicity material** such as brochures, corporate magazines and websites can also be a source of useful background information. Sales brochures show the range of products on offer, and sometimes include price lists, while websites often give more insight into the strategies and philosophies of firms. Typically designed with customers or employees in mind, these publications need critical scrutiny but can be a mine of useful background information.

A company's own **propaganda** – in other words, its public relations activities – can add texture to background statistical information. The need to communicate to shareholders and intermediaries in markets means that frequent marketing or technological initiatives are broadcast widely. A danger here, clearly, is the credibility of the public relations involvement of the competitors. Investigative journalism can lead to more open disclosures but here again usually the press is dependent on the goodwill of a company in providing information. Nevertheless such sources can give a splendid feel for a company's senior executives. In that light it can be akin to the information that great generals try to gather on each other.

An increasingly frequent source of information on a company is **leakages.** These are typically unsanctioned information leakages from employees that get into the hands of press, either intentionally or unintentionally. Since these often have to be newsworthy items such information is usually limited in context but, once again, can give texture to background information. Firms that are more aggressive seekers of information may take positive steps in precipitating the giving of information: for instance, grilling competitors' people at trade shows or conferences, or following plant tours and being a particularly inquisitive member of a party. Increasingly trawling social media is also being used as a source of competitive data (Marshall *et al.*, 2012). Although leakages may involve one of the competitor's employees being indiscreet they do not involve the researching company in unethical activities. Many of the practices that follow hereon may be deemed as less worthy by some.

A company can gather information from **intermediaries** or by posing as an intermediary. Both customers and buyers can have regular contact with competitive companies and can often be a source of valuable information, particularly with the salespeople or buyers from a researching company with whom they have regular contact. It is also possible to pose as a potential buyer, particularly over the phone, to obtain some factual information, such as price, or to obtain performance literature.

Many industries have policies of not recruiting between major companies or, as in the United States, have regulations regarding the nature of an individual's work after they have moved from one company to another. However, a company would be naive if it did not thoroughly debrief **competitors' former employees** if they did join the company and, where there is a strong market leader, it is very frequent for that company's employees to be regularly recruited by smaller companies. For a long time in the United Kingdom, Procter & Gamble and Unilever, for instance, have been a training ground for marketing people in many other industries. When they move they carry with them a great deal of useful information on their previous employers' products, methods and strategies. Many such large employers are very aware of this and often request that people who are leaving clear their desks and leave within minutes once their intention to move is known. Even if competitors' employees are not eventually recruited the interviewing process itself can often provide useful information, particularly since the person being interviewed may be eager to impress the potential employer.

Surveillance is widely used within counter-espionage, but is less common as a means of gathering competitive business information. Some of the methods used can be quite innocuous, such as monitoring competitors' employee advertisements or studying aerial photographs. Others are very sensible business practices, such as reverse engineering, i.e. tearing apart the competitors' products for analysis. Less acceptable, and certainly less hygienic, is the possibility of buying a competitor's rubbish to sift for useful memoranda or components. Bugging is a controversial means of surveillance that is becoming more common now equipment is inexpensive, reliable and small enough to be concealed. Not only were Richard Nixon's presidential campaign organisers found using this method, but also the retailer Dixons, during their acquisition of Currys.

Dirty tricks have always been a danger of test marketing, but with the availability of mini-test markets a new dimension has emerged. Their speed means that while a company is test marketing its products over a matter of months a competitor can buy supplies, put them through a mini-test market, find their market appeal and maybe experiment with alternative defensive strategies, before the test-marketed product is launched fully.

A final means of gathering information is the use of **double agents,** either placed in a competitor's company purposely or recruited on to the payroll while still working for the competitor. One can easily imagine how invaluable such people could be over the long term. We know that such individuals are common within military espionage, although few examples have come to light in business circles. One wonders how many leading companies would be willing to admit that they have been penetrated, even if a double agent was found within them.

5.4.1 Disseminating competitor intelligence

Intelligence itself is an essentially valueless commodity. It becomes valuable only when it researches the right people within the organisation and is subsequently acted on. If no one is analysing, discussing and taking action on data collected, then this is a costly and unproductive exercise. Successful dissemination, however, requires two things. First, the destination must be clearly identified. Basically the question is, who needs to know this? Second, the data must be presented in a manner that the recipient can understand and assimilate. Too many competitive intelligence reports, such as market research reports, are far too detailed and cumbersome for busy executives to extract and use the relevant information.

Bernhardt (1993) suggests the use of a hierarchical approach to dissemination. For senior management (including CEOs and strategy formulation groups) intelligence should be limited to that which is of high strategic value. There is little point burdening top managers with the minutiae of everyday operations. Indeed, too much operational detail in their menu of intelligence may mask the really important issues they need to act on.

Information to senior managers should include special intelligence briefings, typically one- or two-page reports identifying and summarising specific issues and showing where more detailed information can be obtained. Senior managers may also require regular (monthly or quarterly depending on the rate of change in the industry and market) intelligence briefings, which address regularly occurring issues systematically, so that trends can be identified and priorities made.

Middle and junior managers at a more operational level may require more detailed information to enable them to formulate tactical decisions. Here, more detailed profiles of competitor products and services will be required, together with detailed analysis of competitor marketing mix strategies. Increasingly, middle management is becoming conversant with database manipulation, enabling managers to directly interrogate intelligence data rather than simply relying on information specialists to extract and present relevant information (see Fletcher, 1996).

Summary

Just as understanding markets is fundamental to business success, so is a good understanding of competitors, their strengths, weaknesses and likely responses. This chapter suggests that the focus of competitor analysis should be on strategic groups, but should not neglect other firms within the industry with the ability to overcome entry barriers or be potential entrants to the industry. It provides some frameworks for analysing competitors and suggests the importance of thinking through their likely responses. It also suggests that when entering markets and instituting strategies firms should be looking for 'good' competitors that can stabilise markets, provide opportunities and apply downward pressure on performance. Finally, means of gathering and disseminating competitive information are presented. Ultimately the goal is to learn from competitors – their successes and their mistakes – as well as working out how to compete more effectively (Figure 5.11).

Although as important as market information, data on competitors are rarely gathered systematically or comprehensively. There is also such a multiplicity of sources which have to be assessed that there is little chance of doing so on an *ad hoc* basis. There is therefore good reason for incorporating a competitive information system within any marketing information system that exists, and having people responsible for ensuring its maintenance. In competitive

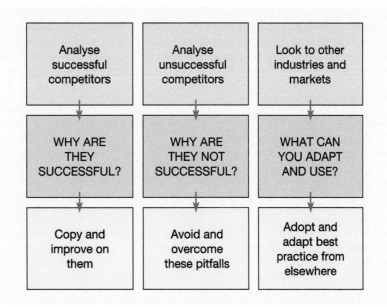

Figure 5.11
Learning from competitors

strategy, just as in war, it is impossible to exaggerate the importance of gathering information on the adversaries a company faces. As Sun Tzu says: 'An army without spies is like a man without ears or eyes' and, because of this, 'to remain in ignorance of the adversary's condition simply because one grudges the outlay of a few hundred ounces of silver in honours and emoluments, is the height of inhumanity'.

Case study Adidas kicks off US drive to close in on Nike

A German sporting goods company is focusing on the global 'epicentre' of the sneaker market to catch up with its rival.

They say a picture paints a thousand words but sometimes a number does it even better.

Nike, the US sporting goods behemoth whose swoosh logo is as instantly recognisable as its name, together with its Jordan brand have built up a share of nearly 60 per cent of the US trainers market. Adidas has just 4.4 per cent.

The German group is far more competitive in sports apparel and markets outside the US. The duo are neck-and-neck in western Europe, Adidas is a long way ahead in Russia, and Nike has a narrow lead in China.

But Nike's dominance in the world's most important sneaker market gives it a painfully sharp edge on Adidas, which is pushing a new strategy to claw back share across key sportswear segments, with a strong emphasis on the US. With such a big gap to close in trainers, Adidas has a mammoth task on its hands.

Outside the US there is much greater parity between Nike and Adidas. 'But the US is the epicentre of the global sneaker/"athleisure" market', says Matt Powell, sports industry analyst at research firm NPD, which calculated the market share data. 'Ultimately to win globally, sneaker brands must win in the US. Nike has a deep and rich understanding of the US sneaker consumer.'

Nike has been a runaway success over the past five years. It is the world's biggest sportswear company by sales and in the year to June 2015 revenues rose 10 per cent, to $30.6bn. Adidas, meanwhile, reported a 6 per cent rise in revenues on a currency-neutral basis to €14.5bn, for the full year 2014.

Profit at Nike has risen at a double-digit rate – and that is despite its overseas business grappling with a strong dollar that has made prices less competitive. Adidas will need to add sales at a brisk pace to even maintain the existing gap with Nike.

The western European market shows how tough this race will be. Over the past three years, the sales growth of the Nike brand has outstripped that of the German group's Adidas and Reebok brands by roughly 10 percentage points on average, once currency fluctuations are excluded, according to UBS analysts.

The result is that Adidas and Nike are now level in the region that has traditionally been the German company's stronghold. Euromonitor, a market research provider, calculates that both groups had a 12.8 per cent share of the western European sportswear market in 2014.

'Alarmingly for Adidas, Nike has caught up in its core western Europe market, and may overtake it in the short term,' says Natasha Cazin, senior analyst at Euromonitor International.

Even maintaining the dead heat in which Adidas now finds itself with Nike could be hard, says Zuzanna Pusz, an analyst at Berenberg. 'Adidas is doing fine in western Europe, but they should be as they are spending 14 per cent of their sales on marketing,' she says. 'The question is whether this is sustainable.'

A recent survey by analysts at UBS also found signs of Nike's surge, particularly among the young. The survey looked at how many times consumers 'liked' Facebook pages associated with different sports brands, and found that Nike was far ahead of its rivals in all the big European markets – and recently overtook Adidas in Germany.

UBS also found that the perception of Nike's brand exceeded that of Adidas in London and Paris, two of the six cities around the world that Adidas is targeting as part of its efforts to regain ground on its US rival.

'Adidas undoubtedly needs to improve brand perceptions among younger consumers. But the good news is that we think it has a big opportunity to achieve this by placing a bigger focus on social media, leveraging its sponsorship asset base, and creating more relevant product for the target teenager,' the analysts wrote.

Adidas's recent overhaul of its football boot offering – it replaced its famous Predator and F50 lines with two newcomers, Ace and X – is seen as one way in which it can renew its appeal among teenagers.

The company has also taken steps to improve its position in the fast-growing area of fitness tracking, snapping up app developer Runtastic. Ms Pusz says focusing on sports software is the right way to go, but adds that Adidas is playing catch up instead of setting the pace.

Nike is already by far the trendsetter in its home market. Not only does it have the financial clout when it comes to endorsements, it was quick off the mark in recognising the importance of social media and advertisements uploaded on YouTube. During the recent women's World Cup in Canada, although Adidas was the main sponsor, Nike emerged victorious in terms of social media engagement. Its #NoMaybes campaign was 121 per cent more associated with the World Cup than Adidas, according to Amobee Brand Intelligence.

But it is an area again where it has the potential to catch up and win over more millennials. It plans to improve marketing, be more innovative with its products and bring them more quickly to market. 'Adidas has made the right decisions to move global product and marketing to the US,' NPD's Mr Powell says. 'Hopefully they will develop a less European-centric point of view.'

It helps Adidas that the so-called athleisure wear trend is only growing stronger. As more people wear casual sports clothes in situations – even work – that were previously considered more formal, there is room for many companies to expand.

This also means there are more companies to overtake it. Under Armour, a relative newcomer, last year sold more trainers, tracksuits and T-shirts than Adidas in the US.

And fashion is fickle. Some analysts question whether sports brands really benefit by overly focusing on chasing trends or working with celebrities – as Adidas is doing with Kanye West after the pop star dropped his relationship with Nike. Paul Swinland of Morningstar says that for a company whose raison d'être is performance – which breeds loyalty – chasing fashion ultimately only gives short-term gains and is 'off brand'.

As Adidas works its new strategy in the US, Nike's challenge is maintaining the pace of growth investors have come to expect. 'They've gotten such strong growth in apparel and basketball, it just can't go on forever; you can't have 15–20 per cent growth forever,' Mr Swinland says.

Yet being Nike's rival must feel a lot tougher. 'Impossible is nothing', or so goes Adidas's well-known slogan. It will be hoping it does not prove itself wrong.

Rivals take different approaches.

When Adidas and Nike make headlines in China, it is often because workers at one of their suppliers in the 'world's workshop' have gone on strike in manufacturing centres such as Dongguan. But as Adidas seeks to make up ground on Nike, the two companies are paying attention to China as an important market in its own right.

In announcing its second-quarter results on Thursday, Adidas highlighted a 19 per cent increase in its Greater China sales.

With second-quarter revenues of €564m ($615m), Greater China is Adidas's third-largest market, after western Europe and North America. But it is also the German company's second-most profitable one, with a second-quarter gross margin of 59 per cent.

Similarly, Nike's Greater China earnings in the three months to the end of June ($266m) were almost as big as western Europe's ($277m), despite a much smaller revenue base – $829m in Greater China compared with $1.2bn in western Europe.

Reflecting the wealth disparities that make China both a manufacturing powerhouse and coveted market, a pair of Nike's LeBron basketball trainers sell for the equivalent of $275 compared with a monthly minimum wage in Dongguan of $210.

Analysts say that Adidas and Nike have adopted different approaches to the China market. 'Nike has gone through the basketball route, focusing on celebrity endorsements, while Adidas has taken a more grassroots focus aimed at youth culture,' says Matthew Crabbe, a retail analyst with Mintel.

Both will have to contend with a tougher retail climate as China's economy is now growing at its slowest annual rate for 25 years.

Source: from 'Adidas struggles to catch up with Nike's runaway success', *Financial Times*, 07/08/15 (Whipp, L. and Shotter, J.).

Discussion questions

1 Why is Adidas focusing on the US market?

2 Why has Adidas seemingly lost ground to Nike?

3 Should Adidas only benchmark itself against Nike? What steps should it follow when conducting benchmarking activities?

CHAPTER 6
UNDERSTANDING THE ORGANISATIONAL RESOURCE BASE

"The most important assets a company has are its brand names. They should appear at the head of the assets list on the balance sheet"

Marketing Director, International Food Marketing Company.

Waterstone's links up with Paperchase

Source: Alamy Images: British Retail Photography.

Waterstone's, the bookseller owned by HMV, has struck a deal with Paperchase to put the stationer's concessions in 20 of its stores.

The deal is in line with Waterstone's strategy of beefing up its stationery range, which it has had in stores for the past couple of years, and which has done well.

Paperchase previously had a relationship with Borders, which has now exited the UK high street.

'We have a number of stores that are closely located to where the original Borders were,' said Dominic Myers, managing director of Waterstone's.

'To partner with Paperchase – who are a good, strong brand with a good offering, well known in those locations – gives us some more immediate scale in our ambitions.'

The Paperchase concessions will open between now and the autumn, primarily in larger stores, although Waterstone's could look to add more concessions at a later date.

It will continue to sell stationery in Waterstone's stores without a Paperchase outlet.

'We have run this sort of gift stationery offer in our stores for two to three years,' said Mr Myers. 'It has been successful, but this will give us a big leg up in the scale of what we will be able to deliver.'

Waterstone's also has about 70 cafés operated by Elior in its stores, and it is putting a small number of larger cafés in some of its stores. Mr Myers said Waterstone's also wanted to expand its electronic book offering.

At the end of March, HMV set out a strategy for reviving Waterstone's, which has been hit by the rise of online book retailers as well as distribution problems after it opened a new distribution centre last year. Among its plans to revive the chain was increasing non-book sales from 6 per cent of sales to 10 per cent by 2013.

HMV is also expanding its product range, with plans to start selling technology, fashion and live music events as part of its three-year strategy to beat the decline in its main markets.

Source: from 'Waterstone's links up with Paperchase', *Financial Times*, 06/05/2010 (Felsted, A.).

Discussion questions

1 What issues is Waterstone's facing?

2 Why is Waterstone's linking up with Paperchase?

Introduction

The attractiveness of opportunities open to the firm depends on the resources available to exploit them. Organisational resources include both tangible and intangible assets, capabilities and competences. This is the base from which organisations build their competitive position, and any marketing strategy needs to be firmly grounded in these resources. Strategies that are not built on resource strength are unlikely to be sustainable in the longer term, and under-utilised resources represent potential wastage. To succeed in a particular market the firm will need specific resources, the key factors for success in that market. If it does not have these, or cannot acquire them, the strategy is likely to fail at the implementation stage.

This chapter is structured around the following issues which provide a framework for assessing organisational resources:

- The role of marketing resources in creating differentiation.
- Insights from the resource-based view (RBV) of the firm, and in particular the more recent emphasis on dynamic capabilities.
- Creating and exploiting marketing assets.
- Deploying dynamic marketing capabilities.
- Developing and exploiting the resource portfolio.

This is shown schematically in Figure 6.1, starting from the most general issues and moving progressively to the more specific.

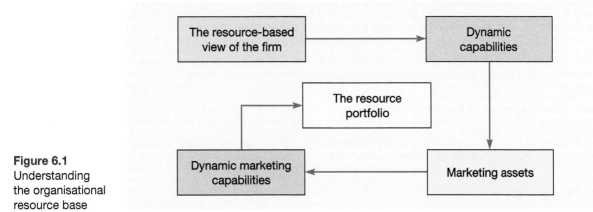

Figure 6.1
Understanding the organisational resource base

6.1	Marketing resources as the foundation for differentiation

While any organisation could produce a long list of the resources at its disposal, what is important is to identify those resources that can help create a competitive advantage, and ideally an advantage that can be sustained into the foreseeable future – sustainable competitive advantage (SCA). Theories developed in the strategic management field can be helpful. Strategic management theorists have shown that a sustainable competitive advantage can be achieved when distinct resources are employed that are resistant to competitor imitation or duplication. The resources that will most likely create sustainable advantage have a number of key characteristics. First, they enable the provision of competitively superior value to customers (Barney, 1991, 1997; Slater, 1997). Second, they are resistant to duplication by competitors (Reed and DeFillippi, 1990; Hall, 1992, 1993). Third, their value can be appropriated by the organisation (Collis and Montgomery, 1995).

Resources, such as brand reputation, relationships with customers, effective distribution networks and the competitive position occupied in the marketplace, are potentially significant advantage generating resources. These have been termed marketing resources as they relate directly to marketing activities and are directly leveraged in the marketplace. Their role in generating value for customers is clear. But how easy are they to protect against competitor imitation (and hence erosion of the advantage)? Some resources, such as capital, plant and machinery, are inherently easier for competitors to copy than others, such as company reputation, brand reputation and competitive position created and reinforced over time. Many marketing resources, as we shall see, are intangible in nature and hence more difficult for competitors to understand and replicate.

The ways in which resources can be protected from duplication have been termed isolating mechanisms (Reed and DeFillippi, 1990) as they serve to isolate the organisation from its competition, creating a competitive barrier. Isolating mechanisms operate at three main levels.

- First, for a competitor to imitate a successful marketing strategy it must be able to identify the resources that have been dedicated to creating and implementing that strategy in the first place. The competitive position created, for example, will include a complex interplay of resources creating difficulties for competitors in identification. Lippman and Rumelt (1982) refer to this problem for competitors as 'causal ambiguity', which can be created through tacitness (the accumulated skill-based resources resulting from learning by doing and managerial experience), complexity (using a large number of interrelated resources), and specificity (the dedication of certain resources to specific activities). For example, a firm enjoying the resource of close relationships with key customers might be more difficult for a competitor to copy than one offering cut-price bargains. The former will require superior customer linking skills, such as customer relationship management (tacit skills), together with the technical skills to serve customer needs. The latter may be based on an effective cost-control system that could be relatively easily installed by a competitor.
- Second, should a competitor overcome the identification barrier it would still need to acquire the resources necessary for imitation of the strategy. Some resources, such as corporate culture or market orientation, may take time to develop (referred to as being 'path-dependent' because they require the firm to go down a particular path to develop them) while others may be uneconomic to acquire, or even protected in some way (for example through patents or copyrights). If resources have transaction costs associated with their acquisition there is likely to be a continuing barrier to duplication. Even where acquisition is theoretically possible some resources may be less effective in the competing firm (for example, managers may be less effective working in one environment than another).
- Third, most resources depreciate over time as competitors are eventually likely to find ways of imitating successful strategies. This is especially true in rapidly changing markets (e.g. where technology is changing swiftly). Again, some resources may depreciate less quickly than others. Reputation, for example, has potential for a longer period

of advantage generation than, say, rapidly depreciating plant and machinery. We say potential because we should always remember that reputations take time to build but could be destroyed overnight if mishandled. BP, the multi-national oil and gas producer, suffered a significant amount of reputational and also financial damage (through large reductions in share price) following the Deepwater Horizon oil rig disaster in 2010. It took some time for them to recover from this, and some commentators suggest that they still have not fully recovered their original position.

In the analysis of resources, therefore, the important question to always bear in mind is: does this resource contribute to the creation of a sustainable competitive advantage for the organisation? Where it does, or it could be leveraged to, the resource should be recognised as the potential source of an effective marketing strategy and protected from both external recognition and internal myopia.

Below we go on to discuss the types of resources organisations may have at their disposal and how these can be identified. In common with current usage, we use the terms resources, assets, competencies and capabilities interchangeably. Conceptually, however, resources could be considered the generic term, while assets and capabilities are different types of resource.

6.2 Value-creating disciplines

Day (1997) points out that

> every business acquires many capabilities that enable it to move its products through the value chain. Only a few of these need to be superior to competition. These are the distinctive capabilities that support a value proposition that is valuable to customers and hard for competitors to match.

In fact, different ways of delivering superior customer value require quite different resources. For example, Treacy and Wiersema (1995) point to three different 'value disciplines', each of which excels at meeting the distinctive needs of one customer type, and each of which requires different resource capabilities (Figure 6.2):

- **Operational excellence** – providing middle-of-market products at the best price with the least inconvenience. Examples include no-frills mass-market retailers such as Aldi and Lidl in groceries, and fast food outlets such as McDonald's, Burger King and KFC. This strategy requires an organisation achieving excellence in the core processes of order fulfilment, supply-chain management, logistics, service delivery and transaction processing.

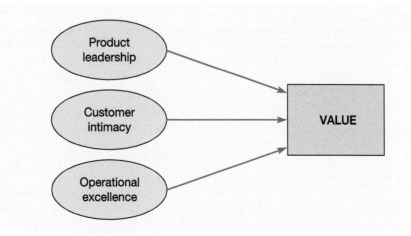

Figure 6.2
Value disciplines

- **Product leadership** – offering products that push the boundaries of product and service performance: Intel is a product leader in computer chips, as is Nike in athletic footwear. A prime example is Hewlett-Packard's computer printer business that once achieved market dominance through major technology advances, rapid product variations, continuous price reductions and a willingness to attack competitors. The core processes that underpin this strategy include market sensing (of latent customer needs), openness to new ideas, fast product development and launch, technology integration and flexible manufacturing. Management and structure will probably be decentralised, team-oriented and loose-knit.
- **Customer intimacy** – delivering what specific customers want in cultivated relationships. The core requirements are flexibility, a 'have it your way' mindset, mastery of 'mass customisation' to meet the distinct needs of micro-segments of the market, and the ability to sustain long-term customer relationships.

Hamel (1996) notes that, in an effective strategy-making process, 'you can't see the end from the beginning'. Organisations need to be flexible enough to change established beliefs about corporate capabilities, as marketing strategy options emerge from analysis (and vice versa); if necessary they need to be able to rethink the attractiveness of strategy options as a result.

In seeking to define key resources however, Porter (1996) points to the dangers of the 'competitive convergence trap'. Porter argues that the danger inherent in the pressure on companies to improve operational efficiency is not simply that we substitute operational efficiency for strategy, but that competing companies become more and more similar: 'The more benchmarking companies do, the more they look alike . . . Continuous improvement has been etched on managers' brains. But its tools unwittingly draw companies towards imitation and homogeneity.' When we attempt to assess corporate capabilities, our search should be for sources of competitive differentiation and advantage in activities and areas that matter to customers, not simply sources of operational efficiency.

We should also be aware that how we group, categorise or label what we see as an organisation's resources can be critical. Strategy does not consist of mere operational improvement, neither does it consist of focusing simply on a few core competencies (especially if they are the same things our competitors would claim as their own competencies). Real sustainable advantage comes from the way the various resources fit together creating a unique resource base for a unique competitive strategy. Porter illustrates this with the example of the car hire business. Companies such as Hertz, Avis and National are the brand leaders, but profitability is generally low – these firms are locked into an operational effectiveness competition, offering the same kinds of cars at the same kinds of airports with the same kind of technology. Enterprise, on the other hand, achieves superior performance in this same industry with smaller outlets which are not at airports, little advertising, and older cars. Enterprise does everything differently. Enterprise employs more experienced staff and operates a business-to-business sales force – it specialises in a temporary car replacement for those whose own vehicle is off the road, and has turned its back on the business travel market at major airports. The point is that on its own each of the Enterprise capabilities is unremarkable; together they comprise a powerful route to a differentiated competitive position and superior performance (Porter, quoted in Jackson, 1997).

In reviewing resources, managers need to search for advantage from the way things fit together, not just the individual resources available. Indeed, the critical question may be how capabilities can be managed successfully across alliances of companies.

An important consideration is whose view of resources to follow – much in this area is subjective and judgemental. Indeed, Hamel (1996) suggests that 'the bottleneck is at the top of the bottle'. Senior managers may tend to defend orthodoxy because it is what they know, and what they have built their careers on: 'Where are you likely to find people with the least diversity of experience, the largest investment in the past, and the greatest reverence for strategic dogma? At the top' (Hamel, 1996).

New perspectives on the resources of the organisation may come from surprising places. Hamel describes how in one company the idea for a multi-million-dollar opportunity came from a twenty-something secretary, and in another some of the best ideas about an organisation's core competencies came from a forklift operator, while in an accounting company the partners learned about virtual reality from a junior employee aged 25.

At the very least, when we are attempting to assess resources we should include the views of those who run the business, and outsiders who may have insights that are valuable. For example, the world-famous Avis campaign 'We Try Harder' came from the advertising agency hired by Robert Townsend to search for a competitive advantage that would enable him to turn around the then ailing Avis company. The agency view was that there was no competitive advantage other than the fact that Avis employees seemed to 'try harder', probably because they had to. This was the core of the highly successful turnaround strategy at Avis – and, it should be noted, it was resisted from the outset by executives who had a more conventional view of the car rental business.

| 6.3 | **The resource-based view of the firm** |

Two main themes dominated thinking about marketing strategy during the 1990s, and influenced much of what is taught today, i.e. the notion of market orientation and the resource-based view (RBV) of the firm. While the market orientation literature emphasises the superior performance of companies with high-quality, organisation-wide generation and sharing of market intelligence leading to responsiveness to market needs, the RBV suggests that high-performance strategy is dependent primarily on historically developed resource endowments (e.g. Grant, 2005).

There is, however, a potential conflict between these two approaches in the sense that one advocates the advantages of outward-looking responsiveness in adapting to market conditions, while the other is inward-looking, emphasising the rent-earning characteristics of resources (Amit and Shoemaker, 1993) and the development of corporate resources and capabilities (Mahoney, 1995). Quite simply, from a marketing viewpoint, if strategy becomes too deeply embedded in existing corporate capabilities, it runs the risk of ignoring the demands of changing, turbulent marketing environments (it is too embedded and inflexible – systemically broken in effect). Yet, from a resource-based perspective, marketing strategies that are not based on a company's distinctive competencies are likely to be ineffective and unsustainable.

However, we argue that competitive positioning provides a way of reconciling this potential conflict. We argue that competitive positioning provides a definition of how the firm will compete by identifying target markets and the competitive advantage that will be pursued in serving these target markets. The attractiveness of markets will depend, in part, on the resources available to the firm to build a strong competitive position. Similarly, the positioning perspective recognises that for corporate resources to be leveraged for economic benefit requires their application in the marketplace. However, it also recognises that, if that application is to be sustainable in the face of competition from rivals, the competitive advantage must be built on the firm's distinctive resources (Hamel and Prahalad, 1994; Webster, 1994). Indeed, market orientation itself may be considered a key corporate resource, accumulated and learned over a substantial time period.

This iterative relationship between the pressures of market orientation and the RBV and the linkage in competitive positioning is shown in Figure 6.3. In this simplified view, the issue becomes one of responding to markets through applying organisational resources to the opportunities and customer needs identified. The outcome is competitive positioning. However, the theories of the RBV of the firm are worth consideration as a further source of insight into assessing corporate capabilities as a basis for competitive positioning.

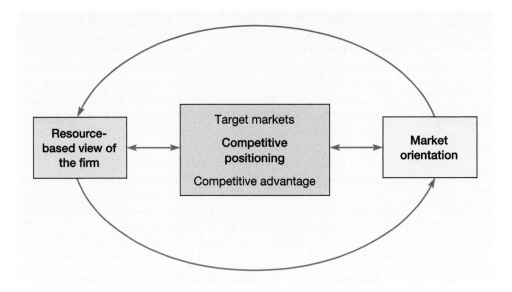

Figure 6.3
Competitive
positioning

6.3.1 Theoretical foundations

The RBV is still present in modern literature of strategy (e.g. see Grant, 2005 for summaries of the main theory). The central tenet of the RBV is that for strategy to be sustainable it must be embedded in the firm's resources and capabilities. Indeed, the potential incompatibility with the principles of market orientation is illustrated by Grant's (1995) view that:

> In general, the greater the rate of change in a company's external environment, the more it must seek to base long term strategy upon its internal resources and capabilities, rather than upon an external market focus.

Grant uses the example of typewriter manufacturers faced with the PC revolution of the 1980s. He suggests there were only two available strategies: pursue the traditional market and attempt to acquire the technology for word processing; or seek other markets where existing competencies and capabilities could be exploited. The move of Olivetti from type-writer to PC is an example of the first strategy. The move of other companies into the printer market to exploit existing resources is an example of the second strategy. However, to assume that these are the only strategies or that they are mutually exclusive is somewhat limited.

Notwithstanding this limitation in perspective, the RBV offers a number of useful insights into the nature of corporate resources. There are a number of different views of how to define and classify resources:

- anything that can be thought of as a strength or weakness of a firm (Wernerfelt, 1984);
- stocks of available factors that are owned or controlled by the firm (Amit and Shoe-maker, 1993);
- a bundle of assets, capabilities, organisational processes, firm attributes, information and knowledge (Barney, 1991).

However, one particularly useful framework for marketing purposes was proposed by Day (1994) in distinguishing between a company's *assets* and its *capabilities*. In Day's terms, organisational assets are the endowments a business has accumulated, such as those resulting from investments in scale, plant, location and brand equity, while capabilities reflect the synergy between these assets and enable them to be deployed to the company's advantage. In these terms capabilities are complex bundles of skills and collective learning, which ensure the superior coordination of functional activities through organisational processes.

In essence the RBV places central emphasis on the role of assets and capabilities in creating competitive advantage. The theory recognises that resources are heterogeneous across firms and that there are barriers to acquisition or imitation that can provide individual firms with ways of defending the advantage created in the short to medium term. Sustainable competitive advantage, the theory suggests, lies in the possession of resources that exhibit certain characteristics: value, rarity, inimitability and non-substitutability (VRIN).

Barriers to imitation, referred to in the literature as isolating mechanisms, include causal ambiguity (difficulty in identifying how an advantage was created), complexity (arising from the interplay of multiple resources), tacitness (intangible skills and knowledge resulting from learning and doing), path dependency (the need to pass through critical time-dependent stages to create the advantage), economics (the cost of imitation), and legal barriers (such as property rights and patents) (Lippman and Rumelt, 1982; Dierickx and Cool, 1989; Reed and DeFillippi, 1990; Hooley *et al.,* 2005).

A major criticism of the RBV, however, has been that it neglects the influence of market dynamism (Priem and Butler, 2001; Wang and Ahmed, 2007). The more rapidly markets change, the more there is a need for firms to renew their resources and develop new capabilities (Ambrosini, Bowman and Collier, 2009).

6.3.2 Dynamic capabilities

In response to the concerns above, recent research broadly in the RBV tradition has focused on dynamic capabilities (see Teece, Pisano and Shuen, 1997; Bowman and Ambrosini, 2003; Ambrosini and Bowman, 2009). For a review of the field of dynamic capabilities see the special issue of *British Journal of Management* edited by Easterby-Smith, Lyles and Peteraf (2009).

Dynamic capabilities have been defined as '*The capacity of an organisation to purposefully create, extend, or modify its resource base*' (Helfat *et al.*, 2007).

This view recognises that as markets change, become more globally integrated, new forms of competition emerge and new technologies are employed, firms cannot rest on their existing capabilities alone (Winter, 2003; Wang and Ahmed, 2007). Firms need to actively seek to recreate themselves through extending and modifying their operations.

It is noticeable that the new focus on dynamic capabilities recognises the need for firms to understand market dynamics more explicitly than the original RBV perspective. From a marketing perspective dynamic capabilities help firms to identify market opportunities and subsequently enter new businesses through the creation of new products and improved services (Teece *et al.*, 1997; Helfat *et al.*, 2007).

Teece *et al.* (1997) suggest that dynamic capabilities have both a coordinating/integrating role and a learning role. The coordination and integration role enables firms to integrate external activities. These activities are related to the capabilities of market-driven organisations that among others need to excel in understanding customer needs and requirements, customer linking and new product development processes (Day, 1994a or b). A customer-linking capability enables the firm to gain the 'inside track' (Penrose, 1959) by establishing a relationship with customers that may enable joint problem-solving activities and the rapid assimilation of new and previously unexploited skills (Zander and Zander, 2005). Product development routines are known to require the integration of diverse skills and know-how from inside and outside the firm. This also suggests that, besides their customer-linking abilities with customers, firms must be able to enhance their knowledge creation process by being capable of developing networks and strategic alliances throughout the value chain (Eisenhardt and Martin, 2000).

Learning enables new opportunities to be identified and can stimulate experimentation and innovation (Bowman and Ambrosini, 2003). More specifically, learning is a core element of dynamic capabilities since it is a 'collective activity through which the organisation systematically generates and modifies its operating routines in pursuit of improved effectiveness' (Zollo and Winter, 2002).

It has been suggested by some researchers (e.g. Ahuja and Katila, 2004) that dynamic capabilities are idiosyncratic and highly dependent on the specific firm–market context. Others, however (such as Eisenhardt and Martin, 2000), seek commonalities across firms. The most recent conceptualisations of dynamic capabilities focus on 'fit' – both technical fit and evolutionary fit. Helfat *et al.* (2007) define technical fit as how effectively a capability performs its intended function (its quality) when normalised by (divided) by its cost, and evolutionary fit as how well a dynamic capability enables an organisation to make a living by creating, extending or modifying its resource base. In this sense, evolutionary fitness includes not only technical fitness but also understanding of competition and market conditions.

Evolutionary fit is central to marketing thinking, ensuring not only that the market offerings are technically fit for purpose, but also that they match changing market requirements in the light of customer and competitor change.

Wang and Ahmed (2007) suggest that resources can usefully be considered at four levels. For our purposes these are conflated to three main levels and types of resource. Figure 6.4 shows these levels in a marketing context.

- At the base level are marketing assets, the resource endowments the organisation has built or acquired over time. Where these exhibit VRIN characteristics (i.e. create value for customers, are rare or unique to the firm, are inimitable or difficult/expensive for other firms to imitate or acquire, and are non-substitutable or easily replaced) they can form the basis of a competitive advantage. Most assets, however, depreciate over time unless they are constantly renewed and refreshed.
- Capabilities, the second level resources of the firm, are the processes that are used to deploy assets effectively in the marketplace. Wang and Ahmed (2007) differentiate between capabilities, which are used to undertake routine tasks, and core capabilities, which are strategically important to creating competitive advantage at a point in time. Core capabilities typically require the bundling together of other capabilities. For example, Zara in the fashion industry has core capabilities in responsiveness to customers, which in turn requires capabilities such as advanced information systems, just-in-time production processes and stock control processes. Core capabilities, therefore, integrate assets and capabilities to enable the firm to

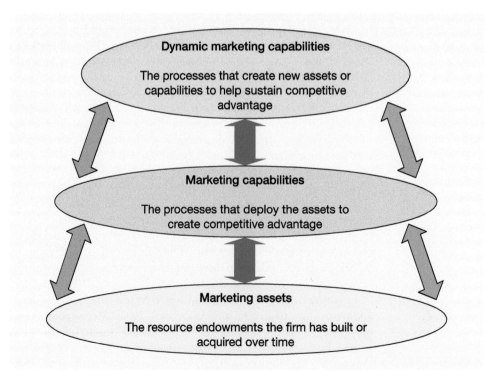

Figure 6.4
Marketing
resources

move in its chosen strategic direction. It has been suggested, however, that core capabilities can become core rigidities when markets change, and they can lock firms into processes that may become less and less relevant (Leonard-Barton, 1992; Tallman, 2003).

- Dynamic capabilities are the highest level of firm resource. They are the capabilities that create new assets and/or new capabilities in response to, or indeed to lead, change in the marketplace (see Ambrosini, Bowman and Collier, 2009).

We now go on to discuss in more detail marketing resources. First we consider marketing assets, then we go on to discuss marketing capabilities, and finally we focus on dynamic marketing capabilities.

6.4   Creating and exploiting marketing assets

The term 'marketing assets' was first used in a series of articles in *Marketing* magazine by Hugh Davidson in 1983. Marketing assets are essentially resources – normally intangible – that can be used to advantage in the marketplace. Davidson also presented the following example of this.

- In the early 1980s the brand share of Kellogg's Corn Flakes, while still in the low 20s, was in long-term decline. The company had spare capacity, but did not produce corn flakes for private label store brands. Kellogg solved this problem by launching Crunchy Nut Corn Flakes which used the Kellogg name and the corn flakes plant. It was priced at a heavy premium, but it gained 2–3 per cent market share, mainly incremental to the share of other Kellogg's brands, at very attractive margins. The new product exploited the existing brand, flake technology and plant, but did so in a way that attracted new customers at high margins.

A wide variety of company properties can be converted into marketing assets. As shown in Figure 6.5, they can be usefully grouped into:

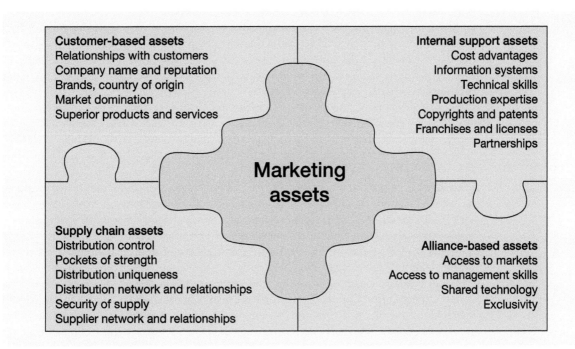

Figure 6.5 Marketing assets

- customer-based and reputational assets;
- supply chain assets;
- internal or marketing support assets;
- alliance-based assets.

6.4.1 Customer-based marketing assets

Customer-based marketing assets are those assets of the company, either tangible or intangible, valued by the customer or potential customer. Often they exist in the mind of the customer and they are essentially intangible in nature. They may, however, be one of the most critical issues in building a defensible competitive position in the marketplace.

Company name and reputation

One of the most important customer-based assets a company can possess is its reputation or image. Companies such as Mercedes, BMW, Land Rover and Rolls-Royce have a clear image of supplying a particular set of customer benefits (reliability, durability, prestige, overall quality) in the markets in which they operate.

Company name confers an asset on all products of the company where it is clearly identified. Indeed, in many cases where the company identity is a strong asset it has been converted into a brand name for use on a wide variety of products (e.g. Virgin Marks and Spencer and Sainsbury are not only company names, but also brands with strong customer franchises).

Image and reputation can also, however, be a negative asset or a liability. This may go far beyond what customers think about product quality. An Ogilvy & Mather study in 1996 contrasted the views of consumers of some companies as 'efficient bastards' compared with the 'Mr Cleans' at the other end of the scale. The top end of the ethical scale was occupied by companies like Marks & Spencer, Boots, Virgin Atlantic, Cadbury and The Body Shop. The other end of the scale was occupied by Camelot (one time UK lottery operator), *The Sun* newspaper, Yorkshire Water utility, William Hill and Ladbrokes (bookmakers) and Sky TV (Bell, 1996). The seriousness of this issue is underlined by evidence that consumers are increasingly reluctant to deal with companies they regard as unethical (Bernoth, 1996). (see Chapter 17 for more detailed consideration of this issue.)

Also important is how firms deal with bad publicity. The reputation of Firestone, the tyre manufacturer, was, for example, badly damaged by public wrangling with Ford over the cause of 170 traffic deaths and hundreds of accidents in the US involving the Ford Explorer, fitted with Firestone tyres. Ford eventually recalled 13 million tyres at a cost of $3 billion (*Marketing Business,* July/August 2001).

Skoda cars were best known in Britain in the mid-1990s as the butt of bad jokes. For example, 'What do you call a Skoda with twin exhaust pipes?' Answer: 'A wheelbarrow.' The jokes merely reflecting widespread and erroneous beliefs that the cars were poor quality. In 1995, Skoda was preparing to launch a new model in the UK, and did 'blind and seen' tests of the consumers' judgement of the vehicle. The vehicle was rated as better designed and worth more by those who did not know the make. With the Skoda name revealed, perceptions of the design were less favourable and estimated value was substantially lower. Subsequent advertising made a joke of this image, showing customers happy with the cars but embarrassed at buying a Skoda. By also showing that Skoda had the strength of VW behind it (visually shown in poster advertisements as a VW shadow behind the Skoda) following acquisition, positive brand values were steadily built. Lidl has recently done something very similar in a recent television campaign. In it, a market stall is seen selling (what seem like) artisan products at very low prices. Indeed some of the customers remark on the low price for the quality of products on sale. The customers are then told that the products they have been raving about are all from Lidl – and of course they are very surprised. Surprise is clearly an erroneous reaction, however this highlights a skewed reputation (or perception), as the quality of products on offer at Lidl is clearly very high.

This leads us from company name and reputation to brands.

Brands

The identity and exploitation of brands remain central to many views of marketing. For example, Interbrand annually reports the most valuable brand names in the world. The top 10 results are presented in Table 6.1 (and are regularly updated by the company on their website at **http://www.interbrand.com**). Building brand value takes time and effort, and it is noticeable how many of the leading brands in the table have been able to retain their position, or close to, over many years. The increased presence of technology-based organisations on this listing is both noticeable and perhaps unsurprising.

For companies where corporate identity is a liability or a non-existent asset, more emphasis is placed on building or acquiring individual brand names as assets. Beechams (now GlaxoSmithKline or GSK), for example, deliberately set out to acquire brands with a marketable reputation. The Bovril brand was purchased to ease the company's launch into the stock cubes market (Bovril being an established brand property in the similar meat extracts market). Companies with little customer-based corporate identity, such as RHM (acquired by Premier Foods) developed various brands into major assets. The Bisto brand, for example, famous as the UK market leader in gravy making, has been used to good effect by in a move into the soups and sauces market.

Branding can operate at the individual level too. For example, sportsmen and sportswomen have begun taking out patents on their names and nicknames, as these are used in merchandising and advertising. Footballers such as David Beckham, Alan Shearer, Paul Gascoigne and Ryan Giggs have, in the past, all registered their surnames and, in some cases, their nicknames e.g. 'Gazza', 'Giggsy'. Recently the trend for individual branding has led to some very impressive financial outcomes indeed. For example, in 2011 Tiger Woods had an estimated income of around $64m of which 'only' £2m was from his tournament earnings; the rest earned largely from endorsements of golf-related products (source *Golf Digest,* 2012). Clearly Tiger's undoubted ability on the golf course allowed him to leverage his personal brand and public profile to great effect (and gain) off the golf course also. Tiger is not alone however, and those with far smaller celebrity media profiles (and hence weaker personal brands) generate significant income from book launches, perfumes and a host of money-making satellite projects.

Table 6.1 The global top ten brands

Rank	2001	2009	2013	Value in 2013 ($USbn)
1	Coca-Cola	Coca-Cola	Apple	98.3
2	Microsoft	IBM	Google	93.3
3	IBM	Microsoft	Coca-Cola	79.2
4	General Electric	General Electric	IBM	78.8
5	Nokia	Nokia	Microsoft	59.5
6	Intel	McDonald's	GE	46.9
7	Disney	Google	McDonald's	41.9
8	Ford	Toyota	Samsung	39.6
9	McDonald's	Intel	Intel	37.2
10	AT&T	Disney	Toyota	35.3

Source: Interbrand (2001, 2009, 2013).

Of course, the overall power and worth of these personal brands is closely linked to the performance, and often behaviour, of the individual concerned; there are many high-profile examples of many millions being wiped off the value of these brands. Tiger Woods lost a number of sponsors following news of his extra-marital affair, and Maria Sharapova (the Russian tennis ace) may lose many millions in sponsorship revenues (from brands such as Tag Heuer, Nike, Porsche and Danone) following a positive test for a banned substance linked to performance enhancement.

Brands can be particularly powerful marketing assets for a number of reasons.

- **Brands are difficult to build.** The leverage highlighted above for the Tiger Woods brand was not built overnight. It was built over many years, and the same is true for successful and profitable commercial brands.
- **Brands add value for customers** – the classic example is that in blind tests 51 per cent of consumers prefer Pepsi to Coca-Cola, but in open tests 65 per cent prefer Coca-Cola to Pepsi. Hence, soft drink preferences are based on brand image, not just taste (de Chernatony and MacDonald, 1992).
- **Brands create defensible competitive positions** – During periods of supermarket price competition, it is not uncommon to see huge discounting on products like baked beans, with own-label baked beans often being priced as low as 3p a can. It is interesting to note that during these periods of discounting Heinz customers are very loyal indeed, and continue to purchase Heinz regardless of much cheaper alternatives. Even though these brand loyal customers are happy to pay around nine times as much as other makes, Heinz have in the past been able to actually increase prices during periods of heavy price competition.
- **Brands build customer retention** – research sponsored by the US Coalition for Brand Equity shows that brand loyalty makes customers less sensitive to competitors' promotions and more likely to try new products and services from that brand. A study of 400 brands over eight years by Information Resources found that with successful brands 30 per cent of the sales increase attributable to new advertising came from new customers, but 70 per cent came from the increased loyalty of existing customers (Kanner, 1996).
- **Brands can transform markets** – the British financial services sector has long been associated with weak branding and low brand awareness. Of late, this sector has been revolutionised by an influx of new brand names (new to this sector) such as Marks and Spencer, Sainsbury's, Tesco and Virgin. All have taken market share away from the incumbents through leveraging their brands and their substantial databases.
- **Brands perform financially** – research study after research study highlight the importance of investment in brands. Those companies that invest in building and maintaining their brands, especially in an economic downturn, outperform those that do not.
- **Brands can cross national borders** – global brands are becoming increasingly common and many firms are attempting to standardise their branding across international markets as their customers also become global. Vodafone, the mobile communications company, for example, has recently 'migrated' regional brands to the one, global brand Vodafone. The Greek subsidiary, formerly Panafon, then Panafon-Vodafone, became simply Vodafone in January 2002. The German brand Vodafone D2 followed in March, and Europolitan Vodafone of Sweden in April. The firm has adopted a dual branding strategy to ease the migration, with the Vodafone name introduced alongside the original for a limited period to build customer recognition (*Marketing Business,* March 2002).

Company and brand are not the only influences on customer perceptions of offerings. The origin of the product may also have a significant impact.

Country of origin (COO)

For companies operating in international markets, the identity of the home country can contribute either as an asset or a liability. Japanese firms, for example, have collectively enjoy a good reputation for quality and value for money. British-made goods, such as Barbour, Burberry, and Church's shoes, have enjoyed a revival in the US due to the favourable image of Britain in this market. Other examples of COO effects include:

- French wine enjoys a strong international reputation, allowing premium pricing. The use of French words (such as 'château' and 'appellation d'origine contrôlée') on labels serves to reinforce the origin. Indeed, wine from specific regions within France can also command a premium even before the wine is sampled. It is noteworthy that wines from Australia depend more on promoting the grape variety (e.g. Pinot Noir, Shiraz, Chardonnay) while French wines promote the region of origin.
- New Zealand successfully promoted itself as a tourist destination following the success of the *Lord of the Rings* movies which were filmed there. The emphasis has now shifted to marketing the country's foods and wines. In 2006, Bacardi paid around $90 million for the luxury vodka brand 42 Below. Originally it was marketed based on New Zealand's reputation for purity, and had gained significant market share on this basis.

Increasingly, consumers in developed markets are concerned about the 'carbon footprint' of their purchases and are starting to question some of their purchasing habits; e.g. items that have travelled long distances at the expense of the environment.

The value of image of home country, company or brand should not be underestimated. Image often takes a long time to build up, but can be destroyed very quickly by mistakes or mishaps. For example, French wine suffered significantly in the US market when France did not support the US-led invasion of Iraq in 2003, and some argue that it has not fully recovered. Conversely, it is often more difficult, though not impossible, for competitors to destroy a company's image-based assets than, say, copy its technology or imitate its products.

Market domination

In addition to image, the domination or apparent domination of the market can constitute an asset. Market presence or domination is used as one of the criteria for valuing brands by Interbrand. Market leaders typically enjoy good coverage of the market, wide distribution and good shelf positions. In addition, market leaders are often believed by consumers to be better in some way than the rest of the market (why else would they be market leader unless they were the best?). Simply being there and highly visible may confer an asset on the product. There is, however, a counter-argument emerging. There is some evidence of an increasing desire among more affluent consumers to demonstrate their independence and sophistication by not buying the same goods and services that others buy. In some product areas this could lead to the situation where being popular and widely used actively discourages some customers who wish to feel they are different from the mass.

For example, in Japan there has been a surge in the sales of unbranded goods in an attempt by conspicuous consumers to stand out from the crowd. The very successful Seibu retail stores, based in Tokyo, selling only *Mujirushi ryohin* ('no brand/ good quality') products, are an example of a retailer that has taken advantage of this. Their labels say only what materials are used and the country of manufacture. The clothes have simple designs, plain colours, high quality and reasonable pricing. Seibu's parent group have also developed the no-brand idea for tinned food and household items in its Seiyu supermarkets.

Superior products and services

It is still worth saying that having superior products and services on the market – products that are, or are believed to be, better in some way (e.g. cheaper, better quality, more stylish and up to date) than the competitors' – can be a marketing asset for the company. Unique products or services, until they are imitated, can provide marketing assets, so long as customers want them and are prepared to pay for them.

6.4.2 Supply chain assets

Assets based in the supply chain are concerned with the manner in which the product or service is conveyed to the customer. They include the distribution network, its control and its uniqueness and pockets of strength.

Distribution network

The physical distribution network itself can be a major asset. In the car hire business, for example, Hertz owes much of its success to a very wide network of pick-up and drop-off centres, especially in the US. This wide network ensures availability of the required services in the right place, increasing convenience of use for the customers.

Distribution control

Investments in dominating some or all of the channels for a product can be a powerful asset. Mars launched the Mars Ice-Cream Bar as a child's treat, transformed into an adult indulgence; a strategy since imitated by countless competitors. However, while having limited success this product has not lived up to expectations in terms of overall sales growth. The Unilever-owned competitor Walls 'owns' the distribution channel that matters: small convenience stores. Indeed, Walls quite literally does own the freezers and display cabinets in many of these outlets, and does not share them with competitors. The critical marketing asset is distribution channel control. Coca-Cola has a very similar approach with its wide distribution of chiller units in retail outlets. These very attractive units do not stock competitor products as a rule, and hence Coke occupies/'owns' retail space that is at a premium in many locations.

Pockets of strength

Selective but close relationships between a company and its distribution outlets can lead to pockets of strength. Where a company is unable, through size or resource constraints, to serve a wide market, concentrating effort, either geographically on specific regions of the market (William Morrison's supermarkets were particularly strong in Yorkshire but spread nationally through acquisition of the Safeway chain of stores), or through specific outlets, can enable a pocket of strength to be developed.

Companies adopting the latter approach of building up a strong presence with selective distributors, or even end users in many industrial markets, often achieve that pocket of strength through key account marketing, i.e. giving full responsibility for each key account development to a specific, normally quite senior, executive. Pockets of strength are typically built up on the basis of strong relationships with those selected distributors and hence require a proactive relationship marketing strategy to ensure their development (see Chapter 15).

Distribution uniqueness

Further distribution-based assets can be built through uniqueness, reaching the target market in a novel or innovative way. For instance, Ringtons sells tea, coffee and other related household items, door to door in the north of England (**http://www.ringtons.co.uk/doorstep**) and the Avon Cosmetics company has built a strong door-to-door business in cosmetics sales (**http://www.ukavonreps.co.uk/**).

Similarly, Dell computers has achieved a uniquely strong position in the personal computer market by using a direct distribution approach, which enables most of the computers sold to be built to the specifications of the customer, while at the same time giving Dell a much faster stock-turn than its competitors.

Delivery lead-time and security of supply

Delivery lead-time is a function of at least three main factors – physical location, order through production systems and company delivery policy. In an increasing number of situations the ability to respond quickly, at no compromise to quality, is becoming more important. Deliberately creating a rapid response capability can constitute a significant marketing asset.

Similarly, particularly in volatile markets, where the supplier's offering is on the critical path of the customer company, the ability to guarantee supply can be a major asset. As with lead-time that ability will be a function of several factors, but perhaps central is the desire on the part of the supplier to meet agreed targets.

The competitive success of fashion clothing retailers such as Primark, Zara and Hennes & Mauritz (H&M) is in large part based on supply chain strengths. These companies can identify fashion catwalk trends and have them in stores in as little as two weeks, sourced from low-cost suppliers, at attractive high-street prices. While they have different competitive positions, these companies are linked by their efficient supply chains and ability to manage the velocity of stock movement rather than focusing on stock levels. They are simply incredibly fast, and their customers expect no less.

Supplier network

At the other end of the supply chain, well-developed or unique links with key suppliers can be important marketing assets. These can help to secure continuity of supply of raw or semi-finished materials at required standards for negotiated prices.

6.4.3 Internal marketing support assets

A resource becomes an asset when it is actively used to improve the organisation's performance in the marketplace. Consider the following examples.

Cost advantages

A cost advantage brought about by employing up-to-date technology, achieving better capacity utilisation than competitors, economies of scale or experience curve effects can be translated into lower prices for products and services in the marketplace. Where the market is price-sensitive, for example, with commodity items, lower price can be a major asset. In other markets where price is less important, cost advantages may not be translated into marketing assets; rather they are used to provide better margins.

Information systems and market intelligence

Information systems and systematic marketing research can be valuable assets in that they keep the company informed about its customers and its competitors. Information is a major asset which many firms guard jealously but until it is utilised to make better decisions it does not convert to a marketing asset. This is an important point, as many organisations collect huge amounts of data, but do not utilise them effectively (or at all). This of course is extremely inefficient and also dangerous, in that they could be missing out on market or customer trends that other competitors, or new entrants, might exploit.

Of particular note is the use of 'data warehouses' of customer information – collected in loyalty schemes or as part of the purchase process, to develop very specific offerings to customers based on their interests and key characteristics. This is why Virgin Atlantic knows which newspapers and seats its frequent fliers prefer, and how Amazon always seems to know the kinds of things you are looking for when you log on (spooky!).

As well as understanding customers better than competitors do, the owners of data warehouses can create marketing strategies that exploit this resource as a differentiating capability. They simply know customers and their markets 'better' than their nearest competitors. Of course, they still have to do something with this knowledge, and one of the key challenges for data-rich organisations is how well (or possibly how quickly) ideas that are informed by data are transferred into actions.

Existing customer base

A major asset for many companies is their existing customer base. Particularly where a company is dealing with repeat business, in consumer and industrial markets, the existence of a core of satisfied customers can offer significant opportunities for further development.

This has been especially noted in the recent development of the direct marketing industry (accounting for around half of all marketing expenditure in the US), where it is recognised that the best customer prospects for a business are often its existing customers. Where customers have been satisfied with previous company offerings they are more likely to react positively to new offers. Where a relationship has been built with the customer this can be capitalised on for market development and employed as a barrier to competitive entry.

The converse is of course, also true. Where a customer has been dissatisfied with a product or service offering they may not only be negative towards new offers, but also may act as 'well poisoners' in relating their experiences to other potential customers. There is an old marketing adage: 'Each satisfied customer will tell 3 others, each dissatisfied customer will tell 33!' Of course, in the digital and social media world this is more like 33,000.

The issue of customer retention and customer loyalty has become extremely important, and we will consider this in more detail in Chapter 14.

Technological skills

The type and level of technology employed by the organisation can be a further asset. Technological superiority can aid in cost reduction or in improving product quality. For example, the high rate of growth of a company such as Amersham plc (specialising in high-technology medical products) is largely based on its ability to stay ahead of its competitors in terms of new product development, but also the capability for distributing highly toxic and radioactive substances safely throughout the world. In the automotive industry, German manufacturers of BMW, Audi and Mercedes-Benz are successfully positioned at the high-quality end of the spectrum on the basis of their superior design, technical engineering excellence and quality controls. The strategy was encapsulated in the famous Audi slogan 'Vorsprung durch Technik' (leading through technology), emphasising the proud German engineering heritage of the cars (country of origin effect).

Production expertise

Production know-how can be used to good effect as a marketing asset. Mars, for example, are particularly good at producing high-quality nougat (a great deal of effort has been put into quality control at Mars, developing their production processes as a core competence). This asset has been turned into a marketing asset in a number of leading products such as Mars Bar, Milky Way, Topic and Snickers, all of which are nougat-based.

Copyrights and patents

Copyright is a legal protection for musical, literary or other artistic property, which prevents others using the work without payment of an agreed royalty. Patents grant persons the exclusive right to make, use and sell their inventions for a limited period. Copyright is particularly important in the film industry to protect films from illegal copy ('pirating') and patents are important for exploiting new product inventions. The protection of copyrights and patents, in addition to offering the holder the opportunity to make and market the items protected, allows the holder to license or sell those rights to others. They therefore constitute potential marketing assets of the company.

Franchises and licenses

The negotiation of franchises or licences to produce and/or market the inventions or protected properties of others can also be valuable assets. Retailers franchised to use the 'Mitre 10' name in hardware retailing in New Zealand, for example, benefit from the strong national image of the licensor and extensive national advertising campaigns.

Similarly, in many countries American Express cards and products are marketed under licence to the American Express Company of the US. The licence agreement is a significant asset for the licensee.

Partnerships

As we shall see in more detail in Chapter 15, increasingly companies are going to market in collaborative or alliance-based strategies. We should not neglect the importance of existing partnerships as marketing assets, and also the management capability to manage marketing strategy in alliance-based networked organisations.

Corporate culture

One of the resources that is hard for competitors to imitate, and particularly distinctive of a company, is its culture. The formation of culture and the capacity to learn are complex issues. None the less, for many successful companies culture represents one of the most unique resources. For example, Hewlett-Packard (HP) has a culture which encourages teamwork and cross-functional and cross-divisional working. This has allowed HP to use its core technologies in many diverse products – printers, plotters, computers, electronic instruments – and to make these products compatible. Competitors can certainly imitate HP's technology relatively easily, but it is far less straightforward to imitate the culture and organisation that underpins HP's marketing effectiveness.

6.4.4 Alliance-based marketing assets

All the assets discussed above can be held internally in the firm itself or gained through strategic alliances and partnerships. Although there are strategic risks involved, alliances can be seen as one way of increasing a company's pool of assets and capabilities without incurring the expense and loss of time in developing them in-house. The importance of strategic alliances and different forms of partnership is discussed in detail in Chapter 15, but for present purposes we should note the significance of such alliance-based marketing assets as:

- **Market access** – for example, alliances with local distributors are frequently the only way open to the exporter to enter protected overseas markets.
- **Management skills** – partnerships may bring access to abilities not held in-house, both in technology management and marketing management.
- **Shared technology** – alliances are often the basis for sharing and combining technologies to create market offerings with higher customer value, which neither partner could achieve alone.
- **Exclusivity** – partnerships may create monopolistic conditions.

6.5 Developing marketing capabilities

All the marketing assets in the world, however, are of little value if they are not actively exploited in the marketplace. The processes and practices that deploy marketing assets are marketing capabilities.

Marketing capabilities are effectively implementation capabilities – the ability to implement marketing mix activities, such as promotions, personal selling, public relations, price deals, special offers to customers, packaging redesign and so on. While the marketing mix is discussed in more detail in Chapter 11, we now briefly describe the main operational marketing capabilities (see Figure 6.6).

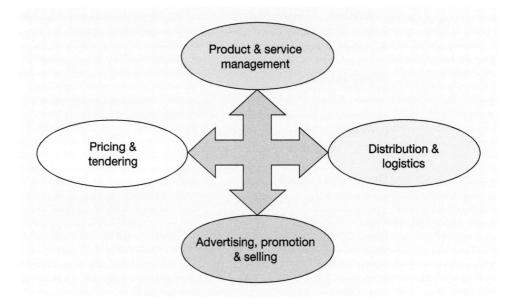

Figure 6.6
Marketing
capabilities

6.5.1 Product and service management capability

Managing existing products, including the ability to influence others in the organisation where their activities impact on customer satisfaction, is basic to effective marketing. This involves the marshalling of all resources (which may cut across traditional organisational boundaries) to deliver customer value. Many firms, following the early examples of Procter & Gamble and Unilever, have designed their organisational structures around the products and services they offer (brand, product and category managers) to ensure that diverse activities such as product design, packaging, pricing, promotions and distribution networks employed all combine effectively. For example, Mercedes cars are clearly positioned as luxury vehicles, often sold into the corporate or fleet market. It is important that all aspects of the marketing are drawn together (price relatively high to denote quality and exclusivity, features to support luxury, distribution through reputable dealers located in business centres) to reinforce the positioning of the car.

6.5.2 Advertising, promotion and selling capability

Effective communications with customers, both current and prospective, take a variety of forms including advertising, public relations, direct marketing, sponsorship and selling (see Chapter 11). Managing the communications process and campaigns, deciding on the mix of approaches to use, and evaluating communications effectiveness are important marketing capabilities.

Increasingly, companies are outsourcing many of these activities to enable them to buy in best practice and expertise from outside. Design consultancies, PR agencies, packaging specialists and the like are emerging as service providers to marketers in these specialist areas of implementation. Within the focal firm, however, the competencies required are increasingly in the selection, management and coordination of specialist outside suppliers.

6.5.3 Distribution capability

Distribution capability is the ability to employ existing channels and/or develop new distribution methods for servicing customer needs. The logistics of delivery can be critical to distribution. A major factor in the success of Amazon as an online retailer has been the capability to accurately and consistently deliver goods bought online to customers through third-party delivery agents such as FedEx. Effective distribution management includes competence for efficient management of traditional distribution channels, but also developing and managing franchising networks and newer electronic channels. This is a broad capability drawing on several organisational competencies such as logistics, production line planning and fleet management. With the growth in mobile, tablet and online retailing, clothing companies such as Charles Tyrwhitt and Hawes and Curtis have built effective and efficient distribution channels in order to make it very easy for loyal customers to buy from them. These companies also have a very substantial high street presence, also fed by their distribution and logistics operations.

6.5.4 Pricing and tendering capability

Pricing decisions are notoriously difficult. Price too high and sales are likely to be low, price too low and the returns to the firm may not provide enough of a margin to enable it to survive or invest in the future. Pricing decisions involve many considerations, including costs of production of physical products or delivery of services, the prices charged by competitors, demand elasticity and the position in the market being targeted. Managing price changes is also a skilled capability requiring judgement about timing, and effective communications. Tendering decisions, used extensively for example in the construction industry, involve a degree of estimation as to who else will tender, and what price they will go in at. Pricing capabilities draw on competencies not only in marketing, but also in finance and operations management.

6.6   Dynamic marketing capabilities

As noted above, the emphasis in the resource-based strategy literature is now on the creation and exploitation of dynamic capabilities (see Bruni and Verona, 2009). While dynamic capabilities in general are the ability to create new resources in changing markets, dynamic marketing capabilities are the ability to create new marketing resources to identify, respond to and exploit change. Ensuring evolutionary fit between market needs in a dynamic competitive environment and market offers is the essence of effective strategic marketing.

Following the typology suggested by Wang and Ahmed (2007), we group dynamic capabilities into three main types: absorptive capability, adaptive capability and innovative capability (see Figure 6.7).

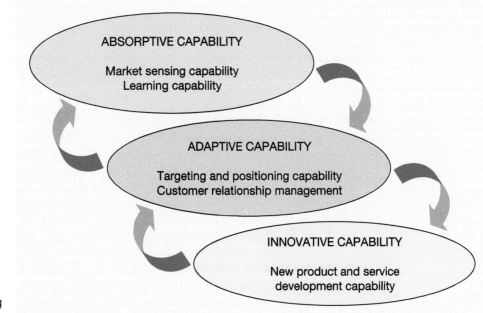

Figure 6.7
Dynamic marketing capabilities

6.6.1 Absorptive marketing capabilities

Absorptive capabilities are the processes that enable firms to recognise the value of new information from the market and to assimilate it. These processes focus on knowledge acquisition and assimilation.

Market sensing capability

The capacity for understanding what is happening in the external environment with respect to demand, customers, competitors and wider macro-environmental change is essential to crafting an effective strategy in a changing market (see Foley and Fahy, 2004).

Specific capabilities include the ability to undertake (or effectively commission) marketing research and competitor analysis, and the ability to ensure dissemination of the resulting information throughout the organisation as a basis for decision making.

Market sensing is not limited, however, to the conduct of formal market research. Famously, Akio Morita, founder of Sony, sensed that there was a potential market for the Walkman when the market research told him otherwise. Market sensing implies being close to the customer, experiencing products and services in the same way that the customer experiences them. Firms operating in business-to-business (B2B) markets may have particular customers that they are especially close to whom they will discuss new product development opportunities with.

Learning capability

Learning processes enable firms to maintain long-term competitive advantages over rivals (Dickson, 1992). In fact, continuous learning is essential for surviving in dynamic and competitive environments as it makes the firm receptive to acquiring and assimilating external knowledge (Zahra and George, 2002). Learning enables new opportunities to be identified and allows for repetition and experimentation, enabling firms to integrate information from the external environment. More specifically, learning is a core element of dynamic capabilities since it is a 'collective activity through which the organisation systematically generates and modifies its operating routines in pursuit of improved effectiveness' (Zollo and Winter, 2002). Prior research has suggested that there are a variety of mechanisms that may be employed to access external knowledge (Almeida *et al.*, 2003). These activities are related to the capabilities of market-driven organisations, that, inter alia, need to excel in 'outside-in' capabilities such as customer linking (Day, 1994).

6.6.2 Adaptive marketing capabilities

Adaptive capabilities centre on the firm's ability to identify and capitalise on emerging market opportunities. Adaptation implies doing things differently in response to external stimuli.

Market targeting and positioning capability

Market targeting and positioning capabilities encompass the ability to identify alternative opportunities and then select appropriate market targets, where the firm's resources and capabilities are aligned for the best effect. Positioning is not just a marketing decision, however. In aligning resources and capabilities with changing markets, the competencies of all aspects of the business (including operations, finance and R&D) as well as marketing need to be taken into account.

As markets change, so the positioning adopted may need to change.

Customer relationship management

Customer relationship management is the ability to acquire, retain, expand and (where necessary) delete customers. Strategic account management skills are becoming increasingly important in business-to-business markets, together with the increased focus in many markets on relationship building through customer service. Direct marketing also has a role to play here. Because of the increasing importance of customer relationship management, we devote Chapter 14 to discussing this in depth.

6.6.3 Innovative marketing capabilities

New product and service development capability

The ability to innovate and develop the next generation of goods and services is the lifeblood of any organisation. Effective new product development requires both an outside-in (customer sensing) capability and appropriate R&D skills. It relies on multi-disciplinary inputs from marketing, R&D, finance, operations and other functional disciplines.

6.7	Resource portfolios

Under the resource-based view of the firm (RBV), organisations are seen as collections of resources, assets and capabilities. These can then be viewed as a portfolio that is available for deployment. When developing strategy the key questions are: how can we exploit our capabilities more fully? What new capabilities will we need to build to enable us to compete in the future?

The interdependence of capabilities and their potential for combination can be the essence of their value.

Hamel and Prahalad (1994) suggest that increasingly firms will define themselves more as portfolios of competencies than as portfolios of products or strategic business units. Indeed, the roots of successful market offerings essentially lie in created and acquired competencies and the key to future strategy is to further develop, extend and deepen them so that they are available for configuration and deployment in new and innovative ways.

Figure 6.8 shows one way of summarising the portfolio of resources the organisation has at its disposal. The two dimensions have been chosen to reflect how far resources contribute

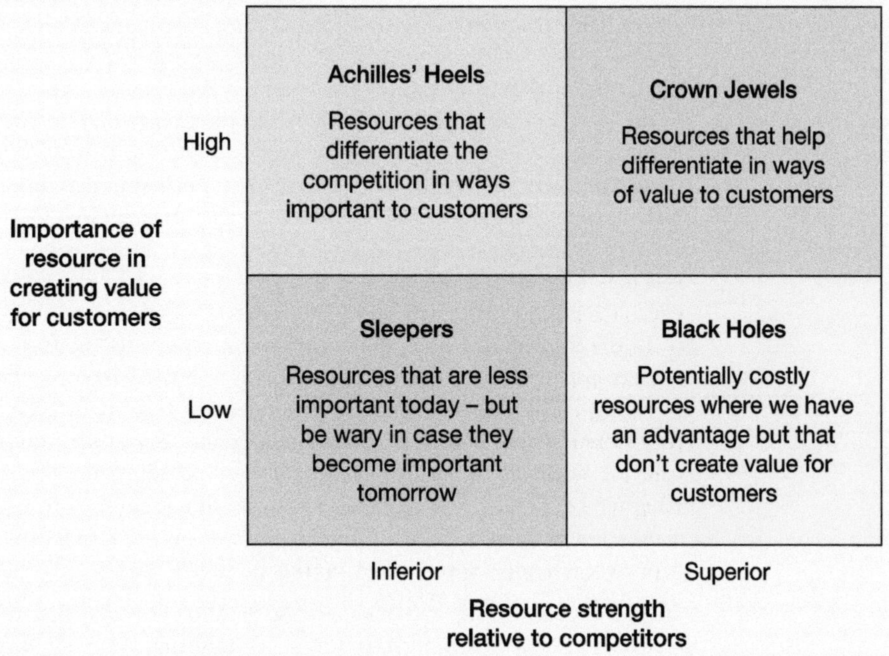

Figure 6.8
The resource
portfolio

to creating value for customers (vertical) and where these resources are superior or inferior to those of competitors (horizontal). Four types of resource can be identified.

- **Crown jewels.** These are the resources where the organisation enjoys an edge over its competitors: they are instrumental in creating value for customers. As the source of differentiation these resources need to be guarded and protected to maintain the competitive edge. At the same time, however, managers need to constantly question whether these resources alone can ensure continued success. The danger lies in resting on the laurels of the past while the world, and customer requirements, move forward.
- **Black holes.** Black holes are resources where the organisation has an edge but which don't contribute to customer value creation. These may be resources that provided customer value in the past but are no longer important. The world and customers may have moved on, rendering them less important at best and obsolete at worst. Managers need to take a long hard look at black holes resources and assess the costs of maintaining them. It could well be that some pruning, or downsizing, of such resources will free up efforts and even cash that can then be deployed more effectively elsewhere.
- **Achilles' heels.** Where competitors are strong but the organisation is weak, and at the same time the resources are important in customer value creation, the clear implication is that resources need to be strengthened. These are resource deficiencies that could prove fatal if not corrected.
- **Sleepers.** Finally, resources that neither constitute a competitive advantage nor are important in customer value creation could be termed sleepers. They are unimportant today but managers do need to watch that they do not become more important in the future.

The resource portfolio model offers a useful summary of the organisation's resources which can be used to highlight areas for attention and development.

6.8 Developing and exploiting resources

While the emphasis above has been on identifying existing resources, organisations also need to ensure they are developing and nurturing the resources that will be required in the future. This involves a degree of forecasting how markets and customers will change over time. Figure 6.9 shows four strategies for development.

The two dimensions shown in Figure 6.9 represent choices open to the organisation in developing and exploiting both the markets in which it operates and the resources it employs.

In the lower left quadrant the focus is on utilising existing resources as effectively as possible in existing markets. The 'fill the gaps' strategy involves looking for better ways of serving existing customers, using the existing strengths of the organisation. In many ways this may be seen as a defensive strategy used to protect existing positions from competitor encroachment.

In the top left quadrant the organisation retains its focus on existing markets and customers but recognises that the resources it will need to serve them in the future will need to change. This requires the next generation of resources to be built and nurtured. Many traditional, bricks and mortar firms have found that to continue to serve their existing customers, they need to develop online services including mobile, tablet and PC offerings (see Chapter 14). This often requires a new set of capabilities to be developed, not just those associated with web-based technology. These new resources do not necessarily enable the firm to reach new customers or markets, but are required to enable it to continue to serve its existing client base. Under this strategy the organisation stays with the markets that it

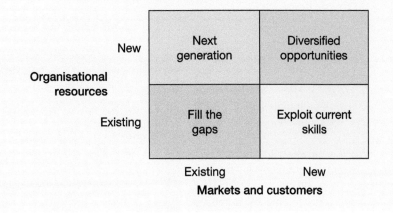

Figure 6.9
Developing and
exploiting resources

Source: Adapted from
Hamel and Prahalad,
1994.

knows and the customers it has built relationships with, but recognises that it must adapt to continue to serve them effectively.

In the bottom right quadrant the organisation seeks new markets and customers where it can 'exploit current skills' more effectively. This quest for new customers, or new markets, is, however, guided by the existing capabilities of the organisation. The acquisition of the UK retailer Asda by the American firm Walmart is a case in point. This enabled Walmart to further exploit its merchandising and purchasing capabilities in the new markets of the UK.

Finally, at top right the organisation looks to serve new customers with new resources through 'diversified opportunities'. This option takes the organisation simultaneously away from its existing markets and its existing resources – a more risky strategy and one that should not be pursued lightly. Firms that take this route often do so through acquisition or merger.

Summary

We started this chapter with a summary of the resource-based view of the firm and the development of ideas surrounding dynamic capabilities. Our focus on competitive positioning (i.e. the choice of target markets and the competitive advantage exploited) provides a mechanism for reconciling the *internal* focus of the RBV with the *external* focus demanded in dynamic markets through the development of dynamic marketing capabilities.

The practical reality faced in building robust marketing strategies is that each company has its own unique strengths and weaknesses with respect to the competition and its own distinctive capabilities. While the overarching imperative is customer focus, a key factor for competing successfully in ever more competitive markets is to achieve an evolutionary fit between capabilities and the environment.

At a fundamental level each organisation needs to understand its resource base. These are the skills and processes at which the company excels, and that can produce the next generation of products or services. At the next level the organisation should be aware of its exploitable marketing assets. The resource-based marketing approach encourages organisations to examine systematically their current and potential assets in the marketplace and to select those for emphasis where they have a defensible uniqueness. Assets built up in the marketplace with customers are less prone to attack by competitors than low prices or easily imitated technologies.

Case study   Family tradition in domestic partnership

Reinhard Zinkann tries to break in to the conversation, but Markus Miele won't let him. 'Just let me finish,' says Mr Miele, a trifle testily. Mr Zinkann shrugs his shoulders, settles back in his chair and waits a few minutes before he gets his say.

This interaction between the men – two halves of an unusual but successful partnership in charge of Miele, the family-owned German manufacturer of upmarket domestic appliances – gives some clues as to how they make their collaboration work.

The pair – both wearing navy suits and red ties – insist the occasional argument is healthy, and that their respective strengths and weaknesses are complementary.

'It would be wrong to say we never have an emotional discussion,' says Mr Zinkann. 'But if this happens, then it does not take too long before either he or I steps in to each other's office to talk about the matter. We always find a joint solution.'

Aged 50, Mr Zinkann, who has a marketing background, is nine years older than his fellow managing partner and both are great-grandsons of the two men who started the business in 1899. They have followed a family tradition: the management of the company has always been handed down to male heirs of the founders, who run it jointly, making the current incumbents the fourth Miele–Zinkann duo to be in charge. The company, which has a long-standing reputation for quality, remains 51 per cent owned by the Miele family, with 49 per cent belonging to the Zinkanns.

Mr Zinkann, the stouter and more relaxed of the two, is expansive to the point of philosophical, on the topic of dishwashers and tumble dryers. In contrast, Mr Miele has the manner and temperament of an engineer, discussing in detail the company's unashamedly expensive products. He is particularly animated when it comes to the special 'honeycomb drums' inside Miele's washing machines that provide a thin film of water, preventing damage from the clothes rubbing too much against the side.

We are talking in the newly opened Miele showroom in central London and surrounded by the company's latest products. Somewhat grandly, the company calls these places 'galleries'. There are about 25 of them around the world, where shoppers can not only look at the latest Miele models but also take part in seminars on how to get the best use out

Source: Getty Images: AFP.

of their cookers or washing machines. For a small fee, they can even cook lunch there under the direction of a top chef.

Mr Miele describes one such 'gallery' in Hong Kong: 'Upstairs from this [showroom] is a very famous hairdresser. While [women] are having their hair done, we will wash the clothes using one of our machines.'

Such showrooms may sound excessive for a domestic appliance maker, but they make sense if one considers the prices. A top-of-the-range, jumbo-sized Miele refrigerator, brimming with speciality controls and sensors, sells in the US for more than $7,000 (£4,400, €4,900) or seven times higher than more standard machines.

This is due in part to the rigour of the company's legendary product testing. To check that the cables in Miele's vacuum cleaners are satisfactory, they are flexed backwards and forwards 100,000 times in the laboratory.

Miele – unlike most other domestic appliance makers, such as Whirlpool of the US or Electrolux of Germany – has only one, top-end brand, rather than a number of names standing for different quality or price levels.

'We put all our power in marketing and engineering into just the one Miele brand,' says Mr Zinkann. 'Perhaps in this way we are a bit like the husband or wife in a monogamous marriage.'

Miele's sales in the year ending June 2009 were €2.8bn, 71 per cent of this coming from outside its home country, where it employs 10,000 of the company's 16,000 workers.

Unlike many of its rivals, who outsource manufacturing to low-cost countries, the company makes many of its own components in its own plants in Germany, even commonplace items such as electric motors.

Mr Zinkann says having an integrated view of production and design – with Germany at the centre – enables Miele to make a better product.

'God creates man with a brain, a heart and a body,' he says. 'Of course, you could design a person with a brain, heart and body that all belonged to someone different, but I think it's better if they all fit with each other.'

The two men say the recession has not hit Miele too badly. While sales in 2008–2009 were slightly down year on year, the company has not had any redundancies.

'I think that in a recession people turn towards quality,' says Mr Miele. 'They are more likely to spend their money on something that's going to last than [an appliance] at the low end.'

Following another family tradition, profits are not disclosed. However, Mr Zinkann says they are buoyant. 'The figures would make the stock market happy. But, unfortunately, if you are outside the company you will never know what they are.'

Mr Zinkann became a managing partner at Miele in 1999, three years before his younger colleague.

After attending Gordonstoun, the Scottish boarding school, famous for having educated three generations of the British royal family, Mr Zinkann had stints at four universities, studying philosophy, history, musicology and business economics. 'I tried to change universities as much as possible just to see new aspects of life. I was interested in a lot of things and my father encouraged me,' he says.

After graduating, he had a three-year spell in the sales and marketing division of the luxury car maker BMW in Munich.

Mr Miele stayed closer to home. He went to school in Gütersloh – the small north German town where the company is based and where both men live within 300 metres of each other – before pursuing a more conventional university career.

The two did not see much of each other until Mr Zinkann was in his 30s and Mr Miele in his 20s. The two families, says Mr Miele, have always made a point of keeping 'a respectful and friendly distance'. Which may explain, he says, how they have 'been able to keep peace and harmony . . . for more than a century.'

Both men were aware from an early age that there was an expectation that they would eventually succeed their fathers and run the business. But they insist there was no pressure on them. 'In Germany, we've seen many examples of family companies where the son or daughter was more or less forced into the top job,' Mr Miele says.

'But then you end up not having success in the market. It's better to leave the [son or daughter] to choose. It is preferable [for them] to become a good lawyer, a good surgeon or a good author, than a bad manager,' he adds.

Source: Peter Marsh, 'Miele focuses on old-fashioned quality', *Financial Times*, 13/11/03.

Discussion questions

1 What are the key resources that have made Miele a successful company so far? Which of these are marketing assets?

2 Miele are now facing more and more competition in a changing market? Do their resources provide them with a sustainable competitive advantage?

3 What new resources might they need to develop/acquire to remain successful in the future?

PART 3
IDENTIFYING CURRENT AND FUTURE COMPETITIVE POSITIONS

Part 3 addresses in more detail the issues and techniques behind segmentation and positioning research.

Chapter 7 discusses the underlying principles of competitive positioning and market segmentation, and their impact on the choice of target markets. The chapter continues by discussing in detail the logic of segmentation as an approach to identifying target markets, and by comparing the alternative bases for segmenting both consumer and business markets. The chapter closes by considering the benefits of identifying and describing market segments, but also the importance of integrating market segment-based strategies with corporate characteristics and competencies, as well as external factors.

Chapter 8 examines the techniques of segmentation and positioning research in detail. Two fundamentally different approaches are discussed. Under the first, termed *a priori,* the bases for segmenting are decided in advance and typically follow product/brand usage patterns or customer demographic characteristics. The second approach, *post hoc* or cluster based, searches for segments on the basis of a set of criteria, but without preconceived ideas as to what structure in the market will emerge. The chapter then discusses methods for collecting segmentation data (relating back to the marketing research methods discussed in Chapter 4), ways of analysing those data to identify and describe market segments, and addresses the issue of validating empirically the segmentation structure uncovered. The chapter next discusses both qualitative and quantitative approaches to positioning research. In the former the use of focus groups and depth interviews to identify images and positions is examined. The chapter concludes with a discussion of quantitative approaches to creating perceptual maps.

Chapter 9 discusses choice of target market following the analysis of options above. Two key dimensions are suggested for making the selection of target markets. First, the relative attractiveness of each potential segment. This will be dependent on many factors, including size, growth prospects, margins attainable, competitive intensity and so on. The second key dimension is the strength of the organisation in serving that potential target market. This is determined by the resources of the organisation, its current and potential marketing assets and the capabilities and competencies it can call on and deploy relative to competitors.

CHAPTER 7
SEGMENTATION AND POSITIONING PRINCIPLES

Focussed competitors dominate their target segments – by fending off broad-coverage competitors who have to compromise to serve the segment, and out-performing rivals with the same focus . . . Focussed strategies also gain meaning from the differences between the segments covered and the rest of the market.

Day (1994)

Jaeger targets younger shoppers

Jaeger, the privately owned fashion chain, is to launch its first young fashion range, in an effort to attract more youthful shoppers.

Boutique by Jaeger aims to compete with high street stores such as Whistles, Reiss and All Saints, but also with diffusion ranges from upmarket designers such as Marc by Marc Jacobs and See by Chloé.

It will be aimed at shoppers aged 20–25 and will be priced 25–30 per cent lower than Jaeger's other ranges.

The move underlines the appeal to retailers of younger shoppers, who have proved more willing to spend through the recession.

Belinda Earl, group chief executive, said the new line may appeal to a 'customer who shops with us maybe only during the sale. It's a way we can attract that customer all the year round . . . it will also bring customers in who can trade up to the main line'.

Jaeger, which started life in 1884 when German doctor Gustav Jaeger extolled the benefits of wearing natural fibres, has been transformed under Ms Earl and Harold Tillman, the entrepreneur who acquired it six years ago.

The Boutique range is based on the Young Jaeger line that Jean Muir designed in the 1950s and 1960s.

Source: from 'Jaeger targets younger shoppers', *Financial Times*, 15/04/2010 (Felsted, A.).

Discussion questions

1 How is the fashion market segmented?

2 Why and how is Jaeger trying to appeal to younger shoppers?

Introduction

Our approach to marketing analysis so far has rested largely on the identification and exploitation of key differences – in marketing capabilities and competitive strengths, for example. Our attention now focuses on two particularly important areas of differentiation: the differences between alternative market offerings as far as customers are concerned, i.e. the **competitive positioning** of suppliers, products, services and brands; and the differences between customers – in terms of their characteristics, behaviour and needs – that are important to marketing decision makers in developing strong marketing strategies, i.e. **market segmentation.**

The distinction between competitive positioning and market segmentation is illustrated in Figure 7.1, which suggests that the key issues are as follows:

- **Competitive positioning:** concerned with how customers perceive the alternative offerings on the market, compared with each other, e.g. how do Audi, BMW and Mercedes medium-price saloon cars compare in value, quality and 'meaning' or image?
- **Market segmentation:** described as how we as marketers can divide the market into groups of similar customers, where there are important differences between those groups, e.g. what are the characteristics of medium-price saloon car buyers that relate to their product preferences and buying behaviour?
- **Customer needs:** while positioning and segmentation are different concepts, ultimately they are linked by customer needs, in the sense that the most robust form of segmentation focuses on the customer benefits that matter most to different types of customer, while the strongest competitive positions to take are those where customers recognise that a supplier or product is the one they choose because it best meets their needs.

In this sense positioning and segmentation are distinct parts of the strategy process and provide us with some extremely powerful tools; but ultimately they are linked by the central issue of focusing on satisfying the customer's needs in ways that are superior to competitors.

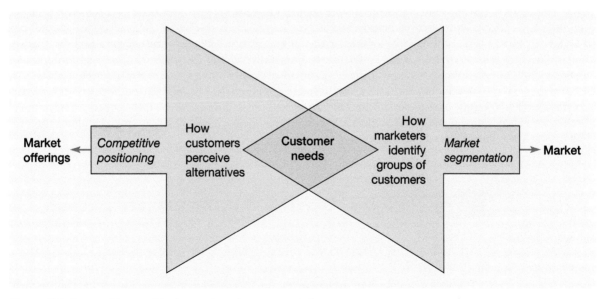

Figure 7.1 Competitive positioning and market segmentation

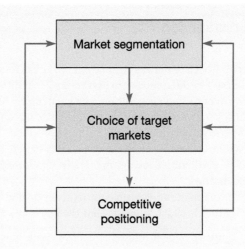

Figure 7.2
Stages in
segmentation and
positioning

Operationally, positioning and segmentation may be linked in the way shown in Figure 7.2. This suggests that the sequence in planning can be the following:

- **market segmentation** – identifying the most productive bases for dividing a market, identifying the customers in different segments and developing segment descriptions;
- **choice of target markets:** evaluating the attractiveness of different market segments, parts of segments (niches) or groups of segments, and choosing which should be targets for our marketing;
- **competitive positioning:** identifying the positioning of competitors (in the market and in target segments or niches), to develop our own positioning strategy;
- **iteration:** understanding competitors' positioning and the possible positioning strategies open to us should influence our thinking about the attractiveness of different market segments and the choice of market targets, and may change the way we segment our market, leading to revised target choices and positioning approaches.

While they are distinct strategy concepts there are important similarities between positioning and segmentation: both start as issues of perception – how customers compare and understand alternative market offerings and how marketers understand the customer benefits different buyers seek from products and services. But both are also susceptible to rigorous research-based analysis.

We approach these issues in the following way. The role of this chapter is to distinguish between positioning and segmentation, and to clarify the underlying concepts and principles. From this foundation we move to an evaluation in Chapter 8 of the technical aspects of developing positioning and segmentation models. The implications for developing marketing strategies are found in Chapter 10 (on creating sustainable competitive advantage in target markets) and Chapter 18 (on the integration of positioning and segmentation to build robust marketing strategies for the future).

7.1 Principles of competitive positioning

Competitive positioning as an issue in developing marketing strategy has been defined in the following terms:

> Positioning is the act of designing the company's offering and image so that they occupy a meaningful and distinct competitive position in the target customers' minds.
> *(Kotler, 1997)*

The essential principle of competitive positioning is that it is concerned with how customers in different parts of the market perceive the competing companies, products/services or brands. It is important to bear in mind that positioning may apply to any of these levels:

- **companies:** for example, in grocery retailing in the United Kingdom the major competitors include Tesco, Sainsbury's and Asda, and positioning is based on these identities;
- **products and services:** positioning also applies at the level of the product, as shown in the example of the Dyson vacuum cleaner compared with similarly priced products from Hoover and Bosch;
- **brands:** competitive positioning is perhaps most frequently discussed in terms of brand identities: Coca-Cola versus Pepsi, and so on.

Indeed, some cases show the importance of these levels as they relate to each other – Virgin, for example, is a company that stands for certain values in customers' minds, which translates to the company's simplified financial services products, and provides the brand identity for diverse products and services.

Competitive positioning may be seen in some ways as the outcome of companies' attempts to create effective competitive differentiation for their products and services. However, Kotler (1997) suggests that not all competitive differences will create a strong competitive position; attempts to create differentiation should meet the following criteria:

- **importance** – a difference should create a highly valued benefit for significant numbers of customers;
- **distinctive and pre-emptive** – the difference cannot be easily imitated or performed better by others;
- **superior** – the difference should provide a superior way for customers to obtain the benefit in question;
- **communicable** – the difference should be capable of being communicated to customers and understood by them;
- **affordable** – the target customers can afford to pay for the difference;
- **profitable** – the difference will command a price adequate to make it profitable for the company.

One way of describing the outcome of the search for differences that matter to target customers, and how we perform them in a distinctive way, is the concept of the value proposition – the promise made to customers that encapsulates the position we wish to take compared with competitors. For example, in the mid-1990s the Korean car company Daewoo gained 1 per cent of the UK car market from a standing start in the fastest time ever achieved by any car manufacturer. There was nothing distinctive about the cars it sold – they were old General Motors designs produced under licence. What was distinctive was an explicit and clear value proposition to its target market segment. The four pillars of this company's distinctive value proposition were:

1 **direct:** treating customers differently by dealing direct instead of through traditional distributors, and staying in touch throughout the purchase and use of the product;
2 **hassle free:** clear communications with customers, and no sales pressure or price haggling;
3 **peace of mind:** all customers pay the same price, and many features traditionally sold as extras are included in the deal;
4 **courtesy:** demonstrating respect for customer needs and preferences throughout the process.

Daewoo quickly established a strong competitive positioning in a specific segment of the car market on the basis of this proposition.

A competitive position may be built on any dimensions of product or service that produce customer benefits in the market, but an important emphasis in positioning is that what matters is customer perception.

In fact the term 'positioning' was brought to prominence by Ries and Trout (1982) to describe the creative process whereby:

> Positioning starts with a product. A piece of merchandise, a service, a company, or even a person . . . But positioning is not what you do to a product. Positioning is what you do to the mind of the prospect. That is, you position the product in the mind of the prospect.

The Ries and Trout approach to the 'battle for your mind' is highly oriented towards marketing communications and brand image while, as we have seen, competitive positioning is somewhat broader in recognising the impact of every aspect of the market offering that is perceived by customers as important in creating distinctive value. One way of summarising the underlying thinking is to focus on customer benefits and positioning in the customer's mind:

> You don't buy coal, you buy heat; you don't buy circus tickets, you buy thrills; you don't buy a paper, you buy news; you don't buy spectacles, you buy vision; you don't sell products, you create positions.

The importance of clear and strong competitive positioning is underlined by Kotler's (1997) warning of the major positioning errors (Figure 7.3) that can undermine a company's marketing strategy:

- **under-positioning:** when customers have only vague ideas about a company or its products, and do not perceive anything special about it, the product becomes an 'also-ran';
- **over-positioning:** when customers have too narrow an understanding of the company, product or brand: Mont Blanc sells pens that cost several thousand pounds, but it is important to that company for the consumer to be aware that a Mont Blanc pen can also be purchased for around £200;
- **confused positioning:** frequent changes and contradictory messages may simply confuse customers about a company's positioning: the indecisiveness of the retailer Sainsbury's about whether or not to have a loyalty card to rival Tesco's launch of its card, and about its price level compared with others, contributed to its loss of market leadership in the 1990s;
- **doubtful positioning:** the claims made for the company, product or brand may simply not be accepted, whether or not they are true: the goal at British Home Stores to position that retail business as 'the first-choice store for dressing the modern woman and family' failed in a market that remains dominated by Marks & Spencer, despite the latter's recent problems.

In essence, positioning is concerned with understanding how customers compare alternative offerings on the market and building strategies that describe to the customer how the company's offering differs in important ways from those of existing or potential competitors. Together with market segmentation, competitive positioning is central to the development of effective marketing strategies (see Chapter 10).

These characteristics of competitive positioning can be compared with the principles of market segmentation.

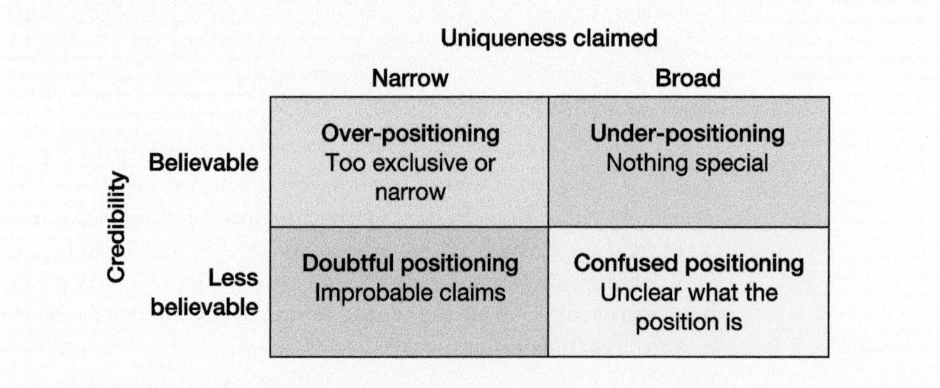

Uniqueness claimed

	Narrow	Broad
Believable	**Over-positioning** Too exclusive or narrow	**Under-positioning** Nothing special
Less believable	**Doubtful positioning** Improbable claims	**Confused positioning** Unclear what the position is

Credibility (axis label)

Figure 7.3
Positioning risks
and errors

> **7.2** **Principles of market segmentation**

Two major features of modern markets are the extent to which they are capable of being segmented (because of growing differences between customers and their demands to be treated as individuals) and the existence of the vastly superior technologies of communication, distribution and production, which allow the pursuit of segmentation strategies. In some cases this leads to 'micro-segmentation' or 'one-to-one marketing', in which each customer is treated as a different segment.

Where there are differences in customer needs or wants, or in their attitudes and predispositions towards the offerings on the market, between groups or individuals in the market, then there are opportunities to segment the market, i.e. to subdivide the larger market into smaller groups (segments) that provide market targets.

The history of thinking about market segmentation can be traced at least as far back as Smith (1956), who distinguished between strategies of product differentiation (applying promotional techniques to influence demand in favour of the product) and market segmentation (adjusting market offerings in various ways to more closely meet the requirements of different customers). Baker (1992) acknowledges this as the first coherent statement of a distinctive marketing view of market structure, representing a compromise between the economist's view of markets as single entities and the behavioural scientist's focus on individual buyer differences. Seen in this light, segmentation is a logical extension of the marketing concept and market orientation (see Chapter 1).

> **7.3** **The underlying premises of market segmentation**

Let us first consider the underlying requirements for market segmentation and take an overview of segmentation issues.

7.3.1 Underlying requirements for market segmentation

Three basic propositions underpin market segmentation as a component of marketing strategy:

1 For segmentation to be useful customers must **differ from one another** in some important respect, which can be used to divide the total market. If they were not different in some significant way, if they were totally homogeneous, then there would be no need or basis on which to segment the market. However, in reality all customers differ in some respect. The key to whether a particular difference is useful for segmentation purposes lies in the extent to which the differences are related to different behaviour patterns (e.g. different levels of demand for the product or service, or different use/benefit requirements) or susceptibility to different marketing mix combinations (e.g. different product/service offerings, media, messages, prices or distribution channels), i.e. whether the differences are important to how we develop a marketing strategy.

2 The operational use of segmentation usually requires that segment targets can be **identified by measurable characteristics** to enable their potential value as a market target to be estimated and for the segment to be identified. Crucial to utilising a segmentation scheme to make better marketing decisions is the ability of the marketing strategist to evaluate segment attractiveness and the current or potential strengths the company has in serving a particular segment. Depending on the level of segmentation analysis, this may require internal company analysis or external market appraisal. The external market evaluation of segments and selection of market targets are discussed in Chapter 9.

3 The effective application of segmentation strategy also requires that selected segments be **isolated** from the remainder of the market, enabling them to be targeted with a distinct

market offering. Where segments are not distinct they do not form a clear target for the company's marketing efforts.

For any segmentation scheme to be useful it must possess the above three characteristics.

7.3.2 Major issues in market segmentation

By way of overview, our general understanding of the issues to be addressed in studying and applying market segmentation falls into the following four areas suggested by Piercy and Morgan (1993):

1 the methodology of market segmentation;
2 the criteria for testing segments as robust market targets;
3 the strategic segmentation decision itself;
4 the implementation of segmentation strategy in the company.

The methodology of market segmentation

The methodological tools available for use in developing segmentation schemes are concerned with two issues. First, there is the question of the choice of the variables or customer characteristics with which to segment the market – the 'bases' of market segmentation. Second, there is the related question of the procedures or techniques to apply to identify and evaluate the segments of the market. The bases for segmentation are considered in the next section of this chapter, and the techniques of market segmentation analysis are discussed in Chapter 8.

Testing the robustness of segments

If segments can be identified using the bases and techniques chosen, then there is the question of how they should be evaluated as prospective targets. In a classic paper Frank *et al.* (1972) suggested that to provide a reasonable market target a segment should be measurable, accessible, substantial and unique in its response to marketing stimuli. These criteria remain the basis for most approaches (e.g. see Kotler and Keller, 2012). In fact, evaluating market segments may be more complex than this suggests.

Strategic segmentation decision

If the market is susceptible to segmental analysis and modelling, and attractive segments can be identified, then the decision faced is whether to use this as the basis for developing marketing strategies and programmes, and whether to target the entire market or concentrate on part of it. These issues of strategy are discussed in Chapter 9.

Implementation of segmentation strategies

Finally, there is the question of the capabilities of the organisation for putting a segmentation approach into effect and, indeed, the extent to which corporate characteristics should guide the segmentation approach in the first place. These questions are considered at the end of this chapter.

7.4   Bases for segmenting markets

Some of the major issues in market segmentation centre on the bases on which the segmentation should be conducted and the number of segments identifiable as targets in a particular market. The selection of the base for segmentation is crucial to gaining a clear picture of the nature of the market – the use of different bases can result in very different outcomes. In fact, the process of segmentation and the creative selection of different segmentation bases can often help to gain new insights into old market structures that in turn may offer new opportunities – this is not merely a mechanical piece of statistical analysis.

In addition to choosing the relevant bases for segmentation, to make the segments more accessible to marketing strategy the segments are typically described further on common characteristics. Segments formed, for example, on the basis of brand preference may be further described in terms of customer demographic and attitudinal characteristics to enable relevant media to be selected for promotional purposes and a fuller picture of the chosen segments to be built.

In the next section we examine the major bases used in consumer markets, and in the following section we turn to industrial and business-to-business markets.

7.5 Segmenting consumer markets

The variables used in segmenting consumer markets can be broadly grouped into three main classes:

1 background customer characteristics;
2 customer attitudes;
3 customer behaviour.

The first two sets of characteristics concern the individual's predisposition to action, whereas the final set concerns actual behaviour in the marketplace.

7.5.1 Background customer characteristics for segmenting markets

Often referred to as classificatory information, background characteristics do not change from one purchase situation to another. They are customer-specific but not specifically related to their behaviour in the particular market of interest. Background characteristics can be classified along two main dimensions (see Figure 7.4).

The first dimension is the origin of the measures. The measures may have been taken from other disciplines and are hence not marketing specific but believed to be related to marketing activity. Non-marketing-specific factors include demographic and socio-economic

	Objective measures	Subjective measures
Non-marketing specific	**Demographics** Sex, age, geography, subculture, etc. **Socio-economics** Occupation, income, education	**Personality inventories**
Marketing specific	**Consumer life cycle** **ACORN** **Media usage**	**Lifestyle**

Psychographics spans between the Objective and Subjective measures columns.

Figure 7.4
Background customer characteristics

characteristics developed in the fields of sociology and demography. Alternatively, measures may have been developed specifically by marketing researchers and academics to solve marketing problems. Typically they have been developed out of dissatisfaction with traditional (sociological) classifications. Dissatisfaction with social class, as a predictor of marketing behaviour, for example, has led to the development of lifestyle segmentation and geodemographic segmentation such as the ACORN (A Classification Of Residential Neighbourhoods) and related classification schemes.

The second dimension to these characteristics is the way in which they are measured. Factors such as age or sex can be measured objectively, whereas personality and lifestyle (collectively termed 'psychographics') are inferred from often subjective responses to a range of diverse questions.

The commonest variables used are as follows.

Demographic characteristics

Measures such as age and gender of both purchasers and consumers have been one of the most popular methods for segmenting markets:

- **Gender:** a basic approach to segmentation of the market for household consumables and for food purchases is to identify 'housewives' as a specific market segment. For marketing purposes 'housewives' can include both females and males who have primary responsibility for grocery purchase and household chores. This segmentation of the total potential market of, say, all adults will result in a smaller (around half the size) identified target. Many segmentation schemes use gender as a first step in the segmentation process, but then further refine their targets within the chosen gender category, e.g. by social class or age. In some markets the most relevant variable is gender preference, e.g. the gay market for certain products and services.
- **Age:** age has been used as a basic segmentation variable in many markets. The market for holidays is a classic example, with holiday companies tailoring their products to specific age groups such as 'under 30s' or 'senior citizens'. In these segmentation schemes it is reasoned that there are significant differences in behaviour and product/service requirements between the demographic segments identified.

  Cadbury Schweppes, for example, has developed new products aimed at young drinkers in pubs. One such product, Viking, is a chocolate-based energy snack that is marketed in Australia as 'the bar with horns'.

  The main reasons for the popularity of age and gender as segmentation variables have been the ease of measurement of these characteristics (they can be objectively measured) and their usefulness for media selection purposes. Widely available syndicated media research studies present data on viewing and reading habits broken down by these characteristics. Matching media selected to segments described in these terms is, therefore, quite straightforward.

  Age may also combine with other characteristics such as social class. For example, Taylor Nelson AGB analysed the alcoholic drinks market into age/social class groups and linked this to drinks consumption (Grant, 1996):

  (a) *Downmarket/young* – favouring alcopops and premium canned lagers.
  (b) *Upmarket/young* – preferences were for premium bottled lagers and cider.
  (c) *Downmarket/older* – favouring stout, and spirits such as rum, brandy and whisky.
  (d) *Upmarket/older* – characteristic preferences for super premium lager and gin.

- **Geographic location:** geographic segmentation may be a useful variable, particularly for small- or medium-sized marketing operations that cannot hope to attack a widely dispersed market. Many companies, for example, choose to market their products in their home country only, implicitly excluding worldwide markets from their targets. Within countries it may also be possible to select regional markets where the company's offerings and the market requirements are most closely matched.

Haggis, for example, sells best in Scotland, while sales of jellied eels are most successful in the East End of London.

- **Subculture:** each individual is a member of a variety of subcultures. These subcultures are groups within the overall society that have peculiarities of attitude or behaviour. For a subculture to be of importance for segmentation purposes it is likely that membership of the subculture has to be relatively enduring and not transient, and that membership of the subculture is of central importance in affecting the individual's attitudes and/or ultimate behaviour.

The major subcultures used for segmentation purposes are typically based on racial, ethnic, religious or geographic similarities. In addition, subcultures existing within specific age groupings may be treated as distinct market segments. For example, targeting 'micro-communities' has become important in relationship marketing – one Canadian bank has focused to great effect on the tightly knit but affluent Filipino community in Canada (Svendsen, 1997).

The major drawback of all demographic characteristics **discussed above** as bases for segmenting markets is that they cannot be guaranteed to produce segments that are internally homogeneous but externally heterogeneous in ways that are directly relevant to the marketer. Within the same demographic classes there can be individuals who exhibit very different behavioural patterns and are motivated by quite different wants and needs. Similarly there may be significant and exploitable similarities in behaviour and motivations between individuals in different demographic segments. As a consequence a generally low level of correspondence between demographics and behaviour has been found in the academic marketing research literature. Despite these drawbacks their relative ease of measurement makes them popular among marketing practitioners.

Socio-economic characteristics

Factors such as income, occupation, terminal education age and social class have been popular with researchers for similar reasons to demographics: they are easy to measure and can be directly related back to media research for media selection purposes. More importantly, the underlying belief in segmenting markets by social class is that the different classes are expected to have different levels of affluence and adopt different lifestyles. These lifestyles are, in turn, relevant to marketing-related activity, such as propensity to buy certain goods and services. Socio-economic measures are best seen in the use of social class groups.

Marketing researchers use several social class stratification schemes. The scheme used in the United Kingdom by the Market Research Society is presented in Table 7.1.

For many marketing purposes the top two and bottom two classes are combined to give a four-group standard classification by social class: AB, C1, C2, DE. In the United States several alternative social class schemes have been used for segmentation purposes (see Frank *et al.*, 1972). The most widely adopted, however, is that proposed by Warner (see Table 7.2).

Social class has been used as a surrogate for identifying the style of life that individuals are likely to lead. The underlying proposition is that consumers higher up the social scale tend to spend a higher proportion of their disposable income on future satisfactions (such as insurance and investments) while those lower down the scale spend proportionately more on immediate satisfactions. As such, socio-economic class can be particularly useful in identifying segments in markets such as home purchase, investments, beer and newspapers.

The financial services industry makes extensive use of socio-economic groups for marketing, such as developing pensions and life assurance products aimed at particular social groups. One company is launching an occupational annuity to pay a higher pension to those in stressful or unhealthy jobs. Premiums and terms for private health insurance are partly determined by social class groupings (Gardner, 1997).

However, as with the demographic characteristics discussed above, it is quite possible that members of the same social class have quite different purchase patterns and reasons for purchase. Consider, for a moment, your peers – people you work with or know socially.

Table 7.1 UK socio-economic classification scheme

Occupation groups		
	A	Approximately 3% of the total population. These are professional people, very senior managers in business or commerce or top-level civil servants. Retired people, previously grade A, and their widows.
Non-manual	B	Approximately 20% of the total population. Middle management executives in large organisations, with appropriate qualifications. Principal officers in local government and civil service. Top management or owners of small business concerns, educational and service establishments. Retired people, previously grade B, and their widows.
	C1	Approximately 28% of the total population. Junior management, owners of small establishments, and all others in non-manual positions. Jobs in this group have very varied responsibilities and educational requirements. Retired people, previously grade C1, and their widows.
Manual	C2	Approximately 21% of the total population. All skilled manual workers, and Manual those manual workers with responsibility for other people. Retired people, previously grade C2, with pensions from their job. Widows, if receiving pensions from their late husband's job.
	D	Approximately 18% of the total population. All semi-skilled and unskilled manual workers, apprentices and trainees to skilled workers. Retired people, previously grade D, with pensions from their job. Widows, if receiving a pension from their late husband's job.
	E	Approximately 10% of the total population. All those entirely dependent on the state long-term, through sickness, unemployment, old age or other reasons. Those unemployed for a period exceeding six months (otherwise classify on previous occupation). Casual workers and those without a regular income. Only households without a chief income earner will be coded in this group.

Source: The Market Research Society.

The chances are they will be classified in the same social class as you. The chances are also that they will be attracted to different sorts of products motivated by different factors and make quite different brand choices.

Concern has been expressed among both marketing practitioners and academics that social class is becoming increasingly less useful as a segmentation variable. Lack of satisfaction with social class in particular and other non-marketing-specific characteristics such as segmentation variables has led to the development of marketing-specific measures such as stage of customer life cycle, geodemographics such as the ACORN classification system and the development of lifestyle research.

Consumer life cycle

Stage of the family life cycle, essentially a composite demographic variable incorporating factors such as age, marital status and family size, has been particularly useful in identifying the types of people most likely to be attracted to a product field (especially consumer durables) and when they will be attracted. The producers of baby products, for example, build (e-) mailing lists of households with newborn babies on the basis of free gifts given to mothers in maternity hospitals. These lists are dated and used to direct advertising messages

Table 7.2 The Warner index of status characteristics

Class name	Description	Consumption characteristics
Upper-upper	Elite social class with inherited social position	Expensive, irrelevant, but purchase decisions not meant to impress; conservative
Lower-upper	Nouveau riche; highly successful business and professional; position acquired through wealth	Conspicuous consumption to demonstrate wealth, luxury cars, large estates, etc.
Upper-middle	Successful business and professional	Purchases directed at projecting successful image
Lower-middle	White-collar workers, small businesspeople	Concerned with social approval; purchase decisions conservative; home and family oriented
Upper-lower	Blue-collar workers, technicians, skilled workers	Satisfaction of family roles
Lower-lower	Unskilled labour, poorly educated, poorly off	Attraction to cheap, 'flashy', low-quality items; heavy exposure to TV

for further baby, toddler and child products to the family at the appropriate time as the child grows.

Stage of family life cycle was first developed as a market segmentation tool by Wells and Gubar (1966) and has since been updated and modified by Murphy and Staples (1979) to take account of changing family patterns. The basic life cycle stages are presented in Table 7.3.

In some instances segmentation by life cycle can help directly with product design, as is the case with package holidays. In addition to using age as a segmentation variable, holiday firms target very specifically on different stages of the life cycle, from the Club Med emphasis on young singles, to Center Parcs family holidays, to coach operators' holidays for senior citizens.

Center Parcs

Source: Image Courtesy of Center Parcs.

Table 7.3 Stages of the family life cycle

Stage	Financial circumstances and purchasing characteristics
Bachelor Young, single, not living at parental home	Few financial burdens, recreation oriented; holidays, entertainments outside home
Newly wed Young couples, no children	Better off financially, two incomes; purchase home, some consumer durables
Full nest I Youngest child under 6	Home purchasing peak; increasing financial pressures, may have only one income earner; purchase of household 'necessities'
Full nest II Youngest child over 6	Financial position improving; some working spouses
Full nest III Older married couples with dependent children	Financial position better still; update household products and furnishings
Empty nest I Older married couples, no children at home	Home ownership peak; renewed interest in travel and leisure activities; buy luxuries
Empty nest II Older couples, no children at home, retired	Drastic cut in income; medical services bought
Solitary survivor Still in labour force	Income good, but likely to sell home
Solitary survivor Retired	Special needs for medical care, affection and security

In the United Kingdom the Research Services Ltd marketing research company has developed a segmentation scheme based on a combination of consumer life cycle, occupation and income. The scheme, termed SAGACITY, defines four main life cycle stages (dependent, pre-family, family and late), two income levels (better off and worse off) and two occupational groupings (white collar and blue collar – ABC1 and C2DE). On the basis of these three variables, 12 distinct SAGACITY groupings are identified with different aspirations and behaviour patterns (see Crouch and Housden, 1996).

Some analysts have pointed out that the Baby Boomer generation has made a significant impact on marketing to the over 50s (Paul Fifield in *Marketing Business,* January 2002). Thirty years ago the 'Boomers' changed the way marketers dealt with the youth market, as they demanded more individualised and tailored products and services. Having now raised families and paid off mortgages they are approaching the 'empty nester' stage of the life cycle but are likely to have very different expectations from previous generations of 50+ consumers. Generally fitter, well educated and more affluent, they pose very significant marketing opportunities for the future.

ACORN and related classificatory systems

As a direct challenge to the socio-economic classification system the geodemographic ACORN system was developed by the CACI Market Analysis Group (**http://www.caci.co.uk/acorn-classification.aspx**). The system is based on population census data and classifies residential neighbourhoods into 36 types within 12 main groups (see Table 7.4). The groupings were derived from a clustering of responses to census data required by law on a ten-yearly basis. The groupings reflect neighbourhoods with similar characteristics.

Early uses of ACORN were by local authorities to isolate areas of inner-city deprivation (the idea came from a sociologist working for local authorities), but it was soon seen to have direct marketing relevance, particularly because the database enabled postcodes to be ascribed to each ACORN type. Hence its use particularly in direct mail marketing.

Other 'geodemographic' data sources are provided by such firms as Eurodirect who developed CAMEO (**http://www.cartogen.co.uk/customersegmentation.htm**) and Experian with their MOSAIC classification system (**http://strategies.experian.co.uk/**).

Personality characteristics

Personality characteristics are more difficult to measure than demographics or socio-economics. They are generally inferred from large sets of questions often involving detailed computational (multivariate) analysis techniques.

Several personality inventories have been used by segmentation researchers. Most notable are the Edwards Personal Preference Schedule (**http://en.wikipedia.org/wiki/Edwards_Personal_Preference_Schedule**), the Cattell 16-Personality Factor Inventory (see, for example, Oxx, 1972) and the Jackson Personality Inventory (see Kinnear *et al.*, 1974). All were developed by psychologists for reasons far divorced from market segmentation studies and have, understandably, achieved only varied levels of success when applied to segmentation problems.

Perhaps the main value of personality measures lies in creating the background atmosphere for advertisements and, in some instances, package design and branding. Research to date, however, primarily conducted in the United States, has identified few clear

Table 7.4 ACORN – a classification of residential neighbourhoods

ACORN group	Description
A	Agricultural areas
B	Modern family housing, higher incomes
C	Older housing of intermediate status
D	Poor quality older terraced housing
E	Better-off council estates
F	Less well-off council estates
G	Poorest council estates
H	Multiracial areas
I	High-status, non-family areas
J	Affluent suburban housing
K	Better-off retirement areas

relationships between personality and behaviour. In most instances personality measures are most likely to be of use for describing segments once they have been defined on some other basis. As with the characteristics discussed **above,** behaviour, and reasons for behaviour, in personality-homogeneous segments may be diverse.

Lifestyle characteristics

In an attempt to make personality measures developed in the field of psychology more relevant to marketing decisions, lifestyle research was pioneered by advertising agencies in the United States and the United Kingdom in the early 1970s. This research attempts to isolate market segments on the basis of the style of life adopted by their members. At one stage these approaches were seen as alternatives to the social class categories discussed above.

Lifestyle segmentation is concerned with three main elements: activities (such as leisure activities, sports, hobbies, entertainment, home activities, work activities, professional work, shopping behaviour, housework and repairs, travel and miscellaneous activities, daily travel, holidays, education, charitable work); interaction with others (such as self-perception, personality and self-ideal, role perceptions, as mother, wife, husband, father, son, daughter, etc. and social interaction, communication with others, opinion leadership); and opinions (on topics such as politics, social and moral issues, economic and business–industry issues and technological and environmental issues).

A typical study would develop a series of statements (in some instances over 200 have been used) and respondents would be asked to agree or disagree with them on a 5- or 7-point agree/disagree scale. Using factor analysis and cluster analysis groups of respondents are identified with similar activities, interests and opinions. Examples include the following:

- In early lifestyle studies Segnit and Broadbent (1973) found six male and seven female lifestyle segments on the basis of responses to 230 statements. These have been used to segment markets by publishers of newspapers (such as the *Financial Times* and *Radio Times*) and manufacturers (Beechams used the technique successfully to segment the shampoo market in the mid-1970s).
- Martini advertising has been directed at individuals on the basis of what lifestyle they would like to have. It appeals to 'aspirational lifestyle' segments.
- Ford Motor Company identified four basic lifestyle segments for their cars: traditionalists (who go for wood, leather and chrome); liberals (keen on environmental and safety features); life survivors (who seek minimum financial risk by going for the cheapest options); and adventurers (who actually like cars and want models to suit their own self-images) (*The Economist,* 30 September 1995).
- Marketing strategy at the House of Fraser department stores group relied on attracting three types of women clothes shoppers to the stores: the 'Follower of Fashion', the 'Smart Career Mover' and the 'Quality Classic – The Woman of Elegance'. The company deliberately decided not to target the 'Young Mum' and other buyers. In the mid-1990s there was some concern that House of Fraser products and merchandising did not attract the target segments (it was found that they tended to shop at House of Fraser only for the concession areas such as Oasis, Alexon and Morgan) (Rankine, 1996).
- B&Q, the UK DIY store, targeted style-conscious consumers with its portfolio of bedroom and office furniture branded 'it'. The range, created by interior designer Tara Bernerd, was modular, allowing customers to choose according to their taste and the dimensions of their home (*Marketing,* 24 January 2002).

The most significant advantages of lifestyle research are again for guiding the creative content of advertising. Because of the major tasks involved in gathering the data, however, it is unlikely that lifestyle research will supplant demographics as a major segmentation variable.

Summary of background customer characteristics

The background customer characteristics discussed above all examine the individual in isolation from the specific market of interest. While in some markets they may be able to discriminate between probable users and non-users of the product class they can rarely explain brand choice behaviour. Members of the same segments based on background characteristics may behave differently in the marketplace for a variety of reasons. Similarly, members of different segments may be seeking essentially the same things from competing brands and could be usefully grouped together. While traditionally useful for the purposes of media selection and advertising atmosphere design, these characteristics are often too general in nature to be of specific value to marketers. They are essentially descriptive in nature. They describe who the consumer is, but they do not uncover the basic reasons why the consumer behaves as they do.

7.5.2 Customer attitudinal characteristics for segmenting markets

Attitudinal characteristics attempt to draw a causal link between customer characteristics and marketing behaviour. Attitudes to the product class under investigation and attitudes towards brands on the market have both been used as fruitful bases for market segmentation.

Benefit segmentation

Classic approaches (e.g. Haley, 1968, 1984) examine the benefits customers are seeking in consuming the product. Segmenting on the basis of benefits sought has been applied to a wide variety of markets such as banking, fast-moving consumer products and consumer durables. The building society investment market, for example, can be initially segmented on the basis of the benefits being sought by the customers. Typical benefits sought include high rates of interest (for the serious investor), convenient access (for the occasional investor) and security (for the 'rainy day' investor).

Nokia recognised that phones are seen by many customers as fashion accessories. The Nokia 5510, for example, was aimed at fashion-conscious young people who used their phones for text messaging and music. While the market in the late 1990s was dominated by first-time purchasers of phones, replacement purchases in Western Europe accounted for 60 per cent of sales in 2001 and were predicted to rise to nearer 99 per cent by 2006. The Samsung A400 phone had a flip-up lid in a red 'feminine' version, called the 'Ladyphone', with special features such as biorhythm calculator, a fatness function that calculates height-to-weight ratio, and a calorie count function which estimates calories burnt for everyday activities such as shopping, cleaning and cooking. Nokia has even launched a subsidiary named 'Vertu', which is marketing platinum-cased handsets with sapphire crystal screens for the very rich (they retail at $21,000) (*Economist*, 26 January 2002). Vertu has increased its product range and in 2015 was starting to make inroads in Asia.

Benefit segmentation takes the basis of segmentation right back to the underlying reasons why customers are attracted to various product offerings. As such, it is perhaps the closest means yet to identifying segments on bases directly relevant to marketing decisions. Developments in techniques such as conjoint analysis make them particularly suitable for identifying benefit segments (Hooley, 1982).

Perceptions and preferences

A second approach to the study of attitudes is through the study of perceptions and preferences. Much of the work in the multi-dimensional scaling area (Green *et al.*, 1989) is primarily concerned with identifying segments of respondents who view the products on offer in a similar way (perceptual space segmentation) and require from the market similar features or benefits (preference segmentation). This approach to market segmentation is discussed further in Chapter 8, where we are concerned with segmentation research.

Summary of attitudinal bases for segmentation

Segmentation on the basis of attitudes, both to the product class and the various brands on offer, can create a more useful basis for marketing strategy development than merely background characteristics. It gets closer to the underlying reasons for behaviour and uses them as the basis for segmenting the market. The major drawback of such techniques is that they require often costly primary research and sophisticated data analysis techniques.

7.5.3 Customer behavioural characteristics for segmenting markets

The most direct method of segmenting markets is on the basis of the behaviour of the consumers in those markets. Behavioural segmentation covers purchases, consumption, communication and response to elements of the marketing mix.

Purchase behaviour

Study of purchasing behaviour has centred on such issues as the time of purchase (early or late in the product's overall life cycle) and patterns of purchase (the identification of brand-loyal customers).

- **Innovators:** because of their importance when new products are launched, innovators (those who purchase a product when it is still new) have received much attention from marketers. Clearly during the launch of new products isolation of innovators as the initial target segment could significantly improve the product's or service's chances of acceptance on the market. Innovative behaviour, however, is not necessarily generalisable to many different product fields. Attempts to seek out generalised innovators have been less successful than looking separately for innovators in a specific field. Generalisations seem most relevant when the fields of study are of similar interest.
- **Brand loyalty:** variously defined, brand loyalty has also been used as a basis for segmentation. While innovators are concerned with initial purchase, loyalty patterns are concerned with repeat purchase. As such, they are more applicable to repeat purchase goods than to consumer durables, though they have been used in durables markets (see the example below). As with innovative behaviour, research has been unable to identify consumers who exhibit loyal behaviour over a wide variety of products. Loyalty, as with innovativeness, is specific to a particular product field.

  Volkswagen, the German automobile manufacturer, has used loyalty as a major method for segmenting its customer markets. It divided its customers into the following categories: first-time buyers; replacement buyers – (a) model-loyal replacers, (b) company-loyal replacers, and (c) switch replacers. These segments were used to analyse performance and market trends and for forecasting purposes.

In the context of e-marketing, companies such as Site Intelligence have devised methods of segmenting website visitors and purchasers using combinations of behavioural (visits) and demographic characteristics.

Consumption behaviour

Purchasers of products and services are not necessarily the consumers, or users, of those products or services. Examination of usage patterns and volumes consumed (as in the heavy user approach) can pinpoint where to focus marketing activity. There are dangers, however, in focusing merely on the heavy users. They are, for example, already using the product in quantity and therefore may not offer much scope for market expansion. Similarly they will either be current company customers or customers of competitors.

Cook and Mindak (1984) have shown that the heavy user concept is more useful in some markets than in others. In the soap market they note that heavy users of soap account for 75 per cent of purchases. However, heavy users account for nearly half the population and constitute a very diverse group. By contrast bourbon whiskey is consumed by around 20 per cent of adults only, and the heavy users account for 95 per cent of consumption, making this a much tighter target market.

In the latter case brand loyalty patterns may be set and competition could be fierce. Companies may be better advised to research further the light or non-users of the product to find out why they do not consume more of the product. In the growth stage of the product life cycle the heavy user segment may well be attractive, but when the market reaches maturity it may make more sense to try to extend the market by mopping up extra potential demand in markets that are not adequately served by existing products.

Product and brand usage has a major advantage over many other situation-specific segmentation variables in that it can be elicited, in the case of many consumer products, from secondary sources. The 'heavy users' of beer, for example, can be identified through the Target Group Index (see Chapter 4) and their demographic and media habits profiled. For this main reason consumption is one of the most popular bases for segmenting consumer markets in the United Kingdom.

Communication behaviour

A further behavioural variable used in consumer segmentation studies has been the degree of communication with others about the product of interest.

Opinion leaders can be particularly influential in the early stages of the product life cycle. Recording companies, for example, recognise the influence that disc jockeys have on the record-buying public and attempt to influence them with free music and other inducements to play their CDs. In many fields, however, identifying opinion leaders is not so easy. As with innovators, opinion leaders tend to lead opinion only in their own interest areas. A further problem with satisfying opinion leaders is that they tend to have fairly strong opinions themselves and can often be a very heterogeneous group (disc jockeys providing a good example).

In addition to information-giving behaviour (as displayed by opinion leaders) markets could be segmented on the basis of information-seeking behaviour. The information seekers may be a particularly attractive segment for companies basing their strategy on promotional material with a heavy information content.

Response to elements of the marketing mix

The use of elasticities of response to changes in marketing-mix variables as a basis for segmentation is particularly attractive as it can lead to more actionable findings, indicating where marketing funds can best be allocated. Identifying, for example, the deal-prone consumer or the advertising-responsive segment has immediate appeal. There are, however, methodological problems in research in identifying factors such as responsiveness to changes in price.

Relationship-seeking characteristics

A related characteristic for segmentation that is attracting some attention in the light of the move towards relationship marketing (see Chapter 4) is the relationship requirements of customers (Piercy, 1997). One initial model suggests that the relationship-seeking characteristics of customers differ in the type of relationship customers want with suppliers (for example, long term versus short term and transactional) and the intimacy customers want in the relationship (for example, close or distant). This suggests the potential for segmenting markets into such groups as the following, and linking this to other variables:

- **relationship seekers,** who want a close long-term relationship with the supplier or retailer;
- **relationship exploiters,** who want only a short-term relationship with the supplier, but are happy with a close relationship, which they will exploit for any advantages on offer;
- **loyal buyers** – those who want a long-term relationship, but at a distance;

- **arm's-length transaction customers,** who do not want close relationships with suppliers and will shop around for the best deal because they see no value in a long-term relationship.

An example of an integrated study of consumer characteristics on a global scale is work done by the US agency Roper Starch (Shermach, 1995). International business has much interest in whether consumer segments cut across national boundaries and may be more useful than traditional geographical approaches to planning marketing. The study identified the following segments from 40,000 respondents in 40 countries:

- **deal-makers:** well educated, aged in the early 30s, with average affluence and employment (29 per cent of the sample);
- **price-seekers:** a high proportion of retirees and lowest education level with an average level of affluence and more females than males (23 per cent of the sample);
- **brand loyalists:** mostly male, aged in the mid-30s, with average education and employment, and the least affluent group (23 per cent of the sample);
- luxury innovators: the most educated and affluent shoppers, mostly male in professional and executive employment; they seek new, prestigious brands (21 per cent of the sample).

The proportions of consumers in these groups varied in interesting ways across the geographic areas: deal-makers predominate in the United States, Asia, Latin America and the Middle East; price-seekers exist mainly in competitive developed markets such as Europe and Japan. Although producing only stereotypes, the study suggests that consumer behavioural and purchase characteristics may be stronger predictors of purchase behaviour than the traditional country-market definitions used in export and international marketing.

Summary of behavioural bases for segmentation

Many variables have been tested as bases for consumer segmentation, ranging from behaviour, to attitudes, to background characteristics. The most often used characteristics are product and brand usage and demographics/socio-economics, primarily because of the ease of obtaining this sort of data from secondary sources. Ultimately, however, for a segmentation scheme to be useful to marketing management it should seek not only to describe differences in consumers but also to explain them. In this respect attitudinal segmentation can offer better prospects.

7.6 Segmenting business markets

As with consumer markets, a wide variety of factors has been suggested for segmenting business markets, but in fact business segmentation variables can be considered under the same headings as those for consumer markets:

- background company characteristics;
- attitudinal characteristics;
- behavioural characteristics.

It should be noted, however, that market segmentation is substantially less well developed in business marketing than consumer marketing, which may affect both the acceptability of different approaches to companies and the availability of information and support to use a particular approach. It should also be noted that in business-to-business marketing it is far more common to find a one-to-one relationship between supplier and customer. In this situation the segmentation approach may best be applied inside the customer organisation. The segmentation structure below follows the model developed in Shapiro and Bonoma (1990).

7.6.1 Background company characteristics

Demographic characteristics of companies can be a useful starting point for business segmentation; indeed, they characterise the approaches most commonly used by business marketing companies. Factors that can be considered here include demographics such as industry type, customer size and location, but also operating variables such as customer technology and capabilities, different purchasing policies and situational factors including product application.

Industry type

Factors such as the Standard Industry Classification (SIC) provide a first stage of analysis, both for identifying target industries and subdividing them into groups of companies with different needs or different approaches to buying. This may be the basis for vertical marketing to industry sectors. Retailers and hospitals, for example, both buy computers, but they have different applications and different buying strategies.

Company size

Size may also be highly significant if, for instance, small companies have needs or buying preferences that are distinctly different from those of larger companies. Typical measures would be variables such as number of employees and sales turnover. Size may be very significant because it impacts on issues such as volume requirements, average order size, sales and distribution coverage costs and customer bargaining power, which may alter the attractiveness of different segments as targets. Company size may be analysed alongside other demographics. Companies, for example, selling ingredients for paint manufacture in the United Kingdom could initially segment the market by SIC to identify paint manufacturers, then by size of company as indicated by number of employees (there are only seven companies employing more than 750 employees and together they account for over 60 per cent of the paint market).

Customer location

The geographic location of customers may be a powerful way of segmenting the market for a business product for several reasons. Domestically, location will impact on sales and distribution costs and competitive intensity may vary if there are strong local competitors in some regions. Increasing concerns over the carbon footprint of sourcing are leading some firms to concentrate their supply, where possible, more locally. For example, leading supermarkets such as Waitrose have developed policies to source as many fresh food products locally as possible.

Product demand may vary also – the demand for chemicals for water softening in operating cooling equipment in factories will vary according to local water hardness conditions. Internationally, product preferences may also be different by location – medical diagnostic products sell to the National Health Service in the United Kingdom, but to private testing agencies and medical practices in the United States, and to hospital laboratories in the developing world, all of whom display very different product and price requirements.

Company technology

The customer's stage of technology development will impact directly on its manufacturing and product technology, and hence on its demand for different types of product. Traditional factories operating mixed technologies and assembly methods require different product and sub-assembly inputs (e.g. test equipment, tooling, components) compared with the automated production unit. High-technology businesses may require very different distribution methods – Tesco requires suppliers to have the capability to cooperate in electronic stock control and cross-docking to avoid retail stockholding. Increasingly, high-technology firms require that their suppliers are integrated to their computer systems for all stages of the purchase process.

Customer capabilities

Business customers may differ significantly in their internal strengths and weaknesses, and hence their demand for different types of product and service. For example, in the chemicals industry customers are likely to differ in their technical competencies – some will depend on their suppliers for formulation assistance and technical support far more than others. For many years in the computer business Digital Equipment specialised in selling minicomputers to customers who were able to develop their own software and systems, and did not need the full-service offering of IBM and others: it targeted a segment on the basis of the customers' technical strength in computing.

Purchasing organisation

How customers organise purchasing may also identify important differences between customers. For example, centralised purchasing may require suppliers to have the capability to operate national or international account management, while decentralised purchasing may require more extensive field sales operations. Depending on a supplier's own strengths and weaknesses, the purchasing organisation type may be a significant way of segmenting the market. IBM, for example, has always maintained a strong position in companies with a centralised IT department, while other suppliers have focused on companies where IT is less centralised.

Power structures

The impact of which organisational units have the greatest influence may also be effective in segmenting a market to identify targets matching a supplier's strengths. Digital Equipment traditionally targeted engineering-led customers, where its strengths in engineering applications gave it a competitive edge.

Purchasing policies

The way different customers approach purchasing may also be a source of targeting information. Customers might divide, for example, into those who want a lease-based deal versus those who want to purchase; those with affirmative action policies versus those dominated by price issues; those who want single supply sources versus those who want to dual-source important supplies; public sector and similar organisations where bidding is obligatory versus those preferring to negotiate price; those actively pursuing reductions in their supplier base compared with others. Indeed, the model proposed **above** of the customer's relationship requirements as a basis for segmenting may be even more useful in the business market, where the demand for partnership between suppliers and customers characterises many large companies' approaches to purchasing.

Product application

The product application can have a major influence on the purchase process and criteria and hence supplier choices. The requirements for a small motor used in intermittent service for a minor application in an oil refinery will differ from the requirements for a small motor in continuous use for a critical process.

7.6.2 Attitudinal characteristics

It is possible also to segment business markets on the basis of the benefits being sought by the purchasers. As we saw, benefit segmentation in the consumer market is the process of segmenting the market in terms of the underlying reasons why customers buy, focusing particularly on differences in why customers buy. Its strength is that it is segmentation based on customer needs. In the business market, the same logic applies to the purchasing criteria of different customers and product applications (see above).

This may be reflected, for example, in urgency of order fulfilment – the urgency of a customer's need to keep a plant in operation or to solve a problem for its own customers may change both the purchase process and the criteria used. Urgent replacements may be bought on the basis of availability, not price. A chemical plant needing to replace broken pipe fittings will pay a premium price for a supplier's applications engineering, flexible manufacturing capacity, speed of delivery and installation skills, while a plant buying pipe fittings to be held in reserve would behave quite differently.

One corporate bank struggled to find a way of segmenting the UK market for corporate financial services; they concluded that the most insightful approach was to examine their customers' own strategies as a predictor of financial service product need and purchasing priorities.

An added complication in business markets, however, is the decision-making unit (DMU) (see Chapter 4). For many business purchases decisions are made or influenced by a group of individuals rather than a single purchaser. Different members of the DMU will often have different perceptions of what the benefits are, both to their organisation and to themselves.

In the purchase of hoists, for example, the important benefit to a user may be lightness and ease of use, whereas the purchasing manager may be looking for a cheaper product to make their purchasing budget go further. Architects specifying installations for new plant may perceive greater benefit in aesthetically designed hoists and maintenance personnel may look for easy maintenance as a prime benefit.

Benefit segmentation is at the centre, however, of conventional wisdom on selling in business markets. Here the emphasis is on selling benefits rather than features of the product or service. In communicating with the different members of the DMU different benefits may be emphasised for each.

7.6.3 Behavioural characteristics

Behavioural issues relevant to segmenting business markets may include buyers' personal characteristics and product/brand status and volume.

Buyers' personal characteristics

Although constrained by company policies and needs, business products are bought by people in just the same way that consumer products are. Business goods markets can be segmented by issues such as the following:

- **buyer–seller similarity:** compatibility in technology, corporate culture or even company size may be a useful way of distinguishing between customers;
- **buyer motivation:** purchasing officers may differ in the degree to which they shop around and look at numerous alternative suppliers, and dual-source important products and services, as opposed to relying on informal contacts for information and remaining loyal to existing personal contacts;
- **buyer risk perceptions:** the personal style of the individual, intolerance of ambiguity, self-confidence and status within the company may also provide significant leverage.

For example, for many years in the computer industry IBM focused on IT buyers in major corporates, providing training information and career development support, to build the 'IBM closed shop' where other suppliers were largely excluded.

Product/brand status and volume

The users of a particular product, brand or supplier may have important things in common that can make them a target. For example, customers may differ in the rate and extent of the adoption of new safety equipment in plants. Companies loyal to a specific competitor may be targeted – for instance to attack that competitor's weaknesses in service or product. Current customers may be a different segment from prospective customers or lost customers.

High-volume product users may be different from medium and low users in how they purchase. Even more than in consumer markets the 80/20 rule (80 per cent of sales typically being accounted for by only 20 per cent of customers) can dominate a business market. Identifying the major purchasers for products and services through volume purchased can be particularly useful. Also of interest may be the final use to which the product or service is put. Where, for example, the final consumer can be identified, working backwards can suggest a sensible segmentation strategy.

The paint market, for example, can be segmented at various levels. At the first level it can be divided into 'decorative paints', mainly used on buildings, and 'industrial paints', used in manufactured products. General industrial paints by volume represented 33 per cent of the UK market, the automobile industry 5 per cent, professional decorative 42 per cent and DIY decorative 22 per cent. Demand for vehicle paints relates to automobile sales (derived demand) and relates closely to demand in this market. In the general industrial paints sector there are various specialist segments such as marine coatings. Here ultimate product use dictates the type of paint and its properties and is the basic method for segmentation.

7.6.4 Summary of bases for segmenting business markets

The segmentation bases available for business marketing follow business buying behaviour as those in consumer marketing follow consumer buying behaviour. Because of the presence, however, of particularly large individual customers in many business markets usage-based segmentation is often employed. For smaller companies geographic segmentation may be attractive, limiting their markets to those that are more easily served. Ultimately, however, in business and consumer markets the basic rationale for segmentation is that groups of buyers exist with different needs or wants (benefits sought) and it is segmentation on the basis of needs and wants that offers the closest approach to implementing the marketing concept.

7.7   Identifying and describing market segments

It will be clear from the above that the first task the manager faces is to decide on what bases to segment the market. If product usage or background characteristics are selected in many markets the segmentation can be accomplished from secondary sources (e.g. from TGI or AGB/TCA in UK consumer markets, or from SIC or Kompass in business markets). Where segmentation is based on attitudes, however, there will often be insufficient data available from secondary sources. In these cases primary research will be necessary.

A typical primary research segmentation study could include initial qualitative research to identify major benefits to users and purchasers of the product or service under consideration. This would be followed by quantitative research to estimate the size of the potential segments and to describe them further in terms of other background characteristics. This methodological approach is described in the seminal work by Haley (1968).

7.7.1 First-order and second-order segmentation

There is a frequent misconception among marketing managers as to what constitutes a market segment.

In consumer marketing, in particular, many managers will describe the segmentation of their market and their selected market targets in terms of customer background characteristics. Thus, for example, a marketer of quality wines might describe the segmentation of the market in terms of social class, the prime target being the ABC1 social classes. From our discussion above, however, it can be seen that this way of segmenting the market is adequate only if all members of the ABC1 group purchase quality wine for the same reasons and in the same way. Where use/benefits of wine purchase differ substantially within a given social class there is the opportunity to segment the market in a more fundamental way.

In reality the most fundamental way of segmenting markets is the market-oriented approach of grouping together customers who are looking for the same benefits in using the product or service. All other bases for segmenting markets are really an approximation of this. The wine marketer assumes that all ABC1s have similar benefit needs from the wines they purchase. Hence use/benefit segmentation can be referred to as **first-order segmentation**. Any attempt to segment a market should commence by looking for different use/benefit segments.

Within identified use/benefit segments, however, there could be large numbers of customers with very different backgrounds, media habits, levels of consumption, and so on. Particularly where there are many offerings attempting to serve the same use/benefit segment concentration on sub-segments within the segment can make sense. Sub-segments, for example, who share common media habits, can form more specific targets for the company's offerings. Further segmentation within use/benefit segments can be termed **second-order segmentation**. Second-order segmentation is used to improve the ability of the company to tailor the marketing mix within a first-order segment.

In the wine example the marketing manager may have identified a first-order segmentation in terms of the uses to which the wine was being put (e.g. as a meal accompaniment, as a home drink, as a social drink, as a cooking ingredient). The quality level of the wine might suggest use in the first segment as a meal accompaniment. Further research would then reveal within this segment further benefit requirements (e.g. price bands individual customers are prepared to consider, character of the wine preferred, etc.).

Having further refined the target through matching the company's offerings to specific customer group requirements the marketer may still find a wide variety of potential customers for their wines. Within the identified first-order segment sub-segments based on demographic characteristics could be identified (e.g. AB social class, aged 35–55, male purchaser), enabling a clearer refinement of the marketing strategy.

7.8   The benefits of segmenting markets

There are a number of important benefits that can be derived from segmenting a market, which can be summarised in the following terms:

- Segmentation is a particularly useful approach to marketing for the smaller company. It allows target markets to be matched to company competencies (see Chapter 6), and makes it more likely that the smaller company can create a defensible niche in the market.
- It helps to identify gaps in the market, i.e. unserved or underserved segments. These can serve as targets for new product development or extension of the existing product or service range.
- In mature or declining markets it may be possible to identify specific segments that are still in growth. Concentrating on growth segments when the overall market is declining is a major strategy in the later stages of the product life cycle.
- Segmentation enables the marketer to match the product or service more closely to the needs of the target market. In this way a stronger competitive position can be built (see Jackson, 2007, for the importance for companies of determining their strategic market position). This is particularly important in the Internet age where companies compete in a large and heterogeneous community (see Barnes *et al.*, 2007).

- The dangers of not segmenting the market when competitors do so should also be emphasised. The competitive advantages noted above can be lost to competitors if the company fails to take advantage of them. A company practising a mass marketing strategy in a clearly segmented market against competitors operating a focused strategy can find itself falling between many stools.

7.9 Implementing market segmentation

It should also be noted that there is evidence that companies often struggle with the implementation of segmentation-based strategies, and fail to achieve the potential benefits outlined above (see, e.g., Piercy and Morgan, 1993; Dibb and Simkin, 1994) – this is the difference between segmentation as a normative model and as a business reality (Danneels, 1996).

7.9.1 The scope and purpose of market segmentation

There is growing recognition that conventional approaches may pay insufficient attention to identifying the scope of market segmentation (Plank, 1985). Indeed, a seminal paper by Wind (1978) proposed that in selecting segmentation approaches it is necessary to distinguish between segmentation that has the goal of gaining a general understanding of the market and use for positioning studies, and segmentation concerned with marketing programme decisions in new product launches, pricing, advertising and distribution. These are all valid and useful applications in segmentation analysis, but they are fundamentally different.

7.9.2 Strategic, managerial and operational levels of segmentation

One approach to making the scope of market segmentation clearer is to distinguish between different levels of segmentation, in the way shown in Figure 7.5 (Piercy and Morgan, 1993).

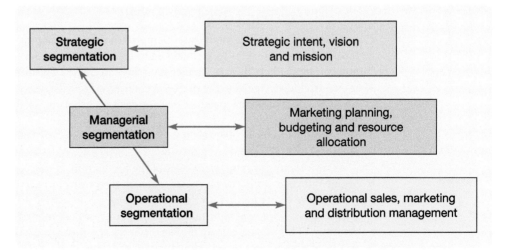

Figure 7.5
Levels of
segmentation

This approach is similar to the first-order and second-order segmentation distinction made above, but goes further in relating the levels of segmentation to organisational issues as well as customer issues. The nature of the different levels of segmentation can be described as follows:

- **Strategic segmentation** is related to management concerns for strategic intent and corporate mission, based on product/service uses and customer benefits.
- **Managerial segmentation** is concerned primarily with planning and allocating resources such as budgets and personnel to market targets.
- **Operational segmentation** focuses on the issue of aiming marketing communications and selling efforts into the distribution channels that reach and influence market targets (and their sub-divisions).

These differences are important to gaining insight into what segmentation can contribute to building marketing strategy and competitive positioning, but also to understanding the sources of implementation problems with segmentation-based strategies. For example, when the manager responsible for marketing replacement car exhausts to car owners groups their customers in terms of their fears, ignorance and transport dependence, rather than their requirements for different product specifications and engineering, they are concerned with creating a new understanding of the market (strategic segmentation), not a model for the detailed application of marketing resources (operational segmentation).

When the corporate banker looks at the corporate banking market in terms of the strategic financial services needs of customers, based on their own corporate strategies (Carey, 1989), the goal is to create a framework for strategy, not a mechanism for advertising and salesforce allocation.

On the other hand, when advertisers and sales managers describe buyers in terms of socio-economic groups, geographic location or industrial sector, they are concerned with the effective targeting of advertising, sales promotion, selling and distribution resources, rather than describing customer benefit-based market segments. Market segmentation studies describing consumer groups in terms of their media behaviour – for example as 'mainstream media rejecters', 'genteel media grazers', '30-somethings', and so on (Laing, 1991) – are concerned with operational effectiveness, not strategic positioning.

Confusing these very different roles for segmentation may be why segmentation is sometimes seen as a failure in organisations:

> Failed segmentation efforts tend to fall into one of two categories: the marketer-dominated kind, with little data to support its recommendations, or the purely statistical type that identifies many consumer differences that aren't germane to the company's objectives.
> *(Young, 1996)*

The implication is that clarifying the role and purpose of an approach to segmentation may be important to avoid unrealistic expectations. However, it is clear that segmentation-based strategies do sometimes fail at the implementation stage.

7.9.3 Sources of implementation problems

The recognition of implementation problems with segmentation-based strategies may be traced back over the years: Wind (1978) noted that little was known about translating segment research into marketing strategies; Young *et al.* (1978) accused marketers of being preoccupied with segmentation technique rather than actionability; Hooley (1980) blamed segmentation failures on the use of analytical techniques for their own sake and poor communication between managers and marketing researchers. Shapiro and Bonoma

(1990) wrote: 'Much has been written about the strategy of segmentation, little about its implementation, management and control', and this would still seem a valid conclusion.

Piercy and Morgan (1993) attempted to catalogue the sources of implementation failure with segmentation-based strategies, and these issues provide a further screening device for evaluating the suitability of a segmentation model generated through market research. Issues to assess include the following:

- **Organisation structure.** Companies tend to organise into functional departments and subunits of one kind or another, depending on their task allocation and how they deal with the outside world. A customer benefits approach to establishing market targets may cut across these internal divisions – they may not 'fit' with the jurisdiction of departments or regional organisations for sales and marketing. Segment targets that fall between departments and regions may be neglected and lack 'ownership', and the strategies built around them will fail. We need to map carefully how segment targets will match the internal organisation structure.

- **Internal politics.** Young (1996) argues that strategic segmentation is essentially a cross-functional activity, requiring expertise and involvement by many functional specialists. If functions cannot collaborate or work together because people are vying for power and withholding their knowledge and expertise, the segmentation strategy is likely to fail. If our segmentation-based strategy relies on internal collaboration and cooperation, we need to be sure this can be achieved or the strategy will fail.

- **Corporate culture.** In some circumstances customer benefit segmentation is unacceptable to people inside an organisation, because it is not how they understand the world. Organisations dominated by strong professional groups frequently have struggles with customer benefit segments – examples are traditional financial service companies and professional service firms such as law and accountancy.

- **Information and reporting.** Novel segmentation schemes may not fit with existing information systems and reporting systems. This may mean it is difficult to evaluate the worth of segment targets, or to allocate responsibilities and monitor performance in doing business with them.

- **Decision-making processes.** If segmentation schemes identify new market targets that are not recognised in plans (they are not currently part of the served market, they are spread across existing segment targets for which responsibility has been allocated, or they are subsumed within an existing segment), then they may be ignored in the planning process and when plans are implemented. Similarly, segment targets that are not recognised by existing resource allocation processes may face difficulty in getting a marketing budget. We should examine carefully how a new segmentation approach can be integrated with planning and budgeting and in evaluation systems.

- **Corporate capabilities.** It is all too easy for marketing researchers and analysts to develop attractive market targets, but a company may have little basis for achieving a competitive advantage simply because it lacks the capabilities for dealing with this type of customer (see Chapter 6).

- **Operational systems.** Segmentation strategy may fail because it underestimates the problems faced at the operational level in translating segmentation strategy into effective reality: can salespeople deal with this target customer? Do we have access to the distribution channels we need? Do we have the expertise to develop and operate segment-based advertising and promotion? Do we have market research organised around the segment targets so we can identify them, measure opportunities and evaluate progress? Do we have the technical facilities to price differently to different customer types if this is required? We should look very carefully at the operational capabilities we have in sales, advertising, promotion and distribution, and question their ability to adapt to a new segmentation-based strategy.

Organisational resource strength

	High	Low
High	**Best prospects** Attractive segments that fit well with organisational resources	**Build strengths first** Attractive markets but with poor fit with organisational resources
Low	**Poor prospects** Unattractive segments that fit well with organisational resources	**Worst prospects** Unattractive segments with a poor fit with organisational resources

Market segment attractiveness

Figure 7.6
Market segment attractiveness and organisational resource strength

Many of these issues are covert and hidden inside the organisation, yet to ignore them is to place the strategy at risk. One proposal is that in addition to the conventional evaluation of market targets each potential target should be tested for internal compatibility, as suggested in Figure 7.6.

This analysis may suggest that some market targets are unattractive because they have a poor 'fit' with the company's structures and processes, or even that the company is not capable of implementing a segmentation-based strategy at the present time, or it may identify the areas that need to be changed if the segment target is to be reached effectively.

Summary

In increasingly fragmented markets, marketers in both consumer and business markets are turning more and more to segmentation methods to identify prime market targets. In approaching market segmentation, companies must confront the sometimes quite sophisticated methodology of segmentation, test the market targets identified and make the strategic segmentation decision of how to use a segmentation model in developing its market strategy.

This suggests that one of the major decisions faced is 'what bases to segment on?' We have seen that there are a great many potential bases for segmentation in consumer and business markets, and for product and service (and non-profit) marketing.

Arguably the segmentation approach closest to extending the marketing concept is use/benefit segmentation originally suggested nearly 50 years ago by Haley (1968). While it does require considerable primary investigation, understanding the benefits customers derive in buying and/or consuming products and services is central to designing an integrated marketing strategy.

There are substantial potential benefits to be gained from basing marketing strategy on rigorous market segmentation. However, the organisational issues impacting on the implementation of segmentation-based strategies should also be evaluated to test for the internal compatibility of segment targets and the costs of organisational change that may be involved in segmentation-based marketing strategies.

The next chapter, on segmentation research, concentrates on the methodology for developing bases for segmentation.

Case study   Nestlé refines its arsenal in the luxury coffee war

Source: Getty Images: Duncan Chard/Bloomberg.

Nestlé has been thinking about how to respond to generic rivals threatening to challenge its spectacularly successful luxury coffee brand, Nespresso. The stakes for the Swiss food multinational are particularly high.

Only last week, Nestlé reported higher-than-expected first-quarter revenues, in large measure thanks to the continued boom in demand for its Nespresso coffee capsules. Since it was launched in 1985, Nespresso has grown at an annual rate of about 30 per cent.

It has become one of the company's so-called 'billionaire brands' with sales last year of SFr2.8bn ($2.6bn). It has also become a compelling case study in developing a global luxury brand in a niche of an otherwise mass-market business and in so doing has created what has been called the Louis Vuitton of coffee.

Under the circumstances, it was only going to be a matter of time before others decided to exploit this business. This month, French retail outlets began selling espresso coffee capsules compatible with Nespresso machines made by Sara Lee of the US under its L'Or Maison du Café label. These are about 10 per cent cheaper than Nespresso capsules and come in four varieties – Delizioso, Decaffeinato, Splendente and Forza.

Next month, another rival product is set to hit the market. This one has been developed by a venture called Ethical Coffee Company set up by Jean-Paul Gaillard, a former Nespresso chief executive.

His capsules, also compatible with Nespresso machines, will be sold by the French retailer Casino.

Why is the competition targeting its first assault against Nespresso in France? Simply because the country, along with Germany, is one of the biggest markets for Nestlé's luxury coffee brand. The latest sales figures show that Europe continues to account for 90 per cent of Nespresso sales with the Americas and Asia each accounting for 5 per cent.

So what is Nestlé going to do? The answer is nothing, or as Richard Giradot, Nespresso's current chief executive, told the French newspaper *Le Figaro* on Tuesday: 'Our response is not to respond.' Rather than engage in a price war and start selling its capsules in mass retailing outlets for the first time, Nestlé has decided to boost even further its luxury marketing approach for Nespresso.

This is based on what it likes to call its 'trilogy concept' – top-quality coffee grandly described like fine wines as 'grand cru', stylish coffee machines and highly personalised customer service. Coffee machines are available in retail outlets but the capsules – there are about 19 varieties – can only be bought online, by telephone or at the 190 or so Nespresso boutiques scattered round the world. Customers are also automatically enrolled as members of the Nespresso club and loyalty programme.

Nestlé plans to open a further 40 boutiques this year and has just started testing a home delivery service in Paris that will eventually be introduced in other countries.

The Swiss multinational's lawyers are also working overtime to see whether the rival capsules infringe one of the 1,700 patents it has filed to protect its Nespresso brand. In so doing it is following the example of litigious luxury goods groups that have traditionally fought tooth and nail to protect their brands.

Source: from 'Nestlé refines its arsenal in the luxury coffee war', *Financial Times,* 28/04/2010 (Betts, P.).

Discussion questions

1 Why is the niche market occupied by Nespresso attractive to generic rivals?

2 Why is Nestlé's response to this onslaught 'not to respond'?

3 What bases could marketers use to segment the coffee market?

CHAPTER 8
SEGMENTATION AND POSITIONING RESEARCH

Researchers are anxious to find a magic formula that will profitably segment the market in all cases and under all circumstances. As with the medieval alchemist looking for the philosopher's stone, this search is bound to end in vain.

Baumwoll (1974)

E-reader market cuts prices again

The e-reader market continues to adjust to brisk sales of Apple's iPad. On Thursday, Amazon slashed the price of its high-end Kindle DX by more than 20 per cent, to $379.

The move follows a wave of price-cutting last week that saw Amazon and Barnes & Noble readjust the prices of their e-readers to better compete with Apple's new tablet computer. Amazon's base-model Kindle now sells for $189, while the Barnes & Noble Nook is $199.

The Kindle DX is Amazon's largest e-reader and was designed for professional and academic environments. Amazon does not release sales figures. It also said the new Kindle DX would come with a better screen, and a free data collection for e-book downloads.

Since it went on sale on April 3, the iPad has sold more than 3m units, with models ranging in price from $499 to $829.

Source: from 'E-reader market cuts prices again', *Financial Times*, 02/07/2010 (Gelles, D.).

Source: Getty Images: Andrew Harrer/Bloomberg.

Discussion questions

1 What are the issues here?
2 How can segmentation and positioning research help solve these issues?

Introduction

While the last chapter was concerned with the underlying concepts and principles for the key strategic issues of competitive positioning and market segmentation, the subject of this chapter is the research and modelling techniques that can be applied to evaluate these issues operationally.

The first section of the chapter focuses on *segmentation research,* in particular the critical questions of whether or not to pursue a segment-based approach, and if so whether these are based a priori on some predefined segmentation scheme, or developed post hoc on the basis of research. The second part of the chapter turns to positioning research, which may often be carried out in parallel to *segmentation research,* applying both qualitative techniques such as focus groups and depth interviews, together with quantitative modelling methods such as perceptual mapping through multidimensional scaling.

The process of identifying potential market targets can be one of the most creative aspects of marketing. However, there is no single 'right way' to segment any market. Different competitors may adopt different approaches in the same market. All may be valid, but each may lead to a different view of the market, and subsequently a different marketing approach and a different strategy. The creative aspect of segmentation research lies in finding a new way to conceptualise your market, and a way that will offer some competitive advantage over the ways competitors choose.

Two broad approaches to segmentation research are typically pursued. First the a priori approach. This entails using an 'off-the-shelf' segmentation scheme, such as socio-economic or geodemographic classifications. Central to this approach is that the segmentation scheme is known in advance and the number of segments predetermined by the scheme chosen. By its very nature, **a priori segmentation** uses schemes that are in the public domain and hence also available to competitors.

The second approach is a **post-hoc** or **cluster-based** approach to segmentation. In this approach the final segmentation scheme is not known in advance, nor is the appropriate number of segments. The criteria on which to segment are defined in advance, but may typically be multidimensional (e.g. usage and attitude data). Data are then collected on these criteria (through the use of qualitative and/or quantitative marketing research) and analysed to identify underlying patterns or structure. The segmentation scheme emerges from the data analysis reflecting patterns identified in response. The data analysis itself is part science (using statistical techniques) and part art (employing judgement on which criteria to include and how to interpret the output). In this way the segmentation scheme emerging is likely to be unique to the specific analysis. This offers potential for looking at the market afresh and identifying new opportunities not necessarily seen by competitors. It also, of course, requires that any segmentation scheme created be rigorously tested to ensure that it is not merely an artefact of the specific dataset or the analytical technique employed.

Following the discussion of segmentation approaches the chapter goes on to examine alternative methods for researching and presenting positions in the marketplace. Two broad approaches are discussed. First the use of **qualitative** research methods to uncover brand, product and company images. These approaches are particularly popular in the development of advertising programmes. Second, **quantitative** approaches to modelling positions are explored, from simple profiling on semantic or similar scales, through the more complex modelling available to multidimensional scaling and correspondence analysis techniques.

To segment or not to segment? That is the question

Although a central part of most marketing programmes, there are circumstances in which segmentation may be inappropriate. It could be, for example, that customer needs and wants in a particular market are essentially homogeneous, and hence similar offerings can be made to appeal across the whole market, or that the costs associated with pursuing individual market segments with tailored marketing programmes outweigh their longer-term economic value.

A company following a segmented approach has either to choose a single market segment at which to aim, and therefore have a marketing mix that is inappropriate for other customers, or develop a series of marketing mixes appropriate for customer segments with different needs.

Both these approaches have limitations depending on the company's longer-term objectives. A single-focus company has limitations, because the market segment itself is limited. If the company has expansion and growth objectives these may be constrained by the size of its target market. This of course, would be much less of a problem for a small- or medium-sized company deliberately trying to stay small and focused. A company taking the multiple segment approach may face diseconomies in managing, supplying and promoting in a different way to each of the segments it has chosen. In some cases an economic alternative is to use an undifferentiated mix designed to appeal to as many segments as possible. The company does not fine-tune offers to any one segment but hopes to attract a sufficient number of customers from all segments with one mix. The company can therefore benefit from economies of scale in a simple operation, but may be damaged by the 'sameness of the mix', not appealing to the customers in each segment completely, or by better targeted competitors.

The appropriateness of segmenting or not segmenting depends on economies of scale, the cost of developing separate marketing mixes and the homogeneity of the needs of different markets – issues that are pursued further in Chapter 9. Such are the similarities in demand for petroleum, for example, that the products being supplied by competitors converge as they all seek to develop a mix with broad market appeal. Certainly segments do exist, but not of significant magnitude or difference to justify separate appeals. The aerospace industry and automobile industry have markets that are diverse but in which development and manufacturing costs are such that it is not feasible to develop products to fit all market needs exactly. The successful companies, therefore, focus on a relatively small product range with variations that appeal to individual customer preferences.

Even in markets whose main body does not demand segmentation, however, there are often small-scale opportunities where companies can thrive by pursuing a focus strategy. Examples include Pagani and Morgan in the sports car market. Therefore, even in markets where the major players may be using a mass strategy, segmentation offers an opportunity for some smaller participants. For small market share companies in particular, the advice is: segment, segment, segment!

Whereas the previous chapter concentrated on the concept of segmentation and possible bases for segmentation, this chapter follows the process of identifying usable market segments. First we discuss a priori approaches to segmentation. The chapter then goes on to discuss post-hoc, cluster-based approaches. For the latter we follow a model originally developed by Maier and Saunders (1990), which takes segmentation research from initiation through to eventual tracking. Within this framework the wide range of approaches and techniques for segmentation are discussed.

8.1   A priori segmentation approaches

8.1.1 Single variable segmentation

A priori, or off-the-shelf, methods are the easiest way of segmenting markets. In their original form this involved searching among demographic or socio-economic characteristics and identifying which of these form significant and useful splits within the marketplace.

Usually the search for appropriate criteria would be guided by some expectation of how the market could be divided.

The major advantage of this approach is that it can be undertaken from secondary sources and can be related directly to advertising media and messages. Consumer markets studies such as the Target Group Index (**http://www.kantarmedia.com/product/tgi-surveys/**) enable managers to identify heavy users of a product group and relate this directly to their media usage and advertising strategy.

There are some clear cases where a priori segmentation has proved a powerful tool. The successful toy company Lego, for example, has carefully developed assembly toys to fit the development of children from birth to mid-teens, segmenting the market on the basis of age. Duplo, their pre-school product, starts with rattles and manipulative toys, which are not immediately intended for assembly but do have fixture mechanisms that allow the child to progress into Duplo proper (chunky and brightly coloured bricks and shapes which can be assembled into all manner of toys). Duplo overlaps with Lego, a system of building bricks upon which the Lego empire was formed. Almost identical to Duplo parts in every other way, the Lego units are half the size, and therefore suitable for a child's enhanced manipulative ability, and allow more detail in construction. They are also cleverly designed to link with the Duplo units and therefore allow relatively easy progression from one to the other. As the children get older so they can progress to Legotechnic, and other specialist variants, which again build on the manipulative, assembly and design skills inculcated with earlier sets.

Age is also used as a powerful segmentation variable in the package tour market. Club 18–30 holidays are aimed at the single or young couples market, while Saga Holidays are aimed at the over-50s.

Despite their ease of use and intuitive appeal, attempts to validate demographic and socio-economic bases in terms of product preferences have met with little success. One of the earliest reported attempts to validate this approach was by Evans (1959), who sought to use demographic variables to distinguish between Ford and Chevrolet owners in the United States. He concluded that:

> demographic variables are not a sufficiently powerful predictor to be of much practical use . . . [they] point more to the similarity of Ford and Chevrolet owners than to any means of discriminating between them. Analysis of several other objective factors also leads to the same conclusion.

In other markets, conclusions have been similar. Some relationships were found, but no more than could have been expected to occur by chance if the data were random. Unfortunately study after study throws doubt on the direct usefulness of demographic characteristics as a predictor for product purchase as they fail to capture the nuances of human behaviour.

These findings do not dispute the certainty that some products with clearly defined target consumers depend heavily on demographic characteristics. For instance, nappies are purchased by families with babies, incontinence pads by older people and sanitary towels by women. However, evidence does seem to show that demographic characteristics alone are incapable of distinguishing between the subtle differences in markets that are not explained by the physiological differences between human beings. Perhaps most limiting, they have been found to be poor differentiators of individual products within the broad categories identified (i.e. brand of nappy).

In business markets perhaps the most often used segmentation variable is the Standard Industrial Classification, or SIC, code. In the United States however, the North American Standard Industrial Classification System (NASICS) is being increasingly used.

By selecting appropriate classification codes business marketers can identify the other businesses that may be most receptive to its offerings. Again, however, for businesses selling products and services that can be used across industry classifications (such as stationery, machine tools or consultancy services) SIC may be of little practical value as a segmentation base. While giving the impression of detail, the codes do not offer many clues as to why specific products are purchased or what is likely to appeal to individual customers.

8.1.2 Multiple variable a priori methods

Recently the traditional demographic and socio-economic means of off-the-shelf segmentation have been supplemented by more sophisticated methods being promoted, in consumer marketing at least, by advertising and market research agencies. These encompass the subjective methods and the marketing-specific objective measures discussed in Chapter 7. The distinction between these and the approaches discussed above is that multiple criteria are considered simultaneously and segments created on the basis of these multiple measures. A number of different consumer classification schemes have been suggested, such as ACORN (http://acorn.caci.co.uk) MOSAIC (http://www.experian.co.uk/business-strategies/mosaic-global.html) and VALS (http://www.strategicbusinessinsights.com/vals). These schemes have been created through analysis of large datasets (in the case of the former, two sets of official census data) using cluster analytical techniques. They are still considered a priori because once formed they are then available for any users off the peg from the agencies concerned.

Earliest of the multiple variable a priori techniques was the extensive use of personality inventories in the 1960s and 1970s. At that time, researchers were seeking to identify personality typologies that could be related, in much the same way as socio-economic factors were, to purchase decisions and consumption patterns. Techniques of personality measurement were borrowed by marketing from psychologists. Standard psychological tests such as the Edwards Personality Preference Schedule and the Catell 16 PF Inventory were tested in a marketing context. Unfortunately these tests showed them to be of little more discriminating power than the less sophisticated demographic and socio-economic methods.

Compared with demographic and socio-economic off-the-peg methods, personality inventories have a slight but insubstantial advantage. They do appear to be able to discriminate to a small extent between some high-involvement products, but even in these cases they leave the majority of variance unexplained. As with demographic and socio-economic methods, they seem to have most power to discriminate in markets where their measurement has a clear role, such as smoking, which reflects a drug dependency, and deodorants, which suggest anxiety. However, the subtlety of personality measurement renders it less useful as an off-the-peg measure in most cases because the personality differences are less strong and obvious than the physiological differences that demographics can measure: introversion and dependency are well-defined personality traits, but they are nowhere near as easily measured or as linked to behaviour as gender or age.

At the same time that personality traits were being explored as potential bases for segmentation, marketers were also experimenting with combining demographic characteristics to create the idea of the consumer life cycle. Under this model, age, marital status and family size were combined to identify a life cycle stage. This approach has been used for the marketing of holidays, insurance, housing, baby products and consumer durables.

The introduction of CACI's ACORN geodemographic database once represented one of the biggest steps forward in segmentation and targeting techniques. Its basis was segments derived from published census information that provides a classification of neighbourhoods based on housing types. The great strength of the service depends on CACI's own research linking the neighbourhood groups to demographics and buyer behaviour, together with the ability to target households. The system, therefore, provides a direct link between off-the-shelf segmenting and individuals, unlike earlier methods that provided indirect means only of contacting the demographic or personality segments identified.

Like the other a priori techniques, the limitation of CACI's approach is the variability within neighbourhoods and the dissimilarity in their buying behaviour for many product classes. English (1989) provides an example of this where five enumeration districts (individual neighbourhood groups of 150 households) are ranked according to geodemographic techniques. Of the five, two were identified as being prime mailing prospects. However, when individual characteristics were investigated, the five groups were found to contain 31, 14, 10, 10 and 7 prospects respectively: the enumeration districts had been ranked according to the correct number of prospects, but neighbourhood classifications alone appeared to be a poor method of targeting. With only 31 prime target customers being in the most favoured enumeration district, 119 out of 150 households would have been mistargeted. To be fair, as with other means of off-the-peg segmentation discussed, geodemographics are powerful when related to products linked directly to characteristics of the neighbourhood districts; for instance, the demand for double glazing, gardening equipment, etc. Even in the case provided, targeting the best enumeration districts increases the probability of hitting a target customer from less than 10 per cent to over 20 per cent, but misses are still more common than hits.

Lifestyle segmentation provides an opportunity to overlay geodemographic data with lifestyle characteristics. These have sometimes been used in conjunction with demographics and form the second part of two-stage segmentation. Third Age Research has done this after first identifying the over-65s as a target market and then breaking them up into lifestyle segments of apathetic, comfortable, explorer, fearful, organiser, poor me, social lion and *status quo*. To anyone who has contact with more than one older person it is clear that these labels provide a much more powerful way of putting a face on the over-65 customer than does their age alone.

Stanford Research Institute in the United States developed a lifestyle segmentation scheme called Values and Lifestyles (VALS) that has seven categories: **belongers** (patriotic, stable traditionalists content with their lives); **achievers** (prosperous, self-assured, middle-aged materialists); **emulators** (ambitious young adults trying to break into the system); **I-am-me group** (impulsive, experimental and a bit narcissistic); **societally conscious** (mature, successful, mission-oriented people who like causes); **survivors** (the old and poor with little optimism for the future); **sustainers** (resentful of their condition and trying to make ends meet). A similar scheme has been developed for use in pan-European marketing including: **successful idealists; affluent materialists; comfortable belongers; disaffected survivors;** and **optimistic strivers** (Hindle and Thomas, 1994).

While the relative merit of demographic variables and lifestyle tends to vary from situation to situation overall, in the comparisons that have been conducted lifestyle comes out worst. It must therefore be concluded that, as with their less sophisticated demographic brethren, lifestyle segments are no panacea for marketing. Although, when added to databases, they provide a powerful means of shifting from target markets to individual customers, their low coverage renders them of limited value. On the other hand, lifestyle segments, where valid, do provide a more graphic portrayal of customers than do demographics, and hence can give suggestions for advertising copy platforms. As with single demographic variables, it is too much to hope that a single classification will work beyond markets for which they are particularly well suited.

To return to the earlier Lego example, that has been so successful in using age as a way of discriminating between sectors in the market for construction toys. Once the individuality of children starts to develop, Lego has found it necessary to develop a wide range of products covering the different needs of children: Lego Basic for 3–12-year-olds, which specialises in using the original Lego components as they were initially contrived; Fabuland, aimed at 4–8-year-old girls, which revolves around a fantasy theme based on animal characters; Legoland for 5–12-year-olds, which are sub-themes of space, medieval life, pirates and modern suburbia; and Legotechnic for 7–16-year-olds, which has a focus on engineering mechanisms. Although the company found demographics as the first basis of segmentation, to go further depended on identifying customer characteristics specific to the product in question.

Additionally, Lego have invested heavily in Lego movies that have proven to be hugely popular and have driven sales and cemented brand image in target segments.

All the above approaches are in the public domain and hence, even where they do offer reliable segmentation schemes of a market, they will rarely offer the marketer any originality in viewing it. The essence of a competitively useful segmentation scheme is that it is fresh, new, original and provides insights into the market that competitors do not have. To achieve this originality requires primary research, where preconceptions about the market structure are put on one side and patterns sought from the original data.

8.2   Post hoc/cluster-based segmentation approaches

Unlike the methods discussed above for segmenting markets, the post-hoc approach does not commence with a preconception of market structure. The analysis is undertaken with a view to uncovering naturally existing segments rather than shoehorning customers into predefined categories.

The remainder of this chapter discusses how firms can go about this more creative approach to segmentation. In doing so it follows a model developed by Maier and Saunders (1990) (see Figure 8.1). The process flows from initiation of the desire, to segment the market creatively, through to the tracking of continuing segment usefulness.

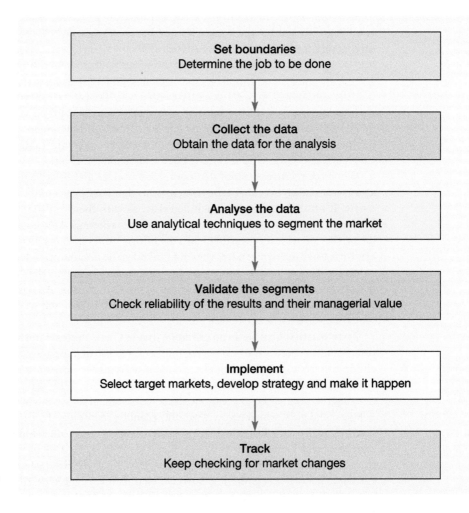

Figure 8.1
A model for segmentation research

Source: Based on Maier and Saunders (1990).

8.2.1 Setting the boundaries

Original and creative segmentation research needs both market and technical expertise. This often necessitates a dialogue between a manager commissioning a segmentation study and an agency or individual conducting the necessary research. The value of the final segmentation results will depend on the effort the individuals concerned have taken in bridging the gap between the technical requirements of segmentation methods and the practical knowledge of marketing and sales management. It is customary to see this bridge-building role as a responsibility of the researcher (who will typically be a modeller or marketing scientist) but, since the marketing manager is going to depend on the results and is going to be responsible for implementing them, he or she has a clear vested interest in ensuring a mutual understanding is achieved. Whereas the expert or modeller faces rejection if the technical gap is not bridged, the marketing manager may face failure in the marketplace if the relationship fails. When employing an agency the marketing manager will certainly need to know how to cross-examine the agency to ensure their methods are appropriate and their assumptions valid.

The entry of the marketing researcher or marketing modeller into the segmentation process is similar to opening a sale. If good initial relationships are not formed the chance of further progress is slight. The researcher has to establish credibility by showing relevant expertise while fitting into the client's culture. As in selling, the prior gathering of information about the industry, the company and the personnel is beneficial. A grasp of terminology popular in the company is particularly useful. This preparation accelerates the formation of the mutual understanding necessary for successful model implementation.

The roles of the salesperson and the marketing researcher should be different because, although a salesperson usually has a limited set of products to sell, the marketing researcher should theoretically be able to choose without bias from a wide portfolio of appropriate techniques. Unfortunately this perspective is an ideal, for many marketing research agencies have a predisposition towards techniques with which they are familiar, or may even have developed in-house. So, in commissioning segmentation research, the marketing manager has to have sufficient knowledge to resist being supplied from a limited portfolio of solutions. Beware the researcher adopting the '*have technique – will travel*' approach!

The major lessons for starting a segmentation project are that the first contact is critical and that successful segmentation depends on the marketing manager and the marketing researcher being sympathetic to each other's needs – not necessarily knowing each other's business perfectly, but certainly having the ability to ask the right questions.

At this initial stage it is essential to agree the focus of the project, the product market to be investigated and the way in which the results are intended to be used. Multi-product companies may choose to start with one application and proceed to others if the trial is successful. There may also be market structures – such as the division between industrial and consumer markets – that suggest a two-stage approach: the first stage breaking the market down into easily definable groups, and the second being involved with the segmentation analysis proper. In their segmentation analysis of the general practitioner (GP) market, Maier and Saunders (1990) used such a process by first dividing doctors into general practitioners and hospital doctors, this distinction being necessary because of the different jobs of the two groups. The second stage then focused on determining the product usage segments within the GP markets.

Agreeing on a focus reduces the chance of initial misunderstandings leading to dissatisfaction with the final results and maximises the chances of the results being actionable.

8.2.2 Collect the data

The data required for segmentation studies can be broken down into two parts: that which is used in conjunction with cluster analysis to form the segments, and that which is used to help describe the segments once they are formed. Cluster analysis will allow any basis to be used, but experience has shown that the most powerful criteria are those that relate to attitudes and behaviour regarding the product class concerned. These could include usage rate, benefits sought, shopping behaviour, media usage, etc.

Before such data can be collected however, it is necessary to be more specific about the questions to be asked. Typically, qualitative techniques, such as group discussions, are used to identify the relevant attitudes, or benefits sought, prior to their incorporation in representative surveys.

For effective benefit segmentation, in particular, it is vital that exhaustive prior qualitative research is undertaken to ensure that all possible benefits of the product or service are explored in depth. The benefits that the firm believes the product offers may not be the same as the ones the customers believe they get. For the subsequent analysis to be valid the customers' perspective is essential, as is the use of the customers' own language in subsequent surveys.

Following qualitative research a segmentation study will usually involve a quantitative survey to provide data representative of the population, or market, under study. The method of data collection depends on the usage situation. Where the aim is to define target markets based on attitudes or opinions the data collection is usually by personal interviews using semantic scales that gauge strength of agreement with a number of attitude statements. The results then provide a proxy to the interval-scaled data, which is the usual basis for cluster analysis.

By contrast, where the segmentation in a study is to be used in conjunction with a database that can rely on direct mailing the data sources are much more limited. For example, the lifestyle classifications mentioned earlier use simple checklists so that consumers can be classified according to their interests. In the database segmentation study conducted by Maier and Saunders (1990) the basis was product usage reports by general practitioners. It is clearly a limitation of database methods that their data collection is constrained by the quality of data that can be obtained from a guarantee card or self-administered questionnaire. There inevitably tends to be an inverse correlation between the coverage in segmentation databases and the quality of the data on which they are formed.

Where surveys are conducted to collect data for segmentation purposes these data are usually of two main types. The primary focus is on the data that will be used to segment the market: the benefits sought, usage patterns, attitudes and so on. In addition, however, the survey will also collect information on traditional demographic and socio-economic factors. These can then be related back to the segments once formed (they are not used to form the segments) to enable a fuller picture of the segments to be painted. For example, a benefit segmentation study may find that a significant segment of car purchasers is looking for economical and environmentally friendly cars. To enable a marketing programme to be directed to them, however, requires a fuller picture of their purchasing power, media habits and other factors. Often age and social class are used as intermediary variables; where these factors discriminate between segments they can be used to select media.

8.2.3 Analyse the data

Once the data on which the segments are to be based have been collected they need to be analysed to identify any naturally occurring groups or clusters. Generically, the techniques used to identify these groups are called **cluster analysis** (see Saunders, 1999).

It should be realised that cluster analysis is not a single analytical technique but a whole class of techniques that, while sharing the same objective of identifying classifications with homogeneity internally but heterogeneity between them, use different methods to achieve this. This diversity of approach is both an opportunity and a problem from the practitioner's point of view. It means that the approach can be tailored to the specific needs of the analysis, but requires a degree of technical expertise to select and implement the most appropriate technique. Not surprisingly, it has been found that cluster analysis is relatively little used and understood among marketing practitioners, but is much more widely used by marketing research companies. In a set of surveys Hussey and Hooley (1995) found that across the top European companies only one in seven (15 per cent) reported regular use of cluster analysis in their marketing analysis, whereas the usage figures rose to three out of five (60 per cent) among specialist marketing research companies. The techniques were seen to be particularly widely used among researchers in the Netherlands (73 per cent), France (68 per cent) and Germany (67 per cent), but less so in Spain (47 per cent) and the United Kingdom (52 per cent).

The most common approach to clustering is called hierarchical clustering. Under this approach all the respondents are initially treated separately. They are then each joined with other respondents who have given identical or very similar answers to the questions on which the clustering is being performed. At the next stage the groups of respondents are further amalgamated where differences are small. The analysis progresses in an interactive fashion until all respondents are grouped as one large cluster. The analyst then works backwards, using judgement as well as the available statistics, to determine at what point in the analysis groups that were unacceptably different were combined.

Even within hierarchical clustering, however, there is a multiplicity of ways in which respondents can be measured for similarity and in which groups of respondents can be treated. Grouping can be made, for example, on the basis of comparing group averages, the nearest neighbours in two groups or the furthest neighbours in each group. Table 8.1 summarises the main alternatives.

Comparative studies consistently show two methods to be particularly suitable for marketing applications: Ward's (1963) method, which is one of the minimum variance approaches listed in Table 8.1; and the K-means approach of interactive partitioning.

Table 8.1 Clustering methods

Favoured name	Method	Aliases
Hierarchical methods		
Single linkage	An observation is joined to another if it has the lowest level of similarity with at least one member of that cluster	Minimum method, linkage analysis, nearest neighbour cluster analysis, connectiveness method
Complete linkage	An observation is joined to a cluster if it has a certain level of similarity with all current members of that cluster	Maximum method, rank order typal analysis, furthest neighbour cluster analysis, diameter method
Average linkage	Four similar measures that differ in the way they measure the location of the centre of the cluster from which its cluster membership is measured	Simple average linkage analysis, weighted average, centroid method, median method
Minimum variance	Methods that seek to form clusters which have minimum within-cluster variance once a new observation has joined it	Minimum variance method, Ward's method, error sum of squares method, H GROUP
Interactive partitioning		
K-means	Starts with observation partitioned into a predetermined number of groups and then reassigns observation to cluster whose centroid is nearest	Non-hierarchical methods
Hill-climbing methods	Cases are not reassigned to a cluster with the nearest centroid but moved between clusters dependent on the basis of a statistical criterion	

Source: Based on Punj and Stewart (1983).

In fact, an analyst does not have to choose between these two, because they can be used in combination, where Ward's method is used to form the initial number of clusters, say seven, and the K-mean approach used to refine that seven-cluster solution by moving observations around. If desired, after finding the best seven-cluster solution, Ward's method can then be re-engaged to find a six-cluster solution that is again optimised using K-mean, etc. This may seem a computationally cumbersome approach, but fortunately packages are available to allow this process to be used. Arguably Ward's method in conjunction with K-means is the best approach for forming cluster-based segments; the analyst has removed the necessity to sort among numerous cluster alternatives and is able to choose between the clustering programs that are available.

While there is plenty of advice available on which techniques to use, the determination of the most appropriate number of segments to select following the analysis is very much more judgemental. The statistics produced will offer a guide as to where amalgamation of groups results in two quite dissimilar groups being joined. The internal homogeneity of the group will suffer. This is a starting point and in some circumstances, where segmentation is very clear-cut, will be the best choice.

Figure 8.2 shows an example where there are three fairly clearly defined segments on the basis of the two dimensions studied. In this case 'eyeballing' a plot of the positions of each object (in segmentation studies the objects are usually individual respondents) shows three clusterings of objects scoring similarly, but not identically, on each of the two dimensions.

In most situations, however, there will be several dimensions on which the clustering is being conducted, and several candidate solutions, possibly ranging from a three-group to a ten-group solution. After narrowing down through examination of the statistics the analyst will then need to examine the marketing implications of each solution, basically addressing the question: 'If I treat these two groups separately rather than together, what differences will it make to my marketing to them?' If the answer is 'little difference' the groups should usually be amalgamated. This is the creative element of segmentation where judgement is crucial!

Finally, it should also be noted that lifestyle and geodemographic databases depend on some form of cluster analysis to group customers who are alike. The results obtained for

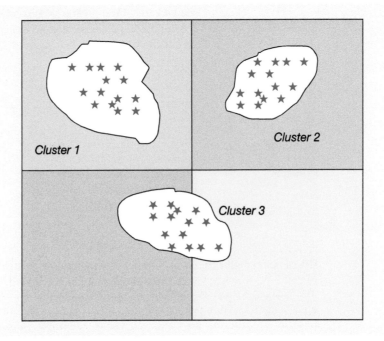

Figure 8.2
Clustering of objects in two-dimensional space

ACORN and MOSAIC, for example, are based on judgement as to how many clusters are needed to represent the population adequately, just as tailor-made approaches are.

Once the segments have been identified, and described across other criteria, there is a need to validate the segments found.

8.2.4 Validate the segments

One of the beauties and problems of cluster analysis is its ability to generate seemingly meaningful groups out of meaningless data. This, and the confusion of algorithms, has frequently led to the approach being treated with scepticism. These uncertainties make validation an important part of segmentation research.

One favoured method of validation was mentioned above. Where product class behaviour or attitude was used to form the clusters, the extent to which those clusters also vary on demographic or psychographic variables is a measure of the cluster's validity. If the cluster is found to describe people with different beliefs, attitudes and behaviour it would be expected that they could also have different demographic or psychographic profiles. Equally, from an operational point of view, if the market segments are demographically and psychographically identical it is going to be very difficult to implement any plan based on them.

Where sample data have been used to suggest segments and there is a hope of extrapolating those results to the fuller population, there is a need to test the reliability of the solution, to ask the question: do the results hold for the population as a whole? The most common way to test for this is cross-validation. This involves randomly splitting the data that have been collected into two, using one set to form the set of clusters and the second set to validate the results. A simple approach is to conduct the same cluster analysis on both samples and to compare them to see the similarity of the clusters in terms of their size and characteristics.

Since comparing two cluster analysis solutions tends to be rather subjective, several authors have recommended using discriminate analysis for cross-validation. This approach once again involves taking two samples and performing a separate cluster analysis on each. One sample is then used to build a discriminate model, into which cases from the other samples are substituted. The reliability is then measured by comparing the allocation using discriminate analysis with the allocation by cluster analysis. Integrated data analysis packages, such as SPSS PC, enable such linked analyses to be conducted quickly and efficiently.

It is necessary to supplement this statistical validation **mentioned above** with operational validation, which checks if the segments have managerial value. At a first level this means the segments having face validity and appearing to provide marketing opportunities. If further endorsement is needed an experiment can be run to test if the segments respond differently or not. For example, Maier and Saunders (1990) used a direct mailing campaign to a sample of GPs to show their segments captured major differences in the doctors' responses to certain self-reported activity.

8.2.5 Implement the segmentation

Implementation is best not viewed as a stage in segmentation research, but should be seen as the aim of the whole research process. Implementation has become one of the central issues in market modelling. A successful (validated) model adequately represents the modelled phenomena, and implementation changes decision making, but a successful implementation improves decision making. In many cases it is worth going beyond the concept of implementation to implantation. By this we mean the results of the exercise not just being used once, but adopted and used repeatedly once the marketing scientist has withdrawn from the initial exercise. This again suggests that implementation not only begins at the start of the segmentation research process, but continues long after the results have been first used by the marketing manager.

Successful implementation, therefore, depends on more than the correct transfer of a model into action. The whole model-building process needs to be executed with implementation in mind. In particular, the segmentation researcher must be involved with the potential user in order to gain their commitment and ensure the results fit their needs and expectations. An unimplemented segmentation exercise is truly academic in its more cynical sense.

Segment selection and strategy development are two critical stages that follow the technical activity of segmentation research. These are managerial tasks that are central to marketing strategy and on which successful implementation depends. Chapter 9 focuses upon these and links them to the broader issues of strategic positioning.

8.2.6 Tracking

A segmentation exercise provides a snapshot of a market as it was some months before the results were implemented. Inevitable time delays mean that, from the start, the results are out of date and, as time goes on and consumers change, it will inevitably become an increasingly poor fit to reality. Modelling myopia (Lilien and Kotler, 1983) occurs when successful implementation leads to the conviction that market-specific 'laws' have been found that make further analysis unnecessary. The converse is true: success means modelling should continue. Customers and competition change. Successful implementation itself may also change the market and competitors' behaviour.

Tracking of segmentation schemes for stability or change over time is essential in rapidly changing markets. As segmentation and positioning strategies are implemented they inevitably change the pattern of the market and customer perceptions, wants and needs. Through tracking the impact of various campaigns on segmentation it may be possible to refine and detail the sort of promotional activity that is appropriate for them. If the segments do not prove to be stable, either showing gradual changes or a radical shift, that itself can create a major opportunity. It may indicate a new segment is emerging or that segment needs are adjusting, and so enable an active company to gain a competitive edge by being the first to respond.

Positioning research is often carried out in parallel with segmentation research. Indeed, the quantitative approaches discussed below typically have as their aim the development of a multidimensional model representing both the positioning of objects (typically brands or companies) and customer segments.

8.3   Qualitative approaches to positioning research

The images of brands, products, companies and even countries have long been of interest to marketing researchers. Qualitative research approaches to this are semi-structured techniques aimed at gaining a more in-depth understanding of how respondents view aspects of the world (or more specifically markets) around them. They include focus groups and depth interviews (see Chapter 4).

Calder (1994) relates a qualitative research study into the image of a for-profit hospital in the United States. The hospital chain was opening a new 100-bed facility in a town with two existing and much larger hospitals. The problem was how to position the new hospital given its relatively small size and lack of established reputation. A number of focus group sessions were held which showed that the relative size was known by respondents but not seen as necessarily negative. Indeed, the smaller size led to expectations of a friendlier, more personalised service. Comments during the discussions included:

Very friendly and you get a lot of good care there. The others are a little big for that kind of care.

From what I hear it has a more personalised service. Mealwise and otherwise. You even get wine [with meals]. It's more of a personalised hospital.

I understand it has quite an excellent menu to choose from. Wine. They have the time to take care of you.

The researchers concluded that the new hospital could be positioned very differently from the existing ones and it built on the friendly, caring image in subsequent marketing.

Through the use of projective techniques during qualitative research images can be uncovered that serve to show how the brand product of the company is positioned in the mind of the respondent. Some of the most popular techniques include the following:

- **The brand or company as animal or person.** Under this approach respondents are asked to name a person or an animal that embodies their view of the product or company under study. Calder (1994) cites the use of the technique to uncover the image of the US Army among potential recruits. Respondents were asked: 'If you were to think of the Army as an animal, which would it most be like?' The answers were, in order: tiger, lion, bull, wolf, bear. The Army was not seen as: mule, horse, dog, squirrel, elephant or cow! The researchers concluded that the Army was symbolised (positioned) as strong, tough, aggressive, powerful and dominating. This positioning had some negative effects on potential recruits who feared failure in the training/induction period. It is interesting to note that more recent recruitment advertising in the United Kingdom has served to stress the 'family' and 'team' nature of military service – an attempt at some repositioning.

- **Role-play.** In role-playing the respondent is asked to assume the role or behaviour of another person, or of an object under research. Tull and Hawkins (1993) give an example of research for a premium brand of Canadian whisky marketed by Schenley, called O.F.C. During a group discussion a member of the group was asked to role-play a bottle of O.F.C. and explain his feelings. The player explained that he didn't think anyone could like him as he didn't have a real name and hence no real identity. Further probing and discussion resulted in the name 'Old French Canadian' being suggested (using the letters of the original name, building on the origin of the liquor in the French-Canadian area of Quebec, and on the favourable image of 'Canadian Club'). The brand was relaunched with the new name, a stronger personality and a clearer positioning in the market.

- **The Friendly Martian.** In this approach the interviewer or group moderator assumes the role of an alien recently landed from space and asks members of the group to explain a particular product and how it is used. By acting as an alien the moderator can ask basic questions to which the respondents would normally assume the moderator knew the answers. In a group discussion for the British Home Sewing and Needlecrafts Association the researcher (a male in a female-dominated market) was able, through use of this technique, to discover that knitting was 'positioned' as a craft hobby that could be undertaken as a background activity while doing other sedentary activities such as watching television. Sewing, on the other hand, was 'positioned' as a thrift activity, undertaken primarily to save money, especially with children's garments, and required full attention to the exclusion of other activities.

A number of stimuli can be used to prompt respondents and aid them in articulating the images they hold of objects. These include the following:

- **Association techniques.** Here respondents are asked for associations with a particular stimulus. They may, for example, be asked what words, or values, or lifestyles, they associate with a BMW car. The words elicited can then be further explored through discussions and other techniques.

- **Concept boards.** Boards with pictures of the brand or the brand logo on them. These are shown to respondents and their reactions sought through probing.

- **Animatics.** Drawings of key frames from a commercial with 'bubble' speech. Respondents are then asked for their reactions and helped to describe the feelings they have towards the items being advertised.

- **Cartoon and story completion.** Cartoons of situations, such as the purchase of a specific brand, where the speech 'bubbles' are left blank for the respondent to fill in. Tull and Hawkins (1993) relate the use of story completion in researching changing drinking habits for Seagram. The unfinished scenario used was:

  > Sarah hadn't seen Jane for a long time. She seemed very sophisticated
  > and self-assured these days. At the bar she ordered . . .

  Completion of the scenario by female drinkers most often had Jane ordering a glass of wine reflecting, as the researchers interpreted it, her higher level of knowledge of drinks and general sophistication. Based on this and further qualitative research the company developed a wine-based drink with a twist of citrus to liven it up – 'Taylor California Cellar's Chablis with a Twist'.

- **Visual product mapping.** This is a qualitative form of the perceptual mapping approaches discussed **below** under quantitative techniques. Here respondents are given a large piece of paper – the size of a flip-chart – with two dimensions drawn at right-angles to each other. Respondents are then given a number of objects (such as brands or companies) on small cards, or in the case of small pack products such as shampoos they may even be given a number of real packages. They are then asked to position the cards or packs on the chart with similar brands close to each other but far apart from dissimilar brands. The dimensions that can be used to explain these differences are then discussed and written on to the maps. Alternatively, the identity of the dimensions may have been elicited from earlier parts of the interview (such as 'price', 'quality', etc.) and respondents are asked to 'position' the objects on the dimensions directly.

Qualitative approaches to uncovering the images and positions of objects in the minds of respondents have been particularly popular among advertising agencies who value the in-depth, rich data that can be derived. The images and positions articulated are in the respondents' own language and hence offer insights for direct communication with them as customers.

The classic concern of qualitative research, however, remains. That is, how representative of the population in their normal everyday shopping and consumption experiences are the responses of a relatively small number of respondents in often very artificial settings completing strange and unfamiliar tasks? In most instances positioning research needs to go beyond the qualitative to develop models of images and positions based on more representative samples in a quantitative study.

8.4 Quantitative approaches to positioning research

While qualitative approaches to image research often focus on the core object (brand, product, company, etc.) in isolation, the more quantitative approaches typically consider positioning relative to the positioning of major competitors and relative to the desires, wants and needs of target customer segments.

As a starting point, therefore, it is necessary to define the competitive set that will be analysed along with the focal brand, product or company. While positioning studies can focus at the level of the company or the product, most typically focus at the brand level.

For example, a company analysing the market for hover-mowers might be interested in how customers perceive competitors' brands (i.e. Flymo, Qualcast and Black & Decker) and the products they sell. When buying such a product a customer is likely to have a reasonable idea about the likely size and cost of the item they wish to buy and, therefore, give most attention to products within that price performance envelope.

Among the competitors the customer is likely to see various dimensions of importance, such as value for money, reliability, safety, convenience, etc., and it is the relationships between the direct competitors with which positioning is particularly involved. If the direct competitors have not been correctly identified the researcher may include within the survey manufacturers of sit-on mowers, i.e. Mountfield or Honda. This would not only add to the burden of respondents whose perceptions are being sought, but could also change the perceptions since, when compared with sit-on mowers, conventional hand-mowers may all look similarly inexpensive, time-consuming and compact.

The mower market is relatively simple compared with some others. Consider the problem faced by a company wishing to launch a low-alcohol lager. Should the competitors be other low-alcohol lagers or should it include low-alcohol beers as well? Or maybe the study should be extended to include other low-alcohol drinks such as shandy, cider or wine. In the United Kingdom the rapid increase in the consumption of soft drinks which has been associated with the concern for the health and safety of alcohol consumption may suggest that they too should be considered as an alternative to low-alcohol lagers, but should diet and caffeine-free versions also be considered? Maybe it is a matter of just taste, and it is more appropriate to low-alcohol drinks with variants with normal alcohol content. Production orientation is a danger when trying to reduce the number of product alternatives. A brewer may well consider low-alcohol lagers or other lagers as the direct competitors, but certain customer groups may easily associate low-alcohol drinks with colas or other beverages. It is clearly necessary to take a customer-oriented view of the direct competitors.

One way of defining direct competitors is to look at panel data to see what customers have done in the past. By tracking the past purchases of customers it may be possible to identify product alternatives when switching takes place. The danger in this approach is the dissociation of the purchasers with the usage situation and the user. For instance, a buying pattern that shows the purchase of low-alcohol lagers, lemonade, beer and cola could represent products to be consumed by different people at different times, rather than switching between alternatives. Another approach is to determine which brands buyers consider. For consumer durables customers might be asked what other brands they considered in their buying process. For low involvement products it may be inappropriate to ask a buyer about a particular purchase decision, so instead they could be asked what brands they would consider if their favourite one was not available.

Day *et al.* (1979) proposed a more exhaustive process as a cost-effective way of mapping product markets. Termed *Item by Use Analysis,* the procedure starts by asking 20 or so respondents the use context of a product, say a low-alcohol lager. For each use context so identified, such as the lunchtime snack, with an evening meal, or at a country pub, respondents are then asked to identify all appropriate beverages. For each beverage so identified the respondent has to identify an appropriate use context. Once again the process is continued until an exhaustive list of contexts and beverages is produced. A second group of respondents would then be asked to make a judgement as to how appropriate each beverage would be for each usage situation, the beverages then being clustered on the basis of their similarity of their usage situation. For instance, if both low-alcohol lager and cola were regarded as appropriate for a company lunchtime snack but inappropriate for an evening meal they would be considered as direct competitors.

Rather than using consumers, it can be tempting to use a panel of experts or retailers to guide the selection of direct competitors. This could be quicker than using customers, but is likely to lead to a technological definition of preference. There can be a vast difference between what is perceived by experts and what is perceived by customers. Since the focus of positioning is to gauge customers' images of offerings and their preferences for them it is difficult to justify using any other than customers to define competitors.

8.4.1 Attribute profiling methods

One of the simplest ways of collecting quantitative position data is through the use of attitude or attribute scaling. Under this approach the dimensions that respondents use to differentiate and choose between alternative offerings are included in a survey (usually personally administered, though it is also possible to collect these data by mail, telephone, or 'e' surveys) and presented as semantic scales for respondents to give their views on.

An example from a survey of store images and positioning is given in Figure 8.3. Here respondents were asked to rate two competing stores on six attributes identified as important in prior qualitative research: quality, price, staff attitudes, range of goods, modernity and ease of parking. Results are shown from one respondent only. Also shown is that respondent's ideal store profile – what he or she would ideally like in terms of the features listed. For most purposes the responses from the sample would be averaged[*] and those averages used to show the differences in positioning and requirements. Where ideal requirements differ across the sample they could be first grouped together (using cluster analysis – see above) to identify alternative segment requirements.

This approach examines each dimension separately, bringing them together in the diagram to enable a more complete image to be drawn. Some dimensions may, however, be more important to particular market segments than others. For instance, in the store positioning example above it might well be that for one segment price considerations outweigh convenience, range and other factors. It is therefore essential to examine the relative importance of the dimensions, either through weighting them differently to reflect importance or through assessing the dimensions simultaneously such that more important dimensions come to the fore.

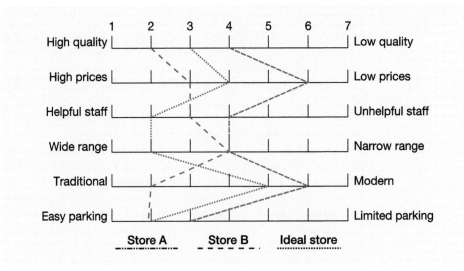

Figure 8.3
Modelling store images through the use of semantic scales

---

[*] Note that where there is wide variation in the evaluations from individual respondents it may be necessary first to group respondents by perceptual segments, i.e. those sharing a common view of the market, prior to analysing alternative segment requirements.

8.4.2 Multidimensional positioning analysis

Increasingly researchers and managers are seeking to create multidimensional models of the markets in which they are operating. The essence of these models is that they seek to look at a number of dimensions simultaneously, rather than separately, in an attempt to reflect more closely the way in which customers view the market.

To explain this approach we shall follow a case involving the positioning of leisure facilities accessible from the east Midlands of the UK. For the sake of simplicity only the major attractions and segments are considered in this case. Interviews with respondents revealed six leisure centres that, although very different in their provision, were all seen as major attractions. These were:

- **The American Adventure theme park:** a modern facility, with a Wild West emphasis but also including other US themes such as GI and space exploration (the park has closed since the case study).
- **Alton Towers:** since 1990 has been acquired by a series of owners including The Tussaud's Group, Merlin Entertainments, Dubai International Capital and Prestbury. This is a large leisure facility based around a derelict country house. It has inherited several natural features, such as the house itself, the gardens and lakes, but particularly focuses on dramatic white-knuckle rides.
- **Belton House:** one of many country houses owned by the National Trust and, as with most of these, has splendid gardens and furnished accommodation, which visitors may see. Atypical of National Trust properties, the house also has a large adventure playground in a nearby wood, this being a venture started by the family who owned the house prior to its being passed on to the National Trust.
- **Chatsworth House:** one of the largest stately homes in the United Kingdom and still the residence of the owning family. Its extensive grounds and the house itself make it a popular place for families to visit.
- **Warwick Castle:** one of the best-kept and most visited medieval castles in the United Kingdom. As with many estates, it has been lived in from medieval times and the current owners have built a country house into the fabric of the building. Now owned by Merlin Entertainments Group, the castle's attractions have been extended beyond the building and its gardens, to include contemporary waxworks within the furnished accommodation, medieval knights, jousting tournaments, medieval torture chambers, etc.
- **Woburn Abbey and Safari Park:** like Chatsworth, still the residence of the family owning the estate. However, the family in this case have developed two distinct attractions, the house and the safari park, the latter also having a fairground, etc.

Although widely different in their appeals, ownership and background, the respondents' interviews clearly indicated that these were direct competitors and were alternatives they would choose between when deciding on an outing.

The positioning research process (Figure 8.4) shows the determination of competitive dimensions, competitors' positions and the customers' positions as parallel phases. This is because there are certain techniques that can be used to extract all these simultaneously. In this case the phases are taken in sequence. Details of other approaches that are available are given later.

Identifying product positions

It is an odd feature of many of the techniques used in positioning research that the competitors' positions can be determined before it is understood how the customer is differentiating between them. Such an approach was used to represent the leisure park market in the east Midlands. The approach is called similarities-based multi-dimensional scaling. In this, respondents were given a shuffled stack of cards that contained all possible combinations

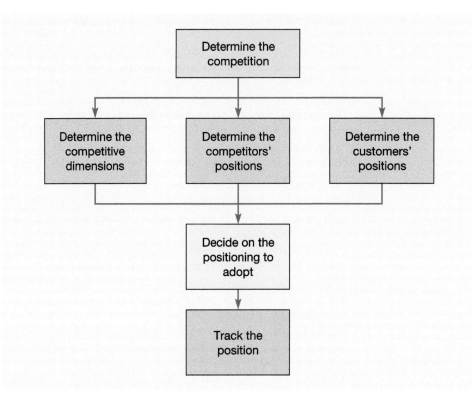

Figure 8.4
The positioning
research process

of the six leisure parks. There were 15 pairs in all, ranging from American Adventure linked to Alton Towers, to Warwick Castle linked with Woburn Safari Park. The respondents were then asked to rank the pairs in accordance with their similarity, the pair most alike being on the top and the pair least alike being on the bottom. Since this can be a rather cumbersome process it is sometimes advisable first to ask respondents to stack the cards into three piles representing those pairs that are very similar, those pairs that are very unalike and a middling group. The respondent then has to rank the pairs within each group.

Figure 8.5 presents the ranking from one such process. It shows that this particular respondent (one of many) thought Belton House and Woburn Safari Park were the most similar. As the next most similar, the pair of Belton House and Chatsworth House were chosen, and so on, until the least similar pair of the American Adventure and Chatsworth House. An indication that the respondent is using different criteria to judge each pair is shown by the judgement that Belton is similar to Woburn and Chatsworth, but Woburn and Chatsworth are not alike. Such are the permutations and combinations of pairs each respondent can choose that it is almost inevitable that each individual's similarity matrix is different.

The objective from this point is to develop a plot of the stimuli (leisure parks) which shows those that respondents said were similar close together, and those that respondents said were dissimilar far apart. Although this is a difficult task to conduct manually,

Figure 8.5
Individual
similarity matrix of
leisure facilities

	(A)	(T)	(B)	(C)	(W)	(S)
American Adventure (A)	–					
Alton Towers (T)	3	–				
Belton House (B)	4	11	–			
Chatsworth House (C)	15	13	2	–		
Warwick Castle (W)	5	12	7	8	–	
Woburn Safari Park (S)	6	10	1	14	9	–

computers are particularly adept at finding such solutions, and researchers in the field of multi-dimensional scaling have produced many computer packages that can be used (for a summary, see Green *et al.*, 1989). A multi-dimensional scaling package called KYST can be used to produce perceptual maps from the similarities matrix provided and many other data formats. The map produced (Figure 8.6) shows some of the detail from a similarity matrix (Figure 8.5). Chatsworth House, Alton Towers and Woburn Safari Park are some distance apart, while American Adventure, Alton Towers and Belton House are somewhat closer together.

There are two reasons why the fit is not perfect.

1   The perceptual map presented in Figure 8.6 is in two dimensions, whereas the customers' perception of the market is rather more complex than that; and
2   the perceptual map is an aggregate of a number of customers' views, whereas the similarity matrix in Figure 8.5 represents the views of one customer.

KYST can produce a perceptual map for a single customer, but it is more common to produce a map that aggregates either all customers or a segment's view.

Uncovering the dimensions of perception

While the map shows a representation of the similarities between objects (leisure attractions) in itself it tells us little of why they are seen as similar or dissimilar. We need to go further to identify and understand the dimensions, or criteria, that were being used by respondents in giving their similarity judgements.

Two methods of determining the dimensions or criteria are not recommended. The first is using experts' judgements as, like their judgements of competitors, it is likely to be different from that of customers. The second is trying to eyeball the perceptual map to try to work out what the dimensions represent. Such maps are often ambiguous and there is a particular danger of researchers superimposing their own views of what is going on. A better, but still imperfect, technique is to ask customers directly how they differentiate the market. The problem here is that customers may give a relatively simplistic answer, which may not represent all the dimensions they may, sometimes subconsciously, use to differentiate product offerings.

More useful is a research-based approach where respondents are asked first to choose two or more similar products and say why they consider them to be alike, then to choose

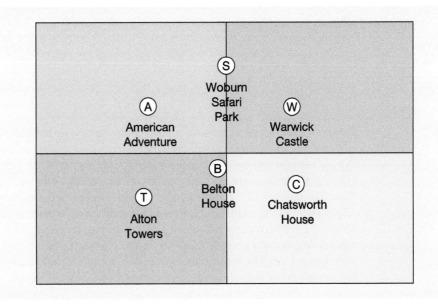

Figure 8.6
Perceptual map of
leisure centres

some products they consider quite dissimilar and say why they see them as unalike. An approach such as this was used to determine the dimensions of the perceptual space for the leisure facilities. The respondents were first asked why they chose the first pair (Woburn Safari Park and Belton House) as most alike. They were then asked what made Belton House and Chatsworth House alike, and so on, until the respondents had difficulty saying that pairs were alike at all. The opposite tack was then taken, where the respondents were asked to explain why they considered pairs to be unalike; first of all, the most dissimilar pair of Chatsworth House and American Adventure, then Chatsworth House and Woburn Safari Park, etc. The result was a long list of attributes, which was reduced to ten after some similar ones were combined and less frequently used ones were deleted. The ones remaining were:

- big rides;
- educational;
- fun and games;
- sophisticated;
- noisy;
- for teenagers;
- strong theme;
- for all the family;
- synthetic/artificial;
- good food.

Kelly Grids are a popular marketing research technique that could also have been used to identify the dimensions underlying the perceptual map. A four-step approach is typically taken.

1 Respondents are presented with three stimuli (in our case, leisure attractions) and asked to state one way in which two of them are alike and yet different from the third.
2 The criteria on which the two were said to be alike (say 'noisy') is labelled 'the emergent pole' and associated dissimilarity (say 'quiet') is labelled 'the implicit pole'.
3 The remaining stimuli (leisure attractions) are then sorted equally between the two poles.
4 Another three stimuli are selected and the process is repeated until the respondent can think of no new reasons why the triad are alike or dissimilar.

To find how the dimensions fit the perceptual map in Figure 8.6, respondents were asked to rank each of the leisure facilities on the basis of the attributes identified. Once again the result is a series of matrices that are difficult to analyse manually and, once again, computers come to our aid. In this case a package called PREFMAP (Chang and Carroll, 1972) was used. This takes the perceptual map of product positions in Figure 8.6 and fits the dimensions as they best describe the respondents' perceptions. To identify the meaning of these vectors, each one can be traced back through the centre of the perceptual map (see Figure 8.7).

The score of each of the leisure centres (stimuli) on the dimension (vector) is measured by their relative position as the vector is traced back through the centre. For instance, the respondents see Chatsworth House as being the most 'sophisticated' (on the east–west dimension), followed by Warwick Castle, Woburn Safari Park, Belton House, American Adventure and Alton Towers. In almost complete opposition to sophistication is the vector representing noisy and rowdy, on which Alton Towers and American Adventure scored the highest. Projecting back the vector that represents a strong theme shows the highest scoring leisure centre to be Woburn Safari Park, followed by the American Adventure and Warwick Castle with an almost equal rating, and finally Belton House, Alton Towers and Chatsworth House. Once again it is likely that the respondents' individual or aggregated scores are not perfectly represented by the map that has been generated. This is inevitable, considering that the picture is now trying to represent even more information in the same two dimensions. The magnitude of this problem can be reduced by resorting to portraying the picture using three or more dimensions, but usually the situation becomes less understandable rather than more understandable as the map goes beyond our normal experience.

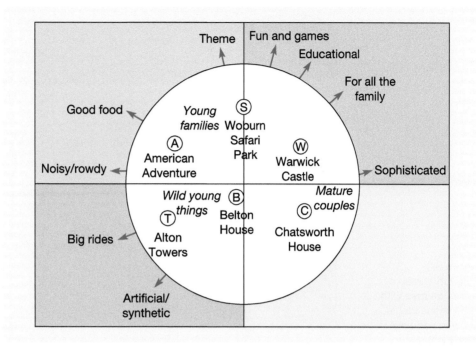

Figure 8.7
Perceptual map
of leisure centres
with dimensions
identified

It may also be that segments of the market have distinctly different views and therefore it is more appropriate to produce maps that represent their different perceptions rather than aggregating the market, as has been done so far.

Identifying market segment locations

A two-stage process was used to add customer positions to the perceptual map of leisure centres. First, respondents were asked to rate the leisure centres in terms of their preference. Cluster analysis was then used to form segments with similar preferences (see above). This indicated the presence of three main clusters. Analysis of their demographic characteristics revealed these to be mature couples or young sophisticates who found Chatsworth House and Belton House most attractive; young families who preferred American Adventure and Woburn Safari Park, and 'wild young things' who were most attracted by Alton Towers and American Adventure.

Once again PREFMAP was used to locate these segments in relation to product position. However, in this case the segments were to be expressed as ideal points within the body of the map rather than as vectors in the way that the dimensions were examined. Figure 8.8 gives the final map. This shows clearly the strategy of American Adventure, the latest of the leisure centres to enter the market. Aimed at the family market, it has big rides, good food and plenty of opportunity for fun and games, particularly for very young children. Although lacking sophistication and being perceived as artificial, it is well positioned for young families and for wild young things. Less successful appears to be Belton House, where the National Trust has found itself running a country estate, with which it is very familiar, and an adventure playground, with which it is unfamiliar. Although the house and gardens may provide the sophistication and tranquillity desired by mature couples, the existence of the adventure playground would make it too rowdy for them. Equally, the direction of so many resources into maintaining the house and gardens to National Trust standards provides facilities that are unlikely to be attractive to the wild young things (which the National Trust probably thinks is good) or young families.

The map also shows the dangers of product positioning without consideration of market segments. The positions of the leisure centres suggest there may be an opportunity to develop one that excels in the provision of an educational experience for the pre-teens,

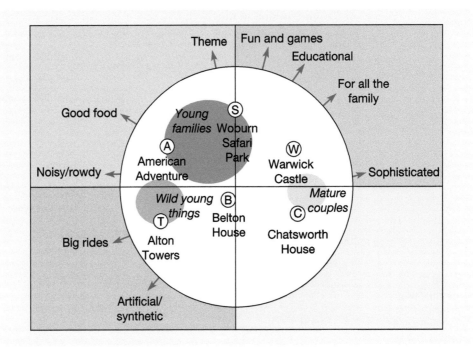

Figure 8.8
Perceptual map of leisure centres with dimensions identified and segment ideal locations

or for all the family. Vacant that position may be, but it is dangerously away from the needs of the three major segments that have been identified in this case. Maybe the mums and dads would have liked such a leisure centre, but the kids would be happier with a less pretentious, synthetic attraction providing fun and games.

8.4.3 Alternative algorithms

In developing positioning maps researchers are spoilt (and possibly confused) by the number of alternative approaches that can be used (see Green *et al.*, 1989). For instance, PREFMAP allows the stage where segments were formed from individuals to be missed out and so produces a map representing the ideal point of each individual. Rather than the picture seen in Figure 8.8, which presents the ideal points of each segment, the map would then show the product positions, the market dimensions and the position of each individual relative to the product. From there it may be possible to eyeball the positions of individual respondents to identify a group that are worthy of being targeted. Another package, MDPREF (Chang and Carroll, 1969), can be used to combine the identification of the perceptual map of product positions and underlying dimensions. This would have required respondents to have rated leisure parks along each of the dimensions, such as 'for all the family' or 'sophisticated', and then aggregating the results to arrive directly at a map similar to Figure 8.7.

A further approach is offered through correspondence analysis. Correspondence analysis (see Carroll *et al.*, 1986, 1987) is a multivariate method for analysing tables of categorical data in order simultaneously to identify relationships between the variables (both rows and columns). It can therefore operate with commonly collected data, such as usage and attitude data, to produce perceptual maps that simultaneously show the positions of objects (brands or segment ideals) and attributes (dimensions). Originally developed in France as an alternative approach to multi-dimensional scaling, correspondence analysis is now available in leading MDS packages such as that provided by Smith (1990).

Anyone who starts to use this diversity of approaches will find that the map produced depends on the approach used. This is because of the differences in the data-gathering techniques and the assumptions and methods used to optimise the results. In that way the use of multi-dimensional scaling to produce perceptual maps is similar to cluster analysis where the results depend on the clustering algorithm used. However, just as in cluster analysis, this should not be seen as a defect but the realisation that there are numerous ways of looking at a market. Life would be more convenient if there was just one map that represented a market, but any attempt to compress the richness of a market into so simple a perspective is likely to result in opportunities being lost, or never seen.

Only a few years ago the access to the packages was difficult, and the programs themselves were poorly documented and hard to use. Now the situation has changed completely, and there are a host of user-friendly and relatively inexpensive packages available – the ones cited and used as examples above are a very small sample. Software is increasingly used by leading market research companies in order to increase levels of decision-making success and marketing effectiveness.

Summary

Considerable research has shown that the naive practitioner of segmentation and positioning research can be easily confused and disappointed. The traditional a priori, off-the-shelf methods of segmentation have proved to be a poor guide to segmenting markets other than those that have a direct and immediate link to the markets concerned, e.g. gender-, age- or race-based products. Although more expensive, and providing a much more graphic view of the marketplace, the more modern psychographic methods appear to provide little advantage. As with demographic bases for segmentation, they do work in certain circumstances, but only when the product class or form and the segmentation criteria are very closely related. Within a product class or a product form, however, they rarely differentiate between brands.

The need to find segmentation bases which are closely associated with the product market in question means that successful implementation often involves a company developing product-specific bases. Here there is a potential barrier because of the perceived complexity of the approach and the confusion that researchers have created by their own misunderstandings. Although once a major block to implementation, sufficient case law on using cluster analysis in marketing has been accumulated to allow some of the confusion to be removed. Comparative studies come down firmly in favour of Ward's (1963) method in conjunction with iterative partitioning.

There is rightly much scepticism about the results from cluster analysis. This is justifiable, given the confusion of the algorithms used, the tendency of cluster analysis to produce results even if the data are meaningless, and the lack of validation of those results. Being aware of these dangers it is vital that validation – both statistical and operational – has a central role within segmentation research. In particular, tests should be done to see if the segments formed can be replicated using other data, that the segments are managerially meaningful and respond differently to elements of the marketing mix.

As with segmentation research there is a wide variety of positioning research approaches and techniques available. Typically they require the collection of primary data relating to brand images and customer requirements. Multi-dimensional scaling techniques can be used to summarise the mass of data collected in visually appealing and easily communicable ways. They are perhaps best seen as visual models of the customer's mind. As such, they should be treated with caution, as any model is a simplification of reality, and used with care. They can never replace the individual manager's insights, which are central to creative marketing decision making. At best they are an aid to that process.

Segmentation and positioning researchers have failed to find a single criterion that will fit all markets, despite the claims of those selling lifestyle segmentation. However, rather than finding a single criterion, researchers have found consistently reliable methods of using product market data to segment customers into groups that are of managerial significance and to represent their views and opinions in visually communicable ways. While Baumwoll (1974) was right in predicting that no philosopher's stone would be found, researchers have perhaps discovered how to make philosophers' stones!

Case study   A passion that became a brand

On the last day of the annual World Economic Forum in Davos, some of Germany's top business leaders meet for a celebrated ski race. Beneath the bonhomie, the mood is ruthlessly competitive, with each participant determined to gain any split-second advantage. Although none is a professional sportsman, all have the money and determination to splash out on anything that might enhance their performance, from the sleekest aero-dynamic ski suits to the slickest skis.

About 100km away in the small Swiss alpine village of Disentis, Simon Jacomet has created a business, Zai, that aims to meet the needs of just such exacting and wealthy potential clients. Last year, Benedikt Germanier, an old friend and former ski teacher turned banker, joined as chief executive to spearhead growth.

In 2003, Mr Jacomet, a former ski instructor who was working on ski development at two established brands, set up Zai, a boutique ski maker that claims to produce the best skis in the world. Costing between SFr3,700 ($3,420, €2,520, £2,220) and SFr9,800 a pair – well above even the top ranges of mainstream brands – they need to be.

Mr Jacomet, a shy, softly spoken 46-year-old, says: 'I'd learnt what the big manufacturers did – and didn't do – making skis. The market is phenomenally competitive. Lots of compromises are made to keep costs down.'

Backed by Thomas Staubli, a close friend and a former Credit Suisse banker with a holiday home nearby, and six other investors, Mr Jacomet created a ski unbound by convention and designed for top performance, irrespective of price. 'The idea was to create a ski that made no compromises,' he says. All the founders, who contributed the start-up capital, were friends united by an interest in skiing.

Mr Jacomet admits he lacked management experience, let alone knowledge of how to run a company, but says: 'We were all passionate skiers, but none of us went into it to lose money. We analysed the market and concluded there was a niche.'

At Zai's small factory, a dozen craftsmen work with high-tech machinery in a snow-bound, mini version of Switzerland's precision watch industry.

Mr Jacomet hired employees for skill, but also for a willingness to innovate. 'We had perfectionists – but,

Source: Zai AG: Zai Rider Simon.

in the end, they weren't always ideal,' he says. Locals were given preference to outsiders partly to create jobs in Mr Jacomet's home town, but also to safeguard intellectual property. 'We reckoned locals were less likely to betray information,' he says. Zai already has many patents. Even today, he declines to employ apprentices, in case they betray trade secrets when they move on, whether by accident or deliberately.

Though similar in appearance to cheaper rivals, Zai's skis combine traditional materials, such as ash, cedar wood and even stone, with high-tech reinforced carbon fibre and rubber to create an unusually light, yet stable and extraordinarily responsive ski.

Sales have climbed from SFr500,000 in 2004–05 to SFr1.9m in 2008–09, and should top SFr2m this year. Surprisingly, Mr Jacomet says the recession has had little impact, with revenues cushioned by the relatively resilient economy in Switzerland, where sales are still concentrated.

Mr Jacomet admits he could probably have continued like this, focusing more on technical prowess than sales growth. Although his business plan aimed for profitability within five years, Zai's backers accepted a two-year delay when Mr Jacomet argued for reinvesting yet more of the already high proportion of sales allocated to research and development.

Last year, however, the investors said it was time for a crucial choice: to stay on the same path, making 700–800 pairs of skis a year and aiming for break-even at about 900–1,000, or to aim for a leap forward via diversification. 'We'd built a strong brand and reputation, largely on word of mouth,' says

Mr Germanier, the extrovert 43-year-old who was appointed to spearhead growth. 'The investors saw potential to expand.'

Central to the decision were Patrick Aisher, a British serial entrepreneur and private equity investor, based in Switzerland since 2000, and Mr Germanier, who last summer quit his job as a UBS currency strategist to take the sales burden off Mr Jacomet, so that his long-standing friend could focus on his passion for applied research and product development.

Mr Aisher became interested after hearing Zai wanted to raise new money on top of its initial SFr450,000 funding. 'I only tested the skis subsequently – fortunately, they were very good,' he says. Mr Aisher also contributed his experience of investing in small companies and even helping to take them public. His two key messages were that the board, which included almost all the investors, was ungainly, and that Zai needed a new, sales-oriented chief executive.

'It's usually a warning sign when there are almost as many board members as employees,' says Mr Aisher. 'All the board members were experts in their fields, but none had any knowledge of running a winter sports company.' His plan involved appointing most of the investors to a non-executive board of directors, and creating a three-strong operating board, comprising Mr Jacomet, Mr Germanier and himself as a link between the two bodies.

Mr Germanier, meanwhile, replaced a former chief executive whose sole focus on financial discipline was no longer appropriate. 'Zai could have remained a "hobby" company for its shareholders for years. But that would have been a shame, as it has built such a strong brand,' says Mr Aisher.

As a former ski instructor, Mr Germanier combined an understanding of the product with the business experience gained from eight years in banking. Moreover, as Mr Jacomet's friend, he knew what he was getting into and, it was hoped, would reduce the potential dangers of management friction with the arrival of an outsider.

'I'd been feeling like a battery hen. I wanted a new challenge and to take on more responsibility', he says. Mr Jacomet adds: 'He had to convince the board he was the right candidate.'

The first fruits of expansion will be seen in May, when Zai unveils a golf club based on the expertise in materials that has already distinguished its skis. The driver – the crucial club most regularly upgraded by golfers – will be priced significantly above rivals, although the margin will be smaller than with the skis. Further ahead, the company is looking at cross-country skiing – another sport with an older, generally affluent, clientele – and accessories, such as sunglasses.

'I'd see this company in two or three years having more than doubled sales, and added 100 per cent again from associated non-skiing products,' says Mr Aisher. 'It then starts to become a "small" sizeable business, with products spread across the seasons and with a particularly international clientele. Our customer database alone would be worth a fortune.'

Toughness designed for luxury

Zen-like simplicity and perfection may be among Simon Jacomet's goals for his ski-making company, but the zen-sounding word 'Zai' in fact means 'tough' in the local variant of Romansh, Switzerland's little-known fourth language, that is spoken in the Surselva region.

Mr Jacomet says the unorthodox mixes of materials such as cedar, ash and stone in Zai's skis are no marketing gimmick but have a genuine basis in the skis' functional needs, notably damping – the ability to translate a skier's movements into a physical response with minimal interference.

Lacking bigger rivals' resources for advertising, Zai has grown by word of mouth. About 80 per cent of sales come via specialist dealers, mostly in Switzerland, but about 20 per cent stem from direct factory visits from customers or special sales events. Apart from its main lines, Zai has produced one-off limited editions for Hublot, a high-end Swiss watchmaker, and Bentley, the luxury carmaker.

Mr Jacomet says the skis' conservative appearance, alongside the often raucous styles of competitors, underlines the brand's sobriety and that its products are meant to last.

Source: adapted from 'A passion that became a brand', *Financial Times*, 24/02/10 (Simonian, H.).

Discussion questions

1 What is Zai's business and why?

2 Why does Mr Germanier want to expand the business? How can segmentation research help?

3 Which quantitative approaches to positioning research might best apply to Zai?

CHAPTER 9
SELECTING MARKET TARGETS

Attacking a fortified area is an act of last resort.

Sun Tzu, c.500 BC. Clavell (1981)

The public image: Kodak

Kodak has revived its long-standing 'Kodak moment' slogan and reinvented it for the Facebook era. Eschewing the megapixel race and technobabble that is usually found in camera marketing, Kodak wanted to re-establish an emotional connection with its customers. The film-cum-camera maker is specifically targeting young women with families who it sees as the guardians of the household photo album. Its new cross-media campaign focuses on a range of cameras that make it easier to e-mail a photo or post it on to Facebook or Flickr.

In the simple, softly lit television ad that leads the campaign, a proud father holds his newborn baby in his arms. He takes a photo of the child and quietly explains how excited his relatives will be to see the picture, an easy process thanks to the camera's share button. His wife smiles approvingly from her hospital bed. 'The real Kodak moment happens when you share,' says a voiceover.

Kodak is already very active in social media, with employees dedicated to listening to customer feedback on Twitter and Facebook. This campaign combines the emotional hit of TV with online engagement through kodakmoments.com. Additional online ads explain how the product works, which balances out some oversimplification in the TV segment.

Source: Photodisc/Jacobs Stock Photography.

Sentimental ads seem to be becoming a trend but this updated Kodak moment pushes the right emotional buttons.

Source: from 'The public image: Kodak', *Financial Times*, 10/05/10 (Bradshaw, T.).

Discussion questions

1 Discuss Kodak's choice of target market.
2 How do social media help Kodak connect with its target market?

Introduction

One of the key decisions a company faces is its choice of market or markets to serve. However, many firms enter markets with little thought as to their suitability in the longer term. They are entered primarily because they appear superficially attractive for the firm's products or services. As we shall see in this chapter, a strong case can be made for choosing markets and industries where the prospects are attractive, but also where the firm can establish a strong, defensible, position. Figure 9.1 suggests that if we compare, in general terms, the attractiveness of markets and the strength of the competitive position we can take, then there are several traps to be avoided:

- **Peripheral business:** areas where the firm can take a strong and secure competitive position, but where the market simply does not deliver the benefits that the company needs. It is easy for those with great enthusiasm for a product or service in which they specialise to drive into these areas, but they will never deliver the margin and growth that is needed and will absorb resources and management time.
- **Illusion business:** areas where the market appears very attractive, because it is large, dynamic, expanding and so on. However, these are areas where the firm can only ever hold a weak position – perhaps because these are typically the markets defended most fiercely by entrenched competitors. It is easy for managers to be seduced into entering these markets because of the potential they offer, without acknowledging that we can never reach that potential.
- **Dead-end business:** markets that are not attractive and where the firm can only take an 'also-ran' position. Few managers will deliberately enter these markets, but this may describe markets from which the firm should exit – they may have been attractive in the past, but have declined, or the firm's competitive position may have been undermined by new competitors and technologies.

Ideally the firm is seeking to position its offerings in:

- **Core business:** markets offering the benefits and returns needed, where the firm can take a strong, defensible, position. Clearly these are the highest priority for investment of time and resources. The major issue here is how well we understand what makes a market attractive for a particular company, and what makes a market position strong (Piercy, 1997).

While the strategic traps are easily described, the importance of the issue is underlined by the fact that market choices are just that – choice may mean ignoring some markets and some customers and some ways of business, to focus on the areas where superior performance and results can be achieved. Making such choices may be difficult. Michael Porter has suggested the heart of the problem:

Figure 9.1
Market attractiveness and competitive position

Source: Adapted from Piercy (1997).

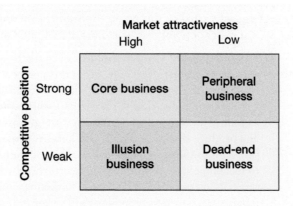

> To put it simply, managers don't like to choose. There are tremendous organisational pressures towards imitation and matching what the competitor does. Over time this slowly but surely undermines the uniqueness of the competitive position.
> *(Porter, quoted in Jackson, 1997)*

Porter's argument is that a key challenge is to make clear trade-offs and strategic choices. The alternative is that a company risks destroying its own strategy:

> They start off with a clear position, and over time they're drawn into a competitive convergence where they and their rivals are all basically doing the same thing. Those kinds of competitions become stalemates.
> *(Porter, quoted in Jackson, 1997)*

However, the importance of market and segment choices must be put in the context of the potential complexity of markets and the consequent uncertainty surrounding the ideal choices to make. Indeed, as we shall see, defining markets and segments is not simply an exercise in statistical analysis, it is also a subjective and highly creative process (e.g. see Aaker, 1995). Considering alternative perspectives on markets and segments is a way to enrich our understanding of the customer, and to establish competitive differentiation in the way we go to market.

The purpose of this chapter can be described as follows. Chapter 7 was concerned with the different ways in which markets could be segmented. Alternative bases for segmentation were examined and the benefits of adopting a segmentation approach discussed. Chapter 8 then looked at the research techniques available to help segment markets. In this chapter market definition and market targeting are discussed in more detail. In particular, the process of identifying the market segments where the company's capabilities can be used to the best advantage is considered, together with the selection of the appropriate marketing strategy.

In deciding on the markets and segment(s) to target, four basic questions need to be asked:

1 How do we define the market – what is its scope and constitution?
2 How is the market segmented into different customer groups?
3 How attractive are the alternative market segments?
4 How strong a competitive position could we take – where do our current or potential strengths lie?

9.1   The process of market definition

The definition of the markets a company serves, or those it is evaluating as possible targets, is partly a question of measurement and conventional competitive comparisons. It is also in part a creative process concerned with customer needs. Stanley Marcus of Neimann Marcus is frequently cited on this point: 'Consumers are statistics. Customers are people.'

A number of points are worth bearing in mind in approaching market definition:

- **Markets change.** The development of marketing strategy takes place in the context of a constant process of change. From this perspective it is unreasonable to assume that a company's definition of markets should remain static.
- **Markets and industries.** We have made the point before that markets are not the same as industries or products. Industries are groups of companies that share technologies and produce similar products. Markets are groups of customers with similar needs and problems to solve. Defining markets around industries and products exposes a company to its competitive position being overturned by competition from outside the conventional industry. Developing robust marketing strategies and strong competitive positions requires not only understanding the existing industry (see Chapter 3), but also the market from the customer's perspective (see Chapter 4).

- **Different definitions for different purposes.** Day (1992) makes the point that we may need different market definitions for different types of marketing decision: tactical decisions such as budgeting and salesforce allocation are likely to require narrow and easily understood market definitions (existing customers, similar products, existing channels), while strategic decisions require broader market definitions (including new market opportunities, changes in technology and substitute products, and potentially new types of competitive entrant).

9.1.1 Different ways of defining markets

Day (1992) suggests that markets can be defined in two ways: on the basis of customers, or on the basis of competitors.

- **Customer-defined markets.** This approach takes us beyond products that are 'substitutes in kind', i.e. the same technology, to 'substitutes in use', i.e. all the products and services which may meet the same customer needs and problems.
- **Competitor-defined markets.** This approach focuses on all the competitors that could possibly serve the needs of a group of customers, and reflects technological similarity, relative production costs and distribution methods.

In general, competitor-based definition will be important for allocating marketing resources and managing the marketing programme – responding to price cuts, salesforce coverage, and so on. On the other hand, customer-defined approaches are likely to be more insightful in understanding the dynamics of the market, the attractiveness of alternative markets, and in developing strong competitive positions.

One practical approach to evaluating the characteristics of markets is the product–customer matrix.

9.1.2 Product–customer matrix

Figure 9.2 suggests that the underlying structure of a market can be understood as a simple grouping of customers and products/services. The challenge is to examine a market using this matrix to identify no more than five or six groups of products and services and

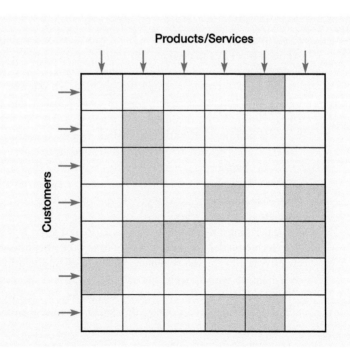

Figure 9.2
The product–
customer matrix

five or six groups of customers, that constitute the market. If this is impossible then this is probably not a single market but several, and the exercise should be subdivided.

The important perspective that can be built using this approach is one which recognises:

- **products/services** – in terms of what they do for customers, not in terms of how they are produced or by whom;
- **customers** – in terms of important differences between groups in needs, preferences, priorities or ways of buying.

For example, vast arrays of retail financial services products provided by banks and their competitors can be reduced to six categories of products by considering what customer benefits they provide. Rather than hundreds of products, the market consists of only six groups of products and services to provide access to cash; provide security of savings; buy-now pay-later; make cashless payments; get a return on assets such as savings; and acquire a range of specialist services. The same process of reduction can be applied to products/services. For example, do not describe the market as 'computers', but as what different mixes of computer hardware, software and services actually deliver to customers in a particular market, such as accounting systems, internal communications, management information and so on.

This approach provides a start in defining markets in such a way that we move past the core market of similar products to find the extended market. This analysis can be used for a variety of purposes, but one advantage of this type of initial approach is that it starts to identify the way a market divides into distinctly different segments.

9.2   Defining how the market is segmented

As discussed in Chapter 7, there are many ways in which markets can be segmented. Often a useful starting point is to ask how management views the market, on the basis of their experience in the marketplace. Management definition of market segments may typically be on the basis of products/services offered or markets served.

9.2.1 Products or services offered

Describing segments on the basis of products or services offered can lead to broad-based segmentation of the market. John Deere, for example, competing against the much larger Caterpillar company in the US crawler tractor (bulldozer) market initially segmented the market into 'large' and 'small' bulldozers. On the basis of its marketing assets (defined in terms of better service support through local dealer networks and lower system price) Deere decided to concentrate its efforts in the small bulldozer market, thus avoiding head-on competition with Caterpillar, which was stronger in the large bulldozer market (where market requirements centred around spare parts availability).

Many market research companies operating in the service sector define their market segments in terms of the services they offer, e.g. the market for retail audits, the market for telephone surveys, the market for qualitative group discussions, the market for professional (industrial) interviewing.

Underlying this product- or service-based approach to identifying markets is a belief that segments defined in this way will exhibit the differences in behaviour essential to an effective segmentation scheme. The strategy adopted by Deere made sense, for example, only because the requirements of purchasers and users of large and small bulldozers were different. Where the requirements of customers are essentially the same, but satisfied by different products or services, this segmentation approach can lead to a myopic view of the market.

9.2.2 Market or markets served

Many companies now adopt a customer-based or markets-served approach to segmenting their markets. Segments are defined in terms of the customers themselves rather than the particular products they buy. In consumer markets, management may talk in terms of demographic and socio-economic segments while in industrial markets definitions may be based on SIC or order quantity. A particularly useful approach in many markets is to segment on the basis of the benefits the customer is seeking in consuming the product or service and/or the uses to which the product or service is put.

Van den Bergh (a subsidiary of Unilever) has been particularly successful in segmenting the market for yellow fats on the basis of the benefits sought by consumers (see Broadbent, 1983). The market, which comprises butter, margarine and low-fat spreads, stood at £600 million at retail selling price in 1979. It was a static market with no overall growth. Within the market, however, there were some important changes taking place. There had been a marked trend away from butter to margarine, primarily because of the increasing price differential (butter and margarine were roughly equivalent prices in the mid-1970s but since then butter prices had increased more rapidly, widening the gap). Coupled with this came increased price sensitivity as the UK economy entered the recession of the late 1970s/early 1980s. Van den Bergh were quick to spot a market opportunity as it segmented the market. There were at least five benefit segments identified:

- **Segment 1** consisted of customers who wanted a 'real butter taste' and were not prepared to forego that taste at almost any price. This segment chose butter, the top-selling brands at the time being Anchor, Lurpak and Country Life.
- **Segment 2** were customers who wanted the taste, feel and texture of butter but were concerned about the price. They were typically not prepared to sacrifice on taste, etc., and not convinced that existing margarines could satisfy them. These customers would typically choose the cheapest butter available, such as supermarket own label.
- **Segment 3** were ex-butter users who were prepared to accept existing margarines as a substitute and even found they offered additional benefits over butter, such as softness and ease of spreading direct from the fridge. Also attractive to this segment was tub packaging and larger packs. They were more price sensitive than Segment 2. The leading brand in this segment was Stork margarine.
- **Segment 4** was a growing minority segment concerned with diet and weight control. In particular they were concerned with calories and with fat content. Outline was a leading brand.
- **Segment 5** were concerned with health in general and particularly the effects of cholesterol. Of special appeal to this segment were spreads low in cholesterol and high in polyunsaturated fats. The market leader in this segment was Flora.

Van den Berghs' had achieved around 60 per cent of the total market in 1980 through recognising the segmentation described above and positioning its brands such that they attracted specific individual segments. Segment 1 was deliberately not targeted specifically. Krona, a block margarine with (in blind tests) a very similar taste to butter, was launched at a premium price and high margins to attract Segment 2 customers as they traded down from butter. Segment 3 was secured by Van den Berghs' leading brand, Stork, while Segments 4 and 5 were served by Outline and Flora respectively. During the 1980s and 1990s competition to serve Segment 2 intensified. Following the initial success of Krona, Dairy Crest launched Clover in 1983 as a dairy spread. In 1991 Van den Berghs launched the amazingly named 'I Can't Believe It's Not Butter' as a brand that gave a butter taste but with much lower fat intake levels. Within just nine months of its launch, ICBINB (as it became to be known in the trade), took 2.3 per cent of the margarine low-fat spreads market. In 1995 it was followed by St Ivel's new brand, positioned directly in opposition, 'Utterly Butterly'. More recently the emergence of 'cholesterol buster' spreads such as Benecol presented a new challenge to Van den Berghs' domination of the market. The launch of Flora pro-activ into this part of the market ensured continued overall leadership. Since its launch in 2000 the brand has gone from strength to strength, outselling its nearest competitor 3 to 1. In 2004 the pro-activ range was enlarged to include a spread with olive oil, a milk drink and low-fat yoghurts.

Central to the success of Van den Bergh and other creative marketers has been an unwillingness merely to accept the segmentation of the market adopted by others. In many fast-moving consumer products markets, and in grocery marketing in particular, there has been a tendency to over-segment on the basis of background customer characteristics or volume usage. By looking beyond these factors to the underlying motivations and reasons to buy, companies can often create an edge over their competitors.

Once the segments have been identified the alternatives need to be evaluated on the basis of market attractiveness and company strength, or potential strength, in that particular market segment. This evaluation is carried out across a number of factors.

9.3 Determining market segment attractiveness

It is clear that many factors may be considered in evaluating market, or specific segment, attractiveness. In Chapter 2 we discussed multi-factor approaches to evaluation in the context of assessing the portfolio of product offerings, while here they are discussed as strategic tools for deciding which markets to enter in the first place. There have been many checklists of such factors, but one way of grouping the issues is as follows:

- market factors
- economic and technological factors
- competitive factors
- environmental factors.

However, it should be noted at the outset that a general checklist of this kind is only a starting point – the factors important to making a market attractive or unattractive to a specific company are likely to reflect the specific characteristics of that company and the priorities of its management. For example, one company may see a market segment that is growing as highly attractive, while in the same industry another company may look for slower rates of growth to avoid stretching its financial and other capacities. Similarly, a company that has cost advantages over its rivals may see a price-sensitive segment as highly attractive, while its competitors do not. In fact, there is a group of factors that impact on judgements of market attractiveness which are wholly subjective.

9.3.1 Market factors

Among the market characteristics that influence the assessment of market attractiveness are the following (Figure 9.3).

Size of the segment

Clearly, one of the factors that make a potential target attractive is its size. High-volume markets offer greater potential for sales expansion (a major strategic goal of many companies). They also offer potential for achieving economies of scale in production and marketing and hence a route to more efficient operations.

Segment growth rate

In addition to seeking scale of operation many companies are actively pursuing growth objectives. Often it is believed that company sales growth is more easily achieved in growing markets.

Market factors Size; growth rate; life cycle stage; predictability; price elasticity; bargaining power of buyers; cyclicality of demand	**Economic & technological factors** Barriers to entry and exit; bargaining power of suppliers; technology utilisation; investment required; margins
Competitive factors Intensity; quality; threat of substitution; degree of differentiation	**Business environment factors** Economic fluctuations; political and legal; regulation; social; physical environment

Figure 9.3
Factors affecting market segment attractiveness

The market for colas within the carbonated drinks market is declining in many Western markets, making it a less attractive market than it has been. In the US, for example, the cola share of the market declined from 72 per cent in 1990 to 60 per cent in 2000. Meanwhile sales of bottled water, juices and sports drinks doubled. This was worrying for Coca-Cola which generated 65 per cent of its sales volume from colas and accounts for one-third of the soft drinks sold in the world (*Financial Times*, 19 September 2001).

Stage of industry evolution

We looked earlier (see Chapter 3) at the characteristics of markets at different stages of evolution. Depending on the company's objectives (cash generation or growth) different stages may be more attractive. For initial targeting, markets in the early stages of evolution are generally more attractive as they offer more future potential and are less likely to be crowded by current competitors (see competitive intensity below). Typically, however, growth requires marketing investment (promotion, distribution, etc.) to fuel it so that the short-term returns may be modest. Where more immediate cash and profit contribution is sought a mature market may be a more attractive proposition, requiring as it does a lower level of investment.

Predictability

Earlier we stressed the predictability of markets as a factor influencing their attractiveness to marketers. Clearly the more predictable the market, the less prone it is to discontinuity and turbulence, the easier it is to predict accurately the potential value of the segment. The more certain, too, is the longer-term viability of the target.

Price elasticity and sensitivity

Unless the company has a major cost advantage over its main rivals, markets which are less price sensitive, where the price elasticity of demand is low, are more attractive than those that are more sensitive. In the more price-sensitive markets there are greater chances of price wars (especially in the mature stage of industry evolution) and the shake-out of the less efficient suppliers.

Bargaining power of customers

Those markets where buyers (ultimate customers or distribution chain intermediaries) have the strongest negotiating hand are often less attractive than those where the supplier can dominate and dictate to the market.

In the UK grocery market the buying power of the major supermarket chains is considerable. Together the top five chains supply around 78 per cent of the nation's food shopping needs. Food manufacturers and processors compete vigorously for shelf space to make their products available to their ultimate consumers. Indeed, some supermarket chains are now moving towards charging food manufacturers for the shelf space they occupy.

Similarly, in the market for military apparel a concentration of buying power (by the governments) dictates to potential entrants on what basis they will compete.

Seasonality and cyclicality of demand

The extent to which demand fluctuates by season or cycle also affects the attractiveness of a potential segment. For a company already serving a highly seasonal market a new opportunity in a counter-seasonal market might be particularly attractive, enabling the company to utilise capacity all year round.

The Thomson publishing group found the package tour market highly attractive, primarily for cash flow reasons. The company needed to bulk purchase paper for printing during the winter months and found this a severe drain on cash resources. Package holidays, typically booked and paid for during the winter months, provided a good opportunity to raise much needed cash at the crucial time. Thomson Holidays, founded originally as a cash flow generator, has gone on to become a highly successful package tour operator.

9.3.2 Economic and technological factors

Issues reflecting the broader economic characteristics of the market and the technology used include the following.

Barriers to entry

Markets where there are substantial barriers to entry (e.g. protected technology or high switching costs for customers) are attractive markets for incumbents but unattractive markets for aspirants. While few markets have absolute barriers to entry in the long term, for many companies the costs of overcoming those barriers may make the venture prohibitively expensive and uneconomic.

Barriers to exit

Conversely, markets with high exit barriers, where companies can become locked into untenable or uneconomic positions, are intrinsically unattractive. Some new target opportunities, for example, may have substantial investment hurdles (barriers to entry) that, once undertaken, lock the company into continuing to use the facilities created. In other markets powerful customers may demand a full range of products/services as the cost of maintaining their business in more lucrative sectors. When moving into high-risk new target markets a major consideration should be exit strategy in the event that the position becomes untenable.

Bargaining power of suppliers

The supply of raw materials and other factor inputs to enable the creation of suitable products and services must also be considered. Markets where the suppliers have monopoly or near-monopoly power are less attractive than those served by many competing suppliers (see Porter, 1980).

Level of technology utilisation

Use and level of technology affects attractiveness of targets differently for different competitors. The more technologically advanced will be attracted to markets which utilise their expertise more fully and where that can be used as a barrier to other company entry. For the less technologically advanced, with skills and strengths in other areas such as people, markets with a lower use of technology may be more appropriate.

Investment required

Size of investment required, financial and other commitment will also affect attractiveness of market and could dictate that many market targets are practically unattainable for some companies. Investment requirements can form a barrier to entry that protects incumbents while deterring entrants.

Margins available

Finally, margins will vary from market to market, partly as a result of price sensitivity and partly as a result of competitive rivalry. In grocery retailing margins are notoriously low (around 2–4 per cent) whereas in other markets they can be nearer 50 per cent or even higher.

9.3.3 Competitive factors

The third set of factors in assessing the attractiveness of potential market targets relates to the competition to be faced in those markets.

Competitive intensity

The number of serious competitors in the market is important. Markets may be dominated by one (monopoly), two (duopoly), a few (oligopoly) or none ('perfect competition') of the players in that market. Entry into markets dominated by one or a few key players requires some form of competitive edge over them that can be used to secure a beachhead. In some circumstances it may be that the existing players in the market have failed to move with changes in their markets and hence create opportunities for more innovative rivals.

Under conditions of perfect, or near-perfect, competition price competitiveness is particularly rife. The many small players in the market offer competitively similar products so that differentiation is rarely achieved (the stalemate environment – see Chapter 3), and it is usually on the basis of price rather than performance or quality. To compete here requires either a cost advantage (created through superior technology, sourcing or scale of operations) or the ability to create a valued uniqueness in the market. In segments where there are few, or weak, competitors there may again be better opportunities to exploit.

In the early 1980s Barratt Developments made a major impact on the house-building market. Its segmentation of the market identified the need for specialist housing at various consumer life cycle phases. The first venture was Studio Solos, designed for young, single people. In the first year of sales Barratt sold over 2,000 (2 per cent of total new home sales in the year). In the United States the same strategy was adopted to spearhead the company's international expansion (70 per cent of Barratt's US sales coming from solos). At the same time in the United Kingdom the company successfully developed retirement housing for pensioners, one- and two-bedroom apartments in blocks featuring communal facilities and wardens. In both retirement homes and solos housing Barratt was among the first to pursue aggressively the markets it had identified. Indeed, it would argue it was among the first to recognise that the housing market was segmented beyond the traditional product-based segmentation of terraces, semis and detacheds.

Quality of competition

Chapter 5 discussed what constitutes 'good' competitors – those that can stabilise their markets, do not have over-ambitious goals and who are committed to the market. Good competitors are also characterised by their desire to serve the market better and hence will keep the company on its toes competitively rather than allow it to lag behind changes in the environment. Markets that are dominated by less predictable, volatile competitors are intrinsically more difficult to operate in and control and hence less attractive as potential targets.

Threat of substitution

In all markets there is a threat that new solutions to the customers' original problems will be found that will make the company's offerings obsolete. The often quoted example is substitution of the pocket calculator for the slide rule, though other less dramatic examples abound. With the increasing rate of technological change experienced in the twenty-first century it is probable that more products will become substituted at an accelerating rate.

In such situations two strategies make sense. First, for the less technologically innovative, seek market targets where substitution is less likely (but beware being lulled into believing substitution will never occur!). Second, identify those targets where your own company can achieve the next level of substitution. Under this strategy companies actively seek market targets that are using an inferior level of technology and are hence vulnerable to attack by a substitute product. Hewlett-Packard's success with laser printers followed by ink jet printers in the PC peripherals market (attacking dot matrix printers) is a classic example.

Degree of differentiation

Markets where there is little differentiation between product offerings offer significant opportunities to companies that can achieve differentiation. Where differentiation is not possible often a stalemate will exist and competition will degenerate into price conflicts, which are generally to be avoided.

9.3.4 The general business environment

Lastly, there is the issue of more general factors surrounding the market or segment in question.

Exposure to economic fluctuations

Some markets are more vulnerable to economic fluctuations than others. Commodity markets in particular are often subject to wider economic change, meaning less direct control of the market by the players in it. For example, the New Zealand wool export industry was badly affected in mid-1990 by an Australian decision, in the face of declining world demand and increasing domestic stockpiles, to lower the floor price on wool by 20 per cent. Australia is such a dominant player in the essential commodity world market that New Zealand exporters were forced to follow suit.

Exposure to political and legal factors

As with exposure to economic uncertainty, markets that are vulnerable to political or legal factors are generally less attractive than those which are not. The exception, of course, is where these factors can be used positively as a means of entering the markets against entrenched but less aware competitors (e.g. when protection is removed from once government-owned monopolies).

Degree of regulation

The extent of regulation of the markets under consideration will affect the degrees of freedom of action the company has in its operations. Typically a less regulated market offers more opportunities for the innovative operator than one that is closely controlled.

Again there is an exception, however. Regulated markets might afford more protection once the company has entered. This might be protection from international competition (e.g. protection of European car manufacturers from Japanese car imports by quotas), which effectively creates a barrier to (or a ceiling on) entry. The warning should be sounded, however, that experience around the world has generally shown that protection breeds inefficiencies and when that protection is removed, as is the current trend in world trade, the industries thrown into the cold realities of international competition face major difficulties in adjusting.

Social acceptability and physical environment impact

Increasingly, with concern for the environment and the growth of 'green' politics, companies are looking at the broader social implications of the market targets they choose to go after. When the company is widely diversified the impact of entering one market on the other activities of the company must be considered.

With increasing concern for the natural world, its fauna and flora, some cosmetics companies are now looking to non-animal ingredients as bases for their products and manufacturers of aerosols are increasingly using non-ozone-depleting propellants in place of CFCs. The Body Shop, a cosmetics and toiletries manufacturer and retailer, has built its highly successful position in the market through a clear commitment to the use of non-animal ingredients, just as Innocent trades on 'natural' values with fruit (and nothing but fruit) drinks.

The Body Shop

Source: Alamy Images: UK Retail Alan King.

The disastrous oil spill in the Gulf of Mexico in the spring of 2010 had major implications for the reputation of the oil giant BP that was responsible for the Deepwater Horizon oil well. Repeated failed attempts to stem the leak led to a loss of confidence in the technical competence of the firm, and indeed the whole oil industry, such that permission for new well drilling in the USA was suspended for a 6-month period while safety procedures were re-examined and revised.

Summary

The quality of a market is dependent on a number of factors. Other factors being equal, segments that are big and growing offer the best prospects for the future. Other factors rarely are equal, however, and size and growth are not the only criteria that should be taken into consideration. Of prime importance is the scope for building a valuable and defensible position for the company in that segment. This will also require a clear identification of the company's strengths with regard to the proposed segment.

9.3.5 Making the criteria clear and explicit

We made the point earlier that the factors making a market or segment attractive to a particular company are likely to be unique to that company, rather than simply reflecting a general checklist of the type discussed above. We also made the point that it is likely that the direction of a decision criterion will also vary – high-growth markets are attractive to some companies and unattractive to others in the same industry.

It is also the case that some of the real criteria for evaluating market/segment attractiveness may be highly subjective and qualitative. For example, a brewery evaluating alternative markets for its by-products identified the criteria of market attractiveness as:

- **Market size:** it defined a minimum market value to be of interest.
- **Market growth rate:** moderate growth was preferred (it did not want to invest large amounts in keeping up with a by-products market).
- **Low competitive intensity:** it wanted to avoid head-on competition with others.
- **Stability:** it wanted a stable income flow.
- **Low profile:** it did not want to invest in any area that would attract media criticism, or regulatory activity by the government.

What we see is a mix of the qualitative and the quantitative, and the objective and subjective. None the less, these are the issues that matter to that management group. There is much advantage in making the real criteria as explicit as possible, notwithstanding that some reflect corporate culture and management preferences rather than economic market analysis.

Indeed, the Virgin Group typically makes explicit the criteria that make further markets attractive to Virgin. The head of corporate development, Brad Rosser, states that Virgin will invest in a market only if it meets at least four out of the following criteria (Piercy, 1997):

1 The products must be innovative.
2 They must challenge established authority.
3 They must offer customers good value for money.
4 The products must be high quality.
5 The market must be growing.

This describes Virgin's original mission of offering 'first-class at business-class prices' and applying the brand to new market opportunities.

9.3.6 The impact of change

It should also be remembered that nothing is static – things change, and sometimes they change rapidly in a number of ways:

- **Company change.** As companies evolve, their views about market attractiveness may develop. In the Virgin example given above these criteria may describe the company's view of how it is developing; they do not describe how it has invested in markets in the past.
- **Markets change.** The attractiveness of a market can alter dramatically. Matthew Clark, the UK drinks group, reported at the end of 1996 that sales of Diamond White and K Ciders had dropped 40 per cent, with declining profits following. The reason was a switch by young drinkers to alcopops like Bass's 'Hooch' brand of alcoholic lemonade. Disparaged by the industry experts, a year after launch alcopops were selling 100 million litres a year. Nevertheless, 10 years later and the cider market was experiencing a boom with a 23 per cent increase in sales in 2006 alone (growth that is continuing to date, albeit at a slower pace). Dubbed the 'Magners Effect' (the brand grew by 225 per cent in 2006), this is attributed to a 'step change in consumer attitudes' (National Association of Cider Makers). The boom in cider sales is now global partly due to the absence of gluten in the drink and increased awareness of gluten-intolerance.
- **Competitors change.** The UK market for household vacuum cleaners had been dominated by Hoover and Electrolux since the 1950s, with very conventional technology. James Dyson offered his new product, 'the world's first bagless vacuum cleaner', to the existing players and was laughed at. After many difficulties he launched his own product – with unknown technology and a high price. He sold £3 million worth of vacuum cleaners in the first year and has tripled sales every 12 months. Hoover's share of the upright vacuum cleaner market has halved, and in the high-margin market for cleaners priced over £180 Dyson in 1995 took 58 per cent of the market compared with Hoover's 14 per cent. The attractiveness of markets and segments within them can change dramatically.

- **Reinventing the market.** Market attractiveness can also change dramatically as a result of those who 'reinvent the business', by establishing new ways of doing business. Daewoo took 1 per cent of the British car market (and a much higher share of its segment) in the fastest time ever, by establishing a new direct distribution channel and a brand proposition of high value and 'hassle-free' car buying. Amazon.com made significant inroads into book retailing through offering sales over the Internet, where additional services (such as online searches, book reviews, etc.) could be offered quickly and cheaply, and Apple iTunes took 80 per cent of the UK digital music market in 2006.
- **Market boundaries change.** The issue of market definition we considered earlier cannot be separated from the question of market attractiveness – attractiveness always means in a specific market. As we saw earlier, a characteristic of many markets is that traditional boundaries and definitions are in flux. Avoiding the investment traps we described at the outset may involve constant awareness of how boundaries are changing as a result of new technologies and new types of customer demand.

9.4 Determining current and potential strengths

The importance of the resource-based theory of the firm, and the practicalities of assessing a company's strengths (and weaknesses) were considered in Chapter 6. The issue to consider now is how those resources, capabilities and competencies can be deployed in a specific market or segment (see Figure 9.4). One approach to this evaluation divides the issue as follows:

- the firm's current market position;
- the firm's economic and technological position;
- the firm's capability profile.

9.4.1 Current market position

A start in evaluating strengths in a particular market or segment can be made with consideration of the following issues.

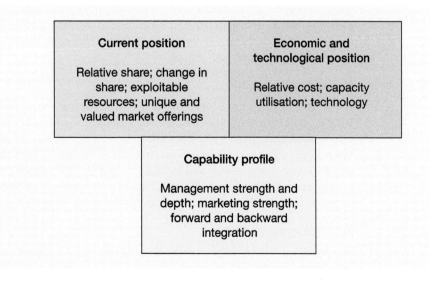

Figure 9.4
Factors affecting
business strength

Relative market share

In markets that the company already targets, market share serves two main functions. First, it acts as a barometer of how well the company is currently serving the target: a higher share will indicate better performance in serving the needs of the customers. Second, market share can, of itself, confer an advantage in further penetrating the market: high share brands, for example, typically have high levels of customer awareness and wide distribution. Share of market is a prime marketing asset that can be used to further develop the company's position.

Rate of change of market share

Absolute market share in itself can confer a strength to the company; so too can rapidly increasing share. Growing share demonstrates an ability to serve the market better than those competitors currently losing share. A company with a low but increasing share of the market can demonstrate to distributors the need for increased shelf space and availability.

Exploitable marketing resources (assets and capabilities)

Central to this text has been the identification and exploitation of the company's marketing resources. In target markets where marketing assets and capabilities have potential for further exploitation (e.g. a favourable image, brand name, distribution network, customer relationships, etc.) the company has potential strength from which to build. Identifying marketing assets and capabilities was discussed at length in Chapter 6. Of interest here is how these affect the strength of the company in serving particular market segments. What may, for example, be a strength with one target segment may be a weakness with another.

Unique and valued products and services

In potential markets where the company has superior products and services which are different in a way valued by the customers, there is potential for creating a stronger competitive position. Similarly, a competitive advantage based on low price relative to the competition is likely to be attractive to price-sensitive segments, but may actually deter segments more motivated by quality.

9.4.2 Economic and technological position

The evaluation should also address the company's relative economic and technological characteristics and resources.

Relative cost position

The company's cost structure relative to competitors was listed as a potential marketing asset in Chapter 6. Low relative production and marketing costs – through technological leadership, exploitation of linkages or experience and scale effects – give a financial edge to the company in the particular market.

Capacity utilisation

For most companies the level of capacity utilisation is a critical factor in its cost structure. Indeed, the PIMS study has shown that capacity utilisation is most crucial to small and medium-sized companies (see Buzzell and Gale, 1987). Few companies can hope to achieve 100 per cent utilisation (there will inevitably be downtime in manufacturing and slack periods for service companies), and indeed running at 'full' capacity may produce strains on both systems and structures. What is clearly important in any operation is to identify the optimum level of utilisation and seek to achieve that.

Technological position

Having an exploitable edge in technology again creates a greater strength for the company in serving a market. That may or may not be leading-edge technology. In some markets a lower technology solution to customer requirements may be more suitable than state-of-the-art applications. Again, the key is matching the technology to the customers' problems or requirements.

9.4.3 Capability profile

The third set of factors affecting competitive strength centres on the resources that can be brought to bear in the market.

Management strength and depth

A major asset, and hence potential strength, of any company is its human resources and particularly its management strength and depth. The skills and competencies of the staff working in an organisation are the tacit strengths on which it can exploit opportunities in the marketplace. In service organisations (such as consultancy companies, health services, etc.) in particular, the strength of the supplier often comes down to the individual skills of the managers who deal directly with the customers.

Marketing strength

Marketing strength stems from experience and synergy with other product areas. Companies operating primarily in consumer markets often believe they have superior marketing skills to those operating in slower moving industrial markets. They then see these markets as areas where they can use the fast-moving consumer goods skills they have learned elsewhere to good effect. Experience of transferring skills from one business sector to another, however, has not been universally successful.

Forward and backward integration

The extent of control of the supply of raw materials (backward integration) and distribution channels (forward integration) can also affect the strength or potential strength of a company in serving a specific target. Where integration is high, especially in markets where supplier and buyer power is high (see above), the firm could be in a much stronger position than its rivals.

Summary

The important point to consider when assessing company or business strength is that strength is relative to competitors also serving the segment and to the requirements of customers in the segment.

9.5 | Making market and segment choices

Conventional approaches suggest the use of portfolio matrices as a useful way of summarising the alternative business investment opportunities open to a multi-product company, and for making explicit choices between markets and segments. While such matrices have been used to assess the balance of the portfolio of businesses the company operates (see Chapter 3), the same techniques can usefully be adapted to help with the selection of market targets.

Classic portfolio techniques include the Directional Policy Matrix developed by the UK Chemical Division of Royal Dutch Shell (Robinson *et al.*, 1978) or the McKinsey/GE Business Screen (Wind and Mahajan, 1981). These are generally considered as methods for modelling existing portfolios; they are actually, in many instances, better suited to deciding

Market segment attractiveness

		Unattractive	Average	Attractive
Current and potential company strengths in serving the segment	Weak	Strongly avoid	Avoid	Possibilities
	Average	Avoid	Possibilities	Secondary targets
	Strong	Possibilities	Secondary targets	Prime targets

Figure 9.5
Target market selection

which markets to target in the first place. An adapted model is presented in Figure 9.5; this is the operational version of the conceptual model we saw in Figure 9.1 at the start of our evaluation of market targets.

Using this approach the factors deemed relevant in a particular market are identified (typically from the factors listed above) and are each assigned weights depending on their perceived importance (using hard data wherever possible). The subjective choice and weighting of the factors to be used in the analysis ensure that the model is customised to the needs of the specific company. The process of selecting and weighting the factors can, in itself, prove a valuable experience in familiarising managers with the realities of the company's markets. Where appropriate, factors can be more objectively assessed through the use of marketing research or economic analysis.

Once the factors have been determined and weighted, each potential market segment is evaluated on a scale from 'excellent = 5' to 'poor = 1' and a summary score on the two main dimensions of 'market segment attractiveness' and 'company business strength in serving that segment' computed using the weightings. Sensitivity analyses can then be conducted to gauge the impact of different assumptions on the weight to attach to individual factors and the assessments of targets on each scale.

The resulting model, such as that shown in Figure 9.6 for a hypothetical company, enables the alternatives to be assessed and discussed objectively.

Ideally, companies are looking for market targets in the bottom right-hand corner of Figure 9.6. These opportunities rarely exist and the trade-off then becomes between going into segments where the company is, or can become, strong, but that are less attractive (e.g. target opportunity 1), or alternatively tackling more attractive markets but where the company is only average in strength (target 2).

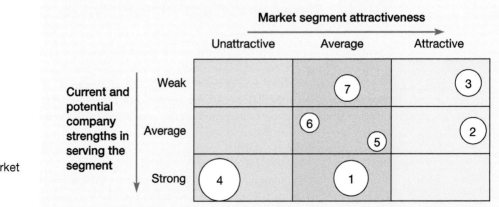

Figure 9.6
Evaluating market targets for a hypothetical company

To develop defensible positions in the marketplace the former (sticking to areas of current or potential strength) often makes the most sense. Indeed, many would argue (see Ohmae, 1982) that most companies are better advised to consolidate in apparently less attractive markets where they have considerable exploitable strengths than to 'chase the rainbows' of seemingly attractive markets where they are only average or weak players.

Where business strength is weak, investment should be avoided in average or unattractive markets (target 7), unless in very attractive market segments where some strengths could be built or bought in through merger/acquisition (e.g. target 3). Similarly, investment in unattractive segments should be avoided unless particular company strengths can lead to a profitable exploitation of the market (target 4). Market segments of medium attractiveness where the company has medium strength should be invested in selectively (targets 5 and 6).

A further factor in selecting target markets for the overall business is how those individual targets add up – i.e. the overall portfolio of businesses or markets the company is operating in (see Chapter 3). Companies are typically seeking to build a balanced portfolio of activities – balanced in terms of cash use and generation, risk and return, and focus on the future as well as on the present.

A prime example of a company using the **above** approach to selecting new market targets on a world scale is Fletcher Challenge Ltd. With assets in 1990 valued at over £6 billion, turnover of £4.11 billion and pre-tax profit of £345 million, it was New Zealand's largest and most successful company. Fletcher Challenge examines opportunities for acquisition or further investment on the basis of two sets of factors – industry attractiveness and potential business strength in serving that market. Industry or target **market attractiveness** is determined by the following key factors: Fletcher Challenge looks for markets with a steady demand growth (growing markets are easier to exit if difficulties arise); which are low in customer concentration (are not dominated by a handful of large customers); where there are substantial barriers to entry (in scale of operations, level of technology employed and control of the inputs and supporting industries); where participants are few and competitors are 'good' (up to two or three major players, in the market for the long haul); where prices are stable (absence of price wars or wild fluctuations); and where there is a steep cost (experience) curve where Fletcher Challenge's scale of operations will yield lower costs. **Company strength** in serving the targets is examined in the following main areas: Fletcher Challenge looks for markets where it is, or believes it can become, the market leader; it seeks to utilise its technological expertise to the full; looks for markets where it can achieve a cost leadership position; seeks markets where it can manage intergroup (competitor) understandings; and markets where it can keep control of the market (especially in pricing). The acquisitions and expansion strategies of Fletcher Challenge from the mid-1980s under the leadership of Stanford MBA Hugh Fletcher consistently met the above criteria. In 2001 the company was divided into a number of more targeted operations: Fletcher Challenge Forests (later renamed Tenon); Fletcher Building (incorporating Fletcher Construction), and Rubicon (New Zealand) (see **http://en.wikipedia.org/wiki/Fletcher_Challenge**).

9.6 Alternative targeting strategies

The classic approach to segmentation or targeting strategies is provided by Kotler, most recently in Kotler and Keller (2012). Kotler's model suggests that there are three broad approaches a company can take to a market, having identified and evaluated the various segments that make up the total (Figure 9.7). The company can pursue:

- **undifferentiated marketing,** essentially producing a single product designed to appeal across the board to all segments;
- **differentiated marketing,** offering a different product to each of the different segments; or
- **concentrated marketing,** focusing attention on one, or a few, segments.

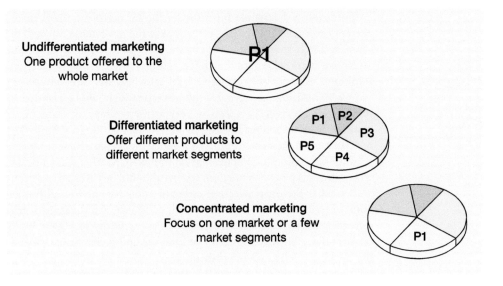

Figure 9.7
Alternative
marketing
strategies

9.6.1 Undifferentiated marketing

An undifferentiated marketing approach entails treating the market as one whole, rather than as segmented, and supplying one standard product or service to satisfy all customers. It is the approach carried out in Porter's (1980) cost leadership strategy. This approach was particularly prevalent in the mass marketing era in the days before the emergence (or recognition!) of strongly identified market segments. More recently, however, as the existence of market segments has become more widely accepted, the wisdom of such an approach in all but markets where preferences are strongly concentrated has been called into doubt.

9.6.2 Differentiated marketing

Differentiated marketing is adopted by companies seeking to offer a distinct product or service to each chosen segment of the market. Thus a shampoo manufacturer will offer different types of shampoo depending on the condition of the hair of the customer. The major danger of differentiated marketing is that it can lead to high costs, both in manufacturing and marketing a wide product line.

Depending on the company's resources, however, differentiated marketing can help in achieving overall market domination (this is the strategy pursued in the yellow fats market by Van den Bergh – see above).

9.6.3 Focused marketing

For the organisation with limited resources, however, attacking all or even most of the potential segments in a market may not be a viable proposition. In this instance concentrated or focused marketing may make more sense. Under this strategy the organisation focuses attention on one, or a few, market segments and leaves the wider market to its competitors. In this way it builds a strong position in a few selected markets, rather than attempting to compete across the board (either with undifferentiated or differentiated products).

The success of this approach depends on clear, in-depth knowledge of the customers served. The major danger of this strategy, however, is that over time the segment focused on may become less attractive and limiting on the organisation.

The Lucozade brand of soft drink was first marketed in the 1920s. It was originally developed by a Newcastle chemist as an energy drink for his son, who was recovering from jaundice. The brand was bought by Beechams in 1938 and marketed in a distinctive yellow cellophane wrapper, with the slogan 'Lucozade Aids Recovery'. During the 1950s and 1960s it was Beechams' biggest selling brand. By the 1970s, however, lower levels of sickness, less frequent flu epidemics and price increases had contributed to a decline in sales. From 1974 to 1978 sales fell by 30 per cent. The company decided that the brand needed to be repositioned.

The first repositioning was as an in-house 'pick-me-up' for housewives in the late 1970s. Sales initially increased by 11 per cent, but growth was not maintained, and by the end of 1979 sales had levelled out. In 1980 a new 250 ml bottle was launched and the new slogan 'Lucozade Replaces Lost Energy' was developed. But by 1982 a usage and attitude survey showed that the brand character had not changed significantly – it was still used primarily for illness recovery.

More radical repositioning was considered. In the carbonated soft drinks market Lucozade was competing head-on with well-established brands such as Coca-Cola and Pepsi. Lucozade also suffered from a poor image at the younger end of the market – it had been given to them by their mums when they were ill! A new positioning was developed around the theme: 'Lucozade is not only delicious and refreshing but can quickly replace lost energy.' The potential of the sports market became apparent and in July 1982 the advertising started to use Daley Thompson, an Olympic decathlete. Initially, however, the target customers liked Daley, but did not connect him with the brand.

The next phase of repositioning was the 'traffic lights' TV commercial, using Daley and the heavy metal music of Iron Maiden to 'portray' rather than 'explain' the message. The advertisements graphically conveyed the energy replacement message in a way younger users immediately identified with. In the first year of the new campaign, sales volume increased by 40 per cent. Qualitative research showed the message getting across to existing users and, crucially, to the younger target market.

Since then Lucozade has enjoyed continued success, and new flavour variants have been launched. The years 1988 saw the launch of the Lucozade Sport isotonic drink and 1995 the launch of the NRG teen drink. The same positioning strategy has been pursued successfully in Ireland, Asia and Australasia. From 1985 to 1995 worldwide sales grew from £12 million to £125 million (Salmon, 1997). In 2002, the brand was promoted through the Lara Croft/Tomb Raider association. At the time of writing Lucozade remains number one in the UK sports and energy drink market, with a share of over 40 per cent.

The most effective strategy to adopt with regard to target market selection will vary from market to market. Certain characteristics of both the market and the company, however, will serve to suggest the type of strategy that makes most sense in a given situation.

The classic statement on how to approach the segmentation strategy choice comes from Frank *et al.* (1972). They propose that the choice of strategy should be based on:

- segment size – to determine its value and prospects;
- the incremental costs faced in differentiating between segments – which may be small, or may be high enough to undermine a full segmentation strategy;
- the extent and durability of segment differences – if segments are only marginally differentiated they may not be worth taking as separate targets, and if the differences are transitory then the viability of a segmentation strategy may be questionable;
- the stability and mutual compatibility of segment targets;
- the 'fit' between segment characteristics and company strengths (see Chapter 7); and
- the level and type of competition in the prospective segment targets.

Summary

The selection of which potential market segment or segments to serve is the crucial step in developing a robust and comprehensive marketing strategy. Until the targets have been clearly identified, their requirements and motivations fully explored, it is not possible to develop a robust competitive positioning.

Case study · No-frills Ryanair faces test with Business Plus

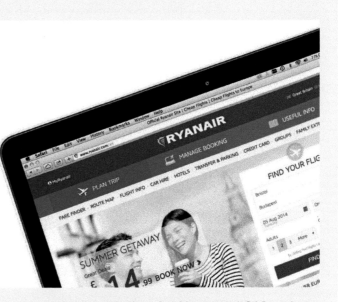

There are no flat bed seats, no free champagne and no left turn. But Ryanair still claims it is offering a business service.

On Wednesday the low-cost Irish airline unveiled Business Plus, a service designed to lure the famously bare-bones airline passengers who usually fly business class on other carriers and are used to curtain dividers, hot towels, free meals and other perks.

None of those frills will be part of the Ryanair package. Instead, according to Kenny Jacobs, the airline's chief marketing officer, what potential business class travellers want are flexible tickets, multiple same-day return flights, fast-track security, priority boarding and seats near the exits and over the wings, which have more legroom.

In other words, Business Plus will be business-class flying – Ryanair style.

'There was no demand for some of the traditional trappings of the business class product – the bad sandwiches, the bad coffee,' says Mr Jacobs. 'What [passengers] wanted us to do was to tweak the schedules to make them more business-friendly. This is a big segment for us, and we want to tailor that service to the needs of business passengers. The numbers stack up from our point of view.'

Ryanair is playing catch-up after admitting that rival easyJet has taken the lead in attracting business passengers. The Irish airline is trying to make inroads into the lucrative market as part of an overhaul to increase its appeal and soften its image for poor service and peremptory treatment of passengers.

The 'caring, cuddly, sharing' Ryanair includes offering allocated seating and mobile boarding passes, revamping its website, as well as giving families some incentives such as discounts and warming babies' bottles.

Enticing business class passengers from their cosseted ways is tough, as easyJet has found. It has lifted the proportion of business travellers it carries from 18 per cent to 20 per cent over the past few years.

Stephen Furlong, an analyst at Davy, the Dublin brokerage, says that for low-fares airlines, winning business passengers 'is a slow, incremental grind'. Moreover, some airlines are moving in the opposite direction. Aer Lingus and SAS no longer offer the full business class service on short-haul flights.

Mr Jacobs says a quarter of the 86m passengers Ryanair has carried over the past year are 'business travellers', but they are paying standard fares, which start at €19.99.

Ryanair will have to convince more of them to pay the higher fare – the cheapest Business Plus ticket will cost €69.99. That is less than the business ticket on traditional carriers, but it does not include incentives such as loyalty programmes.

'It will be tough to get business class passengers on the flag carriers to come across to Ryanair,' says David Holohan, who follows the company for Merrion Capital in Dublin. He says that if the Ryanair offering succeeds in luring more higher-paying passengers, the rewards could be significant given the gap between Business Plus and regular fares.

But he says the airline would be doing well to get 5 per cent of its passengers to pay the higher business product fare regularly.

One factor that may count against Ryanair is that it often flies to out-of-the-way airports. EasyJet has been building positions at primary airports for years; they now account for 70 per cent of its destinations. Ryanair is trying to increase its share of primary airports, and says it will move from 35 per cent to 45 per cent within two years.

But Michael O'Leary, chief executive, says Ryanair will not fly to Europe's three main business hub airports – London Heathrow, Paris Charles de Gaulle and Frankfurt. The toughest challenge then for Ryanair may be to make its business product work even if it does not serve Europe's main business airports.

Oliver Sleath, airlines analyst at Barclays, says: 'Ryanair is coming at this with a brand that will take some time to improve, and a network/frequency offering that is fundamentally less attractive, although evolving quickly.'

'Wait and see if easyJet can materially drive up their share of business passengers before assuming Ryanair will be successful.'

Mr O'Leary does not sound entirely convinced that being nice will make Ryanair more money, but he is willing to give it a try. In Dublin last week to announce new routes, he said his staff had assured him that if he kept up his efforts to be 'caring, cuddly and sharing', Ryanair would win more business passengers from Aer Lingus, its local rival.

'So I am doing my level best, and funnily enough it's working,' he said.

That boast is about to be put to the test.

Ride of private equity heavyweight Bonderman

David Bonderman, the 71-year-old chairman of Ryanair, has been an ever-present figure at the Irish low-cost airline.

The co-founder of Texas-based buyout group TPG Capital, who has chaired the company for 18 years, personally invested £1m for a 20 per cent stake in the low-cost airline in 1996, when the founding Ryan family was looking for a partner to boost the company's expansion internationally.

Airlines have always been the sweet spot of the private equity financier. The former lawyer rose to prominence in the US with the turnround of Continental Airlines in 1993, making almost 12 times his original investment.

Back in 1996, Ryanair's founders managed to get Mr Bonderman to drop a planned venture he was negotiating with Richard Branson to back their company instead, writes Siobhan Creaton in her book, 'Ryanair: How a small Irish airline conquered the world'. The financier participated in a refinancing of the company and bought a stake alongside the family and the management.

A year later, Ryanair became a public company and Mr Bonderman's stake was worth £60m. Since then the company's share price has surged from €0.4 to €7.1, bringing its market capitalisation to €9.6bn. The US financier, whose private equity firm is now seeking $10bn for a new leveraged buyout fund, has since sold down his stake to 0.55 per cent, which is worth €54m.

However, addressing the International Air Transport Association in 2006, Mr Bonderman said: 'It's time to sell, ladies and gentlemen,' he told his audience in Paris. 'This is as good as it gets in the airline industry. It's only going to get worse.'

Source: from 'No-frills Ryanair faces test with Business Plus', *Financial Times*, 27/08/14 (Boland, V. and Wild, J.).

Discussion questions

1 What is the rationale behind Ryanair's decision to compete in the business segment?

2 How attractive do you assess the business segment to be to Ryanair and why?

3 What targeting strategy is Ryanair trying to pursue? What difficulties do you anticipate Ryanair will face in following such a strategy?

PART 4

COMPETITIVE POSITIONING STRATEGIES

Part 4 looks at the main ways in which firms strive to create a competitive advantage.

Chapter 10 discusses ways of creating sustainable competitive advantage once the target market has been decided. Routes to achieving cost leadership and differentiation are examined, both as alternative and as complementary strategies. The dangers of falling between these strategies, and not executing either effectively, are also addressed. The chapter then goes on to discuss how competitive positions can be communicated effectively to customers, as well as the characteristics of sustainable competitive advantage through positioning. It concludes by examining strategies for building position, holding position, harvesting, niching and divesting.

Chapter 11, considers the new marketing mix including recent developments in e-business and e-marketing and their impact on marketing strategies. Following the early hype of the dot.com boom, and the equally spectacular dot.com bust (or dot.bomb as it is being referred to), the chapter takes a more measured view of the opportunities and threats Internet-based technologies have to offer organisations and looks at how they integrate with the more traditional elements of the marketing mix.

Chapter 12 assesses the role of innovation and new product/service development in creating competitive positions. The critical factors for success in new product development are identified, together with common reasons for failure. The processes of new product development are discussed along with suggestions for speeding up and enhancing the likelihood of success. The chapter concludes by considering organisational issues in new product development and innovation.

Chapter 13 looks at the role of service and relationship marketing in building stronger competitive positions. The goods and services spectrum is introduced to show the increasing importance of the service element in the marketing implementation mix, even for goods marketers. Relationship marketing is discussed in the context of building and maintaining long-term relationships with key customers and customer groups. Techniques for monitoring and measuring customer satisfaction are presented with particular emphasis on the use of gap analysis to track problems in customer satisfaction back to their root causes.

CHAPTER 10
CREATING SUSTAINABLE COMPETITIVE ADVANTAGE

> Competitive Strategy is the search for a favourable competitive position in an industry. Competitive Strategy aims to establish a profitable and sustainable position against the forces that determine industry competition.
>
> Michael Porter (1985)

Samsung to launch new mobile payment service in the US

Samsung Pay, the mobile payment service of Samsung Electronics, is to debut in the US on Monday, as the South Korean group looks to diversify its features to revive slowing phone sales.

The world's largest smartphone maker hopes its platform will have an edge of rival services from Apple and Google in the annual $67bn mobile payment market, as Samsung's technology is designed to work with existing credit card readers.

Samsung rolled out the payment service in its home market last month and the South Korean company said its adoption was 'beyond our expectations' with about $30m transactions in its first month.

Samsung plans to expand the service to the UK, Spain and China, and is expected to adopt the payment feature to enhance its new low-to-mid-end smartphones next year.

However, analysts remain doubtful of the prospects of Samsung Pay abroad, given the company's relatively late entry market and weaker software ecosystem. Apple is leading the field but even the US company is still struggling to turn the mobile phone into a mainstream method of payment, with

Apple phone users complaining that the service gets rejected at many merchants.

'In the US, Samsung is facing stiff competition by coming late to the mobile payments scene,' said Siyun Zeng, analyst at IHS. 'Apple Pay has established a lead in the US and Google is revamping Google Wallet to Android Pay.'

While Apple has accumulated 800m payment card accounts associated with iTunes, Ms Zeng said Samsung lacks a critical element for its payment service to gain traction. She also cautioned that Samsung Pay's co-existence with Android Pay, which was launched in the US earlier this month and works with a broader range of Android devices, could create friction as Android users could get confused by the two payment options.

Still, Samsung is hopeful its payment system will become a popular choice, given its compatibility with existing magnetic-strip card readers – Apple Pay and Android Pay require retailers to instal new equipment compatible with their near-field communication technology.

However, such advantage is poised to disappear as a new US standard requires merchants and banks to switch from a card system using magnetic strips towards chips until next month to prevent fraud.

Analysts said that the diversification of services is a meaningful step for Samsung – one that could set its Galaxy smartphones apart from rival devices in the crowded handset market, although the new service will not generate direct revenues for the company.

'Samsung's handset revenue has been declining [since] 2014; investment into software is a step for Samsung to offset [such] loss,' said Ms Zeng. 'Samsung doesn't have to rely on Samsung Pay as its core revenues [maker] but [it is] a means to tie users into the ecosystem.'

The company has been struggling to defend its market share, squeezed between premium maker Apple and lower-cost Chinese rivals such as Huawei and Xiaomi. Samsung's global market share fell from 26.2 per cent a year earlier to 21.9 per cent in the second quarter, according to research group Gartner.

Source: from 'Samsung to launch new mobile payment service in the US', *Financial Times*, 25/09/15 (Jung-a, S.).

Discussion questions

1 What issues is Samsung trying to address?

2 Why is Samsung launching Samsung Pay in the USA?

Introduction

Chapter 9 discussed the choice of target market suited to the strengths and capabilities of the firm. This chapter focuses on methods for creating a competitive advantage in that chosen target market. While few advantages are likely to last forever, some bases of advantage are more readily protected than others. A key task for the strategist is to identify those bases that offer the most potential for defensible positioning.

10.1 Using organisational resources to create sustainable competitive advantage

In Chapter 6 we assessed organisational resources. These we classed as three main types: organisational culture; marketing assets; and marketing capabilities. Any organisation will be able to create a long list of its resources, but some of these will be more useful than others in creating competitive advantage. Fortunately, research under the resource-based view of the firm suggests that there are three main characteristics of resources which, when they coincide, help create a sustainable competitive advantage (SCA): that the resource contributes to creating value for customers; that the resource is rare, or unique to the organisation; and that the resource is hard for competitors to imitate or copy (Figure 10.1) (Collis and Montgomery, 1997).

10.1.1 Contribution to creating customer value

The prime consideration of the value of any resource to an organisation lies in the answer to the question: does this resource contribute to creating value for customers that can be leveraged to create value for the organisation? Value creation may be direct, such as through the

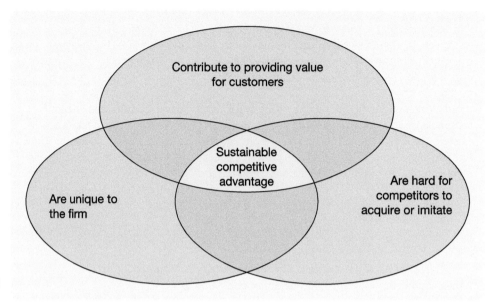

Figure 10.1
Advantage-creating
resources

benefits conveyed by superior technology, better service, meaningful brand differentiation and ready availability. The resources that contribute to these benefits (e.g. the technology deployed, skilled and motivated personnel, brand name and reputation, and distribution coverage) create value for customers directly they are employed. Other resources may, however, have an indirect impact on value for customers. Effective cost control systems, for example, are not valuable to customers in and of themselves. They only add value for customers when they translate into lower prices charged, or by the ability of the organisation to offer additional customer benefits through the cost savings achieved.

The value of a resource in creating customer value must be assessed relative to the resources of competitors (Chapter 5). For example, a strong brand name such as Nike on sports clothing may convey more value than a less well-known brand. In other words, for the resource to contribute to sustainable competitive advantage it must serve to distinguish the organisation's offerings from those of competitors.

10.1.2 Uniqueness or scarcity

Where resources do contribute to customer value their uniqueness to the organisation also needs to be assessed. Some resources, e.g. distribution outlets used, may offer little differentiation from those available to competitors. In the grocery business, for example, distribution through the major multiple grocery stores is essential for the companies such as Unilever and Procter & Gamble, but the outlets are not unique to either company and hence do not create sustainable competitive advantage for either. Those competence resources that are unique to the organisation have been termed **distinctive competencies** in contrast to **core competencies** by some commentators (e.g. Collis and Montgomery, 1997). For an advantage to be sustainable the rarity of the resources used to create it must be sustained over time.

10.1.3 Inimitability

Even resources that are unique to the organisation run the risk in the longer term of imitation or substitution by competitors (see Figure 10.2). In addition, competitors may find ways of acquiring or appropriating critical resources. In service organisations, for example, key staff may be 'poached' from a competitor with offers of enhanced salaries, better working conditions, and so on. In the advertising industry the danger of losing clients when key staff move to competing agencies has been long recognised and agreed codes of practice have been drawn up, including 'golden handcuffs' to minimise the damage caused by lost resources.

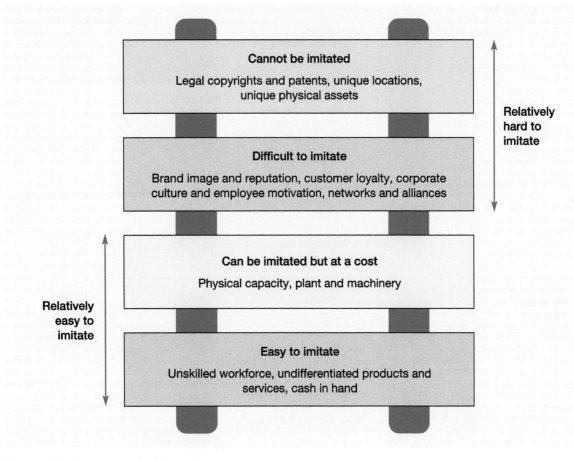

Figure 10.2 Resource imitability ladder
Source: Adapted from Collis and Montgomery (1997).

In Chapter 6 the ways of protecting resources from competitor copy, or isolating mechanisms, were discussed. These include enhancing causal ambiguity (making it hard for competitors to identify the underlying value-creating resources in the first place), building economic deterrence (making resource acquisition uneconomic), establishing legal protection (through patents and copyrights) and creating path dependency (the need to devote time and effort to the establishment and/or appropriation of resources). In the longer term, however, few resources can be effectively protected against all competitor attempts to imitate.

10.2   Generic routes to competitive advantage

As noted in Chapter 2, Porter (1980) identified two main routes to creating a competitive advantage. These he termed cost leadership and differentiation. In examining how each can be achieved Porter (1985) takes a systems approach, likening the operations of a company to a 'value chain' from the input of raw materials and other resources through to the final delivery to, and after-sales servicing of, the customer. The value chain was discussed in the context of competitor analysis in Chapter 5 and was presented in Figure 5.5.

Each of the activities within the value chain, the primary activities and the support functions, can be used to add value to the ultimate product or service. That added value, however, is typically in the form of lower cost or valued uniqueness. These options are shown in Figure 10.3.

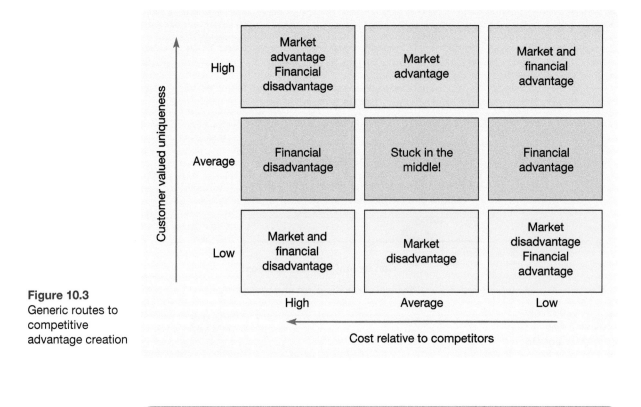

Figure 10.3
Generic routes to
competitive
advantage creation

10.3 Achieving cost leadership

Porter (1985) has identified several major factors that affect organisational costs. These he
terms 'cost drivers'; they are shown in Figure 10.4 and each is reviewed briefly below.

10.3.1 Economies of scale

Economies of scale are perhaps the single most effective cost driver in many industries. Scale
economies stem from doing things more efficiently or differently in volume. In addition,
sheer size can help in creating purchasing leverage to secure cheaper and/or better quality
(less waste) raw materials and securing them in times of limited availability.

There are, however, limits to scale economies. Size can bring with it added complexity
that itself can lead to diseconomies. For most operations there is an optimum size above or
below which inefficiencies occur.

The effects of economies of scale are often more pronounced in the manufacturing sector
than in services. While manufacturing operations such as assembly lines can benefit through
scale, the advantages to service firms such as advertising agencies are less obvious. They
may continue to lie in enhanced purchasing muscle (for the ad agency in media purchasing
for example) and spread training costs.

10.3.2 Experience and learning effects

Further cost reductions may be achieved through learning and experience effects. Learning refers to increases in efficiency that are possible at a given level of scale through an
employee's having performed the necessary tasks many times before.

The Boston Consulting Group (BCG) extended the recognised production learning
curve beyond manufacturing and looked at the increased efficiency that was possible in
all aspects of the business (e.g. in marketing, advertising and selling) through experience.

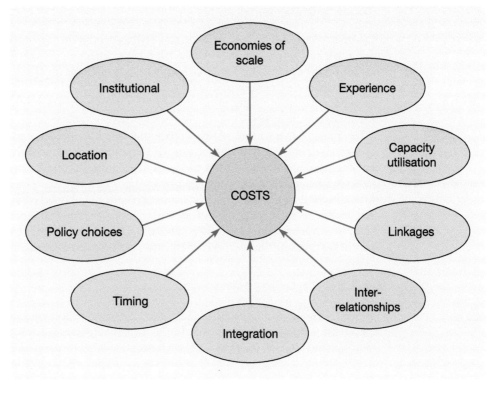

Figure 10.4
Cost drivers

BCG estimated empirically that, in many industries, costs reduced by approximately 15–20 per cent each time cumulative production (a measure of experience) doubled. This finding suggests that companies with larger market share will, by definition, have a cost advantage through experience, assuming all companies are operating on the same experience curve.

Experience can be brought into the company by hiring experienced staff, and be enhanced through training. Conversely competitors may poach experience by attracting away skilled staff.

The experience curve as an explanation of costs has come under increasing scrutiny. Gluck (1986) argued that when the world changed from a high growth 'big is beautiful' mentality to low growth 'big is bust' realisation the experience curve fell into disfavour. He concludes that in today's business environments competitive advantages that rely too heavily on economies of scale in manufacturing or distribution are often no longer sustainable. In addition, a shift in the level or type of technology employed may result in an inexperienced newcomer reducing costs to below those of a more experienced incumbent, essentially moving on to a lower experience curve. Finally, the concept was derived in manufacturing industries and it is not at all clear how far it is applicable to the service sector.

10.3.3 Capacity utilisation

Capacity utilisation has been shown to have a major impact on unit costs. The PIMS study (see Buzzell and Gale, 1987) has demonstrated a clear positive association between utilisation and return on investment. Significantly, the relationship is stronger for smaller companies than for larger ones. Major discontinuities or changes in utilisation can add significantly to costs, hence the need to plan production and inventory to minimise seasonal fluctuations. Many companies also avoid segments of the market where demand fluctuates wildly for this very reason (see Chapter 9 on factors influencing market attractiveness).

10.3.4 Linkages

A further set of cost drivers are linkages. These concern the other activities of the firm in producing and marketing the product that have an effect on the costs. Quality control and inspection procedures, for example, can have a significant impact on servicing costs and costs attributable to faulty product returns. Indeed, in many markets it has been demonstrated that superior quality, rather than leading to higher costs of production, can actually reduce costs (Peters, 1987).

External linkages with suppliers of factor inputs or distributors of the firm's final products can also result in lower costs. Just in time (JIT) manufacturing and delivery can have a significant impact on stockholding costs and work in progress. Beyond the cost equation, however, the establishment of closer working links has far wider marketing implications. For JIT to work effectively requires a very close working relationship between buyer and supplier. This often means an interchange of information, a meshing of forecasting and scheduling and the building of a long-term relationship. This in turn helps to create high switching costs (the costs of seeking supply elsewhere) and hence barriers to competitive entry.

10.3.5 Interrelationships

Interrelationships with other SBUs in the overall corporate portfolio can help to share experience and gain economies of scale in functional activities (such as marketing research, R&D, quality control, ordering and purchasing).

10.3.6 Degree of integration

Decisions on integration, e.g. contracting out delivery and/or service, also affect costs. Similarly the decision to make or buy components can have major cost implications. The extent of forward or backward integration extant or possible in a particular market was discussed as one of the factors considered in assessing target market attractiveness to the company (see Chapter 9).

10.3.7 Timing

Timing, though not always controllable, can lead to cost advantages. Often the first mover in an industry can gain cost advantages by securing prime locations, cheap or good-quality raw materials, and/or technological leadership (see Chapter 12). Second movers can often benefit from exploiting newer technology to leapfrog first mover positions.

As with other factors discussed above, however, the value of timing goes far beyond its impact on costs. Abell (1978) has argued that a crucial element of any marketing strategy is timing, that at certain times 'strategic windows' are open (i.e. there are opportunities in the market that can be exploited) while at other times they are shut. Successful strategies are timely strategies.

10.3.8 Policy choices

Policy choices, the prime areas for differentiating (discussed below), have implications for costs. Decisions on the product line, the product itself, quality levels, service, features, credit facilities, etc. all affect costs. They also affect the actual and perceived uniqueness of the product to the consumer and hence a genuine dilemma can arise if the thrust of the generic strategy is not clear. The general rules are to reduce costs on factors that will not significantly affect valued uniqueness, avoid frills if they do not serve to differentiate significantly, and invest in technology to achieve low-cost process automation and low-cost product design (fewer parts can make for easier and cheaper assembly). The policy choices pursued by Ryanair, for example, of reducing service levels and charging for all extras, enable the company to offer consistently low air fares. In 2013, following growing customer discontent, the company embarked on a customer experience improvement programme ('Always Getting Better') and introduced a business service in 2014. Nevertheless, their unrelenting commitment to lower costs and to keep fares low remains, when their competitors are putting their prices up.

10.3.9 Location and institutional factors

The final set of cost drivers identified by Porter (1985) are location (geographic location to take advantage of lower distribution, assembly, raw materials or energy costs), and institutional factors such as government regulations (e.g. larger lorries on the roads can reduce distribution costs but at other environmental and social costs). The sensitivity of governments to lobbyists and pressure groups will dictate the ability of the company to exercise institutional cost drivers.

10.3.10 Summary of cost drivers

There are many ways in which a company can seek to reduce costs. In attempting to become a cost leader in an industry a firm should be aware, first, that there can only be one cost leader and, second, that there are potentially many ways in which this position can be attacked (i.e. through using other cost drivers). Cost advantages can be among the most difficult to sustain and defend in the face of heavy and determined competition.

Cost leadership in itself does not give the customer a reason to buy unless translated into low prices in the marketplace. It is essentially an internally focused strategy based on efficiency rather than effectiveness.

That said, however, it should be a constant objective of management to reduce costs that do not significantly add to ultimate customer satisfaction.

> ## 10.4   Achieving differentiation

Most of the factors listed above as cost drivers could also be used as 'uniqueness drivers' if the firm is seeking to differentiate itself from its competitors. Of most immediate concern here, however, are the policy choices open to the company. These are summarised in Figure 10.5.

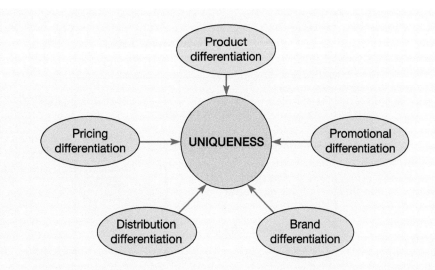

Figure 10.5
Uniqueness drivers

10.4.1 Product differentiation

Product differentiation seeks to increase the value of the product or service on offer to the customer. Levitt (1986) has suggested that products and services can be seen on at least four main levels. These are the core product, the expected product, the augmented product and the potential product. Figure 10.6 shows these levels diagrammatically. Differentiation is possible in all these respects.

At the centre of the model is the core, or generic, product. This is the central product or service offered. It is the petrol, steel, banking facility, mortgage, information, etc. Beyond the generic product, however, is what customers expect in addition, the expected product. When buying petrol, for example, customers expect easy access to the forecourt, the possibility of paying by credit card, the availability of screen wash facilities, air for tyres, radiator top-up and so on. Since most petrol forecourts meet these expectations they do not serve to differentiate one supplier from another.

At the next level Levitt identifies the augmented product. This constitutes all the extra features and services that go above and beyond what the customer expects to convey added value and hence serve to differentiate the offer from that of competitors. The petrol station where, in the self-serve 2000s, one attendant fills the car with petrol while another cleans the windscreen, headlamps and mirrors, is going beyond what is expected. Over time, however, these means of distinguishing can become copied, routine, and ultimately merely part of what is expected.

Finally, Levitt describes the potential product as all those further additional features and benefits that could be offered. At the petrol station these may include a free car wash with every fill-up, gifts unrelated to petrol and a car valeting service. While the model shows the potential product bounded, in reality it is only bounded by the imagination and ingenuity of the supplier.

Peters (1987) believes that while in the past suppliers have concentrated on attempts to differentiate their offerings on the basis of the generic and expected product, convergence is occurring at this level in many markets. As quality control, assurance and management methods become more widely understood and practised, delivering a performing, reliable, durable, conforming offer (a 'quality' product in the classic sense of the word) will no longer be

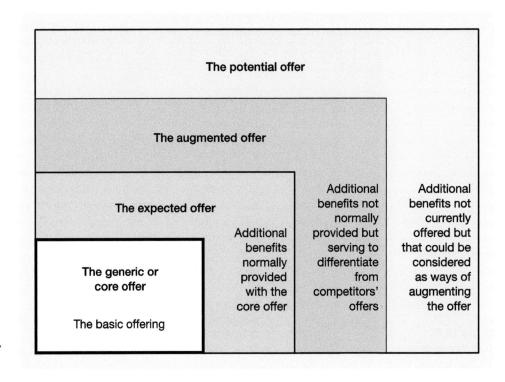

Figure 10.6
Levels of product/
service offering

adequate. In the future he predicts greater emphasis on the augmented and potential product as ways of adding value, creating customer delight and hence creating competitive advantage.

Differentiating the core and expected product

Differentiation of the core product or benefit offers a different way of satisfying the same basic want or need (see Figure 10.7). It is typically created by a step-change in technology, the application of innovation. Calculators, for example, offered a different method of solving the basic 'calculating' need from the slide rules they replaced. Similarly the deep freeze offers a different way of storing food from the earlier cold stores, pantries and cellars. A new strain of grass that only grows to 1 inch in height but never wears out could replace the need for a lawnmower.

Augmenting the product

Differentiation of the augmented product can be achieved by offering more to customers on existing features (e.g. by offering a seven-year guarantee as Kia do for their cars, rather than the more usual three-year guarantee most other manufacturers provide) or by offering new features of value to customers. There are two main types of product feature that can create customer benefit: performance features and appearance features.

Analysis of product features must relate those features to the benefits they offer to customers. For example, the introduction of the golf ball typewriter did not change the core benefit (the ability to create a typewritten page of text or numbers). It did, however, allow different typefaces and different spacing to be used, thus extending the value to the customer who wanted these extra benefits. The ink jet printer extended those benefits even further, offering virtually unlimited fonts, sizes and other effects.

In estimating the value to the consumers of additional product features and their resulting benefits, conjoint measurement (see Green and Wind, 1975) can be particularly useful. This technique has been successfully applied, for example, to decisions on product features by companies operating in the audio market and to service features offered by building societies in high-interest accounts.

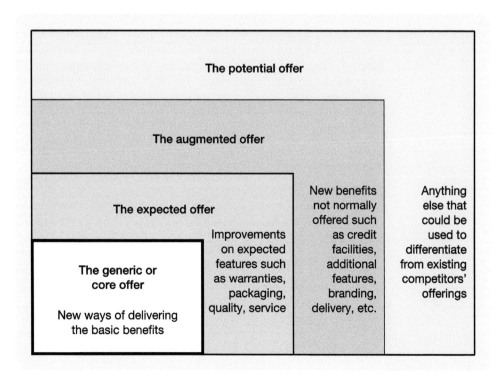

Figure 10.7
Product/service
differentiation

In the lawnmower market Flymo introduced the rotary blade hover mower as a means of differentiating from the traditional rotating cylinder blade. In some markets, especially where lawns were awkwardly shaped or steeply sloping, the ease of use of the hover mower made it a very attractive, differentiated product. In other markets, however, the market leader, Qualcast, was able to retaliate by showing the advantage of the conventional mower in having a hopper in which to catch the grass cuttings. Under the Flymo system the cuttings were left on the lawn. More recent developments have seen the introduction of rotary hover mowers with hoppers.

Quality

A prime factor in differentiating the product or service from that of competitors is quality. Quality concerns the fitness for purpose of a product or service. For manufactured products that can include the durability, appearance or grade of the product while in services it often comes down to the tangible elements of the service, the reliability and responsiveness of the service provider, the assurance provided of the value of the service and the empathy, or caring attention, received (see Parasuraman *et al.*, 1988). Quality can reflect heavily both on raw materials used and the degree of quality control exercised during manufacture and delivery.

Of central importance is consumer perception of quality, which may not be the same as the manufacturer's perception. Cardozo (1979) gives an example of where the two do not coincide:

> The marketing research department of a manufacturer of household paper goods asked for consumer evaluation of a new paper tissue. The reaction was favourable but the product was not thought to be soft enough. The R&D department then set about softening the tissue by weakening the fibres and reducing their density. In subsequent usage tests the product fell apart and was useless for its designed purpose. Further tests showed that to make the product 'feel' softer required an actual increase in the strength and density of the fibres.

Quality has been demonstrated by the PIMS project to be a major determinant of commercial success. Indeed, Buzzell and Gale (1987) concluded that relative perceived quality (customers' judgements of the quality of the supplier's offer relative to its competitors) was the single most important factor in affecting the long-run performance of a business. Quality was shown to have a greater impact on ROI level and be more effective at gaining market share than lower pricing.

Closely related to perceptions of quality are perceptions of style, particularly for products with a high emotional appeal (such as cosmetics). In fashion-conscious markets such as clothes, design can be a very powerful way of differentiating. Jain (1990) notes that Du Pont successfully rejuvenated its market for ladies' stockings by offering different coloured tints and hence repositioned the stockings as fashion accessories – a different tint for each outfit.

Packaging

Packaging too can be used to differentiate the product. Packaging has five main functions, each of which can be used as a basis for differentiation.

1 Packaging **stores** the product, and hence can be used to extend shelf life, or facilitate physical storage (e.g. Tetra Paks for fruit juice and other beverages).
2 Packaging **protects** the product during transit and prior to consumption to ensure consistent quality (e.g. the use of film packs for potato crisps to ensure freshness).
3 Packaging **facilitates use** of the product (e.g. applicator packs for floor cleaners, wine boxes, domestic liquid soap dispensers).
4 Packaging helps **create an image** for the product through its visual impact, quality of design, illustration of uses, etc.
5 Packaging helps **promote** the product through eye-catching, unusual colours and shapes, etc. Examples of the latter are the sales of wine in carafes rather than bottles (Paul Masson California Wines) and the sale of ladies' tights in egg-shaped packages (L'eggs).

Branding

A particularly effective way of differentiating at the tangible product level is to create a unique brand with a favourable image and reputation. As discussed in Chapter 6, brand and company reputation can be powerful marketing assets for a company.

Brand name or symbol is an indication of pedigree and a guarantee of what to expect from the product – a quality statement of a value-for-money signal. Heinz baked beans, for example, can command a premium price because of the assurance of quality the consumer gets in choosing the brand. Similarly, grocery retailers such as Waitrose and Sainsbury's are able to differentiate their own branded products from other brands because of their reputation for quality that extends across their product ranges. Branding is also a highly defensible competitive advantage. Once registered, competitors cannot use the same branding (name or symbol).

Service

Service can be a major differentiating factor in the purchase of many products, especially durables (both consumer and industrial). Certainly enhanced service was a major factor in the success of Wilhelm Becker, a Swedish industrial paints company. Becker developed 'Colour Studios' as a service to its customers and potential customers to enable them to experiment with different colours and combinations. Volvo, the Swedish auto manufacturer, used the service in researching alternative colours to use on farm tractors and found that red (the colour used to date) was a poor colour choice as it jarred, for many farmers, with the colours of the landscape. Changing the colour scheme resulted in increased sales.

In domestic paints, too, there has been an attempt to add service, this time provided by the customers themselves. Matchpots were introduced by a leading domestic paint supplier to allow customers, for a small outlay, to try different colours at home before selecting the final colour to use. In this case, however, unlike Becker's Colour Studios, copy by competitors was relatively easy and the advantage quickly eroded.

Service need not be an addition to the product. In some circumstances a reduction can add value. The growth in home brewing of beers and wines is a case where a less complete product (the malt extract, hops, grape juice, yeast, etc.) is put to market but the customer is able to gain satisfaction through self-completion of the production process. Thus the customer provides the service and becomes part of the production process.

Providing superior service as a way of creating a stronger link between supplier and customer can have wide-reaching consequences. In particular, it makes it less likely that the customer will look for alternative supply sources and hence acts as a barrier to competitor entry.

To ensure and enhance customer service Peters (1987) recommends that each company regularly conducts customer satisfaction studies to gauge how well it is meeting customers' expectations and to seek ways in which it can improve on customer service.

Further elements of the augmented product that can be used to differentiate the product include installation, credit availability, delivery (speedy and on time, when promised) and warranty. All can add to the differentiation of the product from that of competitors.

Deciding on the bases for product differentiation

Each of the elements of the product can be used as a way of differentiating the product from competitive offerings. In deciding which of the possible elements to use in differentiating the product three considerations are paramount.

First, what do the customers expect in addition to the core, generic product? In the automobile market, for example, customers in all market segments expect a minimum level of reliability in the cars they buy. In the purchase of consumer white goods (fridges, freezers, washing machines, etc.), minimum periods of warranty are expected. In the choice of toothpaste, minimum levels of protection from tooth decay and gum disease are required. These expectations, over and above the core product offering, are akin to 'hygiene factors' in Hertzberg's Theory of Motivation. They must be offered for the product or service to be considered by potential purchasers. Their presence does not enhance the probability of consumers choosing products with them, but their absence will certainly deter purchase.

The second consideration is what the customers would value over and above what is expected. In identifying potential 'motivators' the marketer seeks to offer more than the competition to attract purchasers. These additions to the product beyond what is normally expected by the customers often form the most effective way of differentiating the company's offerings. Crucial, however, is the cost of offering these additions. The cost of the additions should be less than the extra benefit (value) to the customers and hence be reflected in a willingness to pay a premium price. Where possible an economic value should be placed on the differentiation to allow pricing to take full account of value to the customer (see Forbis and Mehta, 1981).

The third consideration in choosing a way of differentiating the product from the competition is the ease with which that differentiation can be copied. Changes in the interest rates charged by one building society, for example, can easily be copied in a matter of days or even hours. An advantage based, however, on the location of the society's outlets in the major city high streets takes longer and is more costly to copy.

Ideally, differentiation is sought where there is some (at least temporary) barrier precluding competitors following. The most successful differentiations are those that use a core skill, competence or marketing asset of the company which competitors do not possess and will find hard to develop. In the car hire business, for example, the extensive network of pick-up and drop-off points offered by Enterprise, the market leader, enables them to offer a more convenient service to the one-way customer than the competition. Emulating that network is costly, if not impossible, for smaller followers in the market.

Peters (1987) has argued that many companies overemphasise the core product in their overall marketing thinking and strategy. He suggests that, as it becomes increasingly difficult to differentiate on the basis of core product, greater emphasis will need to be put on how to 'add service' through the augmented (and potential) product. This change in emphasis is shown in Figure 10.8, which contrasts a product focus (core product emphasis) with a service added focus (extending the augmented and potential products in ways of value and interest to the customer).

A focus away from the core product towards the 'outer rings' is particularly useful in 'commodity' markets where competitive strategy has traditionally been based on price. Differentiation through added service offers an opportunity for breaking out of an over-reliance on price in securing business.

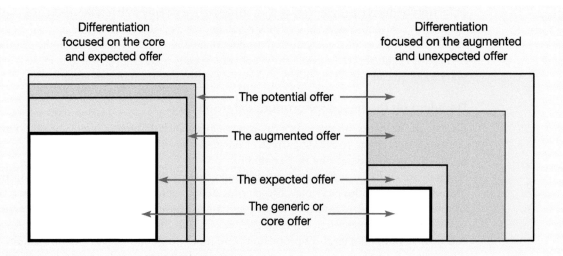

Figure 10.8 Alternative emphases for differentiation

In summary, there are a great many ways in which products and services can be differentiated from their competitors. In deciding on the type of differentiation to adopt, several factors should be borne in mind: the added value to the customer of the differentiation; the cost of differentiation in relation to the added value; the probability and speed of competitor copy; and the extent to which the differentiation exploits the marketing assets of the company.

10.4.2 Distribution differentiation

Distribution differentiation comes from using different routes to market, having a different network or a different coverage of the market.

Nespresso differentiates itself through all the elements of the marketing mix but more specifically in the way it distributes its products. It emphasises its aspirational luxury positioning with its exclusive Nespresso boutiques and concessions in top department stores, as well as its online club. This has the added advantage of allowing Nespresso full control on its customers' experience.

The growth of the Internet has made significant changes to the distribution strategies of many firms. Particularly for firms offering bit-based products such as information, or music, direct delivery to customers through their Internet connections is instant (see Chapter 11). Again, first mover advantages afforded short-term differentiation but competitor copy has been rapid. Protecting an advantage in e-marketing, be it a distribution advantage or a communications advantage, is proving particularly difficult and innovative companies such as Amazon.com are having to constantly find new ways to add value for their customers in an attempt to remain differentiated.

10.4.3 Price differentiation

Lower price as a means of differentiation can be a successful basis for strategy only where the company enjoys a cost advantage, or where there are barriers to competing firms with a lower cost structure competing at a lower price. Without a cost advantage, starting a price war can be a disastrous course to follow.

Premium pricing is generally only possible where the product or service has actual or perceived advantages to the customer and therefore it is often used in conjunction with, and to reinforce, a differentiated product.

In general, the greater the degree of product or services differentiation, the more scope there is for premium pricing. Where there is little other ground for differentiation, price competition becomes stronger and cost advantages assume greater importance.

10.4.4 Promotional differentiation

Promotional differentiation involves using different types of promotions (e.g. a wider communications mix employing advertising, public relations, direct mail, personal selling, and social media and permission marketing via e-mails), promotions of a different intensity (i.e. particularly heavy promotions during launch and relaunch of products) or different content (i.e. with a clearly different advertising message).

Many companies today make poor use of the potential of public relations. Public relations essentially consists of creating relationships with the media and using those relationships to gain positive exposure. Press releases and interviews with key executives on important topical issues can both help to promote the company in a more credible way than media advertising.

A small, UK-based electronics company brilliantly exploited a visit by Japanese scientists to its plant. The company gained wide coverage of the event, presenting it as an attempt by the Japanese to learn from this small but innovative firm. The coverage was in relevant trade journals and even the national media. The result was a major increase in enquiries to the company and increasing domestic sales of its products. The PR had two major advantages over media advertising. First, it was very cheap in relation to the exposure it achieved (the company could never have afforded to buy the exposure at normal media rates). Second, the reports appearing in the press attracted credibility because they had been written by independent journalists and were seen as 'news' rather than advertising (*source: The Marketing Mix,* television series by Yorkshire TV).

Using a different message within normal media advertising can also have a differentiating effect. When most advertisers are pursuing essentially the same market with the same message an innovative twist is called for. Most beers are promoted by showing gregarious groups of males in public houses having an enjoyable night out. Heineken managed to differentiate its beer by using a series of advertisements employing humour and the caption 'Heineken refreshes the parts other beers cannot reach'. Similarly an innovative campaign for Boddington's Bitter, emphasising the down-to-earth value of the beer and its creamy, frothy head, served to mark it out from the crowd.

When Krona was launched by Van den Bergh into the margarine market (**see** Chapter 9) it was aimed at consumers who were increasingly sensitive to the price of butter but who still required the taste of butter – and the company had a major communications problem. Legislation precluded it from stating that the product tasted like butter (Clark, 1986) and the slogan 'Four out of five people can't tell the difference between Stork and butter' had already been used (with mixed success) by one of the other company brands. The solution was to use a semi-documentary advertisement featuring a respected reporter (René Cutforth) which majored on a rumour that had circulated around a product of identical formulation in Australia (Fairy). The rumour had been that the product was actually New Zealand butter being dumped on the Australian market disguised as margarine to overcome trade quotas. The slogan selected was 'The margarine that raised questions in an Australian parliament' and the style of the advertisement, while never actually claiming taste parity with butter, cleverly conveyed the impression that people really couldn't tell the difference.

More recently Van den Bergh has promoted the margarine Flora as the spread bought by women who care about the health of their men, while their originally branded 'I Can't Believe It's Not Butter' returns to Stork's old taste appeal.

10.4.5 Brand differentiation

Brand positioning places the customer at the centre of building a maintainable hold on the marketplace. It shifts from the classic idea of companies developing a 'unique selling proposition' (USP) to establishing a 'unique emotional proposition'.

Competing products may look similar to the hapless parent buying a pair of Nike trainers, but not to their children. They want Nike trainers, and the parent is pressured to pay the extra to get them. Nike's success at brand differentiation flowed from its Air Jordan range, which built upon the USP of air cells in the heels and their unique emotional proposition of being associated with top athletes. So powerful did this combination become that even in relatively crime-free Japan people paid huge price premiums for their Air Jordans but would not jog in them for fear of being mugged (called jugging) for their Nikes. Adidas and Reebok promote their products using athletes and air in their heels, but Nike has won the battle for the minds of teenagers and their parents' pockets.

Nike is an exemplary case of gaining market strength by using Ries and Trout's (1986) ladder of awareness. Even though there may be numerous products on the market consumers are rarely able to name more than a few. This was the problem faced by Audi when they realised that people mentioned Mercedes, BMW and Volkswagen as German cars, with all the connotations of quality and reliability that entails, but often omitted Audi (now owned by VW). The result was the 'Vorsprung Durch Technik' campaign which concentrated on the German pedigree of the product and, through rallying and the Quatro, on their technical excellence.

Source: Alamy Images: Niall McDiarmid.

Ries and Trout noted that the second firm in markets usually enjoys half the business of the first firm, and the third firm enjoys half the business of the second, etc. This flows through into profitability and return on investments where, in the long term, profitability follows the market share ranking of companies. Leading companies can also achieve major economies in advertising and promotion (Saunders, 1990). Part of the reason for this is the tendency for people to remember the number 1. When asked who was the first person to successfully fly alone across the Atlantic most people would correctly answer Charles Lindbergh, but how many people can name the second person? Similarly with the first and second people to set foot on the moon, or climb Mount Everest.

The importance of being number 1 is fine for market leaders such as Nike in sports shoes, Mercedes in luxury cars, Coca-Cola in soft drinks and Nescafé in coffee, but it leaves lesser brands with an unresolved problem. Positioning points to a way of these brands establishing a strong place in the mind of the consumer despite the incessant call for attention from competing products. This involves consistency of message and the association of a brand with ideas that are already held strongly within the consumer's mind.

10.4.6 Summary of differentiation drivers

Where the route to competitive advantage selected is differentiation the key differentiating variables, those that offer the most leverage for differentiation using the company's skills to the full, should be identified. Where possible, differentiation should be pursued on multiple fronts for its enhancement. In addition, value signals should be employed to enhance perceived differentiation (e.g. building on reputation, image, presence, appearance and pricing of the product). Barriers to copying should be erected, through patenting, holding key executives and creating switching costs to retain customers.

10.5   Sustaining competitive advantage

It will be clear from the above that there are a variety of ways companies can attempt to create a competitive advantage for themselves. Some of these will be easier for competitors to copy than others. The most useful ways of creating defensible positions lie in exploiting the following.

10.5.1 Unique and valued products

Fundamental to creating a superior and defensible position in the marketplace is to have unique and valued products and services crafted through the use of scarce and valuable organisational resources to offer to customers.

Dow Jones maintains high margins from unique products. *The Wall Street Journal* is a product that customers want and are willing to pay for. Central to offering unique and valued products and services is the identification of the key differentiating variables – those with the greatest potential leverage.

Uniqueness may stem from employing superior, proprietary technology, utilising superior raw materials, or from differentiating the tangible and augmented elements of the product.

Unique products do not, however, stay unique forever. Successful products will be imitated sooner or later so that the company which wishes to retain its unique position must be willing, and indeed even eager, to innovate continually and look for new ways of differentiating (see Chapter 12). This may mean a willingness to cannibalise its own existing products before the competition attacks them.

10.5.2 Clear, tight definition of market targets

To enable a company to keep its products and services both unique and valued by the customers requires constant monitoring of, and dialogue with, those customers. This in turn requires a clear understanding of who they are and how to access them. The clearer the focus of the firm's activities on one or a few market targets, the more likely it is to serve those targets successfully. In the increasingly segmented and fragmented markets of the 2010s the companies that fail to focus their activities are less likely to respond to changing opportunities and threats.

10.5.3 Enhanced customer linkages

Creating closer bonds with customers through enhanced service can help establish a more defensible position in the market (see Chapter 13). As suggested above, a major advantage of JIT manufacturing systems is that they require closer links between supplier and buyer. As buyers and suppliers become more enmeshed, so it becomes more difficult for newcomers to enter.

Creating switching costs, the costs associated with moving from one supplier to another, is a further way in which customer linkages can be enhanced. Loomis, writing in *Fortune* (1984, April 30), pointed to the success of Nalco in using its specialist expertise in the chemicals it markets to counsel and problem solve for its customers. This enhancement of the linkages with its customers makes it less likely they will shop around for other sources of supply.

10.5.4 Established brand and company credibility

Brand and company reputation are among the most defensible assets the company has, provided they are managed well and protected.

> Worthington Steel in the US have an enviable reputation for superior quality workmanship. The company also has a high reputation for customer service. Combined they make it hard for customers to go elsewhere.
> *(Peters, 1987)*

The rate of technological and market change is now so fast, and products so transient, that customers find security and continuity in the least tangible of a company's assets: the reputation of its brands and company name. Brand, styles and products change year on year, but people the world over desire Nike, Sony, Mercedes, Levi's and Rolex. They 'buy the maker', not the product (Sorrell, 1989).

10.6   Offensive and defensive competitive strategies

Successful competitive strategy amounts to combining attacking and defensive moves to build a stronger position in the chosen marketplace. A number of writers, most notably Kotler and Singh (1981), James (1984) and Ries and Trout (1986), have drawn an analogy between military warfare and competitive battles in the marketplace. Their basic contention is that lessons for the conduct of business strategy can be learned by a study of warfare and the principles developed by military strategists. Indeed, the bookshelves of corporate strategists around the world now often contain the works of Sun Tzu (Trai, 1991; Khoo, 1992) and von Clausewitz (1908).

Similarly, much can be learned from the approaches used in competitive sports, pastimes and team games, where brains as well as (or instead of) brawn are important for success. Successful sportsmen and women, such as Olympian rower Sir Steve Redgrave and coach Sir Clive Woodward, have made successful second careers through speaking about strategy and motivation at corporate development seminars.

There are five basic competitive strategies pursued by organisations. These include build (or growth) strategies, hold (or maintenance) strategies, niche (or focus) strategies, harvest (or reaping) strategies and deletion (divestment) strategies. The structure of the discussion draws from both Kotler (1997) and James (1984).

10.6.1 Build strategies

A build strategy seeks to improve on organisational performance through expansion of activities. This expansion may come through expanding the market for the organisation's offerings or through winning market share from competitors.

Build strategies are most suited to growth markets. In such markets it is generally considered easier to expand, as this need not be at the expense of the competition and does not necessarily provoke strong competitive retaliation. During the growth phase of markets companies should aim to grow at least as fast as the market itself.

Build strategies can also make sense in non-growth markets where there are exploitable competitor weaknesses or where there are marketing assets that can be usefully deployed.

Build strategies are often costly, particularly where they involve a direct confrontation with a major competitor. Before embarking on such strategies the potential costs must be weighed against the expected gains.

Market expansion

Build strategies are achieved through market expansion or taking sales and customers from competitors (confrontation). Market expansion, in turn, comes through three main routes: **new users** (attracted as products progress through their life cycles from innovators to laggards via a trickle-down effect), **new uses** (introduced to existing or new users), and/or **increased frequency of use** (by encouraging existing users to use more of the product).

For products that have reached the mature phase of the life cycle a major task is to find new markets for the product. This could involve geographic expansion of the companies' activities domestically and/or internationally. Companies seeking growth but believing their established market to be incapable of providing it roll out into new markets.

Market share gain through competitor confrontation

When a build objective is pursued in a market that cannot, for one reason or another, be expanded, success must, by definition, be at the expense of competitors. This will inevitably lead to some degree of confrontation between the protagonists for customers. Kotler and Singh (1981) have identified five main confrontation strategies (see Figure 10.9).

Frontal attack

The frontal attack is characterised by an all-out attack on the opponent's territory. It is often countered by a fortification, or position, defence (see below). The outcome of the confrontation will depend on strength and endurance (see Figure 10.10).

The requirement of a similar 3 to 1 advantage to ensure success in a commercial frontal attack has been suggested (Kotler and Singh, 1981), further calibrated (Cook, 1983) and questioned (Chattopadhyay *et al.*, 1985). All agree, however, that to defeat a well-entrenched competitor who has built a solid market position requires substantial superiority in at least one key area of the marketing programme. For a frontal attack to succeed requires sufficient resources, a strength advantage over the competitors being attacked, and that losses can be both predicted and sustained.

Flanking attack

In contrast to the frontal attack, the flanking attack seeks to concentrate the aggressor's strengths against the competitor's weaknesses (see Figure 10.11).

A flanking attack is achieved either through attacking geographic regions where the defender is under-represented or through attacking underserved competitor segments. The principle is to direct the attack at competitors' weaknesses, not their strengths.

Segmental flanking involves serving distinct segments that have not been adequately served by existing companies. Crucial to a successful flanking strategy can be timing. The Japanese entry into the US sub-compact car market was timed to take advantage of the economic recession and concerns over energy supply. The strategy requires the identification of competitor weaknesses, and inability or unwillingness to serve particular sectors of the market. In turn, identification of market gaps often requires a fresh look at the market and a more creative approach to segmenting it.

- Frontal attack
- Flanking attack
- Encirclement attack
- Bypass strategy
- Guerrilla tactics

Figure 10.9
Market challenger
strategies

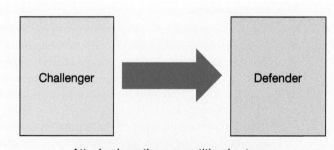

Attack where the competition is strong
and rely on outweighing them for victory

Figure 10.10
Frontal attack

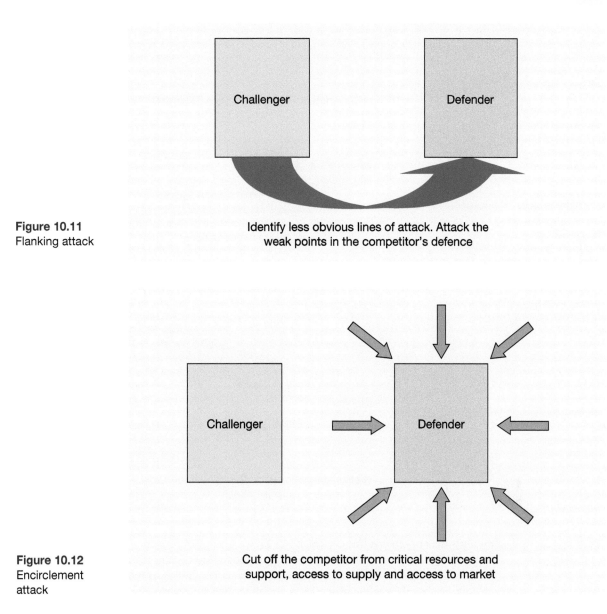

Figure 10.11
Flanking attack

Identify less obvious lines of attack. Attack the
weak points in the competitor's defence

Figure 10.12
Encirclement
attack

Cut off the competitor from critical resources and
support, access to supply and access to market

Encirclement attack

The encirclement attack, or siege, consists of enveloping the enemy, cutting them off from routes of supply to force capitulation (see Figure 10.12).

There are two approaches to the encirclement attack. The first is to attempt to isolate the competitor from the supply of raw materials on which they depend and/or the customers they seek to serve. The second approach is to seek to offer an all-round better product or service than the competitor.

Bypass strategy

The bypass strategy is characterised by changing the battleground to avoid competitor strongholds (see Figure 10.13).

Bypass is often achieved through technological leapfrogging.

Guerrilla tactics

Where conventional attacks fail or are not feasible guerrilla tactics may be employed. In chess a player in an apparently hopeless situation may sacrifice a piece unexpectedly if it

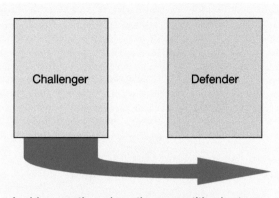

Figure 10.13
Bypass strategy

Avoid competing where the competition is strong.
Go around to new positions

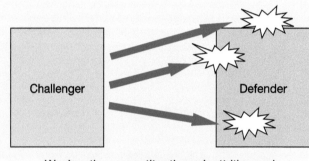

Figure 10.14
Guerrilla tactics

Weaken the competitor through attrition and
surprise attacks

disrupts the opponent's line of attack (see Figure 10.14). In boxing it has been known for a contender on the ropes to bite the ear of his opponent to disrupt the onslaught!

Unconventional or guerrilla tactics in business are employed primarily as 'spoiling' activities to weaken the competition. They are often used by a weaker attacker on a stronger defender. Selective price cuts, especially during a competitor's new product testing or launch, depositioning advertising (as attempted by the Butter Information Council Ltd in its campaign against Krona margarine), alliances, executive raids and legal manoeuvres can all be used in this regard. Guerrilla tactics are used by companies of all sizes in attempts to soften up their competitors, often before moving in for the kill. Their effectiveness lies in the difficulty the attacked has in adequately defending against the tactics due to their unpredictability.

10.6.2 Holding and defensive strategies

In contrast to build strategies, firms already in strong positions in their markets may pursue essentially defensive strategies to enable them to hold the ground they have already won.

For market leaders, for example, especially those operating in mature or declining markets, the major objective may not be to build but to maintain the current position against potential attackers. It could also be that, even in growing markets, the potential rewards judged to be possible from a build strategy are outweighed by the expected costs due, for example, to the strength and nature of competition (Treacy and Wiersema, 1995).

A hold strategy may be particularly suitable for a business or product group designated as a cash generator for the company, where that cash is needed for investment elsewhere.

Market maintenance

The amount and type of effort required to hold position will vary depending on the degree and nature of competition encountered. When the business dominates its market it may have cost advantages through economies of scale or experience effects that can be used as a basis for defending through selective price cutting. Alternatively, barriers to entry can be erected by the guarding of technological expertise, where possible, and the retention of key executive skills.

Defensive strategies

While in some markets competitor aggression may be low, making a holding strategy relatively easy to execute, in most, especially where the potential gains for an aggressor are high, more constructive defensive strategies must be explicitly pursued. Kotler and Singh (1981) suggest six basic holding strategies (see Figure 10.15).

Fortification strategies and position defence

Market fortification involves erecting barriers around the company and its market offerings to shut out competition (see Figure 10.16).

In business a position defence is created through erecting barriers to copy and/or entry. This is most effectively achieved through differentiating the company's offerings from those

- Position defence
- Flanking defence
- Pre-emptive strike
- Counter-offensive
- Mobile defence
- Contraction defence

Figure 10.15
Defensive
strategies

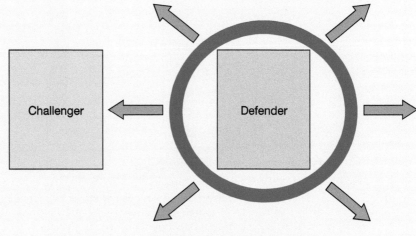

Figure 10.16
Position defence

Plug the gaps and fill the holes

of competitors and potential competitors. Where differentiation can be created on non-copyable grounds (e.g. by using the company's distinctive skills, competencies and marketing assets) that are of value to the customers, aggressors will find it more difficult to overrun the position defended.

For established market leaders, brand name and reputation are often used as the principal way of holding position. In addition, maintaining higher quality, better delivery and service, better (more appealing or heavier) promotions or lower prices based on a cost advantage can all be used to fortify the position held against a frontal attack.

A fortification defence may also involve plugging the gaps in provision to shut out competitor attacks.

Flanking defence

The flanking defence is a suitable rejoinder to a flanking attack. Under the attack strategy (see above), the aggressor seeks to concentrate strength against the weaknesses of the defender, often using the element of surprise to gain the upper hand (see Figure 10.17).

A flanking defence requires the company to strengthen the flanks, without providing a weaker and more vulnerable target elsewhere. It requires the prediction of competitor strategy and likely strike positions. In food marketing, for example, several leading manufacturers of branded goods, seeing the increasing threat posed by retailer own-label and generic brands, have entered into contracts to provide own-label products themselves rather than let their competitors get into their markets.

The major concerns in adopting a flanking strategy are, first, whether the new positions adopted for defensive reasons significantly weaken the main, core positions. In the case of retailer own labels, for example, actively cooperating could increase the trend towards own label and lead to the eventual death of the brand. As a consequence many leading brand manufacturers will not supply own label and rely on the strength of their brands to see off competition (effectively a position, or fortification, defence).

The second concern is whether the new position is actually tenable. Where it is not based on corporate strengths or marketing assets it may be less defensible than the previously held positions.

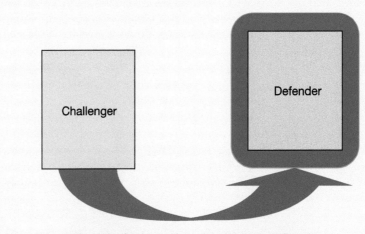

Figure 10.17
Flanking defence

Defend the flanks against attack by extending the
defences to cover peripheral weaknesses

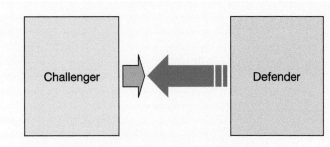

Figure 10.18
Pre-emptive strike

Attack the competition before they attack you

Pre-emptive defence

A pre-emptive defence involves striking at the potential aggressor before they can mount their attack (see Figure 10.18).

The pre-emptive defensive can involve an actual attack on the competition (as occurs in the disruption of competitor test marketing activity) or merely signal an intention to fight on a particular front and a willingness to commit the necessary resources to defend against aggression.

Sun Tzu (Khoo, 1992) summed up the philosophy behind the pre-emptive defence: 'The supreme art of war is to subdue the enemy without fighting.' Unfortunately it is not always possible to deter aggression. The second-best option is to strike back quickly before the attack gains momentum, through a counter-offensive.

Counter-offensive

Where deterrence of a potential attack before it occurs may be the ideal defence, a rapid counter-attack to 'stifle at birth' the aggression can be equally effective. The essence of a counter-offensive is to identify the aggressor's vulnerable spots and to strike hard.

When Xerox attempted to break into the mainframe computer market head-on against the established market leader, IBM launched a classic counter-offensive in Xerox's bread-and-butter business (copiers). The middle-range copiers were the major cash generators of Xerox operations and were, indeed, creating the funds to allow Xerox to attack in the mainframe computer market. The IBM counter was a limited range of low-priced copiers directly competing with Xerox's middle-range products, with leasing options that were particularly attractive to smaller customers. The counter-offensive had the effect of causing Xerox to abandon the attack on the computer market (it sold its interests to Honeywell) to concentrate on defending its copiers (James, 1984).

The counter-offensive defence is most effective where the aggressor is vulnerable through overstretching resources. The result is a weak underbelly that can be exploited for defensive purposes.

Mobile defence

The mobile defence was much in vogue as a military strategy in the 1980s and 1990s. It involves creating a 'flexible response capability' to enable the defender to shift the ground that is being defended in response to environmental or competitive threats and opportunities (see Figure 10.19).

A mobile defence is achieved through a willingness to update and improve the company's offerings to the marketplace continuously. Much of the success of Persil in the UK soap powder market has been due to the constant attempts to keep the product in line with changing customer requirements. The brand, a market leader for nearly half a century, has gone through many reformulations as washing habits have changed and evolved.

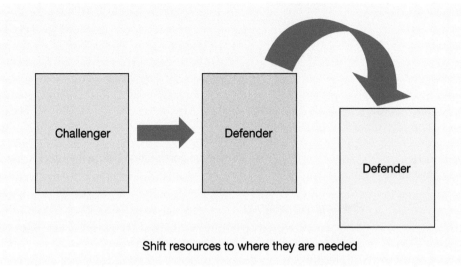

Figure 10.19
Mobile defence

Shift resources to where they are needed

Reformulations for top-loading washing machines, front loaders, automatics and more recently colder washes, have ensured that the brand has stayed well placed compared with its rivals.

Interestingly, however, Persil went too far twice in recent years: first, when it was modified to a 'biological' formula. Most other washing powders had taken this route to improve the washing ability of the powder. For a substantial segment of the population, however, a biological product was a disadvantage (these powders can cause skin irritation to some sensitive skins). The customer outcry resulted in an 'Original Persil' being reintroduced. A few years later Persil came back again with the even more disastrous Persil Power with its magnesium accelerator. Initially Unilever denied its competitor Procter & Gamble's claim that Persil Power damaged clothes in many washing conditions. However, within months 'Original Persil' was back again.

The mobile defence is an essential strategic weapon in markets where technology and/or customer wants and needs are changing rapidly. Failure to move with these changes can result in opening the company to a flanking or bypass attack.

Contraction defence

A contraction defence, or strategic withdrawal, requires giving up untenable ground to reduce overstretching and allow concentration on the core business that can be defended against attack (see Figure 10.20).

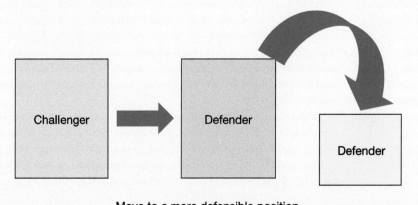

Figure 10.20
Contraction (focus)
defence

Move to a more defensible position

For example, in response to both competitive pressures and an adverse economic environment, Tunnel Cement rationalised its operations. Capacity was halved and the workforce substantially reduced. Operations were then concentrated in two core activities where the company had specialised and defensible capabilities: chemicals and waste disposal.

Strategic withdrawal is usually necessary where the company has diversified too far away from the core skills and distinctive competencies that gave it a competitive edge.

10.6.3 Market niche strategies

Market niche strategies, focusing on a limited sector of the total market, make particular sense for small and medium-sized companies operating in markets that are dominated by larger operators. The strategies are especially suitable where there are distinct, profitable, but underserved pockets within the total market, and where the company has an existing, or can create a new, differential advantage in serving that pocket.

The two main aspects to the niche strategy are, first, choosing the pockets, segments or markets on which to concentrate and, second, focusing effort exclusively on serving those targets (see Figure 10.21).

Choosing the niche

An important characteristic of the successful nicher is an ability to segment the market creatively to identify new and potential niches not yet exploited by major competitors. The battleground, or niches on which to concentrate, should be chosen by consideration of both market (or niche) attractiveness and current or potential strength of the company in serving that market.

For the nicher the second of these two considerations is often more important than the first. The major automobile manufacturers, for example, have concentrated their attentions on the large-scale segments of the car market in attempts to keep costs down, through volume production of standardised parts and components and assembly-line economies of scale.

This has left many smaller, customised segments of the market open to nichers where the major manufacturers are not prepared to compete. In terms of the overall car market these segments (such as for small sports cars) would be rated as relatively unattractive, but to a small operator such as Morgan Cars, with modest growth and return objectives, they offer an ideal niche where its skills can be exploited to the full. The Morgan order book is full, there is a high level of job security and a high degree of job satisfaction in manufacturing a high-quality, hand-crafted car.

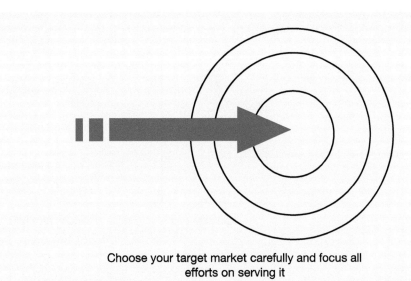

Choose your target market carefully and focus all
efforts on serving it

Figure 10.21
Niche strategies

Focusing effort

The essence of the niche strategy is to focus activity on the selected targets and not allow the company blindly to pursue any potential customer. Pursuing a niche strategy requires discipline to concentrate effort on the selected targets.

Hammermesh *et al.* (1978) examined a number of companies that had successfully adopted a niche strategy and concluded that they showed three main characteristics:

1 **An ability to segment the market** creatively, focusing their activities only in areas where they had particular strengths that were especially valued. In the metal container industry (which faces competition from glass, aluminium, fibrefoil and plastic containers) Crown Cork and Seal has focused on two segments: metal cans for hard-to-hold products such as beer and soft drinks, and aerosol cans. In both these segments the company has built considerable marketing assets through its specialised use of technology and its superior customer service.

2 **Efficient use of R&D resources.** Where R&D resources are necessarily more limited than among major competitors they should be used where they can be most effective. This often means concentrating not on pioneering work but on improvements to existing technologies that are seen to provide more immediate customer benefits.

3 **Thinking small.** Adopting a 'small is beautiful' approach to business increases the emphasis on operating more efficiently rather than chasing growth at all costs. Concentration of effort on the markets the company has chosen to compete in leads to specialisation and a stronger, more defensible position.

Nearly four decades on, these three guidelines for nichers remain as relevant as they have ever been.

10.6.4 Harvesting strategies

Building, holding and niche strategies are all applicable to the products and services of the company that offer some future potential either for growth or revenue generation.

At some stage in the life of most products and services it can become clear that there is no long-term future for them. This may be because of major changes in customer requirements, with which the offering as currently designed cannot keep pace, or it may be due to technological changes that are making the offer obsolete. In these circumstances a harvesting (or 'milking') strategy may be pursued to obtain maximum returns from the product before its eventual death or withdrawal from the market (see Figure 10.22).

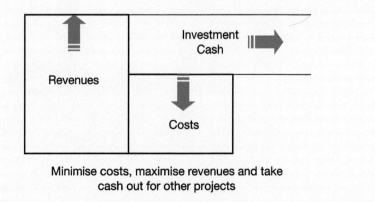

Figure 10.22 Harvesting strategies

Minimise costs, maximise revenues and take cash out for other projects

Kotler (1997) defines harvesting as:

a strategic management decision to reduce the investment in a business entity in the hope of cutting costs and/or improving cash flow. The company anticipates sales volume and/or market share declines but hopes that the lost revenue will be more than offset by lowered costs. Management sees sales falling eventually to a core level of demand. The business will be divested if money cannot be made at this core level of demand or if the company's resources can produce a higher yield by being shifted elsewhere.

Candidate businesses or individual products for harvesting may be those that are losing money despite managerial and financial resources being invested in them, or they may be those which are about to be made obsolete due to company or competitor innovation.

Implementing a harvesting strategy calls for a reduction in marketing support to a minimum, to cut expenditure on advertising, sales support and further R&D. There will typically be a rationalisation of the product line to reduce production and other direct costs. In addition, prices may be increased somewhat to improve margins while anticipating a reduction in volume.

10.6.5 Divestment/deletion

Where the company decides that a policy of harvesting is not possible, for example when, despite every effort, the business or product continues to lose money, attention may turn to divestment, or deletion from the corporate portfolio (see Figure 10.23).

Divestment – the decision to get out of a particular market or business – is never taken lightly by a company. It is crucial when considering a particular business or product for deletion to question the role of the business in the company's overall portfolio.

One company, operating both in consumer and industrial markets, examined its business portfolio and found that its industrial operations were at best breaking even, depending on how costs were allocated. Further analysis, however, showed that the industrial operation was a crucial spur to technological developments within the company that were exploited in the consumer markets in which it operated. The greater immediate technical demands of the company's industrial customers acted as the impetus for the R&D department to improve on the basic technologies used by the company. These had fed through to the consumer side of the business and resulted in the current strength in those markets. Without the industrial operations it is doubtful whether the company would have been so successful in its consumer markets. Clearly, in this case, the industrial operations had a non-economic role to play and divestment on economic grounds could have been disastrous.

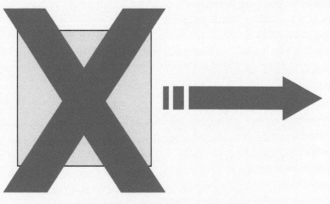

Figure 10.23
Divestment
strategies

Minimise costs and get out quick!

Once a divestment decision has been taken, and all the ramifications on the company's other businesses have been carefully assessed, implementation involves getting out as quickly and cheaply as possible.

10.6.6 Matching managerial skills to strategic tasks

The **above** alternative strategies require quite different managerial skills to bring them to fruition. It should be apparent that a manager well suited to building a stronger position for a new product is likely to have different strengths from those of a manager suited to harvesting an ageing product. Wissema *et al.* (1980) have suggested the following types of manager for each of the jobs outlined above.

Pioneers and conquerors for build strategies

The pioneer is particularly suited to the truly innovative new product that is attempting to revolutionise the markets in which it operates. A pioneer is a divergent thinker who is flexible, creative and probably hyperactive. Many entrepreneurs, such as Jeff Bezos at Amazon.com and James Dyson of vacuum cleaner fame, would fall into this category.

A conqueror, on the other hand, would be most suited to building in an established market. The conqueror's main characteristics are a creative but structured approach, someone who is a systematic team builder who can develop a coherent and rational strategy in the face of potentially stiff competition.

Administrators to hold position

The administrator is stable, good at routine work, probably an introverted conformist. These traits are particularly suited to holding/maintaining position. The administrator keeps a steady hand on the helm.

Focused creators to niche

This manager is in many ways similar to the conqueror but in need, especially initially, of more creative flair in identifying the area for focus. Once that area has been defined, however, a highly focused approach is necessary at the expense of all other distractions.

Economisers for divestment

The diplomatic negotiator (receiver, or hatchet man!) is required to divest the company of unprofitable businesses, often in the face of internal opposition.

Summary

While two basic approaches to creating a competitive position have been discussed it should be clear that the first priority in marketing will be to decide on the focus of operations: industry-wide or specific target market segments. Creating a competitive advantage in the selected area of focus can be achieved through either cost leadership or differentiation. To build a strong, defensible position in the market the initial concern should be to differentiate the company's offerings from those of its competitors on some basis of value to the customer. The second concern should then be to achieve this at the lowest possible delivered cost.

A variety of strategies might be pursued once the overall objectives have been set. The strategies can be summarised under five main types: build; hold; harvest; niche; divest. To implement each type of strategy different managerial skills are required. An important task of senior management is to ensure that the managers assigned to each task have the necessary skills and characteristics.

Case study   Volvo's heart will 'remain in Sweden'

Volvo's safe, trusted cars – a mainstay of affluent suburban enclaves in the US and Europe – have been called many things.

However, the Swedish brand has rarely been compared with a predator of the forest – at least until now.

Li Shufu, the colourful chairman of Chinese car maker Geely, Volvo's new owner, on Sunday likened Volvo to a tiger penned in a zoo that needed to be let loose to run free in the broader world. 'I think we need to liberate this tiger,' Mr Li declared.

At a ceremony in Volvo's hometown of Gothenburg, Mr Li's company signed a deal to buy Volvo for $1.8bn from Ford Motor, marking the US carmaker's last disposal of an overseas brand and China's first purchase of a premium western car marque.

Mr Li told reporters that the Volvo tiger's 'heart' would remain in Sweden, where it has two plants, and in Belgium, where it has one.

Geely's boss vowed to keep Volvo's manufacturing footprint in Europe, but said that the tiger's 'power should be projected across the world,' giving new life to its operations in mature markets.

Volvo sits in the 'near-luxury' or 'only-just-upscale' part of the car market, alongside rival Swedish brand Saab and Fiat's loss-making Alfa Romeo – a subsection of the premium market under attack from luxury leaders BMW, Mercedes-Benz, and Audi since the car industry's crisis began in 2008.

The German brands' superior sales and higher prices have allowed them to outspend Volvo on research and development, and ride out the crisis in fitter shape.

Volvo's signature contribution to car industry history is the three-point seatbelt, which it claims has saved more than 1m lives since it pioneered it in 1959, prompting other car makers to follow suit.

The Swedish brand celebrated the belt's 50th birthday last year – a fitting event for a car maker

Source: Alamy Images: Oleksiy Maksymenko Photography.

with a solid reputation for safety, but a dull and worthy image among some consumers and an urgent need to raise its game.

The brand is still seen as an industry leader in safety technology, though rival German brands and Toyota's Lexus have recently matched or outdone it in pioneering some safety features.

However, Volvo's reputation for building safe cars could help its business in China as safety becomes an increasing priority in the world's largest car market.

In design, Volvo is moving away from making boxy, square cars into more edgily fashioned, smaller and alternative fuel models – an area where Geely, which is developing electric cars, can help it.

Source: from 'Volvo's heart will "remain in Sweden"', *Financial Times*, 29/03/10 (Reed, J.).

Discussion questions

1 How has Volvo achieved differentiation over the years?

2 Why did Geely acquire Volvo?

3 Suggest strategies for Volvo to build upon its unique strengths.

CHAPTER 11

COMPETING THROUGH THE NEW MARKETING MIX

[An executive is] a mixer of ingredients, who sometimes follows a recipe as he goes along, sometimes adapts a recipe to the ingredients immediately available, and sometimes experiments with or invents ingredients no one else has tried.

(Culliton, 1948)

When building a marketing program to fit the needs of his firm, the marketing manager has to weigh the behavioural forces and then juggle marketing elements in his mix with a keen eye on the resources with which he has to work.

(Borden, 1964)

Black Friday breaks records at John Lewis

The lure of Black Friday bargains lifted weekly sales at John Lewis to the highest levels ever recorded in its 150-year history, with one tablet computer being sold every second as consumers sought pre-Christmas bargains.

Sales data released by the retailer on Tuesday recorded sales of £179m last week, an increase of nearly 22 per cent on Black Friday last year, and surpassing the previous weekly record of £164m set in the week before Christmas last year.

The employee-owned partnership matched prices on electricals, accessories and fashion ranges offered by high street rivals who embraced the US tradition of holding a flash sale on the Friday after Thanksgiving. This is known as Black Friday in America as it is traditionally the day when retailer's accounts go 'into the black' as they recoup the cost of buying Christmas stock.

John Lewis saw sales of electrical goods rise by nearly 41 per cent last week, saying that on

Black Friday, it had sold one Samsung TV every minute and one De'Longhi coffee machine every three and a half minutes as it matched the prices of its rivals.

Weekly online sales rose more than 42 per cent year-on-year. The John Lewis website saw a 300 per cent increase in traffic in the early hours of Friday morning, and between the hours of midnight and 8am, 70 per cent of this came via smartphones and tablets. More than 13,000 online orders were placed between 8am and 9am on Friday, and on the following Saturday there was an 87 per cent rise in the number of online parcels processed in its distribution centres.

'The year-on-year gain was all the more impressive given that John Lewis had also taken Black Friday very seriously in 2013,' said Howard Archer, chief economist at IHS Global Insight. 'The spectacular John Lewis performance highlights just how keen consumers have been to take advantage of Black Friday bargains . . . [the desire] has undoubtedly been heightened for many people by the extended squeeze on purchasing power coming from prolonged low earnings growth.'

The retailer said that its stores in London's Oxford Street, York, Southampton and Liverpool were among those that achieved record takings on the day.

Fashion sales rose over 16 per cent year-on-year, with menswear and sport the 'standout categories' with Barbour, Ted Baker and Polo Ralph Lauren achieving record sales, the retailer said.

Sales of handbags had a record week, with sales up 37 per cent year-on-year, and the retailer said brands such as Mulberry and Michael Kors included in its price match promotion were 'very popular'.

'While the sales figures are attention grabbing, for me our biggest achievement was delivering an operation which ran like clockwork,' said Dino Rocos, operations director of John Lewis. 'Our website coped well with exceptional demand whilst the atmosphere in our shops remained both seasonal and calm with customers enjoying extended opening hours and the great offers to be had.'

Mr Rocos' comments tacitly referred to the scenes of chaos around the UK as police were called to supermarkets offering cut-priced electrical goods as customers scuffled to grab the best bargains.

Despite the record-breaking performance, retail analysts have warned that Black Friday sales are merely cannibalising Christmas trading and reducing sales margins for UK retailers as consumers bring forward seasonal purchases.

'John Lewis can certainly be pleased with their operational success in handling all the extra volume of business last week and they look to have got more than their share of Black Friday spending, but how much has been pulled forward from December and how much was pulled away from other High Street retailers by that huge Black Friday spike remains to be seen,' said Nick Bubb, the independent retail analyst.

Source: from 'Black Friday breaks records at John Lewis, *Financial Times*, 02/12/2014 (Barrett, C.).

Discussion questions

1 What are the issues facing John Lewis here?
2 How do they impact on the marketing mix?

Introduction

In the early 1960s one of the leading US marketing writers, Neil Borden (1964), coined the term 'marketing mix' to cover the main activities of firms that were then thought to contribute to the marketability of their products and services. These were classified under the famous '4Ps' of marketing: product, price, promotion and place.

Recent thinking, spurred on through the development of relationship marketing (see Chapter 13), has extended the four Ps to include people, processes and physical evidence. In addition, as the service sector has grown in many developed economies, a new 'dominant logic' is emerging in marketing (see Vargo and Lusch, 2004; Lusch *et al.*, 2006), in which service provision rather than the exchange of goods has centre stage. This has further encouraged a rethink of the traditional elements of the marketing mix and their relevance to twenty-first century marketing.

Particularly significant has been the increasing use of the Internet for marketing purposes. The advent of the Internet as a major marketing medium has had impacts right across the spectrum of activities of the marketing mix. Initially seen primarily as a communications tool for reaching prospective customers, it is clear that the impact of the Internet has been far more pervasive, affecting the ways in which customers shop, how they gather and use information, and also their expectations of the type and level of service they should receive. Not least, the Internet has resulted in new forms of product. The music retailer iTunes, for example, now sells more tracks for download electronically than its largest high-street competitor sells tracks on conventional CDs. New 'bit-based' products, immediately and cheaply downloadable, are affecting many markets.

In this chapter we summarise the main ingredients of the new marketing mix and examine the opportunities brought about by Internet technology.

11.1 The market offer

Most market offers are combinations of physical, tangible product and intangible service (see Chapter 13). For ease of presentation here we refer to 'product' as the mix of physical, emotional, tangible and intangible elements that go to make up the overall market offer. It is important to always bear in mind that the product is what it does for the customer. Customers do not buy products; they buy what the product can do for them.

11.1.1 Key product/service concepts

Products are best viewed as solutions to customers' problems or ways of satisfying customer needs. American Marketing guru Philip Kotler (1997) put this neatly when he said that customers do not buy a quarter-inch drill bit – they buy the hole that the drill bit can create. In other words customers buy the benefits a product can bring to them, rather than the product itself.

That has two particularly important implications for marketing. First, it follows that customer perceptions of the product – what they believe about it – can be as, or even more, important to them than objective reality. If customers believe that a product gives them a particular benefit (for example enhanced attractiveness from using a particular cosmetic), that is what is likely to motivate them to purchase. Second, most if not all products are likely to have limited lives; they will only exist as solutions to customer problems until a better solution comes along. There is some evidence that product life cycles are shortening, with new offers coming to market more rapidly than in the past, and existing products becoming obsolete more quickly. That has implications for new product development (Chapter 12).

11.1.2 Product/service choice criteria

The reasons why customers choose one product over another can be simple ('it's cheaper') or far more complex ('it feels right for me'). In seeking to understand choice criteria it is useful to distinguish two main sets, the rational and overt; and the emotional and covert (Figure 11.1).

When questioned about their purchase decisions in market research surveys most customers will rationalise their choices. They will articulate objective reasons for their actions that they feel can be logically justified. These might include the practical benefits of the product, belief about value for money, the availability of the product and perhaps habit. These are reasons customers can give without loss of self-esteem, demonstrating that they are in control of the buying situation.

For many products, however, emotional reasons may play as big as, or even a bigger role. The purchase of branded goods, for example, may be prompted by the reassurance that a well-known and respected brand can bring. The physical product may be no better, a 'rational' comparison may show no differences, but customers will pay more to have the reassurance of the brand. Similarly, products may be chosen because they are believed to

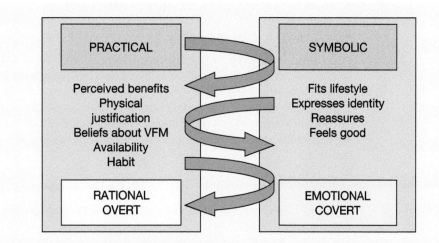

Figure 11.1
Product choice
criteria

fit the lifestyle of the customer more closely, or make a statement about the purchaser (why else would someone pay thousands of pounds for a watch, such as a Rolex, when a cheap alternative can be as accurate in delivering the overt, rational benefit of telling the time?).

While conventional quantitative market research may uncover the rational and overt motivations of customers, more in-depth, qualitative and often projective research is needed to uncover emotional and covert motivations. Famously, researchers in the USA trying to understand why more people did not fly between major cities rather than driving found through direct questions that reasons given were rational (cost of flying, greater convenience of driving) but when projective techniques were used (asking respondents why others did not fly more) fears of flying and concerns for safety began to emerge.

Most purchases are a combination of the rational and the emotional. The balance between the two, however, will vary significantly across products and it is an important task for marketers to understand the balance for their particular market offering.

11.1.3 Product/service differentiation

Central to successful marketing is product differentiation – ensuring that the total market offer is different and distinct from competitor offerings in ways that are of value to the target customer. This was discussed in more detail in Chapter 10.

With the convergence of manufacturing technology, and the widespread application of total quality management (TQM) methods, it is increasingly difficult for firms to differentiate on their core products. Differentiation in most markets now focuses on the augmented product (see Chapter 10), and in particular on ways of tailoring to individual customer requirements. In automobiles, for example, using basic building blocks of sub-frames, engines, body panels and interior options, there is now the opportunity for new car buyers to create near unique cars, matching their requirements or tastes very closely. Indeed, the industry's quest in the 3DayCar Programme is to find ways to customise the vehicle to the buyer's exact preferences and to deliver it three or four days after it is specified and ordered.

11.1.4 Diffusion of innovation

New products (those new to the market) require careful management as they enter the product life cycle. A theory of the diffusion of innovations (of which new products are one type) was proposed by Rogers (1962) (see Chapter 3). He suggested that the rate of diffusion of any innovation depends on a number of factors including:

- the relative advantage of the innovation over previous solutions to the customer's needs;
- the compatibility of the innovation with existing values and norms;

- a lack of complexity (ease) of using the innovation;
- the divisibility of the innovation facilitating low-risk trial; and
- the communicability of the advantages of the innovation (see Chapter 12 and Figure 12.3).

In considering these factors with regard to the adoption of the Internet and e-business techniques, for example, it can be seen that some of those techniques are likely to diffuse more rapidly than others.

Parasuraman and Colby (2001) introduced the concept of 'technology readiness' as a measure of customers' predispositions to adopt new technologies – based on their fears, hopes, desires and frustrations about technology. They identify five types of technology customers:

1 Explorers – highly optimistic and innovative.
2 Pioneers – the innovative but cautious.
3 Sceptics – who need to have the benefits of the technology proven to them.
4 Paranoids – those who are insecure about the technology.
5 Laggards – those who resist the technology.

Rogers (1962) identified five adopter groups – innovators, early adopters, early majority, late majority and laggards – which were further developed by Moore (1991, 2004, 2006) in his discussion of the adoption of high-technology products and services. We add a sixth and final adopter group, the sloths (see Figure 11.2).

- Innovators are the first to adopt a new technology or product. Often they are technology enthusiasts and adopt because the technology is new and they wish to be, and be seen to be, up to date. Initial demand for Apple's iPad, launched in the UK in May 2010, and the iPhone 4, launched in June 2010, was in large part driven by the desire to be seen as an innovator and first user of the new technologies. It is often the novelty value of the technology that drives their adoption. Many innovations fail because they are technology-driven rather than meeting the real needs of customers. Once the novelty value has worn off, and newer technologies have been substituted by the innovators, the product dies a natural death.
- Early adopters are similar to the innovators, but often demonstrate a more visionary reason for adopting the new technology. In business markets, for example, early adopters often see significant advantages from adoption and ways in which the new technology can enable them to change the way a market works, to the benefit both of themselves and of customers. Early adopters of e-business approaches, for example, include Jeff Bezos

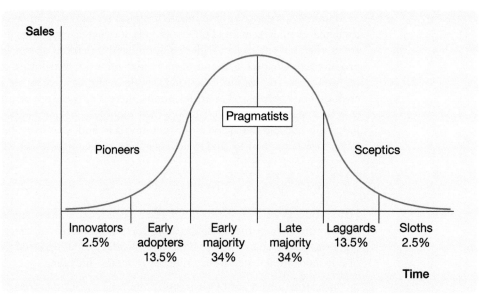

Figure 11.2
The diffusion of
innovation

at Amazon.com who saw in the use of the Internet a whole new way of retailing books and other products that could add value for customers. Vision such as this can lead to spectacular success, as well as spectacular failure.

- Early majority adopters are even more pragmatic than the early adopters. Typically they are less likely to see ways of revolutionising their markets, more likely to see incremental possibilities for improvement. They may, for example, take a particular aspect of the supply chain, such as purchasing, and use Internet technologies to improve the efficiency of this activity. Early majority adopters are often efficiency driven while the early adopters had seen opportunities to improve effectiveness.

- Late majority adopters have been described as 'conservatives' (Moore, 1991) who often enter a market or adopt a technology largely because others in the market have done so and they fear being left behind. More reluctant in their adoption than the early majority, and in greater need of support and direction in use of the new technology, these adopters are often confused about how the technology can be beneficial to them and wait until the technology has been tried and tested before adopting it. But they are sure that they need to embrace it or be overtaken by competitors.

- The laggards have been described as 'sceptics' who do not really see the potential for the new technology, will resist its adoption as long as possible, but may eventually be forced into adoption because all around them, including their suppliers, distributors and customers, have adopted.

- Finally, the sloths are the very last adopters of new technologies, often going to great lengths to avoid adoption. In some instances they change the way they operate to isolate themselves from the innovations taking place around them, and may even make a virtue of non-adoption. Some accountants still use the quill pen in preference to the spreadsheet! Some firms will never adopt e-business technologies, and may actually carve viable niches for themselves serving similarly minded customers.

Moore (1991) argued that in the adoption of new high-technology products, a gulf existed between the early adopters and the early majority that he referred to as the new product chasm, into which many fall (Figure 11.3). This is essentially the transition from a technology for enthusiasts and visionaries to a technology for the pragmatists. While the enthusiasm of the innovators and early adopters is often sufficient to carry an innovation forward, its

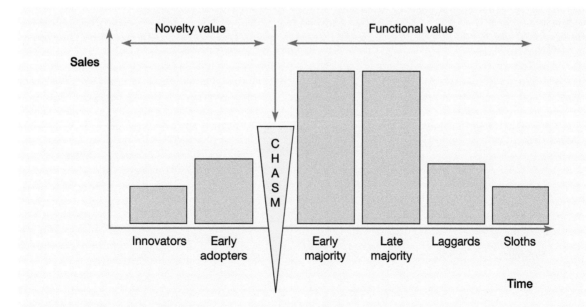

Figure 11.3 The new product chasm

Source: Based on Moore (1991), p. 17.

ultimate success depends on its ability to convince the pragmatists of the productivity and process enhancements it can deliver. Apple seem to have pulled off the enviable trick of both attracting innovators and early adopters to their new products, but also providing value beyond novelty that bridges the chasm and delivers adoption beyond the technology geeks.

11.1.5 Managing the product over its life cycle

The concept of the product life cycle was introduced in Chapter 3 (see Figure 11.4). With changing market conditions over the life cycle it is important that product and service strategies are designed to match. It will also be apparent that different adopter groups (see above) are likely to form key target markets at different stages of the product life cycle.

Pre-launch

In the pre-launch phase, before the product has appeared on the market, the main emphasis of the organisation will be on research and development, as well as gearing up production capacity for launch. The development costs for the Airbus A380, for example, have been put at around €11bn. High levels of expenditure may be incurred before any returns are seen through sales receipts. Also important at this stage is market research to identify likely early adopters of the product (see Chapter 12) and to develop key sales messages demonstrating the benefits of the new offering relative to the current solutions to customers' problems.

Market research into wholly new products can be notoriously inaccurate. Sony's formal market research into the Walkman concept showed that there was little potential demand for a mobile music player, but the Chairman, Akio Morita, went ahead anyway and created a whole new market now dominated by Apple's iPod. The lesson is that customers may not know what they want, or what they could find useful, before they see it. We refer to these as 'latent markets' – waiting for creative marketers to discover and exploit them.

Launch

The launch phase of the life cycle is the major opportunity for the organisation to shout loudly about the benefits the new product can offer. This will often take the form of explaining to customers the new benefits over and above those enjoyed from the products they currently use to satisfy their needs.

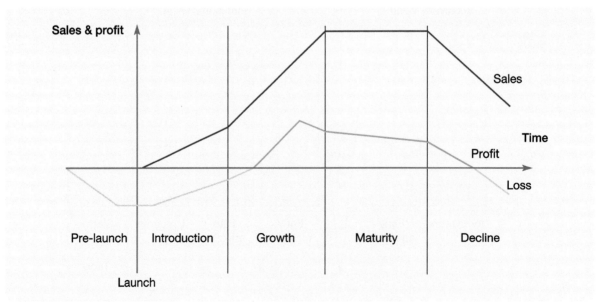

Figure 11.4 The product life cycle

At this stage, by definition, there is one product in the market and the real task is one of convincing the best prospect customers (the innovators identified through research during pre-launch) of the value of the new offering. The launch period offers significant opportunities for creative communication with prospective customers while the product is novel and newsworthy. Public relations (PR) can be particularly effective at this stage, as can the use of exhibitions and conventions.

Expenditures can be very high during launch and returns in the form of sales not yet realised. Significant budgets may need to be assigned to give the launch the best prospects of success. Classic examples include the launch of new movies or new car models where high advertising spend prior to and during launch excites interest and stimulates demand. The launch by Apple of their watch in 2015 was attended by significant media coverage.

Introduction

The introduction phase following launch is crunch time for the new product. Many new products do not get beyond this phase. During the introductory phase sales begin to take off but expenditures on marketing remain high to establish the new product as a superior alternative to previous offerings.

It is at this stage that competitors are likely to take increasing interest in the new product, attempting to gauge whether it will be a success, and hence present opportunities for copy or further improvement, or a costly failure. As the success of the new product becomes more certain, so competitive products will begin to appear as 'me too' products or improvements on the market pioneer. In digital portable music the pioneering iPod was soon joined in the market by rival MP3 players from iRiver, Sony, Philips and others.

Growth

The growth phase of the PLC is often considered the most exciting. Most brand and marketing managers prefer to operate in growth markets. At this stage the product is becoming readily accepted on the market, sales are growing rapidly and returns begin to outstrip expenditures. Other things also happen during this phase that significantly affect marketing strategies. First, the success and growth are likely to attract more competitors into the market, especially those that have adopted a 'wait and see' attitude during launch and introduction. Now that the market is proven, risks are lowered and potential returns beckon.

With further competitor entry comes greater product differentiation among offerings, and typically greater segmentation of the market. The early majority, the new macro-target, are likely to be diverse in their exact wants and needs, offering greater opportunities for micro-targeting. Expenditures continue to be high in researching market opportunities and

iPod range

Source: Corbis: © Everett Kennedy Brown/epa.

product improvements, second generation and so on. In the MP3 player market, for example, by Christmas 2006 there were several different versions of the iPod available (from Shuffle to Nano to Video). For Apple a problem began to emerge as the innovators, primarily younger and more fashion-conscious purchasers, saw their parents' generation buying the bigger, 60GB iPod Videos. In response Apple launched coloured versions of the iPod Nano, with additional add-on features and skins, to retain the younger market.

It is at this stage that returns peak and surplus cash can be diverted into developing and launching the new generation of new products (see portfolio theory section).

Maturity

The mature phase is reached when growth slows and the bulk of the market (late majority) have entered. This phase can be characterised by particularly fierce competition as those who entered the market during the growth phase fight for market share rather than market expansion to improve performance. Price wars are common, profit margins are squeezed, and expenditures on marketing and research and development scrutinised more critically.

Decline

The decline, and eventual death, phase sees profits squeezed even more as the next generation of products takes over the market. Figure 11.5 shows the sales of cameras in the USA. The sales of traditional, film-based cameras peaked around 2000 but since then have been in steep decline due to the growth of digital versions. Surprisingly, the market downturn for film-based cameras has been even more dramatic in countries like China. This switch in market has been fuelled by technological advances (Figure 11.6) where the cost of sharper definition in digital pictures (as measured by the number of megapixels) has plummeted, allowing the quality of digital pictures to rapidly challenge that of film.

Turning points

The phases of the product life cycle are notoriously difficult to predict, and especially difficult to identify are transitions between stages (Figure 11.7). First, the transition from introductory phase to growth. Here the danger is being left behind as the market takes off. Second, the transition from growth to maturity. The clear danger here is being left with over-capacity, or high stock levels, of difficult to move products (as happened with the over-supply of mobile phones when the market became mature in the early 2000s). This is another reason why the mature phase is so competitive – firms often have excess capacity and stock available that they need to move. Finally, transition from steady state maturity to decline can leave some firms wedded to old technology and unable to embrace the new.

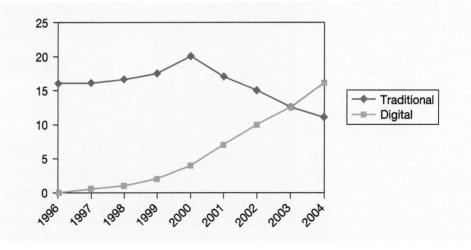

Figure 11.5
US amateur
camera sales

Source: New Scientist,
2004, October 16.

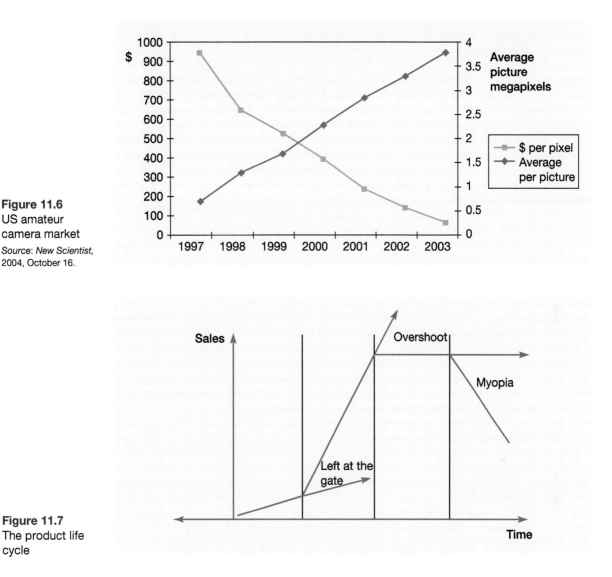

Figure 11.6
US amateur
camera market
Source: New Scientist,
2004, October 16.

Figure 11.7
The product life
cycle

The product life cycle concept has also been criticised for encouraging tunnel vision in marketers (Moon, 2005). Moon suggests that managers slavishly following the PLC see only an inexorable advance along the curve, and because they all see the cycle in the same way they all adopt similar positions for products and services during each of the life cycle stages. To counter this convergence of strategies Moon suggests three alternative positioning strategies for breaking free of the life cycle: reverse positioning; breakaway positioning; and stealth positioning.

- Reverse positioning involves stripping down the augmented product to its core, and then seeking new ways to differentiate. This strategy recognises that in the quest to augment core products firms may have added so many additional features that they become the expected, rather than the exception that differentiates. The example of toothpaste is cited where the core product has been augmented with whitener, fluoride, plaque preventative, breath freshener etc. to the extent that all these now feature in leading brands and no longer serve to differentiate. Ikea have adopted this approach in their successful self-assembly furniture stores. Rather than adopt the strategy of other furniture retailers of carrying enormous product lines, varied inventories, high-pressure sales operations and seemingly permanent 'sales' and 'special offers', Ikea offers stores with play areas for children, Scandinavian restaurants, no high-pressure sales staff, very little in-store support or service, self-collection (rather than delivery weeks or months after order), self-assembly and now home delivery.

- Breakaway positioning is where a product is deliberately moved from one product category to another. The category a product occupies is determined by the way customers perceive that product – the competing products they associate it with, the messages that are employed to promote it, the price charged, the channels through which it is distributed – in short, the entire marketing mix employed. By switching categories products can gain a new lease of life beyond the existing PLC. Swatch, for example, is an example of breakaway positioning. Before its launch in 1983 Swiss watches were sold as jewellery and most customers rarely bought more than one model. Swatch changed that by defining its watches as playful fashion accessories, fun, ephemeral, inexpensive and showy. Impulse buying was encouraged and customers typically bought several watches for different outfits.

- Stealth positioning involves shifting to a different product category in a covert way, rather than overtly as practised through breakaway positioning. This may be appropriate where there is prejudice about a product or the company which needs to be overcome. Moon stresses this is not the same as deceit and can backfire if customers believe they are being cheated or exploited. Sony have been highly successful in the games console market with their PlayStation product but its market penetration has been limited to a narrow customer base – primarily males in their late teens and early twenties. The company wished to broaden its platform for home entertainment and communications but found that the PlayStation format did not appeal beyond the narrow customer focus. In response, in July 2003 it launched a PlayStation product in Europe called EyeToy: Play (http://www.eyetoy.com/index.asp?pageID=18). This included a video camera (EyeToy) and game software (Play) that plugged into the PlayStation 2 console but allowed the user to become part of the game, appearing inside the television where they interact with objects on the screen by moving their bodies, rather than using hand-held controllers. The product sold 2.5 million units in the first seven months, crucially engaging a much wider target market including parents and even grandparents (Moon, 2005).

11.1.6 The impact of the Internet on market offerings

With the advent of marketing over the Internet, two types of market offering became apparent: the so-called 'atom-based' and 'bit-based' products.

Atom-based products are physical offerings that have a separate presence and form for the customer. While they may be promoted over the Internet they need to be physically shipped to the customer, are subject to returns where they are not satisfactory and can be resold by customers. Typical examples include books and videos (Amazon.com), clothes and appliances. For the customer the product at the end of the day is the same as that purchased through a bricks and mortar retailer, but the experience may be enhanced through the additional services, convenience and low price available through Internet purchase. For the retailer the logistics of delivery represent significant challenges.

Bit-based products, on the other hand, do not have a physical presence. They can be represented as digital data in electronic form. They are typically non-returnable but do not require separate shipping and can be transferred online. Bit-based products include music, news, information services, movies and TV programmes. Similarly, online lessons and tutorials are proving increasingly popular (e.g. http://www.onlinelessonvideos.com/home.php). These products are ideally suited to marketing over the Internet as the complete supply chain, from procurement through sales and marketing to delivery, can be conducted online. This synergy provided the logic for the global merger in 2000 of AOL (a leading Internet service provider) with Time Warner (an entertainment and news conglomerate) as a foundation for online provision of enhanced information and entertainment products (though integration of the two business cultures proved more problematic).

For both atom- and bit-based products sold over the Internet, the power of the customer is significantly greater than in purchases from bricks and mortar suppliers. Put simply, the information available to the customer is far greater, enabling wider search of competitor offerings, online recommendations and greater price comparisons. The online customer can decide at the click of a mouse to buy or bypass a firm's offerings, whereas in a face-to-face situation a vendor may rely more on personal selling and persuasion. For offerings to be consistently chosen over competing offerings they need to offer greater value to customers, through lower prices, greater convenience, additional valued features, speed, or whatever. Hence the driver of web-based marketing is increasingly to look to the augmented product for differentiation (see Chapter 13).

The Internet has also facilitated integrated marketing of bit-based and atom-based products. In December 2001 New Line Cinema launched their epic movie *The Lord of the Rings: The Fellowship of the Ring* (LOTR) based on the bestseller books by J.R.R. Tolkien. More than 100 million copies of the books have been sold in 45 languages prior to the movie launch. To heighten interest in the movie New Line created a website in May 1999 (**www.lordoftherings.com**). A trailer for the movie became available on the website in April 2000 and was downloaded more than 1.7 million times. The site was updated three to four times per week as part of a four-year editorial schedule spanning the life of the three films in the trilogy (the second was released in December 2002, the third in December 2003). The aim was to create an online community as a hub for the 400 fan sites devoted to LOTR. This type of integrated marketing started a trend now regularly followed.

Merchandising associated with the movie is extensive with toys and 'collectibles' based on the film sculpted by WETA, the New Zealand-based firm that created the creatures and special effects of the film. There have also been marketing partnerships with restaurants (Burger King), consumer products manufacturers (JVC, General Mills), book sellers (Barnes and Noble, Amazon – sales of the books are up 500 per cent since the launch of the film), theatre shows in London which attracted over 700,000 people by the end of 2008, and even the New Zealand Post Office (in December 2001 a set of New Zealand stamps was issued with images from LOTR on them – see **http://www.newzeal.com/Stamps/NZ/LOTR/Rings.htm**). In addition, AOL Time Warner launched a new version of AOL (version 7) with an LOTR sweepstake which generated 800,000 entries in its first two weeks.

Customer service and support

Potentially the Internet offers many opportunities for customising and tailoring the service offered to the needs and requirements of individual customers. Jeff Bezos, CEO and founder of Amazon.com, is reported as saying that if Amazon has 4.5 million customers it should have 4.5 million stores, each one customised for the person who visits (Janal, 2000). When customers make initial purchases from Amazon they are invited to give information, such as billing details and address shipping address, which will be stored and used for future transactions. On logging into Amazon the customer is greeted by a 'personalised' greeting, recommendations for books based on previous purchases, and one-click ordering for new books. The system is automated for efficiency, but from the perspective of the customer, tailored to their individual needs and requirements.

The interactivity of the Internet makes it possible to establish two-way relationships with customers so that feedback on product performance or operational problems can be received, as well as advice for solving problems provided. Firms offering bit-based products, such as software, often use the Internet as a way of providing product upgrades and patches. Norton Antivirus, for example, update subscribers' software automatically. Similarly popular personal navigation systems such as TomTom offer map upgrades and safety camera locations over the Internet to subscribers (**http://www.tomtom.com/products/maps/**).

Some firms offer added value services by encouraging chat rooms and online communities through their sites. Reebok, for example, established an online community where potential customers could 'chat' with famous sports personalities. They regularly post articles and news items of interest to their target customers. All these activities are designed to help build the brand and establish its credentials with the target market (Janal, 2000).

Deise *et al.* (2000) identify five types of website that allow or encourage customers to interact with the company. Content sites provide customers with basic information about the company, its products and its services. FAQ sites answer frequently asked questions and can help customers with common queries. Knowledge-based sites have knowledge bases, or databases, that can be searched by customers. These require a greater degree of involvement from the customer but may be more convenient than making a service call. Trouble ticket sites allow customers to post queries or problems and then receive personalised feedback or problem solving (often from other users). Interactive sites facilitate interaction between the firm and its customers. Often these are part of an extranet where customers are given access to proprietary information.

Again, however, it should be noted that the power lies with the customer. Online, as in the physical world, customers are only likely to be attracted by services that provide value for them. The key to successful service online will remain identifying what gives customers value, and what can be uniquely offered through the Internet. Because of the ease of competitor copying, however, service benefits need to be constantly upgraded.

A related issue which may complicate matters is broader concerns for issues like customer privacy, which may hold some back from Internet relationships with companies, as well as the enormous potential for dissatisfied customers to quickly spread news of their dissatisfaction through social media.

11.2 Pricing strategies

Setting prices can be one of the most difficult decisions in marketing. Price too high and customers may not buy, price too low and the organisation may not achieve the profit levels necessary to continue trading or invest in its future. In the 1960s British Leyland had major product success with the Mini, a small car aimed at a growing market of increasingly affluent consumers. Part of the market success was down to relatively low prices being charged. Unfortunately, however, the margins achieved were very thin and the company did not generate enough profits from the Mini to put back into R&D to develop the next generation of cars, and cars for other market segments. The company was financially crippled in 1975 by falling sales (brought about by strong competition from Japan and elsewhere), the first OPEC oil crisis which saw the price of fuel increase significantly, and high levels of UK inflation.

11.2.1 Pricing considerations

A number of factors need to be taken into account when setting price levels (Figure 11.8).

- **Production costs.** The simplest, and most often used, pricing method is to set price at cost plus a percentage mark-up (e.g. cost plus 20 per cent). Provided the product sells in sufficient quantities at this price, this strategy ensures a given level of profitability and a good degree of predictability. It also ensures that products are not sold at below cost – a strategy that is not sustainable in the long term without subsidy. In practice costs should be seen as a floor below which prices should not be allowed to fall.
- **Economic value to the customer (EVC).** The value of the product to the customer over its lifetime gives a ceiling above which prices would be unacceptable to customers. Doyle and Stern (2006) explain how EVC can be calculated with an example from B2B marketing (see below).
- **Competitor price levels.** Also important to consider are the prices set by competitors. Where two or more product offerings are similar on other characteristics, price can become the final determinant of choice. Firms may decide to price higher than competitors (as a signal of superior quality), at similar prices (and compete on other features), or lower prices (and compete primarily on price). In the UK market for petrol (gas) there

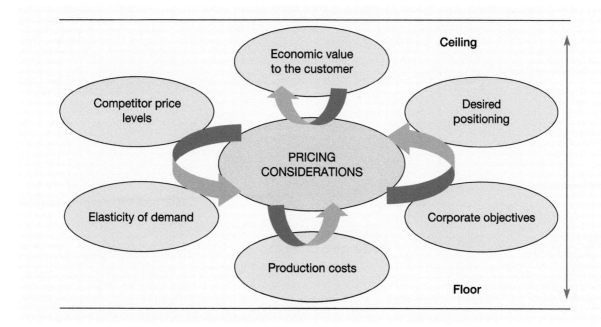

Figure 11.8 Pricing considerations

is very little price differentiation between competitors. This is in part due to the high level of taxation (VAT and duty) on petrol, at around 70 per cent in 2015, leaving little margin for price differences.

- **Desired competitive positioning.** The price charged can be a powerful signal to the market of the quality and reliability of the product. Too low a price may suggest poor quality rather than good value for money. In the hi-fi market Bose have deliberately priced their offerings significantly higher than competitors as a signal of superior product quality. Other brands, such as LG, price below competition to attract the more price-sensitive consumer. In between these extremes brands such as Sony, JVC and Samsung compete at similar prices but offering different features, styles and other customer benefits.
- **Corporate objectives.** Are the objectives to grow the market rapidly (which might argue for a relatively low price), to harvest (which might argue for prices at the high end), or to maximise profit (which would indicate marginal cost pricing)?
- **Price elasticity of demand.** A further consideration in setting prices is the extent to which demand will vary at different price levels. Some products, such as luxury goods, are highly price elastic – changes in price affect quantity demanded to a great extent. Others, such as essentials, are relatively price inelastic, with price having little effect on demand.

11.2.2 Price elasticity of demand

The price elasticity of demand is the effect of changes in price on demand for the product. Most demand curves slope downwards from top left to bottom right (see Figure 11.9). In other words, the lower the price, the more of a product is purchased, and conversely, as prices rise, less is demanded. Price elasticity is defined as:

Price elasticity = (% change in demand) ÷ (% change in price)

Where price elasticity >1 we term this 'elastic demand' (a change in price generates a greater change in quantity demanded); where price elasticity <1 we term this 'inelastic demand' (a change in price generates a smaller change in quantity demanded).

The extent to which quantity demanded is affected by differences in price varies from market to market. Where there is a steep slope to the demand curve (a in Figure 11.9) a change in price has relatively little effect on quantity demanded; demand is 'inelastic'. A price rise

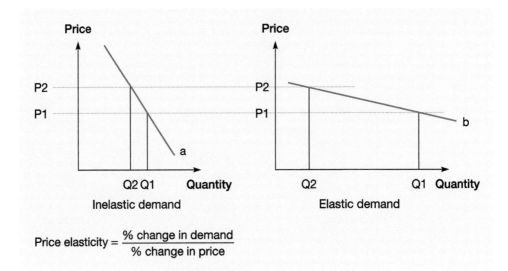

Figure 11.9
Price elasticity of
demand

$$\text{Price elasticity} = \frac{\% \text{ change in demand}}{\% \text{ change in price}}$$

from P1 to P2 results in a reduction in quantity demanded from Q1 to Q2. By multiplying price by quantity we can see that revenue changes from P1 × Q1 to P2 × Q2. The loss of quantity demanded is offset by the higher prices and revenues will increase. Markets which enjoy inelastic demand are often monopoly or near monopoly supply where customers have little or no choice about how much of a product they use and where switching costs are high.

A shallow demand curve (b in Figure 11.9) occurs where a relatively small change in price stimulates a more significant change in demand; demand is 'elastic'. An increase of price from P1 to P2 results in a much more significant reduction of demand from Q1 to Q2. Similarly, price reductions are likely to have a more significant effect on stimulating demand. Markets where demand is more price elastic are generally characterised by greater levels of competition, more customer choice and the easy ability of customers to switch from one supplier to another.

11.2.3 Assessing value to the customer

Economic value to the customer (Forbis and Mehta, 1981) and customer value propositions (Anderson *et al.*, 2006) are central concepts in pricing of industrial products such as plant and equipment. This approach entails attempting to identify the lifetime value to the customer of the purchase, taking into account all costs (e.g. purchase price, running costs, maintenance etc.) and all benefits.

Doyle and Stern (2006) show the example of a market-leading machine tool selling at €30,000. In addition to the purchase price the customer will incur €20,000 start-up costs (including installation, training of operatives etc.), and post-purchase running costs over the life of the machine of €50,000. In total, the lifetime cost is €100,000. Of this the initial purchase price is less than one-third. A new competitor coming into the market might be tempted to charge less for the product, but the effect of that lower price over the life will be considerably less. A 20 per cent reduction in initial price, for example, of €6,000 is in effect only a 6 per cent reduction in lifetime costs.

A more productive approach might be to estimate the total output value to the customer over the life of the machine. This could be done by estimating the number of outputs from the machine tool over its life together with an assessment of likely defects. If the new machine is an improvement on the existing one, with say 20 per cent greater efficiency, it can be expected to save 20 per cent of total costs or produce 20 per cent more output (both equivalent to €20,000 added value for the customer). Hence there is scope to actually increase the initial purchase price to, say, €40,000 while still offering an overall saving of €10,000 to the customer. In this case a higher price might also be needed to signal a higher quality product that can deliver the 20 per cent savings claimed. A lower price might raise doubts on ability to deliver the savings.

In markets where lifetime value may be less easy to demonstrate (e.g. consumer markets for appliances) the perceived value of the product can be used as an alternative to EVC. Using techniques such as Vickrey auctions, value to the customer can be estimated. In normal auctions the item will go to the highest bidder. There can be times, however, where bidders will bid below the perceived value of the item in an attempt to get a bargain (this happens regularly on eBay!). Vickrey auctions are a technique to get to the true value the bidder places on the item. They are sealed bids to purchase where bidders submit written bids without knowledge of who else is bidding for the same item. While the highest bidder wins, they pay the price bid by the second highest, not the price they bid. This creates a powerful incentive for bidders to bid the real value they place on an item rather than gamble on getting it for a bargain, lower price (see **www.wikipedia.org**).

Trade-off analysis (also called conjoint analysis) can also be used to estimate the 'utility' of different price levels, and how customers will trade-off between alternative configurations of benefits (features) at different prices (see Green *et al.*, 1981; Orme, 2005).

11.2.4 Pricing methods

A number of alternative pricing methods are used by organisations, sometimes in combination.

- **Cost plus pricing.** This is the simplest approach to setting prices and requires little understanding of customers and their needs. Prices are set at cost plus a percentage mark-up. Prices therefore reflect directly the costs of creating and delivering the product. The disadvantage of this method, of course, is that it takes no account of the value of the product to the customer. If the value to the customer is greater than cost plus mark-up, the product will be attractive, but if the value to the customer is lower, sales are likely to suffer.
- **Going rate pricing.** In some markets, such as petrol and diesel, prices are typically set on a 'going rate' basis – at what others set – and there is little price competition between suppliers. Competition takes place on other factors such as availability, location and convenience.
- **Perceived value pricing.** Pricing products at their perceived value to customers requires sophisticated research methods to identify value. When customers are asked direct questions about value (e.g. 'how much would you pay for . . . ?') few would vote for high prices! Projective techniques and other approaches such as trade-off, or conjoint, analysis (see above) can be more useful. Under these approaches customers are put into simulated purchasing situations and their behaviour is observed to gauge the value they perceive in the market offer.
- **Sealed bids.** In many industrial purchasing situations, especially in capital projects, a number of potential suppliers may be invited to bid to supply. Normally at least two stages will be employed. First, a specification stage where suppliers need to demonstrate their ability to supply to specification and on time. This stage will reduce the number of potential suppliers to a manageable number. Second, a sealed bid which indicates the price each selected supplier would charge. Deciding how to bid under competitive situations can be highly sophisticated. Typically firms will take into account not only their own costs but also their predictions of the prices competitors will bid at (based on their costs and expectations of competitors). Game theory may be useful in this context. Game theory refers to a set of techniques and approaches that study situations where players choose different actions in an attempt to maximise their returns. It provides a formal modelling approach to situations in which decisions are not made in isolation, and where the decisions of one party can be influenced by the decisions of others. Hence the need to model and predict the intentions of others (see **http://www.gametheory.net/**). The growing use of Internet auctions that ask suppliers to bid prices online to a purchaser's product specification is the newest approach to this situation.

11.2.5 Promotional pricing

- **Loss leaders.** Used extensively by retailers and other suppliers as a means of attracting customers into their stores, or on to their websites, loss leaders are products sold below cost for promotional purposes. Once customers have been attracted in by the loss leader the retailer will attempt to sell other market offerings at a profit. Manufacturers also use this tactic where the lifetime cost of a product is considerably greater than the initial purchase price. Home photograph printers, for example, are sold at very low prices with little margin because the manufacturers and retailers can make their profits through selling ink cartridges, photo-quality paper and other consumables.

- **Special events.** Seasonal sales, special price promotions and 'once in a lifetime' deals are ways in which price is used to gain customers. Sales originated as a means of moving old stock to make way for new season offerings. Some organisations now appear to have near permanent sales, suggesting that really they are offering products at prices lower than the 'ticket price' but, because they do not want the product to appear low quality, justify this through discount.

- **Cash rebates.** Money-back offers and coupons are popular among marketers of fast moving consumer goods. Coupons can be most cost effective as not all are cashed in, and only when another purchase is made. Money back can be more expensive as claims are more likely to be made.

- **Low interest finance.** For the purchase of significant goods such as furniture and automobiles, some suppliers will offer low, or 'zero' interest on hire purchase deals. In effect this gives a discount on price when net present values are calculated and can be powerful inducements to customers to move to higher price points.

- **Psychological pricing.** Pricing just beneath psychological barriers (e.g. €2.99 rather than €3 or at €9,995 rather than €10,000) is common practice. The assumption (rarely tested) is that customers have a psychological price threshold and will group prices in broad bands for comparison purposes. A car priced at €19,995 is seen in a lower price band than one priced at €20,000. Increasingly with Internet searches set to look for products at 'prices up to . . . ' psychological pricing is likely to be employed.

11.2.6 The effects of the Internet on pricing decisions

The Internet makes it far easier for customers to compare prices than in the past. Not only can prices be compared between manufacturers (for example, the price of a BMW compared with the price of an equivalent model Mercedes) but also the prices of alternative suppliers of the same product or model. And the latter is no longer confined to the immediate geographic vicinity – comparisons can be made nationwide and even globally. The advent of a single currency in some parts of the EU has made price comparisons across the euro-zone even easier.

Kerrigan *et al*. (2001) report that in B2B markets customers experience price savings of around 10 per cent for commodity products and up to 25 per cent for custom purchases. These result from the increased choice customers enjoy, coupled with increased price competition between suppliers. P&G, for example, is reducing its supply costs by conducting 'reverse auctions' with suppliers and estimates annual savings in the order of 20 per cent on supplies of around $700 million.

In addition, customer-to-customer (C2C) communications or chat lines between customers help to spread information about competitive prices, as well as product and service recommendations or warnings. Through customer-to-business (C2B) communications reverse auctions are now taking place where buyers post what they are looking for and invite suppliers to bid to supply them.

Overall, the Internet has made customers more, rather than less, price sensitive as they have access to greater amounts of information, easily searched, and not controlled by the sellers.

11.3 Communications strategies

For many people advertising is synonymous with marketing. In practice, advertising is one (albeit an important one) of the ways in which firms communicate with their customers and prospective customers. The range of communications tools available is increasing as new technologies present new opportunities. Podcasting and vodcasting (blogging) are becoming new and popular communications tools. Very soon they will become standard tools in the communications toolbox, and other approaches will be developed.

11.3.1 The communications process

Communications are about two-way exchanges between sender and recipient (see Figure 11.10).

All marketing communications take place under 'noisy' conditions. Other communicators, both direct competitors and others with different market offerings to communicate, are also bombarding the same audience with messages. It has been estimated, for example, that US consumers are subjected to some 5,000 advertising messages each day. It is therefore important to ensure that the message is clear as well as effectively communicated. A starting point is to be clear about what the communications objectives are. These are best viewed using a simple model of marketing communications.

Figure 11.10
The communications process

Source: Developed from Doyle and Stern, 2006.

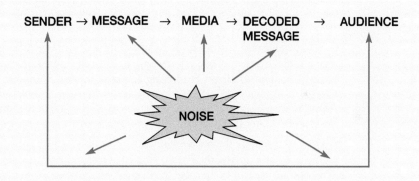

11.3.2 A basic communications model

A number of models of how communications work have been developed. Most, however, come back to a basic model called AIDA – Awareness → Interest → Desire → Action.

- **Awareness.** At a very basic level marketing communications set out to create or raise awareness of the market offering among the selected target market. If customers are not aware of the existence of the offer they are very unlikely to purchase! Awareness raising is particularly important at the launch and introductory stages of the product life cycle. In the early stages of the MP3 player market, for example, the communications task was to explain to the market what an MP3 player was and what it did.
- **Interest.** Once awareness has been created the communication goal changes to creating interest in the market offer. Customers are bombarded by many messages every hour of every day and may have an awareness of many products and services. Relatively few will interest them, however. Key to creating interest is demonstrating how the offer is relevant to the wants and needs of the customer. In the case of the MP3 player, the advantages of music on the move beyond the personal cassette player (Walkman) and personal CD player were stressed (e.g. does not skip tracks or mangle the tape, is smaller and more convenient, batteries last longer, there is no need to carry libraries of cassettes or discs as they are already loaded etc.).

- **Desire.** Once interest has been stimulated, communications seek to create desire for the offer ahead of other offers in the market. Rather than demonstrating the benefits of the generic product group the emphasis is now on creating a desire for this particular brand or offering. Much of Apple's promotion of the iPod MP3 player centres on creating a cool image for iPod as the only MP3 player to own. So successful has this been that iPod has now moved from its original target market of 15- to 30-year-olds to a more mature market. This is in danger of weakening its position among the original market (see above).
- **Action.** Awareness, interest and desire are of little value to a supplier unless they result in purchases or other forms of support. Communications aimed at taking the customer to the next stage, creating action, include offers, promotions and deals to stimulate purchase, as well as the use of personal selling.

11.3.3 Communications decisions

A number of decisions need to be made regarding communications.

- **What message to convey.** First and foremost the message to be conveyed needs to be clearly understood and accepted by those responsible for sending it. Confused messages create confusing signals in the minds of customers. The most effective communications have a single but clear message they are trying to get across. This has been referred to as the USP (unique selling proposition) of the market offer. Communications centring on conveying the key benefits of the product in a novel and attractive way (see copy, below) help not only to raise awareness but also to create a powerful position for the product in the mind of the customer.
- **What communications tools to use.** There are many different communications tools available. These include advertising, public relations, sales promotions, personal selling (see Chapter 14), direct marketing and sponsorship. Each has advantages and disadvantages (discussed below). Some are better at creating awareness (e.g. advertising) while others focus more on creating desired actions (personal selling). The various tools are used in combination at different stages in the communications process.
- **How to translate the message in copy.** Not only is it important for the communicator to know what message they are trying to convey, they must also translate it into effective words and symbols that the recipient of the message can understand and decode. Too subtle, or complicated, translations can result in a confused message being received, or even the wrong message being received. Early anti-drug use advertisements in the UK were criticised for actually making drug taking look glamorous, rather than getting across the message that drugs can seriously damage your health.
- **Which media to use.** The media available for marketing communications vary across different countries, as do their effectiveness. Relevant media include press, television, cinema, posters, Internet, radio, post box (e-mail inbox as well as the physical letterbox still used for direct mail), point of sale, fax machines, mobile phones.
- **How much to spend on communications.** Setting communications budgets is notoriously difficult. Years ago a marketing executive said, 'Half my advertising budget is wasted – the trouble is, I don't know which half!' Advertising effectiveness modelling by leading firms such as Millward Brown can assess the levels of awareness created through promotional campaigns (see Maunder *et al.*, 2005) by surveying the target audience regularly and modelling the relationship with advertising activity.

11.3.4 Communications tools

- **Advertising.** Advertising is particularly effective at creating awareness. It can have high visual impact, wide reach and is easily repeated to reinforce messages. Its disadvantages are that it is impersonal, lacks flexibility, is generally not interactive with the customer

Table 11.1 UK ad spending, by media, 2005–2014

Millions	2005	2010	2011	2012	2013	2014
Internet*	$1,862	$5,507	$6,377	$7,036	$7,732	$8,509
TV	$5,539	$5,223	$5,275	$5,301	$5,407	$5,515
Newspapers	$6,685	$4,404	$4,036	$3,969	$3,972	$3,943
Magazines	$2,577	$1,463	$1,341	$1,315	$1,320	$1,314
Outdoor	$1,222	$1,199	$1,207	$1,266	$1,279	$1,292
Radio	$836	$713	$725	$743	$750	$758
Cinema	$215	$248	$240	$245	$256	$265
Total	$18,934	$18,758	$19,202	$19,876	$20,717	$21,595

Note: Converted at the exchange rate of US$ = £0.62; numbers may not add up to total due to rounding; *classifieds, display and paid search
Sources: ZenithOptimedia, 'Advertising Expenditure Forecasts', June 2012; provided by Starcom MediaVest Group, June 2012; www.eMarketer.com.

(questions cannot be answered, objections cannot be overcome) and has a limited ability to close the sale on its own. Table 11.1 shows the proportion of advertising expenditure in each of the main media in the UK in 2014.

- **Public relations.** PR can be more credible than advertising as it uses a third party, the reporter and the medium used, to convey the message – the final message to the customer does not come directly from the marketer. As such it can have a higher impact than advertising for a fraction of the cost, and may also reach audiences that would be difficult or impossible to reach otherwise. The major disadvantage, however, is the loss of control. Once a press release has been issued there is no guarantee that it will be taken up and acted on by the media, and it is quite possible that the message will be distorted so that it does not get across as intended. It may also reach the wrong audience.

- **Sales promotions.** Sales promotions include money off, bonus packs, three for the price of two, free samples, coupons, loyalty cards, prizes, bulk discounts, competitions, allowances and any other creative 'deal' that firms can dream up. Their advantages are that they can have a very direct effect on behaviour and those effects can generally be directly monitored and evaluated. The disadvantages are that their effects may be short-lived and hence they could be a costly way of achieving sales. Excessive use of promotions may also weaken the image of a brand ('it can't be very good if they are always giving it away!').

- **Personal selling.** One of the most effective tools for closing a sale is personal selling (see Chapter 13). It is flexible, can be adjusted to individual situations, can be used to build relationships with customers, and can be used to understand, address and overcome barriers and objections to purchase. It can, however, be costly, is highly dependent on the skills of individual salespeople, and in some markets may incur customer resistance.

- **Direct marketing.** At its best direct marketing can offer a highly personalised service, tightly targeted to those customers who are prime targets for the offers made. Thus there is less wastage of the promotional budget. At its worst, however, direct mail can be indiscriminate, can generate high levels of scepticism among customers and result in message and material overload. As with all communications tools, effective targeting is the key to ensure the messages are directed effectively to the target market.

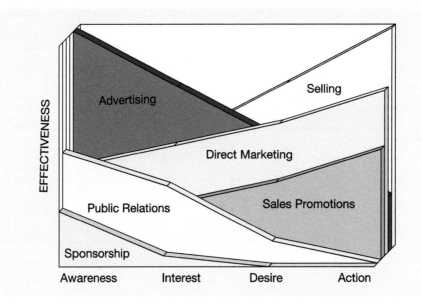

Figure 11.11
Communications
effectiveness

- **Sponsorship.** Sponsorship of sporting, social, cultural and other events, or of teams, causes or facilities, can be an effective way of targeting potential customer groups through their wider interests and concerns. This can help with credibility building and reputation enhancement. It is perhaps the most difficult communications tool to measure the impact of, however. It can be expensive, and may not be particularly effective in achieving awareness goals. Sponsorship of the London Olympics achieved very low levels of recall among target audiences. It can also be subject to 'ambush' – competitor products achieving placement in sponsored events.

Communications tools effectiveness

Figure 11.11 shows the effectiveness of each of the above across the four stages of the communications model. In general, advertising, PR and sponsorship are better at raising levels of awareness and interest than creating desire or action. Personal selling, direct marketing and sales promotions are more effective at inducing action. An effective communications campaign will determine first what the objectives are, then select an appropriate mix of tools to achieve that objective.

11.3.5 The use of the Internet for marketing communications

In 2001 it was estimated that advertising over the Internet totalled $9.6 billion. By 2006 that had risen to $27 billion. In 2006 that represented approximately 5 per cent of worldwide advertising expenditure, but is expected to rise to around 20 per cent over the next few years (*The Economist*, 25 November 2006). By 2010 it is expected to rise to over $60 billion.

In the UK over £2 billion was spent on Internet advertising in 2006 (up 41 per cent on 2005), accounting for 11.4 per cent of all advertising spend. For the first time Internet advertising overtook newspaper advertising (10.9 per cent of all spend). Of that the biggest sectors were recruitment ads (25 per cent), finance and banking (14 per cent), technology (13 per cent) and motors (13 per cent) (*The Observer*, 1 April 2007, quoting PricewaterhouseCoopers).

As noted above, a significant feature of the Internet is the shift in power away from manufacturers and retailers towards customers. While the period to the middle of the twentieth century saw power concentrated in the hands of manufacturers and suppliers (due to demand typically outstripping supply in many industries), a major feature of the last quarter of that century was the shift in power to retailers. It was the retailers who controlled the connection between manufacturers and customers, and crucially managed the information flows to customers. Customers who wanted to gather information about competing products could do so, but the process was often time-consuming and cumbersome, resulting in choices being made with limited, imperfect information. A major characteristic of the Internet-based marketplace of the twenty-first century is the 'information superhighway' that makes comparative information far more easily available to customers. Indeed, the customer now typically initiates information search, whereas in the past the manufacturer or the retailer initiated and controlled this.

For example, powerful retailers like Tesco and Walmart participate in global online exchanges based on the Web. They can source products from the cheapest suppliers anywhere in the world. They can also pressure their suppliers to switch sources for raw materials and components to cheaper alternatives located on the exchange (though not obliged to adopt such suggestions, suppliers find that their prices are adjusted down as though they had). This represents a significant change in the marketing communications process, and shift in power from seller to buyer. Information search is more likely to be triggered by customers than by marketers, despite the large sums being spent on online advertising.

Customers are becoming information seekers rather than passive recipients as evidenced by the extensive use of search engines such as Google and Yahoo. Coupled with this are changes in media viewing habits brought about by the explosion in channel availability through cable and satellite, and media merging as the boundaries between phones, television and Internet technologies become blurred.

One of the potential benefits of communicating over the Internet is the possibility of relating sales to promotions more accurately. These are reflected in a number of new marketing communication methods emerging to take advantage of the particular characteristics of the Internet. Among these are banner advertising and viral marketing.

Banner advertising and pay-per-click

Banner advertising is the use of advertisements on web pages that have click-through options to take browsers through to company websites. They are currently the main form of advertising on the Internet. Advertisers bid on key words they believe potential customers will use in their searches (using Google, Yahoo or other Internet search engines). The search engines then display advertisements next to the results of the Internet search. While irritating to some customers they have proven very successful when linked to the page content being viewed. For example, search engines such as Yahoo and Lycos will flash links to commercial sites offering goods and services related to the items that are the subject of searches. Much of the early success of Amazon was attributed to the banner advertising it enjoyed on the AOL website which directed purchasers to books on the topics of interest. The effectiveness of banner advertisements in general, however, is questionable, with Timmers (1999) reporting that click-throughs (visitors clicking on banner ads to link through to the corresponding website) can be as low as 0.5 per cent (one in two hundred). As users of the Internet become more sophisticated and experienced it is likely that the click-through rate will fall rather than increase. To be effective a banner advertisement must make an immediate impact on an often crowded computer screen, as well as conveying in a few words reasons to click through.

Most rapidly growing, and predicted to account for more than half of Internet-based advertising by 2010, is pay-per-click advertising. The advertiser only pays when a customer clicks on their advertisement and is taken to their website. As only interested customers are likely to click through, the quality of the leads generated is very high and can therefore cost between $0.10 and $30 (average in 2006 was $0.50) depending on the keyword (*The Economist*, 25 November 2006).

Viral marketing

Viral marketing involves creating a marketing message with the intention that people will forward it to friends. This has a significant advantage over 'spam' messaging in that the friend will have some level of credibility which may cause the message to be viewed more sympathetically. While not unique to the web, Internet-based technologies have greatly facilitated easy use of this type of marketing.

The paint maker Dulux, for example, wanted to sell more paint to British women. Rather than indiscriminately bombarding women with e-mail messages to 'buy more paint' the company created a website featuring a 'belly fluff' game and e-mailed 10,000 women invitations to play. In the event, 13,000 did play. The company estimates that one-third of the people entering the competition received the e-mail forwarded from a friend (*The Guardian*, February 2002).

Forrester Research (**www.forrester.com**) estimates that a high-quality e-mail distribution list should generate a response rate (purchase) of around 6 per cent. A list created through panning will generate 1 per cent. Viral marketing, on the other hand, has achieved response rates of between 25 and 50 per cent (Forrester Research, quoted in *The Guardian*, February 2002).

Nestlé uses viral marketing for its Nescafé products including Blend 37. In one campaign 20,000 Nescafé drinkers were e-mailed invitations to click onto a weblink to enter a prize draw for tickets to the Silver Historic Festival in August 2001. The top 36 scores won VIP passes to an event at the Silverstone racing circuit (*Precision Marketing*, 29 June 2001).

Pre-launch promotion

The Internet can be an ideal vehicle for 'teaser' ads prior to new product launches (see for example *The Lord of the Rings* movie above). Before launching its new Crest Whitener into the US market, P&G set up a pre-retail launch website which attracted 1.2 million visitors and actually sold 140,000 units (worth over $6 million retail). The company estimated that the initiative created around 500,000 buyers before the launch advertising and retail distribution began (*Marketing Business*, July/August 2001).

Advertising audience measurement

In order to standardise the ways in which measurements of advertising reach and effectiveness are made the UK advertising industry has established a Joint Industry Committee for Web Standards (JICWEBS). The committee has now agreed definitions of 'users', 'page impressions', 'visits' and 'sessions'. JICWEBS is addressing circulation issues, but there has been little attention to date to audience profiling through panels and surveys, as exists for other media such as television (BARB) and the press (JICNAR).

11.4 Distribution strategies

Distribution strategy focuses on how products and services will be physically delivered to the customer. The distribution network used or created will depend on a number of factors including whether the final customers are consumers or other businesses.

11.4.1 Channels of distribution

The main choice facing most marketers is whether to sell through intermediaries or direct to customers. Intermediaries, such as wholesalers and retailers, can have a number of advantages. The most significant advantage is that they have direct relationships with customers that may be helpful.

In UK consumer grocery markets, for example, retailers such as Tesco, Sainsbury's, Asda, Morrisons and Waitrose have loyal customers who regularly shop in their stores. Products sold through the stores gain credibility in the eyes of the customer because of where they are sold. The disadvantage, however, is that the retailer has many competing products on their shelves, and has little incentive to promote one brand over another. Suppliers attempt to counter this through either a 'push' or a 'pull' strategy. A push strategy is one where the retailer is given incentives to stock the product (for example, bulk discounts or additional promotional offers that might encourage additional shoppers into the store). A pull strategy, on the other hand, is where the supplier encourages customers to go into the store demanding the product. In this way the product is 'pulled' through the distribution channel rather than being 'pushed'.

In business markets intermediaries may also be used (usually trade wholesalers) but it is more common to find direct sales through the firm's salesforce. The advantages of direct selling through a salesforce are discussed above. The obvious disadvantage is the cost incurred, though this is generally offset by the higher prices that can be charged. In addition many firms may hire a contract salesforce to help with special activities, such as the launch of a new product, or peak demand periods.

11.4.2 Effects of the Internet on distribution strategies

The Internet has greatly facilitated the distribution of bit-based products such as information, music and video. Indeed, in the recorded music industry, many now suggest that physical products like the CD are on the point of obsolescence because of the attractiveness of downloading music from the web. In 2005 there were more sales of albums as music downloads in the UK from iTunes than through the leading high-street CD retailer. The challenge for the music companies is to find ways of generating income from music downloads in the face of competition from pirate sites providing the music free.

With atom-based products the key to success has often rested with efficient and effective distribution systems and logistics. Every book sold by Amazon online must be delivered to the customer, and customers increasingly accustomed to rapid access via the Internet also expect rapid physical delivery once they have made purchases. The traditional '28-day delivery' period is no longer acceptable to many customers. Failures in distribution destroyed many of the dot.coms – eToys found, for example, that the 'virtual business' is an illusion, when you have to operate warehouses full of toys. The fulfilment strength of Amazon.com is proving a core competence, driving many of its alliances, for example with Toys 'R' Us.

Increasingly, the distribution issue becomes one of multi-channels – numerous ways in which the same products and services reach the customer. For example, one major strength of the Tesco.com Internet grocery offering was that it recognised that Internet grocery purchasing is not a substitute for store visits; it is a supplement. Managing complex multi-channel systems will be a substantial challenge for many companies. The critical tension will be between what companies want from multi-channel strategies and how customers react to them.

For example, PC market leader Dell Computers aimed to get the majority of sales onto the web because of the huge economies this achieves. However, the company also has internal and external salesforces to promote new products with corporate customers and to win business from the competition. Their view is that, if you want to buy a few PCs, then you buy on the web or go elsewhere. If you want to buy for a whole company, then you buy through the direct salesforce. If you are another Boeing with a potential installed base of 100,000 PCs, then the founder Michael Dell will come and see you. To make this multi-channel work, Dell has grasped the nettle of paying salespeople commission for sales through the web, and even offering salespeople additional bonuses for moving smaller buyers on to the web.

However logical multi-channel models may be, they can be reinterpreted by customers in other ways. One leading financial services company in the UK designed its channel system with three main options: the Internet, the branch network, and postal/telephone banking.

They saw customers as either Internet customers or branch customers. Customers, on the other hand, tended to redefine the model in their own terms: why not go to the branch to open a deposit account and get a passbook, then do all the transactions through the post or on the telephone, and then operate the current account on the Internet? The company's multi-channel strategy was wrong-footed (along with all the cross-selling and promotional plans in each channel), but they are learning to cope with the fact that this is how their customers want to use different channels.

11.5	The extended marketing mix – people, processes and physical evidence

11.5.1 People

While important in any business, the quality, training and enthusiasm of the people employed in the organisation are absolutely critical to service businesses. Happy, skilled and motivated staff are much more likely to serve customers well and effectively, and establish an ongoing relationship that can be mutually beneficial. A number of factors are important in designing the staffing strategy:

- **Job design and description.** The starting point is to have a clear idea of the job roles and tasks that staff will be required to carry out. This will include identifying the level of technical competence required, as well as the softer skills for dealing with people in a manner that will leave them satisfied (or better still, delighted). In service firms, however, jobs rarely conform to exact specifications. There is a need for flexibility to adapt the job as conditions change and as customer requirements also change.
- **Selection.** Choice of which staff to employ is largely driven by the job specification. If a 'bouncer' is being hired for a nightclub, the job specification will include an ability to physically defend himself and others. In hiring an accountant, however, other technical qualifications will be more important.
- **Training.** While staff may be highly skilled on appointment, ongoing training is essential to ensure that skills are maintained and enhanced in the light of changing circumstances. Much training may occur on the job but it can also be important to allow time out for reflection and to sharpen specific skills.
- **Appraisal.** Also important is regular appraisal and feedback to staff on their performance. Provided this is done in a constructive manner most staff welcome feedback on their performance and suggestions as to how it can be improved. Also part of the appraisal process is revisiting the job description and updating it in the light of experience.

Because the people employed have the direct contact with customers it can be problematic when staff leave. In some instances they make take the customers with them if they move to a rival organisation (e.g. account executives being poached from one advertising agency to another). The human resource management strategy needs to ensure the firm is not over-vulnerable to changes in personnel. This may be through rotation of customer contact staff, or through team approaches to serving particularly valuable customers or clients. In some instances 'golden handcuffs' might be appropriate to stop particular staff leaving and taking key clients with them.

11.5.2 Processes

The systems and processes involved in delivering the product or service to customers will not only impact on the ability of staff to effectively serve customers, they will also affect how customers judge the level of service they have received. Staff need to be given the tools to do the job. This may include ICT tools such as customer relationship management (CRM) packages (see **http://en.wikipedia.org/wiki/Customer_relationship_management**), as well as more basic order processing and delivery techniques.

CRM covers all the methods and technologies used by companies to manage their relationships with customers and clients. Information held on existing customers (and potential customers) is analysed and used to create a stronger and hopefully mutually beneficial relationship. Amazon.com use automated CRM processes to generate automatic personalised marketing (such as book and CD suggestions or recommendations) based on the customer information, including recent purchases, stored in the system. Using this technology advantage, Amazon is becoming a general trading platform for diverse products and services beyond books and CDs.

An effective CRM system helps organisations to acquire customers, build closer relationships with them, provide better customer services and hence retain valued customers. By tracking customer contacts through the CRM the organisation is able to ensure appropriate levels of contact are maintained, and to monitor the effectiveness of specific interactions.

In the public sector, universities are increasingly using CRM packages to track contacts with students through initial enquiry, decision to study, course performance and progress, on to graduation, career progress and alumni status. In this way additional opportunities can be pursued for improving the overall student experience through a complete life cycle, as well as maximising the return to the university by way of repeat business, donations and endowments from the student.

CRM applications often track customer interests and requirements, as well as their buying habits. This information can be used to target customers more selectively. In addition, the products a customer has purchased can be tracked throughout the product's life cycle, allowing customers to receive information concerning a product or to target customers with information on alternative products once a product begins to be phased out. Baby products companies now have sophisticated CRM packages that alert them to stages in the baby's development when, for example, there is a need to change from one type of nappy to another, or from baby food to toddler food. In some cases they even trigger automatic birthday cards.

11.5.3 Physical evidence

As discussed in Chapter 13, a key aspect of service delivery evaluation is tangibles, or the physical evidence that accompanies the offer. In the marketing of physical, atom-based, products the appearance of the product itself and its packaging, together with the surroundings in which it is marketed, can have an impact on the overall attractiveness to customers. For example, sophisticated retail facility design pays detailed attention to the smells and sounds that comprise part of the retail experience, as well as the sound and feel of the floor underfoot, and the space allowed to avoid the 'butt brush' (when one shopper brushes against another and disturbs their purchase consideration), and the effect of lighting on mood and ambience. In service encounters the appearance and demeanour of staff can be equally important.

Customers take many cues to the quality of the product or service they are purchasing from the physical evidence that surrounds it. When lecturing to MBA students or executives on management development programmes, most faculty members will dress in a more 'business-like' fashion than when teaching undergraduates. The formalities of dress code are used to establish rapport with the audience and are varied depending on the particular audience. Packaging for products may also vary to give cues as to quality. For example, the Sunday Times Wine Club distributes to members some of its fine wines in wooden crates while more everyday wines are dispatched in cardboard boxes.

11.6	New businesses and business models

In the wake of the uncertainty and undoubted opportunities generated by the Internet, two distinct types of firms are emerging: Internet pioneers and Internet pragmatists.

11.6.1 Internet pioneers

The Internet pioneers have set up radically new types of business to exploit the benefits of the new technology to do business in very different ways. Straub and Klein (2001) refer to these as 'omega'-level firms and note that the successful ones have harnessed the power of the new technology to gather information about customer preferences and to tailor products and services specifically to the needs of individual customers. These firms, however, are relatively rare but do include the likes of Amazon.com in consumer goods retailing, eBay in online auctions and Monster.com in the jobs market.

eBay is a prime example of an Internet pioneer. In the late 1990s it became the preferred place on the web to trade collectibles, building its position largely through word of mouth rather than media advertising, and creating a virtuous circle whereby more buyers attracted more sellers, who in turn attracted more buyers. In 2016 eBay has 162 million users worldwide. In 2015, eBay sold $82 billion worth of goods, 60 per cent of which was outside the US, and had more than 800 million listings.

A further example of an Internet pioneer is Egg, the UK's first Internet bank. The bank was launched with a positioning as both innovative and tailored to customer needs (the brand statement was 'Egg is your ground breaking partner, who is always there for you offering simple, smart financial solutions'). Within a week of its launch it had received 1.75 million visits to its website. By the end of 2001 it had gained 9 per cent of the UK credit card market and brand awareness has risen to a staggering 88 per cent. By then it had 1.58 million customers, on a par with many of the high-street banks. This was all achieved through the use of innovative technologies, which effectively lowered the entry barriers to a once well entrenched market (*Marketing Business*, September 2001).

11.6.2 Internet pragmatists

The second type of firm to emerge has been termed 'Internet pragmatists' (Fahy and Hooley, 2002). These firms have embraced the opportunities of the Internet to enhance their existing business models. Dell, for example, uses online ordering to enhance its direct marketing operations, FedEx uses the technology to enable personalised tracking of customer packages during transit (3.1 million packages per day with 99 per cent on time, accurate delivery), and Cisco saves US$700 million annually through offering customer support over the web. These pragmatists have used the Internet to enhance the services they already offered to their customers, and also to reduce costs, but have not completely thrown out their existing business models. Rather, these have been adapted to the new environment.

The national roll-out of Tesco's Internet grocery service in 2000 followed almost five years of preparation and piloting, and that preparation means Tesco.com leads the Internet quality measurements published by the Chicago-based Gomez company, and is regarded by many US companies in this field as a world leader. Certainly, Tesco.com was the world's largest e-grocery business with over $1bn in online sales in the UK alone by September 2008 (**http://www.davechaffey.com/E-commerce-Internet-marketing-case-studies/Tesco.com-case-study**). The formulation of Tesco Direct's value proposition and business model was based on close study of what customers wanted from Internet grocery shopping. Contrary to expectations that online shoppers would want to abandon traditional stores, they found customers liked to visit stores to examine fresh produce personally and to see what new products were available, and trusted their local stores to provide quality goods at fair prices. Most customers did not see online shopping as a substitute for traditional shopping, but as a complement. For this reason the online shopper uses the same store that they visit in person, choosing from the same regional product selection and buying at the same prices. The proposition was to 'shop online from my store'. The Tesco model integrates online and offline business – online sales are part of branch sales and feed into store-based replenishment. The value proposition is convenience and time-saving, but also greater personalisation – the software remembers previous purchasing and gives 'reminders', and can also warn those vulnerable about things like nut allergies and food choices. The relatively low start-up costs (£35 million) and fast national coverage reflect use of the conventional stores as 'mini-depots' where pickers can make up six online orders a time using a special trolley. Company estimates are that the average online shopping order is 2 or 3 per cent more profitable than the average in-store order, because Internet shoppers tend to select the higher margin products on offer.

The difference between the pioneers and the pragmatists can clearly be seen by the stage of diffusion at which they adopted the newer technologies. It seems that we are now firmly in the majority phase of diffusion of the Internet as an enabling technology (possibly even late majority stage) where the majority of adopters are pragmatists, using the new technology to enhance and improve existing business models, rather than to revolutionise them.

Many of the pragmatists represent the much-maligned 'old economy'. These are companies that, in some instances, were slow to join the information technology revolution and also includes those firms that are selective in their use of the Internet. For example, firms like IBM and Cisco Systems have moved most of their customer service online and customers now serve themselves from the menus of options available on their websites. These companies claim cost savings of the order of $500–700 million per annum through providing service online. Some of the kinds of online customer service currently available include customised web pages, targeted information, customer-service provider interaction, customer-to-customer interaction, customised products and rewards and incentives (Walsh and Godfrey, 2000).

Similarly, right through the business system, pragmatists are using the Internet to enhance what they are currently doing (Porter, 2001). For example, Compaq Computer Corporation is increasingly distributing software online rather than on CD and floppy disk. They have pioneered a 'try it and buy it' distribution system where customers use the software for a trial period and then the licence is extended should a customer wish to purchase. Sales conversion rates have increased significantly using this system. Many of the basic organisational activities are now being outsourced electronically. Mobile phone companies like Vodafone offer fleet management services for corporate clients while corporate health plans can be managed off-site by companies like BUPA. Corporate training services can be managed remotely by e-learning companies like Smartforce and even basic corporate R&D activity is enhanced by vast stores of information now available electronically. In summary, Internet pragmatists are those that have adopted the Internet to enhance existing products and processes. These are frequently labelled 'bricks and clicks' operations, meaning that the company sees the Internet as an additional channel which complements existing activities. Dell Computer Corporation found that its make-to-order model was very well suited to the Internet and consequently more than 50 per cent of its business is now being conducted through this medium. Allied Irish Banks examined the option of setting up an Internet-only bank to compete with the likes of First-e but dropped the idea in favour of improving its Internet banking facilities for existing customers.

While the Internet pioneers have grabbed the headlines, it is likely to be Internet pragmatists who eventually dominate the use of the Internet as a business channel.

Summary

The 'new' marketing mix is constantly changing. New ingredients are being added all the time by creative marketers. The most significant development over the last decade, however, has been the coming of age and greater exploitation as a marketing tool of the Internet. This has significantly impacted on all aspects of the marketing mix, from product and price through to promotions and distribution. A number of conclusions (and possible warnings) emerge:

1   Don't assume that the Internet will cure all your marketing ills. Firms that are poor at marketing in the bricks and mortar world are unlikely to suddenly succeed in the virtual world of the Internet. For creative, Internet-savvy firms, however, the new technologies may offer ways of leapfrogging more conventional competitors and adding value for customers in innovative ways.

2 Remember that atom-based products will still need efficient and effective distribution systems to physically get them to customers. Indeed, the logistics and distribution systems of online retailers may need to be even more effective than those of bricks and mortar firms as expectations of speed are greater for Internet-based firms.

3 Beware of assuming that today's atom-based products will be tomorrow's atom-based products. Increasingly, physical products (such as music CDs, videos, newspapers, magazines) are being turned into bit-based products. Because of the Internet the market for TVs and PC monitors is blurring; PDAs and mobile telephones can now access broadcast material.

4 Continue to base your competitive advantage on the marketing resources you possess that can be protected from competitor imitation. Actively develop the new resources, skills and competencies necessary to take advantage of the new technologies.

Case study   Sensory ploys and the scent of marketing

We have all heard of the estate agent tricks to help sell a property: baking bread in the oven or simmering a fresh pot of coffee on the stove. But marketing assaults on peoples' senses go far beyond a simple house sale. Global brands have become increasingly aware of the power of sight, smell, touch and sound to influence purchasing behaviours.

McDonald's has trialled scents for use in its restaurants in the knowledge that this not only draws in customers but also improves their perception of their overall dining experience.

Lynx, the popular deodorant for men, has spent considerable sums perfecting the sound of its aerosol can to amplify its brand message of strength and effectiveness. This has led to a spray that is noticeably louder than their 'female' deodorants.

Singapore Airlines even has a signature scent, which is worn by its aircraft crew and sprayed on to its steaming hot towels.

All these sensory ploys look to play on the limitations of the human brain, which is unable to cope with sensory overload. When this happens it uses cognitive short-cuts to reduce the amount of information it needs to process information. So a subtle scent or a particular sound can be just enough to awaken positive past associations or simply alter our other sensory perceptions.

Charles Spence, professor of experimental psychology at Oxford University and a sensory consultant to brands, points to research conducted by Unilever about 15 years ago. The fast-moving consumer goods group discovered that by adding a fragrance to clothes, they were perceived by users as whiter even when they weren't.

Scent in washing detergents has now become a powerful weapon in engendering brand loyalty. Indeed, sensory marketing has evolved into a multimillion dollar global industry. Diageo, the drinks group, which sets aside close to £2bn for its annual global marketing budget, invests heavily on managing the emotional responses of its consumers to many of its key drinks brands, and employs more than 180 people worldwide in innovation roles. Jeremy Lindley, Diageo's global design director, highlights examples such as 'the pop of the cork when you open a bottle of whisky or the particular sound a Baileys [Irish Cream liquor] makes as you pour it' as powerful emotive tools to boost sales. 'It's kind of hard-wired into our understanding of drinks and our understanding of the emotional connection that our consumers have to them,' he says. 'It's a topic that marketers and designers have become more aware of over the years.'

This understanding goes far beyond the drinks industry. From the reassuring clunk of a BMW car door to the subdued lighting in some shopping outlets, many sensory experiences are no accident. They are often the fruits of extensive market research and hours of work from behind-the-scenes scientists such as Diageo's own 'liquid development team', which sits inside its innovation centre.

Prof Spence says a push towards sensory marketing has accelerated in recent years following the growth in – and wider availability of – consumer research. 'If tests say [your brand] does not taste better than a white label, what can you do? You can start selling the experience of the bottle,' he says.

Drinks brands are also increasingly looking to improve the experience of customers in bars and pubs as ways to further engender brand loyalty. He points to a recent trend in Latin America of drinking gin and tonic in balloon glasses, which has led more drinks brands to roll out their own branded glassware for bars and pubs. 'By developing a signature glass you can change the drinker's behaviour by changing their experience,' he says, pointing to research that shows that a particular glass 'can add 20 per cent to the enjoyment'.

Francis McGlone, professor of cognitive neuroscience at Liverpool John Moores University, notes that some butchers use special fluorescent lighting: 'Lighting meat with certain wavelengths makes it look redder.'

But there can be measurable practical benefits to sensory research too. Toyota is looking to introduce a vibrating warning signal in its car headrests on the back of research which indicates that we respond more quickly to alerts in this area. In a car accident scenario, every millisecond counts. And in the world of trading, every millisecond has a financial value. Prof Spence is also working with a major bank to introduce sensory signals on its trading desks with the aim of shaving fractions of a second off the average trade.

Certainly, the advertising world appears to need little convincing of the emerging science behind sensory marketing. In March, JWT, the international ad group, formed a strategic alliance with Prof Spence as it seeks to push its consumer understanding beyond 'data, questionnaires and focus groups'. JWT says physical experiences and human senses will become even more important in the digital world as 'more people feel disconnected with the physical world'.

Some brands are encountering their own particular challenges as their customers migrate online. Splendid, a US clothing retailer that built its brand by using particularly soft materials, has introduced online tools that allow shoppers to listen to the texture of a material with the roll of a mouse.

Other tricks, such as using high-pitch music, can drive people towards the top of a website, Prof Spence says. Meanwhile, by simply changing the background colour on their website, companies can increase trustworthiness. This is of particular value, for example, when asking customers to enter their credit card details.

But brands do not always get it right. Back in 2008, Frito-Lay knew that consumers responded positively not only to crunchier crisps but also to noisier packaging. So it introduced new noisy packaging for its SunChips. So loud that they reached as high as 105 decibels, louder than a lawnmower or food processor.

Two years later it withdrew the packaging following widespread consumer complaints. There was even an active Facebook page entitled: 'Sorry but I can't hear you over this SunChips bag.'

There can be advantages in tapping into consumers' senses. But brands can clearly go too far, says Prof McGlone: 'People just don't like their world to be too dislocated sometimes.'

Source: from 'Sensory ploys and the scent of marketing', *Financial Times*, 03/06/13 (Budden, R.).

Discussion questions

1 Why are marketers interested in scent and other sensory stimuli?

2 How can sensory stimuli be integrated in the marketing mix?

3 What issues can you envisage in the use of such stimuli in marketing?

CHAPTER 12
COMPETING THROUGH INNOVATION

Self-driving cars . . . 3-D printing . . . the Internet of Things . . . the Apple Watch . . . legal marijuana . . . plants that glow in the dark to replace street lights . . . up-market office supplies for addicts . . . printable make-up . . . mobile light switches for the home . . . a vegan condom . . . a vacuum cleaner that uses ultraviolet rays to kill bacteria in carpets . . . light-producing walls to replace light bulbs . . . sensors in floors to measure gait and diagnose health problems . . . health spas for 5-year-olds . . . printable electronics to produce Harry Potter-style live newspapers . . . the world is full of novelties and new products.

Dyson to double numbers in UK engineering team

This article dates from 2010 and since that time Dyson has increased to over 2,000 engineers at their Malmesbury site and launched the robot vaccuum cleaner in 2015.

Sir James Dyson, the businessman behind the best-selling bagless vacuum cleaner, hand dryers and bladeless fan, is to double the numbers of its UK engineering team from 350 to 700 at its headquarters in Malmesbury, Wiltshire.

The recruitment drive will cover a range of engineering disciplines but focus particularly on a new generation of electrical motors being developed by Dyson to power a range of domestic and commercial devices.

Recent initiatives by the company include the worldwide launch of its D26 mini-vacuum cleaner and last autumn's launch of a bladeless 'Air Multiplier' fan.

Last year, Dyson patented an all-in-one kitchen appliance kit designed to accommodate a range of so-far undetailed kitchen appliances.

Sir James declined to comment on whether his expanded staff of R&D engineers would be looking to develop alternatives to traditional kitchen devices. But he confirmed that the development and consumer launch of a robotic vacuum cleaner was on Dyson's agenda.

'We are very much looking at a robotic vacuum cleaner – we made one five years ago – it'll be part of our future,' he said.

Source: Courtesy of Dyson.

Sir James, a longstanding champion of British engineering and recently recruited business tsar for the Conservative party, caused controversy in 2002 when he announced plans to shift production abroad to Malaysia with the loss of 800 jobs.

But Sir James said that employment at the Wiltshire site, set to rise from about 1,300 to 1,700, now exceeded the level employed before manufacturing went offshore.

The company, he said, had had a good recession and had steadily increased its R&D investment and staff throughout the global downturn while it remained 'the second-largest filers of patents in the UK after Rolls-Royce'.

The company hopes to recruit a range of graduating and postgraduate staff in fields ranging from microbiology, fluid, mechanical, electrical, acoustic and software engineering to work in new product lines.

Accounts for Dyson, published in September 2009, showed turnover rose from £611m to £628m as pre-tax profit fell from £89m to £85m in the year to December 2008, as R&D spending held steady at £49m.

Source: from 'Dyson to double numbers in UK engineering team', *Financial Times*, 26/04/10 (Kavanagh, D.).

Discussion questions

1 Why is Sir James Dyson set to double the numbers of his engineering team?

2 How successful would you expect Dyson to be at innovation?

Introduction

A recent report by McKinsey predicts that after decades of expansion, global economic growth will slow dramatically as the world's population ages. Their data suggest that the rate of gross domestic product will decline by 40 per cent over the next 50 years. They fear that today's feeble growth rates, collapsed oil prices and low interest rates may mark the start of a new era of austerity and low growth. However, the bright spot in the McKinsey work is that they conclude that with pro-market reforms and radical technological innovation, growth may accelerate again. Economic growth can be driven by creativity and, above all else, by innovation (cited in Tett, 2015). The priority for companies to compete through innovation has probably never been higher.

Certainly, many companies are experiencing the squeeze between investor demands for sustained earnings growth, and shrinking and fiercely contested post-recessionary markets. It is a problem that in the past, marketing has tended to fixate on serving and retaining current customers, which has been reinforced by company rewards and incentives that emphasise short-term market share and profitability. Marketing should be central to corporate growth but it is in danger of being marginalised in important decisions about growth strategy – some see marketing and sales only as the people responsible for selling what is produced and hitting volume targets. Instead, marketing's real role is to contribute to a firm's growth through better anticipation of market opportunities and evaluation of risks, tighter linking of technological possibilities with market concepts, and faster adjustment to shifting market needs and competitive moves (Day, 2003). The key has become **competing through innovation.**

There are many factors that encourage a company to innovate. These factors include internal pressures to exploit existing and new technologies to the full, together with the desire to use the organisation's resources, its assets and capabilities, as effectively as possible. External pressures include the push from intense competition, increasingly demanding customers whose priorities have changed through the recession, and the technological drive of shortening product life cycles (see Chapter 3).

We examine the mandate to compete through innovation at two levels in this chapter (see Figure 12.1). First, we examine key issues in innovation strategy, industry change driven by innovation, and the impact of disruptive innovation initiatives, leading to an emphasis on value innovation achieved through new business models and global innovation networks. Second, we turn our attention to the operational aspects of new product development, which are driven by a company's innovation strategy.

Certainly, new systematic product planning is a vital activity for every company, and it applies as much to services as it does to physical products. Generally, companies that are successful with new products follow a step-by-step process of new product planning combined with effective organisation structures and processes for managing new products. Experience

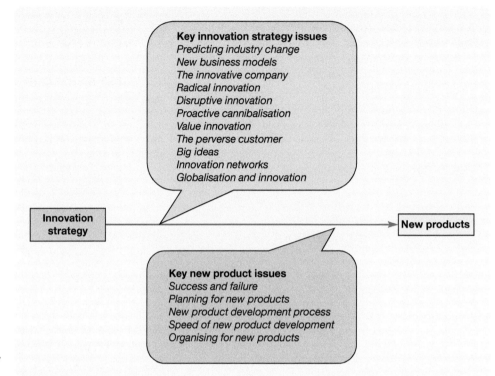

Figure 12.1
Innovation strategy
and new products

and learning helps these firms to improve product planning over time. Importantly, however the process is organised, the corporate cultures of companies like Apple, IBM, Facebook and Google actively encourage and reward innovation. It is imperative for executives to understand the reasons for new product failure and to avoid these pitfalls. By understanding the drivers of new product success, managers can check if their firm has the requirements for effective product innovation. If it does not, they should develop means by which the essentials of successful innovation are acquired to minimise the likelihood of market failure.

12.1   Innovation strategy

One of the most critical issues facing executives is the need for radical innovation in the value they provide to their customers. In many practical situations while true innovation addresses superior customer value, many of existing bureaucratic processes in corporate marketing are geared towards making only marginal changes in products and brands, and in avoiding mistakes rather than taking risks (Vence, 2007). Real innovation means more than producing new products which are marginally different to their predecessors. It is about the quest for delivering superior value to customers. Accordingly, before turning to the tactical and operational aspects of managing new product development, as part of marketing strategy and enhanced competitive positioning, it is worth considering some of the broader arguments supporting innovation as an essential key point of focus for executives.

12.1.1 Innovation predicting industry change

A powerful argument developed by Clayton Christensen and his colleagues is that understanding innovation patterns and emergent events is key to predicting the direction and extent of change in an industry – simply 'seeing what's next' (Christensen *et al.*, 2004). They suggest that major recurring questions for managers include issues such as: whether a new start-up will succeed or fail; which emerging technologies will be accepted by consumers; whether a new entrant is a serious threat to existing competitors; whether government regulation will affect competition significantly; whether company managers are making good or short-sighted decisions; which firms are likely to come out on top. Answering such questions correctly is fundamentally important to making effective strategic decisions. Christensen's work suggests that theories of radical and disruptive innovation provide a basis for addressing these questions (see sections below).

For example, in the IT sector, Google is reshaping the industry based on the strength of its search strengths, but particularly through the impact of cloud computing. Google's 'cloud' is a network of hundreds of thousands – by some estimates 1 million – cheap servers, each storing huge amounts of data, to make search faster. Unlike its predecessor, the supercomputer, Google's system never ages – as individual computers die, they are replaced individually with newer, faster boxes. This means the cloud regenerates as it grows, almost like a living thing. As the concept of computing clouds spreads, it expands Google's footprint way beyond search, media and advertising, and Google could become, in effect, the world's primary computer. IBM's head of research operations notes that 'compared to this, the Web is tiny'. No corporate computing system can match the efficiency, speed and flexibility of resources like Google's cloud. It is estimated that Google can carry out a computing task for one-tenth of what it costs a typical company. A move towards cloud computing represents a fundamental change in how we handle information. It is almost the computing equivalent of the evolution in electricity supply from a hundred years ago, when farms and businesses closed down their own power generators and bought power instead from efficient industrial utilities (this illustration is based on 'The clouds raining on the computer business', in Piercy, 2009a, pp. 162–167). But there is already fierce competition for Google from Amazon.com, IBM and salesforce.com to dominate cloud computing. By contrast, in the pharmaceuticals sector the new product pipelines of the major pharmaceutical companies have largely run dry – there are no new blockbuster drugs in prospect from conventional R&D, and current blockbusters are losing out to generic drugs as patents expire. Instead, the drug treatment innovation is being driven by small biotechnology start-ups based on less conventional science and technology in which big pharma has been slow to invest. Small biotechnology firms are commanding massive premiums as they sell out to big pharma (who have belatedly recognised that this new technology will shape the future of their industry) (Cookson, 2006).

An interesting area of speculation at present is whether Silicon Valley companies (Google, Apple) will challenge Detroit (Ford, General Motors) for control of the automotive industry. As Google and Apple are pioneering self-driving cars, they are in partnership with companies like Bosch, Continental and Delphi – leading suppliers to the industry. The growing technology content of the vehicle – about 40 per cent of the cost of the average vehicle already – creates a potential shift in power away from traditional brands and manufacturers to technology-led groups. While speculative for the moment, executives need to be constantly aware that innovation may reshape their industries in dramatic and unexpected ways (Gapper, 2015).

Increasingly the challenge facing executives is not simply to launch new and better products and services but to grasp how fundamental change is reshaping the industry and how to respond to this challenge.

12.1.2 Developing new business models

The business model, or business design, describes how a company makes money – how it generates revenue and profit by delivering value to customers – including the infrastructure and processes needed to achieve this goal. One of the hardest decisions for executives to confront is when the established business model has become obsolete, and how to change.

Tackling inefficiencies and developing better internal organisational processes is an important part of a manager's role, but coping with inefficiencies is ineffective if the business model has been displaced by something better.

The inevitable displacement of the recorded music CD by digital music downloads and now music streaming; the unbeatable challenge of the low-cost budget airlines to the established full-service flyers; the superiority of agile fast-fashion companies like H&M and Zara in speed and cost over established fashion clothes retailers; Google's attempts to make the value chain in wireless mobile like that in the broadband Internet market (where applications are developed independently of device manufacturers and network operators) may relegate operators to a minor and unprofitable role; the impact of open-source (free) computer software from Linux and Sun on conventional software producers like Microsoft – all are examples of new business models displacing the old by offering better value to customers.

A prime example of the power of a new business model is provided by the revolutionary Uber taxi service business model. Uber is already disrupting transport services in 230 major cities in more than 50 countries across the world and has quickly achieved a market value of $40bn. Uber provides an online platform supported by mobile apps to allow a taxi booking, linking the user to an independent contractor driver in his or her own vehicle, with the goal that the ride is never more than five minutes away. Prices reflect demand levels, and the ride is prepaid. Uber is reinventing the concept of the taxi ride and delivering superior customer value, in the face of resistance and hostility from regulators and conventional taxi companies. Uber owns no vehicles, but conventional taxi use in its first site in San Francisco has fallen by two-thirds in less than two years. What is more, the basic Uber concept is already spreading so that online platforms don't just coordinate hundreds of thousands of freelancers to drive taxis (Uber), but also rent rooms (Airbnb), clean laundry (Washio), provide massages (Zeel), and perform other services. These are all businesses that create a platform by combining the characteristics of companies and markets, in which the supply chain operates as a marketplace. The Uber phenomenon is about the creation of new business forms that replace the tired, unresponsive, clumsy, slow structures of conventional companies as a better way of delivering value to customers. Traditional organisations are increasingly unable to support the innovation and radical change demanded by the marketplace.

It is increasingly the case that competition is between business models rather than products and companies. It follows that companies require a capacity for continuous reconstruction or resilience to overcome forces which do no more than perpetuate the past, to seek out innovation for the future (Hamel and Välikangas, 2003). This explains the swapping of workers between Google and Procter & Gamble – the goal is to stimulate innovation in taking consumer products into online value chains.

The organisational changes at successful companies like Procter & Gamble and IBM in their search for valuable innovations that benefit customers, underline the fact that real innovation, that taps into new value creation opportunities, is likely to be disruptive and challenging, not incremental and predictable. Indeed, although innovation in marketing often refers to technology and products, the most important innovations may actually be in how we think about management and implement organisational change – management innovation changes how we work and is directly linked to sustainable competitive advantage. The constant search for better ways of managing underpins outstanding successful innovation at companies like Toyota and Procter & Gamble (Mol and Birkinshaw, 2007). In many ways the 'innovative company' has become the critical aspiration for management (see next section).

For example, several car makers are looking at 'pay-as-you-go' plans for younger consumers, as well as participating in new car sharing schemes, which aim to free urban dwellers from the need for car ownership in any form. Daimler, for instance, is working on a new 'pay-as-you-drive' business model that makes car use more like using a mobile phone than owning a vehicle in the conventional way. In the cosmetics sector, L'Oréal is pursuing a new business model based on 'accessible innovation' to expand its base into new and emerging markets. In the retail sector, new value chain models include 'pop-up shops' – temporary retail outlets operated by firms like Prada and Harvey Nichols, or by Internet fashion houses, to provide a new offer to their online communities. Marmite, for example, had a novel temporary store on London's Regent Street. These are innovations in business models, not simply in products.

These broad strategic issues should be addressed operationally in considering the link between effective marketing strategy and positioning and innovation. In several important ways, the most appropriate words to describe modern markets are revolution, reinvention and renewal:

- **revolution** – in the ways industries and markets operate and the sources of competition which become important, and consequently in the strategies that successful organisations pursue;
- **reinvention** – in the creation of new business models that make traditional ways of doing business obsolete as routes to delivering and sustaining superior customer value; and,
- **renewal** – in the strategies of change and repositioning by companies whose business models have become outdated, as they rebuild and respond to change. Increasingly the priority is not just short-term performance but building the robustness to bounce back, to change, to survive, to turn things around (Cravens *et al.*, 1998).

In using the structure in Figure 12.2 to analyse a company situation, we accept that the changes in the market amount to a **revolution**. It is inevitable that radical market and customer change provides disruptive pressures for the established players in the market. The challenge for them is to understand the specific changes unfolding and where they are going, and to respond with coping and adaptation mechanisms – **renewal.** The same market changes identify the new opportunities to create superior value for customers by designing new business models, i.e., to develop new ways of doing business which are aligned with market change – **reinvention.** Tracking the specifics of fundamental market changes and the disruptions created is the basis for developing effective responses and evolving new business models.

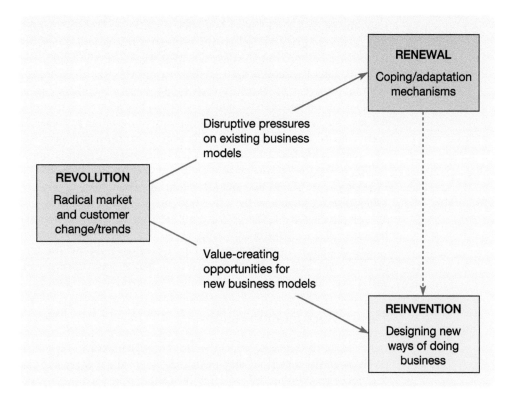

Figure 12.2
Innovation drives
strategy renewal
and reinvention

Source: Adapted from
Nigel F. Piercy (2017).

One interesting question in using this approach is whether the existing competitors in a market are capable of reinvention, or whether emerging value-creating opportunities will instead be exploited by new entrants to the market. It is quite possible that the new entrant, unencumbered by existing ways of doing things, will take the strongest position. When the laptop computer market became obsessed with the size and weight of the machines, the first sub-three pound laptop did not come from Dell, IBM or Hewlett-Packard – it came from Sony. Sony had no real track record or capabilities in the computer business, but is just very good at making things smaller. In the move to develop electric and hydrogen-powered vehicles as an alternative to high-pollution petrol fuels, it is small start-ups, notably in Silicon Valley, which are driving innovation, not the big car makers who have been reluctant to invest and slow to respond (Reed, 2008).

Increasingly, it looks like success goes to the company which can invent a whole new category of products – brewing coffee at home from expensive pods in expensive coffee-makers has taken the market away from traditional but cheaper ways of making coffee; Microsoft's Xbox live gaming system combines a traditional video game with a subscription-based online service; the creation of Spanx has revolutionised the underwear business by the creative use of a new fabric type. Companies which create new categories show high performance compared to their competitors.

12.1.3 The innovative company

Increasingly, and in most industrial sectors, one key survival factor is the ability to build creative, innovative companies. A new corporate model is taking shape in successful organisations, which focuses on creativity and innovation to provide new pathways to growth. As technology and information become commoditised and globalised, so the advantage of making things cheaper, faster and better diminishes and profits decline. Design strategy begins to play a key role in product differentiation, decision making and understanding the consumer experience. Creative innovation becomes the key driver of growth, because companies create products that address consumers' unmet and often unarticulated needs. The successful creative corporation emerges with a new 'innovation DNA' and a fast-moving culture that routinely beats the competition because of high success rate in innovation (Nussmaum, 2005). The transformation of software company Intuit came from the creation of the company as 'a design-driven innovation machine' and its 'Design for Delight' initiative to produce the most user-friendly software in the world.

Companies like Apple, Google, Toyota and General Electric are regularly rated as the most innovative in the world ahead of their competitors (McGregor, 2007). The move by Apple from computers to the music and movie business; the evolution of Google from Internet search to advertising, to data organisation, to online software, to mobile phones; the dominance of Toyota in hybrids and the quest for the first plug-in electric car; GE's search for 'imagination breakthroughs' has led into emerging market initiatives and green technology – all represent the power of ideas in changing markets and achieving step-changes in performance. Breakthrough ideas represent new market power. Steve Jobs at Apple achieved a step-change in the music business because of the iPod – not even a new product, but one which was a better-conceived and better-designed version of an existing product – because Jobs had the power to attract customers with his superior ideas (Colvin, 2007).

The challenge for marketing is to drive creative and powerful innovations that make a difference and reshape markets. Innovation that creates superior value provides a route to above-average earnings, even in turbulent markets (Henry, 2006).

12.1.4 Radical innovation

Importantly, the strategic imperative for effective innovation is not incremental change to products and services, but deep-seated change in the way we approach the market, and a deep focus on customer value – everything else is just variation on a theme (Vence, 2007). By contrast, it should be noted that it is estimated that minor innovations make up 85–90 per cent of most companies' development portfolios, but rarely generate the growth that companies seek – in effect, at a time when companies should be taking bigger, but smarter, risks, their bias is in the other direction (Day, 2007). The failure to innovate at this level has been tracked to: (1) paying too much attention to the company's currently most profitable customers, (2) creating products and services that do not do the jobs customers want done, and (3) the misguided application of financial analysis as an accomplice in the conspiracy against innovation (Christensen *et al*., 2008).

In fact, authors like Daniel Pink argue that the very basis of value creation is shifting from the disciplines of logic, science, and linear thinking to the intuitive, non-linear processes of creativity and imagination (Pink, 2006). Terms like the 'imagination economy' describe the move from technology and services to create value to creativity and imagination (Colvin, 2006). The focus is on innovation so radical it may even frighten customers – for example, a major concern at companies like Samsung and LG, who are worried that the growing sophistication of their products will put off buyers (Gowers *et al*., 2005).

When you identify the world's most innovative companies, the top five usually include Apple, Google, Microsoft, IBM and Toyota, but in fact when you look more closely at the list, 15 of the top 50 are Asian companies and the majority of the top 25 are based outside the US. *BusinessWeek* concludes: ' . . . we're starting to see the beginning of a new world order. The developed world's hammerlock on innovation leadership is starting to break' (Arndt and Einhorn, 2010).

1 Apple
2 Google
3 Samsung
4 Microsoft
5 IBM
6 Amazon
7 Tesla Motors
8 Toyota Motors
9 Facebook
10 Sony.

> *Source*: https://www.bcgperspectives.com/Images/Most_Innovative_Companies_ 2014_Oct_2014_tcm80-174313.pdf, accessed 2015, October.

These companies are managing deep-seated change, not just in products but in their business models.

Examining the issue of radical change in value offered to a market highlights issues like: **disruptive innovation** – innovation that changes the way an industry operates; **cannibalisation** – the resulting forces that drive successful companies to compete with themselves; **value innovation** – the companies that pioneer change with increasingly perverse customers; **big ideas** – nurturing the big ideas that will change an industry; and, **innovation networks** – the shift in managing innovation to open business models and cross-boundary collaboration. Importantly, **globalisation** may be one of the most important sources of radical innovation. We consider each of these questions briefly.

12.1.5 Disruptive innovation

The failure of many major organisations to innovate and change is in some important ways explained not because managers are complacent, but because they follow conventional wisdom in their industries. Clayton Christensen has described what he calls the 'innovator's dilemma' (Christensen, 1997). His research question concerned why major companies get left behind. Why, he asked, when the computer market moved from mainframes to minicomputers, was IBM left behind, and then when the market moved again from mini-computers to personal computers, were the makers of mini-computers (Digital, Wang, Nixdorf, and the rest) left behind in their turn? Could it be that these companies were too short-sighted to see how the market was changing, or was there something else at work?

Christensen argues that the PC was an example of a 'disruptive technology'. Generally, new technologies tend to do things better from the customer's viewpoint – these are 'sustaining technologies', because they allow us to sell similar things to current customers, but better, cheaper and faster. But, the distinguishing characteristic of the disruptive technology is that it does the job **worse** than the existing technology – but it is cheaper. However, as disruptive technologies improve over time, and get to do the job adequately, then their lower prices drive the existing technology out of the market. Disruptive technologies are fundamentally different to conventional or 'sustaining' technology.

For example, until the 1920s, the established technology for excavators was the steam shovel. This was followed by the machines powered by the internal combustion engine, which did the job better, and was a sustaining technology. Most large steam shovel excavator manufacturers made the transition successfully. In 1947, J.C. Bamford developed the hydraulic shovel, or backhoe. This did a poor job – it could only handle small bucketsful of earth, far smaller than was demanded by the big contractors in mining and sewage construction. The JCB was, however, cheap, because it worked off the back of a tractor. Initially its market was restricted to digging narrow trenches in the street. As its technology became more robust, backhoes attacked the main excavator market. Few of the traditional manufacturers survived.

Established manufacturers are bad at coping with these breakthroughs *because* they are so good at serving their customers. These companies knew about the innovations in question; the reason they did not adopt them was that their customers did not want them. The new technology appeals to less sophisticated, lower margin customers. The product is not as good as what went before. It is not what our (currently) most profitable customers want.

In other words, sticking to tried-and–tested strategies with our major customers may blind a company to changing market needs and competitors with new technologies. The risk faced is that established firms, excelling in the core competencies that keep their biggest customers happy, fail to see the threat of disruptive innovation in time because their customers do not see it, need it, want it, or ask for it (Donath, 2000). It is also the case that while the disruptive innovation undermines some business models, it may at the same time be a sustaining technology for others. The Internet, for example, disrupted Compaq's distributor-based approach to computer marketing, but was an important sustaining technology for the direct marketers Dell and Gateway – the Web allows them to serve customers in the same way they always did, but faster and cheaper.

Christensen also tells us that few established firms succeed in adapting to disruptive innovation. The best hope is to create an independent business with a completely new business model designed to attack the competition including its parent company. It also has to ignore the wishes of existing major customers – he calls this 'agnostic marketing', or the 'innovator's solution' (Christensen and Raynor, 2003).

More recently, Downes and Nunes have coined the term 'big-bang disruptors' to describe innovations which do not start at the bottom of the market with a lower-priced and inferior alternative to existing products. Big bang disruptors can come out of nowhere and instantly be everywhere, and once launched they are hard to fight. Navigation-product makers like TomTom, Garmin and Magellan were completely wrong-footed by the free navigation apps now pre-loaded on every smartphone, which are cheaper and much better than stand-alone devices. Consumers in every segment defected in a matter of weeks.

Faced with existing or potential disruptors in your market, the advice is to (1) identify the strengths of the disruptor's business model, (2) identify your own relative advantage, and (3) evaluate the conditions that would help or hinder the disruptor from beating your current advantages in the future – the goal is to develop a disruption of your own before it is too late, to participate in new, high-growth markets while you still can.

It may be that responding to such radical, game-changing market shifts requires an equally radical change in a company. One view, for example, is that resilience comes from two different efforts: first, repositioning the core business by adapting its current business model to the changed marketplace, and second, creating a separate, disruptive business to develop the innovations that will become the source of your future growth. Apple and IBM both took this twofold approach to adapting to changed markets. IBM rethought its mainframe business, shifting from proprietary systems to servers running open standard software, while creating a Global Services organisation that became the source of future growth. Apple repositioned its struggling computer business, trimmed the offering and focused on design; it was then ready to launch the iPod, open the iTunes store, and proceed with the 'i-revolution'.

Executives should constantly bear in mind that the evidence is that in the volatile markets we now deal with, disruption can occur anywhere – and likely will.

An interesting example of large-scale disruptive innovation is the television business. The once-dominant cable companies face new online and digital competition to which the existing providers find it difficult to respond. Cable and satellite operators compete to gain viewers, while services like Netflix try to draw them away. The likely response is mega-mergers to create giant media companies providing all services from conventional television to video-on-demand and streaming of programmes and movies (Gapper, 2014).

Even in a more traditional area, utilities companies in countries like the United States fear a 'death spiral' as more businesses and homeowners produce their own electricity with solar and wind power. They fear that the power company will go the same way as the telephone landline. DIY electricity is spurred by falling costs for solar panels and government incentives, so US homes and companies are producing more of their own power. Utilities fear this will squeeze their revenues while leaving them to bear the costs of maintaining the electricity grid. European utilities, notably in Germany, have already been battered by weaker demand and the EU's support for renewable energy. Responding effectively to disruption on this scale is challenging (Crooks, 2015).

Responding effectively to disruptive innovation also identifies the challenge of innovations that compete with what we already do – cannibalisation.

12.1.6 Proactive cannibalisation

(This section draws from Cravens *et al.*, 2002.) One of the strongest conventional arguments against radical innovation is that we end up simply competing with ourselves – we cannibalise our own sales to our existing customer base. Executives often believe that it is unproductive for a company to compete with its own products and services, rather than targeting those of competitors – it risks under-exploiting existing investments for no gain in sales (or probably profits). However, the idea of 'proactive cannibalisation' has taken grip of many strategists' minds. At its simplest the logic is compelling – someone is going to compete with you and attack the sales of your products and services, so you might as well do it yourself and retain the customer. More elegantly expressed:

> What causes some firms to be radically innovative over long periods of time, whereas many others ossify and perish? We suggest that the answer lies in the extent to which firms are prepared to give up the old and embrace the new. Firms must break out of the natural human trait that propels them to use yesterday's bag of tools to solve tomorrow's problems. They must do so today, while they still have options, not tomorrow, when they will have nothing left but a useless bag of tools. They must be willing to cannibalise before there is nothing left of value to cannibalise
> *(Chandy and Tellis, 1998a)*

These researchers conclude that, although it is counter-intuitive for many managers and organisations, willingness to cannibalise is one of the most powerful drivers of radical product innovation (Chandy and Tellis, 1998b).

For example, Volkswagen's multi-brand strategy (VW, Audi, Seat and Skoda) leads to some competition between its brands in the middle of the market (all the brands have similar hatchbacks built on a similar engineering platform), but enabled VW to break Fiat's control of the European car market and achieve leadership, until the faked emissions test scandal of 2015 weakened the company's position.

Nonetheless, considerable care is required. Faced with the invasion of the British and European internal flight market by 'no frills', low price operators like easyJet and Ryanair, BA needed to respond to stop the decline in market share. Having looked at buying their new competitors or putting them out of business, and being prevented by the European regulators from doing either, BA's response was to establish its own 'no frills' airline – Go. However, from the start Go was priced substantially higher than the 'no frills' operators, but offered less service and convenience than BA's regular flights. Predictably, the major effect of Go was to cannibalise sales of BA flights, but with little impact on the 'no frills' operators, who continued to expand. By 2001, BA was ready to sell Go (for much less than the original asking price). Go was sold to venture capitalists 3i for £110m, who promptly resold the business to easyJet, the rival low-cost airline. It seems a conventional full-cost airline lacked the will or the ability to operate a 'no frills' operation, and BA had simply established a stronger competitor for itself. A similar result was achieved by Buzz, launched by KLM as its low-cost brand, which was bought by Ryanair in 2003 for £15m (based on O'Connell, 2003).

Less extreme is defensive cannibalisation – or at least cannibalisation resulting from defensive strategies – which is different to proactive cannibalisation, when the price of innovation is to compete with your own products. For example, Intel's continuous improvement of computer chips and Gillette's continuing introduction of improved shaving technology show cannibalisation that has positive benefits at relatively low risk.

12.1.7 Value innovation

The growing challenge for companies is to focus innovation thinking on customer value. Broad-based innovation is increasingly critical – extending far beyond new products and services to include ideas, processes, business practices and designs (Shervani and Zerrillo, 1997) – and is not just concerned with conventional new product development, and minor brand extensions. Gary Hamel is critical, for example, of the type of product-led, incremental change led by marketing departments in the past – his challenge is that we should be creating radical new products, concepts and business models or face the alternative of 'crash and burn' He says. 'Radical, non-linear innovation is the only way to escape the ruthless hyper-competition that has been hammering down margins in industry after industry' (Hamel, 2000). For example, in one major research programme, the study of 100 major new business launches found that 86 per cent were 'me-too' launches, or incremental improvements, but these generated only 62 per cent of launch revenues and 39 per cent of profits. By contrast, the other 14 per cent of launches – those radical enough to create or re-create markets – generated 38 per cent of revenues and a massive 61 per cent of profits (Kim and Mauborgne, 1998).

The reality is that as products tend to converge and become more similar, it is no longer possible to beat the competition by making incremental improvements and changes, because they will be instantly copied, and in modern markets you quickly reach the point of diminishing returns (Jones, 2000).

An important insight comes from the work of W. Chan Kim and Renee Mauborgne at INSEAD. Their observation is that between 1975 and 1995, 60 per cent of the *Fortune 500* companies disappeared. The reason was that in industry after industry, companies building innovative businesses raced ahead by replacing established firms who were focused on improving existing businesses. Their research suggests that the really high-performing companies in every sector are those who achieve 'value innovation' – they do not just imitate competitors, or invest for competitiveness against established rivals, they innovate in new value for customers. They suggest that one useful exercise is to assess our portfolios of products and service on their 'Pioneer-Migrator-Settler' map, because innovation linked to value determines our real growth prospects. They argue that we should examine and predict the competitive offerings and entries in terms of the categories:

- **Settlers** – these offer 'me-too' value, based on equalling what their competitors do, usually in the same way that they do it, but often cheaper.
- **Migrators** – these offer conventional value improvements over competitors, e.g., in product function improvements or design.
- **Pioneers** – these are the businesses that represent real value innovations, e.g., the Sony Walkman, the Dyson bagless, cyclone carpet cleaner, the Swatch watch, and so on. Apple's iPhone is a pioneer, because by introducing the App Store and linking app developers and app users, Apple created a platform, not just another phone product (Van Alstyne *et al.*, 2016).

A portfolio that is heavy with settlers leads to a company's decline. One dominated by migrators offers some growth potential, but is vulnerable to the strength of a value innovator. The issue is whether we are gearing our planning towards pioneers, or merely settling for the *status quo*. The challenge is to continuously shift the portfolio away from settlers. This may produce very different conclusions to those based on just looking at current numbers like market share, sales revenue, customer satisfaction and profitability – because these numbers all represent the past, not the future (Kim and Mauborgne, 1997, 1998).

The underlying principle is that 'understanding the needs of customers is what distinguishes innovation from novelty . . . pioneers are routinely pushed aside by rivals whose skills are in the marketplace rather than the laboratory' (Kay, 2009). For example, Apple's achievements are less about its new technology and more about deploying existing technology in ways that meet consumer needs and attracting buyers through beautifully designed devices which are user friendly. The issue is creating superior customer value through innovation and this is the critical challenge for marketing strategy.

12.1.8 The perverse customer

One further driver of value innovation is the truculent or perverse post-recessionary customer. A weakness of much of the literature of marketing and management, and perhaps even more of economics, is the assumption of the compliant and acquiescent customer who responds predictably to price and other marketing stimuli, and is a willing partner in the consumption process. In reality, we face the sophisticated consumer who rejects traditional marketing messages. One overarching impact of economic downturn and recession is a wholesale loss of confidence in institutions, both public and commercial, and in particular a loss of trust in business and the professions, which takes consumer sophistication much further. Hence, we have the perverse customer.

It is not so much that we have to deal with the sophisticated customer who is more demanding in relatively conventional ways, but a customer who is actually perverse and maven-like in their dealings with business and with authority in general. The perverse customer is the one who takes a positive delight in confounding the attempts by their political masters, lobbyists, or by business to change their behaviour. In other words, the customer who delights in being awkward and who changes the rules. Consider the pressure placed on consumers to adopt electric/hybrid cars promising environmental benefits. In spite of all the hoopla and policy pressure it took Toyota a decade to sell the first million Prius vehicles, in a world with more than a billion vehicles on the road. The evidence is that the customer decisions on vehicles regarding size and fuel-efficiency have more to do with oil prices than environmental conscience. With the plunge in oil prices, companies like Tesla in the electric car market are suffering badly, because car buyers are going back to fast sports saloons and 4×4s, because they like them more than clunky and expensive electric cars.

The real point is that in the tough, cynical post-recession markets in which we have to survive, we have to identify new value-creating and profit-generating opportunities and innovate in the areas that customers value. Consider the following examples of the perverse customer, but importantly, what comes out in business opportunities:

- **Train fares.** The confusion pricing policies adopted by some railway companies create anomalies – buying two single tickets may be cheaper than a return; splitting journeys into segments and buying a separate ticket for each segment can often produce a cheaper total fare. Confusion pricing only works if customers cannot be bothered to untangle the confusion, and most times they cannot or will not. However, that untangling is really easy for a computer algorithm. The opportunity is underlined by Trainsplit.com which already offers the online service of splitting journeys into legs to minimise fares, even though it requires a whole set of tickets for a single journey. Most consumers will not bother with this and will go on paying higher fares. The perverse customer is the one who will go for the ticket splitting, and moreover will take pleasure in beating the train company.

- **Cigarettes.** Governments and the anti-smoking lobby have mandated the placement of lurid pictures on cigarette packets and now dingy, generic pack designs as a ploy to discourage smokers. Other ploys include forcing retailers to hide the cigarettes they quite legally sell, behind covers, lest an innocent and unknowing consumer should suddenly start smoking because they have seen the product on the shelf. These are crude policies and crude policies often have unintended consequences – e.g., it seems that anti-smoking ads actually remind smokers that it is time for a cigarette, which was not the intended outcome. The opportunities are starting to emerge. It is almost inevitable that by the time there are generic ugly cigarette packs, there will also be a range of attractive and decorated sleeves into which those unattractive packages will slide. There will be a resurgence in the use of cigarette cases and boxes. More importantly, digital channels will become a more significant value chain as people buy whole cartons of cigarettes to avoid playing guessing games with shop assistants who are not allowed to show them what cigarettes are available. The perverse consumer does not like being coerced and is likely to respond accordingly. There is money to be made here.

- **Bin collections.** The environmental 'green' lobby is pushing harder and harder on local authorities, and using more and more tricks to get their own way, to reduce the number of household rubbish collections, and local authorities are complying to save money. Consumers, however, generally want their rubbish collected every week – particularly perishables, which smell and attract vermin – whatever the environmental lobby thinks. As a result, we are already seeing the launch of private bin collection services which will collect household waste on a weekly basis for a small fee. Expect also a rapid growth in household waste disposal units as people decide to put their food waste direct into the public sewer on a daily basis, in spite of environmental considerations. It seems that the perverse consumer just will not be cooperative when they are inconvenienced. There is money to be made here.

- **Medicine.** Writing prescriptions for medicines and diagnostic tests has long been a monopoly of doctors and a few other clinicians. But doctors often do not do what they are told by patients and generally make the process of getting things you want difficult – including waits of up to a month to get to see a GP, forcing people to sit in a waiting room full of ill people, and making them wait weeks for test results. Most consumers put up with this. Some do not. Companies like Direct Laboratory Services and WellnessFX in the United States have already leapt on the opportunity provided by perverse customers – they sell diagnostic tests direct to consumers, cutting out the barrier of the doctor. You want a battery of blood tests or a thyroid function measurement – there you go, all yours, no doctor interfering. Rapid and at-home diagnostics are a very attractive and growing niche in the global health care business. Similarly, 23andMe provides the consumer direct with genetic testing based on DNA analysis (Piercy, 2017). And that is before you even consider the potential for self-prescription and the growing purchase of pharmaceuticals on the Internet. This will grow even faster when quality assurance is more advanced. Consumers are cutting the doctor out. It may not be wise, but it seems to be what is happening. There is money to be made here.

- **Privacy.** It is clear that privacy and the rights of the individual provide one of the hottest issues in the twenty-first century. The state has taken upon itself unprecedented rights to observe and track citizens and monitor their behaviour, all the way from intense coverage of public areas by cameras through to checking phone calls and e-mails and exploiting health and bank data. Similarly, there are a growing number of business models which rely on using personal and individual data for commercial advantage. For example, Facebook and Google are advertising-supported businesses that use member social interactions and search behaviour to sell behaviour-directed advertising – that is how they make money. For others it is a lucrative by-product – retailers track consumers through their mobile phones; gaming machines and smart TVs observe and monitor users in their homes; the NHS sells patient data; and so on (Piercy, 2017). Some consumers simply do not care. Others are really quite miffed and definitely interested in products and services which make it difficult or impossible for others to invade their privacy. We are already seeing the launch of encryption software to prevent e-mail monitoring; secure mobile phones that cannot be monitored; walled-garden social networks to avoid Facebook; people refusing to supply their personal data when they do not have to or submitting false data; and growing pressure to assert the right to anonymity. There is even a resurgence in sales of manual typewriters in some areas where privacy is paramount – try hacking a typewriter! In fact, privacy will become one of the biggest products in the twenty-first century, as people become prepared to pay to avoid being observed, monitored and targeted. There is money to be made here.

Governments and powerful lobby groups cannot resist tinkering with markets in their desire to change other peoples' behaviour. Often, they get it wrong. Decades of persuading people not to eat butter because it is 'bad' for them turns out to have been based on bad science and possibly even harmful to peoples' health, as well as severely damaging to the dairy industry. Nonetheless, even after tinkering and intervention, markets adjust and identify dissatisfied customers who will be responsive to new offers. Markets always adjust in the end. As mature markets become more fragmented or granular, the perverse customer is becoming an interesting target in a growing number of situations. Observing the diverse ways in which perverse customers get their own way, and smart companies make more money as a result, is an interesting exercise for any manager. Learning to deal with a defiant, awkward, yet sophisticated customer, who does not plan to be cooperative and docile any time soon, is a major challenge for suppliers of all kinds, but that is where the money will be made. The search for value innovation opportunities may lead in surprising directions.

12.1.9 Big ideas

The heart of radical innovation is the search for 'big ideas', rather than settling for 'small ideas'. To stay relevant and to succeed, companies need bold, innovative strategies. But this relies on the ability to create and resource big ideas, and to overcome inertia, narrow-mindedness and risk aversion that provide barriers to true innovation – what Bernd Schmitt calls 'big think strategy' (Schmitt, 2007). For example, the launch of the iPhone by Apple – an attractive mobile phone, though based on out-of-date technology – achieved mixed sales results. On the face of things, the iPhone was a straightforward extension of the iPod and iTunes music business, with the prospect of competing against the BlackBerry in the business market. In fact, as the underlying iPhone strategy unfolded, a very big idea became apparent. By allowing software manufacturers to create applications or 'apps' custom-built for the iPhone – freed by the iPhone's breakthrough touch screen from the constraints of fixed buttons and small screens – the goal was to allow the iPhone to develop into the 'third great platform' for software makers, after the personal computer and the Internet. This is a 'big idea', not just another mobile phone (Allison, 2008).

In another example, after a history of missing out on some of the most important big ideas when they arrived, IBM is putting some of its brightest and best talent behind new ventures that break free of the existing business. Because new ideas fall between organisational boundaries and sometimes conflict with existing business units, they are managed differently. 'Horizon Three' businesses, as opposed to Horizon One businesses (mature businesses like mainframe computers) or Horizon Two businesses (current growth businesses), are protected from the rest of the organisation. They are put in separate organisational units with dedicated teams, providing visibility and management sponsorship. The young Horizon Three business units are insulated from traditional management methods and performance yardsticks – efficiency measures can squeeze the life out of a promising new idea. There is a clear understanding that Horizon Three businesses benefit from personal sponsorship by senior managers, to prevent middle managers using their power to block new developments that might not fit their personal agendas (Waters, 2001).

There is also a compelling argument that sustainability is, and should be, a key driver of innovation. For example, Nidumolu and colleagues argue that sustainability is linked to lowering costs and increasing revenues and should be part of all thinking about innovation. They believe that only companies that make sustainability a goal will achieve competitive advantage (Nidumolu *et al.*, 2009). Certainly, sustainability is one of the big ideas which executives should consider in planning and making innovation choices.

Generally, growing emphasis is being placed on developing an 'ideas culture' in companies (Overell, 2005). However, in IBM as in many other companies, the search for big ideas as the basis for radical innovation increasingly relies on collaboration with others and open source approaches, rather than relying on in-house development.

12.1.10 Innovation networks

The growing emphasis on collaboration and cooperation (**see** Chapter 15) in radical innovation strategies is underlined by Lynda Gratton's research into 'hot spots' of energy and innovation in companies (Gratton, 2007). Gratton sees hot spots as points where people work together in exceptionally creative and collaborative ways. For hot spots to emerge, they need: (1) a cooperative mind-set, (2) an ability to span boundaries, and (3) a successful igniting of purpose – following by making productive capacity available to create real value. The old, protective barriers set up by businesses around themselves are increasingly a barrier to the new open business models that underpin radical innovation (Chesbrough, 2006).

For example, Procter & Gamble sets high targets for the proportion of its new products developed with external partners, and there are many other examples of effective innovation partnerships demonstrating how open innovation can power growth:

- **Nike+** – Nike worked with Apple to develop a sensor that can transmit data from the heel of its running shoes to the wearer's iPod or iPhone, launched in 2006.
- **Little Swimmers Sun Care** – Kimberly-Clark created adhesive plasters for children that use ultraviolet sensitive material to warn parents of the risk of sunburn, developed and marketed in partnership with Sunhealth Solutions in the US and launched in 2007.
- **Aquafresh White Trays** – GlazoSmithKlein's Consumer Healthcare's entry into the tooth whitening strip market in 2007 came through a partnership with Oratech, a private manufacturer supplying dental products (Birchall, 2010).

Further insight into new forms of collaboration and open source innovation comes from Don Tapscott's *Wikinomics* (Tapscott and Williams, 2007). A 'wiki' is a piece of software that allows thousands of people to edit the same website. Tapscott's view is that if people from all over the world can get together to create an encyclopaedia – Wikipedia – there are no limits to what they can create. Wikinomics brings people together on the Web to create a giant new brain. Companies are exploiting this in the form of 'crowd-sourcing'. When

Procter & Gamble needed a new chemical to remove red wine stains from clothing, instead of turning to their own R&D department, they created a website called InnoCentive, where anyone could come up with a solution and be paid. The logic is that 1.5 million people on the Web are more likely to come up with the solution than 9,000 chemists in the company.

Many companies have realised that going 'open source' or collaborating and sharing ideas means many innovations can be created and developed outside the company. At Procter & Gamble, in a massive turnaround of a business that had stalled, under A.G. Lafley the company abandoned its reliance on in-house R&D. The classic corporate drive to research and develop was replaced by a 'connect and develop' strategy of working with outside partners. By 2007, 35 per cent of P&G's new products came from outside the company. Under Mr Lafley, P&G's performance saw a step-change improvement, and rival Unilever was left behind. This is an 'era of open innovation' (Ancona and Bresman, 2007).

Indeed, for many major organisations, reduced spending on traditional R&D activities has encouraged a broad global search for new ideas from any source. Companies like Intel are locating satellite research facilities close to leading research universities to tap into academic expertise. In some cases the breakthrough ideas come from research-based collaboration. For example, Xerox has broken with its tradition to look to outsiders to help develop optical-network technology. One result is the inclusion of Xerox's imaging technology expertise in a joint project with Intel, to produce a new microprocessor tailored to document imaging. In complex and rapidly changing markets, many companies are exploring new and faster ways to capture new ideas from diverse sources as the basis for developing new products and services (Greene et al., 2003).

Worldwide innovation networks are increasingly central to maintaining and enhancing competitiveness. This may involve a worldwide research and development organisation. Microsoft is tapping into a new talent pool with its advanced technology centre outside Beijing. IBM has major labs in China, Israel, Switzerland, Japan and India. For smaller companies, global innovation networks involve loose structures of in-house engineers, contract designers and manufacturers, university scientists, and technology suppliers brought together around a single project. At a time when technology crosses borders faster than ever – because of the Internet, cheap telecoms, and advances in interactive design software – the location of R&D matters less than who controls the networks (Engardio, 2004).

12.1.11 Globalisation and innovation

The examples above emphasise the global perspective needed to understand how innovation is changing.

For example, Indian company Mahindra & Mahindra, has opted to design and manufacture its latest motor scooter in the United States, turning conventional wisdom on its head. The company aims for an 'all American product' generated by its 'global new-product manufacturing set-up'. Emerging market companies are rapidly evolving their traditional business models (Mallett and Crabtree, 2015).

The broader implications are interesting. A number of influential global companies, like General Electric and Procter & Gamble, are adopting strategies of 'reverse innovation', i.e., turning products created for the emerging markets into low-cost products for developed world customers (Govindarajan and Trimble, 2012). The new approach is also known as 'trickle-up innovation'. GE, for example, has created a portable ultrasound business, stemming from products originally designed for China, which has achieved growth rates of 50–60 per cent a year in its early stages (*BusinessWeek,* 2009).

In another example, consumer goods company Nestlé is bringing sales and packaging techniques pioneered in emerging markets to improve its position in problematic markets in Europe. Marketing innovations developed in countries like Thailand and Russia are being applied in stressed European markets like Greece, Spain and Ireland to familiarise less affluent consumers with Nestlé brands. Innovations include smaller packs for Nescafé instant coffee and 'refill' coffee packs, and Maggi soup powders sold in individual units (Simonian, 2010).

It is clear that emerging markets are not only providing multi-nationals with faster growth prospects, but also new products, services, manufacturing methods and business processes. For example, Pulpy is a drink developed by Coca-Cola's Chinese offshoot which is being launched in eastern Europe, after a successful entry to Latin American markets. Similarly, Levi Strauss, makers of Levi's jeans, has brought its Denizen brand of jeans, nurtured in China, back to its home US market. A mobile payment system which has revolutionised business and banking in sub-Saharan Africa is being brought to Europe by Vodafone. These are examples of emerging markets spawning new products with global potential. While once business solutions flowed only from the West to the East, they are now flowing from East to West as well (Wagstyl, 2011).

The underlying point is that the model that companies like GE have followed in the past – developing high-end products for the home market and adapting them for export – does not work as growth slows in the developed markets. The goal is to develop products in markets like China and India, and then distribute them globally to tap into value-based segments across the world (Immelt *et al.*, 2009).

Indeed, some argue that the real revolution in business is doing more with less. For example, Radjou and Prabhu make a compelling case for 'frugal innovation', learning from the emerging markets, where engineers move away from plentiful resources in a rich market to constrained resources and value-hungry customers (Radjou and Prabhu, 2015). When Renault found its expensive cars were outsold in India by the $6,000 locally produced Lada, they created the no-frills $6,000 Logan. Designed for India but selling well in Europe, Renault developed a line of low-cost vehicles that today constitutes nearly half its global sales. A similar view is adopted by Charles Leadbeater in his work on 'shoestring innovation', emphasising reuse and recycling in low-cost innovation (Leadbeater, 2014). Frugal innovation has produced ultra-cheap laptops, mobile phones, refrigerators and even ECG machines (Coy, 2015).

Earlier, Radjou and his co-authors used the Hindi word 'jugaad' to describe the approach of entrepreneurs in India and other emerging markets, where innovation is driven by finding opportunities in scarcity and developing smart ways to make more from less. They argue that businesses in the richer Western world have lost their innovation edge and executives should study and learn from jugaad innovation. The focus should be on simplicity, not endless new product features (Radjou *et al.*, 2012).

The globalisation of innovation suggests new approaches and models from which to learn. Certainly, it is likely that radical innovation will lie at the heart of strategic thinking in many companies and the new context is global. Indeed, as we noted earlier, the most important innovations may be in how we change the ways in which we work, organise and manage (Mol and Birkinshaw, 2007) – the issue is not just a new product, but a new business model.

We turn attention now to the innovation process – or new product development – within a company.

12.2 New products

Studies that compare new product successes with failures are consistent in their observations of the key factors that influence a new product's success in the marketplace. Getting to grips with these helps executives to understand successful product innovation. For example, one interesting way of categorising the new products that firms produce is as follows:

- **Dinosaurs** are products that have missed their niche, the market has moved on and the demand for them has passed. Where product development times are overly long, there is a danger that even well-researched products take too long to come to market. By the time they are launched the market has moved on, customer requirements have changed, and/or competitors have more successfully met those needs.

- **Flamingos** are products that are beautiful but unsaleable. The development process has resulted in products with well-designed features and a multitude of characteristics – but unfortunately the costs of producing are too high, due to over-specification, that customers cannot afford to buy. Unless there are enough potential customers willing and able to buy, the flamingo runs the risk of early extinction.

- **Ostrich** products are blind to the future. They may meet today's market needs but take no account of future changes in the market, and are not well placed to adapt and change as customer requirements and competitive pressures evolve. An example is the Iomega PocketZip drive which saved on a disk and was launched just when self-sufficient flash memory cards came on the market.

- **Pearls** are the constant quest of effective new product development. A pearl will always be of value, and even if its popularity wanes it can be modified into jewels or traded for other resources required. The pearl offers the source of a profitable future for a foreseeable period.

12.2.1 Successful new products

Successful new products provide better performance than existing products and often they succeed despite being offered at higher prices than competitors. In fact, most failures offer price parity or inferior value. Successful products offer advantages that matter to customers (see Figure 12.3). Failures too have performance advantages, but in fringe areas where customers see little benefit.

As well as price and performance advantage, successful new products often provide benefits that are dramatically different from current offerings. For example, Innocent fruit smoothies (which contain nothing else but fruit) provided a uniquely healthy snack/drink. New products need to have a significant advantage over existing products.

Conventional thinking also suggests it is almost always better to be first to market.

Despite the inevitable risk of being a pioneer, first to market is often best for several reasons. The news value of an innovation peaks in the early stages, and this offers maximum communication impact and a chance for widespread consumer trial. The innovator catches consumers first; this means that competitors who follow must improve their market positioning and produce better and/or cheaper products to make consumers switch. This may not be easy to achieve once the pioneer has secured strong consumer loyalty and a reputation for innovation in the marketplace.

For example, Richard Branson explains: 'A good idea for a new business tends not to occur in isolation, and often the window of opportunity is very small. So speed is of the essence' (Hamm, 2006). In many companies, the time to bring new products to market has halved in recent years: at Nissan, the development time for new cars used to be 21 months, now it is 10½ months; Nokia and Motorola used to take 12 to 18 months to develop new mobile phone models, now it is 6 to 9 months; H&M can get fashion clothes from sketch pad to the racks in its stores in just three weeks; Samsung partnered with XM Satellite Radio to bring the first portable satellite radio combined with music player to store shelves in 9 months from the partners shaking hands on the deal. Similarly, by closely aligning design, R&D and marketing,

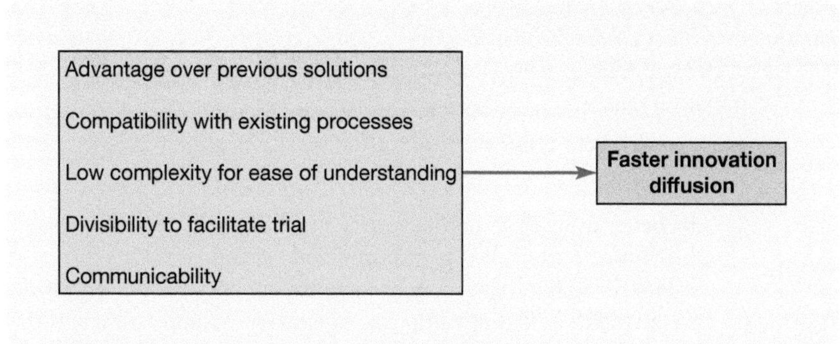

Figure 12.3
Accelerated
diffusion of
innovations

Advantage over previous solutions

Compatibility with existing processes

Low complexity for ease of understanding → **Faster innovation diffusion**

Divisibility to facilitate trial

Communicability

appliance maker Electrolux cuts product launch times by a third compared to competitors (Matlack, 2013). At the other end, it also follows that fast innovators like Virgin and Google are also fast to get out of a venture when things underperform (Hamm, 2006).

Nonetheless, it should be noted that first mover advantage is not always the best goal. In some situations strategy may be more about 'active waiting', rather than speed and trying to establish a first-mover advantage. Donald Sull argues, for example, that really attractive business opportunities are quite rare, and their timing is almost never under the control of an individual company, suggesting that we should be ready when the big opportunities emerge and protect resources during the long periods of business as usual. He argues that successful businesses often falter because managers experienced in stable, familiar markets stumble when they enter less certain, volatile markets – they fail to create a long-term strategy that will produce sustainable advantage. Active waiting involves anticipating, making preparations, ready to seize opportunities and deal with threats, when they arise (Sull, 2005).

Making a reasoned decision on how quickly to move and the type of business model appropriate to deliver the speed required has become a key part of strategic thinking. The most obvious answers are not necessarily the most useful ones. The strategic issue is not just what to do, but when and how quickly.

12.2.2 The case of business products

Studies of new business-to-business product successes and failures make the following distinctions between successes and failures: product uniqueness (innovativeness) or superiority; management's possession of market knowledge and marketing proficiency; and, presence of technical and production synergies and proficiency.

The first dimension – industrial product uniqueness/superiority – is very close to that for consumer products. In this respect industrial and consumer products are similar. It is likely that industrial and consumer products are similar in other ways too. Successful industrial innovators study their customers and market well. They carry out market research to gain knowledge of customer's requirements/needs; they are sensitive to price as well as to the intricacies of buyer behaviour.

Successful innovators acquire as much of the required information as possible to enable them to forecast market size and determine potential demand for their new product. They test the market prior to product launch. There is strong and often well-targeted sales support, which recognises the need for forceful communications to stimulate primary demand and to prise open new markets.

Successful industrial innovations are clearly not the result of sophisticated technology alone. Mismanagement of technical and technological resources can have a detrimental effect on new product performance. Successful industrial innovators ensure there is synergy between the firm's engineering and production capabilities and the new product project. They also undertake a range of technical activities and do these proficiently – preliminary technical assessment, product development, prototype testing with customers, production start-up, with facilities well geared for launch. Their technical staff know the product technology well. They are familiar with the product design.

12.2.3 New product failures

One question central to manager interests in innovation strategy is, in what ways do new products fail? Answering this question helps us appreciate what actions the firm should take to avoid different types of product failure. One way of classifying new product failures is shown in Figure 12.4.

1 **The better mousetrap no one wanted** is the classic 'technology-push' type innovation for which little or insufficient market demand exists. Customers do not perceive they have a real need for the technology and, consequently, are not prepared to buy the innovation. Sinclair's C5 electric car falls firmly into this category – an innovation without an obvious market.

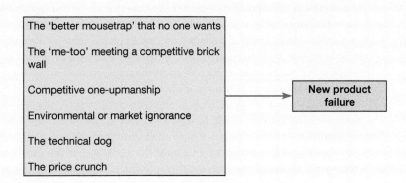

Figure 12.4
Some reasons
for new product
failures

2 **The me-too meeting a competitive brick wall** is the result of followers failing to reconcile with the market leader's or established competitors' strengths. Nokia's attempts to gain position in the smartphone market may be in this category.

3 **Competitors** can spring surprises and come up with a better product that is preferred by customers. 'Competitive one-upmanship' is not easy to predict but can be seen in the case of Apple's iPhone upstaging Nokia, Samsung and the others in the mobile phone business, or Google wrong-footing the automotive industry with its advances in autonomous vehicles (self-driving cars). Innovations may achieve great short-term advantage, but if competitors can easily and simply imitate the innovation (and have other advantages as well), then the innovator is likely to achieve little long-term value.

4 **Environmental or market ignorance** occurs when the innovating firm fails to study market or customer requirements or to monitor and scan its external environment for signals of change. Socio-economic, technological, political and/or legislative conditions and/or changes are ignored, overlooked or misunderstood, resulting in poor sales after launch.

5 **The technical dog** product does not work or users are dogged by technical problems (e.g. Jaguar Land Rover vehicles were frequently seen in this way, until the take-over by Tata and a major investment in quality improvement).

6 **The price crunch** comes when the innovating firm sets too high a price for a new product whose value is not perceived by target customers to be better or greater than existing products. Often if competition offers a lower-cost product the innovating firm has to cut its price so fails to obtain the required return on investment from the innovation. Even Apple's innovative iPhone was priced too high at launch and disappointing sales led to an early price reduction and refunds to early purchasers.

12.3 Planning for new products

The fact that innovation is so uncertain raises the question whether innovation can be managed? Certainly it seems that using formalised new product development processes achieves greater new product success in some situations than does an *ad hoc* approach to product innovation. There is, however, a distinction between invention and innovation. The former is the discovery of a new device or a new process. It is fair to say that managers cannot specify deadlines for the discovery of new ideas or predict when a particular invention will occur or, indeed, when exactly a scientific discovery will be made. Invention cannot be planned. Often it is left to chance, or the perseverance and ingenuity of the scientist/inventor. Innovation is different. Once the new scientific or technical discovery is made, or a novel product idea has been conceived, its chances of being successfully commercialised rest predominantly on the astuteness of the firm's management in new product planning and strategy determination, as well as the proficiency with which certain new product developments and launch activities are undertaken. From discovery/conception of the idea to marketplace, management and employees of the firm have direct control and influence over the fate of the discovery/idea.

Businesses can reduce the risk of product innovation while improving the likelihood of success by adopting a planning orientation and sophisticated new product development process. There was nothing accidental or *ad hoc* about the results achieved by Glaxo for Zantac in the anti-ulcer drugs market, or McDonald's in fast foods – they succeeded through careful preparation of the strategies for product development and market entry.

Nonetheless, one important caveat is that some of the most innovative companies in the world achieve their success through far less organised behaviours. The bureaucracy of conventional product planning plays little role in creating and managing innovation at Google. Indeed, innovation at Google appears to the outsider to be almost anarchic – disordered, in disarray and embroiled in uncomfortable uncertainty, living on the edge of chaos (Lashinsky, 2006) – but it is effective for that company. There are many risks in how Google manages innovation, but it is how the company has built the capability to handle multiple, simultaneous, radical innovation initiatives. Similarly, in a famous statement to *Fortune* magazine, Steve Jobs of Apple stated: 'We do no market research. We just want to make great products' (quoted in *Fortune,* 2008, March 17), which is what Apple appears to have done. Formal product planning procedures may be useful but they do not guarantee success.

12.3.1 The new product planning process

Nonetheless, many successful innovating companies develop a new product process, such as that shown in Figure 12.5, which is linked to their company's overall longer-term planning process.

First, the process suggests companies should define their business mission by asking: What business are we in? And what business do we want to be in? By considering the

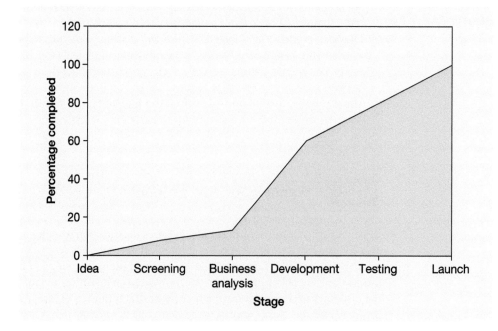

Figure 12.5
New product
development
stages and time
lapse

Source: Adapted from
Booz *et al.*(1982).

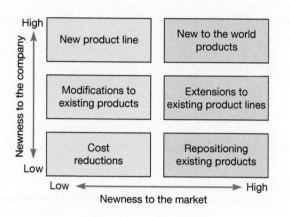

Figure 12.6
New product
innovation

growth potential of the sales and market share and profitability of the company's current range of products, and the extent to which growth objectives will be fulfilled, management can begin to identify gaps in achievable and desired growth. The role of new products and how the firm's portfolio of businesses might be changed to achieve planned growth can be determined.

Firms also have to decide on the types of new product that are to be developed. It is usual to classify new products according to the degree of newness to the company and to the customers (Figure 12.6).

Six categories of new products emerge, each one taking the company further and further away from its current activities and, therefore, being more risky.

1 **Cost reductions,** which provide similar performance at lower cost.
2 **Repositionings,** which are current products targeted at new customer segments or new markets. For example, Lucozade, a soft drink, traditionally aimed at the 'convalescent', then targeted the youth and sports user segment as an energy drink.
3 **Modifications,** in the form of improvements or revisions to existing products, which enhance performance or perceived value and replace existing products. For example, car manufacturers tend to upgrade existing models, supplying 'new products' with improved performance and/or more features, as opposed to developing radically new models from scratch.
4 **Extensions** to existing product lines that supplement a firm's established product lines.
5 **New product lines,** which enable a company to enter an established market for the first time, such as Virgin's financial services products.
6 **New-to-the-world products,** which create an entirely new market.

Depending on the sales, market share and financial objectives set by the firm, and the overall strength of its current range of products, management has to select the appropriate type, or combination of types, of new product to develop. Usually a firm would have to invest in various types of new product development to maintain a healthy and balanced portfolio of products. The firm's functional capabilities and available resources have to be considered when deciding the strategic direction to be taken. Figure 12.7 shows the various strategic roles for new products and the types of new product that are likely to fulfil each of these roles. The magnitude of the risk attached to innovation alters with the type of new product being developed. Planning can help; failure to do so increases the risks, while decreasing the chances of new product success.

Strategic role	New product type
Maintain technology leadership ⟶	New to the world New product line
Enter new markets ⟶	New to the world
Meet competitive threat or segment the market ⟶	New to the world New product line Repositioning
Maintain market share ⟶	New product line Repositioning Extensions to existing product line
Defend market position/prevent decline ⟶	Repositioning Cost reduction Modifications to existing product line
Exploit technology in a new/novel way ⟶	New to the world New product line
Make most of distribution strengths ⟶	Extensions to existing product line

Figure 12.7
Strategic role of
new products

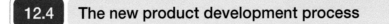

12.4   The new product development process

12.4.1 Idea generation

For new products, a firm has to find novel ideas, do new things and do things differently. This is the essence of product innovation. New ideas trigger the innovation process and the development of new products. Ideas are where all new products start. Both the creativity of individuals and the methods of idea generation can be employed to obtain novel ideas.

Creativity and productive ideation – really innovative ideas come out of inspiration and use appropriate techniques. Because of the high mortality rate of new ideas it is desirable to generate and consider a large number of ideas. The use of appropriate methods to generate new product ideas can improve the productivity of in-house ideas generation. A company can also facilitate the generation of innovative new product ideas by creating an environment that will induce and facilitate creativity. How can the creative potential of individuals be harnessed, and what techniques aid the creative ideas generation process?

Defining creativity – creativity is the combining of previously unrelated parts into a useful whole so that one can get more out of the emergent whole than one has put in (Miller, 1996). This explanation of creativity suggests that one condition has to be satisfied for really novel ideas to emerge, which is that many widely disparate ideas must coexist long enough in the individual's mind to combine, to yield a 'useful whole'.

The creative process is not easily implemented and many managers would assert that creativity cannot be supervised, as can the pursuit of quality or other functional operations. It is not possible to predict when a creative person will generate a novel idea. It is almost as if management should leave outbursts of creative thinking to nature and chance. However, contrary to conventional wisdom, creativity can be managed. Rather than spotting creative individuals within the firm and encouraging them to tap their creative potential, the manager would do better by asking if barriers to creative thinking exist and, if so, how these barriers might be overcome.

Nonetheless, there may also something in the view that fresh thinking about important issues should not be the preserve of conventional executives skilled in running the existing business. Companies need to think about attracting unconventional people with unconventional ideas – possibly 'weird' people – to become in-house mavericks. However, managing mavericks will be far from easy, every one a prima donna, because 'stars don't work for idiots' and they need a 'maverick-friendly' environment in which to operate. Google is a high performer which employs such people, but this is not just about the new economy – companies like IBM and Procter & Gamble are also exploring ways of capturing maverick creativity and innovation to channel it into mainstream business (Taylor and LaBarre, 2008). Dan Cable argues that if your goal is to create something that is valuable, rare and hard to imitate, then compared to your competitors, your people need to be downright strange (Cable, 2007). He argues that far from benchmarking against competitors, we should aim to accentuate differences in our thinking, even to the point of becoming a little strange. That way you can focus on an obsession with commitment to doing things differently (and better) than anyone else. Strange is weird but good in thinking strategically about innovation.

For example, some product designers are turning to 'extreme users', from obsessive cleaners to dominatrices to get new ideas: a cocktail expert shares tips on the quality and complexity of ice with a home appliance maker; dominatrices share the secret of how to avoid blisters from wearing uncomfortable high-heeled shoes; and skateboards were developed and branded after sports equipment manufacturers spotted teenagers improvising their own. Designers are finding that mavericks, outliers and obsessives can provide ideas for new products and valuable improvements (Clegg, 2014).

Aids to idea generation – some of the many techniques that can help creative thinking are shown in Table 12.1. The best approach is to use a variety of approaches, where possible; leeway is a must; try out, adapt and fit approaches to the problem at hand. There are many other approaches: suggestion boxes, competitive products analysis or negative engineering, patents searches, customer need assessment and problem-detection studies; there are almost as many techniques as there are creative people.

12.4.2 Screening

If you take ten new product ideas, the chances are that two will pay, seven will fail, and only one will be a big winner. New product idea screening and selection is not about dropping bad ideas but identifying the winner. Picking a potential winner is not an easy task. What should managers take into account when evaluating new product ideas? What are the critical screening criteria? How do managers choose the best from among a pool of apparently viable ideas?

Systematic screening

If resources are committed to the development of a new product idea, management should assess the commercial potential and technical (including production) feasibility of the idea. If there are alternative ideas or projects competing for development funds and management time, these have to be screened and the more viable and attractive ideas selected.

Ideas screening is, therefore, an important component of the product innovation process. Screening can take up management's time. It is often tempting for the management team to devote a minimum amount of time and effort to it, and even to skip the exercise, in the rush to get idea development started and new products out to market quickly. An idea coming from a senior manager in the firm may sometimes also escape thorough screening and

Table 12.1 Aids to thinking

Thinking aid	Process	Blocks confronted
Question the problem (ask a lot of questions about the problem at hand)	Inculcate a questioning attitude; ask questions about the problem to gain familiarity with it rather than hiding ignorance	• Perceptual (overcomes problem of having narrow viewpoints, clarifies problem) • Emotional (addresses fear of looking like a fool, betraying ignorance – individual is forced to ask questions instead of hiding ignorance by not questioning) • Intellectual (questions about the problem stimulate generation of information/ideas that later help conception of solution to problem)
Listing (force individual to make a list of ideas to facilitate generation of many ideas)	Encourage problem solvers/ideas generators to make a list of the ideas, whatever comes to mind. Once the individual's thoughts are flowing, this simple but disciplined ideas-listing exercise can facilitate 'fluency' of thought (i.e. aid individual to generate many ideas)	• Emotional (attacks inflexibility of thinking and triggers creation of a large volume of ideas)
Attribute listing	Break a product into its main components. For each component list all the physical attributes or functions and then examine possible alternatives for fulfilling each of these in isolation	• Perceptual (helps individual examine the problem from a variety of angles/see it more clearly)
Applied imagination checklist	Use an explicit checklist to identify new product opportunities. Questions act as triggers: Can the product be used in any new way? What else is like it and what/whom could we copy? Can the product be changed in meaning, function, form, usage pattern? What can be added to the product? To make it bigger; stronger; longer; thicker; etc.? What can be deleted from it? How to make it smaller, lighter, etc.? What can be substituted? Other material, process, ingredient, etc.? Can we rearrange its components? Can it be combined with other things?	• Perceptual (by encouraging problem solver to extend thinking/look at problem from a variety of perspectives) • Emotional (pushes the imagination)

evaluation because of the assumed credibility of the source – which could turn out to be a costly error of misplaced confidence. Or ideas may not be systematically evaluated because management regards screening as a superfluous exercise given the lack of concrete data, in the early stages, on what are still apparently vague and ill-formed ideas.

Whatever the barriers, it pays to give serious attention to screening. There are good reasons for doing this. Screening helps avoids potentially heavy losses by reducing the possibility of bad ideas being accepted, and raises the chances of good ideas being developed. It encourages more efficient resource allocation by directing the firm's attention to the 'best' ideas and encourages firms to pursue those ideas that build on its core strengths. Also, as screening experience accumulates, it improves the managers' precision in ideas selection, so increasing the chances of success.

Initial screen

Screening can be conducted at different levels of detail. The preliminary screening may be treated as a coarse filter, enabling managers quickly to separate out useful ideas for further investigation. Figure 12.8 shows the key screening questions. Remember that the initial screen is only a crude filtering device. Sometimes a new product idea might hit a legal, technical or marketing barrier which might not be particularly insurmountable. It is therefore important for the management team to use the tool cautiously, taking on board internal company, as well as market and technological, developments that could be exploited to avoid premature closure of new product opportunities.

Formalised screening system

Potentially viable ideas should be evaluated more thoroughly for selection purposes. It is important for management to appreciate that full screening requires identification of specific information and the investment of resources to obtain these data. Formalised screening means that new product ideas are evaluated logically and within a systematic structure. It is less impressionistic than initial screening and attempts to increase the objectivity of idea selection.

When actual data are unobtainable the management team doing the screening must exercise subjective, qualitative judgements. It is important to record all major assumptions and quantitative estimates so that they can be used as control standards for future reference.

The screening devices are not a panacea for a poor innovation record. The analyses rely on the ability of the firm's management team to combine high-quality subjective judgements with good objective data. The tools do not absolve management using them from exercising creativity, nor are these techniques a substitute for management vision.

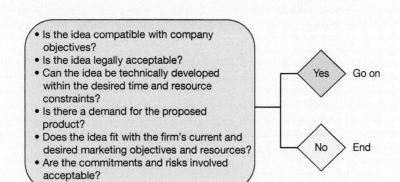

Figure 12.8
Initial screening
of ideas

The analyses are time- and resource-consuming. The many uncertainties at the early stage of ideas selection make detailed and sophisticated evaluation somewhat meaningless. This encourages rejection of screening. But it is certainly misguided to make no attempt to consider the determinants of project success and failure, or the attendant risk and uncertainty when committing resources to major product innovation programmes.

The output of screening and evaluation is only as good as the input data. This means that, to benefit from utilising screening systems, management must commit time and resources to building an information system geared to supporting ideas screening, evaluation and selection decisions. As with building any management information system, this takes time but, if implemented properly, yields a lasting and positive effect.

Screening based on the opinions and judgements of staff within the firm can be highly biased. Judgements can be distorted because of undue pressure applied on individuals, information sparseness/inaccuracy, psychological pressures, personal influences, etc. The market viability of an idea should always be tested against criteria judged important by the customer/potential customer.

12.4.3 Business analysis

Business analysis considers the attractiveness of the market for the proposed new product idea and the company's capabilities and whether it has the business skills required to cater to the needs of the market in a way that gives it a distinct edge over the competition.

Sales, costs and profit projections for a new product show whether they satisfy the company's objectives. To estimate sales, the company looks at the sales history of similar products and surveys market opinion. Estimates of minimum and maximum sales give the range of risk. Starting with a sales forecast, the expected costs and profits for the product, including marketing, R&D, manufacturing, accounting and finance costs, are calculated.

Management has to decide which criteria are the most critical and what level of accuracy in the data is needed for decision making. This is to avoid wasting resources on refining information pertaining to factors to which the project's viability is relatively insensitive. While the desired criteria may vary according to the nature of the industry and the circumstances of the individual firm, some criteria are likely to be relevant to most companies. With measures of market attractiveness and business position decided, the process becomes similar to segment selection described in Chapter 9. If the market is attractive and the company has a sufficiently strong position relative to the competition, the product can move to the product development stage.

12.4.4 Product development

At this stage R&D or engineering convert the concept into a physical product. So far the new product development process has been relatively inexpensive; the product has existed only as a word description, a drawing or perhaps a crude mock-up. In contrast product development calls for a large jump in investment. It will show whether the product idea can he turned into a working product.

The R&D department will develop physical versions of the product concept: a prototype that will satisfy and excite consumers and which can be produced quickly and at budgeted costs. Depending on the product class, developing a successful prototype can take days, weeks, months or even years. Nonetheless, new technologies like 3-D printing are drastically reducing the prototyping time for some products.

Prototypes must have the required functional features and convey the intended psychological characteristics. When the prototypes are ready they must be tested. Functional tests are then conducted under laboratory and field conditions to make sure that the product performs safely and effectively. A new car, for example, must start easily; it must be comfortable; it must be able to corner without overturning. Consumer tests are conducted, in which consumers test drive the car and rate its attributes.

When designing products the company needs to look beyond simply creating products that satisfy consumer needs and wants. Too often companies design their new products without enough concern for how the designs will be produced – their main goal is to create customer-satisfying products. The designs are then passed along to manufacturing, where engineers must try to find the best ways to produce the product.

Increasingly, businesses use Design For Manufacturing and Assembly (DFMA) to fashion products that are both satisfying *and* easy to manufacture. This often results in lower costs while achieving higher quality and more reliable products. For example, using DFMA analysis Texas Instruments redesigned an infrared gun-sighting mechanism it supplies to the Pentagon. The redesigned product required 75 fewer parts, 78 per cent fewer assembly steps and 85 per cent less assembly time. The new design did more than reduce production time and costs; it also worked better than the previous, more complex version. Thus DFMA can be a potent weapon in helping companies to get products to market sooner, while offering higher quality at lower prices.

12.4.5 Market testing

By this point in the product innovation process there is a physical product or complete specifications for a new service. The product has passed a use test which has suggested that the product works and fulfils the need as originally expressed in the concept. The next phase is market testing or trial sell. Test marketing is not one, but a range of techniques, from a simulated sale using carefully selected customers to a full test market in one or more regions of a country.

Up to this stage in the overall new product development process testing has not been conducted under realistic market conditions. It is dangerous to trust any customer judgement completely until it is made under typical market conditions. This is where market testing plays a role in helping the firm to gauge whether its marketing plan for the new product will work and to confirm that the product, with its attendant claims, does, in fact, motivate customers to buy it and that they keep on doing so, if repeat purchase is an important factor. Market testing could be regarded as a form of 'dress rehearsal' that enables management to gather information to forecast new product sales and test effectiveness of the marketing plan (i.e. pricing, advertising and promotion, distribution). It checks that all key operations fit with each other and are adequately geared up for launch, and provides diagnostic information to help managers revise/refine the marketing plan. Full test markets can test competitive response and gauge if their efforts affect the judgements of customers. This is a mixed blessing since full test markets can be deliberately spoilt by competitors and give them an early warning of intended activities.

12.4.6 Commercialisation

Commercialisation is often the 'graveyard' of product innovation, not because new products die here but because real innovation often stumbles at this point of the process. By this we mean that things are going wrong and the product concept that seemed so feasible in the beginning is now tarnished and facing considerable pressure of compromise because of time, cost and other resources. Managers who are impatient to get the product to market fail to allocate sufficient time and resources to developing an effective launch campaign. Surprisingly, after all that has gone into development, products often fail because they are launched with insufficient marketing support. Most new products fail, not because of any inherent deficiency, but because the market launch strategy and tasks were poorly conceived and executed.

The launch managers should work closely with sales and other operating staff to achieve good coordination of the timing and scheduling of all these activities. Every effort must be made to ensure that critical activities (e.g. salesforce training, sales and promotions materials) are completed proficiently to secure launch success. In conjunction with key operating personnel, the launch manager has also to put together a launch plan, which consists of a programme outlining the sequence of tasks to be performed, a schedule that relates the programme to a time sequence, and budgets for the programme and schedule.

Launch programmes easily turn into a complicated and unwieldy task. There is little point in turning out project control or milestone events charts hundreds of pages long because this is bound to break down, providing hardly any basis for effective project control. Except for the most complex technological developments, as found in car, aerospace and defence projects, complex, computer-based systems for project control are usually not necessary. For the small- to medium-sized company simple checklists may suffice. Remember, there is also 'eyeball control', which relies on managers being constantly on the go, visiting every area of the firm (daily, if possible), gathering their own information, and becoming 'expert' enough to exercise sound judgement and keep launch tasks under control.

12.5   Speeding new product development

Managers must appreciate the value of being fast at innovation. A company that takes less time to develop and commercialise a new product can be expected to be more competitive than a slower competitor. The firm would be able to launch more new products in a given period of time, therefore building a strong innovation leadership image. Speedy companies are also able to respond faster to changing customer requirements, thereby securing sales and building customer loyalty. Also, by increasing the frequency with which it introduces new products into the market, the firm could pre-empt competition, thereby creating and maintaining a market leadership position.

At the same time, fast efficient processes also allow an earlier decision on which new product projects to kill. There are advantages in culling weak projects at the earliest reasonable opportunity to contain costs and avoid 'organisational creep' leading to growing commitment to continue with weak ventures simply on the basis of the time and resource invested to date.

The cost of new product development could be reduced by undertaking innovation of an incremental, as opposed to radical, nature, with substantial reduction in the risks of innovation. Companies should, however, ascertain if they have the capabilities for accelerating new product development. Also, management should ensure that the firm supports a balanced innovation programme such that opportunities are not forgone because of failure to fund more radical (and longer-term) product innovation programmes in view of the obsession with speed.

Speeding the new product development process needs action at all stages of the process. At the start, avoid delays in approving budget for developing product idea and pay early attention to 'snagging' at the end of the process. Overlapping product and process design and development phases has two benefits. It means that processes take place in parallel and forces the formation of multi-functional project teams (design, engineering, production, sales, marketing, etc.). Big technological breakthroughs are not necessary to make big commercial gains, so take an incremental approach to product improvement and development, making many small steps rather than attempting giant leaps forward. New product innovation often clashes with the systems and controls designed to make firms 'well managed'. To overcome this, successful businesses adapt operational and organisational procedures to give the flexibility and freedom that new product innovation needs.

12.6   Organising for new product development

There may be a variety of roadblocks and barriers to innovation in a company. The nature and intensity of these blocks vary from individual to individual, but organisations that innovate effectively recognise and avoid them (see Figure 12.9).

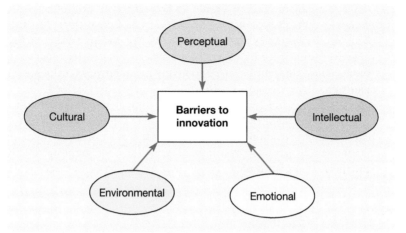

Figure 12.9
Barriers to
innovation

12.6.1 Blocks and bugs

- **Perceptual blocks** prevent the person from perceiving clearly either the problem itself or the information needed to solve the problem (e.g. problem isolation difficulty; narrow definition of problem; limited viewpoints examined).
- **Cultural blocks** are acquired as a result of exposure to a given set of cultural values or patterns (e.g. tradition is preferable to change; intolerance of subjectivity; fantasy/reflection/playfulness is a waste of time; humour is 'out of place' where problem solving is concerned).
- **Environmental blocks** are imposed by our immediate social and physical environment and are, therefore, closely linked to cultural barriers (e.g. autocratic boss; lack of trust/cooperation among colleagues; distractions; unsupportive organisation; lack of financial support to implement ideas).
- **Emotional blocks** interfere with the freedom with which we explore and play with ideas, and prevent us from communicating them effectively to others (e.g. fear of failing or looking like a fool; intolerance of ambiguity; preference for judging ideas rather than generating them; inability to incubate and 'sleep on it').
- **Intellectual and expressive blocks** arise because intellectual capabilities are limited and verbal/writing skills needed to communicate ideas, not only to others but to yourself, are deficient (e.g. lack of information; incorrect information; poor language skill; failure to apply appropriate mental problem-solving tactics).

12.6.2 Organisational support for innovation

It is people, not plans or committees, who create ideas and achieve innovation. It is their efforts that truly determine whether businesses succeed or fail. If managers have grand visions for their business the surest way of bringing these to fruition is to have their staff on their side, to encourage, enthuse and motivate them and, above all, to reward them for their achievements.

Three conditions are required for a firm to innovate successfully:

1 **closeness to customers:** managers must know their customers and understand their needs and requirements well;
2 **cross-functional communications:** innovation in most companies (except the 'one-man-band', which is not stereotypical of the average established small/medium-sized firm anyway) is about the flow of information between key functions;
3 **multi-functional teamwork:** successful product innovations are almost invariably the result of people in the firm working together in teams rather than independently.

These are three deceptively simple criteria for innovation success. In practice, they are often very difficult for a firm to achieve. Large, bureaucratic firms face this problem most of all. Small companies that can still maintain a cohesive unit may find criteria 2 and 3 easy to achieve, but, if led by excessively product-oriented technocrats, frequently drift away from 1. The manager of a small company must, however, take note of the 'fast-forgetting' syndrome: as the business grows and the organisation expands the three principal requirements for innovation become increasingly difficult to preserve, frequently resulting in management losing sight of the very factors that brought success to the business in the first place. Entrepreneurship, although highly desirable, is, on its own, insufficient for successful innovation, especially continual innovation. To remain successful innovators, business managers must continually review their firm's ability to meet the above three conditions for effective innovation.

12.6.3 Organisational alternatives

Although marginal product changes can be managed within conventional organisations, radical innovations need suitably radical organisations. Six broad approaches are suggested that differ in their isolation from day-to-day business activities. All help small groups escape from entrenched departments and attitudes.

1 **The functional approach** has people from different business areas (such as finance or marketing). Tasks are carried out by the various departments. Individuals meet to make the necessary decisions. Usually a new products or product planning committee reviews project progress. Members do not commit all their time to the project, which must mesh with their normal duties.

2 **A taskforce** consists of several individuals who either are hand-picked by the boss or have volunteered to join the team. Taskforce members come together more regularly to work on the project, which they pursue with slightly greater urgency than in the previous approach. The taskforce should have a balance of engineering, production and marketing talents. Members' primary commitment is still very much to their function rather than the project.

3 **A project team–functional matrix** is appropriate when project demands are high. Team members commit themselves to the project as much as to their normal functional responsibilities. However, this type of 50:50 thinking often results in indecision and delay because members involved still need to see to their regular job, while project needs require greater 'push'. There may also be a conflict between what the project team needs to achieve and their parent function's main interests.

4 **Venture teams** are mostly associated with very small firms that have few people and no entrenched departments. The venture group should contain a mix of people with different functional skills, not just specialists. For bigger companies the venture option is used to free people from current functional pressures so that they can focus their entire effort on the project. The group is given complete autonomy and power to forge ahead, and incentive compensation for taking the risks.

5 **Spin-outs** are completely detached from the parent company. Big companies use this option to support very risky product innovation projects that do not currently fit the corporation's core business. Outside capital could be sought. The venture is sold off for an equity stake in the new start-up firm. For small firms, spin-offs are not a logical route for nurturing innovation but they could consider another type of venture approach – the joint venture.

6 **Inside–outside venture** approaches fit both big and small/medium-sized firms. Smaller firms with the advantages of advanced technology, flexibility, vigour and/or entrepreneurial flair could team up with larger firms with the capital, distribution network and marketing muscle to gain market entry. The big firm gains through achieving entry into promising technologies that were too risky and ill-fitted to their mainstream business (the alliances between pharmaceuticals and biotechnology firms are a case in point).

The more radical the new product project (which means higher risk), the greater the need for project focus and its protection from current departmental and operational influences and constraints. The functional and taskforce options are therefore appropriate for low risk, incremental product innovations (e.g. improvements, repositionings, new sizes, etc., involving present product lines).

A project team–functional matrix is most suitable for marginally riskier projects, involving expansion in the number of product lines. Venture teams, spin-outs and inside–outside venture options are for radical, high-risk projects where internal constraints and opposition are expected to be very high.

The proposed radical structures help large firms capture the benefits of a small firm. Ironically, the idea that 'small is good' stems from the observations that large, innovative firms work in non-bureaucratic, smaller settings. They try to gain the advantages of being small. But, of course, size is not a determinant of innovation success. Many new products introduced by small firms fail because they should never have come about – it may be that they were badly conceived, they failed to meet market needs, or that the company lacked the marketing skills required to prise open new markets.

Summary

In this chapter we approach innovation at two levels: strategic innovation issues and the mechanics of new product development processes.

Innovation strategy is driven by the goal of creating the innovative company and achieving real value innovation that drives effective strategy and positioning in a market. Issues examined include: the link between innovation patterns and fundamental change in an industry; the creation of new business models to drive effective value innovation; the impact of radical and disruptive innovation on competitive patterns; the possibilities for proactive cannibalization strategies; and, the creation of innovation networks often on a global basis to encompass collaborative and open source innovation.

We then turned attention to the product development process in companies. Importantly, we saw that product innovation is not a one-off activity. A successful, profitable innovation can see a firm through for a while, but long-run survival depends on new products to balance its future portfolio (Chapter 2), replace declining products and cater for new customer needs.

Many businesses are caught out because management has failed to use the profits from current innovations to develop more innovations for future markets. Today's breadwinners will eventually dry up as competitive forces intensify over the product's life cycle. New products – tomorrow's breadwinners – are necessary to maintain the firm's position in the marketplace. One win is insufficient; multiple wins are necessary for corporate longevity.

The more the firm innovates, the greater the experience accumulated; the greater the experience gained, the better it gets at innovation; the better the firm becomes at this daunting activity, the greater its chances of competitive survival. A virtuous cycle of innovation is established.

Increasingly, a multi-disciplinary, team-based approach to product innovation is required. Team work is important and has been one of the most significant organisational factors behind companies' ability to accelerate new product development in the drive to achieve lasting competitive advantage, as observed, for example, in the consumer electronics, computer and motor vehicle markets.

There are many factors that affect new product performance. Neglect of one factor alone can bring about failure. Management should check that their firm is pursuing a balanced and realistic new product development strategy, that customer/market needs are clearly identified and well understood and that requisite technical and technological skills are married with a market orientation to ensure success.

Case Study   Apple moves into fashion business with Watch launch

Apple launches new products

Google is investing hundreds of millions of dollars in self-driving cars and prolonging life. Amazon is testing deliveries by drone. Facebook is toying with virtual reality and flying internet access into far-flung places in solar powered planes.

Apple, meanwhile, is going into the fashion business.

In spite of the seemingly different scales of ambition and complexity, all have something in common: they are long-term bets that will take many years to make a significant dent in these vast companies' bottom lines.

After years of speculation, Apple's new Watch was launched by Tim Cook, chief executive, in Cupertino on Tuesday. As the unusual group of *Vogue* editors and other fashion journalists invited to the event attests, Apple sees the device as more than just technology: 'It's something functional yet incredibly beautiful,' Mr Cook said.

While others in Silicon Valley may try to bring forward a science-fiction vision of the future, Mr Cook says that Apple wants to create products that help people's everyday lives, such as through the smart-watch's health-tracking apps, and solve more personal technological challenges.

'We wanted to create something that was very personal. We felt that the wrist was the best place to do that,' Mr Cook told the *Financial Times*.

'We can help people live a better day with this. But we love innovating around things that require seamless innovation of hardware, software and services. You can see all those together in the watch.'

As well as these technological achievements, Apple stands to profit handsomely from its Watch if it proves anywhere near as popular as the iPod, iPad and iPhone.

The device will cost upwards of $350 when it goes on sale early next year – a price that is higher than many analysts had predicted, and one that will jump for the gold version with a leather strap.

That cost may limit how many customers can afford Apple's Watch, but of the 200m people who already own compatible iPhones, many affluent consumers may shell out for Apple's latest gadget purely for early-adopter kudos.

'Tim Cook has been under a lot of pressure the past 12 months,' said Geoff Blaber of CCS Insights. 'They needed to get a toe in the water.'

After seeing the Watch, Citi predicts that Apple will sell 14m in its first year and 15m in its second. That overshoots its forecast for Samsung to sell 4m smartwatches and fitness bands this year, and will add $12bn to Apple's revenues over the next two years.

But given the vast scale of Apple's existing iPhone business, which has sold more than 550m devices to date, Citi sees the Watch making up just 3 per cent of its annual sales.

With pent-up demand from Apple customers with older models, analysts see the iPhone 6 kick-starting a huge upgrade cycle. Many see the jumbo-sized 5.5-inch iPhone 6 Plus, which costs $100 more than previous models, as driving higher margins, although that may be offset by Apple increasing the memory it provides for the same price in more expensive models.

Concerns linger about Apple's ability to meet consumer demand for the iPhone 6 Plus in the run-up to Christmas. Nonetheless, IHS, a researcher, predicts that the new iPhone will propel Apple ahead of Microsoft's Nokia as the world's second-largest maker of mobile phones after Samsung – including all phones, not just smartphones.

'The introduction of larger-screen iPhones eliminates a key differentiator that has insulated Samsung, Sony, HTC and LG large-screen flagship smartphones from iPhone competition,' IHS said.

For the Watch to move the financial needle – and impress Wall Street, which left Apple shares broadly flat after Tuesday's announcements – the tech group will need to convince more than just early adopters that its pricey bracelet belongs on their wrists.

That is something Apple's competitors have failed to do, analysts say. Some have chastised Apple for being slow to catch up with arch-rival Samsung, which launched its first smartwatch more than a year ago, but Mr Cook is unruffled by such complaints.

'We ship things when we believe they are ready,' he said. 'For us, it's much more important to be the best than to be the first.'

Apple did not have the first MP3 player, smartphone or tablet, either, he continued. 'You could say we had the first modern one of all of those, and I think you can make the same point today that we have the first modern smartwatch.'

Some analysts watching Apple's event on Tuesday seemed to agree.

'They got the design right,' said Carolina Milanesi of Kantar Worldpanel, a market research unit of WPP. 'They've taken the technology out of it, which is not what everyone else is doing. They made it much more appealing to a wider audience.'

Many noted that Apple packed a lot more ideas in to its smartwatch than the first version of the iPhone, which lacked seemingly key features such as 3G wireless and an app store.

'I've seen a lot of smart watches – this one was really polished,' said Richard Doherty of Envisioneering.

But some complained that Apple had lost its famous focus by trying to sell consumers on something that is part jewellery, part sports device, part communicator, part wallet and even, according to Mr Cook, a remote control for the Apple TV box.

'I'm underwhelmed,' said Om Malik, a tech blogger turned investor with True Ventures, a San Francisco group that counts fitness band maker Fitbit among its portfolio.

'I feel that they should have tried to do a few things well. Apple is missing its editor,' Mr Malik added, in a reference to Apple co-founder Steve Jobs' capacity to axe features and products even at late stages of development.

Many are looking to the app developer community to come up with something to convince consumers to buy the Watch. Here, Apple retains an advantage over rival app stores such as Android's Google Play.

Mr Cook said that part of the reason for launching the Watch months in advance of its release to consumers was to get developers working.

If they do not come up with the substance, Apple will have to fall back on the Watch's style until they do, analysts say.

'Every wearable device we've seen to date has been in search of a reason to use it,' said Mr Blaber. 'This is a step in a long journey.'

Source: from 'Apple moves into fashion business with Watch launch', *Financial Times,* 10/09/14 (Bradshaw, T. and Waters, R.).

Discussion Questions

1 Why would Apple want to move into the fashion business?

2 What type of innovation is Apple's new watch?

3 What role does innovation play for a company such as Apple?

CHAPTER 13

COMPETING THROUGH SUPERIOR SERVICE AND CUSTOMER RELATIONSHIPS

Companies still have much to learn about the true meaning of service . . . If the two characters on my doorstep really had come to instal my broadband connection, why did they have the appearance and demeanour of a pair of burglars? I asked them to identify themselves. One fished in his sweatshirt and produced a plastic card on a silver necklace. The other chortled that he had lost his identification . . . Those first impressions can be so misleading, can't they? Not really . . .

Michael Skapinker, *Financial Times*, 2003

The customer is more right than you know

At SuperJam, the old adage that the customer is king has been extended a little. The jam maker's customers are also asked to act as the marketing department and have found hundreds of independent shops to sell its products.

The reason for this is simple: despite selling half a million jars of preserve a year, amounting to 1 per cent of all UK jam sales, SuperJam is actually a one-man business run by Fraser Doherty.

'You could say that they are doing a job that I would otherwise have employed someone to do,' Doherty says.

The customers are arguably even more effective in that they give warm sales leads Doherty could never hope to muster on his own by cold calling shops.

The use of customers is just another extension of Doherty's complete outsourcing of his company's activities, from the manufacturing operations in

Source: Super Jam

Dundee to the sale of the product through Waitrose, Asda and Morrisons.

But larger businesses have also found value in engaging their customers.

Event promotion business Triumphant Events classifies its 1,148 customers as 'affiliates', encouraging them to promote the company's activities through Twitter, Facebook, emails and blogs.

Daniel Priestley, Triumphant's founder and chief executive, says: 'We believe that our customers are our marketing team.'

Wonga.com, a flexible loans service, enables its customers to control where the business does charitable work by letting them vote on potential support to entrepreneurs in the developing world.

The company also landed the Webby People's Voice Award, beating Bank of America among others, by asking customers to vote for it in the banking and bill payment category.

Z-Card, a marketing company specialising in information sheets that can be folded up to fit in a pocket, offers complimentary rates to customers who share the results of their first campaign with the company. It recently did a deal with the Dublin Bus Company, which used Z-Card's system to attach route maps to the back of its new contactless ticketing system.

Rachel Blair, Z-Card's assistant manager, says: 'Through using product champions we can ensure our offerings are tailored to market requirements, a good value service for our clients.'

A similar approach is taken by Donseed, which provides workplace management systems for the construction industry. In several cases, it has given discounts to customers who agree to act as a case study for the company.

Vincent Lynch, Donseed's chief executive, says this avoids any confusion further down the line if the company asks for a case study. It also allows him to approach other peer companies to show what their competitors are able to achieve.

'When negotiating a deal, I find it important that a concession being given by me should be met with a concession from the other side,' Lynch says. 'Call it my definition of fair trade.'

Ajay Mirpuri says he broke into new markets and developed new products by following advice and support from clients at his bespoke tailoring business.

One example was the company's move into Israel on the basis of a single client reference, which immediately brought another 100 clients to the business.

'I had never thought I would go to Israel in my life,' Mirpuri says. 'Now I love the country.'

Customer feedback has also stopped Mirpuri from making changes to his suits. For instance, Mirpuri had been keen to end his tailors' practice of stitching spare buttons into the right hand side of suits.

However, when he asked his clients from across the company's London, New York and Geneva shops, he found that many valued the design quirk because it meant they had spare buttons if one fell off during a business trip.

'I hated that design, but 100 per cent of the people we asked said not to change it,' Mirpuri says.

Engaging with customers also proved profitable for Pauley Creative, a specialist digital marketing group for the construction industry.

Founder Nick Pauley went through his customer database and pulled out 30 companies that he felt would give frank and honest answers. Using the online questionnaire tool Survey Monkey, he asked them whether they would promote his company and, if they would, what they would say.

Pauley's intention was to find out what customers felt about his company's service, but the act of asking customers encouraged several of them to actually make a referral to another company.

One customer had given Pauley Creative a very low score, so Pauley made a point of approaching the company's owner when the two were at a conference later that week.

The meeting had a dramatic effect: the very next day, the customer recommended Pauley Creative to a key decision maker within a national building company.

As a result, Pauley Creative is now on the building company's approved supplier list, something which might have otherwise taken several months to achieve.

Pauley believes that the referral was entirely down to the fact that he had made the effort to reconnect with the customer, meaning that the business was fresh in the customer's mind when an opportunity came up to recommend it.

'We hadn't even discussed the low score fiasco,' Pauley notes.

Source: from 'The customer is more right than you know', *Financial Times,* 19/05/10 (Moules, J.).

Discussion questions

1 What are the issues here?

2 How are the companies cited trying to deal with these issues?

Introduction

The pressure on companies to compete through superior service and effective customer relationships has never been higher. But achieving appropriate competitive positioning based on service and relationships investments has never been harder. Certainly, the post-recession consumer is more demanding than has ever been the case before. Equally, the case for 'lean consumption' built by leading operations experts is compelling:

> The concepts underlying lean consumption boil down to six simple principles
>
> 1 Solve the customer's problem completely by insuring that all the goods and services work, and work together.
> 2 Don't waste the customer's time.
> 3 Provide exactly what the customer wants.
> 4 Provide what's wanted exactly where it's wanted.
> 5 Provide what's wanted where it's wanted exactly when it's wanted.
> 6 Continually aggregate solutions to reduce the customer's time and hassle.
>
> *(Womack and Jones, 2005)*

Similarly, from a marketing perspective, Barwise and Meehan (2004) put the central competitive strategy issue nicely when they underline the fact that as products have become more difficult to differentiate (largely because there are few real differences between them), companies have resorted to excessive branding and marketing, leaving customers less satisfied now than they were a decade ago. Their appealing logic is that customers do not want bells and whistles and trivial brand differences – they just want quality products, reliable services, and fair value for money (Barwise and Meehan, 2004). It may even be that 'consumer decadence' is dead and that marketing must focus on the basics of value, practicality and durability – even luxury car brand Lexus in the US has run ads with the tagline 'lowest cost of ownership' to emphasise fuel economy and resale value rather than extravagance (Burt, 2008). Indeed, Price and Jaffe (ex-Amazon executives) argue in their book, *The Best Service Is No Service* (2008) that most customers do not want a relationship with a company, they just want things to work.

For example, a recent multi-national survey concludes that many consumers find the rising volume of marketing messages on the Internet and in the mobile-enabled world to be simply overwhelming. It seems that rather than attracting customers and building loyalty and effective relationships, marketers are pushing them away with relentless and ill-conceived efforts to engage with them. It seems that what customers want most is 'decision simplicity' – ease in gathering trustworthy information about a product so they can confidently and efficiently weigh their purchase options and choose. It seems what customers want from marketers is actually simplicity, not more complexity and confusion (Spenner and Freeman, 2012).

Similarly, it has been argued that companies should stop trying to 'delight' their customers and just focus on solving their problems. While the rewards for over-the-top service are small (if they exist at all), the loss of customers because you do not solve their problems is likely to be large. Customers punish bad service but may not reward good service. The link between service and loyalty is not straightforward. So, telling staff to exceed customers' expectations is liable to produce confusion, wasted time and effort, and expensive giveaways (Dixon *et al.*, 2010).

Indeed, while customer loyalty has long been a central tenet of marketing, it is increasingly being called into question. The modern customer may increasingly be a 'serial adulterer' rather than conventionally loyal (Hill, 2014). Perhaps customer loyalty does not really matter anymore? Loyal customers may not actually be cheaper to serve as conventionally suggested. For example, one study that goes against the conventional marketing grain divides customers into: **true friends** (long term and highly profitable), **butterflies** (transient but profitable), **strangers** (with the lowest potential for profit) and **barnacles** (who create 'additional drag' and need to be removed or converted into better customers). Conventional loyalty programmes may just attract butterflies – less than a third of Tesco shoppers are 'highly loyal' (spend 50 per cent of their grocery budget there), while for Sainsbury's the figure is 9 per cent, and for M&S Food less than 3 per cent. Grocery customers appear to be overwhelmingly disloyal in spite of all attempts to gain their affections.

Far from customers providing a devoted, monogamous relationship, Simonson and Rosen (2014) suggest the customer relationship has become an 'open marriage', where customers evaluate each new model of the camera, car or computer on merit rather than on marketing messages or prior preference. This opens the way for upstarts to challenge with better products – as Asus laptops did successfully when they took on Dell and Hewlett-Packard. Traditional measures of customer loyalty become meaningless, as do attempts to measure customer lifetime value, if consumers spend their lifetime flitting between brands. The key issues become not loyalty, but quality, service and consistency (Simonson and Rosen, 2014).

It is important that executives should rigorously evaluate the controversies surrounding issues like customer loyalty, satisfaction and service/relationship investments with a critical perspective. Many conventional assumptions may be misleading.

Nonetheless, more conventionally, one of the most significant changes in contemporary marketing thinking and practice was the shift in focus from achieving single transactions to establishing longer-term relationships with customers (see, for example, Vargo and Lusch, 2004). While transactional marketing is concerned with making a single sale, relationship marketing is more concerned with establishing a rapport with the customer aimed at achieving higher customer satisfaction, more repeat business, greater word-of-mouth referral, more opportunities for further business development, and enhanced revenues and profitability for the supplier.

Certainly, in a post-recessionary environment, many markets in developed countries can be regarded as mature, or at best growing only slowly, suggesting that there are fewer new customers for which to compete. Demographics emphasise this condition – an ageing population coupled with high youth unemployment in the West constrains market growth in many markets. Competition is increasingly intense, particularly in the new competitive landscapes which are the legacy of economic downturn, and the costs of attracting new customers are high. It has been estimated that the costs of attracting new customers can be up to five times as much as the costs of adequately serving existing ones to ensure that they stay with you.

Ideas like lean, waste-free consumption and fair value for money resonate with the demands of the post-recession consumer. Appropriate service and relationship strategies are critical issues for executives to address in developing robust marketing strategies for the environment we all now face.

Note that conventional logic suggests that customer retention is a key predictor of profitability. Support for this view dates back to Reichheld and Sasser (1990), who claimed to show the value to companies, operating in a variety of markets, of cutting customer defections (lost customers) by as little as 5 per cent; for an automobile service chain a 5 per cent cut in customer defections resulted in a 30 per cent increase in profits; for an industrial laundry a 47 per cent increase in profits; for an insurance brokerage a 51 per cent increase; and, for a bank branch a staggering 84 per cent increase. Customers that have been with a company longer tended, on average, to spend more on each transaction, offer more opportunities for cross-selling (selling them other products and services), and give better recommendations to their friends and colleagues. In the bank, customer relationships of ten years or more accounted for 29 per cent of the account base but 71 per cent of the profits. Nonetheless, while the logic appears compelling, there are some suggestions that there are limits to its universal applicability. Some companies are placing more emphasis on making choices between customers based on profitability and future prospects rather than simply longevity of relationship. Maintaining some customer relationships may become expensive compared to the value of the customer in question to the company.

Indeed, in all this, it is important that we distinguish between customer retention and customer loyalty, together with the relationship each of these has with customer satisfaction. There is a danger, in practice, that these concepts become confused. Customer retention is essentially a measure of repeat purchase behaviour, and there are many reasons why customers may come back even if we have failed to provide them with a high level of satisfaction – they may have no choice or they may not know any better. Fraser (2007), for example, warns of 'conflicted consumers' who buy your product and appear highly satisfied, but in fact are a stealth segment ready to defect as soon as a viable alternative appears. Customer loyalty, however, is more to do with how customers feel about us: do they trust us? Do they actively want to do business with us? Will they recommend us to others?

To confuse retention and loyalty can be dangerous. Retention may be achieved through a 'bribe' – discounts for repeat purchase, additional exclusive value-added services, and so on. Achieving high customer loyalty is likely to be far more difficult and requires greater long-term investment. The practical difference is great.

For example, 'customer loyalty' card schemes offered by many retailers are more about customer retention than loyalty and satisfaction, and it is likely that their effects will last only until there is a better offer available. On the other hand, the John Lewis Partnership achieves high customer loyalty through satisfaction building above and beyond such 'loyalty cards'. This is expressed in their long-term strategic principle: 'The Partnership aims to deal honestly with its customers and secure their loyalty and trust by providing outstanding choice, value and service' (**http://www.johnlewispartnership.co.uk/about/our-principles/generating-loyalty-through-choice-value-and-service.html** , accessed 2015, October 15). John Lewis has been rated as the most admired British company for honesty and trust and wins many awards for customer satisfaction. Indeed, as airlines have discovered, for example, if all competitors offer the same thing, then customer 'loyalty' programmes such as frequent flyer awards become a cost of being in business rather than a differentiator. Many frequent fliers will have loyalty cards with several airlines or alliances.

To build customer retention, anticipating the major financial benefits it brings, let alone longer-term customer loyalty, requires companies to invest in strategies focused on these goals, not just on sales volume. But it is suggested that retention is not enough as an absolute concept and that these strategies should also be about correcting any downward migration in customers' spending habits long before they defect. A two-year study of attitudes of US households about companies in 16 diverse industries showed that 'improving the management of migration as a whole by focusing not only on defections, but also on smaller changes in customer spending can have as much as ten times more value than preventing defections alone' (Coyles and Gokey, 2005).

This may involve brand building (of the type practised at Virgin) or specific programmes (such as the 'loyalty' schemes or product innovation), but increasingly it involves emphasis on achieving excellence in the service activities that augment the basic product offering. Nonetheless, for the reasons given above, a company faces an important strategic decision about the level of service and relational investment it should make in a given market or customer group, compared to the value of that market and its service delivery capabilities. Low-service strategies are a viable option where non-service benefits such as low price are key value drivers for some customer groups.

This chapter explores the concept of 'service' and examines methods for competing through service as an important element of marketing strategy and competitive positioning, in which executives face making some challenging choices. Figure 13.1 sets out the structure we are following to provide systematic appraisal of the key issues in competing through superior service and customer relationships.

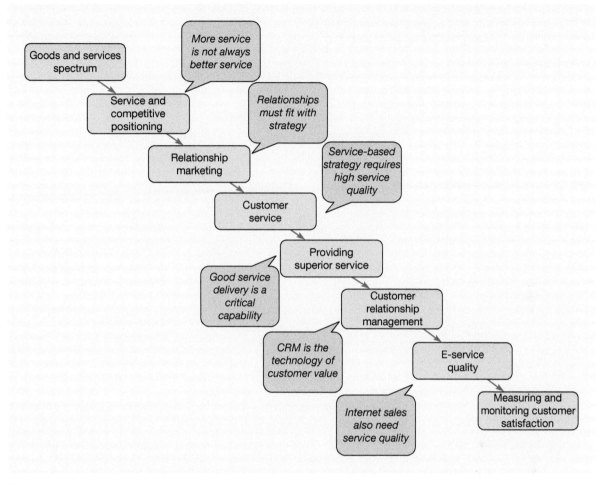

Figure 13.1 Key issues in competing through superior service and customer relationships

13.1   The goods and services spectrum

It is important to recognise that most offerings in a marketplace represent some combination of tangible and intangible elements, as illustrated in Figure 13.2.

The tangible elements of what people buy can be seen, touched, smelled, heard or tasted. They constitute the physical aspects of the offer, such as the product itself and the surroundings in which it is bought or consumed. The intangible elements are often more elusive. They comprise the level of service offered in support of the tangible elements, and the image, associations or beliefs that surround the product.

At the left-hand end of the spectrum, the offer to customers is primarily physical and hence tangible. Examples include packaged goods such as baked beans and batteries, and consumer durables such as stereos and tablets. From the customers' perspective, however, the benefits derived from purchase and consumption may well be less tangible – baked beans defeat hunger, batteries provide portable light, stereos provide entertainment and tablets provide access to online media. The distinguishing factor is that these benefits are primarily delivered by the physical features and characteristics of the product. There are also, of course, even less tangible elements to these purchases. Physical products are sold through retail outlets where sales staff may provide advice and demonstrations. Individual brands, through their media advertising and other promotional activities, may have established images and reputations in the minds of customers that will enhance value to them.

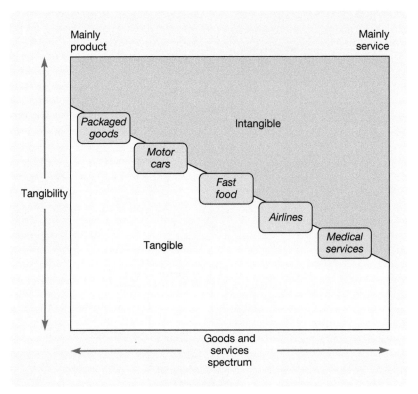

Figure 13.2
Goods and
services

At the right-hand end of the spectrum the relative importance of intangibles and tangibles is reversed. In medical services, for example, the essence of the 'offer' is intangible. It is concerned with the service provided to the patient and the way in which the patient interacts with doctors, nurses and technology. There are some tangible, physical elements involved, such as medicines, prosthetics, written instructions, and the physical surroundings. The essence of medical services, however, is the intangible process that takes place in the diagnosis and treatment of the medical problem. Ultimately the success of the medical services process is determined by the way the patient responds to, and interacts with, the services provided.

It is also worth bearing in mind that the services sector now accounts for some three-quarters of the gross domestic product of the EU countries and over three-quarters of EU jobs (see **http://ec.europa.eu/trade/creating-opportunities/economic-sectors/services/**, accessed 2015, October). Services are growing quickly in the world economy, making up almost 64 per cent of gross world product, suggesting huge potential in emerging markets (see The World Factbook, **https://www.cia.gov/library/publications/the-world-factbook/geos/xx.html** and **https://www.cia.gov/library/publications/the-world-factbook/fields/2012.html**, accessed 2015, October).

Between these two extremes lie offers that combine tangible and intangible elements in more equal proportions. In fast-food outlets, for example, the offer is a combination of the physical food (tangible) together with the ambience of the restaurant and the speed of the service provided (intangibles).

As more companies have embraced quality control and assurance techniques in the production of their physical products, so the scope for differentiation between one supplier and another on the tangible elements of offer has diminished. Total quality management has been increasingly applied to the physical element of products, reducing variability, tightening tolerances and ensuring fewer defects (or even approaching the cherished goal of zero). Increasingly, companies operating at the left-hand end of the spectrum are looking to enhance differentiation through focusing on the intangible elements of offer. These efforts include branding the offer and the delivery of service to augment the physical product offer. At the right-hand end of the spectrum companies and other service providers are recognising that the type and quality of the service they offer is their major means of differentiation. The line between tangible and intangible elements is becoming blurred and moving downwards, so that the intangible elements like service are becoming increasingly important across the whole spectrum.

For example, Vargo and Lusch (2004) have pioneered a 'service dominant logic' (SDL) that has attracted huge attention globally. SDL proposes that organisations, markets, and society are fundamentally concerned with exchange of service – the applications of competences (knowledge and skills) for the benefit of another party. That is, 'service is exchanged for service', such that all firms are service firms; all markets are centred on the exchange of service, and all economies and societies are service-based. Consequently, marketing thought and practice should be grounded in service logic, principles and theories. SDL embraces concepts of the 'value-in-use' and 'co-creation of value' rather than the 'value-in-exchange' and 'embedded-value' concepts. Instead of firms being informed how to *market to* customers, they are urged to *market with* customers, as well as other value-creation partners in the firm's value network. Traditional assumptions about differences between marketing goods and services are severely challenged by SDL. The fuller implications of SDL continue to unfold (for example, see **http://www.sdlogic.net/** for updates and further insights).

The practical implications of choices on product and service mix are considerable. In industrial product manufacturing, increasingly the highest added-value lies in technically complex products. Advanced manufacturing processes produce items that require considerable engineering or scientific skills, or special marketing capabilities. Shifting towards advanced manufacturing offers a way of developing strong positions in niche markets globally, although the investment required may be considerable (Marsh, 2009).

For example, aero-engine manufacturer Rolls Royce's strategy has been to expand after-sales service, instead of relying on sales of new engines, selling airlines outsourcing packages in which it takes responsibility for maintaining their engines. As new generations of complex 'low carbon' engines become available, it is likely the outsourcing business will expand further – currently around half Rolls Royce's income is from servicing engines (O'Connell, 2009).

13.2　Service and competitive positioning

A critical starting point in building a strategy is the issue of what level of service provision is to be offered and how this defines a company's positioning in the market or market segment in question. Of course, into this choice must also be factored the capabilities of the company to deliver the service level being offered, but a first question is how we want to be perceived in terms of service level and quality compared to the alternatives in this market.

In many modern markets the base-level requirement for service is higher than ever before. Without meeting this minimum level of service provision, it is unlikely we can be a significant player in this market – this is the cost of being in this business. But importantly,

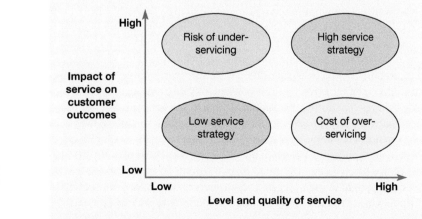

Figure 13.3
Service and competitive positioning

beyond this point significant choices exist. It is competitively risky and very expensive to assume that all service is good service, so the more we provide the better. In fact, important strategic choices should be addressed by executives.

Figure 13.3 suggests some important positioning choices as they relate to service provision. The attractions of a high service strategy are in enhancing customer retention and satisfaction through hard-to-imitate added-value in the form of intangibles. Much conventional wisdom supports this as an attractive option. However, it is important to recognise that there are choices. In many situations a low service strategy may be an effective alternative which defines a distinct space in the market and delivers high customer value through lower prices or other factors.

13.2.1 Low service strategy

Low service strategy is a component of the positioning of budget hotels like Accor's Formula 1. By stripping out the services typically provided by a two-star hotel and focusing on a better sleeping environment, Accor found a successful way to deliver a two-star hotel level of comfort for a one-star hotel price. The model is based on the observation that people trade-up from one-star to two-star for the better sleeping environment, not for the other services provided by conventional two-star hotels, and trade down from two-star to one-star just for the lower price.

Low service strategies have been particularly successful in some sectors during the economic downturn and recession of the 2010s and what has followed since. For example, low-cost retailers Aldi and Lidl have made significant inroads into Tesco's market leadership during the toughest of economic conditions. While high service strategies at Sainsbury and Waitrose have to a degree protected their competitive position, low service and very low price strategies at Aldi and Lidl have also been incredibly effective. Market leader Tesco has been left looking increasingly 'stuck in the middle' of the UK grocery market (Piercy *et al.*, 2010a).

A prime example of an effective low service strategy is the European no-frills airline Ryanair. It is the most successful of the European 'no-frills' airlines, based on the model of Southwestern Airlines in the US – offering very low fares but stripping out many of the expensive services provided by conventional airlines. Aggressive Chief Executive, Michael O'Leary, even plans to go from being a 'low-cost airline' to a 'no-cost airline', by making tickets free, while earning more from additions like food and luggage charges. In some promotions, Ryanair has offered to pay people £1 to sit in a seat on the aircraft (i.e., deduct £1 from the airport taxes and charge no fare). Ryanair has given new meaning to the 'art of cheap': a quarter of seats are already 'free' except for airport charges and taxes; the planes are stripped down with seats that don't recline (you can fit in more passengers instead, and worse, reclining seats break and have to be fixed, which slows things down); no window shades (flight crew have to waste time opening them to land); no seat-back pockets (less cleaning costs); no entertainment; advertising on seat-back trays; tickets sold online (along with insurance, hotels, car rentals and even online bingo); flight attendants selling digital cameras and MP3 players; and soon flights providing onboard gambling and a cell-phone service. O'Leary's view is that 'You want luxury? Go somewhere else.' Passengers who want even minimum services are required to pay extra for them. Employees are encouraged in O'Leary's low-cost thinking. Flight crews must buy their own uniforms and staff at Ryanair headquarters must buy their own pens. Staff are banned from charging their mobile phones at work. Faced with economic downturn, Mr O'Leary said his 'only one response to any consumer uncertainty' would be to intensify a price war, with moves 'to slash fares and yields, stimulate traffic, encourage price-sensitive consumers, and promote new routes and base developments'. He believes that during recessions travel does not get cut back, but people do look for cheaper alternatives (Piercy, 2009d). Nonetheless, 2015 saw Ryanair's 'Always Getting Better' customer experience programme operating to counter the company's reputation for low customer services levels, and concessions being made to customers (Thomas *et al.*, 2015).

Relatedly, a recent argument is that actually 'the best service is no service' because if you get things right in the first place, customers do not want your service (Price and Jaffe, 2008). In this sense, 'the size of a company's customer service operations is in inverse proportion to the quality of its underlying operations' (Mitchell, 2008). According to research by Price and Jaffe, customer contacts come in **four categories:**

About 1 in 7 customer contacts:	Are triggered by basic quality defects – 'it doesn't work'	Which have to be addressed by quality improvements
Another 25% or so:	Take the form of 'How do I?' questions	Which means the company has failed to communicate properly or its processes are confusing, and these are the issues to address
About 40%:	Are 'Where can I get?' queries	If the web page or other self-service options are done properly customers should be able to answer these for themselves
The last 20%:	Are people who want to buy stuff	The more the first 80% can be reduced, the more the company can invest in helping customers when they actually need and value it.

Making assumptions is dangerous, even though sometimes the evidence is highly counter-intuitive. A Canadian study of shop assistants found that in luxury shops, the 'snooty' attitude of assistants may actually boost sales – consumers may react in a positive way to rude and rejecting behaviour. It seems those who value designer labels want to be accepted by assistants in expensive shops. In an experiment the researchers found that consumers who felt rejected when shopping liked the brand and were willing to pay more for it than those who were treated well. The researchers reason that social rejection drives people to conform and work harder in an attempt to be accepted – though in the context of shopping for luxuries, not routine shopping (Macrae, 2014).

13.2.2 Under- and over-servicing traps

Examining links between service level and quality and customer impacts also highlights the potential problems of under- and over-servicing. Over-servicing occurs when services are provided to an extent and at a quality level which exceeds customer needs and has little impact on outcomes like customer retention or satisfaction. The same effect can occur when service efforts are concentrated in activities which matter little to the customers in question and do not create value. The low cost operations described above exploit the over-servicing and wrong-servicing of conventional competitors.

To understand the idea of 'wrong-servicing', consider, for example, US retail giant Walmart's experiences in the European market. Walmart is the world's biggest supermarket retailer. Its US value proposition of lowest price and highest service has been incredibly successful domestically. As part of its global expansion, in January 1998, Walmart arrived in Germany. However, this is a country where the rules of retailing seem to be 'the grumpier the better', the 'customer comes last', and 'shopping is boring', and the emphasis is on efficiency. Walmart arrived determined to pamper every customer in sight. Walmart's 'ten-foot rule' states that if a customer comes within ten feet of an employee, the latter must smile and offer to help. Complaints/requests must be dealt with 'by sundown'. In fact, the result was a major culture clash. The Walmart tactics infuriated consumers and aroused their suspicions – if someone takes hold of their purchases at the checkout (to pack them in a bag), they think someone is trying to steal from them. Locally employed shop-workers have been found hiding in the lavatories to avoid the embarrassing but mandatory morning Walmart chant. By late-2000 Walmart's losses were running in excess of £150 million a year in Germany from its 95 stores, and the company was ranked bottom of all retailers in Germany in an annual customer satisfaction survey. Analysts blamed Walmart's reluctance to adjust its retail model to the demands of German customers. In April 2001, the company announced it was scrapping its expansion plans in Germany and would not be launching the planned 50 new stores by the end of 2002. In 2006, after 8 years of losses, Walmart beat a retreat from Germany, selling its stores to Metro, Germany's leading retailer, losing $1 billion in the process. Walmart admitted it had completely misjudged German shopping tastes and habits. Being excellent at the wrong service is very expensive (Piercy, 2009d).

Correspondingly, offering a low level of service to a customer group where service has a high impact on the outcomes desired (sales, retention, satisfaction) is also risky unless a new market position can be defined and defended around a low service offer. In many situations, an under-serviced position indicates the need to invest more in service level and quality.

Increasingly, in harsh economic conditions and with more demanding customers, the conclusion is that we should think in terms of *appropriate* service and quality strategies, that match the most important needs of our target customers but also our ability to deliver. The map in Figure 13.3 may assist in looking at our competitors and their service-based positioning and how well they are doing, and comparing their performance to our own. Before reaching conclusions about what works and what does not, it is useful to examine the distribution and spread of service-based competition – is high customer satisfaction achieved through service and quality or other issues (and if so, which dimensions of service and quality or other issues), is low customer satisfaction associated with high or low service provision, or is there no clear relationship? Indeed, we might then look at which types of firms are doing best in market share and profitability terms.

There is a danger that executives confuse customer satisfaction, customer loyalty and the goals of customer service. Unsurprisingly, the result is many unsatisfied customers, disloyal customers and criticisms of customer service delivery. What is worse is a failure to identify what levels of customer satisfaction, loyalty and service are needed to implement our marketing strategy with these customers. In some cases, the obvious conclusion from a company's performance is that its strategy has failed because poor customer service is linked to low customer satisfaction and loyalty, and a poor reputation, with adverse effects on its performance (sales, growth profitability). But in other cases, high performance may be driven by low service levels (typically coupled with lower prices and other benefits).

Dealing effectively with the service/competitive positioning issue rests on understanding what aspects of customer service are important to the customers who are important to us, and aligning service capabilities with these priorities. This relates to where a company wants to be in the market compared to competitors and the type of value to be offered to different customers. The risk is that not challenging assumptions about service and value means we provide services to customers who do not value them, or deny services to our target customers because we spread our efforts over all customers. The critical issue is alignment between service capabilities and delivery and marketing strategy.

13.3 Relationship marketing

In conventional efforts to improve the probability of retaining customers, many organisations have turned to the techniques and philosophy of relationship marketing. The focus of relationship marketing is on building bonds and ties between the organisation and its customers to improve feedback and ultimately enhance the prospects of customer loyalty.

Figure 13.4 shows the classic 'relationship marketing ladder', originally developed by Payne et al. (1995). The ladder shows a number of identifiable stages in relationship building. At the bottom of the ladder is the prospect, or the target customer. The initial emphasis will be to secure the prospect as a customer. To achieve this, marketing effort is concentrated on customer catching. Once the customer has been caught, however, the emphasis

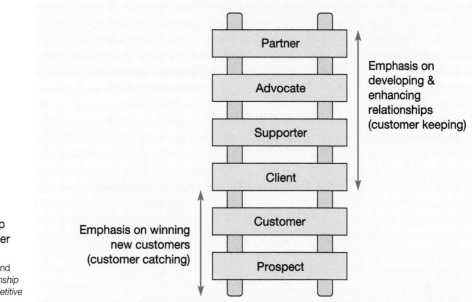

Figure 13.4
The relationship
marketing ladder

Source: Payne,
Christopher, Clark and
Peck (1995) *Relationship
Marketing for Competitive
Advantage*.

shifts to securing a longer-term, ongoing relationship. While a customer may be essentially nameless and have done business with the company once or only occasionally, a client is more individual and does business on a repeat basis. Clients may, however, be ambivalent or neutral towards the supplier company. Relationship marketing seeks to convert clients into becoming supporters, those who have positive feelings towards the supplier, and even advocates (those who may actively recommend the supplier to others). The top rung of the ladder is partner. At this level the supplier and the customer are working together for mutual benefit. The focus of relationship marketing is moving customers up the ladder, finding ways of enhancing the value both parties get from the relationship.

Clearly, not all prospective customers will be equally worth the effort needed to move them up the ladder. Critical to a successful relationship marketing strategy is targeting customers of sufficient value (current or potential) to warrant the investment in creating a relationship with them. IBM, for example, has identified its top 1,000 customers and puts great effort into identifying their current and future needs. The firm has combined its customer relationship management processes with its opportunity management system and ranked these customers according to their estimated lifetime value to IBM. When a high-ranking customer launches a big project with opportunities for IBM to tender, it is given highest priority across the organisation (Eisenstat *et al.*, 2001).

Nonetheless, effective relationship marketing requires sound reasons for the relationship on both sides (Figure 13.5). In some markets, such as rail travel, customers may not see advantages in becoming 'partners' and may prefer to stay at arm's length from the supplier. One respondent filling in a customer satisfaction questionnaire on a train was overheard to say: 'I wish I could go back to being just a passenger rather than a customer!'

Indeed, in some cases there may be an element of spuriousness about the relationship offering made by some companies. From the customers' perspective, the British Airways relationship does not offer more seat room, and the Sainsbury's relationship does not offer much more than a bribe to come back next time. The only tangible aspect of the customers' relationship with these companies seems to be becoming the target of large quantities of mail selling financial services (Piercy, 2009a). These inappropriate and often ineffective approaches to relationship marketing can be the result of poorly designed programmes based on weak value propositions (see Capizzi and Ferguson, 2005). In fact, a survey conducted by IBM of about 1,000 customers of 10 major retailers uncovered that factors relating to overall customer experience were far more relevant to customer satisfaction than price and value (Chu, 2002).

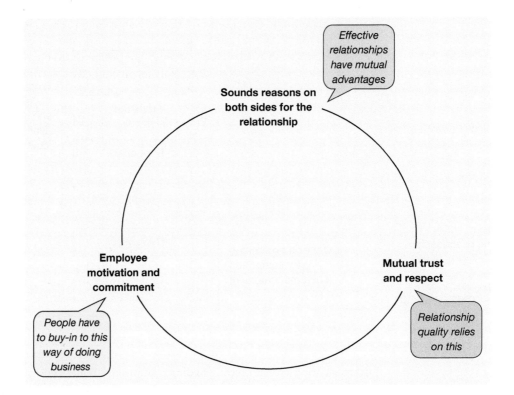

Figure 13.5
Foundations
of relationship
marketing

In other markets firms may misjudge the value customers put on relationship. In financial services, for example, attempts to create closer relationships with individual clients may have been naive in assuming the client will automatically see a value in having a 'personal banking manager'. Fundamental to establishing a relationship is to determine what each party gets, or could get, from that relationship. Too many organisations still look primarily from their own perspective, recognising the value to them of customer retention or loyalty, but not thinking through clearly what value the customer will get from the deal that would motivate them to participate.

In contrast, other firms are now coming to realise that the type of relationship customers want with a supplier can in itself be an effective way of segmenting markets around fundamental customer needs. This can lead to focusing relationship-building resources on those customer groups where this is mutually advantageous, and significantly cut the cost and the ill-will created through more scatter-gun approaches. In business markets, for example, Narayanda (2005) suggests four types of customers depending on their location on the loyalty ladder and the sellers' costs of serving them.

- **Commodity buyers** are only interested in obtaining the lowest price and are unlikely to be worth investments to move them up the relationship ladder.
- **Under-performers** should not be allowed to remain in that position as they have low loyalty and are expensive to service.
- **Partners** are expensive to run but high on the ladder and normally rewarding financially. Their management requires ongoing care to prevent them from becoming underperformers.
- **Most valuable customers** (normally accounting for less than 10 per cent of revenues) are as loyal as partners but cheaper to service.

Essential for more advanced relationships such as partnering, or awarding most valuable customer status, is the establishment of mutual trust and respect between the parties. This involves being prepared to share sometimes commercially sensitive information.

The core message is that effective relationship marketing focuses on choosing the 'right' customer as the target for service and relational investments – this may not be those who currently generate most revenue, but those who unlock the most value in the company. So, for example, Amazon has four very different types of customer: consumers, sellers, enterprises, and content providers. But Amazon devotes maximum resources to pleasing consumers – even if it means sellers or content providers sometimes feel short-changed. The unwavering focus on consumers has resulted in unparalleled consumer loyalty and incredibly high stock valuations (Simons, 2014).

Indeed, research in the United States suggests that the challenge to companies in business-to-business markets is no longer simply to sell, but to become the 'outsource of preference', through a collaborative relationship between vendor and customer. The customer expects the vendor to know the customer's business well enough to create products and services that the customer could not have designed and created, and to give proof in hard evidence that the supplier has added value in excess of price. The excellent suppliers are those which add value to the customer's business by being close enough to measure the customer's needs, develop added value services to improve the customer's business performance, and prove to the customer that this has been done. This is a long way removed from simple, transaction-based business (Chally, 2006). We consider this particular issue in more detail in strategic customer management (Chapter 14).

The third cornerstone of relationship marketing stems from employee involvement and commitment to the relationship building and maintaining process. While companies may set strategies in the boardroom for relationship marketing, the success of those strategies ultimately rests with the employees who are charged with putting them into practice. Employees, from front-line sales staff through accounts personnel to car park attendants, need to understand their role in relationship building, be committed to it and be motivated to achieve it. In many situations, as far as the customer is concerned, the employee they meet at the point of sales or service delivery *is* the company and its brand. We will consider the importance of this relationship in examining the growing importance of internal marketing in Chapter 16.

13.3.1 Building relationships with customers

Various approaches have been suggested for building closer links with customers, and hence moving them higher up the relationship marketing ladder. These can be grouped into three main categories: building enhanced benefits of loyalty; creating structural ties; and creating delighted customers.

Building enhanced benefits of loyalty

One basic approach to building relationships is through the development of enhanced benefits of loyalty for customers. These might be financial or social benefits.

Financial benefits give the customer a financial reason to enter into a longer-term relationship and remain loyal to the supplier. These might include discounts for bulk or repeat purchases or other rewards for loyalty. Typical examples include store loyalty cards, where shoppers build credits towards free purchases, or the collection of Air Miles through the use of credit cards.

Social benefits might include the establishment of regular social groupings, and increasingly companies now use Internet-based blog sites and specialised social networks to create such benefits. Sermo is a US online social networking site for doctors, with no advertising and open unedited interactions between members. Pfizer works in collaboration with Sermo's Internet-based social network to establish how drug makers can best communicate with doctors online. Mothercare launched Gurgle.com, a social networking site for parents of babies. Unilever's Dove brand operates an online community around its natural beauty concept and products.

On the other hand, social benefits might include corporate hospitality or social events sponsored by a firm where its clients can meet other clients with a view to developing their mutual business interests or technical knowledge, e.g., through seminars and workshops on product technology and industry change.

Creating structural ties and bonds

Through offering enhanced benefits companies may create structural ties with their clients, which then make it difficult, or costly, for their clients to defect. Professional medical equipment supply companies, for example, provide hospital surgeons with the equipment needed to help perform knee and hip implants with their own make of implant. The equipment works poorly with competitors' implants and is hence a major incentive for the surgeons to remain loyal. Sponsorship of the surgeons at symposia and conferences to enable them to stay up to date with medical advances also helps to strengthen their relationship with the supplier and build corporate goodwill, although there are important ethical constraints on some such actions.

In some industries the structural ties might be based on legal agreements and commitments, particularly where the use of protected patents is concerned. Ties are also created through the sharing of knowledge and expertise to which the client would otherwise not have access.

When structural ties are strong even dissatisfied clients may stay loyal due to the high switching costs involved. Some experts discuss 'strategic bundling', whereby companies build barriers to customer defections through offering groups of interrelated products. Banks, for example, may offer several different types of accounts, together with mortgage and loan facilities. Despite dissatisfaction with one or more of these services the costs to the customer of switching to a competitor may be substantial when all the services are taken into account. The growing significance of collaborative relationships with customers and the formation of networks of collaborative organisations is discussed in more detail in Chapter 15 on strategic alliances and networks.

Creating delighted customers

One view is that the most fundamental basis for establishing a lasting relationship with clients, and moving them up the ladder to become supporters, advocates or even partners is by ensuring that customers get more from the relationship than they were originally looking for. We expressed some reservations about this view earlier.

Historically, research has suggested that merely satisfying customers is rarely enough to give them a reason for staying loyal and becoming advocates rather than merely clients (Jones and Sasser, 1995; Reichheld, 1993). Depending on the level of competition in the market and hence the level of choice available to the customer, and the degree of involvement the customer feels with the product or service, customer retention rates among 'satisfied' customers may vary dramatically. Some time ago, British Airways found, for example, that its retention rate was exactly the same among satisfied and dissatisfied customers. As noted earlier, customer retention is not the same thing as customer satisfaction and loyalty. Reichheld (1993) reports that 65–85 per cent of customers who defect say they were satisfied with their former supplier. Among dissatisfied customers (with freedom of choice) retention rates rarely exceed 20 per cent, and among the seriously dissatisfied, 'terrorists' or 'well poisoners' can pose a significant threat to the business as they tell others about their poor experiences.

The concept of customer delight receives some support, though. For example, Guy Kawasaki, an Internet entrepreneur who worked on the marketing of Apple Macs in the 1980s, uses the word 'enchantment' to describe the 'process of delighting people with a product, service, organisation or idea'. He claims that the outcome of enchantment and delighted customers is 'voluntary and long-lasting support that is mutually beneficial' (Kawasaki, 2012).

It appears to follow that to improve the probability of customer retention it may be necessary to go beyond what is expected and deliver even greater value to customers. Among very satisfied or delighted customers retention rates are significantly higher, and they are more likely to become 'apostles', or advocates, telling others of their good experiences. Creating delighted customers demands that a high priority be given to customer service, both in the strategies the organisation designs and the actions it takes in the marketplace.

Nonetheless, there remains controversy in this area, and some authorities would suggest that delighting customers is a fast route to losing money, since many customers will happily receive and demand benefits which are not justified by their value to the seller:

> The idea that companies must 'delight' their customers has become so entrenched that managers rarely examine it . . . loyalty has a lot more to do with how well companies deliver on their basic, even plain-vanilla promises than on how dazzling the service experience might be. Yet most companies have failed to realise this and pay dearly in terms of wasted investments and lost customers.
> *(Dixon* et al., *2010)*

Recall the views of Barwise and Meehan, considered earlier (p. 334), on the power of providing customers with good value for money rather than gimmicks.

It is clear that some considerable care is needed in assessing the investment required to retain a customer compared to the actual benefits achieved by retaining them. We consider this further in a business-to-business context in Chapter 14.

13.4   Customer service

Where customer service is seen as key to competing effectively, conventional wisdom is that there are three critical ingredients to successful service provision. These have been called the 'three S's of service': strategy, systems and staff.

First, there is a need to have a clear service strategy that is communicated throughout the organisation, so that everyone knows their role in providing service to customers and clients. The strategy needs to demonstrate the company's commitment to service and its role in overall corporate strategy. Increasingly companies are using customer satisfaction measures alongside financial and other criteria for measuring overall performance, signalling the higher priority they now give to creating customer satisfaction. Indeed, some of these companies now promote and reward staff on the basis of customer satisfaction ratings achieved.

Second, not only do firms need to be committed to superior service in their strategies, but they need to put in place the systems to enable their staff to deliver service to their clients.

Third, and perhaps most important of all, the staff must recognise the importance of customer service and be committed to providing it. That means recruiting, training and empowering employees to provide the levels of service that will create customer delight and then rewarding them appropriately. Central is the provision of information, both on what customers require and how well the organisation is doing in providing that level of service. Also important is the power for employees to make decisions that will affect the level of service provided. One analyst advises executives: 'Remember there are two groups of people who know the business better than you do. They are customers and the people who deal with them. You need to talk to them both, often' (Skapinker, 2003).

13.5   Providing superior service

If superior service is an important element of competitive positioning, accepting this is not always the case, then understanding the requirements for providing better service becomes an important management concern. In fact, there is a long-standing research literature published in the United States (e.g. Berry and Parasuraman, 1991) and in Europe (e.g. Gummesson, 1987; Grönroos, 1994; Payne *et al.*, 1995), which looks at the nature of 'service' and what constitutes excellent or superior service in the eyes of customers.

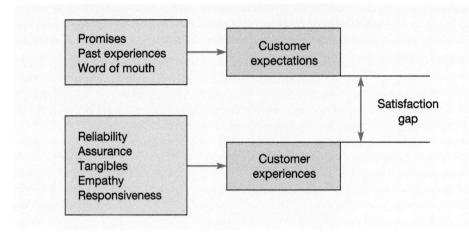

Figure 13.6
Assessing cus-
tomer satisfaction.

Source: Adapted from
Parasuraman, Zeithaml
and Berry (1985).

Much of the literature on customer satisfaction measurement (e.g. Berry and Parasuraman, 1991) concludes that customers measure their experiences against a benchmark of the service they expect to receive. The quality of service provision, and subsequently the level of satisfaction of the customer, is directly related to the difference (or 'gap') between expectations and experiences (see Figure 13.6). This has become the conventional wisdom in assessing service quality, though it should be noted that some recent research challenges the notion that buyers have pre-formed expectations of this kind, and looks for other approaches to measuring service quality, such as comparing the importance of a service attribute to its performance, or simply the measurement of performance alone (e.g., see Caruana *et al*. 2000).

13.5.1 Expectations

In the conventional approach to service quality measurement, Berry and Parasuraman (1991) discuss two different ways in which expectations may be used as comparison standards. First, there are expectations of what customers believe will occur in a service encounter. These they call predictive expectations. Second, there are what customers want from the service encounter – their desires. These two levels indicate adequate and desired levels of service. Between these two levels Berry and Parasuraman (1991) suggest there is a 'zone of tolerance'. A performance level above the zone of tolerance will pleasantly surprise the customer and strengthen loyalty, while performance below the zone of tolerance will create customer dissatisfaction, frustration and may ultimately lead to decreased customer loyalty (see Figure 13.7). Their research showed that both types of expectations are dynamic – over time expectations generally increase. There was some suggestion, however, that desired levels change more slowly than adequate levels.

Several factors have been found to influence expectations, ranging from the personal needs of the customer, through to the alternative services considered, and to the specific promises made by service providers in their bid to win business in the first place. Word-of-mouth communications with influencers and the customers' past experiences also affect service level expectations.

Prior experiences with the service provider, or with similar providers, are often the starting point in creating expectations. When customers step into a restaurant they are often judging the experience based on other restaurants they have visited. They typically make verbal comparisons: 'It was more relaxed than . . . ' 'The food was better than it was at . . . ' In addition to their own prior experiences expectations are also often affected by the opinions of friends, relatives or colleagues, who have related their own experiences. Depending on the standing of these opinion makers in the customer's esteem, they can have a significant influence on what is expected, and even deter trial of a particular service.

A third major determinant of expectations is the promises the company itself makes prior to customers using it. These promises, by way of advertising messages, sales pitches and general image created through pricing strategies and so on, set standards up to which the company is expected to live. Pitching them can be difficult. Promising too little may result in failing to attract the customers in the first place (they may be seduced by more attractive competitor promises); promising more than can be delivered may result in dissatisfied customers. The smarter companies manage their customers' expectations at each of the steps of the service encounter so expectations align with what the firm can actually deliver (Coye, 2004).

Managing and exceeding customer expectations

From Figure 13.7 it can be seen that, in order to create delighted customers, organisations need to exceed customer expectations. There are two main ways to achieve this: provide an excellent service or manage customer expectations downwards so that they *can* be exceeded. They are not, of course, mutually exclusive but should be used together. Berry and Parasuraman (1991) offer a number of suggestions for managing customer expectations:

- **Ensure promises reflect reality:** explicit and implicit promises are directly within the control of the organisation, yet many promise what they can never deliver in the desire to win business. Promises should be checked beforehand with the personnel responsible for delivering them, to ensure they are achievable, and attention paid to methods that might be employed to demonstrate to customers that promises have been kept (or exceeded).
- **Place a premium on reliability:** we discuss below the main elements of service evaluation. A key aspect of most services is reliability: doing what you say you will do when you say you will do it. Where services are reliably performed they may fall down on other criteria (e.g. the manner of their performance), but overall evaluation is likely to be acceptable. Where services are reliably performed they also reduce the need for rework, or redoing the service, a highly visible indicator of poorly performed service. During rework customer expectations are likely to be raised and the chances of successful completion diminished.
- **Communicate with customers:** keeping in touch with customers to understand their expectations and to explain the limits of service possibilities can be a powerful way of managing their expectations. Communication can encourage tolerance, demonstrate concern for the customer and may serve to widen the tolerance zone. Phoning ahead to warn a customer of being late for an appointment is a simple example of communication being used to reduce the probability of customer frustration (though not a guarantee it will be eliminated altogether).

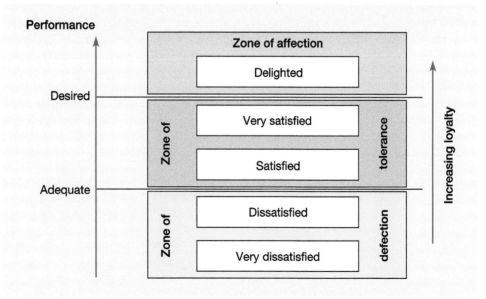

Figure 13.7
Performance, satisfaction and customer loyalty

13.5.2 Evaluation

Customers evaluate the performance of a service provider against expectations. Again, there are a number of factors that customers typically take into account when evaluating the service they have received. The most enduring classification is the five-dimensional model proposed by Parasuraman *et al.* (1988) and easily remembered by the acronym RATER: Reliability, Assurance, Tangibles, Empathy and Responsiveness:

- **Reliability** is the ability of the provider to perform the promised service dependably and accurately. In other words it is conformance to specification – doing what you said you would do when you said you would do it. In many service situations reliability has been shown to be the single most important aspect to many customers. Besides contributing to customer satisfaction, reliable service reduces the costs of redoing the service and can contribute to higher employee morale and enthusiasm (Berry and Parasuraman, 1991).

- **Assurance** stems from the knowledge and courtesy of employees and their facility to convey trust and confidence in their technical abilities. Customers want to be assured that the chef in the restaurant can cook without endangering their life, that the garage mechanic can fix the car, and that their accountant will not have them convicted for tax evasion. Assurance stems from professional competence. It is not enough, however, merely to have a high level of competence. It must also be demonstrated to the customers, often through the use of tangible cues.

- **Tangibles** are the appearance of physical features: equipment, personnel, reports, communications materials, and so on. Chartered accountants, for example, are critically aware of the impression their physical appearance creates with their clients. Care and attention is exercised when choosing company cars for partners and managers. Too expensive or luxurious a car might signal to clients that they are paying too high a fee for the services they are getting, while too cheap a car might signal that the firm is not particularly successful. Tangibles can be used in this way as indicators of professional competence.

- **Empathy** is the provision of caring, individualised attention to customers. It is the quality good doctors have of being able to convince patients that they really care about their welfare beyond addressing the current ailment. Empathy implies treating customers as individual clients and being concerned with their longer-term interests.

- **Responsiveness** is the ability of the organisation to react positively and in time to customer requests and requirements. Some businesses, such as Richardson Sheffield Ltd which makes kitchen knives under the Laser brand, have built their positions on being more responsive to the customer than their competitors. The company claims to respond to written enquiries within the day, electronic enquiries within minutes, and telephone enquiries instantly. They can also provide samples of products the next working day, even to new specifications. In some markets instantaneous, or near-instantaneous, responsiveness is critical. In Japan, for example, a key factor for success in the elevator business is the speed with which faults are fixed, as the Japanese particularly hate to get stuck in a faulty lift. Responsiveness typically requires flexibility. Customer requests can often be offbeat, unexpected. The highly responsive organisation will need to predict where possible, but build into its systems and operations capacity to respond to the unpredictable.

These five main dimensions of service quality have been found in many different service situations, from banking to restaurants, construction to professional services (Parasuraman *et al.*, 1988). The relative importance of each might vary, and the way in which each is manifested in any situation will be different, but time and again these factors have been shown to be relevant to customers in their evaluation of the services they receive.

13.6 Customer relationship management

The importance of enhanced customer relationships has led to large investments by many companies in formalised customer relationship management (CRM) systems – most commonly manifested in call centres, customer service/loyalty programmes and data warehousing. In fact, CRM is better understood as a cross-functional core business process concerned with achieving improved shareholder value through the development of effective relationships with key customers and customer segments (Payne and Frow, 2005).

For example, the French hotel group Accor links CRM data to its guest survey information in its Sofitel and Novatel hotels, to anticipate the preferences of frequent users. The Vice President for Sales and Marketing for Accor North America notes:

> It takes us back to the time when there were small inns and the owner knew every customer and treated them as an individual. It should help streamline check-in and accommodate preferences for guests who, for example, request the same room every time. The group will be able to market with a microscope instead of a telescope.
> *(Edmunds, 2000)*

The goal of CRM systems is to form and sustain valuable customer relationships (Kale, 2004). CRM encourages a focus on customer loyalty and retention, with the goal of winning a large share of the total lifetime value of each profitable customer. However, one of the primary conclusions of research concerning CRM performance is that achieving desired customer outcomes requires the alignment with the entire organisation, and avoiding the narrow and incomplete perspective of viewing CRM just as the technology of call centres and data warehousing.

It is clear that successful CRM initiatives are guided by a carefully formulated and implemented organisational strategy. CRM offers sellers the opportunity to gather customer information rapidly, identify the most valuable customers over the relevant time period, and increase customer loyalty by providing customised products and services (Cravens and Piercy, 2009). This has been described as 'tying in an asset', when the asset is the customer and CRM supports a customer-responsive strategy. The logic is that CRM expertise gains competitive advantage for a company when it:

- Delivers superior customer value by personalising the interaction between the customer and the company.
- Demonstrates the company's trustworthiness and reliability to the customer.
- Tightens connections with the customer.
- Achieves the coordination of complex organisational capabilities around the customer (Day, 2000).

Nonetheless, there have been many criticisms of the operation of CRM systems in practice, and questions raised about their real impact. Call centres are frequently disliked by customers. The recent case of a call centre in the UK making 6 million cold calls in a single day – selling debt consolidation and PPI claims – illustrates the source of some consumer annoyance (Davies *et al*., 2015).

Moreover, the reputational damage from crude culling of apparently less valuable customers may be substantial. Barclays Bank has attracted negative publicity and lost customers by shifting customers from one account to another because they did not meet an income threshold – effectively suggesting they were too poor to merit a paid-for account (Black, 2015). Similarly, private banks like Deutsche Bank Private Wealth Management have been 'managing out' lower margin customers, even those with portfolios worth hundreds of thousands of pounds – they are rich, just not rich enough (Cumbo, 2012). Similar approaches have led to good payers on credit cards having their cards withdrawn because the card operator makes low margins from such customers (Ashton and Watts, 2008). The gain from tactical customer culling should be weighed carefully against the threat to the company's competitive position and ability to deliver its marketing strategy.

Generally, the successful implementation of CRM is linked to the following factors:

- A front office that integrates sales, marketing, and service functions across all media (call centres, people, retail outlets, value chain members, Internet).
- A data warehouse that stores customer information and the appropriate analytical tools with which to analyse that data and learn about customer behaviour.
- Business rules developed from the data analysis to ensure the front office benefits from the firm's learning about its customers.
- Measures of performance that enable customer relationships to continually improve.
- Integration into the firm's operational support (or 'back office' systems), ensuring the front office's promises are delivered (Knox *et al.*, 2003).

However, research by consultants Bain & Co. suggests that there are four significant pitfalls to avoid in CRM initiatives:

1 Implementing CRM before creating a customer strategy – success relies on making astute strategic customer and positioning choices, and this outweighs the importance of the computer systems, software, call centres, and other technologies.
2 Putting CRM in place before changing the organisation to match – CRM affects more than customer-facing processes, it impacts internal structures and systems that may have to change.
3 Assuming that more CRM technology is necessarily better, rather than matching the technology to the customer strategy.
4 Investing in building relationships with disinterested customers, instead of those who value them (Rigby *et al.*, 2002).

From the perspective of marketing strategy and competitive positioning, it is important to consider the CRM interface as a key element of the capability of a company to manage customer relationships effectively. CRM capabilities and investments need to be examined in formulating and implementing effective customer strategies.

13.7 E-service quality*

The rapid and pervasive growth in online trading by both consumers and businesses underlines the need to include online service and relational issues in executive thinking. This is relevant in both the pure-play or Internet-only operations (e.g., Amazon.com) and to companies combining 'bricks and mortar' and online channels in their value chains (e.g., Tesco stores and Tesco Direct).

13.7.1 Online versus offline

In fact, Internet retailing is a multi-billion pound industry that continues to experience double-digit growth rates. Intense competition and increasingly demanding customers make the delivery of high-quality services vital for success in this marketplace. There has been wide-ranging research into online services quality. The first wave of early research focused on simple measures such as website usage statistics. From this researchers moved on to look specifically at the website as the key aspect of online service. In the past several years focus has shifted again to consider measuring the online service experience as a whole. There remains little consensus on the exact dimensions of online service quality, with many studies

---

* The section of this chapter concerning e-service has been contributed by Dr Niall C. Piercy, University of Bath, UK, from unpublished sources.

providing different results (see, for instance, Parasuraman *et al.*, 2005 or Wolfinbarger and Gilly, 2003), However, it is possible to identify several broad themes in online research. First, the core delivery of products and services is the foundation of quality service in any context online or offline. This said, two major differences emerge in comparing online to offline service: the company–customer interface becomes technologically-mediated and the role of trust is accentuated as the service provider is more separated from the customer.

The continuing importance of service fulfilment

Some important differences do exist in the customer service experience when shopping online – for example, those buyers with the technological competence to shop online are attracted to a wider range of products and the opportunity to shop at any time from home, as well as lower prices than traditional retail. Nonetheless, despite these unique characteristics of online purchasing, service fulfilment and delivery reliability remain the most important aspects of service quality and strongest predictor of customer satisfaction online. Offering better quality service can enable online and offline retailers to achieve significant competitive advantage, charge higher prices and benefit from customer recommendations.

Service fulfilment covers a range of customer service issues. For instance, Parasuraman *et al.* (1988) emphasise reliability, responsiveness and willingness to help customers as the critical elements in customer service. On the other hand, Warrington and Eastlick (2003) highlight product range and pricing as vital when dealing with physical products, while Dabholkar *et al.* (1996) propose product quality and availability as the most important issues. Pragmatically, these issues concern the delivery of the core product or service of the nature described and at the time promised to the customer. In Internet commerce, this basic mission remains the foundation for service delivery. This includes accurately displaying and describing products, the required items being in stock, delivery of what is ordered when promised, and accurate billing. When problems occur, responding to customer issues effectively is also increasingly important.

Change at the customer–company interface

The clearest difference in online versus offline service is the technology-mediated nature of the customer–company interface. Traditional service quality issues related to human-to-human interactions (such as responsiveness or empathy), as well as the context of service delivery (tangible elements), are replaced with customer experiences via the website. Offline, the design, quality and surroundings of the physical retail store and the knowledge, nature and actions of sales staff all send signals to customers about the quality of products and services on offer. These important sensory cues about the reliability of the product and store are absent online. The website therefore takes on a dual role as substitute for both physical context and human interaction in signalling the potential credibility and quality of the business prior to purchase. Such signals become more important online where the customer is dislocated from the business and requires greater reassurance.

Online customers also place greater importance on information about products and companies prior to purchase online. The Internet makes information location easier but the computer screen provides a smaller viewing window than a traditional retail store, so information must be concisely and usefully conveyed in a customer-friendly format.

The website also takes on a role in providing personal service. Internet purchasing lacks the feedback of face-to-face or telephone human interactions, making it harder for Internet sellers to customise service offerings. Technology does allow for customised service by remembering customers' previous purchases to make recommendations of potential products to buy that can drive sales. Nonetheless, the website plays a crucial role in online service but remains only one part of the broader service bundle.

An increased role for trust and assurance

Interestingly, offline evaluations of service quality have paid relatively little attention to customer trust issues. Major offline service studies such as the ServQual measure of Parasuraman *et al.* (1988), or the retail adaptation by Dabholkar *et al.* (1996), include no specific dimension on trust or security. However, the separation of the customer from the company in Internet buying suggests a significantly greater importance for trust in effective online strategies.

However, trust in the online environment is multi-faceted and complex. Three key trust issues appear in online retail: that the company will deliver products as promised; that the company will respect customer privacy, not disclosing personal details to third parties; and that the company will securely handle financial information. These issues affect both new and long-term Internet users. Some research has found that trust in the company can be a major driver of customer loyalty, far more than in the case with offline selling (Harris and Goode, 2004).

As Internet commerce continues to mature and online companies establish brand names that become as recognised as those in offline operations, trust issues may decline in importance. Research is already identifying a role for trust that is reduced from the early pivotal role suggested by some analysts (Wolfinbarger and Gilly, 2003). However, online service quality cannot be evaluated without major attention being placed on trust issues.

It is important that management thinking about customer service quality perceptions and relationships with sellers should recognise important differences in their growing online channels compared to more conventional offline operations. Not least among the reasons is that customers who become disaffected because of online experiences with a company may easily transfer their negative perceptions to the company's offline business.

13.8   Measuring and monitoring customer satisfaction

One start to measuring customer satisfaction can be made through complaint and suggestion systems. These catch those highly dissatisfied customers who bother to complain. The problem, of course, is that it may be too late to retrieve the situation, though swift attention to customer problems has actually been shown to help bond closer relationships – what Berry and Parasuraman (1991) refer to as 'doing the service *very* right the second time'.

For every dissatisfied customer who complains, however, it is estimated that around 12 others will be equally dissatisfied but not bother to complain. They will simply take their business elsewhere and may even tell others about their bad experiences (the 'well poisoners'). There is, therefore, a need for a more systematic assessment of customer satisfaction rather than sitting back and waiting for problems to emerge.

A more systematic approach is the use of regular customer satisfaction surveys, as now used by many service providers from railway companies to the leading international accounting firms. A four-step approach is typically adopted (Figure 13.8).

1 Identify the factors that are important to customers. These are not necessarily the same as the factors that managers think are important. Qualitative research techniques such as group discussions and depth interviews can be useful here. Depth interviews with the

Figure 13.8
Monitoring
customer
satisfaction

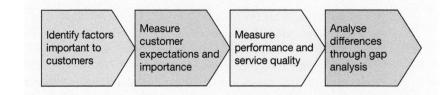

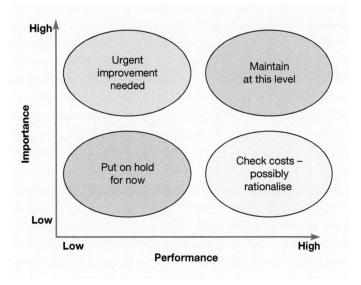

Figure 13.9
Performance and
importance

clients of a large accountancy firm showed that partners demonstrating that they really cared about the development of the client's business (showing empathy) was critical to building a long-term relationship.

2   Assess the relative importance of the factors identified and measure customer expectations on those factors. While some clients may expect their problems to be dealt with immediately, others may have more relaxed expectations. While for some reliability may be paramount, for others cost could be more critical.

3   Assess performance of the service provider on the factors important to the clients. Here it can be useful to assess performance relative to expectations directly (Parasuraman *et al.*, 1994). Did performance live up to, fall short of, or exceed expectations? At this stage a useful summary can be made of the factors under consideration in a performance–importance comparison (Figure 13.9). Here the factors are plotted in terms of their importance to customers and the performance of the firm on them.

A typical example is shown in Figure 13.10 for a firm of chartered accountants (disguised data). The evaluations were made by a client, a finance director of a large national company. The factors were identified through depth interviews and the evaluations of performance made against 'what would be expected of a leading firm of accountants'. The matrix can be used to focus attention on those aspects of the service of particular importance ('essential') to the client but where performance is judged to be below par.

In the example five elements of service were identified as being 'essential' to this client. On three of the factors performance exceeded expectations, while on two it fell below. Technical competence ('assurance' of technical ability to perform the audits), efficient use of the client's time ('reliability' in taking the time originally specified) and discussing charges in advance (and 'reliably' keeping to them) all constitute differentiators for this firm with their client. Where they fall down, however, is in showing an interest in the client's business (a lack of 'empathy') and some problems in the punctuality of staff or reports ('unreliable' delivery). Clearly these factors need to be addressed as a priority.

At the next level of importance the firm is poor at demonstrating flexibility ('responsiveness' to client requirements, especially when they change) and in being readily available to help when needed (again, a lack of 'responsiveness' to the client). On the other hand, they are well organised and have a good standard of written documents ('tangibles'). Again, areas for action are suggested.

Finally, the chart also shows that the firm excels in areas less important to the client. They rate highly on showing creative thinking and in providing detailed invoices. It may

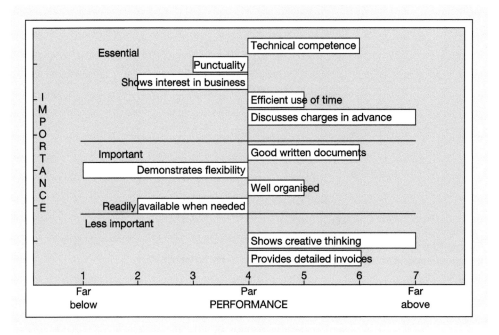

Figure 13.10
Performance
summary
(chartered
accountant)

be that providing these less important aspects of service is distracting attention from getting the basics right on the more important factors, and hence might be candidates for rationalisation. As a warning, however, we should note that sometimes factors are not important to customers until they start to go wrong. If the detailed invoices were not provided, for example, it could be that they start to become essential!

4 Analyse the differences between expectations and performance through gap analysis. For important factors, where there is a significant gap, there is a need to identify the reasons behind it and identify suitable remedial action.

13.8.1 Gap analysis

Figure 13.11 shows the ways in which a satisfaction gap could have arisen. By working systematically through the framework the root causes of dissatisfaction can be identified and dealt with.

A starting point is to determine whether the provider really understood the expectations and needs of the client in the first place. The market intelligence gap is the difference between customer expectations and supplier understanding, or perception, of those expectations. This could be brought about through inadequate research of customer wants and needs, or through arrogance on the part of the supplier in assuming knowledge of the customer. It could also be brought about through poor internal communications such that customer requirements are not passed on from the marketing researchers through to those responsible for designing the service that will be provided.

Where customer expectations are understood, they may still not be adequately catered to in the service specification. The design gap is the difference between what the supplier believes the customers expect and the service specification. This could typically be caused by resource constraints, where a service provider is too stretched to provide the service he or she knows the customer expects. Rather than increase the resource, or admit that the expected service cannot be provided, the service provider attempts to get as close as possible to customer expectations.

Even where the service specification is closely aligned to customer expectations there is a possibility that the actual service delivered falls short. The production gap is the difference between the service specification and the service that is actually delivered to the customer. There are a number of reasons why there may be a gap here. First, the service

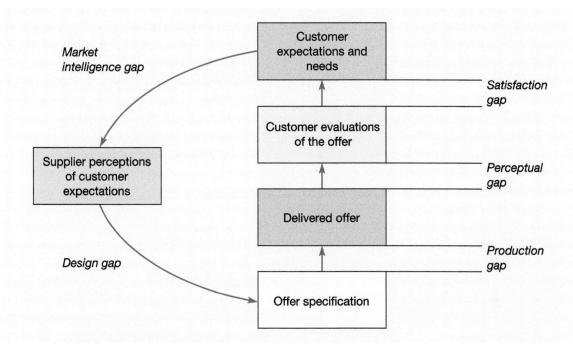

Figure 13.11
Quality gap analysis

Source: Adapted from Parasuraman, Zeithaml and Berry (1985).

design might be so complex as to make accurate delivery unlikely. Service promises may be unrealistic given the resources put into them. Response times planned for telephone enquiries, for example, may be unrealistic given the number of staff available to answer the phone or the number of lines available to take the calls. Second, staff may not have the skills or the systems back-up to deliver the service as specified. Poor employee training, poor technology provision or even inadequate internal communications can result in frustrated employees unable to deliver the service as specified to the customer. Third, a major problem in service provision is the very heterogeneity of services. The quality of service can vary from employee to employee, and from time to time for the same employee. Quality control systems are more difficult to implement in services than in manufacturing; they can be no less important, however.

The final gap that can lead to a satisfaction gap is the perceptual gap. Here it may be that the service has been delivered to specification and that the specification was in tune with customer expectations, but that the client, for one reason or another, does not believe the service has been delivered as expected. This could be brought about through poor use of tangible cues, lack of reinforcement of delivery, poor delivery manner or through the intercession of external influencers. In many ways a perceptual gap is the easiest to rectify. It requires the service provider to demonstrate to the client that the service really has been delivered to original expectations.

Summary

There is growing controversy surrounding conventional prescriptions of high customer service and relationship-building investments that executives should consider. Nonetheless, this chapter focuses on the idea that for many companies successful competitive positioning is about creating ongoing relationships with selected target customers rather than relying on more sporadic transactions. However, an important strategic choice exists regarding the appropriate or 'right service' level and quantity for a specific firm. In general terms, relationship marketing seeks to build longer-term relationships with selected customers, moving them up the relationship marketing ladder from customers to clients to supporters to advocates and ultimately, where applicable, to partners. A major factor in creating longer-term relationships is often the provision of superior service, beyond original customer expectations.

Customer satisfaction monitoring is a means of assessing the quality of the service offered. Where there is a gap between expectations and customer evaluations of the service provided, a systematic gap analysis can be used to identify and eliminate the causes. Renewed attention is being given to service quality and customer satisfaction issues in the context of online trading and the mix between 'bricks and mortar' and online offers in new types of value chain.

Case Study   Property portals hand control to homeowners

One of Britain's least popular professions, the high street estate agent, is facing a shake-up as the digital revolution finally reaches the business of selling and renting bricks and mortar.

The growing popularity of property portals Rightmove and Zoopla has made it possible for homeowners to take control out of estate agents' hands.

It has enabled the rise of online estate agencies, which offer sellers and landlords a way of advertising on the portals without having to pay the high fees that traditional high street agents charge. Portals do not allow individual sellers to list properties directly but they do permit them to list through online agencies.

A recent survey by analysts Jefferies found that 79 per cent of consumers would list their homes directly if they were allowed to. Three-quarters said estate agents' fees were too high.

Most high street estate agents charge between 1 and 2 per cent of the property's sale value, plus value added tax at 20 per cent of the fee. With the average British home now worth £265,000, that could cost the seller more than £6,000.

Online agents such as emoov, Hatched and House-network charge roughly £300–£600 for their main packages and have a sliding scale of fees, depending on which optional services a seller chooses. Options include photography, floor plans, and help with appointments and negotiations.

Yet to date they have only claimed a tiny slice of the market – just 2 per cent of home sales. By contrast they make up more than 10 per cent in the US, France, Canada and Germany.

Even the most established sites have sold only a few thousand homes so far; in total there are 1m properties for sale or rent every day on Rightmove.

But in recent months there has been a flurry of activity in the online agency sector – spurred in part by rising house prices and transaction volumes – that is creating more business for all parts of the estate agency industry.

This week veteran fund manager Neil Woodford backed start-up Purplebricks with a £7m investment. And next month entrepreneur Stelios Haji-Ioannou will launch his new site, easyProperty.

'Traditional agents have got to wake up to the modern world – it's adapt or die,' says Robert Ellice, chief executive of easyProperty.

'The portals have enabled people to know as much about a property as the owner does, before they even view it. Sellers are better-educated than ever before and they want flexibility but the existing agents don't allow that. The industry is absolutely ripe for disruption, it's a model that hasn't changed in 30 years.'

Traditional estate agents argue that the new brand of online disrupters do not offer the same levels of customer service. Ed Mead, a director of London chain Douglas & Gordon, says 'selling a property is not like selling a car'.

'Eighty per cent of the work done in selling is after an offer is agreed, and involves a lot of hand-holding and time,' he says. 'The internet provides many things, a personal service is not one of them.'

More than a third of all deals fall through before completion and it takes agents three months on average to close a sale, Mr Mead adds.

In an important test case last year, Country Properties, a high street agent, complained to the Advertising Standards Authority about Hatched.co.uk, alleging that it was misleading advertising for Hatched to claim to offer 'a complete estate agency service at a fraction of the cost'.

Hatched won that case, with the ASA ruling that the online agent did provide a complete service that was comparable to high street agents.

Adam Day, director of Hatched, says its model fuses the best of the old with technology to customise services.

'We offer everything a high street agent does, if the client wants it,' he says. 'But it is a waste of a client's money to advertise in a newspaper or having a window display or paying the rent on a prime high street office.'

This, however, makes online agents very dependent on portals – something which not all businesses are keen on. Other start-ups are bypassing Rightmove and Zoopla to create standalone sites.

Aidan Rushby and Logan Hall launched Movebubble in June, using travel website Airbnb as an inspiration.

'Yes Rightmove and Zoopla are great channels but from a business perspective it makes you quite vulnerable,' Mr Rushby says. 'It's then a race to the bottom, who can be cheapest. That kind of business model isn't a fun one to be in – low margins, high risk and ultimately you're not the one who is finding your customers.'

Instead, Movebubble matches landlords directly with potential tenants. It is free for landlords and charges tenants a flat £50 fee if they take up a rental through the site.

'This is the age of the collaborative customer,' Mr Rushby says. 'There is a very big shift in all areas of consumer business towards openness and transparency. People love the fact that they can deal directly with each other [on the Internet].'

While Movebubble focuses on the rental market, the Little House Company helps homeowners to find buyers directly. One of Britain's oldest portals, first set up in 2000, it will relaunch with a new name and ambitious growth plans later this year.

Miles Shipside, Rightmove's commercial director, said the emergence of online agents was still only a small part of the total market: 'Consumers now have more choice than ever before with a record number of agents in the market, and ultimately they will decide what level of service they want or need.'

The disrupter: Stelios Haji-Ioannou, easyProperty

Now that budget airlines have become industry stalwarts, it is hard to remember how disruptive the arrival of easyJet was.

Founded almost two decades ago, the airline aimed to 'make flying as affordable as a pair of jeans' and made direct booking popular, cutting travel agents out of the equation.

Since then, easyGroup has brought this corporate insurrectionism to other industries including hotel rooms, car rental, bus services, office rental and gyms.

Now it aims to take its tried-and-tested formula to the real estate market.

Easily the biggest brand name yet to enter the online business, easyProperty will launch in September as a rentals site, with a sales site planned for next year.

Having raised an initial £5m from friends and family in February, easyGroup founder Stelios Haji-Ioannou and easyProperty chief executive Rob Ellice have just launched a second funding round targeting ultra-high net worth individuals and individual private City figures.

With 10,000 properties already pre-registered, the site aims to be letting around 4,000–5,000 homes a month by the end of this year and is considering expanding across Europe within three years.

'We have very aggressive targets, we are going into the market in a very big way,' Mr Ellice said. 'The main problem with high street estate agents is wastage – only around 25 per cent of the deals that agents pitch for actually generate cash for their bottom line. It's a very inefficient model.'

By contrast easyProperty plans to avoid upfront fees but users will pay for optional extras. Services such as hosting viewings, drawing up floor plans and advising on pricing will be carried out by its network of 400 freelancers.

The big spender: Neil Woodford, Purplebricks

The face of Invesco Perpetual for more than a quarter of a century, Mr Woodford's new £2.3bn fund invests in small, rapidly growing companies.

His latest – taking a £7m stake in newly launched online estate agency Purplebricks – marks the biggest investment to date by a major investor into the emerging digital home sales market.

Launched in April, Purplebricks only operates in parts of southern England, and has sold fewer than 500 homes. But it has plans to roll out to the Midlands this autumn and aims to build to national scale and a £100m turnover within two years.

Chief executive Michael Bruce previously ran a traditional high street estate agency chain. Seeing the scope for 'a more cost-effective, convenient and transparent means of selling property', he sold his business in 2011 and invested an initial £1.5m in creating a software platform and website.

Since then he has put together a staff of 80 people, which will rise to 500 by the time the site is fully national. Four-fifths of these are 'boots on the ground' workers whose job it is to present a friendly and experienced face to potential clients.

'People aren't yet ready to go entirely online,' Mr Bruce says. 'They still want guidance from an expert on pricing and some local presence [in the property market].'

Purplebricks represents a fusion of old and new; its key goal is to make property selling into a 24-hour business. 'You can book a restaurant or a hairdresser 24 hours a day, but you can't currently do that with an estate agent,' Mr Bruce said.

The veteran: Sarah Beeny, Tepilo

Television personality and veteran property developer Sarah Beeny was one of the first on the digital home-selling scene, launching Tepilo.com in 2009.

Initially set up to cut estate agents out of the sales process completely, letting sellers and buyers interact directly with each other, it relaunched last autumn taking on a more traditional intermediary role.

That move, says Ms Beeny, was entirely driven by the need to get properties on to online property portals Rightmove and Zoopla.

'Our customers wanted to be there, the vast majority of people buying a house will be looking on those sites,' she said.

But expanding into estate agency does not necessarily mean taking on all the trappings. 'The old model of having a high street shop with branded cars and an in-house coffee shop and all those costs is part of the reason why estate agents have had to charge so much for so long,' cautions Ms Beeny. 'We felt there should be an option for people not to have to pay £6,000–10,000 just to get their home seen by buyers.'

Tepilo is selling around 50 homes a month and aims to reach £1m in turnover in its first year as an agent. It has about 25 employees, with a register of freelance local surveyors who visit advertised properties.

Ms Beeny is a serial digital entrepreneur, having also set up dating website Mysinglefriend. She first got the idea for a property-selling website while working as a developer.

'All my businesses have started from a sense of irritation that nobody else has done something that I've wanted,' she says. 'Tepilo was born when I thought that I don't understand why I'm having to pay up to 2.5 per cent plus VAT to sell a house.'

The experience is now feeding back into her day job – this autumn she will host a Channel 4 show called *Clicks And Mortar*, in which families try to sell their homes online.

Source: from 'Property portals hand control to homeowners', *Financial Times*, 22/08/14 (Allen, K.)

Discussion questions

1 How can 'customer service' be a differentiator in the service industry?

2 How can a company such as easyProperty ensure 'e-service quality'?

3 Do you agree with Ed Mead that 'the internet provides many things, a personal service is not one of them'? Explain your reasons.

PART 5
IMPLEMENTING THE STRATEGY

Part 5 examines a number of the most topical and relevant issues emerging in marketing practice, which have a profound influence on a company's decisions about marketing strategy and competitive positioning. These topics are linked by a focus on the challenges of implementing or executing marketing strategies.

We feature here two areas not extensively covered in traditional approaches to marketing strategy: the management of strategic customer relationships through sales and account management processes (Chapter 14), and the topical question of corporate social responsibility and ethical standards and their links to competitive positioning and advantage (Chapter 17). The logic for these additional points of focus is that these are topics proving of substantial and growing significance to the shaping and implementation of marketing strategy, particularly in the new post-recession environment which we now face.

In the earlier parts of the text, we have provided extensive coverage of the analytical and theoretical underpinning of marketing strategy: planning market-led strategy; analysis of the competitive marketplace and organisational capabilities; and market segmentation and competitive positioning. However, the focus now changes from the content of strategy to the context – the organisational and environmental realities in which marketing strategy must be put into effect. Nonetheless, the conventional dichotomising of strategy and implementation is largely unproductive. Both issues are interdependent parts of the same process of strategic development and market performance. It is also intriguing that in each area of strategy context that we examine, there are both challenges and obstacles for executives to meet, but also importantly new opportunities to compete more effectively and develop new types of competitive advantage.

Chapter 14 is concerned with strategic customer management. The focus here is the strategic role of the sales organisation and the development of strategic account management approaches to handle relationships with large, powerful, dominant business-to-business customers. We examine the role of strategic sales capabilities in managing business-to-business customer relationships and the evolution of the strategic sales organisation to enhance and apply these new types of capabilities. Strategic customer management is concerned both with the strategic management of investment of resources in different parts of the customer portfolio, but relatedly also with the management of relationships with strategic customers. Very large (or more strictly, very important) customers provide the domain of strategic account management – moving from transactional and relationship marketing approaches to major accounts, toward the partnering with a small number of key accounts. This strategy has potential gains in locking-in relationships with the most dominant customers in the portfolio, but also carries substantial risks from dependence and customer opportunism, which should be carefully weighed. Nonetheless, strategic account management approaches are highly topical and a balanced case should be established prior to making decisions and commitments.

Our concern with key external dependencies continues in Chapter 15, which examines the role of alliances and networks in marketing strategy, as the organizational forms developed by many organisations to take their strategies to market. Environment change and complexity has heralded for many organisations an era of strategic collaboration. We examine the drivers of collaboration strategies and the types of networks, alliances and partnerships which result. Our emphasis is in the emergence in many sectors of alliances as the way in which we compete, but we also underline the risks in strategic alliances. Competing through strategic alliances offers many potential benefits, but requires attention to the underlying rationale and priorities for collaboration and investment of effort in managing and appraising alliances, which pose quite different challenges to conventional organizational structures.

Chapter 16 turns explicit attention to strategy implementation and internal marketing, where our focus is more on key internal dependencies than external ones. We review the sources of the continuing implementation or execution challenges in marketing, and examine internal marketing as a set of tools, or a template, for structuring and managing the implementation process. The development and scope of internal marketing has been associated with enhancing service quality, improving internal communications, innovation management, and internal markets, but our focus is on strategic internal marketing as a parallel to external marketing, which focuses on the organisational and behavioural changes required to effectively implement strategy. A particularly vital purpose of strategic internal marketing is achieving cross-functional collaboration and seamlessness in delivering value to customers.

The last chapter in Part 5 – Chapter 17 – focuses on the rapidly emerging area of corporate social responsibility and ethics, and the impact on the ways organisations must adapt to new societal demands, but also how it is creating new areas to consider in developing different kinds of competitive strength. Corporate social responsibility and ethical issues are linked in their relationship with corporate reputation. This chapter is concerned with an important relationship between external and internal dependencies. At one level, attention to corporate social responsibility concerns is mandated by customer pressures, both in consumer and business-to-business markets. However, a fuller consideration of the scope of corporate citizenship suggests that the drivers of social responsibility go much further than moral obligation and are linked to the ability of companies to compete effectively. We look at defensive social responsibility initiatives in responding to competitor and customer pressures. However, what emerges is a view of corporate social responsibility as a route to competitive advantage. This view emphasises a strategic perspective on social responsibilities, where a social dimension becomes part of the company's value proposition to its customers. The goal becomes not altruism for its own importance, but the combination of business and social benefits. It is clear that this challenge will be extremely important to management thinking in the current business environment.

CHAPTER 14

STRATEGIC CUSTOMER MANAGEMENT AND THE STRATEGIC SALES ORGANISATION

. . . Selling is changing fast and in such a way that sales teams have become strategic resources. When corporations strive to become customer focused, salespeople move to the foreground; engineers recede. As companies go to market with increasingly complex bundles of products and services, their representatives cease to be mere order takers (most orders are placed online, anyway) and become relationship managers.

(Thomas Stewart, writing in the *Harvard Business Review* in 2006)

Letting go can cut both ways

A sad by-product of any recession is the painful process of having to let people go. This should always combine the realities of the company's performance with an assessment of an individual's contribution. You should also consider going through exactly the same process with your customers.

Inexperienced or poorly managed salespeople tend to go after any piece of new business. However, the cost of the sale alone can render this business uneconomic. In a difficult market, it is much better to focus on generating extra revenue from your existing customers, ensuring that you focus your best efforts on the most profitable accounts.

Phil Jesson is an expert in strategic account management. He advises a wide range of companies, including Pirelli, Bass and Tarmac.

Jesson explains that once a commercial relationship becomes established, your customers will inevitably spend more time with your delivery people. As time goes on, there is a risk that the profitability of the account begins to suffer.

It is common for your customers to enjoy an increasing number of discounted products and free services.

The underlying causes of unprofitable accounts are fundamental; as well as the usual pre and post-sales

of
KEY ACCOUNT MANAGEMENT
Written by
Phil Jesson

www.philjesson.com

Source: Phil Jesson: A-Z logo reproduced by permission of Geographers' A-Z Map.

activity, there is a specific requirement for a third pair of eyes. These are people who manage the entire sales process, not just measure the performance of your people.

While the motivational elements of sales management are important, this has to be backed by a detailed review of your best accounts, very similar to formal staff appraisals.

Jesson has a three-stage process for instilling best practice into companies. He always starts at board level, encouraging the board members to be personally involved in account management.

The next stage is in the training room, providing the right tools for account managers. The final and most important part is out in the field, coaching account managers as they work with their customers.

In the 1990s, one of the management fads was the 360-degree review where employees rated the performance of their bosses. Jesson recommends the same process with your key accounts, following the 80:20 rule, where 80 per cent of the value comes from 20 per cent of the accounts.

Formal, two-way customer reviews can be cathartic, but just as the client may use this to highlight deficiencies in your products and services, the evidence may show that some clients are no longer profitable. The only solutions are either to raise your prices or let these customers go.

Hard times often require tough action, and Jesson recommends backing up action with evidence, not sentiment. While it can be difficult to renegotiate terms with your longest-serving customers, the alternative can be insolvency.

The natural tendency of the entrepreneur is to say 'yes' to everything, and this is a good approach in the early days. But every successful entrepreneur also talks about the hardest part of their journey, the day they had to let go some well-loved but non-performing members of staff.

The same is true with your customers. Jesson suggests that the best strategy is to work only with those customers that fit your business profile, and let your competitors work with the rest.

Source: from 'Letting go can cut both ways', *Financial Times*, 29/06/09 (Southon, M.)

Discussion questions

1 Why are companies such as Pirelli, Bass and Tarmac embracing strategic customer management?

2 What stages are advocated to improve customer management and why?

Introduction

Many of those concerned with marketing strategy or competitive positioning pay relatively little attention to issues concerning the salesforce or strategic account management structures. The view has generally been that marketing executives and business planners make strategic decisions, and create value through product and brand innovation and make strategic choices, while sales and account managers are really concerned only with the implementation of the plans created by the strategic decision makers. However, this over-simplified view of the world does not stand up to the scrutiny of managers who have to develop and implement strategy in the complex and highly competitive conditions that characterise most business-to-business situations. It is illustrative that a growing number of companies are making appointments such as director of Strategic Customer Management, or Strategic Customer Manager or making other organisational changes to reflect new realities.

For example, Proctor & Gamble under A.G. Lafley's leadership was transformed from the stodgy, slow-moving, inward-looking bureaucracy in the 1990s into a nimble, innovative and aggressive competitor beating the rest in the 2000s. A significant and enduring part of that transformation was the creation of Customer Business Development (CBD) organisations at the front of the business. The goal of CBD was to transform the old, narrow idea of buyer-seller relationships with customers, into a multifunctional, collaborative approach designed to achieve mutual volume, profit and market share objectives. CBD teams work with customers to develop the customer's plans and strategies to the advantage of both customer and P&G. CBD team members work collaboratively with experts from finance, management systems, customer service and brand management to develop and implement business strategies that deliver sustainable competitive advantage for P&G brands (Piercy and Lane, 2009a).

The ability of organisations to achieve superiority in how they manage customer relationships to create value and to sustain profitable relationships is increasingly recognised as a core capability – but a capability which has often been ignored in the literature of marketing strategy (Piercy and Lane, 2009a). This chapter seeks to explain why the sales organisation and related strategic account management activities should form an important element for executives considering the development of marketing strategy – and how they define important implementation capabilities (see Chapter 16).

Indeed, many marketing strategy implementation failures can be explained by the poor alignment of strategy with sales capabilities. One problem is that many traditional marketing and sales approaches were not designed for complex, consultative and collaborative, technology-based customer relationships where, for example, the 'product' is being created jointly by buyer and seller as it is being 'sold'. Sales capabilities provide a critical resource which differentiates suppliers from each other in the eyes of professional purchasers. There have been calls to recognise sales as the key to business success and worthy of a 'corner office' (Delves Broughton, 2012).

For example, it is apparent that in many sectors, traditional sales models are obsolete as a result of growing customer sophistication. Indeed, in the pharmaceuticals business, high sales pressure placed on doctors to prescribe new drugs has resulted in formal training courses in medical schools to teach future doctors how to resist sales pitches (Weintraub, 2008). This is symptomatic of the search by the pharmaceutical industry for new and better ways to get to market. Companies like Pfizer, Wyeth, Novartis and GlaxoSmithKlein recognise that the era of 'hard sell' is over in their sector and are working to develop new, more appropriate, business models. Fundamental changes in the requirements of business customers mandate a strategic response from sellers that is more robust than simple acquiescence to demands for lower prices and higher service levels. The challenge is to reposition sales as a core part of a company's competitiveness, where the sales organisation is closely integrated into a company's business and marketing strategy (Stephens, 2003).

The pressure is on to achieve a better alignment between marketing strategy and sales and customer management capabilities. The idea of 'marketing and sales fusion' is gaining traction in many situations as a way of overcoming organisational separation and problems of coordination (Chartered Institute of Marketing, 2011). Certainly, better alignment between marketing and sales has become a priority for many companies (Act-On Software, 2015). According to a study by Aberdeen Group in 2011, highly aligned organisations achieved a 32 per cent year-on-year revenue growth, while less aligned competitors saw a 7 per cent decline in revenue (Aberdeen Group, 2013).

Of particular importance to strategic decision makers, the financial and reputational costs of some sales-related behaviours may be enormous, acting to undermine a company's market positioning and destroy its strategic credibility. In 2014, leading drugs company GlaxoSmithKlein was fined £297 million by the Chinese authorities for paying incentives to doctors to prescribe the company's drugs. The company quickly moved to stop paying its sales representatives volume-based commission and to stop paying doctors to speak on its behalf at medical conferences (Griffiths, 2014). The company was accused of systemic bribery over a sustained period of time (Anderlini *et al.*, 2014). In some ways the company was a scapegoat for a traditional sales approach in this market – a former salesman comments, 'I never met a doctor who refused a handout unless it was too little' (Ward and Waldmeir, 2014). Nonetheless, GSK has seen a 60 per cent collapse in sales in China resulting from the corruption probe (Griffiths, 2014).

The crisis in China follows fines for pharmaceutical companies in the United States related to their sales and marketing policies: GSK paid $3 billion to the Department of Justice to settle claims including 'cash payments disguised as consulting fees, expensive meals, weekend boon-doggles and lavish entertainment'; Abbott paid $1.6 billion for illegal marketing of a bipolar disorder drug; Johnson & Johnson paid $181 million to settle claims over marketing of an anti-psychotic drug, and the final bill could reach \$2.2 billion (Andrew and Waldmeir, 2013). US estimates are that payments and gifts by pharmaceutical companies to physicians add up to \$19 billion a year (Weintraub, 2007). Pharmaceutical companies are not alone in being criticised for their sales and marketing approaches – financial services, public utilities, and social media are very much in the firing line. Banks in the UK have been warned that they are failing to shed their aggressive, bonus-led sales culture, and the regulators are taking a close interest (Arnold, 2014).

Sales and marketing activities are under intense scrutiny on a global basis. Aside from simple damage to corporate reputation and brand equity, the danger is that crises of these kinds reduce a company's ability to implement its marketing strategy and undermine its competitive position. This underlines the strategic significance of the front-line of the business.

In this chapter, we first examine the factors which should encourage executives to re-examine the salesforce as a strategic capability, and the marketplace demands which are reinforcing these efforts. Then, we examine the strategic sales organisation – the new forms of organising the front-line resources that impact on customer relationships and deliver superiority in customer value.

This brings us to the issue of 'strategic customer management'. In the same way that companies have come to recognise the strategic aspects of operations management (for example, in total quality deployment, and business process reengineering initiatives), and in supply chain management (supplier relationship management approaches rather than simpler notions of transportation and warehousing), there is now an increasing priority for a strategic perspective on the management of customer relationships.

There are two aspects of strategic customer management. The first relates to the strategic management of the customer portfolio – making investment choices between different types of customer to deliver the goals of marketing strategy, but also to shape that strategy. The second aspect relates to the management of strategic customers – building relationships with the dominant customers in the company's portfolio, some of which may be classified as strategic accounts and handled differently in a new type of partnership-based business model. These are important strategic decisions which impact directly on the profitability and risk profile of the company's business. The structure we have adopted to cover these issues is illustrated in Figure 14.1.

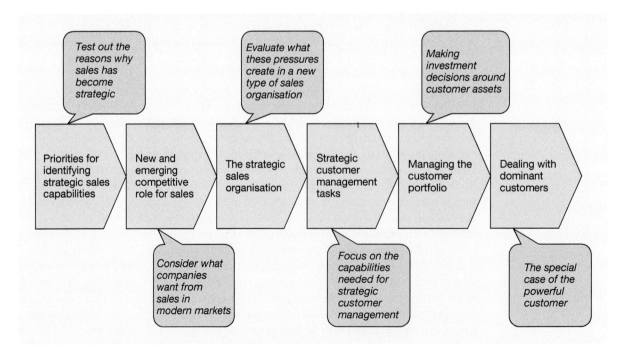

Figure 14.1 Key issues in strategic customer management

14.1   Priorities for identifying strategic sales capabilities

To begin, consider the factors encouraging executives in many major organisations to re-examine the role of salesforce capabilities in the context of developing and implementing marketing strategy. This is an important starting point in understanding the potential role of strategic customer management approaches to enhancing the development and implementation of marketing strategy.

Traditional views suggest that marketing and sales should be considered separate entities in the organisation because, according to Levitt, 'Selling focuses on the needs of the seller; marketing on the needs of the buyer' (Levitt, 1960). The conventional subordination of sales (tactical) to marketing (strategic) was elaborated in statements like Drucker's view that 'the aim of marketing is to make selling superfluous' (Drucker, 1973). However, it should be noted that Levitt was writing more than 50 years ago, and Drucker more than 40 years ago, underlining the risk that their views may have dated somewhat. Consider the following issues in reaching a view about the strategic significance of sales capabilities in a particular company situation. Figure 14.2 summarises the approach we are taking.

Customer relationships

Clearly, in many companies channels development has included the establishment of direct channels, such as those based around Internet websites – in consumer marketing by 2014 almost a third of British household purchases apart from groceries were made online (Poulter, 2014b), and Internet shopping was blamed for the closure of 16 high street stores a day (Poulter, 2014a). The proportion of spending going online is much higher for many business-to-business sellers. At the same time, there is a growing trend towards outsourcing routine sales operations to third parties (Anderson and Trinkle, 2005). In the US, Proctor & Gamble has a 200-person team wholly dedicated to Walmart (the single customer that constitutes 20 per cent of P&G's business); it is relatively straightforward for P&G to outsource routine sales visits to stores to a third- party sales organisation. For example, Acosta in the US provides the third party sales team for Kellogg's, P&G and Nestlé in American supermarkets, and their clients include the number one and number two brands in most grocery categories (Boyle, 2011). Similarly, global corporate expenditure on customer relationship management (CRM) technology is measured each year in billions of dollars, and individual spends by companies can be in tens of millions of dollars. CRM explicitly aims to automate many of the functions traditionally associated with the salesforce.

However, this leaves the vital issue of whether a company's most important business-to-business customer relationships can really be managed to full advantage through a website, a third party seller, or a call centre? Answering this question is important to understanding the strategic role of sales for a company, rather than considering only the routine activities involved in taking and processing orders, For instance, Dell Computers is an Internet-based company – the majority of sales and service provisions are on the Web. Nonetheless, Dell maintains both account executives in the field as well as internal salespeople in branches, because the view is that the technology exists to free salespeople to sell and

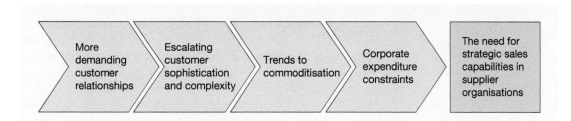

Figure 14.2 Pressures on sales capabilities

develop customer relationships, not to process orders (which the technology generally does better and cheaper). As Dell struggles to rebuild its weakened market position, its multi-channel sales capabilities are critical to success.

There is a substantial business and competitive risk in underestimating the role of the salesforce in defending and sustaining a competitive position. Consider the case of a $210 million manufacturer of specialty industrial lubricants, based in Atlanta. Expecting in an Internet-enabled world that the 400 person salesforce would be increasingly irrelevant, the company spent $16 million on its website, e-portals, call centres and an integrated CRM system. When the new sales model went live, the anticipated 35 per cent sales increase in sales turned out to be an 18 per cent decline, with falling margins (largely because of the cost of the new Internet infrastructure). In addition, nearly a third of the salesforce resigned in just over a year (including 17 of the top 20 salespeople), because there was a general feeling that there was no point in staying to compete with the new website, after spending years developing personal relationships with their customers. There had been no customer involvement in developing the new sales model – the company had not bothered to ask customers how they wanted to do business. When asked, customers identified this company's only real competitive advantage as the expertise of its salesforce and their ability to design solutions to solve technical problems for customers. The new sales model deploys salesperson expertise in the specification and design phases, and in negotiating prices and terms, and uses the Web for routine repeat purchases and order tracking, and the competitive situation is being retrieved (Friedman, 2002).

Understanding and enhancing the ways in which sales resources add value and protect customer relationships is becoming of strategic importance in markets being driven towards commoditization (see below). To the extent that a marketing strategy depends upon strong and sustained customer relationships, there is an implicit reliance on sales capabilities. To the extent that a salesforce has built and sustains strong customer relationships by creating value for customers, this provides a strategic resource for the company, which should impact on its strategic choices.

Customer sophistication and complexity

The growing sophistication and aggressiveness of purchasers in business-to-business markets has also escalated the strategic importance of effectively managing buyer-seller relationships (Jones *et al.*, 2005). For a company like IBM, for example, how can traditional marketing cope with consultative selling, when the product is being designed as it is being sold? The challenge to the seller is to implement effective marketing strategy in a dramatically changed world of sophisticated buyers (Shapiro *et al.*, 1998). This change is underlined by the shift in the traditional role played by purchasing functions in customer organisations.

Increasingly, purchasing has become a strategic function linked to the customer's strategic plans, with a major level of responsibility for profitability, cost control and enhanced shareholder value (Janda and Seshandri, 2001). Professional purchasing managers use complex sourcing metrics to select the 'right' suppliers, and to dictate terms on how they will be supplied, so more than ever supplier profitability is determined at the point of sale, where the sales organisation interacts with the customer (De Boer *et al.*, 2001; Talluri and Narasimhan, 2004). Correspondingly, the sales task has become much more complex and the stakes much higher.

Sellers in business-to-business markets increasingly face much more complex decisions about their marketing and sales investments in customer relationships. Historically, seller profits were generally in line with account size, because prices tended to be cost-based, sales costs were relatively low, and the size of accounts did not vary dramatically. However, consolidation by merger and acquisition and attrition through recession has changed this situation in many markets. In industrial markets, sales situations are increasingly characterised by fewer, larger and more complex purchasing organisations, and in consumer markets there has been a massive shift in power to retailers (Shapiro *et al.*, 1998). Unsurprisingly, very large customers are powerful and demand customised sales and account management, and are challenging in terms of profitability for the supplier. Other customers also demand special treatment, but it is likely to be different. Small and medium-sized accounts require yet more different approaches, mainly because of the cost of serving them. The strategic challenge is to match sales efforts and approaches to different parts of a complex portfolio of customers, to balance revenue and profitability with business risk. These choices impact substantially on corporate performance.

Market trends of this kind have elevated the importance of the effective deployment of sales capabilities to a strategic issue. In particular, we will explore the themes of the customer portfolio and the impact of dominant customers as the chapter develops.

Commoditisation

One impact of the revolutions which have taken place in operations management and supply chain design has been to reduce product and service differentiation in many sectors. Competing products are frequently built on near-identical modularized platforms, and supply chains are designed for maximum speed and lowest cost. Benchmarking systems encourage suppliers to achieve similar performance against the same metrics. It is unsurprising that the result is growth in product similarity rather than differentiation.

In parallel, customer organisations increasingly pursue aggressive commoditization strategies with their suppliers – if all competitive offerings are essentially similar, then differentiation can only be achieved through price, because that is how commodities are sold. This may be the preferred situation for the purchaser, but not usually for the seller. The chief purchasing officer's modern armoury includes: RFPs (Request for Proposal or an invitation to suppliers bid for business on a specific product or service); Internet auctions; purchasing consultants; and, buying consortiums. These mechanisms all seek to reduce purchasing to a comparison of prices and product technical specifications. The challenge to sellers is to constantly expand the scope and value of the offering to the customer, and the impact of the offering on the customer's business performance. Achieving differentiation with strategic customers requires new types of buyer-seller relationships that assist customers in implementing their own strategies. This underlines the need for the sales organisation to take a more strategic and less tactical role in developing and implementing business and marketing strategy.

Indeed, it may be that the sales/customer interface is the place where competitive differentiation is actually achieved. Research by the US consultancy, H.R. Chally, suggests that salesperson effectiveness accounts for as much as 40 per cent of business-to-business customer choice of supplier, because technology has made products increasingly substitutable (Stephens, 2003).

For example, SKF is the world's largest maker of industrial bearings – a business highly susceptible to commoditization. SKF's fight to overcome commoditization threats relies on the company's 5,000 sales engineers developing close relationships with customers and liaising with technical experts deep inside their own business. The goal for sales is to align customer needs with complex technical solutions, often involving customised products. In several important ways, the sales engineer stands between the company and commoditization (Marsh, 2007).

Corporate expenditure

Recall also that corporate expenditure on sales operations is estimated to greatly exceed that on higher profile advertising and sales promotion activities. Indeed, it is also clear that sales activities are frequently among the most expensive in the marketing budget. Research in the US finds that while in some sectors companies spend as little as 1 per cent of sales on their salesforce (e.g., banking, hotels), the average company spends 10 per cent of sales revenue on the salesforce, and some spend as much as 22 per cent (e.g., printing and publishing) (Dartnell Corporation, 1999). Indeed, it is not uncommon for sustained salesforce costs to be as high as 50 per cent of sales in some cases (Zoltners *et al.,* 2004).

In addition, the sales function employs more people and in many companies is a much larger function than marketing. Interestingly, estimates in both the UK and the US suggest that sales employment is expected to continue to increase. Indeed, the economic recession saw aggressive companies like Hewlett-Packard, Southwest Airlines and FedEx actually adding to their sales resources to attack competitors weakened by the economic down turn (Piercy *et al*. 2010a). The 'death of the salesman' forecast as a result of the expansion in Internet marketing and other direct channels appears to have been greatly exaggerated.

Expenditure levels and the growth in employment suggest that managers are likely to continue asking questions about the full utilisation of these resources to add value to the company. Indeed, evidence in the US suggests that many senior managers are dissatisfied with the productivity of their sales organisations, and many see salesforce cost poorly aligned with strategic goals (Deloitte Touche, 2005) These indications support the view that the sales organisation is becoming a substantially higher priority issue for strategic decision makers. However, notwithstanding the cost of the salesforce, the changing role of the sales organisation is driven by more than cost, and reflects the power of salesforce capabilities to change a company's competitive position for better or worse.

> ## 14.2 The new and emerging competitive role for sales*

Understanding the evolution of the sales organisation, and the strategic capability it represents, as well as the forces shaping this capability, has become an important issue for strategic decision makers in marketing.

14.2.1 The evolution of the sales organisation to strategic importance

There is little doubt that the role of the sales organisation has gone through major changes in many companies in recent years, and it is likely that this change process will continue and escalate. However, what should not be underestimated is the extent to which such changes are increasingly radical and disruptive to traditional business models and theories (Shapiro *et al.*, 1998).

For example, in identifying priorities for sales, Thomas Leigh and Greg Marshall (2001) wrote that 'The sales function is undergoing an unparalleled metamorphosis, driven by the plethora of changing conditions' (Leigh and Marshall, 2001). They suggested that this metamorphosis was seeing the selling function shift its role from selling products and services to one emphasising 'increased customer productivity', through enhanced revenues or cost advantage. They support the transformation of the traditional sales function to a pan-company activity or process, driven by market pressures: 'customers indicate that the seller's organisation must embrace a customer-driven culture that wholeheartedly supports the salesforce' (Leigh and Marshall, 2001). Interestingly, they also underline the parallel between the transformation of the sales organisation and other company-wide marketing developments, such as: market orientation (Jaworski and Ajay, 1993), market-orientated organisational culture (Homburg and Plesser, 2000), and marketing as a cross-functional process rather than a functional department (Workman *et al.*, 1998).

---

* This section of the chapter draws on Piercy and Lane, *Strategic Customer Management: Strategizing the Sales Organization,* Oxford: Oxford University Press, 2009.

Another analysis suggested that:

> the sales function is in the midst of a renaissance – a genuine rebirth and revival. Progressive firms are becoming more strategic in their approaches to the sales function . . . Enlightened firms view their customers as assets, and are entrusting their salespeople to management of these assets.
> *(Ingram et al., 2002)*

These authors call for joint action by sales managers, educators, trainers, consultants and professional organisations to improve the conceptualization and practice of sales management. Certainly, there appears growing consensus that traditional approaches will fail, and that 'the shaping of the selling function has become a strategic corporate issue', requiring clarity about the new sales role, new structures and new management approaches (Shapiro *et al.,* 1998).

Many suggest that this revolution has already arrived, even if marketing executives (and educators) have yet to notice. One British commentator has suggested that: 'sales functions are in the early stages of a transformation comparable to that which reshaped manufacturing 20 years ago' (Mazur, 2000). The evolution of the sales organisation is already becoming apparent in studies of marketing organisation and there is growing evidence of the expanding influence of sales over strategic decisions. For example, research findings suggest that the sales department has more influence than the marketing department on many so-called 'marketing' decisions (Krohmer *et al.,* 2002), and that 'primary marketing coordinators increasingly reside in sales rather than the marketing organisation' (Homburg *et al.,* 2000), while sales plays a growing role in formulating as well as executing marketing strategies (Cross *et al.,* 2001). In fact, even the success of marketing initiatives like market orientation may depend in large part on the sales organisation – for example, one study shows the impact of market orientation on performance to be fully mediated by the adoption of customer-orientated selling by the salesforce (Langerak, 2001). Similarly, the sales organisation may have a decisive influence on shaping the direction of new product innovation through the intelligence collected and how it is interpreted (Lambert *et al.,* 1990), and in assessing and accessing targeted key market segments (Maier and Saunders, 1990).

A more strategy-oriented salesforce has to cope with a range of interfaces with internal functions and departments, and increasingly partner organisations, to deliver value seamlessly to customers. For example, when Sam Palmisano took over as CEO at IBM, he conducted a painful overhaul of the 38,000 person salesforce (see Hamm, 2005, 2008). In the 1990s salespeople representing the various IBM business units were essentially on their own – looking for good opportunities to sell individual products or services. Palmisano 'reintegrated' IBM in front of customers by bringing together specialists from computers, software, consulting and even research into teams that meet with customers to help solve their business problems and develop new business strategies. Collaborating with customers, suppliers and even rivals was part of his plan to invent new technologies and to create new markets. IBM's new sales capabilities underpin a strong performance during the economic recession by focussing on technical services rather than selling hardware.

These arguments suggest an urgent need in many companies to consider the transformation of the traditional sales organisation and its more strategic role as a focus for strategic customer management (Piercy and Lane, 2009a).

14.2.2 Shaping forces for the new sales organisation

Clearly, the sales organisation has for some time been subject to powerful company and customer forces that have re-shaped its role and operation (Jones *et al.,* 2005). The forces acting to reshape the sales function in organisations are summarised in Figure 14.3. As we have already seen, the implementation of new types of marketing strategy requires the realignment of sales processes with the strategy. At the same time, multi-channelling and the growth in Internet-based direct channels are substituting for many traditional sales activities.

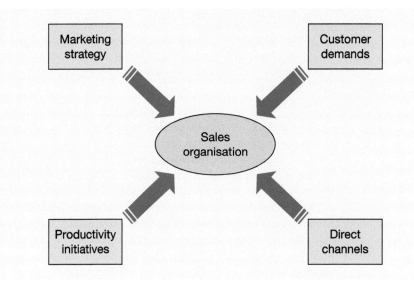

Figure 14.3
Forces
acting on the sales
organisation

Perhaps most telling in business-to-business marketing has been the dramatic escalation in the demands for enhanced service and added-value by customers. As a consequence, one study calls on management to abandon their fixation of process compliance in sales (scorecards, activity metrics, and so on), and adopt a more flexible approach to selling driven by salespeoples' reliance on insight and judgement – 'insight selling' is one response to customers demanding new and better engagement with their suppliers (Adamson *et al.*, 2013). Put this in the context of the Chally Group finding that nearly 40 per cent of business-to-business buyers select a supplier because of the skills of the salesperson rather than price, quality or service features, to understand the importance of selling quality (Fogel *et al.*, 2012).

Further, the H.R. Challey consultancy's *World Class Sales Excellence Research Report* (2006) lists the views of corporate purchasers and their expectations for the relationship with the salesperson from a supplier:

1 *Be personally accountable for our desired results* – the sales contact with the supplier is expected to be committed to the customer and accountable for achievement.
2 *Understand our business* – to be able to add value, the supplier must understand the customer's competencies, strategies, challenges and organisational culture.
3 *Be on our side* – the salesperson must be the customer's advocate in their own organisation, and operate through the policies and politics to focus on the customer's needs.
4 *Design the right applications* – the salesperson is expected to think beyond technical features and functions to the implementation of the product or service in the customer's environment, thinking beyond the transaction to the customer's end state.
5 *Be easily accessible* – customers expect salespeople to be constantly connected and within reach.
6 *Solve our problems* – customers no longer buy products or services, they buy solutions to their business problems, and expect salespeople to diagnose, prescribe, and resolve their issues, not just sell them products.
7 *Be creative in responding to our needs* – buyers expect salespeople to be innovators, who bring them new ideas to solve problems, so creativity is a major source of added value.

These qualities characterise how world class salesforces are distinguished in the eyes of their customers. They describe a customer environment which is radically different from the transactional approaches of the past, and which poses substantially different management challenges in managing business-to-business customer relationships. However, at the same time, business constraints in seller organisations suggest that in most companies there is considerable pressure to reduce costs and enhance productivity in the salesforce.

One example of changing customer demands is the development of 'social selling' – the coming together of online, mobile and social media with personal selling in how customers make purchase decisions and how sellers are engaging customers and building stronger customer relationships. Customers have much more control over the sales process than in the past. The emergence of new technologies to create a new digital and social media age places emphasis on a strong, multi-skilled sales team able to integrate technology with selling. The requirement in a new digital buying environment is for sellers to build their sales processes around the new customer buying process. Effective salesforces are escalating their use of social media to engage customers throughout the buying process (Giamanco and Gregoire, 2012; Green, 2013).

While the ways in which traditional sales organisations are likely to transform to meet these contrasting forces to reshape will vary considerably between different industrial and commercial sectors, one way of integrating the outcomes in general terms is in a model of the strategic sales organisation.

14.3 The strategic sales organisation

The importance of strategic customer relationships mandates a strategic response from sales and account management. The strategic sales organisation is an attempt to capture the range of changes which may transform the traditional sales organisation into a strategic force, impacting both on the ability to implement marketing strategy, but also providing leadership in the shaping of that strategy.

Most attention given to the sales and account management area in the past has been largely concerned with tactical and operational issues, and has failed to adopt a strategic perspective on the management of customer relationships. Interestingly, similar comments would have applied in the operations and supply chain strategies prior to the revolutions in thinking and practice experienced by those disciplines in the 1990s and early 2000s. The sales and account management field is in the early stage of a similar and related revolution, characterised by a shift in approach from tactical to strategic. There can be little further doubt that, as Shapiro and his colleagues at Harvard asserted some time ago, once again: 'Sales is a board room topic' (Shapiro *et al.*, 1998), and that the strategic sales organisation is positioned on the top management agenda in many organisations.

However, the new processes and structures needed to enhance and sustain value delivery to customers through the sales organisation are likely to require careful evaluation and appraisal that extends to domains far beyond those traditionally associated with selling activities (Ogbuchi and Sharma, 1999). To support this analysis and to provide a framework for management action, we propose the framework shown in Figure 14.4 and identify several tools for practical application (Piercy and Lane, 2009a).

The framework suggests the following imperatives for management focus:

- *Involvement* – placing the sales organisation in the centre of the business and marketing strategy debate in companies and aligning sales operations with strategic direction.
- *Intelligence* – building customer knowledge as a strategic resource critical both to strategy formulation and to building added-value strategies with major customers.
- *Integration* – establishing cross-functional relationships necessary to lead the processes which define, develop and deliver superior value propositions to customers, and managing the interfaces between functions and business units impacting on service and value as it is perceived by customers.
- *Internal marketing* – using sales resources to 'sell' the customer across functional and divisional boundaries within the company and across organisational boundaries with partner companies, to achieve seamless value delivery.

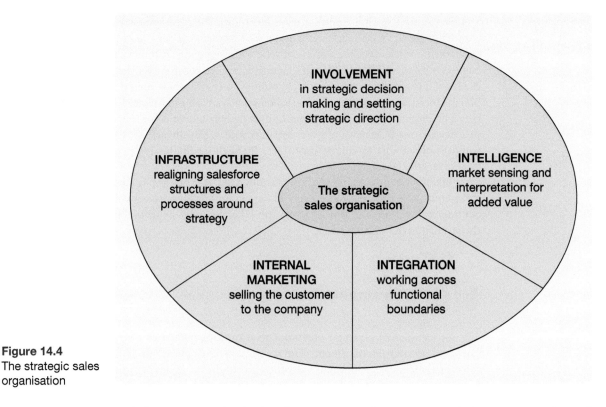

Figure 14.4
The strategic sales
organisation

- *Infrastructure* – developing the structure and processes needed to manage sales and account management organisations to match customer relationship requirements and to build competitive advantage.

14.3.1 Involvement in strategic decision making

As customer demands for superior seller relationships continue to evolve and escalate, then a distinct new role is becoming critical in selling organisations – the strategic management of the relationship with the customer. While harsh economic conditions and the search for competitive edge mandate cost reductions to increase margins, sales revenues and profits are derived not only from finding new customers and sales channels, but from growing relationships with existing customers and sales channels. However, conventionally, sales organisations manage customers for short-term revenues, which in highly competitive markets often results in declining margins and commoditisation (Lombardi, 2005). Underpinning a strategic response to radical market change is the challenge of repositioning sales as a core part of the company's competitiveness, where the sales organisation is closely integrated into marketing strategy (Stephens, 2003).

In calling on companies to put sales at the centre of strategy, Frank Cespedes (2014) suggests that too often management embarks on a strategy without considering the realities facing the people who must execute the strategy with paying customers, and notes that 'Strategists, years removed from customer contact, often have an obsolete vision of the company-customer interface' (p. 24). He concludes that logically the sales organisation should be part of every conversation about strategy.

Involvement of the sales organisation in strategy has two aspects. The *first* strategic sales issue is concerned with developing a perspective on the sales organisation which does not focus simply on the tactical management of transactional sales processes, but examines the relationships formed with different types of customers as the basis for long-term business development (Olson *et al.*, 2001). This implies a new appraisal of the activities and processes required to enhance and sustain value delivery to customers through the sales organisation. It is also increasingly the case that major customers require a highly specific value proposition built around 'unique value' for the customer.

The *second* strategic sales issue is concerned with the role of sales and account management in interpreting the customer environment as a basis for strategic decisions. As the costs of dealing with major customers continue to increase, companies face major choices in where they choose to invest resources in developing a customer relationship, and where they choose not to invest. With large customers in particular, the risks in investment or disinvestment are high, and it likely that the intelligence-gathering and market sensing capabilities of the sales and account organisation will play a growing role in influencing strategic decisions about resource allocation in the customer portfolio. The shift in thinking required is from the tactical management of sales transactions to focus on the relationships formed in different ways with different types of customers as the basis for long-term business development (Olson *et al.*, 2001). We will consider below the customer portfolio as a tool for surfacing these issues.

14.3.2 Intelligence to add value

One clear and repeated demand by corporate buyers is salespeople should demonstrate deep knowledge of the customer's business, such that they can identify needs and opportunities before the buyer does (Chally, 2006). The deployment of such superior knowledge and expertise is a defining characteristic of the world class sales organisation in the buyer's eyes. The buyer logic is straightforward: if the seller cannot bring added-value to the relationship by identifying new opportunities for the buyer to gain competitive advantage in the end-use marketplace, then the seller is no more than a commodity supplier, and can be treated as such (the product will be purchased on price and technical specification).

This represents a challenging change in focus in the way sales organisations interact with major customers. While traditional selling activities focus primarily on the need to convert product and service into cash flow, conventional marketing shifts the focus from seller need to buyer need and developing the customer relationship. However, in many situations now faced by suppliers, strategic customers demand that the seller displays not simply a superior understanding of the customer's own organisation, but detailed and insightful knowledge of the customer's end-use markets. The strategic sales role is becoming one of deploying end-use market knowledge to enhance the customer's competitive position and cost efficiency. This is summarised in Figure 14.5, which provides a framework for evaluating where a company's salesforce is currently focusing efforts and how this compares to customer demands.

Even in the consumer goods sector, retailers continue to report that their suppliers perform inadequately in key areas which help differentiate them to the consumer, such as consumer insight development. Major retailers emphasise that trade relationships are no longer based on buyer-seller roles, and characterise the best-in-class supplier as one that has a firm understanding of the retailer's position, strategy and ambitions in the marketplace – they require consumer insight from their suppliers (IBM, 2005).

Successful business models like those at companies as diverse as Dell Inc. in computers, Johnsons Controls in automotive controls, and Kraft in groceries display this type of end-use market perspective in strategic sales relationships. Major customers evaluate their suppliers on the seller's success in enhancing the customer's competitive position, and increasingly expect proof of this achievement.

The challenge to suppliers from an increasing proportion of their major customers is to understand the customer's business and the customer's end-use markets, to leverage that knowledge to create competitive advantage for the customer. The alternative is to face growing commoditisation and declining margins. Meeting this challenge with major accounts and strategic accounts is a central element of strategic sales choices. The corresponding challenge for the reformed sales organisation is to develop, deploy and sustain new skills and capabilities in market sensing.

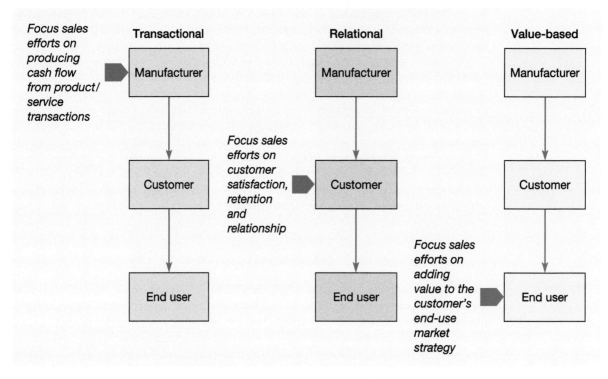

Figure 14.5 Changing focus in buyer–seller relationships

14.3.3 Integration across functional boundaries

Turbulent and demanding markets create new challenges for managers in supplier organisations. Powerful customers increasingly demand problem-solving and creative thinking about their business, requiring the commitment of, and access to, the supplier's total operation. One European executive describes this as 'the convergence of strategic management, change management and process management, all critical elements of transforming the sales function to meet today's customer requirements' (Seidenschwartz, 2005). Certainly, in some cases programmes of value creation around major customers have been plagued by problems of 'organisational drag' – where the seller's organisational functions are not aligned around processes of creating and delivering customer value (Koerner, 2005). Similarly, retailers emphasise supplier organisational structure and culture as key obstacles to improving customer management effectiveness (IBM, 2005).

Success in the new marketplace increasingly demands the integration of a company's entire set of capabilities into a seamless system that delivers superior customer value – what has been called elsewhere 'total integrated marketing' (Hulbert *et al.*, 2003). This logic is based on the observation that superior performing companies share a simple characteristic: they get their act together around the things that matter most to their customers, and they make a totally integrated offer of superior value in customer terms. Management attention must focus on the actual and potential contributions of functional units and departments, and third party suppliers in alliances and networks, in delivering superior value to customers, and how to improve the integration of these activities.

One of the developing roles of the sales organisation will be in managing processes of value definition, development and delivery that cut across functional interfaces to build real customer focus. Many of the barriers to developing and delivering superior customer value come from the characteristics of supplier organisations. One challenge of strategic customer management mandates effective approaches to cross-functional integration around value processes. Rather than managing only the interface with the customer, the reformed sales-force must cope with a range of interfaces with internal functions and departments, and increasingly partner organisations, to deliver value seamlessly to customers. We discuss the issue of cross-functional partnership further in Chapter 16.

14.3.4 Internal marketing of the customer

It seems inevitable that a strategic approach to the role of sales in managing customer value will simultaneously impose the problem of positioning and 'selling' the customer value strategy inside the organisation.

For example, consider the issue of service quality, which has proved to be a decisive competitive weapon in many industries (see Chapter 13). Service quality is normally evaluated in the customer marketplace in terms of the perceived delivery of the product or service confirming or disconfirming customer expectations to create satisfaction or dissatisfaction (Berry and Parasuraman, 1991). However, those same dimensions of attitudes and beliefs are mirrored in the internal marketplace of company employees and managers.

In the internal marketplace, expectations are concerned with anticipations by people inside the company of external customer preferences and behaviour, and perceived delivery is about differences between internal and external criteria of what 'matters' – priorities of people in the 'back office' or the factory may conflict with those of the external customer. Confirmation/disconfirmation relates not to consumption of the product, but to judgements people inside the company make about the external customer. When external customers 'disappoint' employees by their adverse reaction or complaints, this may easily have a negative effect on the future behaviour of employees in dealing with customers (Piercy and Lane, 2009a).

The risk of undermining the competitive position with a major customer as a result of such internal market factors is too serious to be ignored. One role of the reformed sales organisation is likely to be 'selling' the customer to employees and managers, as a basis for understanding customer priorities and the importance of meeting them, as an activity that parallels conventional sales and marketing efforts, as suggested in Figure 14.6. Internal marketing is discussed further in Chapter 16.

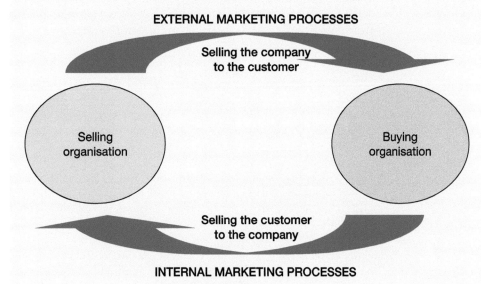

Figure 14.6
The internal marketing challenge for sales

14.3.5 Infrastructure for the new sales organisation

The role of the transforming sales organisation is unlikely to be implemented effectively through traditional salesforce structures and processes. Shapiro and his colleagues suggest that 'most established salesforces are in deep trouble. They were designed for a much simpler, more pleasant era . . . The old salesforce must be redesigned to meet the new needs' (Shapiro *et al.,* 1998). New definitions of the sales task will require substantial shifts in the way that the sales organisation is managed. Turbulent markets mandate constant attention to alignment between sales processes and the goals of market and business strategy (Strelsin and Mlot, 1992). Certainly, research suggests that the move from transactional relationships with customers (selling on the basis of price and product advantages) to value-added relationships is proving extremely challenging for many organisations striving to pursue this strategy (*American Salesman,* 2002).

Change in the infrastructure supporting the strategic sales organisation is likely to span organisation structure, performance measurement systems, competency creation systems, and motivation systems – all driven by the definition of the new task and role of the sales operation (Shapiro *et al.,* 1998).

Figure 14.7 suggests some of the areas where particular attention is required, and where new research into sales organisation effectiveness indicates some of the productive approaches to be explored. The Figure 14.7 logic is that the overall result on which attention should focus is the effectiveness of the sales organisation in implementing business strategy and meeting organisational goals. Traditionally management attention has focused on outcome performance as the main indicator of effectiveness (i.e., meeting sales volume and revenue targets). However, if strategy requires the development of closer customer relationships and the implementation of a value-based strategy, then salesperson behaviour performance may be a more productive point of focus (i.e., not simply what salespeople sell, but the behaviours they undertake to achieve their goals and to build customer relationships).

If salesperson behaviour performance is key to delivering the outcomes and overall effectiveness required as marketing strategy moves towards a relationship focus, then this has several important implications for the competencies and behaviours to be developed in salespeople, and against which to evaluate their performance. This in turn, has major implications for the type of people to be recruited to sales and account management roles, as well as for the way in which they are managed (Baldauf *et al.,* 2001a, b), . Particular controversy is reserved for the move from outcome-based control (primarily in the form of compensation-based incentives such as sales commission and bonus) towards behaviour-based control (direct manager intervention in how salespeople do their jobs, and greater reliance on fixed salary compensation packages) (Piercy *et al.,* 2004a, b).

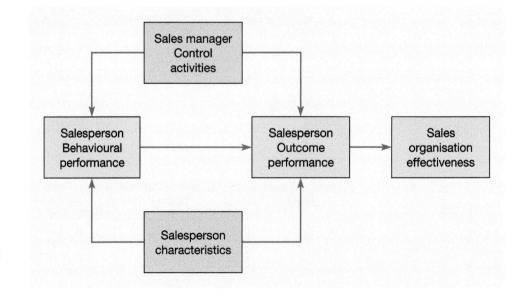

Figure 14.7
Realigning sales
structures and
processes

The process of 'reinventing' the salesforce to meet the challenges of new markets and new strategies is likely to require attention to several critical issues:

- Focus on long-term customer relationships, but also assessing customer value and prioritising the most attractive prospects.
- Creating sales organisation structures that are nimble and adaptable to the needs of different customer groups.
- Gaining greater ownership and commitment from salespeople by removing functional barriers within the organisation and leveraging team-based working.
- Shifting sales management from 'command and control' to coaching and facilitation.
- Applying new technologies appropriately.
- Designing salesperson evaluation to incorporate the full range of activities and outcomes relevant to new types of sales and account management job (Cravens, 1995).

For example, when the then-new CEO of Hewlett-Packard began that company's remarkable performance improvement, he found that there were as many as 11 layers between him and a customer. Correspondingly, H-P was slower to respond to customers than its competitors, and of the 17,000 people working in corporate sales, only 10,000 directly sold to customers – the rest were support staff or managers. His overhaul of H-P's vast corporate salesforce involved: closing a large sales group that sold a broad portfolio of products and reallocating salespeople to product-specific groups, so they could master the products they sold; cutting hundreds of under-performing salespeople; removing three levels of sales management; and paring back internal meetings so salespeople could spend more time with customers. H-P's salesforce now spends more time in front of customers, responds faster to their needs, and is winning more corporate sales deals (Tam, 2006).

While beyond the scope of this present review, a study of the antecedents and consequences of sales management control strategy reveals several issues, which are commonly neglected in leveraging change and superior performance in the salesforce as part of aligning sales efforts with strategic direction (Baldauf *et al.*, 2005). It should be quite apparent, however, that new business and marketing strategies and an evolving role for the sales organisation in leading strategic customer management will inevitably require considerable re-evaluation of the management of the sales organisation.

While the agenda above provides a framework for examining the operational characteristics of the strategic sales organisation and evaluating organisational needs, by defining the new domain for the strategic sales organisation, it is important to note that research also suggests the need to place developments into a broader context of shaping factors as well. This logic is summarised in Figure 14.8. The context for the strategic sales organisation includes factors such as:

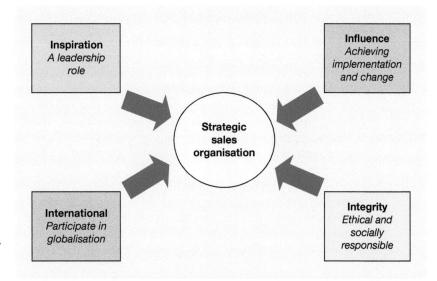

Figure 14.8
Shaping factors for the strategic sales organisation

- **Inspiration** – part of the outcome of reinventing the traditional sales organisation should be to renew the ability of those who manage key external relationships with customers to inspire and provide broader leadership within the business.
- **Influence** – a test of whether the strategic sales organisation is taken seriously is the degree to which it exerts influence over the company's strategic agenda and the key strategic decisions which are made.
- **Integrity** – there has never been a time when scrutiny of the ethical and responsible behaviour of companies was greater, and when the cost of being judged unethical or irresponsible was higher. Managing relationships with customers, partners and suppliers with integrity is a huge challenge, but not one that can be ignored. Increasingly, major customers cannot do business with people who they cannot trust, or whose poor corporate reputations carry a danger of contamination by association. This may be among the highest priorities in new types of buyer-seller relationship (Galea, 2006).
- **International** – the globalisation of markets, the emergence of global customers, and the spread of international competition mandates an international perspective on how we manage customer relationships in domestic and overseas markets. We expand on this fuller agenda in more detail and with operational tools elsewhere (Piercy and Lane, 2009a).

14.4 Strategic customer management tasks

The transformation of the traditional sales organisation into a strategic force, that should feature centrally in the analysis that underpins strategic choices by marketing executives, may be achieved by moves towards at least some of the characteristics of the strategic sales organisation. However, the larger goal we pursue is a strategic customer management perspective, which may be achieved through the strategising of sales processes and structures. The key distinguishing features of a strategic customer management (SCM) approach are summarised below and developed further in the sections that follow. The domain for strategic customer management is described in Figure 14.9.

14.4.1 Alignment of sales processes with strategy

At one level, the SCM mandate is concerned with the issue of marketing strategy implementation. To many business-to-business customers, the salesperson who visits *is* the supplier company, and has far more impact on customer perceptions of the supplier than promotional and other communications approaches. The interface between the customer and the supplier managed by the salesforce has long been recognised as a major source of implementation failures. We consider implementation issues in Chapter 16, but particular problems relating to the sales/marketing strategy interface which are frequently encountered include:

- Marketing strategies which aim to build strong competitive positions through superior customer relationships fall foul of sales organisations where salespeople are rewarded by volume-based commission paid for sales transactions – traditional evaluation and reward systems often value highest sales activities that run counter to strategic goals of customer-orientation and relationship-building and favour short-term volume.
- Strategies are built around vertical markets and customer-focus, but salespeople struggle to implement these approaches because they are organised into geographical areas or product divisions.
- Sales managers do not 'buy in' to marketing strategies, and cling to traditional leadership behaviours and performance management in controlling sales operations.
- Traditional conflicts of interests between marketing and sales executives (they are frequently rewarded for different achievements and evaluated against different measures) spill over into lack of cooperation and coordination.

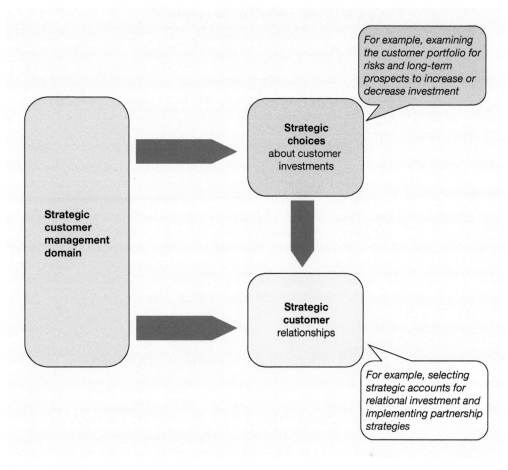

Figure 14.9 The domain of strategic customer management

- Marketing strategies are developed in isolation from the customer and competitor insights provided by salespeople and account managers, and without any understanding of the company's sales capabilities compared to competitors.
- Salespeople and sales executives experience job ambiguity and conflict in attempting to implement strategies that fit poorly with the systems and structures in the sales organisation, experiencing lower motivation, job satisfaction and perhaps higher levels of stress and burnout (Hulbert *et al.*, 2009).

Poor alignment of the realities of existing sales processes and structures and the intent of marketing strategy is likely to make effective implementation difficult to achieve. Nonetheless, it must be recognised that changing issues like evaluation and reward systems, leadership and control strategies, and organisational structures in the salesforce is usually not a minor undertaking.

14.4.2 Providing the real customer perspective in marketing strategy

The importance of understanding the sales/customer interface is vital to strategy analysts and decision makers for another reason as well. In most business-to-business situations, the salesforce represents a key market sensing capability, or source of intelligence. However, research evidence suggests that this resource is generally poorly used or applied by marketing decision makers (Fitzhugh and Piercy, 2006). A high priority is emerging for the better management of market sensing processes which involve the salesforce and account management teams as one of the primary sources of intelligence.

14.4.3 Managing the customer portfolio

Our earlier comments on changing customer relationship requirements and demands for service enhancement suggest that different customer groups should be evaluated very differently in terms of their potential attractiveness and the supplier's cost to serve them. Choices regarding the customers in which to make investments of selling efforts of different types, and where not to make such investments, will shape the future of a business and merit senior management attention. We will consider the customer portfolio in the next section of this chapter.

14.4.4 Developing effective positioning with dominant customers

Currently, one of the most troublesome issues for developing effective strategy in business-to-business companies is the impact of powerful customers and the demands that they can make on their suppliers – whether the consumer goods manufacturer dealing with very large retailers like Tesco and Walmart, or the components manufacturer dealing with automotive companies. One response to this has been the growth in strategic (or key) account management approaches, to 'partner' with the most important customers. However, it is clear that some customers do not provide good partnership prospects – while they may be large, they are transactional customers, not collaborators. The last section of the chapter turns to the issue of dominant customers.

14.5	**Managing the customer portfolio**

In much the same way that we can examine a portfolio of products or brands, the importance of customers as assets and investment centres mandates a similar portfolio analysis. Figure 14.10 shows an approach to mapping the number of customer accounts held by a company or business unit, by their sales level and potential, and their service and relationship requirements from the supplier. This categorisation can be initially made simply by the number of accounts, but can be subsequently enhanced by examining the profitability and stability of business in the different account categories. Identifying the categories is the important first step.

The *direct channel* is typically the route to market for smaller accounts with low relationship/service requirements, e.g., the Internet, telemarketing. Importantly, customer development strategy may also involve moving some accounts towards the direct channel, because they are consuming more service/relationship resources than they merit, but also moving some out of the direct channel, based on changing prospects and the costs of serving the account. Such considerations illustrate the potential importance of shifting some salesforce resources from a short-term transactional focus, to longer-term business development issues in line with business and marketing strategy.

The *middle market* contains customers with varying prospects, but generally with moderate relationship/service requirements. These are the most conventional buyer-seller relationships. Those with promising potential may be moved into the major account area over time, while those with relationship/service requirements which are excessive compared to their potential, may be moved towards the direct channel.

Major accounts are usually large in the supplier's terms and have high relationship/service requirements, but they are customers in a conventional buyer-seller relationship. While major accounts are important to the supplier, it is quite possible that the supplier is of far less importance to the customer (if accounting for a relatively small part of the customer's expenditure, or capable of being replaced reasonably easily). However, major account size and prospects identifies the need to develop appropriate salesforce approaches to deliver added value to these customers. Nonetheless, it is likely that appropriate salesforce strategies will be, and should be, substantially different between major accounts and strategic accounts.

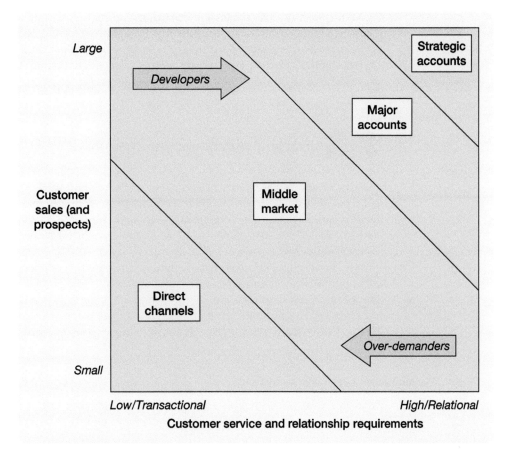

Figure 14.10
The customer portfolio

Strategic accounts are those where collaborative and joint problem-solving approaches are appropriate to win status as a strategic supplier. Strategic account management strategies and structures have developed in many companies as a way of developing close, long-term and collaborative relationships with the most important customers and meeting their needs in ways which the traditional salesforce did not (Homburg *et al.*, 2002a). Important questions surround the selection and management of relationships with strategic accounts, who may be the most expensive customers to serve. Growing buyer concentration in many markets mandates collaborative relationships with these accounts as strategic suppliers, but the costs of partnership and the growing dependence involved underlines the need for careful choices and evaluation of performance.

The distinction between major accounts (conventional customers) and strategic accounts (collaborators or partners) underlines several strategic choices. Plans may include the movement of accounts between these categories – developing a closer relationship with a major account to develop a new strategic account relationship, or moving away from a close relationship that is ineffective to move a strategic account to major account status.

This customer portfolio mapping process is a screening device for identifying the most appropriate relationship to offer a specific account and the choices to be made in allocating scarce salesforce, account management, and other company resources, as well as evaluating the risks involved in over-dependence on a small number of very large accounts.

Underlying the strategic sales issue is the question of developing the capability of the sales organisation to deliver added-value in different ways to various categories of customers. It unlikely that a traditional, transaction-focused salesforce will be able to deliver added value required by some customers. However, the deployment of expensive resources to develop added-value sales strategies for particular customers implies choices and investment in creating new types of salesforce resource and capability, which should be confronted at a strategy level in an organisation.

Major accounts and strategic accounts are normally the supplier's largest customers (although it may be more appropriate to consider prospective sales rather than just existing sales). These accounts constitute the dominant customers whose impact can be massive on the supplier's performance and ability to implement marketing strategies. We now turn more detailed attention to the dominant customer issue.

14.6 Dealing with dominant customers*

One important insight from the customer portfolio analysis is the recognition of the different types of customer in the company's portfolio, and their differing demands for value and relationship. Particular questions are raised about the largest and most influential customers – perhaps, the 20 per cent of customers who may account for 80 per cent (or more) of the supplier's business.

It is important for strategic decision makers in marketing to understand the basis for the different types of customer relationship which exist in the portfolio, and particularly the idea of a transition from traditional transactional relationships to much closer links between the seller and the most dominant buyers. Figure 14.11 summarises some of the commonest business-to-business buyer-seller relationships, and the critical differences between them.

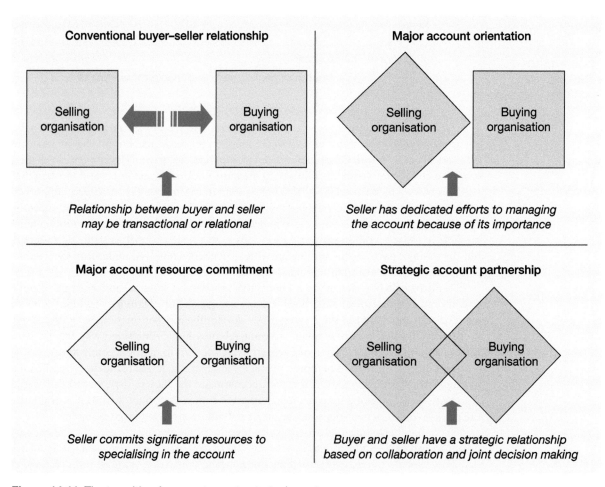

Figure 14.11 The transition from customer to strategic partner

* This section draws on Piercy and Lane, 2006a, b, 2007, 2009a.

The *conventional buyer-seller relationship* is the most familiar – it typifies the middle market. Links are between salespeople and purchasers, and the relationship may be purely transactional (depending largely on the importance of the purchase to the customer, or the way in which the customer chooses to do business), or it may involve a higher level or closer relationship being built between buyer and seller. This is the type of relationship which most traditional salesforces were created to manage.

However, the existence of larger, more dominant customers requires different approaches. The *major account orientation* case is where the size and impact of a customer requires that sales and management efforts should be refocused to provide a dedicated approach to a particular customer. This may involve the appointment of an account manager, or a national account specialist, and the development of plans around this customer's specific needs. Nonetheless, the relationship remains largely a conventional buyer–seller format.

The *major account resource commitment* situation takes things substantially further in terms of dedicated efforts around the major account. Substantial teams of people may now work around the single account and offerings may be substantially different for this customer. Nonetheless, the resource commitment remains essentially one-sided. Proctor and Gamble's 200-person team for the Walmart account is P&G's investment in that customer. Correspondingly, while Dell Computers has a dedicated team for its major customer, Boeing, this does not suggest that Boeing makes decisions about Dell's business. At the end of the day, these relationships remain buyer–seller transactions. The investment is essentially one-sided – it is made by the seller.

The big difference is with the *strategic account partnership*. This type of account relationship is based on collaboration and joint decision making between the buyer and seller. It is a two-sided relationship – both buyer and seller invest time and resources in the relationship. This relationship has much in common with the strategic alliances discussed in Chapter 15. The impact of strategic account relationships and management merits more detailed attention.

14.6.1 Strategic account management

Growth in management attention given to strategic account management (SAM)[*] as a way of developing and nurturing relationships with a company's most important customers is unprecedented. While currently given relatively little attention in the mainstream strategy literature, a Google search reveals hundreds of Web pages detailing managerial books about SAM, countless consultants eager to offer advice, numerous training courses for executives, and a growing number of business school programmes in SAM in universities across the world. The underlying concept is the shift from adversarial buyer–seller relationships towards collaborative or partnership-based relationships, with the company's most important customers.

Many major international companies have made SAM an important element of how they manage relationships with their largest customers. For example, IMI plc is a major UK engineering group, whose published strategy statement identifies SAM as a key theme in achieving its goal of 'leading global niche markets'. The company is investing heavily

> to enhance our ability to create and manage close customer relationships with our clients [and] provide IMI business managers with the skills to create and develop close and successful relationships with major customers . . . which places key account management among the central elements of IMI's business approach.
> *(IMI, 2010)*

---

[*] For purposes of discussion we regard the terms strategic account management and key account management as interchangeable, and our commentary generally applies to what some designate as national account management and global account management.

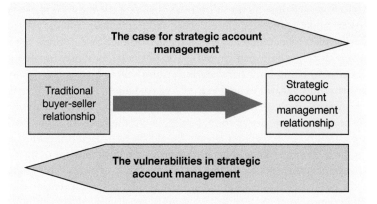

Figure 14.12
The case for
and against
strategic account
management

For a growing number of companies, SAM is a deep-seated strategy for customer partnering, often on a global basis.

At the same time, many major buyers have adopted radical strategic supplier strategies. For the last decade, Ford Motor Company has been in the process of consolidating its supply base for its $90 billion components purchases from 2,000 suppliers to 1,000 globally. Moreover, the first seven 'key suppliers' constitute some 50 per cent of Ford's parts purchases, and will enjoy superior access to Ford's engineering resources and product planning. Ford will work closely with its key suppliers, giving them access to key business plans for new vehicles and committing to give them business (Mackintosh and Simon, 2005).

On one hand, a compelling case can be made for the attractiveness of SAM as a strategy of collaboration and partnership with major customers. However, there are several assumptions and propositions underpinning the case for SAM, which appear to have been largely ignored by its adopters and advocates. As suggested in Figure 14.12, balancing these issues is an important challenge for strategic decision makers in marketing.

14.6.2 The case for strategic account management

One study suggests that strategic/key account management is one of the most fundamental changes in marketing organisation (Homburg *et al.*, 2000), and yet one in which a sound research foundation to guide management's strategic decisions remains almost completely lacking (Homburg *et al.*, 2002a). Indeed, while there is a long stream of research in the areas of national and key account selling starting in the 1960s, this research has been largely descriptive and conceptual, and has not addressed the long-term impact of SAM on buyer-seller performance (Workman *et al.*, 2003).

The rationale for SAM is that demands from large customers have caused suppliers to respond with dedicated organisational resources to concentrate on these 'key' or 'strategic' accounts and to incorporate special value-adding activities (e.g., joint product development, business planning, consulting services) into their offering to the customer (Dorsch *et al.*, 1998). Fundamental to the logic of SAM is the suggestion of an inevitable concentration effect whereby a small number of customers provide a disproportionately large share of a seller's sales and profits (the so-called '20:80 rule'). Almost as a natural consequence, suppliers frequently dedicate most of their resources to the core portfolio of buyers who represent the highest stakes and are identified as 'strategic accounts' or 'key accounts' (Pardo, 1997).

SAM is a strategic development which has become increasingly widespread in response to a variety of customer and market pressures, which may be summarised as:

- escalating levels of competition in most markets and consequently higher selling costs for suppliers;
- increased customer concentration resulting from merger and acquisition activity, as well as competitive attrition in many markets during the recession;

- growing customer emphasis on centralised strategic purchasing as a major contributor to enhancing the buyer's cost structure and building competitive success in their end-user markets;
- active strategies of supplier base reduction by larger buyers to reduce purchasing costs; and
- increasing exploitation by large customers of their position of strategic importance to their suppliers to gain lower prices and enhanced terms of trade (Capon, 2001).

Importantly however, SAM is not seen simply as an organisational response that focuses on meeting growing demands from dominant customers, it is seen as progression towards a form of 'partnership' with those customers, characterised by joint decision making and problem solving, integrated business processes and collaborative working across buyer–seller boundaries, described as a process of 'relational development (Millman and Wilson, 1989). However, while we have discussed the strengths in effective strategic account relationships, decision makers should also recognise the growing evidence that ineffective strategic account relationships may create a range of strategic vulnerabilities for sellers.

14.6.3 Vulnerabilities in strategic account relationships

There are a number of potential flaws in the underlying logic for SAM which may make it unattractive for sellers in some situations, and which should be made explicit in strategic choices.

Investing in strategic weakness

There is a case that SAM involves the seller investing in strategic weakness, in the sense that it may be unattractive to institutionalise dependency on major customers as a way of doing business. The SAM approach rests on the notion that the '20:80 rule' produces a situation for the seller which is attractive, or at least inevitable. Conversely, it can be argued that any company which has reached a situation where a '20:80' position exists – i.e., 80 per cent or more of profits and/or revenue come from 20 per cent or less of the customer base – has already witnessed the failure of its business model. The business model has failed because it has led to such a high degree of dependence on a small number of customers, that the company's strategic freedom of manoeuvre has been undermined, and much control of the supplier's business has effectively been ceded to its major customers. The eventual outcome for selling companies in this situation is likely to be falling prices, commoditisation of their products, and progressively lower profits as major customers exert their market power.

Clearly, many practitioners would argue that in businesses like grocery there is no choice other than to deal with the major retailers who dominate the consumer marketplace, because there is no other route to market, and little choice other than to accept the terms they offer. Similarly, suppliers of automotive components would point to the limited number of automobile manufacturers in the world, and producers of computer components would argue that if you want Dell's business, then you do business on Dell's terms, robust though those terms may be. Such responses at least clarify that in many 'strategic account' situations, the real issue is less partnership and more about one party dictating terms to the other, which is not the concept of 'collaboration' normally advanced to justify SAM investments by suppliers.

If it is conceded that powerful customers will ultimately exploit that power to their own advantage, then their business carries a disproportionately higher risk than that of less powerful, less dominant customers, and it is less attractive as a result. If it is inevitable that major customers will demand more concessions and pay less, then it is likely they will also be substantially less profitable than other customers. There is little consistent empirical evidence, but there are suggestions that for many sellers, strategic or key accounts are the least profitable part of their business.

The importance of the understanding the balance of power

Notwithstanding the importance of strategic buyer–seller relationships, there seems a strong case that the party in the supply chain enjoying the balance of power will use that to their advantage. For example, in spite of surging raw material costs, the pricing power of suppliers has continued to deteriorate in many markets. Producers may have to absorb most cost increases because they are unable to pass them fully through the supply chain, simply because powerful buyers will not permit it (Cave, 2005). It is illustrative that in the automotive components market, notwithstanding escalating steel and raw material prices faced by producers, Volkswagen told its parts suppliers in 2005 it wanted 10 per cent cost savings over the following two years. At Chrysler, the CEO demanded an immediate 5 per cent price cut by suppliers, with a further 10 per over the following three years (Mackintosh, 2005).

For example, a study of Tesco suggested that at one point it had some 2,600 suppliers providing £9 billion worth of goods. The largest supplier had less than 3 per cent of Tesco's total sales and the median supplier less than one-hundredth of a per cent. If a contract is lost, the absolute maximum impact on Tesco's sales would be 1–3 per cent, and normally far less. For the supplier, it could mean a loss of sales of 10–30 per cent of total revenue, without an alternative sales outlet (Giles and Tricks, 2005). Consider the negative impact on Premier Foods' profitability and share price, when Tesco elected to de-list 11 out of 18 bread product lines that Premier produces, rather than accept a price rise (Kavanagh, 2011). This neatly defines the relative power of buyer and seller.

For such reasons, in sectors like automotive components, suppliers are actively seeking to diversify their customer bases and to change product portfolios to reduce dependence on a small number of powerful accounts (Simon, 2005). The issue is becoming one of staying close to key customers, but reaching out to other customers groups as a route to reduced dependency on a few and enhanced profits (Witzel, 2005b). Indeed, this shift in dependency may be one of the highest strategic priorities impacting on survival.

The real buyer–seller relationship

The critical issue is interdependence between buyer and seller, or perhaps more aptly the balance of dependence, since it is rarely symmetrical. The question is 'who is dependent on whom?' in the buyer–seller relationship. Failure to grasp the simple issue of the direction of dependency is likely to blind the seller to a critical vulnerability of SAM, while simultaneously souring relationships with the account in question – professional purchasers find it difficult to work with suppliers who misunderstand the nature of the relationship they really have with the buyer. Sellers with an exaggerated view of their strategic importance to a buyer have unrealistic expectations of the customer, with the potential for growing frustration because the customer does not behave in the way expected, and ultimately leading to conflict between buyer and seller.

Figure 14.13 illustrates a buyer perspective on supplier types – the professional purchaser distinguishes on the basis of risk (substitutability) and impact (reduced costs or improved competitive advantage in the end-use marketplace). From a purchaser perspective, suppliers with significant impact on the buyer's business, but who can easily be replaced, are mainly targets for pressure on price and terms, while those with low impact, who can be easily substituted, are likely to be treated as commodities, where the goal is to routinise transactions to reduce supply chain costs. With suppliers who cannot easily be replaced, but have limited impact, the goal is to reduce the customer's risk exposure (e.g., to negotiate guaranteed supplies). Only where a supplier cannot easily be substituted by a competitor, and has a major impact on the customer's business, is the customer likely to work towards a strategic supplier relationship. At any time, for most buyers it is likely that very few suppliers will have strategic importance. It is important to understand the relationship defined by the customer, before assuming that the buyer should be treated as a strategic account.

The risks of dependence

A related point is that SAM exposes the seller to another type of risk, which is derived from the strategic account's own end-use markets. The closer the relationship becomes to strategic account/strategic supplier status, the higher this risk becomes for the supplier.

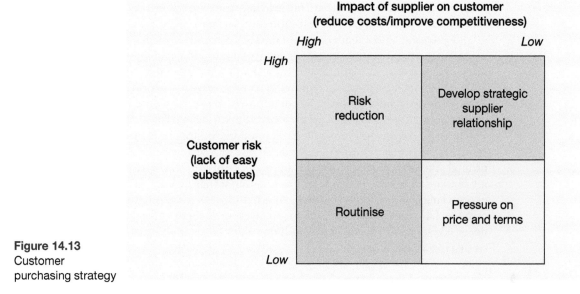

Figure 14.13
Customer
purchasing strategy

Quite simply, if the key account's performance declines, or if its business fails, its strategic suppliers will suffer businesses losses which are likely to be substantial, and over which they have little control.

Consider the dilemma faced by tyre manufacturer Dunlop, and many other smaller suppliers, created by the 2005 collapse of MG Rover – it is believed some 15–20 per cent of Dunlop's UK business was lost with Rover's demise. Further, the value of Dunlop's investment in a long-term collaborative relationship based on new product development for Rover was also lost. The impact was equally serious for some 1,500 small car parts manufacturers who supplied Rover, both in lost business and bad debts (Quinn, 2005a). Focus on a strategic account creates a shared business risk for suppliers, which may be uncontrollable, unrecompensed and unattractively high.

The paradox of customer attractiveness and competitive intensity

Advocates of SAM strategy argue that this model should only be applied to the customers who are most 'attractive' to a particular supplier (Capon, 2001). Setting aside the issue of how a company defines its criteria of attractiveness, the paradox is that the customers who are most attractive to one supplier will probably at the same time be the most attractive to competitors. While there will be situations of 'fit' which make a customer attractive to one supplier and unattractive to others, this is likely to be the exception rather than the rule. Accordingly, the most 'attractive' customers for a SAM strategy are also likely to be those where competitive intensity is highest and consequently where the ability of the customer to substitute one supplier for another is highest. The likelihood seems that competitive intensity will deny strategic supplier status for any seller and place all in the routinised, commodity supplier category. The most 'attractive' customers become the least 'attractive' through processes of competitive convergence of suppliers on the same customers as strategic accounts (Saunders *et al.*, 2000).

The case for strategic account investment

This brings us to a critical question – if strategic accounts are less profitable for a supplier and impose higher levels of risk on the supplier's business, then how is it possible to make a case for increasing dependence on such accounts, and to invest in SAM systems to further reinforce the dependence of the company on low-profit, high-risk business? There may be no choice, certainly in the short term, other than to meet the requirements of dominant customers for special treatment, but to regard this element of the business as the highest investment priority for the longer-term may be questionable. Indeed, the more rational course might be to find ways of ring-fencing such customers and diverting resources to develop more profitable parts of the customer portfolio.

SAM strategy also carries the substantial opportunity cost that management focus on key accounts reduces the attention given to other customers, who in reality offer higher margins and lower risk. Indeed, there is a significant danger that having invested in SAM with a customer, even as the account becomes progressively less profitable because of excess demands, inertia and reluctance to admit failure may easily cause the supplier to cling to the key account relationship regardless of disappearing margins.

There is a strong, and for some companies urgent, argument that investment priorities should be reconsidered in many customer relationships, with an emphasis on long-term profitability and balanced risk exposure, and less on the short-term characteristics of existing markets. The logic is that if the business model has failed, then the issue becomes one of searching and developing a new business model, not persisting with the old model until commercial failure ensues. The goal is to invest in strength and enhanced future earnings, not to invest in positions of weakness and to maintain the *status quo*, only to enjoy progressively reduced earnings.

Understanding customer relationship requirements

The European purchasing manager with a leading engineering company observes that:

> I love it when a supplier tells me I am a key account – I make a lot of fuss of them. However, most times all I really do is to get concessions on price and terms. I almost feel guilty, it is so easy, but it's my job.
> *(Piercy and Lane, 2006a)*

Underpinning the weakness of SAM strategy in potentially mismanaging critical inter-organisational dependencies is the observation that suppliers frequently tend to have exaggerated views about the relationship that major customers want to have with their suppliers.

It is likely that SAM can only be an effective strategy from a supplier perspective where there is a close match between seller and buyer relationship requirements. Consider the scenario in Figure 14.14. Frustration results for the supplier attempting to build closer

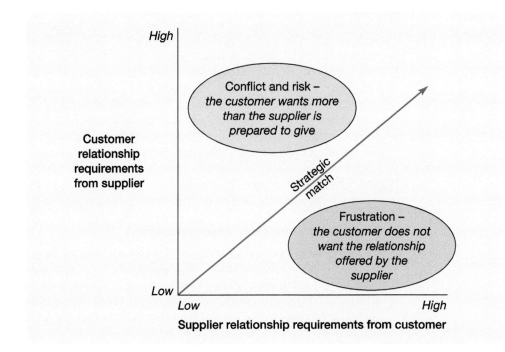

Figure 14.14
Buyer and seller relationship strategies

relationships with customers who mainly want efficient transactions – from the buyer perspective the supplier is not important enough to justify strategic supplier status, or this may simply not be how this company does business with its suppliers. On the other hand, conflict arises when a customer looks for a close relationship with a supplier prepared only to offer more limited engagement – this customer does not warrant a larger relationship investment by the supplier. Only where there is continuous alignment between buyer and seller relationship requirements is there potential for effective SAM. The problem facing suppliers seems to be recognising how rare alignment may be in practice, as well as how transitory.

Distinguishing large (major) customers from strategic accounts

The tendency among sellers is to equate large customers with strategic accounts. We commented earlier on the importance of distinguishing major accounts from strategic accounts in the customer portfolio. The danger of not distinguishing these types of customer is three-fold: first, confusing the major account with the real strategic account prospect, leading to unproductive investments in the relationship; second, diverting attention from developing new and profitable major accounts growing out of the traditional middle market; and, third, neglecting the productivity enhancements available by moving over-demanding customers from the traditional middle market to the direct channel. Identifying major customers wrongly as strategic accounts is capable of undermining the management of the whole portfolio of accounts being serviced by the seller, with likely further negative effects on overall performance and profitability.

Furthermore, some major customers may be relatively unattractive because they offer little profit or future growth. The fact that such customers may presently be large buyers does not alter this fact. On these grounds, simply being a large customer does not justify supplier relationship investments like SAM. There is no logic in building stronger relationships with unattractive customers, particularly if this reduces opportunities to invest more productively elsewhere. As noted earlier, in many ways, the large low-profit customer should encourage ring-fencing to minimise additional investment to the lowest level that retains the business, and the diversion of resources to more profitable applications elsewhere in the business.

Understanding the reality of customer loyalty

Much of the attraction of SAM lies in the promise that collaborative relationships with key customers will enhance the retention of that business – i.e., strategic accounts will reciprocate by offering loyalty to their long-term strategic suppliers. This promise may not be fulfilled.

Consider the long-term textile and clothing suppliers who believed their relationship with Marks & Spencer was secure, only to discover that when their customer was under pressure, purchasing transferred to cheaper off-shore sources. Examine the current US situation for clothing manufacturers for whom Walmart is a 'key account' – Walmart is now the eighth largest purchaser of Chinese products at incredibly low prices, which matters more than long-term relationships with domestic suppliers. Alternatively, view the Dell Inc. situation – a company renowned for its strategic account strategy, acting almost as an outsourced IT department for major customers. Dell Inc. does not extend the same philosophy to its suppliers – a company remains a Dell supplier only as long as it has better technology than the rest.

Recent research suggests that while relational exchanges between suppliers and customers frequently benefit customers in performance improvements, generally the customers concerned do not reward suppliers with a higher share of their expenditure or long-term contractual commitments (Fink *et al.*, 2007). The mutual benefit and long-term relationship building implicit in strategic account management approaches may have been exaggerated.

If SAM is seen as a model of collaboration that has many similarities with strategic alliances (both involve agreement for partnership and joint decision making, with no transfer of ownership), then it perhaps worth considering the evidence that the majority of strategic alliances fail, and in the view of many executives do not deliver the benefits they promised. The success of alliances seems to depend on conditions of mutuality and symmetry between partners. Those conditions do not appear to exist in many SAM situations.

Underestimating the rate of change

Even if a customer is willing and eager to offer a seller the status of a strategic supplier and is treated as a strategic account, with all the additional investment that this is likely to require, some sellers mistakenly believe that strategic relationships with these accounts will be stable and long term.

The more likely truth is that as a seller's own strategy changes, the importance of a particular supplier will change – possibly dramatically and quickly. As the recorded music business transforms to one based on Internet downloads instead of physical products, strategic suppliers will be those with expertise in the new technology, not those offering CDs and support for the old technology. Indeed, supplier switching may increasingly be an explicit element of a company's business strategy. In 2005, Apple announced it was teaming up with Intel to provide the components suitable for new generations of Apple products, effectively bringing an unexpected end to long-term supplier relationships with IBM and Freescale (formerly Motorola) (Morrison and Waters, 2005; Witzel, 2005a). Apple's goal was to build on the momentum created by its iPod digital music player and to meet the lower prices demanded in the mass consumer market. Supplier switching may be an inevitable consequence of strategic change.

The reality is that the strategic supplier relationship for many suppliers will be temporary and transitory, as customers develop their own market strategies and adopt new technologies. This leaves the supplier investing heavily in the strategic account relationship, only to see that relationship disappear as the customer moves on. Customers rarely offer recompense to a supplier to cover the costs of dismantling a redundant SAM system.

Even more traumatic is the sudden collapse of a key account/strategic supplier relationship. Changes in customer businesses may end relationships that had taken years to build – the key account is taken over and the acquiring company imposes its own supplier arrangements on the acquired business; there is a change in supply strategy from the top of the customer organisation, for example the move from single sourcing to multiple-sourcing; the customer learns technology and process from its strategic supplier, enabling it to undertake production of the product in-house; or, customer personnel move on and their replacements do not have a close relationship with the supplier and maybe do not want one. The collapse of a strategic account relationship will have a major negative impact on sales volume, which may not have been predicted. The end of a SAM relationship may impose additional and substantial costs – adjusting operations capacity to allow for short-term volume reduction, disentangling integrated systems, rebuilding processes previously shared with the key account, reallocating or removing personnel previously dedicated to the key account, putting in place new arrangements to retain whatever residual business there may be in the account.

The failure of a strategic account relationship may be very public and create additional vulnerability. If a company's shares are written down because of the collapse of business with a strategic account, then the supplier becomes vulnerable to a predator – perhaps even the customer in question, who has the opportunity to in-source the product by buying the supplier; possibly a competitor; or possibly a stalker from outside the sector. The point is that the cost of a failed key account relationship may not simply be losing the customer, it may be losing the company as well.

Consider the experiences of Marconi in its strategic relationship with British Telecom. Marconi was the rump of the former GEC and through the 1990s focused investment heavily on the telecommunications sector. Marconi was one of British Telecom's largest suppliers of network equipment for several decades. By 2004 BT represented a quarter of Marconi's total sales – as much as the next nine customers put together. Notwithstanding being described as a 'terrific partner' by the chief executive of BT Wholesale, in 2005 Marconi was shut out of BT's £10 billion '21st Century Network' project. BT's decision was based on price, not technology or relationships, and Marconi could not equal the prices of overseas competitors from eight countries ranging from France to China. Under BT pressure, Marconi had even lowered prices to a level that would have represented substantial losses in its UK operation, but not enough to satisfy BT. With the loss of a quarter of its sales base, shares falling 60 per cent in value, and substantial job losses in prospect, Marconi's experience underlines the risks of over-reliance on one customer, and the critical error of believing that a customer would be a loyal partner. The loss of the BT business fundamentally weakened Marconi's ability to compete globally in new areas like Internet Protocol networks. Within months of the BT decision, it was clear that investors were looking for Marconi to sell the business or merge to survive. Marconi's Chinese joint venture partner, Huawei, gained two parts of the BT contract, and BT even hoped it would get access to Marconi's technology through this lower price channel. In 2006 the main Marconi business was sold to Ericsson, leaving Marconi only a smaller services business working on maintenance of legacy systems (Ashton, 2005; Brummer, 2005; Durman and Box, 2005; Grande, 2005).

Challenging the regulator

SAM strategy is akin to a full-blown merger between buying and selling organisations – in buyer and seller making joint investment decisions, the exchange of proprietary information, the exclusion of third parties, and so on. SAM strategy creates a potential for anti-trust violation. Competition regulators are increasingly taking the view that such close collaboration between buyer and seller is potentially anti-competitive.

Believing that SAM is easily implemented

Lastly, there appears inadequate recognition of the implementation barriers and organisational issues faced in SAM strategy. To assume that this is a strategy that can be made effective easily underestimates the degree to which this is a quite radical new business model. Even if a SAM strategy is appropriate for a supplier to manage strategic relationships with certain critical customers, there remains the issue of whether the supplier has the capabilities and resources to make the strategy real, in ways which matter to the customer.

14.6.4 Balancing the case for strategic account management

We have attempted to contrast the apparently compelling case for strategic account management (SAM) models that develop collaborative and integrative relationships with major or dominant customers, with the serious flaws in the underlying assumptions of those models and the potentially damaging traps for the unwary. In many situations, it appears that the adoption of SAM models is based on the suspect logic that the best use of a company's resources is to invest heavily in that part of the business (the largest most dominant customers) which has the lowest margins and the highest business risk.

Defenders of the SAM model argue that this scenario reflects not the weakness of the model, but poor choice of key accounts by companies. There is some merit in such a response. However, since the apparent reality is that companies choose as strategic accounts those customers to which they sell most, or respond to the demands of large customers for special treatment, then suggesting that the weaknesses inherent in the SAM model can be overcome by better choice of strategic accounts seems somewhat unrealistic.

One logic is that the search should be for alternative strategies that avoid the trap of high dependence on a small number of powerful dominant accounts. Some would probably suggest that this is a search doomed to failure – the most powerful customers control markets and are unlikely to surrender this control willingly. Yet, on the other hand, consider the potential disruption of the *status quo* in a market by the introduction of a new business model. For example, consumer and business computer users have voiced numerous complaints over the years about the product functionality of Microsoft offerings, and struggled in vain against the massive Microsoft market share in areas like operating systems and server software. In 2005, we saw the dramatic impact of Linux software – available free or cheaply – developed through a peer-to-peer network, in a business model that appears uninvolved with concerns like profitability. Microsoft increasingly looks like a company with a mid-life crisis, that has no effective response to competitors like Google, Amazon and Sony, and open-source software suppliers . However, more interesting yet is the fact that much of the Linux revolution has been driven and facilitated by IBM, Sun Microsystems and Dell, who are dramatically reducing their dependence on the old adversaries at Microsoft. Actively managing dependence between buyer and seller may be one way out of the trap.

For example, Heinz is attempting to reduce its heavy dependence on traditional retailers (Tesco, Sainsbury's) by making products available in petrol stations, convenience stores chains, Mothercare stores for baby-foods, and garden centres (Wiggins, 2009). The same logic explains the involvement of Amazon.com in the grocery business in the UK – supported by big brands who are tired of poor treatment and low returns from the dominant supermarkets (Felsted, 2010). Similarly, the strategic relationship between Google and Procter & Gamble involving the exchange of knowledge on how to develop P&G online is illustrative (Byron, 2008).

It is noteworthy that 2006 saw the Proctor & Gamble/Gillette merger to create the world's largest consumer brands group. The combined portfolio of brands provides a much stronger hand in dealing with major retailers (Quinn, 2005b). However, the merger also represents a fundamental change to P&G's business model. The goal is serve not only the world's most affluent one billion consumers in developed countries, but to serve the world's other six billion consumers, with a new focus on lower-income consumers in such markets as China and India. In developing these emerging markets, P&G is deliberately not partnering with global retailers like Walmart and Carrefour. Instead, in China P&G will offer Gillette access to a huge distribution system staffed by an army of individual Chinese entrepreneurs – what P&G calls a 'down the trade' system ending up with a one-person kiosk in a small village selling shampoo and toothpaste. The effect should be that stable growth in Asian markets will reduce the combined company's dependence on mature markets dominated by powerful retailers (Grant, 2005). As noted, more recently P&G has been developing a relationship with Google, expected to be a precursor to an aggressive value chain innovation of selling products direct to consumers and bypassing powerful conventional retailers (Piercy *et al.*, 2010b).

New business models that will be effective in avoiding the dominant customer trap will probably share some of the following characteristics:

- reducing critical dependencies and risks by developing alternative routes to market – consider the example of the automotive manufacturers developing direct channel strategies to take back control of the value chain and reduce dependencies on independent distributors;
- developing alternative product offerings to rebuild brand strength as a counter to the power of the largest;
- emphasising the need for high returns to justify taking on high risk business, not the other way around;
- reducing strategic vulnerabilities created by excessive levels of dependence on a small number of customers or distributors;

- clarifying the difference between major accounts and key accounts and developing appropriate ways of managing these different types of relationship profitably;
- actively rejecting business from some sources because the customer is unattractive in terms of profitability and risk, even if the business on offer is large;
- managing customer accounts as a portfolio (**see** Figure 14.5) using criteria of attractiveness and prospective performance, not simply customer size.

There are situations when SAM is an effective strategy to manage relationships with major buyers and to develop collaboration and partnership rather than adversarial transactions. However, what requires careful management consideration is under what conditions this is true, and whether these are truly the conditions they face. There is potential insight in evaluating the customer portfolio and its changing composition, and to consider not simply the quantity of business offered by the largest accounts, but also the quality of that business. The quality of business with major accounts includes the profitability of the business, but also the business risk involved, the impact of increased dependence on a small number of customers, and the opportunities given up. A balanced evaluation of this kind provides the basis for a more informed decision, but may also be the trigger for the search for strategic alternatives that may avoid the downside of dependence on powerful key accounts. This balanced evaluation and search for new business models appears urgently needed in many organisations.

Importantly, strategic sales capabilities define in a number of important ways the strategic options available to a company and its ability to implement them. The realities of buyer–seller relationships cannot be underestimated in understanding strategic strengths and weaknesses, and the ability to exploit market opportunities.

Summary

Strategic sales capabilities are an increasingly vital resource in adding value and sustaining effective customer relationships, which executives need to consider when formulating marketing strategy. Better alignment between marketing and sales is a high priority for many companies, as well as recognition of a more strategic role for sales and account management. This new relationship is important to the development and effective implementation of marketing strategy. Strategic customer management is a broad term describing the sales and account management relationships that link buyers and sellers in business-to-business markets. In particular, it focuses on the choices companies face in how they allocate selling and marketing resources between different customer types and the approaches taken to implementing effective relationships with powerful, dominant customers. The growing attention given to these issues reflects both internal company pressures to reform and reshape the traditional sales organisation so that it can deliver the value and the customer relationship upon which marketing strategy implementation rests. However, the strategic sales organisation elevates attention from the salesforce as the route to implementing strategy, to a force that participates in shaping strategy around the realities of the marketplace. Analysis of the customer portfolio provides the basis for distinguishing between customers in a direct channel and in the traditional middle market, but importantly major account and strategic accounts. Strategic account management represents a new business model based on collaboration and joint decision making between buyer and seller. It provides a mechanism for managing some dominant customer relationships. Nonetheless, while there is a compelling case for strategic account management, there is a balancing case of the vulnerabilities and risks in this model. Managers need to balance these factors carefully in deciding whether to implement strategic account management models. The analysis of choices in marketing is closely related to strategic sales capabilities in the business-to-business marketing company.

Case Study   Power of the 'mummies' key to Nestlé's strategy in DR Congo

Kinshasa's women traders hold the key to corporate strategy. Hervé Barrère is an amiable Tahitian with an easy smile and a flair for Congolese dance. He also has an eye for the 'mummies on the table tops'. These are the women traders at markets across the Democratic Republic of the Congo, and Mr Barrère, the country director for Nestlé, the Swiss consumer group, believes these women are key to understanding local tastes and purchasing decisions.

At 'Petit Pont', Kinshasa's main spice market, one of the 29 open-air markets in the capital, a sprawling array of wooden tables are topped with loose garlic, onions and red chillies, near to a rickety bridge that gives the market its name. Mummies are pitching cartons of Maggi's red and yellow-wrapped stock cubes – the Swiss company's flagship brand – against cheaper competitors from Spain's Jumbo and China's Top.

Mr Barrère believes Maggi is now winning thanks to four strategic aspects – taste, margins, marketing and trade organisation. 'We had to work on trade and consumer insight; you need to immerse yourself in this understanding,' says Mr Barrère, who regularly visits the markets to talk to the mummies.

As attempts to cash in on the 'Africa rising' phenomenon go, picking DR Congo must be among the bravest. For all the allure posed by untapped African markets and consistently impressive growth rates, few multinationals set their sights on the vast sprawling country at the heart of the continent. It might have a population of 70m with growth rates close to 9 per cent a year, but poor roads, poor legal frameworks and poorer customers – 60 per cent exist on less than $2 a day – make it a tough market to crack.

Since Nestlé took the plunge, investing $43m in a new factory in Kinshasa that started producing in 2011, the company has set about overcoming the hurdles in a fashion reminiscent of a smaller, more nimble business. But it is far from plain trading. The Swiss corporate is already in court over tax issues there and sales have been disappointing. It sells the same number of its Maggi stock cubes in neighbouring oil-producer Republic of Congo, a country of 5m people, as it does in DR Congo, a country of 70m albeit with a per-capita income 15 times as small.

The Kinshasa factory site remains spacey: only a few machines fill the void. Mr Barrère, however, is confident that the factory will be furnished with more equipment in the future. 'I am waiting for the [growth]

wave to come; we need to be ready before the others,' he says. 'Consumption will come if the country is growing, if the people [have] money. Since we got a better understanding of the market we are growing very fast.'

Senior executives credit Mr Barrère with turning around prospects in DR Congo. The company is now selling 100 tonnes of Maggi a month, up from 30 tonnes when he arrived two years ago, and sales in the country are growing at 30 per cent a year. It is this expansion that gives Nestlé – which also sells dairy products in the country – the confidence to bill Maggi as the market leader.

Mr Barrère says it is all down to a better understanding of how DR Congo's markets work, with ragtag stalls and profit-seeking micro-entrepreneurs, and structuring sales to match.

To this end he goes into people's homes to see how women cook and what families like to eat, in an attempt to develop the right product as well as encourage higher usage. While Kenyans like their stock cubes filled with salt and coriander, and Nigerians go for a more fermented soya taste, DR Congo has a more eclectic palate, based on spices Nestlé has tried to replicate in its products. Even its 'standard' flavour is adapted to the market, with extra doses of nutmeg and garlic, and in others, extra aubergine and dried fish. Five years ago, Nestlé even developed the green 'pondu' tablet, a flavour made specifically from cassava leaves to match the beloved Congolese stew made from the same.

'In Lubumbashi they cook with tomatoes and in Kisangani they cook with pondus,' says Mr Barrère, keenly aware that tastes vary throughout this forested country the size of western Europe.

Developing a successful sales chain to sell the stock cubes, which start at 50 francs (three pence) for two individually wrapped 4-gram portions, has been the hardest task. Although open-air markets take only a quarter of sales, he believes their role in the trading chain and their potential reach into the population makes them critical to Nestlé's expansion in DR Congo.

'The mummies are really at the heart of what we are doing in terms of our business. I have been married so many times with them!' he jokes, saying social interactions in DR Congo must be 'super energetic' and 'extremely positive' if they are to succeed. He refused to cut his hair this year until he made his first-half sales target, prompting laughter from women traders in a country where long hair on men is more commonly a sign of madness than market determination.

'For the mummies on the table top, if you don't have the right margin you're out of the market; they have to be clear how much they will earn and be clear what the demand is,' says Mr Barrère.

That is why, under their new director, Nestlé overhauled its sales approach. Previously, it sold to both retailers and wholesalers, which made pricing chaotic. In order to impose order and discipline on prices and the distribution chain, Mr Barrère now sells only to wholesalers. The company sends agents to oversee the chain, ensuring the mummies secure daily credit to buy fast-selling stock, meaning they can repay the loan by lunchtime. They even oversee such minutiae as the arrangements of merchandise on the table tops.

The company puts on regular Maggi neighbourhood promotions – Mr Barrère frequently jumps up on stage and dances at such events. It also holds cookery demonstrations, encouraging women to use three stock cubes, which Mr Barrère says is more healthy than the women's typical method – using two plus extra salt.

Following Nestlé's market reorganisation, Beatrice Betuma is now one of only two wholesalers in the whole of Kinshasa. In the past two years, sales at her shop at a crossroads where women cook stews in huge vats on the ground have gone from $30,000 a month to $170,000. 'I have a lot more customers; now my name is famous,' says Ms Betuma, once a 'mummy on a table top' herself. Loyalty programmes, targets and incentive schemes – Nestlé took Ms Betuma on a holiday to South Africa as a reward for increased sales – are key. 'Now I want to go to Canada,' says the 51-year-old mother-of-three, whose husband lives in neighbouring Angola.

Penetrating DR Congo beyond Kinshasa is a further feat. Due to hazards such as theft, damage and red tape, sending cargo by train to Lubumbashi takes two months. But Mr Barrère insists it is worth doing, claiming to have tripled sales in Lubumbashi in the past year and a half. In the east, access was so prohibitive, and the road over-run by rebels at the time, that he took to airfreighting the goods to Goma until only two months ago, making them 'the most expensive stock cubes in the world'. Last month, he managed to deliver a consignment by the huge, bending Congo River for the first time. 'It is so amazing,' says Mr Barrère. 'It is like, how do we conquer the full Congo.'

Further reading: Emotional appeal

Supporting the local economy appeals to market-women, and Nestlé draws on this, says Hervé Barrère, the company's Congo director. Unlike Nestlé's products, competitors' stock cubes are made and imported entirely from abroad.

However, some of Mr Barrère's toughest competition, he discovered, came from Nestlé itself: its stock cubes had been smuggled from Nigeria and Kenya. In both cases the taste and the packaging – in English – were not adapted to a French-speaking market with a more eclectic palate. Several tours to the factory, which employs 60 people, convinced the women to switch. 'It was very emotional: one of the mummies cried because . . . she realised she has a role to play to develop the country.'

Source: from 'Power of the "mummies" key to Nestlé's strategy in DR Congo', *Financial Times*, 01/10/14 (Manson, K.)

Discussion questions

1 How does strategic customer management differ from selling? How is it strategic?

2 How is Nestlé using strategic customer management in the Democratic Republic of the Congo? What are the benefits of such an infrastructure?

3 How is such an approach also helping with the rest of the marketing mix?

CHAPTER 15
STRATEGIC ALLIANCES AND NETWORKS

Good relationships between companies are of crucial importance. They represent the effective teamwork that allows partners to create value for customers and shareholders that could not possibly be created by individual firms.

(Gibbs and Humphries, 2009)

But, on the other hand . . .
We have no permanent allies, we have no permanent enemies, we only have permanent interests.

(Attributed to Henry John Temple, Viscount Lord Palmerston 1784–1865, Foreign Secretary and Prime Minister during Queen Victoria's reign)

MasterCard cashes in on smart transit

MasterCard is building a network of partnerships to realise the potential of contactless and mobile payments to make urban transit systems work more efficiently, as it looks to the trend for 'smart cities' as a means of expanding the market for its cards.

In tests from Philadelphia to Gujarat, MasterCard has begun to integrate payment systems for train, metro, bus and road toll systems.

'85 per cent of the world's payments are still in cash. To me that's our largest opportunity,' Ajay Banga, MasterCard's chief executive, told the *Financial Times*.

Mastercard analysis found that transit systems – along with coffee and newspapers – were one of the largest markets in which cash dominates payment cards. 'It's $200bn a year in different cities around the world, which has the opportunity to be transformative for our business,' he said.

The company announced a partnership in March with Cubic Transportation Systems, which uses traffic data to advise network operators from London to Chicago whether they need to change routes or pricing to cope with rush hour demand, and to alert commuters through their smartphones of the best options.

Other new partners include Masabi, which allows users to buy tickets through their mobile devices, and Parkeon, a parking company with which MasterCard this week announced a plan to turn parking meters into kiosks that offer coupons for local businesses.

Mr Banga said MasterCard's aim in cities such as Philadelphia, where a pilot programme is due to expand into a full consumer launch later this year, was to cut the time train passengers spend buying a separate bus ticket, and 'intelligent personal routeing', using data to advise users of their best routes home.

'All transit systems are built for the peak of the peak. If you could find a way to take 5–7 per cent of the peak of the peak traffic off to less used routes you could reduce the cost of how you build and plan transit systems enormously,' he said, estimating that large urban transit systems could save $150m–$200m by being able to delay upgrades to their infrastructure.

Citing the example of Transport for London, which has opened up its ticketing systems from depending on its Oyster Card contactless payment system to accepting ordinary bank cards, Mr Banga said MasterCard could save transit system operators the cost of maintaining their own systems. 'It's actually cheaper for them' than maintaining their own systems and handling cash, he said. 'It takes out the friction.'

Mr Banga said that getting transit systems to accept payment cards could be a 'critical factor' in expanding MasterCard's market. It processed more than 11bn transactions in the first quarter from the 2.2bn MasterCard and Maestro cards in issue.

Mr Banga added that most MasterCard users are in cities, which are home to more than half of the world's population and about half of the world's 'financially excluded' – a group MasterCard has been targeting through separate initiatives with the UN, the World Bank and others.

The company is among several, including IBM and Google, to have identified the business potential in the rise of 'smart cities' – increasingly automated and connected urban areas whose authorities use data to inform the provision of public services.

More public–private partnerships would be needed as urbanisation puts a strain on cities' networks, Mr Banga added, saying the challenges transit systems face were 'too vast, too deep' to tackle alone.

Source: from 'MasterCard cashes in on smart transit', *Financial Times*, 02/07/15 (Edgecliffe-Johnson, A.)

Discussion questions

1 What are the issues facing MasterCard?

2 How is the company attempting to address these issues?

Introduction

In developing marketing strategy it is important for executives to consider the new organisational forms and routes to market which are developing, and in particular the impact of strategic alliances and networks as a way of competing. However, from the outset, two points are important: first, what matters are your strategic objectives – alliances and networks are a means to an end, not an end in themselves; and second, if partnership and alliance is your way forward, then you need to take a strategic approach to managing these new types of business relationships, or they will fail – one estimate is that between 60 and 70 per cent of alliances fail (Hughes and Weiss, 2007).

Thus, this chapter adopts a critical perspective that examines the following issues as a framework for competing through strategic alliances and networks:

- the implications of an era of strategic collaboration for our strategic choices;
- the types of partnership, collaboration and strategic alliance which are emerging in the marketplace, as important ways of building networks;
- the forms which networks of collaborating organisations take, and the development of new organisational forms for marketing based on networks;
- the importance of strategic alliances as a competitive force in global markets;
- the risks involved in strategies of collaboration and alliance.

A clear management agenda in needed which details the issues that should be addressed in evaluating alliance-based strategies as a way for us to go to market. Figure 15.1 shows the structure of our coverage of this topic.

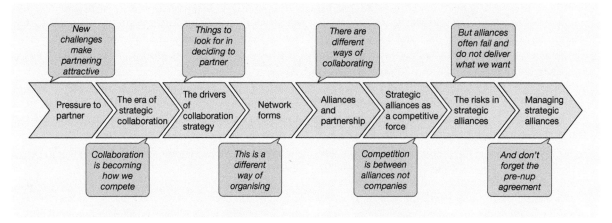

Figure 15.1 Key issues in evaluating strategic alliances and network organisations

It is important from the outset to recognise that alliances and networked organisations may be the basis for driving new business models and new marketing strategies in markets everywhere. For example, Chinese e-commerce phenomenon Alibaba became the world's largest stock market flotation in 2014, with a $22 billion valuation on the New York stock exchange, which some see as heralding the end of US dominance in e-commerce. Alibaba is the world's largest online marketplace for trade between companies and has built an unrivalled online retail platform in China. It ships around £90 billion worth of goods a year, and handles more packages annually than Amazon and eBay combined. Its Taobao website has been the engine of growth by linking consumers together on a peer-to-peer model. More recent emphasis is on the Tmall website that hosts large retailers selling to consumers. Alibaba operates on a net margin of 50 per cent because its model is to connect buyers and sellers and leave others with the costly business of moving goods around. Helping merchants to market their goods in China accounts for half of Alibaba's sales; sellers' commissions account for a quarter; and most of the rest comes from the wholesale business and international commerce. Cost of sales is incredibly low. The wall around Alibaba's business is the network effect – the company has the most buyers and sellers, giving current users an excellent reason to stay and new users reasons to come. Alibaba has created multiple sites – each tailored for a different style of transaction, and each with the potential for massive global reach. Alibaba is a global channel in a way that Amazon is not, because it facilitates so much business into and out of China (Collack and Armstrong, 2014). Alibaba is a compelling example of the strength of a networked competitive model.

15.1 Pressures to partner

The topicality of alliance and network concerns reflects the fact that the environment in which businesses go to market has changed radically in most sectors and continues to be turbulent and higher risk than ever before. We will consider the nature of this revolution and its profound implications further in Chapter 18. For the moment we note that the new environment for business is increasingly characterised by:

- **scarcer resources** – both in the physical environment, but also in terms of the down-sized, leaner, strategically focused corporations;
- **increased competition,** frequently from new sources, new types of competitor, and new technologies, at home and overseas;

- **escalating customer expectations** for higher service and quality from more sophisticated and better informed customers, which demands higher levels of expertise at the market level;
- **pressures from strong distributors** like retailers in consumer goods marketing, to achieve ever-greater economies in supply-chain costs;
- **high levels of customer concentration** in many business-to-business markets shifting power from seller to buyer;
- the pervasive onslaught of the **internationalisation of markets and competition**, driven by technology like the Internet;
- **faster rates of change in markets and technologies**, demanding higher levels and more rapid responsiveness in organisations;
- a **post-recession environment** characterised by lack of trust in business and an unprecedented emphasis on customer value; and,
- **more turbulent, unpredictable markets,** where change is greater in magnitude and very difficult to anticipate with a high degree of certainty.

Importantly, business environment changes of this kind, and the new business models they demand, continue to be associated with the evolution and growth of new organisational forms. This process sees the displacement of traditional, hierarchical, free-standing monoliths by flexible, agile, responsive organisational forms. Over a substantial period it is clear than many of these new forms will depend on inter-organisational collaborations or alliances and hollow organisations with a virtual Internet-based form. Importantly, often these new types of organisational arrangements completely reverse historical trends of aggregation and integration into large conventional structures, in favour of disaggregation and devolution of functions:

> Organisations of the future are likely to be vertically disaggregated: functions typically encompassed within a single organisation will instead be performed in independent organisations. The functions of product design and development, manufacturing, and distribution . . . will be brought together and held in temporary alignment by a variety of market mechanisms.
> *(Miles and Snow, 1984)*

The realignment of company resources with the demands of new and more challenging business environments – characterised by the post-recession era – has seen the widespread emergence of strategies of collaboration and partnership with other organisations as a key element of the process of going to market. While precise terminology does not exist, these new organisational forms and network arrangements have been variously been termed marketing partnerships, strategic alliances and marketing networks (Cravens and Piercy, 2013).

For example, Prahalad and Krishnan (2008) have described a fundamental transformation of business structure taking place in numerous industries. Their argument is that this fundamental transformation is being driven by two main factors. First, they argue that the age of mass production is over and customers demand unique value: 'value is shifting from products to solutions and experiences', in such a way that relationships are taking over as the central element of exchange. Second, they argue the consequence is that increasingly no single business is likely to be big enough to cope with the complexity and diversity of customer demands that is emerging. In turn this underlines the importance of alliances and networks to deliver customer value – constellations of suppliers that can be configured in different ways to meet different customer needs. Success will increasingly rely on abandoning the business models of the past and managing through new collaborative networks.

The effects may be dramatic. For instance, already more than a third of Proctor & Gamble's new products come from external alliances and more broadly P&G is a prototype of a multi-national corporation that has transformed itself through collaboration. For example, P&G has a strategic relationship with Google whereby P&G aims to enhance its

Web capabilities and Google looks to gain a higher share of P&G's advertising. P&G has also taken a stake in Ocado in the UK, as a testing ground for new online concepts. With insights gained from its partners, P&G has already started selling its brands direct to the US consumer from its 'eStore' site (Birchall, 2010).

Some partnerships may be surprising. Apple and IBM were once fierce rivals, but have struck a deal to sell iPads, iPhones and apps deeper into the corporate marketplace. In collaboration they are developing more than 100 apps for a range of industries. Apple hopes that IBM's vast network of corporate clients will win it business customers, while IBM will use Apple devices to sell more of its software and services (Stock, 2014). New strategies built around attractive business opportunities outweigh traditional rivalries.

Indeed, IBM itself has been transformed into a borderless organisation working globally with numerous partners to enhance the value of its offerings to customers on a worldwide basis. IBM is a highly internationalised business. It has over 50,000 employees in India – IBM's second biggest operation outside the US. Interestingly, the company has moved its head of procurement from New York to Shenzhen in China (*Economist*, 2007; Palmisano, 2007). In fact, IBM's former Chairman and CEO, Samuel Palmisano, defined a vision for the globally integrated enterprise (GIE), as the twenty-first century successor to the multinational corporation. Palmisano argued that businesses are changing in fundamental ways – structurally, operationally and culturally – in response to imperatives for globalisation and the impact of new technology. The emerging GIE is a company that shapes its strategy, management and operations in pursuit of a new goal: the integration of production and value delivery worldwide. Shared business practices and connected business activities make it possible for companies to transfer work from in-house operations to outside specialists. Global integration forces companies to choose where they want work performed geographically, and whether they want it performed in-house or by an external partner. The centre of the GIE is global collaboration both with commercial partners and governments.

Along similar lines, Hagel and Seely-Brown (2005) suggest that lowered barriers to international trade and technological developments mean companies have no choice but to concentrate on their areas of expertise, while collaborating globally with others specialising in different activities. The goal is to find ways of working with suppliers not simply to cut costs but to collaborate on product innovation. Li & Fung is a Hong Kong-based clothing supplier that Hagel and Seely-Brown describe as a 'process orchestrator'. The company produces goods for Western companies drawing on a network of 7,500 partners – yarn from Korea, dyed in Thailand, woven in Taiwan, cut in Bangladesh, assembled in Mexico, with a zip from Japan. Importantly, these companies are partners to Li & Fung rather than simply suppliers. By operating as a network, the partners help each other innovate in both design and manufacture (Hagel and Seely-Brown, 2005). Nonetheless, Li & Fung's reliance on alliances has unnerved investors and what is now the world's largest sourcing company is subject to drastic overhaul (Hughes and Kirk, 2013; Sevastopulo, 2014).

Working with partners to create enhanced customer value creates a need for flexible yet effective integration of inputs to deliver seamless value to customers. While building effective customer relationships has always depended on understanding and predicting customer needs, the additional role is to work with a set of providers of different parts of the value offering – some internal and some external to the company – to construct and deliver a coherent value offering to the customer.

Nonetheless, by way of balance, it should be recognised that the challenges in working effectively with external partners mean that this is not always the best route to superior customer value. Rolls-Royce runs a global service network providing a real-time support and maintenance service to airlines operating planes with Rolls-Royce engines – there are more than 50,000 Rolls-Royce engines flying and the support extends decades after the original purchase. Conventional wisdom was for aero-engine makers to license out much support and maintenance – that is, to collaborate with third party suppliers – and their aftermarket business was restricted to spare parts and distress repairs. To align the interests of airlines with its own, Rolls-Royce runs its own operations centres, in a move which has revolutionised the industry. Support and maintenance grew to generate 55 per cent of Rolls Royce revenues by the late 2000s (Pfeifer, 2008). Partnership strategies are not always the best, or only, response to complex customer and market situations. Similarly, many European producers are moving outsourced production back closer to home because of disappointing results in working with overseas partners in emerging markets. One reason is that managing across organisational and national boundaries is frequently not straight-forward (Milne, 2008).

In a growing number of markets, however, it is clear that complex networks of partner-ships will be the way in which business is done. The transition to working across traditional organisational boundaries identifies a new and possibly complex integration challenge. Responding effectively to that challenge is a growing part of the marketing strategy and implementation problem (see Chapter 16).

Certainly, it is likely that the strategic internal relationships, which will be vital to achieving effective integration in networked companies, will be between the organisational units and processes that manage key external relationships. As customer demands for more complex value offerings grow, the ability to work collaboratively to create solutions will emphasise the need for close coordination between suppliers, partners and sellers. The management of that coordination will require the effective management of relation-ships between those responsible for strategic marketing and sales, those who manage rela-tionships with suppliers, and those who are tasked with the management of alliance and joint venture relationships with external organisations. In many companies these strategic internal relationships may be one of the core value-creating processes (see Chapter 14). Furthermore, these strategic internal relationships will often have to cope with complex markets where there are also links between our suppliers and our partners and between them and our customers, in the way suggested by Figure 15.2.

Indeed, in some interesting ways, the trend towards inter-organisational collaboration in the route to market provides the other face of relationship marketing. While the priority of managing better customer relationship remains, for a growing number of companies this is accompanied by the need for efforts to be made in managing the relationship with the

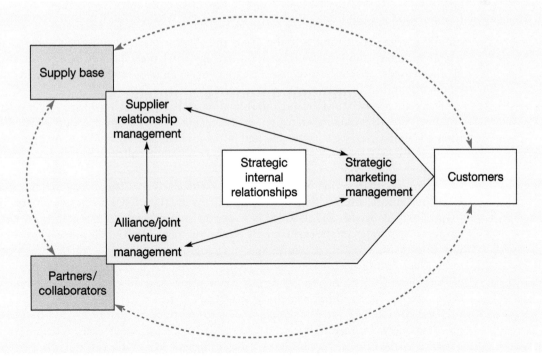

Figure 15.2 Strategic internal relationships and value chain collaboration

collaborator as well. Importantly, these new collaborative and networked organisations are distinctive and different to conventional structures. They are, for example:

> characterised by flexibility, specialisation, and an emphasis on relationship management instead of market transactions . . . to respond quickly and flexibly to accelerating change in technology, competition and customer preferences.
> (Webster, 1992)

Correspondingly, it is important to recognise that in many industries the emergence of networks of collaborating organisations, linked by various forms of alliance, has become a dominant platform for strategic development.

The growing importance of alliance and inter-organisational collaborative forms means it is important that our thinking about the implementation of our own strategies, and also our understanding of the emerging forms of competition we face in the market, should embrace the strategic alliance and the resulting growth of networks of organisations linked by various forms of partnering relationship. It is also important to emphasise that some of the strategic issues faced in alliances and networks go far beyond simple inter-organisational cooperation, and are leading to new ways of doing business with the customer, as shown by the Alibaba example above (also see Chapter 14).

15.2 The era of strategic collaboration

Executives should be aware that collaborative forms characterise competitive behaviour in many sectors, with major implications for strategic choices. For example, Cravens and Piercy (2013) argue that factors like the emergence of new value-enhancing opportunities, rapidly changing markets, a complex array of technologies, shortages of important skills and resources, and more demanding customers, present organisations with an unprecedented set of challenges. Importantly, one central feature of developing an effective response to these challenges has been the recognition by many business executives that building relationships with other companies is essential to compete effectively in the turbulent and rapidly changing post-recession era confronting the developed world economies, and in working with the rapidly-growing opportunities in the Asian and Chinese markets. Indeed, in some sectors like automotive, conventional acquisition strategy has largely been dropped in favour of alliance-based ventures. In effect, we are experiencing an important change from an era of competition to an era of strategic collaboration.

There are a variety of inter-organisational relationships which we have to consider in building effective marketing strategies: vertical channel relationships and supplier/manufacturer collaborations (see Chapter 14), and horizontal relationships in the form of strategic alliances and joint ventures, all share a growing emphasis on collaboration and partnership rather than simple contractual obligations.

These new collaboration-based relationships with customers, suppliers, distributors and even competitors, are resulting in a variety of new organisational forms, which are commonly grouped together and classified as 'networks', where members may constitute 'virtual corporations' (for example, existing only on the Internet). Many of the pioneers have been in the services sector, but networks spanning complexes of supply chains are becoming more usual. In fact, the network paradigm may become the dominant organisational form of the twenty-first century, but the reality we face may be a complex mix of collaborative organisational forms with conventional structures.

We shall examine a variety of examples of network organisations below, but the characteristics of network organisations can be discussed in the following terms. A defining characteristic of the network organisation is the performance of marketing and other business functions by different independent organisations and individuals – the process of 'vertical disaggregation'. The network is a flat organisational form, involving interaction between network partners rather than the multi-layered functions of the traditional hierarchical organisation. In fact, dramatic changes have taken place in the traditional hierarchical forms of organisations as a result of alliance and network strategies. Although in some ways similar to channel of distribution networks (e.g. suppliers/producers, marketing intermediaries and end-users), network organisations may display both horizontal and vertical structures (e.g. collaborations between suppliers as well as supply-chain linkages). Moreover, networks are frequently complex and liable to change more frequently than traditional distribution channels.

Typically, network operations are guided by sophisticated information and decision support systems, often global in their scope, which perform many of the command and control functions of the traditional hierarchical organisation. The resulting network is flexible and adaptable to change, and the more successful network designs are customer-driven – guided by the needs and preferences of buyers – but may be complex and unfamiliar to executives.

The inter-organisational ties in a network may span organisations from suppliers to end-users, and/or actual or potential competitors. The network may also include service agencies, such as advertising, research, consulting services and distribution specialists. The relationships among the firms in a network may include: simple transactional contracts of the conventional buyer–seller type; supplier–producer collaborative agreements, strategic alliances or partnerships, consortia, franchising and distribution linkages, joint ventures or vertical integration. We shall examine these relationships in more depth below.

Starting from these general points about alliances and networks, this chapter builds a framework for evaluating, designing and managing alliance and network-based organisations as part of the implementation of marketing strategy and as a fundamental change in the competitive scenario. Nonetheless, it should be remembered that limited knowledge and often the absence of effective management capabilities for managing in these new organisational forms is illustrated by the continued high failure rate of strategic alliances.

15.3   The drivers of collaboration strategies

A starting point is to identify the potential drivers or motivating factors that lead organisations towards collaboration in delivering their strategies to market. Such driving forces include factors such as those outlined in Figure 15.3 and discussed below.

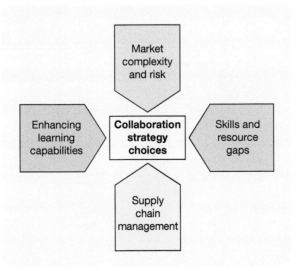

Figure 15.3
Drivers of collaboration strategy

15.3.1 Market complexity and risk

Modern markets are frequently characterised by complexity and high degrees of risk. One way of coping with that complexity and reducing (or sharing) risk is through collaboration. Complexity and risk may be exhibited in various situations:

- **Blurring of market boundaries** – conventional market definitions may become outdated and expose a company to new types of customer demand and new types of competition. The information industry is a prime example, where we see the convergence of Internet companies, telecommunications, consumer electronics, entertainment media, publishing and office equipment industries. A converging industry greatly increases the complexity for a single firm trying to compete in the face of a widening range of customer requirements and technologies to satisfy customer needs. Many of the products required are likely to be beyond the design, manufacturing and marketing capabilities of a single company, thus driving companies to pool their skills. This pooling of capabilities may be very effective. Technological convergence making the mobile telephone both a camera and a music player have had severe disruptive effects for the traditional photography and music businesses. High technology businesses of this kind have seen many alliances formed, though often lasting only a short period of time as competitive priorities change.

- **Escalating customer demands** – in many markets buyers are demanding increasing value but also uniqueness in their purchases: one-to-one marketing, or micro-segmentation, is becoming a reality. To respond positively to this demand may be beyond the scope of a single company in terms of expertise and economy, and may require new ways of doing business. For example, the taxi firm Uber, and other firms growing in the 'sharing economy', have revolutionised their sectors. Uber's car-sharing model provides an online, pre-paid, online-tracked taxi ride, but by using freelance drivers with their own cars, Uber avoids owning vehicles or taxi depots and yet provides a greatly superior model (see Figure 15.4). Its 'product' is to connect passengers to pre-existing fleet and car owners through its smartphone app. Uber started with $307 million from a group of backers

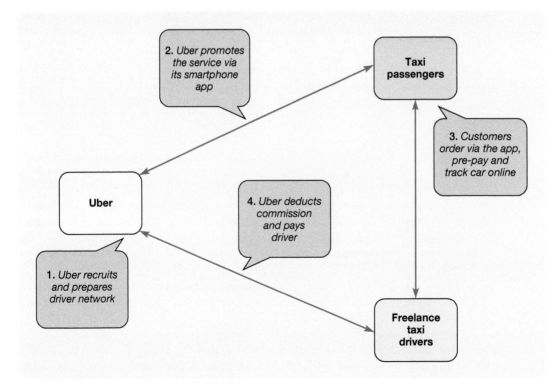

Figure 15.4 Uber's network organisation

including Google Ventures and Jeff Bezos, founder of Amazon. The Uber concept is to make booking a taxi as easy as making an online dinner reservation or checking a price on Amazon. By 2014, Uber was operational in 246 cities in 46 countries, and was valued at $40 billion. Models like Uber are springing up in many sectors – people can rent out spare rooms or holiday homes on Airbnb or HomeAway, and get Gesty or UrbanBellhop to welcome the guests and clean up after them. There are Uber-type models for laundry (Washio), massages (Zeel), alcohol (Minibar), and many more – the network concept is a powerful response to escalating customer demands.

- **A borderless world** – It is more than 25 years since Ohmae (1990) wrote about the interlinked economy of *The Borderless World*. Companies are increasingly driven to compete globally, and collaboration offers an attractive alternative to competing alone in a new environment. We mentioned earlier the global networks being developed at IBM to reflect changing international connectedness. Another global initiative is the long-standing partnership between competitors General Mills from the US and Nestlé from Switzerland. They created a joint venture – Cereal Partners Worldwide – to market General Mills' cereal brands in 130 countries outside North America. General Mills contributes its high quality cereal brands and Nestlé provides its extensive international distribution channels and local market knowledge, for an effective and enduring global collaboration (see 'General Mills: Joint Ventures', 2015).

15.3.2 Skills and resource gaps

It follows that there are growing pressures on firms to collaborate to compete effectively in globalised, technology-driven markets. The costs of developing internally the full range of skills and capabilities needed to compete effectively may be beyond the resources of a single company, or simply more cheaply available through alliances with specialised partners – where each partner can concentrate on applying its own core competencies, i.e. what it does best.

This may be of most importance with strategic accounts – the powerful major customers upon whom we have greatest dependence as a seller (see Chapter 14). Strategic customers generally seek 'solutions-oriented' packages that relate to their business problems and opportunities, and will accept nothing less from their strategic suppliers. Selling products or services is not acceptable. The problem faced is that constructing the appropriate 'solution' for the strategic customer may involve expertise and technology that forces the seller to partner with others. Johnson Controls, for example, is the highly successful seller of automotive seating and electrical switching. While Johnson manufactures seat and switches, it has had to partner with others to provide the simple 'bolt-on', modularised seating and electronics components systems required by modern car assembly plants.

Filling skills and resource gaps may also involve the creation of new brands and new business forms in surprising ways. For example, some years ago Honda Motor and Hong Kong Disneyworld formed a strategic alliance. As part of the alliance, Honda sponsors the Disneyworld's Autopia attraction, which allows visitors to 'drive to the future' in electric cars and experience 'outer space', and supports the park's safety features. Honda gets exclusive rights to use Disneyland images to promote their cars, motorcycle and power equipment products in Hong Kong and China. The partners are looking for further opportunities for both brands to collaborate, and interestingly appear have to found ways to merge automotive and entertainment industry interests. Disney has similar corporate alliances with Siemens, Coca-Cola, Hewlett-Packard and others to share the Disney brand.

In other cases, an alliance may provide enhanced market access and open new ways of trading. For example, the fast-food chain McDonald's has an alliance with Sinopec, the state-owned oil company in China that operates 30,000 petrol stations (and adds around 500 more every year). The alliance is to support McDonald's strategy of expanding drive-through restaurants in China. The strategy is based on changing eating habits in heavily populated Chinese cities, which are becoming more Westernised, with more widespread car ownership and mobile lifestyles among the young, which favour purchases directly from vehicles. McDonald's believes that Sinopec will provide a platform to build its China business around drive-through restaurants.

Much of the growth strategy at Alliance Boots is based on partnering – Boots and Waitrose sell each other's products in the UK and the company has merged with Walgreens in the US to achieve global expansion. Alliance Boots' goal of expanding sales of its emerging skincare brands is supported by a deal with P&G, which markets and distributes Alliance Boots' Laboratories Serum 7 skincare range to pharmacies in Italy, Spain, Germany, Austria and Switzerland (Felsted, 2011). The partnership puts the power of P&G's distribution network and marketing expertise behind Alliance Boots' products, while giving P&G (the maker of Olay) a more exclusive brand to expand the skincare product portfolio it sells in these markets (Rigby and Felsted, 2010a, b).

15.3.3 Supply-chain management

One recent manifestation of the pressure to collaborate has come through the proposal for the 'lean enterprise' (Womack and Jones, 1996), which involves partnering between companies at different stages of the supply chain. The Efficient Consumer Response programme of 'cooperative partnerships' between retailers and manufacturers, who have committed to reducing costs in markets like grocery, is illustrative.

When Google launched Android as a key part of its mobile phone strategy, the package of open-source software was designed to make it easier and cheaper to build the next generations of smartphone services. However, on a broader front, Google also launched its Open Handset Alliance to attack Nokia and Microsoft. The alliance had 34 mobile and technology company members at the outset, including handset makers Samsung and Motorola and mobile operators NTT, DoCoMo and T-Mobile. Importantly, open handsets running any applications desired by the user weakens the existing mobile phone companies' business model. Google is trying to make the value chain for wireless mobile like that in the broadband Internet market – where applications are developed independently of the device manufacturer and network operators, thus relegating operators to a minor role (Waters and Taylor, 2007). Google's gamble is that redesigning the value chain will reshape the mobile phone business to its advantage (Taylor *et al.*, 2007).

Sometimes supply-chain collaborations may be problematic, as discovered when the French train operator Société Nationale des Chemins de Fer and network operator Réseau Ferré de France acquired a fleet of trains too wide to fit French railway station platforms – 1,300 platforms have to be trimmed to fit the new trains at a cost of almost $70 million (Horobin, 2014). On a broader scale, Boeing's 787 'Dreamliner' relied on a key strategy of outsourced manufacturing. Only 10 per cent of manufacturing is done by Boeing, the rest is supplied by 40 partners – wings built in Japan, the carbon composite fuselage in Italy and the United States, and the landing gear from France. The Dreamliner has 367,000 parts sourced from a global network of 900 suppliers. Managing a collaborative supply chain this complex has severely stretched Boeing's capabilities, and there have been major problems with poorly fitting components, and delays leading to cancelled orders (Weitzman, 2011).

15.3.4 Enhancing learning capabilities

One reason for alliance may be to learn and acquire new capabilities. For example, as mentioned above, consumer products giant Procter & Gamble has recently taken a shareholding in Internet retailer Ocado, seen as a testing ground for P&G to evaluate its ability to sell direct to the consumer and challenge the power of major 'bricks and mortar' retailers. Other P&G projects include swapping executives with Google to learn more about search behaviour and Internet use, in developing a new business model in the conventional value chain (Piercy *et al.,* 2010b).

With the promise of biotechnology to provide new generations of drugs at a time when many pharmaceutical companies have clung to more traditional areas of R&D, big pharma companies like Novartis and Merck are rapidly forming alliances with small biotechnology companies to strengthen their position in the race to develop new cancer immunotherapies. This category is expected to be worth $40 billion a year within a decade, and the large companies cannot afford to miss out and must tap into the knowledge of others (Ward, 2015).

These developments cannot be ignored as they provide powerful pressures towards collaboration between companies conventionally viewed as having only a buyer–seller relationship, or who were traditionally competitors. It is important that in evaluating our markets and our strategies for the future we should carefully and systematically consider the emergence of factors like those listed above, which may drive our competitors' and our own strategies into collaborative network forms.

The next questions to consider relate to the types of networks which can be identified and the nature of the links which hold them together. As strategic alliances have become one of the most important organisational forms in modern business, managers are frequently faced with decision choices in terms of which type and form of alliance should be adopted (Pansiri, 2005).

15.4	**Network forms**

There is no broadly accepted typology of network organisational forms. However, the approach **below** is useful in clarifying our ideas about the types of network which exist and may emerge in our markets. Cravens and Piercy (2013) report the integration of the perspectives offered by Achrol (1991), Powell (1990), Quinn (1992) and Webster (1992) to propose the model of network organisation types shown in Figure 15.5. They argue that there are different kinds of networks which can be classified in two important respects:

1 **The type of network relationship,** which can vary from the highly collaborative (involving various forms of inter-organisational cooperation and partnership), to the mainly transactional (the traditional buyer–seller transaction, for example).
2 **The volatility of environmental change** – the argument that in highly volatile environments, external relationships with other organisations must be flexible enough to allow for alteration – and possibly termination – in a short time period. On the other hand, when the environment is more stable, more enduring forms of collaboration are more attractive.

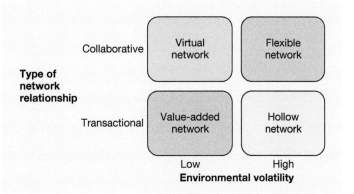

Figure 15.5
Type of network organisation

Using these dimensions to classify networks produces the model in Figure 15.5, which suggests that there are at least four types of network prototype:

1 **The hollow network** – a transaction-based organisational form, associated with highly volatile environments. The term 'hollow' emphasises that the core organisation draws heavily on other organisations to satisfy customer needs. For example, organisations that compete in this way are often specialists that coordinate an extensive network of suppliers and buyers. One example of this type of network is Monster.com, the online recruitment and careers company. Monster connects job seekers with employers, as well as providing them with careers advice online. Some 75 million individuals have established personalised accounts with Monster, which operates in 36 countries with 4,200 employees. The hollow organisation offers a buffer against the risks in a frequently changing environment.

2 **The flexible network** – associated with conditions of high environmental volatility but characterised by inter-organisational links which tend to be collaborative and long term in duration, where the network coordinator manages an internal team that identifies customer needs and establishes sources of supply to satisfy customer requirements. For example, as noted earlier, many of the multi-national pharmaceutical firms are tied to core competencies in organic and inorganic chemistry and are seeking to establish alliances with entrepreneurial biotechnology firms. The larger firms have too much invested in their current technology to switch completely to biotechnology, but want to exploit partnerships to ensure they have a source of biotechnology-based products. The Uber example discussed earlier also provides a model of a flexible network, where Uber acts as a hub promoting and defending the service and providing the smartphone software, but using a network of external partners (drivers) to provide the taxi ride to the customer.

3 **The value-added network** – associated with less volatile environments and based mainly on transactional relationships between network members. For example, the network coordinator may use a global network of suppliers, but still maintain substantial internal operations – the core organisation may contract for many added-value functions such as production, but retain responsibility for innovation and product design. Industries using this type of network are clothing manufacture, furniture, eye-glasses and some services – the link is that the value-added network fits situations where complex technologies and customised product offerings are not required.

4 **The virtual network** is associated with situations where environmental volatility is relatively low, and the core organisation seeks to establish collaborative relationships with other organisations. This is similar to what has been called the 'virtual corporation', which seeks to achieve adaptability to meet the needs of segmented markets through long-term partnerships rather than internal investment. In these cases market access and technology access are the key drivers, and as with the flexible network, formal strategic alliances are the most common method for collaborating. The virtual network provides a buffer against market risks and access to new technology.

A broader and more complex view of network types was been provided by Achrol (1997), who attempted to reflect three important characteristics that may differentiate different types of network: whether they are single-firm or multi-firm, whether they are single-industry or multi-industry; and, whether they are stable or temporary. Achrol's (1997) view of networks identifies the following types:

- **Internal market networks** – this describes the reformation of major companies to break free of the restrictions of traditional hierarchies and multi-divisional forms, by organising into internal enterprise units that operate as independent profit centres. For example, at one stage General Motors reorganised rigid and inefficient component manufacturing units into eight internal market units, each specialised in an automotive system area and able to sell its products on the open market as well as to GM, including sales to GM's competitors in automotive manufacture.

- **Vertical market networks**, or **marketing channel networks**, reflect the traditional view of vertical channel relationships, but go further to recognise the focal firm that co-ordinates upstream supplier firms and downstream distributor firms. Often the integrator special-ises in marketing functions and uses specialists for manufacture and distribution. Early forms included the 'hollow corporation', for example Casio, Nike, Liz Claiborne. In such networks, the typical pattern is that the integrator is the firm which owns the brand and which specialises in the marketing function, while alliance partners are specialised resource centres providing some aspect of product or production technology. An exam-ple is provided by IKEA, the retailer of Swedish furniture, which successfully operates a global sourcing network of 2,300 suppliers in 67 countries, to get 10,000 products on the shelf at prices up to 30 per cent cheaper than traditional rivals.
- **Intermarket or concentric networks** – this is largely the province of the Japanese and Korean economies – the well-known *keiretsu* and *chaebol* 'enterprise groups' represent-ing alliances among firms operating in a variety of unrelated industries. The intermar-ket network involves institutionalised affiliations among firms operating in different industries and the firms linked in vertical exchange relationships with them. They are characterised by dense interconnections in resource-sharing, strategic decision-making and culture and identity. The centre may be a trading company – possibly functioning as the marketing arm of the network – associated with manufacturing affiliates, which in turn have large vertical clusters of subcontractors, distributors and satellite companies, and are often involved in technology alliances with competitors. For example, Toshiba has around 200 companies in a direct exchange relationship, and another 600 'grandchild companies' below them.
- **Opportunity networks** – this is represented as a set of firms specialising in various prod-ucts, technologies or services that form temporary alignments around specific projects or problems. Characteristically, the hub of the network is a marketing organisation specialising in collecting and disseminating market information, negotiating, coordi-nating projects for customers and suppliers, and regulating the network. Achrol (1991) has described this as the 'marketing exchange company'. One prototype is the direct marketing company using media like the Internet to market a wide variety of consumer products and novelties.

This review illustrates the diversity and potential complexity of network organisational forms as they are emerging and as we are trying to classify and understand them. How-ever, even with 20 years' experience with these innovations it remains true that our general understanding is not well developed: 'network and virtual organisations have been here for a long time, although our ability to define them and communicate their true content is still limited' (Gummesson, 1994).

We may be able to improve that understanding in practical terms by turning attention next to the nature of the links which tie organisations together in these various forms of collaboration.

15.5   Alliances and partnerships

It is useful to think about networks in terms of relationship marketing, where the relation-ships between network partners go beyond those that would be defined by contract or written agreement or buyer–seller exchanges in the channel of distribution. Achrol argues that 'the mere presence of a network of ties is not the distinguishing feature of the network organisation', but that 'the quality of the relationships and the shared values that govern them differentiate and define the boundaries of the network organisation' (Achrol, 1997).

This said, one starting point in understanding the dynamics of the network organisa-tion, and its attractiveness or otherwise in developing a specific marketing strategy, lies in

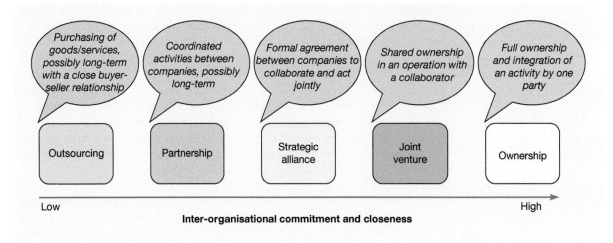

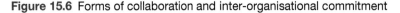

Figure 15.6 Forms of collaboration and inter-organisational commitment

analysing partnership. It is important that we do not see strategic alliances and network formation as ends in their own right, but as a means to an end – the implementation and regeneration of our marketing strategy and the enhancement of our process of going to market – to be used selectively and appropriately based on our objectives and our capabilities for managing collaborations with other organisations.

One way of categorising collaborative relationships is shown in Figure 15.6. These relationships form a spectrum running from a largely traditional, transactional relationship to full-scale vertical integration. The relationships shown in Figure 15.6 have the following characteristics.

15.5.1 Outsourcing

At one extreme is an 'arm's length' relationship, where we may simply buy-in goods and services from outside, as the alternative to producing them internally. This might involve outsourcing for services like advertising, market research, the salesforce, and direct marketing expertise. It may also describe how we buy-in goods for resale, or handle relationships with our distributors. However, increasingly even at this end of the spectrum people may see suppliers and distributors as partners and use terms like 'strategic alliance' to describe what appear to be no more than conventional, though close, buyer–seller relationships. This may be inaccurate, but underlines the point above that networks are about more than the nature of the legal ties between partners. Transactional relationships of this kind also characterise what Cravens *et al.* (1996) described as value-added and hollow networks (see above). It is also true that in many situations, arm's length relationships are reshaping into closer collaborative relationships. What starts as outsourcing may acquire many of the collaborative characteristics of a formal strategic alliance.

However, it is worth noting that the general growth of outsourcing may have peaked because of several factors. For example, many German companies that outsourced work to countries like Poland and Romania are retreating and taking work back to the home market because of lack of loyalty and broken contracts in outsourced markets (Woodhead, 2007). Similarly, while in 2007 NCR decided to outsource the production of its bank ATMs to cut costs, by 2009 it was bringing production back in-house and describing outsourcing as 'an enormous and costly exercise', that led to product delays and upset customers (Engardio, 2009). Certainly, the economics have changed in many situations – outsourcing IT functions to India and China has to be placed in the context of higher wage costs, making Vietnam, China and Brazil more attractive locations (Leahy, 2007). Indeed, India's Wipro Technologies began reverse offshoring by sending work from its Indian clients to offices in Egypt (Leahy, 2009).

Companies make different choices where the outsource/insource decision is a key strategic choice. For example, Jeff Immelt, CEO of General Electric, has declared that outsourcing is 'mostly outdated as a business tool' (Mallaby, 2013). Certainly, Lenovo has decided to keep production in-house as a competitive strength, while competitors in smartphones, tablets and Internet televisions outsource manufacturing (Chao, 2012).

Nonetheless, outsourcing models remain central to the strategic choices faced in going to market and achieving an effective competitive position. For example, a crucial strategic difference between rivals Sony and Samsung in the emerging 3D television business is that Sony has gambled on outsourcing its television production, while Samsung is dedicating its resources to its own manufacturing capacity (Ihlwan, 2010). Certainly, the use of outsourcing strategies by government has greatly expanded in the UK, and outsource firms look forward to continued good earnings (Plimmer, 2015).

In supply chain management, the use of third-party logistics providers (3PLs) is illustrative of successful long-term outsourcing. A growing number of firms outsource some or all of their logistics to 3PLs, such as FedEx Logistics or DHL Logistics. In fact, a group of 3PLs dominate logistics outsourcing around the world. Manufacturers need absolutely reliable sources of supply. Retailers need flexible links to suppliers with low-cost production, but these suppliers are often in remote regions. At the same time, retailers need rapid delivery channels for an ever-expanding distribution network of consumers. These global 3PLs provide transportation, consolidation, forwarding and customs brokerage, warehousing, fulfilment, distribution and virtually any logistics and trade-related services that their international customers need. In a global 3PL market worth $270 billion a year, the top three companies turn over around $42 billion a year. The global market leaders are Excel (UK), Kuehne + Nagel (Switzerland) and Schenkler (Germany). Unsurprisingly, the top seven global 3PL providers are European, since 3PL use is more widespread in Europe than America. Companies use 3PL providers for several reasons. First, because getting the product to market is their main focus, these providers can often do it more efficiently and at lower cost. Outsourcing typically results in 15–30 per cent in cost savings. Second, outsourcing logistics frees a company to focus more intensely on its core business. Finally, integrated logistics companies understand increasingly complex logistics environments.

15.5.2 Partnerships

These are collaborations that involve a closer relationship between organisations, but stopping short of a formal strategic alliance agreement, shared ownership in a joint venture or vertical integration. Lambert *et al.* (1996) suggest that partnerships vary in the degree and type of integration. They suggested that: (1) some partnerships are short term in focus and involve limited coordination; (2) other partnerships have a longer-term focus and move beyond coordination to integration of activities; and, (3) the closest partnerships are viewed as 'permanent' and each party views the other as an extension of its own firm.

For example, in one strategic alliance, Dell Inc. and EMC had a partnership relationship in the data storage business, providing advanced networked storage solutions for organisations of all sizes. The partnership made Dell the fastest growing disk storage systems seller, and EMC the mid-tier market share leader in revenue. The combined capabilities of Dell and EMC made a major impact on the data storage business. Dell and EMC leveraged a unique model of sales, marketing, engineering and manufacturing collaboration to exploit each other's strengths and deliver superior value to customers, but the relationship had a fixed term (*Al Bawaba*, 2006). Interestingly, Dell has more recently shown interest in buying EMC to re-establish the relationship.

A different form a marketing alliance was shown by the Jigsaw Consortium formed by Cadbury Trebor Bassett, Unilever and Kimberly-Clark. The consortium was managed for the members by direct marketing agency OgilvyOne. The members of the consortium owned brands like Persil, Flora, Lynx, Huggies, Cadbury Creme Egg and Flake. The alliance created a consumer database covering the purchasing behaviour and brand attitudes of nine million consumers. Importantly, while retailers like Tesco and Sainsbury's have the strength of consumer purchase data through point-of-sale scanning, the consortium database included attitudinal data for additional insight and predictive power.

In the same sector, excess capacity in British supermarkets is driving them to collaboration in the form of placing concession stores within major supermarkets. With rapid expansion now a thing of the past, supermarkets are looking to high street retailers and leisure operators to take up their unproductive floor space. The first two Argos stores opened in Sainsbury's in 2015, with more to follow. Sainsbury's has also signed agreements with Jessops, the photographic retailer, and Western Union, to begin global money transfer services to its stores. Asda has partnered with French sports retailer Decathlon, while it is expected that Tesco will bring Sports Direct into its stores. Deals between supermarkets and dentists, opticians and hairdressers are expected to follow. These horizontal collaborations have not always been successful in the past, but it looks like they will expand, driven by the excess selling space in large supermarkets, which face tough competition from discounters and convenience stores (Shubber, 2015).

15.5.3 Strategic alliances

Strategic alliances are more formal arrangements, sometimes under contract, for companies to collaborate and act jointly. The defining characteristics of strategic alliances are that (1) two or more companies unite to pursue a set of agreed goals, but remain independent even though in an alliance; (2) the alliance members share the benefits of the alliance and control over the assigned tasks; and (3) the firms in the alliance contribute on a continuing basis to one or more strategic areas (e.g., technology sharing, product development or marketing) (Taylor, 2005; Todeva and Knoke, 2005).

In some sectors, such as airlines, strategic alliances have become the dominant way of doing business. Most of the world's big airlines are members of one of the alliances. The three major airline alliances are Star Alliance (United Airlines, Lufthansa and 25 others); SkyTeam (Delta, Air France/KLM, and 17 others); and Oneworld (American Airlines, British Airways, Cathay Pacific and 12 others). Between them the big three alliances carry almost two-thirds of all passengers flying in the world and control more than half the global fleet of commercial passenger aircraft. While these alliances offer airlines advantages in code-sharing, loyalty programmes and marketing, they are also fragile as members move allegiances. It is also noteworthy that many of the world's rapidly growing airlines (e.g., Emirates, Etihad) are not alliance members and most of the successful no-frills fliers are unaligned (easyJet, Ryanair, Southwest). Some analysts predict a fracturing of the existing alliances and a fresh wave of consolidation in the airline industry. While alliance-based competition brings strengths, alliances may not last (Tovey, 2015).

15.5.4 Joint ventures

These are relationships where the ownership of a project or operation is shared between the parties concerned. For example, Mercedes, the German car company, and Swatch, the Swiss watch company, entered into a short-lived joint venture to produce the Smart mini-car, supported by partnership sourcing by its ten key suppliers, which relocated their operations to a 'smart ville' in France. This relationship focused on partners from different industries sharing innovative design abilities, technological expertise and marketing capabilities to innovate. The concept was that the partners were selling 'mobility' as a total product not just a car – the overall market offer included the ability to borrow larger cars when needed for particular mobility needs. The joint-venture became a wholly-owned subsidiary of Daimler Chrysler and is now owned by Daimler AG.

Joint venture collaborations have proved highly problematic in some cases. BP's growth strategy of partnering with companies in resource-rich countries like Russia is illustrative. The relationship between BP and its Russian partners in TNK-BP was plagued with problems and conflicts of interest, culminating in the Russian security services raiding the joint venture offices, withdrawing visas for BP executives, and chasing the BP-TNK CEO out of the country, from where he continued to run the business in hiding (White and Chazan, 2008). TNK-BP accounts for around a quarter of BP's total global oil production and reserves. Eventually, BP had no choice but to concede the demands of its Russian partners and accept it was no longer the 'senior partner'. Suggestions are that what appeared a strategic triumph for BP had turned into a costly trap.

15.5.5 Vertical integration

An activity in another part of the value chain is fully owned by the core organisation, although the relationship may still be seen as a strategic alliance, even though strictly one company owns another. Apple Inc. provides an interesting example of a company which is vertically integrated using both outsourcing and direct financial ownership. Apple designs the computer hardware, accessories, operating system, and much of the software itself, but does not manufacture. Production is outsourced to specialist suppliers like Foxconn. Apple established a chain of high-profile, up-market retail outlets to protect its consumer market position, using forward vertical integration to retain control over its product presentation in the marketplace.

In another sector, for example, Italian company Luxottica is the world's largest eye-wear business. The company produces many famous eyewear brands – including its own Ray-Ban and Oakley brands and licensed brands such as Burberry, Chanel, Polo Ralph Lauren, Dolce & Gabbana, Donna Karan, Prada, Versace, and Bulgari. It then sells these brands through some of the world's largest optical chains – LensCrafters, Pearle Vision and Sunglass Hut – that it also owns. In another example, integrating the entire distribution chain, from its own design and manufacturing operations to distribution through its own managed stores, has turned Spanish clothing chain Zara into the world's fastest-growing fast-fashion retailer (*Economist*, 2012; Berfield, 2013).

It is important that executives carefully consider the strengths and weaknesses of these different degrees and types of partnership in developing appropriate alliance strategies, and that we recognise that, in reality, networks may contain a mix of different partnership styles. It should also not be assumed that inter-organisational relationships are static – collaborative forms may change or be removed during the course of a project, for example if one partner is gaining benefits while the other(s) is/are not. For example, BMW and Rolls-Royce operated an alliance in the form of a joint venture – BMW Rolls-Royce GmbH – for some ten years in the aerospace industry, focused on advanced aero engine development. The partners succeeded in producing a commercially successful family of advanced engines. The alliance provided Rolls-Royce with a stronger product strategy, but after ten years BMW withdrew to concentrate on automotive and the business became wholly owned by Rolls-Royce as Rolls-Royce Deutschland (Smith, 2003).

| 15.6 | Strategic alliances as a competitive force |

It is important that we recognise in our marketing strategy development that in some markets, competition is increasingly based on the relationship between alliances and the networks they create and no longer simply between individual companies or brands. We saw this in the airline industry example above. This is particularly true in global businesses. Consider the following examples:

- Increasingly, the global automotive business is characterised by global networks, rather than free-standing manufacturers. This sector is characterised by a fast-moving and flexible array of alliances: 2012 saw Nissan and Daimler partnering to build engines together in the US (Reed, 2012); GM and Peugeot have a broad alliance for European car operations as GM seeks to improve its European performance (*Wall Street Journal*, 2012); Ford and Toyota have teamed up on hybrid car and truck development in response to higher emissions standards in the United States (Bennett and Ramsey, 2011); and the highly successful entry of Western carmakers to China has been mainly through joint ventures with local firms (Mitchell, 2014).

- In the aerospace industry, a strategic alliance between Boeing and Lockheed Martin means that by working together the companies can leverage their expertise in air traffic management and aircraft-focused solutions to transform air traffic control system products. Lockheed-Martin brings air traffic route management experience, while Boeing contributes expertise in aircraft systems, avionics and airspace simulation and modelling (*Airline Industry Information*, 2007).

- In the rapidly evolving biotechnology industry, companies like Novartis and Merck are forging alliances with biotechnology firms to stake a claim for part of the $40 billion market for new breakthrough cancer treatment drugs. Partnerships around immunotherapy developments offer traditional pharmaceutical companies access to new areas of growth. This is only one example of numerous technology-based alliances between traditional pharmacists and biotechnology ventures. Competition is increasingly between alliances rather than individual companies (Ward, 2015).

- In a completely different business, Coke and Pepsi are fighting over the growing Ready to Drink Coffee market. But this is a battle between partnerships – Pepsi has partnered with Starbucks, and Coke with Illycaffe from Italy to respond and counter Pepsi's initiative.

- Meantime, the media and communications sector shows a constant flurry of alliances and networks – many of which are short-lived. For example, Apple's strength is integration of hardware and software and its network of apps developers. In response, Google teamed up with Motorola and Microsoft with Nokia to emulate Apple's integrated hardware and software strategy – neither alliance was effective or sustainable. More generally, we are seeing Web worlds of Internet search and social networks collide in a war for followers with an alliance between Facebook and Microsoft's Bing as the first salvo, along with a Google and Yahoo partnership replacing an earlier Microsoft and Yahoo alliance. Many inter-organisational relationships in this sector are transitory. Apple and Google were once allies (with cross-board memberships) but now they are rivals. Apple and IBM were once rivals, but now have a collaboration to push Apple's digital devices into IBM's corporate heartland.

- Similarly the 'Internet of things' is bringing together search, software, apps and hardware manufacturers in novel ways as the fight is on to dominate this new category of products – no one can move fast enough alone, which encourages acquisitions, partnerships and alliances. The battle to shape the 'Internet of things' is rapidly hotting-up, as technology and telecoms companies race to build the infrastructure to connect billions of devices in homes and offices. For example, in 2014 Google bought Nest Laboratories for $3.2 billion – twice what it paid for YouTube. Nest makes smart thermostats and smoke alarms, but has redesigned these appliances as connected, digital devices for the smartphone age. Google intends to provide the resources for Nest's technology to run peoples' smart homes, which is a huge market. Underpinning this move is the battle for whose service – Google, Amazon, Apple, Microsoft, or others – will coordinate the new 'smart home'.

Nonetheless, alliances and networks are a means to an end – delivering a strategy to the market and achieving the companies' goals. The strategy matters more than the specific structures used to implement it. But, at the very least, our analysis of competitive structures would possibly be misleading if we did not account for the potential impact of strategic alliances – both existing and potential – on our ability to successfully implement a strategy.

15.7 | The risks in strategic alliances

We stressed earlier that strategic alliances are no panacea. They may be an important way to achieve the things we need, but there are significant risks also. To begin with, we should be aware that, for one reason or another, strategic alliances sometimes simply do not work, and they may crash spectacularly. Consider the airline alliance and information technology examples examined above. Strategic alliances may be transitory. For example, an early study by Cravens *et al.* (1993) found that in 82 large multi-national corporations, fewer than half the companies operating strategic alliances were satisfied with the effectiveness of those alliances and other evidence concurs with this finding of a dismal failure rate for strategic alliances (Hughes and Weiss, 2007). The underlying concern is that the greater the reliance of a company and its strategy on alliance and network, the greater is the associated risk.

It has never been wise to overestimate the strength and durability of strategic alliances. Quinn noted some time ago:

> Like earlier decentralisation and SBU concepts, some of these newer organisational modes have been touted as cures for almost any managerial ill. They are not. Each form is useful is certain situations, and not in others. But more importantly, each requires a carefully developed infrastructure of culture, measurements, style and rewards to support it. When properly installed, these disaggregated organisations can be awesomely effective in harnessing intellectual resources for certain purposes. When improperly supported or adapted, they can be less effective than old-fashioned hierarchies.
> *(Quinn, 1992)*

Indeed, as well as the outright failure of an alliance and the crash of the network involved, there are a number of other important issues to bear in mind as potential limitations to the application of strategies of collaboration.

Achrol (1997) argued that we should consider the following factors as key elements of designing and operating network organisations:

- **Power:** we need to take a careful look at the relative dependence and power within a network, both in terms of whether the relative position we take is acceptable to us and if we are going to be able to cope with the way power is likely to be exercised in the network, and how vulnerable this may make us.
- **Commitment and interdependence:** at its simplest, are the people in the partnering companies going to be behind the alliance, and what mechanisms may be needed like interlocking directorships and exchange of personnel or other liaison mechanisms? In the *keiretsu*, the Japanese refer to what is necessary to 'keep each other warm' – their example suggests we should not underestimate the importance of people's commitment, or lack of it, in an effective network organisation.
- **Trust:** the network organisation requires that each partner gives up some influence or control over important issues and becomes vulnerable to ineffective or hostile actions by other network members. This is a key aspect of relationship management in a network. The cases of network failure discussed earlier illustrate the vulnerability involved. Compare this to the risk of lack of commitment to a collaboration through an unjustified lack of trust in the partner organisation, and the significance of the issue becomes clearer.
- **Social norms:** it is suggested that network organisations should be considered in terms of behavioural issues like (a) solidarity – the unity of action among network members, (b) mutuality – network partners acting in the common good and receiving a payoff in terms of benefits from the collaboration, (c) flexibility – the willingness of partners to change the joint arrangements as conditions change, (d) role integrity – clarity in what each partner organisation is to do, (d) conflict handling – agreement on how conflicts will be handled in the network. The important point to bear in mind is that while organisations are familiar with how to handle these questions in conventional, independent,

hierarchical structures, we are still learning how best to manage them in the very different setting of the collaborative network of organisations.

In a transparent, brand-oriented world, we can add to this concerns about **damage by association**: the performance of an organisation in terms of its competitive behaviour and social responsibility stance may make it a more or less attractive partner because of the association. For example, one surprising consequence of BP's disastrous oil spill in the Gulf of Mexico in 2010 is that its partner company – Anadarko – finds its existence and future plans in jeopardy because it is tainted by its relationship with BP (Klump and Reed, 2010).

The stability or instability of an alliance may also reflect **changing strategic priorities**: when an ally becomes a rival because its strategies change over time, then alliance may no longer work. For example, while Apple and Google had maintained a cooperative relationship for a number of years (primarily against the common enemy Microsoft), 2009 saw Eric Schmidt, CEO of Google, resigning from Apple's board. As the two companies' products have begun to overlap, cooperation is giving way to competition, and Google membership of Apple's board is no longer appropriate (Menn, 2009).

Moreover, we need to consider the attractiveness of a collaborative or alliance-based strategy in terms not simply of the pressures of factors like resource gaps and market access, but also in the light of whether we can design and implement an effective network, and whether we have the skills and capabilities to manage through a network of relationships with other companies.

We shall consider these points in more detail in the managerial agenda **in the next section**. Issues like trust, commitment and power may hold the key to identifying the large business risks involved in reliance on strategic alliances. As situations change, so may the commitment of a partner to an alliance. The risk of opportunistic behaviour by a partner is an important issue to be monitored (Kale *et al.*, 2000).

15.8   Managing strategic alliances

The discussion above and the examples examined in this chapter suggest that the managerial issues that should be addressed carefully and systematically in evaluating the strategy of collaboration and alliance as a route to market are the following (the key management issues are summarised in Figure 15.7 and discussed below).

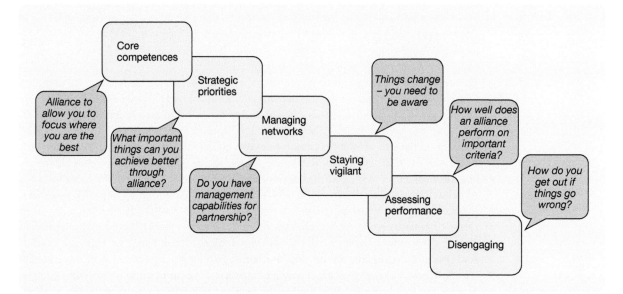

Figure 15.7 Issues to consider in managing strategic alliances

15.8.1 Core competencies

One of the fundamental attractions of collaboration and partnership with other organisations is that it allows each organisation to focus on its own core competencies and to benefit from the specialisation of other organisations in their own areas of expertise (Achrol, 1991; Webster, 1992). Quinn (1992) noted: 'If one is not 'best in world' at a critical activity, the company is sacrificing competitive advantage by performing that activity internally or with its existing techniques'. Certainly, research by Buffington and Frabelli (1991) in the telecommunications industry suggests that when partners in a collaboration do not contribute their core competencies, then the probability of success for the alliance is substantially reduced. This suggests that clarity in defining those core competencies may be critical to negotiating and sustaining effective inter-organisational relationships of this type.

However, there are two problems. First, it is clear that the identification of core competencies may be far from straightforward within an organisation or between partners (e.g. see Piercy and Cravens, 2013). Second, we have to factor in not just existing and recognised core competencies, but issues of complementarity and 'fit' between potential partners, and the potential for synergy through collaboration. This is a complex and largely subjective evaluation which executives must make.

15.8.2 Strategic priorities

The issue of core competencies also raises important questions about competitive strategy and the choices faced in when, where and how to compete (Prahalad and Hamel, 1990). While networking offers a company the opportunity to focus on and exploit its core competencies, only rarely will it rarely create such capabilities for a company.

However, this focus and concentration may create vulnerabilities. For example, some years ago the British Airways alliance with USAir collapsed before the new alliance with American Airlines was approved. This left BA with no US-based collaborator and highly exposed to competitive attack by other alliances. While there is much current favour in corporate thinking for strategic focus and concentration, using collaborations as a vehicle, we should be aware of the risks involved in this prioritising. Reliance on partners to perform critical activities involves risks if the partnership fails or underperforms, and may leave us without the capacity to develop new competencies.

15.8.3 Managing networks

It is apparent from the case examples **above** that organisations differ markedly in their ability to manage effectively in networks or alliances. Forming and managing networks calls for a different set of management skills and issues compared to the conventional organisation.

Research suggests that lack of success in business partnerships and alliances is frequently because companies pay inadequate attention to planning. Lack of careful planning leads to conflicts about strategy, problems with governance and missed opportunities (Bamford *et al.*, 2004). The latter suggest forming a team dedicated to exposing tensions as early as possible, and to deal with four challenges: (1) to build and maintain strategic alignment across the partner companies; (2) to create a shared governance system; (3) to manage the economic interdependencies between the partner organisations; and (4) to build a cohesive organisation.

Indeed, many of the problems which have emerged in the management of alliance-based organisations were captured in Bensimon's (1999) executive guidelines:

- Assimilate the competencies of your partner;
- Think of your partner as today's ally and tomorrow's competitor;
- Share power and resources, but share information wisely; and
- Structure your alliance carefully.

Before making the commitment to enter an alliance, we should consider the following factors:

- **Drivers** – which of the drivers of collaboration strategies apply in this case? What does a collaboration strategy offer us in terms of: asset/cost efficiencies; customer service improvements; marketplace advantage over the competition, profit stability/growth?
- **Choice of partners** – which potential partners are available, and what basis do we have for believing that we could create an environment of trust, commitment and cooperation between the members of the alliance (Cravens *et al.*, 1997)?
- **Facilitators** – are the circumstances and environment favourable for a partnership? Lambert *et al.* (1996) suggest that partnerships are more likely to be successful if the following conditions prevail:
  - *corporate compatibility*: the cultures and business objectives of the partners must mesh;
  - *managerial philosophy and techniques*: are the partners' organisational structures, attitudes towards employees and method of working compatible?
  - *mutuality*: are there equally important benefits for both partners?
  - *symmetry*: are the partners similar types of company who understand each other?
  - *exclusivity*: are partner organisations willing to shut out others who are not part of the network?
  - *shared competitors*: partnerships work best as an alliance against a common foe;
  - *prior history*: experience in successful collaboration is a plus;
  - *shared end-user*: when partners serve the same customer, collaboration is likely to be more successful.
- **Components** – these are the activities and processes that management establishes and controls throughout the life of the partnership, and effective partnerships understand these from the outset. This includes arrangements for joint planning, joint operating controls, communications between partners, equitable risk/reward sharing, facilitating trust and commitment between partner organisations, a contract acceptable to both sides, the definition of the scope of the partnership and clarity about the financial investments to be made by partners.
- **Network effectiveness** – we saw earlier that it has been found that many companies pursuing alliance-based strategies are dissatisfied with the results. Defining realistic expectations at the outset and evaluating progress against them is required. We may have to think in terms of somewhat different measures to the conventional evaluation of effectiveness – network stability and sustainability, relationship strength, network synergy, and the like. If we cannot provide convincing evidence that the network provides a superior way of going to market, it is unlikely to endure. We consider the evaluation and appraisal process in more detail below.
- **Organisational change** – it is highly likely that the formation of network organisations will be stimulated by, and in turn lead to further changes in, alliance companies' internal organisational structures and processes. The requirements for effectiveness here may be complex and currently outside the experience of many senior managers in traditional organisations. The complexity of this issue was underlined early on by Gummesson (1994): 'organising a network business requires continuous creation, transformation and maintenance of amoeba-like, dynamic processes and organisational structures.'
- **Market orientation and customer service** – a particular point of concern for the marketing strategist is the impact of networked operations on the market orientation of the new type of organisation and its ability to deliver the required levels of customer service and superior customer value. Where the primary motivation for collaboration is technological or supply-chain efficiency, this may be a particularly significant concern. For example, some companies in the airline business are moving towards the concept of the 'virtual airline' which owns no aircraft or facilities and exists primarily as a brand and information system with a small core staff. Some executives suggest that while the core organisation is highly market-oriented and committed to high service quality, in a networked organisation they lack the means to share these imperatives with their partners. Quite simply, we may believe in service quality at the core airline, but is this shared by the people who

run the operation the customer experiences at check-in (Piercy and Cravens, 2013)? This suggests that one of the major questions we need to consider is what mechanisms we may need to create to drive goals like service and quality through a network to the end-user.

- **The role of marketing in network organisations** – there is some lack of clarity about how marketing is located and operated in a network organisation. Some suggest that the critical role for marketing in the alliance-based network is applying relationship marketing skills to managing the links between partners in the network (see Chapter 16 and our discussion of internal marketing as an implementation approach in partnerships). Certainly, there is a compelling argument that the concepts and processes of relationship marketing are pivotal to the management of networks. Relationship marketing involves the creation and distribution of value through mutual cooperation and interdependence and we have seen that cooperation and interdependence are central features of network organisations. It is too early to reach conclusions about the role that marketing can and will take generally in these new organisational forms, although it is highly likely that there will be some redefinition of its role which may be radical.

15.8.4 Staying vigilant

As experience grows in the advantages and pitfalls of going to market or operating key processes through strategic alliances, it is apparent that there may be temptations to persist with alliance relationships way past the point where this makes sense. The benefits of some inter-organisational relationships may be transitory, and the relationship may need to be reconsidered on a regular basis. Indeed, one of the attractions of networked organisations is that they may be designed to be temporary and to exploit a given opportunity, and then be dissolved. However, there is evidence that recognising the point when the alliance should end and managing the dissolution or disengagement process may pose some problems.

For example, there is some evidence that managers may be reluctant to end alliance relationships, even though they have evidence that the alliance is failing to meet its purposes and there is little chance that things will improve. This appears to be most likely with large joint ventures when closing costs may be high, sunk costs may have escalated, and where the alliance has high visibility – terminating large expensive partnerships may impact negatively on management careers and prospects (Delios *et al.*, 2004).

While an early concern about strategic alliances was that they could be unstable and unreliable because of the nature of inter-organisational, non-ownership relationships, it has been suggested, for example, that alliances may be too stable. Companies are urged now to routinely review and re-think their alliance arrangements. Rather than waiting for a crisis to emerge, a company should scan its major alliances to see which need restructuring, to understand the root causes of the venture's problems, and to estimate how much each problem is costing the company (Ernst and Bamford, 2005).

Indeed, there may be greater risks, which emerge in some situations, which are even more threatening than inertia allowing underperforming alliances to stay in place. The outsourcing or contract manufacturing area provides an illustrative example of the risks to be considered. Contract manufacturing is attractive to an original equipment manufacturer (OEM), the traditional brand owner, because it reduces labour costs and frees up capital to outsource manufacturing, leaving the OEM free to focus on product research, design and marketing. This practice started in the computer business, and has spread to areas as diverse as toys, clothing, footwear, beer and pharmaceuticals. Even in the automotive sector, Finland's Valmet Automotive assembles the Porsche Boxer, and Austria's Magna Steyr assembles cars for Mercedes, BMW and Saab. However, research suggests that the outsource relationship may develop in threatening ways, where the contract manufacturer displays:

- **Promiscuity** – the contract manufacturer (CM) seeks business with the OEM's competitors.
- **Infidelity** – the CM becomes a competitor by selling to the OEM's retailers and distributors.

- **Betrayal** – the CM shares the OEM's intellectual property with competitors or retains it for its own exploitation.

Meanwhile, the OEM cannot terminate the outsourcing because there are no alternative sources of product. Considerable care is required in making outsourcing decisions and deciding when they should end (Arruñada and Vázquez, 2006).

It is likely that as reliance on strategic alliances continues to increase, but as situations change companies will need to consider what is involved in effective disengagement from an alliance.

15.8.5 Assessing the performance of strategic alliances

It is perhaps symptomatic of the relative lack of maturity of the strategic alliance organisational model that it is claimed that a major reason for the high failure rate of alliances is that relatively few have developed and implemented formal performance measures. Appropriate control mechanisms will depend upon the underlying rationale for the alliance relationship, i.e., the strategic intent of the partners; the form of the alliance relationship; and the strategic objectives of the relationship. This context provides the basis for selecting evaluation criteria and methods of evaluation and implementing an alliance evaluation plan. For example, the evaluation criteria for a global airline alliance, reflecting the 'Balanced Scorecard' approach (Kaplan and Norton, 1996), and the several stages of management control activity is shown in Table 15.1.

Table 15.1 Selecting the evaluation criteria for a global airline alliance

Management control activities	Balanced Scorecard dimensions			
	Financial	*Customer focus*	*Internal business process*	*Learning and growth*
Planning	Profit by route and coverage of destinations	Identify potential customer groups not served by existing routes	Identify partner responsibilities	New ideas for the extension of the collaboration
Coordinating	Potential income from network	Use of airline lounges by partners' passengers	Savings from shared services	Increase in market share from collaborative routes
Communicating	Detailed financial reports by segment for passengers using alliance network	Potential increase in load factors from partners' customers	Process improvements initiated by partners relative to the alliance	Employee satisfaction regarding alliance
Evaluating	Revenue per seat mile from collaboration relative to potential	Repeat and new customer passenger miles by customer type and route	Provision of comparable service for customers on collaborative routes	Employee productivity by function and general service activity for collaborative routes
Deciding	Operating profit per seat mile from collaboration	Market share on collaborative routes	On-time performance on collaborative routes	Demand information by segment on collaborative routes
Implementing	Percentage contribution of collaboration load factor	Customer complaints from collaborative routes	Performance improvement and complaints reduction on collaborative routes	Staff turnover relative to collaborative routes

Source: Adapted from Cravens *et al.*, 2000.

This provides a generic template, but one which should be adapted and refined for specific application. The goal of establishing and clarifying the performance criteria for an alliance and evaluating performance against those criteria is, however, a general requirement.

15.8.6 Disengaging from alliances and networks

Vigilance and more thorough appraisal are likely to identify situations where it is desirable to end an alliance relationship. Research suggests that companies face important challenges in withdrawing or disengaging from alliances that are underperforming or have outlived their usefulness. For a start, companies may not recognise the life cycle underlying the alliance relationship, and treat alliances as though they were permanent organisational arrangements (Taylor, 2005). The problem is compounded because typically disengagement is not agreed at the outset of the alliance. It is highly desirable to negotiate exit options while still at the alliance formation stage, with clarity about the events or contingencies which will trigger the termination of the alliance.

It appears that part of the problem is that without clear agreement on how to withdraw from an alliance relationship, when tensions arise between partners, managers may be reluctant to report problems, fearing they will be blamed for the alliance's failure. Instead, they tend to blame their alliance counterparts. The typical outcome is likely to be a dysfunctional strategic alliance characterised by deep animosity between alliance managers, making negotiation of alliance termination highly problematic. It may be more effective to handle alliance disengagement with a core team of senior managers, chosen in part because they were not involved in the original alliance. A strong communications plan also assists in avoiding damage to the company's reputation during the break-up (Gulati *et al.*, 2007).

Summary

We have argued in this chapter that there are many factors compelling organisations to collaborate and form alliances with others, rather than to compete independently – we may be in an era of collaboration rather than competition. The network paradigm is impossible to ignore for two reasons: it may be how we take our strategy to market; and it may be how our competitors build their market power. The factors driving this process include market complexity and risk, skills and resource gaps, supply chain management imperatives, and the strategic priority of focusing on core competencies and outsourcing to partners for other activities and resources.

We attempted to identify the types of networks which are emerging in the modern marketplace. One approach looks at the type of relationship on which alliance is based and market volatility in order to identify the hollow network, the flexible network, the value-added and the virtual network. A broader view suggests that there are internal market networks, vertical market networks, intermarket or concentric networks and opportunity networks (Achrol, 1997). Related issues concerned the type of relationship ties between network members, ranging from outsourcing, through partnership, to joint venture and vertical integration.

The conclusion we reached at this point was that strategic alliances are a major competitive force, which in some industries like airlines, computing and telecommunications is replacing conventional competition between individual companies. However, the cases and studies available to date suggest that while the potential gains may be great, strategic alliances and networks carry major risks.

This led us to an important management agenda to be considered in evaluating the importance of strategic alliances and networks as part of marketing strategy. We suggest that in considering a strategy of alliance, managers should focus on the issue of core competencies brought to the alliance by each partner, and the benefits and vulnerabilities associated with focus and outsourcing, and the capabilities that a company has to manage its strategy through a very different organisational environment. Questions to raise regarding those managerial capabilities include: understanding the underlying drivers favouring collaboration strategies, the choice of partners, the facilitators and components important to effective collaboration, the ability to define and evaluate network effectiveness in achieving marketing goals, and the capacity of a network to deliver the customer value on which our marketing strategy is based. The redefinition of the role of marketing also falls into this area. Maintaining vigilance regarding changing circumstances and an effective alliance appraisal approach are priorities for managing in networked strategies. Managing disengagement or withdrawal from ineffective or damaging alliances may be a necessary consequence of improved appraisal and control.

Strategic alliances and networks are not a panacea for strategic problems. They are an important development with many potential benefits. They also carry major strategic risks and vulnerabilities, and demand new managerial skills. This is an issue requiring particularly careful and detailed analysis.

Case study UPS and FedEx turn focus to consumer behaviour

On the ground floor of United Parcel Service's $2.2bn Worldport Hub, workers are stuffing into huge airfreight containers some of the roughly 1.1m packages that the centre in Louisville, Kentucky, handles every night.

Most of the containers have sped through Worldport's maze of whirring conveyor belts and been reloaded in less than four hours. At 2.30am, some of the 100 or so flights that will carry the packages around the US and the world are starting to leave.

Amid the dazzling efficiency, however, is evidence of the significant challenge that UPS and FedEx, its main US rival, are facing. Many of the boxes bear the logo of Zappos.com, the internet footwear retailer. Another box contains frozen artificial skin for use in surgery, while one bears the simple legend, 'Live Tropical Fish'.

Online retailing and business-to-business ordering are driving up traffic volumes for both UPS and FedEx but also making flows harder to predict.

The question for both companies is whether management changes and technology investments can help them to avoid a repeat of the chaos that engulfed UPS last Christmas, when demand surged more than anticipated. Volumes on its busiest day, December 23, were 13 per cent up on 2012's peak and the network was clogged. Many packages were delivered after December 25.

The problems reflect the behaviour of the individual consumers who increasingly drive big operators' deliveries worldwide, according to Alan Braithwaite, a UK-based logistics consultant. They are more likely than logistics operators' corporate customers to order at the last minute.

'The peaks are getting even peakier,' he says.

Fewer goods are being delivered in bulk via single stops on vehicles' routes to retail outlets, according to Henry Maier, chief executive of FedEx Ground, the company's road-delivery division.

'Now those individual items get boxed up and sent to somebody's house, so that creates a stop,' Mr Maier says. 'The challenge across the industry is managing the stops.'

UPS is improving its management systems and investing $500m in extra capital spending this year to boost capacity, according to Kurt Kuehn, the group's chief financial officer.

'We're very focused on expanding capabilities and capacity to meet the current growth, not to mention the peak season,' Mr Kuehn says. 'We have what is in many ways an enviable problem.'

One of UPS's efficiency-boosting investments is on display at the Louisville Centennial Hub, a base for UPS's ground operations near Worldport. Jerry Durham, a driver, each morning consults a bank of computers running Orion, a new computer system, to work out the most efficient route between his scheduled drop-offs.

The technology has raised the average number of drop-offs per mile from 1.9 when drivers devised their own routes to 2.2 now, says Roger Hicks, UPS's business manager for Louisville East.

The system has overcome his initial scepticism, according to Mr Durham.

'I've gotten to like it a lot more,' he says.

Mr Maier praises new hand-held scanners for boosting FedEx's efficiency. The scanners know the GPS co-ordinates of every address in the US and will alert drivers if they appear to be delivering in the wrong place. Such technology helps to cut down worker errors, especially among temporary staff taken on for the peak season.

'It makes our temporary resources much more effective,' Mr Maier says.

An innovation at Centennial typifies UPS's approach. In the past year, sorters have been given technology that scans package labels and tells them into which delivery bag they should post them. The technology has cut down on wasteful 'mis-sorts'.

Mr Kuehn says most investments are focused on such local hubs, rather than the efficient Worldport, and predominantly into computer systems.

Yet, for UPS, last Christmas's biggest failing may have been in communication rather than in technology. UPS failed to spot its customers' higher than expected order volumes in time. Much of the short-term effort has focused on ensuring future volume forecasts and communications with customers are better than last year's. FedEx says that such forecasting also plays a key role in its peak-season planning.

'We're working with some large customers to get enhanced visibility,' Mr Kuehn says.

In the long run, meanwhile, both companies expect to overcome the challenges partly through making more of their facilities operate like Worldport.

FedEx already operates all 33 of its ground network's hubs in the US on Worldport's highly automated model, with minimal handling by humans. Mr Maier says it expects to start introducing such advanced technology in still more, smaller facilities.

For UPS, meanwhile, Worldport, the world's biggest fully automated package-handling facility, remains noticeably more advanced than smaller hubs such as Centennial, where much sorting is still by hand.

As the company adapts to the challenges of handling more shoes, medical supplies and fish, that will have to change, Mr Kuehn says.

'[Worldport is] a highly automated, incredible asset, driven by technology,' he says. 'There are several other generations of buildings around the country that we're going to be renovating to look more like Louisville.'

Customised needs

In the middle of a warehouse near the end of Louisville Airport's runway stands a line of heavy-duty freezers, an electronic stopwatch sitting on the lid of one. The stopwatch is intended to protect the delicate sheets of artificially-grown skin inside the freezers, used to treat diabetics' foot ulcers. Supervisors time how long each freezer is open when stocks are being retrieved, to ensure the temperature stays low enough.

The business in the warehouse illustrates how thoroughly UPS and other logistics companies have involved themselves in some customers' operations. Next to the skin freezers, workers are preparing to ship batches of influenza vaccine. In another section of the building, workers are putting together packages of mobile telephones for Sprint, the mobile telecoms company. They customise devices for customers with special requirements, including government departments that want employees' phone cameras disabled.

Such supply chain business is separate from the flagship express parcel operations of UPS, FedEx and other logistics operators but adds a vital extra dimension to the services they can offer companies. According to Rich Shaver, division manager for healthcare in UPS's Americas Central District, the growing popularity of outsourcing reflects the increasing pressure on healthcare companies to save money and compete more effectively.

'The customers have to have a competitive advantage,' he says. 'The only way they can have a competitive advantage is if they have a very nimble, flexible supply chain that at the same time is looking for what regulations and changes are coming.'

The healthcare business, unlike high technology, remains relatively conservative and goods are shipped mostly to retail outlets, hospitals and other corporate customers.

However, the Louisville warehouse already employs pharmacists to handle prescriptions for some goods heading direct to customers. The company is receiving increasing numbers of requests to suggest ways that customers can deliver more healthcare products direct to consumers, according to Mr Shaver.

'Most times, it's going to be a progressive, step-by-step process,' he says.

Source: from 'UPS and FedEx turn focus to consumer behaviour', *Financial Times,* 12/08/14 (Wright, R.).

Discussion questions

1 What issues are UPS and FedEx facing here?

2 How do UPS and FedEx contribute to their clients achieving a competitive advantage?

3 What are the drivers for collaboration in the examples given?

CHAPTER 16
STRATEGY IMPLEMENTATION AND INTERNAL MARKETING

Drawing a line between strategy and execution almost guarantees failure . . . It's a commonly held idea that strategy is distinct from execution, but this is a flawed assumption. The idea that a strategy can be brilliant and its execution poor is simply wrong.

(Martin, 2010)

Where is the value zone? . . . In the interface between employee and customer . . . So what business should the management of the company be in? Enthusing, enabling, encouraging and creating an environment so employees can create value.

(Nayar, 2010 – CEO of HCL Technologies and author of *Employees first, customers second* quoted in Davidson, 2010)

GM backs away from drive to end use of 'Chevy'

General Motors was forced into an embarrassing U-turn on Thursday, distancing itself from an internal memo that had instructed employees to stop using 'Chevy' as an abbreviation for the Detroit carmaker's flagship Chevrolet brand.

After being pilloried for what it described as 'a poorly worded memo', GM said in a statement: 'we love Chevy . . . In no way are we discouraging customers or fans from using the name.'

Bloggers and other commentators not only poked fun at the attempt to stop the usage one of America's most affectionate abbreviations for a brand but also questioned whether the instruction was a sign of widening turmoil under GM's new chairman and chief executive, Ed Whitacre.

Since he took over six months ago, Mr Whitacre has made a series of management changes and other moves designed to encourage speedier decision-making and greater accountability.

The memo, first published by the *New York Times*, was signed by two senior Chevrolet managers.

Source: Getty Images.

'We'd ask that whether you're talking to a dealer, reviewing dealer advertising, or speaking with friends and family, that you communicate our brand as Chevrolet moving forward,' the memo said.

'When you look at the most recognised brands throughout the world, such as Coke or Apple . . . one of the things they all focus on is the consistency of their branding,' the authors added, apparently forgetting that Coke is an abbreviation for Coca-Cola.

The memo ended by telling employees that anyone using Chevy instead of Chevrolet would have to put a 25-cent coin into a plastic can. The proceeds would be used for 'team-building activities'.

The Chevy monicker is part of US folklore, mentioned in songs and even in GM's own advertising.

The carmaker recently launched a review to devise a more coherent marketing strategy. Mark Reuss, head of GM's North American operations, told the

Financial Times last month that 'Chevrolet needs to stand for a few things that everyone can understand. We need to be very concise and understandable.'

Source: from 'GM backs away from drive to end use of '"Chevy"', *Financial Times*, 10/06/10 (Simonin, B.).

Discussion questions

1 What can the impact of an internal memo be on marketing?

2 What could GM do now?

Introduction

This chapter takes marketing strategy further by considering strategy implementation, and particularly the role of internal marketing in enhancing and sustaining a company's ability to compete. There are several different models of internal marketing which overlap to a degree and require clarification (since as a consequence there are a number of different roles that internal marketing can play in a company's strategic development in different situations). There are important linkages to consider between internal marketing and certain of the issues we have examined earlier. Our focus in this chapter is on a company's implementation capabilities and the essential fit between strategic choices and the ability to execute those choices. The ability to execute is perhaps the most critical capability of all.

In an interesting example, in 2011 Google set out to build a value chain in mobile phones to challenge Apple's business model, integrating software and hardware businesses. Google acquired Motorola's mobile phone business for $12.5 billion – its largest ever acquisition. As creator of the fast-growing Android operating system, Google wanted to be able to make its own smartphones and tablet computers. Motorola's 17,000 patents were also important, for example getting Google into the consumer living room via Motorola's TV set-top boxes. However, as a software company, Google now faced the challenge of running manufacturing plants, controlling inventory, and managing relationships between carriers and retailers. The move also took Google into competition with existing Google partners already licensing its Android operating system. Google had earlier attempted to manufacture laptops running its Chrome software to rival Microsoft's Windows, but the execution problems forced it to work instead with brand-name hardware manufacturers like Acer and Samsung. With Motorola, the companies were separated by half a continent, a different legacy (Google is a software company and Motorola is an 80-year-old hardware operation), and very different corporate cultures. By 2012, Google was looking to reduce Motorola staffing by 20 per cent to regain profitability in the business, and its intentions for the business had become unclear. Early in 2014, Google sold Motorola's mobile phone operations to Lenovo for $2.91 billion, getting the world's dominant mobile operating systems company out of the business of making mobile phones. The implementation risks in the Google strategy had always been high, and they ended up walking away (Fitzgerald, 2012; Berman, 2012). Implementation capabilities are a critical consideration in making strategic choices.

Much thinking and practice in strategic marketing is concerned with *managing relationships:* with the customer (**see** Chapter 13), and with partners in strategic alliances (see Chapter 15). However, a further aspect of relationship management and relationship marketing is the relationship with the employees and managers, upon whose skills, commitment and performance the success of a marketing strategy unavoidably relies. This is the *internal market* inside the company. The thinking in an increasing number of companies is that building effective relationships with customers and alliance partners will depend in part (and possibly in large part), on the strengths and types of relationships built with employees and managers inside the organisation. The goal may be for all employees to become 'brand ambassadors' – brand owners such as Unilever, SABMiller, and BT are among those with established internal marketing excellence programmes to pursue this goal (*Brand Strategy*, 2006). At Honda, for example, all new staff receive the *Book of Everything* containing the normal employee handbook information but also extensive explanation of the Honda brand philosophy – 'spreading 'Honda-ness' and turning people into brand ambassadors' (Croft, 2007). In some companies, the emphasis has turned from internal communications to internal branding to build employee understanding and buy-in to corporate brand values (Dowdy, 2001). For instance, faced with a drain of key employees to Google, Microsoft appointed a Chief Happiness Officer, to focus on retention of key 'Microserfs' and improve morale (Conlin and Greene, 2007).

While some of these approaches may seem extreme, employee buy-in becomes particularly significant in times of change and repositioning, as well as in recovery from the economic downturn and adjusting to more demanding customers whose priorities fundamentally changed in recession. For example, fast food giant McDonalds pursued a 'balanced lifestyles' positioning to counter links between its products and obesity (MacArthur, 2005). Part of this strategy was aiming the global 'I'm Loving It' slogan at employees as well as consumers (Grant and Foster, 2005). Cynics parodied McDonald's campaign as trying to suggest to employees that 'It's not a McJob, it's a McCalling' (Helm and Arndt, 2007). Nonetheless, with a stronger employee buy-in, clearer competitive positioning, competitive prices and new menus, as well as challenges to Starbucks as a coffee shop, McDonalds performed strongly through economic downturn, although is doing less well in recovery.

Similarly, recovery of market position for Heinz's UK division was based not simply on launching new products but also on reinvigorating employee and manager morale and engagement with the business: Monday morning product tasting sessions; monthly meetings with all employees to obtain their views on issues; managers expected to work in the factories and watch how food is produced; a *Dragons' Den* programme for staff to pitch their ideas for new products (Waples, 2008).

Importantly, it should be noted that there are various indications that employees in companies worldwide show evidence of detachment from their work – they simply do not care very much about the job in hand (Stern, 2008). Conversely, the characteristics of organisations which display high levels of employee engagement are that they: have high ethical standards; show clear core values; have employees who respect management and are treated with respect; and, where management seeks the opinions of employees (MacLeod and Brady, 2007). For example, it has been suggested that one of the worst outcomes of the attacks on Nike for their use of Asian 'sweatshops' to produce their sports shoes was the negative impact on employee morale. It is perhaps surprising that many organisations fail to meet these basic criteria and consequently suffer in their ability to deliver their strategies to the marketplace.

Further, it is worth recalling from the commentary in Chapter 15, concerning strategic relationships and the increasing dependence of company on cross-boundary collaboration, that building and sustaining effective ties with allies is a major challenge. We saw that the field of strategic alliances and partnerships is full of failed relationships. The reliance on third parties brings significant political, reputational and logistical risks for a company (Beattie, 2005). Yet, as we have seen, networked organisations based on collaboration are core to the success of companies like IBM and Procter & Gamble. While internal marketing is normally framed in terms of winning the support of managers and employees inside the company for strategic change, increasingly that internal marketplace will extend to partner organisations, whose buy-in is also needed to make strategy implementation effective.

We have also emphasised the importance of *competitive differentiation* to build market position. Yet truly exploiting a company's potential competitiveness and its capabilities in reality is often in the hands of what Evert Gummesson (1990) called the 'part-time marketers', i.e. the people who actually run the business and provide the real scope for competitive differentiation. Indeed, in some situations, the employees of a company may be the most important resource that provides differentiation. Certainly, research at Northwestern University found internal marketing to be one of the top three determinants of a company's financial performance – companies with better integration of internal and external marketing report better financial results (Chang, 2005).

In a similar way, the growing emphasis on competing through superior *service quality* relies ultimately on the behaviour and effectiveness of the people who deliver the service, rather than the people who design the strategy. For example, when the Hampton Inn hotel chain in the US was ready to roll out 122 changes to its products and services, its new marketing campaign was 'Make It Hampton', but it was aimed at hotel managers and employees not guests. Building internal brand enthusiasm and employee motivation involved: a giant model of a hotel to showcase the improvements and allow employees to experience them, motivational conference calls, focus groups, targeted newsletters and training materials. The end of the first phase of 'Make It Hampton' saw a five per cent increase in market share, and a similar growth in the percentage of highly satisfied customers (Drake *et al.,* 2005).

Increasingly it is recognised that one of the greatest barriers to effectiveness in strategic marketing lies not just in a company's ability to conceive and design innovative marketing strategies or to produce sophisticated marketing plans, but in its ability to gain the effective and enduring *implementation* of those strategies. One route to planning and operationalizing implementation in strategic marketing is 'strategic internal marketing' (Piercy 2009a).

Practical applications suggest that, depending on the particular circumstances, the internal marketing process might include the following types of activity and programmes:

- Gaining the *support* of key decision makers for our plans – but also all that those plans imply in terms of the need to acquire personnel and financial resources, possibly in conflict with established company 'policies', and to get what is needed from other functions like operations and finance departments to implement a marketing strategy effectively;
- Changing some of the *attitudes and behaviour* of employees and managers, who are working at the key interfaces with customers and distributors, to those required to make plans work effectively (but also reinforcing effective attitudes and behaviour as well);
- Winning *commitment* to making the plan work and 'ownership' of the key problem-solving tasks from those units and individuals in the firm whose working support is needed; and
- Ultimately, managing incremental *changes in the culture* from 'the way we always do things' to 'the way we *need* to do things to be successful' and to make the marketing strategy work.

The potential importance of internal marketing to relationship marketing strategies, to strategic alliances, to competitive differentiation, to delivering superior service quality and above all to effective marketing implementation is underlined by the growing emphasis placed by companies on this issue. Nonetheless, studies suggest that many organisations reveal an inadequate state of internal marketing – they cannot deliver their brand propositions, for example, because of lack of investment in the internal company marketplace (*Marketing Week,* 2003).

Certainly, it remains true that internal marketing means very different things in different companies and different situations. If we are to evaluate the potential contribution of internal marketing to building and implementing our (external) marketing strategy and achieving our chosen position in the market, then we need to consider such issues as the following:

- the types of internal marketing practice in companies;
- how internal marketing can be planned as part of our competitive strategy;

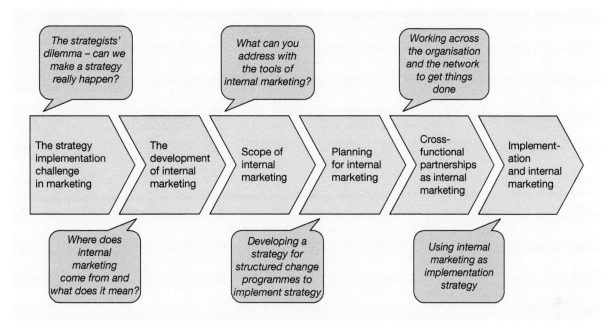

Figure 16.1 Key issues in looking at strategy implementation and internal marketing

- the implication for other significant relationships such as the potential partnership between marketing and human resource management within organisations to achieve the effective implementation of marketing strategies; and
- building implementation capabilities as a long-term marketing resource.

However, first we place internal marketing in the context of strategy implementation, and the challenge that execution poses for marketing managers. Our view of internal marketing is that it provides a model to facilitate a company's effective execution of marketing strategies.

Attention to marketing strategy and competitive positioning decisions by executives needs to be placed in the context of implementation capabilities and the need for effective change management in execution. The structure of our approach to these issues and the key questions to be raised are summarised in Figure 16.1.

16.1   The strategy implementation challenge in marketing

Achieving more effective implementation or execution of marketing strategies remains a high priority for many organisations, because of the long history of strategy implementation failures which has been experienced by many. For example, on the general strategy front, Miller (2002) suggests that organisations fail to implement more than 70 per cent of their new strategic initiatives.

It is apparent that implementation is not generally well understood, as compared to the issues in strategy generation, and one large-scale international study suggests that the problem is compounded by the myths surrounding strategy implementation:

- **Myth 1 – Execution equals alignment** – actually companies seem pretty good at cascading goals down the organisation but less so at managing coordination across the units and functions in the company.
- **Myth 2 – Execution means sticking to the plan** – companies invest heavily in formal planning and budgeting, but are less skilled at real-time adjustment to changed circumstances and agility to achieve effective implementation.

- **Myth 3 – Communication equals understanding** – managers are shocked at how poorly their strategy is understood throughout the organisation in spite of large investments in 'communicating', which results in messages which are unclear and change too often.
- **Myth 4 – A performance culture drives execution** – in reality execution is not just about performance-orientation; a culture that supports execution must recognise and reward other things as well, such as agility, teamwork and ambition.
- **Myth 5 – Execution should be driven from the top** – in fact, in complex organisations, execution lives and dies with 'distributed leaders' – the middle managers and technical experts who run critical parts of the business. They are the ones who represent management to most employees, partners and customers. Execution should be driven from the middle but guided from the top (Sull *et al.*, 2015).

The authors of this study suggest we should think carefully about what is really needed to achieve strategy implementation and the worry that several widely-held beliefs about how to implement strategy are actually misleading.

In fact, there are many pitfalls faced in moving from strategies and plans to effective implementation and the changes that are usually involved for an organisation, its people, and its partners. One listing of implementation pitfalls likely to resonate with managers' experiences identifies the following issues:

- **Strategic inertia** – things never get started because executives resist change or fail to give it priority.
- **Lack of stakeholder commitment** – not having everyone on board, particularly at middle management levels, where progress can be blocked.
- **Strategic drift** – a lack of focus on where the strategy should end up, leading to failure to reach that destination.
- **Strategic 'dilution'** – an absence of strong drive behind the strategy means that managers give more priority to operational decisions than strategic goals.
- **Failure to understand progress** – not having the appropriate metrics to monitor progress towards strategic goals.
- **Initiative fatigue** – too many 'top priority' projects lead to cynicism and inadequate emphasis on the strategy.
- **Impatience** – expecting results too quickly, and giving up when the reality is slower.
- **No celebrating success** – failing to recognise and reward milestones that lead towards the strategic goal (Freedman, 2003).

Indeed, there is a strong argument that much of the implementation problem comes from the fact that generally managers are trained to plan, not to execute, and frequently are judged on their capabilities for managing day-to-day operations rather than strategic initiatives. The problem is likely to be worse when execution is seen as a low-level responsibility in the organisation (Hrebiniak, 2006). In fact, the reality is that strategy and implementation are interdependent – strategic choices should be linked to implementation capabilities, and implementation capabilities should be developed in line with strategic imperatives, and the dichotomy between strategy and implementation is false and unproductive (Cespedes and Piercy, 1996).[2] Martin (2010) describes this as the 'execution trap', and argues that drawing a line between strategy and execution almost guarantees failure. Nonetheless, the tendency to separate strategy from implementation remains in organisations and creates obstacles and challenges in executing strategic initiatives.

Hrebiniak (2006) draws on a range of research studies and discussions with managers to identify the following factors as the top obstacles to effective strategy execution:

- **Inability to manage change effectively and overcome resistance to change** – managing change well is vital to effective strategy implementation. Nonetheless, where change impacts on corporate culture, then moving too fast may be dangerous.
- **Poor or vague strategy** – good implementation capabilities cannot compensate for a strategy which is weak or ambiguous. Strategy drives execution, and if strategy is unclear or weak, then implementation is irrelevant.

- **Not having guidelines or a model to guide strategy implementation efforts** – managers want a logical model to guide implementation efforts and actions, particularly in translating strategic imperatives into practical actions.
- **Poor or inadequate information sharing among individuals/units responsible for strategy execution** – poor sharing of information or poor knowledge transfer and unclear responsibility and accountability make it unlikely strategy implementation will be effective.
- **Trying to execute a strategy that conflicts with the existing power structure** – working against the power structure presents a major obstacle to implementation effectiveness, and underlines the importance of gaining the support of the influential in the organisation and forming coalitions to share implementation responsibility.
- **Unclear responsibility or accountability for implementation decisions or actions** – lack of clarity in responsibility for implementation and the achievement of measurable progress presents another obstacle to effective implementation (Hrebiniak, 2006).

Similarly, it has been suggested that:

One key reason why implementation fails is that practicing executives, managers and supervisors do not have practical, yet theoretically sound, models to guide their actions during implementation. Without adequate models, they try to implement strategies without a good understanding of the multiple factors that must be addressed, often simultaneously, to make implementation work.
(Alexander, 1991)

Implementation capabilities

It emerges from the debate about execution that there is a corporate resource that we can label as 'implementation capabilities'. Certainly, the capability of people and organisations that allows them to get things done is not neatly defined by academics, but is instantly recognisable by executives. However, it is also apparent that a company's implementation capabilities may be:

- **time-specific** – things change, sometimes radically;
- **culture-specific** – what works in one organisation may not work elsewhere;
- **partial** – being good at doing one type of thing does not necessarily transfer to others;
- **latent** – we may not have learned how to do things;
- **internally inconsistent** – some parts of the organisation are better at execution than are others;
- **strategy-specific** – we are good at doing one type of business; and,
- **person-specific** – some individual managers may be the ones who are best at getting things done (Piercy, 1998).

Careful thought is needed in identifying the location of implementation capabilities in the organisation and particularly the people most likely to drive change effectively. It is interesting that one of the first management matrices was produced by Helmuth von Moltke, head of the Prussian army a century-and-a-half ago. He divided his officers on two criteria: clever versus dim, and lazy versus energetic, to identify the following categories:

- **Dim and lazy** – good at executing orders.
- **Dim and energetic** – very dangerous because they take the wrong decisions and drive them forward.
- **Clever and energetic** – excellent staff officers.
- **Clever and lazy** – top field commanders who get results (Kellaway, 2015).

Evaluating and assessing executives for implementation capabilities is an important stage in preparing for effective execution.

The important point is that implementation capabilities are not a given that should be taken for granted, but something to be evaluated carefully and enhanced where possible. One implication is that trying to create and execute a strategy for which a company lacks implementation capabilities carries a high risk of failure and loss – consider the Google–Motorola example discussed earlier. Further, enhancing and sustaining implementation capabilities may be one of the most important elements of managing strategic change in a company.

While it is not a complete answer to overcoming implementation obstacles, internal marketing provides us with a set of tools to address some of the major barriers faced to the effective implementation of marketing strategies, and managing the associated organisational changes. It provides us with a model for structuring and managing the implementation process, defining responsibilities, evaluating progress, and managing the cross-functional relationships important to strategy execution. It provides a way of enhancing and applying implementation capabilities.

16.2 The development of internal marketing

Conventional training and development of marketing executives, quite reasonably, focuses primarily on the *external* environment of customers, competitors and markets, and the matching of corporate resources to marketplace targets. The internal marketing logic is that while analysing markets and developing strategies to exploit the external marketplace is quite appropriately the central focus, it is frequently not enough on its own to achieve the effective implementation of marketing strategies. In addition to developing marketing programmes and strategies aimed at the external marketplace, in order to achieve the organisational change that is needed to make those strategies work, there is a need to carry out essentially the same process for the *internal marketplace* within companies.

However, because it is still relatively new, the term: 'internal marketing is difficult to pin down to a specific definition', which suggests a dilemma:

> What to call this emerging area of internal alignment, engagement or whatever. Clearly, the new discipline is holistic. It must be inclusive. It is cross-functional and not just involve selling, service and operations. Most importantly, it must focus on delivery of corporate promises, both internally and externally.
> *(Schultz, 2006)*

In essence, the internal marketplace is made up of the people, the culture, the systems, the procedures, the structures and developments inside the company, where skills, resources, participation, support and commitment are needed to implement marketing strategies. The internal marketplace extends to include our partners in alliances and network organisations (see Chapter 15).

It seems that the reality in many organisations is that an assumption is made by executives that marketing plans and strategies will 'sell' themselves to those in the company whose support and commitment are needed. When made explicit in this way, it is apparent that this is just as naive as making similar assumptions that, if they are good enough, products will 'sell themselves' to external customers. It is often surprising that those same executives who have been trained and developed to cope with behavioural problems – like 'irrational' behaviour by consumers and buyers, or the problems of managing power and conflict in the distribution channel, or the need to communicate to buyers through a mix of communications vehicles and media, or the problems of trying to outguess competitors – have taken so long to arrive at the conclusion that these same issues have to be coped with *inside* the company. Real commitment to strategic marketing must involve a managerial role of creating the conditions necessary to permit strategic change to happen.

What we are calling strategic internal marketing here has the goal of developing a marketing programme aimed at the internal marketplace in the company that *parallels* and *matches* the marketing programme aimed at the external marketplace of customers and competitors. This model comes from the simple observation that the implementation of external marketing strategies implies changes of various kinds within organisations – in the allocation of resources, in the culture of 'how we do things here', and even in the organisational structure needed to deliver marketing strategies to customer segments. In practical terms, those same techniques of analysis and communication, which are used for the external marketplace, can be adapted and used to market our plans and strategies to important targets within the company and to alliance partners. The goals of the internal marketing plan are taken directly from the implementation requirements for the external marketing plan, and the objectives to be pursued.

There is certainly well-established historical precedent for use of the terms 'internal marketing' and the 'internal customer' in the marketing and services literature. We see these developments as important for two main reasons. First, the internal marketing paradigm provides an easily accessible mechanism for executives to analyse the organisational issues which may need to be addressed in implementing marketing strategies. Quite simply, concepts of marketing programmes and targets are familiar to marketing executives and they are 'comfortable' with them. And second, the internal marketing model provides a language which actually legitimises focusing attention on issues like power, culture and political behaviour which appear quite often to be avoided by executives as somehow 'improper'.

16.3   The scope of internal marketing

It follows from the emergence of the internal marketing paradigm from diverse conceptual sources that the practice of internal marketing and its potential contribution to marketing strategy are similarly varied. It is possible to consider the following 'types' of internal marketing, although they are probably not equal in importance:

- internal marketing that focuses on the development and delivery of high standards of *service quality* and customer satisfaction;
- internal marketing that is concerned primarily with development *internal communications programmes* to provide employees with information and to win their support;
- internal marketing which is used as a systematic approach to managing the *adoption of innovations* within an organisation;
- internal marketing concerned with providing products and services to users *inside the organisation;* and
- internal marketing as the *implementation strategy* for our marketing plans.

16.3.1 Internal marketing and service quality

The original and most extensive use of internal marketing was in efforts to improve the quality of service at the point-of-sale in services businesses, like banking, leisure, retailing, and so on – the so-called 'moment of truth' for the services marketer. Some call this 'selling the staff', because the 'product' promoted is the person's job as a creator of customer service and value. This tends to impact on customer care training programmes and similar initiatives. These types of internal marketing programme are, in practice, essentially tactical and often restricted to the operational level of the organisation.

The logic is that marketplace success is frequently largely dependent on employees who are far removed from the excitement of creating marketing strategies – service engineers, customer services departments, production and finance personnel dealing with customers, field sales personnel, and so on. As we noted earlier, these are all people Evert Gummesson (1990) called 'part-time marketers' – they impact directly and significantly on customer relationships, but are normally not part of any formal marketing organisation, nor are they typically within the marketing department's direct control.

Indeed, US research suggests we should think more carefully, for example, about the impact of the organisation's external marketing communications on employees – as 'advertising's second audience' (Gilly and Wolfinbarger, 1996). Actually, the chances are that employees are aware and influenced by our advertising as much as our external customers, so the suggestion is that we should use that awareness productively to deliver messages to employees.

There are a growing number of cases of companies whose service quality excellence has been driven by explicit attention to internal marketing. Southwest Airlines is the much-admired originator of the 'no frills' airline model, and has achieved not only outstanding profit performance in a difficult sector, but has also regularly won industry awards for service quality and low levels of customer complaints. From the outset, Southwest's mission statement said, 'Above all, employees will be provided the same concern, respect and caring attitude within the organisation that they are expected to share externally with every Southwest customer'. The company uses high employee morale and service quality to achieve excellent profitability. Tactics include offering employees a vision that provides purpose and meaning to the workplace, competing aggressively for the most talented people, providing skills and knowledge, but also emphasising teamwork and motivation, and ensuring that organisational management understands the internal customer. The effect is an integrated internal marketing approach that drives service quality. Southwest shows the positive impact of internal marketing on employees, external customers and performance. Southwest's success is based in large part on its employees' positive attitudes, high productivity, and customer orientation (Czaplewski *et al.*, 2001).

Similarly, Marriott is a company that stands out in the luxury hotel business for the way it treats its employees to bolster its higher service strategy. Its approach includes pre-shift dance sessions for housekeepers, Oscar-style award nights, free travel for some, and clear career development opportunities, and consequently employee retention is high. The company believes that a seasoned workforce does a better job and costs less money (Gallagher, 2015).

It can be argued that there is no one 'right' strategy in any given product market situation, but there are certainly good and bad ways of *delivering* market strategies, which determine if they succeed or fail. The critical issue is becoming the consistency between strategies, tactics and implementation actions. This suggests that real culture change is a central part of the process of going to market effectively. At its simplest, the disgruntled employee produces the disgruntled customer. Bonoma (1990) summarised this point succinctly: 'treat your employees like customers, or your customers will get treated like employees'.

However, it is apparent that successfully exploiting the linkage between employee and customer satisfaction may not always be straightforward. Research into the way in which customer satisfaction is measured and managed in British companies is revealing (Piercy, 1995). Studies suggest that:

1   There is a need to create *clarity* for all employees regarding customer service quality policies and customer satisfaction targets. It is not enough to pay lip-service to these ideals and to expect success in attaining them. The starting point must be to identify what has to be achieved in customer satisfaction to implement specific market strategies, and to position the company against the competition in a specific market. It is unlikely that achieving what is needed will be free from cost. We need to take a realistic view of the time needed and the real costs of implementation in aligning the internal market with the external market.

2   *Internal processes and barriers* suggest the need to consider both the internal and external markets faced in implementing customer satisfaction measurement and management systems. To ignore the internal market is to risk actually damaging the company's capacity to achieve and improve customer satisfaction in the external market. If, for example, management uses customer feedback in a negative and coercive way, then it may reduce

employee enthusiasm for customer service, or create 'game-playing' behaviour where people compete for 'Brownie points' in the system at the expense of both the company and the customer. This said, we have also to recognise not just the complementarity between internal and external markets, but the potential for conflict of interest. Achieving target levels of customer service and satisfaction may require managers and employees to change the way they do things and to make sacrifices they do not want to make. This may take more than simple advocacy or management threat.

3 Related to the above argument, recognising the internal market suggests that there may be a need for a structured and planned *internal marketing programme* to achieve the effective implementation of customer satisfaction measurement and management. This has been described elsewhere as 'marketing our customers to our employees' (Piercy, 2009a), and can be built into the implementation process to address the needs of the internal customer and to confront the types of internal processual barrier we have encountered.

4 Also related to the recognition of the internal market is the need to question the *relationship* between internal and external customer satisfaction. This can be discussed with executives using the structure shown in Figure 16.2. This suggests four possible scenarios that result when internal and external customer satisfaction are compared:

(a) **Synergy,** which is what we hope for, when internal and external customer satisfaction are high, and we see them as sustainable and self-regenerating. As one hotel manager explained it: 'I know that we are winning on customer service when my operational staff come to me and complain about how I am getting in their way in providing customer service, and tell me to get my act together!' This is the 'happy customers and happy employees' situation, assumed by many to be obvious and easily achieved.

(b) **Coercion** is where we achieve high levels of external customer satisfaction by changing the behaviour of employees through management direction and control systems. In the short term this may be the only option, but it may be very difficult and expensive to sustain this position in the longer term, and we give up flexibility for control.

(c) **Alienation** is where we have low levels of satisfaction internally and externally, and we are likely to be highly vulnerable to competitive attack on service quality, and to the instability in our competitive capabilities produced by low staff morale and high staff turnover.

(d) **Internal euphoria** is where we have high levels of satisfaction in the internal market, but this does not translate into external customer satisfaction – for example,

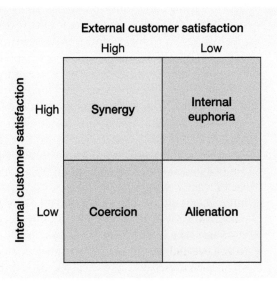

Figure 16.2
Customer
satisfaction in the
internal market and
the external market

if internal socialisation and group cohesiveness actually shut out the paying customer in the external market. These scenarios are exaggerated, but have provided a useful way of confronting these issues with executives.

5 A critical mistake is to ignore the real *costs and challenges* in sustaining high service quality levels and the limitation which may exist in a company's capabilities for improving customer satisfaction levels. While advocacy is widespread and the appeal is obvious, achieving the potential benefits requires more planning and attention to implementation realities than is suggested by the existing conventional literature.

16.3.2 Internal marketing as internal communications

As well as customer care training and a focus on service quality, internal marketing may also be seen as internal communications. In fact, the largest growth in this area has been investment by companies in broader internal communications programmes of various kinds – where 'communications' is understood as providing our employees with information and delivering messages which support the business strategy. The goal of internal communications is normally to build both understanding and commitment. Often, these activities tend to be a responsibility of the human resource department. One industry study (Pounsford, 1994) suggested that managers saw the role of internal communications in the terms and with the advantages shown in Table 16.1.

The manifestations of this form of internal marketing include: company newsletters, employee conferences and training, video-conferencing, satellite TV transmissions, interactive video, corporate social media platforms, e-mail, and so on. Increasingly, creating dialogue within an organisation and encouraging employee involvement can involve approaches like web-based internal blogs (Hathi, 2007). These delivery mechanisms are important, but are in danger of obscuring an important point. Instructing and informing people about strategic developments is not the same as winning their real involvement and participation. Real communication is a two-way process – listening as well as informing. This may be why internal communications appear ineffective in some companies. There is a risk that internal communications programmes become about telling and persuading, not listening. This may be said to be internal *selling* not internal *marketing*.

Indeed, large companies like Microsoft and Germany's SAP have an organisational role for a 'Chief Storyteller' to promote storytelling as internal communication related to management, innovation and change to staff and investors, although some commentators are sceptical about their value (Hill, 2014).

An interesting illustration of the gains from two-way communications comes from Dana Corp, the US car parts manufacturer. At that company, the 'suggestions box' is described by the CEO as 'a core part of our value system'. Employees contribute ideas to improve operations and service, and 70 per cent are actually used. Dana is an example of an organisation where employees have taken a share of the responsibility for keeping the company competitive. This underlines the important practical difference between producing company newsletters and taking internal communications seriously.

Indeed, some major companies, such as Procter and Gamble and Cisco Systems, are actively seeking out the employees who are most influential inside the organisation because of their social links and social media communications. The logic is to harness the clout of these influencers to identify new product opportunities, get other employees on board with big changes, and spread information throughout the organisation. The twenty-first century is very much the era of the network (Feintzeig, 2014; Mattu, 2011). Others use 'reverse mentoring' to have employees mentor managers – for example informing them about the reality of social media or bridging the 'generation gap' so managers understand younger consumers and employees better – an established practice at Tesco, Deloitte's and GE (Jacobs, 2013).

Table 16.1 The role of internal communications

Perceived role	Illustrative comments
Team building	Educate employees about breadth and diversity of the organisation.
	Assist cooperation between divisions.
Damage control	Prevent managers getting communications wrong.
	Suppress bad news.
	Counter pessimism.
Morale builders	Build confidence.
	Increase motivation.
Involvement	Represent employee opinions upwards.
	Create channel to share problems/values.
	Increase people recognition.
Change management	Increase understanding of the need for change.
	Test new ideas.
	Help people relate to rapidly changing environment.
Goal-setting	Help organisation steer in a coordinated direction.
	Provide focus on corporate goals.
	Generate support for policies.

16.3.3 Internal marketing and innovation management

Somewhat different is the use of the internal marketing framework to place, and gain use of, innovations like computers and electronic communications in the IT field. These applications use tools of market analysis and planning to cope with and avoid resistance and to manage the process of change. This may be particularly important where the effectiveness of a marketing strategy relies on the adoption of new technologies and ways of working. The argument here is that people in an organisation are 'customers' for our ideas and innovations. This view encourages us to consider:

- **looking at customer needs** – even in hierarchical companies people are not robots waiting to be told what to do, so making the effort to understand their needs increases the likely effectiveness of innovation;
- **delivering the goods** – the needs of customers tell us what matters most to them;
- **raising unrealistic expectations** – is as dangerous with internal customers as it is with external customers (Divita, 1996).

For example, the use of technology by a geographically dispersed salesforce in one company was guided by the analysis of the 'internal market' using the classic diffusion of innovation model to identify opinion leaders as key influencers in the adoption process. Similarly, the BT problem of marketing its information systems and services to its internal customers was addressed through the same principles used to market solutions to the organisation's external customers: segmentation, targeting, and positioning IS solutions to the internal customer base (Morgan, 2004).

16.3.4 Internal markets instead of external markets for products and services

The terms 'internal market' and 'internal marketing' have been applied to internal relationships between different parts of the same organisation – making them suppliers and customers as a way of improving the focus on efficiency and value. This is common in total quality management programmes, and in wider applications like attempted reforms of the UK National Health Service.

This can lead to some interesting issues. For example, work with the R&D division of a major brewery suggested that the internal customer issues were really about the type and degree of dependence between the internal supplier (in this case the provider of R&D solutions to process problems in the brewery) and the internal customer (here the production and sales units of the brewery), which in turn reflects the freedom of either internal supplier or customer to deal with third parties outside the company.

16.3.5 Strategic internal marketing

Strategic internal marketing (SIM) is an approach to the structured planning of marketing strategy implementation, and analysis of underlying implementation problems in an organisation. This form of internal marketing is a direct parallel to our conventional external marketing strategy and marketing programme, which aims at winning the support, cooperation and commitment we need inside the company, if our external market strategies are to work. This is a somewhat different view of internal marketing compared to those discussed **above,** although it is informed by the other types of internal marketing which have a longer history. The key underlying issue here is the organisational and cultural change needed to make marketing strategies happen.

A structure for an internal marketing programme is shown in Figure 16.3. The underlying rationale is that the easiest way to make practical progress with this type of internal marketing, and to establish what it may achieve, is to use exactly the same structures that we use for planning *external* marketing. This suggests that we should think in terms of integrating the elements needed for an internal marketing mix or programme, based on our analysis of the opportunities and threats in the internal marketplace represented by the company with which we are working. This is shown in Figure 16.3 as a formal and legitimate part of the planning process.

In this model, we take the internal marketing programme not only as an *output* of the planning process and the external marketing programme, but also as an *input*, i.e. constraints and barriers in the internal marketplace should be considered and analysed as a part of the planning at both strategic and tactical levels. For the proposals to make sense in practice, we rely on this iterative relationship.

The starting point for this approach is that the marketing strategy and the planning process may define an external marketing programme in the conventional way, and less conventionally the internal barriers suggest that some external strategies are not capable of being implemented in the time-scale concerned, and we have to feed back into the planning process the message that some adjustments are needed while there is still time to make those adjustments to plans.

More positively, however, it is equally true that our analysis of the internal market may suggest new opportunities and neglected company resources which should be exploited, which in turn impact on our external marketing plan and thus on the planning process. What we are trying to make explicit for executives is the need to balance the impact of both internal and external market attributes on the strategic assumptions that they make in planning.

The structure of such an internal marketing programme is suggested in Figure 16.4 and can be presented to executives in the following terms:

- **The product.** At the simplest level the 'product' consists of the marketing strategies and the marketing plan. Implied, however, is that the product to be 'sold' is those values, attitudes and behaviours which are needed to make the marketing plan work effectively. These hidden dimensions of the product may range from increased budgets and different resource allocations, to changed control systems and criteria used to evaluate

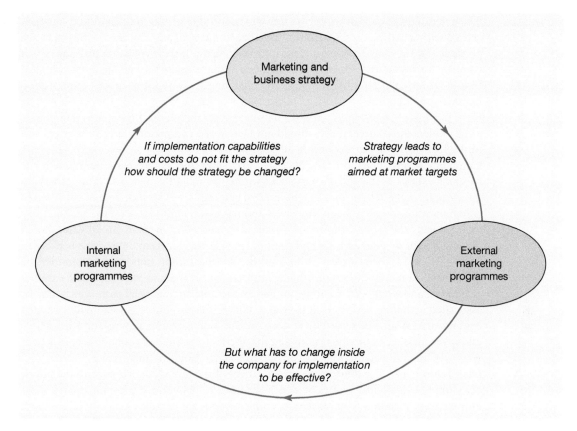

Figure 16.3 Internal and external marketing

Figure 16.4
Content and
structure of
internal marketing
programmes

Source: Adapted from
Piercy (2009a).

Programme	Contents	Examples
Product	The strategy and the plan, including the values, attitudes and behaviours needed to make them work	*For example, the written plan, the new company initiative*
Price	What we are asking internal customers to 'pay' – other projects abandoned, personal and psychological adjustment to change	*For example, stepping out of comfort zones for new types of operations*
Communications	Media and messages to inform and persuade	*For example, reports, plans, presentations, videos, roadshows*
Distribution	Physical and social venues for delivering the product and communications	*For example, meetings, workgroups, training sessions and workshops, informal meetings, social occasions*

performance, to changed ways of handling customers at the point of sale. At the extreme the product is the person's job – as it is redefined and reshaped by the market strategy so it will make people's working lives more enjoyable. There may also be negatives – changes people will not like, which brings us to price.

- **The price.** The price element of the internal marketing mix is not *our* costs, it is concerned with what we are asking our internal customers to 'pay', when they buy in to the product and the marketing plan. This may include the sacrifice of other projects which compete for resources with our plan, but more fundamentally the personal psychological cost of adopting different key values, and changing the way jobs are done, and asking managers to step outside their 'comfort zones' with new methods of operation. The price to be paid by different parts of the internal marketplace, if the marketing plan is to be implemented successfully, should not be ignored as a major source of barriers and obstacles of varying degrees of difficulty.

- **Communications.** The most tangible aspect of the internal marketing programme is the communications media and the messages used to inform and to persuade, and to work on the attitudes of the key personnel in the internal marketplace. This includes not only written communications, such as plan summaries and reports, but also face-to-face presentations to individuals and groups who are important to the success of the plan. Broadly, we should remember that to assume that simply 'telling' people will get them on our side is likely to be as naive inside the company as it is outside. We suggest it is important to consider the full range of communications possibilities and associated goals, as we would with external customers, and we should not forget to budget the time and financial costs which may be associated with these activities. At the simplest level, the purpose of our internal marketing communication may be served by a video presentation explaining things, or a roadshow taking the message out to the regions and the distributors. But real communication is two-way – we listen, we adapt, we focus on our audience's problems and needs.

- **Distribution.** The distribution channels element of the mix is concerned with the physical and socio-technical venues at which we have to deliver our product and its communications: meetings, committees, training sessions for managers and staff, seminars, workshops, written reports, informal communications, social occasions, and so on. Ultimately, however, the real distribution channel is human resource management, and in the lining up of recruitment training, evaluation and reward systems behind marketing strategies, so that the culture of the company becomes the real distribution channel for internal marketing strategies. In fact, as long ago as the 1990s, Ulrich (1992) made some radical points about this, which are worth confronting. He said that if we really want complete customer commitment from our external customers, through independent, shared values and shared strategies, then we should give our customers a major role in our:

  - staff recruitment and selection decisions;
  - staff promotion and development decisions;
  - staff appraisal, from setting the standards to measuring the performance;
  - staff reward systems, both financial and non-financial;
  - organisational design strategies; and
  - internal communications programmes.

In effect this means using our human resource management systems as the internal marketing channel, thus taking the internal and external customer issue to its logical conclusion. Companies developing such approaches include General Electric, Marriott, Borg-Warner, DEC, Ford Motor Company, Hewlett Packard and Honeywell.

In many important ways, the revitalisation or transformation of a company as well as the implementation of a new strategy, may be in large part dependent on incorporating employees fully in the challenge to change the ways they deal with conflict and learning; leading differently to maintain employee involvement; and instilling the disciplines that will help people learn new ways of behaving and sustain that new behaviour (Pascale *et al.*, 1997). Managers who fail to get employees to understand what they are doing and why, and to

Table 16.2 Internal marketing in a computer company

Internal market targets *(1) Business unit management*
(2) Product group management
(3) Salesforce

Internal marketing programme	Internal marketing levels		
	Formal	Informal	Processual
Product	Marketing plan to attack a small industry as a special vertical market, rather than grouping it with many other industries as at present, with specialised products and advertising	Separation of resources and control of this market from the existing business unit	Change from technology-oriented management to recognition of differences in buyer needs in different industries - the clash between technology and customer orientation
Price	Costs of developing specialized 'badged' or branded products for this industry	Loss of control for existing business units	Fear of 'fragmentation' of markets leading to internal structural and status changes
Communications	Written plan Presentations to key groups	Support for plan by key board members gained by pre-presentation 'softening up' by planners	Action planning team formed, including original planners, but also key players from business unit and product group – rediscovering – the wheel to gain 'ownership' Advertising the new strategy in trade press read by company technologists and managers
Distribution	Business unit board meeting Product group board meeting Main board meeting Salesforce conference	Informal meetings	Joint seminars in applying IT to this industry, involving business unit managers and key customers Joint charity events for the industry's benevolent fund

build their enthusiasm, should not be surprised when strategy execution fails. Indeed, one argument is that the real role of management should be to connect employees better with end users of the product or service, because they can energise the workforce far better than can managers (Grant, 2011).

For example, a simple internal marketing analysis for two companies is illustrated in Tables 16.2 and 16.3. These examples concern a key customer account strategy in a financial services organisation and a vertical marketing strategy in a computer company. In both cases we can see a 'formal' level of internal marketing which concerns the marketing plan or strategy, but also levels of internal marketing concerned with the informal organisation and the processes of decision-making and change inside the company. In the computer company, vertical marketing is not a simple strategy because it is linked to changing resource

Table 16.3 Internal marketing in a financial services organisation

Internal market targets	(1) Branch managers of retail banks and finance company offices (2) Divisional chief executives for the banks and the finance		

Internal marketing programme	Internal marketing levels		
	Formal	Informal	Processual
Product	Integration of selling efforts around key customers, as a key marketing strategy	Head office group-based planning and resource allocation with greater central control	Change in the individual manager's role from independent branch entrepreneur to group-based collaborator
Price	Branch profit/commission from independent selling to smaller customers, to be sacrificed to build long-term relationships with key accounts	Loss of freedom/independence of action in the marketplace Potential loss of commission-earning power	Time, effort and psychological 'pain' of collaborating with former 'competitors' with different ethnic/educational/professional backgrounds–the 'banker versus the hire purchase salesman' Fear that the other side would damage existing customer relationships
Distribution	Written strategic marketing plans Sales conferences	Written communications Informal discussion of chief executive's 'attitude' Redesign of commission and incentives systems in both companies	Joint planning /problem-solving teams for each region–built around central definition of target market segments Combining/integrating management information systems, and changing its structure to reflect new segments
Communications	Formal presentation by chief executive at conferences Written support from chief executive Redesign market information systems to be more up-to-date	Sponsorship by chief executive - 'the train is now leaving the station, you are either on it or . . . ' (written memo sent to all branches)	Social events Joint training course Redefinition of markets and target segments

allocation and departmental responsibilities, and also to a change of management culture. In the financial services company, a key account strategy involves not simply a new marketing direction, but a change in line management freedom and ways of doing business. These cases are indicative of the types of implementation and change problem which can be addressed by internal marketing.

It also follows that we can use conventional market research techniques inside the company to get to grips with who has to change, in what way, how much and what the patterns are in our internal marketplace.

Finally, as with the external marketing programme, we should not neglect the importance of measuring results wherever possible. This may be in terms of such criteria as people's attitudes towards the market strategy and their commitment to putting it into practice, or customer perceptions of our success in delivering our promises to them – or, perhaps more appositely, our lack of success as presented by complaints, and so on.

Again, in exact parallel with the conventional external marketing plan, our internal marketing programmes should be directed at chosen targets or segments within the market. The choice of key targets for the internal marketing programme should be derived directly from the goals of the external marketing programme, and the types of organisational and human changes needed to implement marketing strategies. The internal marketplace may be segmented at the simplest level by the job roles and functions played by groups of people, e.g. top management, other departments and marketing and sales staff.

Alternatively, we might look beyond job characteristics to the key sources of support and resistance to the external marketing plan which are anticipated, to identify targets for reinforcement, or for persuasion and negotiation. Perhaps at the deepest level we might choose our targets on the basis of the individual's attitudes towards the external market and customers, and the key values that we need communicated to external customers, together with people's career goals.

It can be seen, therefore, that internal marketing can be used in different ways, and that the role may vary from developing customer care and service quality programmes to improve and maintain service standards and customer satisfaction at the point-of-scale, through to internal communication programmes, to providing a structured approach to planning the full implementation of marketing strategy. We noted also that internal marketing may be of particular importance in the alliance-based network organisation.

16.4   Planning for internal marketing

There are a variety of situations when strategic thinking about competitive strategy should address the possible role of internal marketing:

- where performance in critical areas of customer service are unsatisfactory and not sufficient to establish a strong competitive position;
- where customer satisfaction is consistently low and complaints suggest that the underlying causes are employee attitudes and behaviour, rather than poor product standards or inadequate support systems;
- when market conditions and customer requirements have shifted, so that continuing the standards and practices of the past will no longer bring success;
- when new marketing strategies require new skills and ways of behaving – a 'stretch' strategy;
- when bridging the gap between planning and implementation has proved problematic in the past.

In such situations, we may wish to consider an internal marketing strategy with the following components:

Internal market orientation

Some attention has been given to internal market orientation as the foundation for success, in the same way that external market orientation has been linked to the effectiveness of external marketing strategies. The logic is that internal market orientation increases the effectiveness of a market-oriented company to external market conditions, because it allows management to better align external market objectives with internal capabilities. However, this symmetry relies on assessment of internal market orientation as a precursor to action (Gounaris, 2006). Lings and Greenley (2005) propose that assessing internal market orientation should encompass directly parallel measures to those associated with external market orientation, thus internal market orientation involves the generation and dissemination of intelligence pertaining to the wants and needs of employees, and the design and implementation of appropriate responses to meet those wants and needs.

Internal market strategy

In broad terms what is needed to gain the successful implementation of an external market strategy. It is here that we need to confront the real implications of our external market strategy for the internal customer – the decision makers, managers, operatives and others without whose support, co-operation and commitment, the external strategy will fail. This is the most critical question in the whole internal marketing exercise. It may be worth consulting the people directly concerned – doing internal market research. It is certainly worth incorporating some diversity of opinion. As we learn more, we can come back and redraft and rethink our conclusions here. It is here that we should take a view of what it is likely to cost us to achieve these things and the deadline for achieving them to implement the external marketing strategy on time.

Internal market segmentation

This is about identifying the targets in the internal marketplace around which we can build internal marketing programmes, which are different in what we have to achieve and how we are going to do it. This may not be straightforward, but is the route to real insights into the internal market problem and effectiveness in how we cope with that problem. The most obvious way of identifying internal segments may be by role or function, or location, and this may be sufficient. It might be more productive to think of who are the innovators and opinion leaders who will influence others. We might approach this more directly in terms of the role that different people will play in implementing the external strategy and the problems they may face in this, or simply how much different people will have to change to get the external strategy to work.

For example, one argument is that we should consider the employer as the brand, and then the same underlying bases can be used in segmenting employees as are used externally with consumers: potential profitability, product-feature preferences, influential reference groups, bargaining power, choice barriers. Then the internal market segmentation model will include:

- **Potential profitability** – employees who have the skills, experience or knowledge that are strategically important to the company, who should get resources for recruitment and retention.
- **Product-feature preferences** – employees grouped according to the career benefits they value most highly, to identify the bundles of benefits with most value to these groups.
- **Reference groups** – people generally want to work for companies with good reputations, as judged by the people whose opinions they value. This supports efforts to reinforce the brand with those who influence employee perceptions.
- **Bargaining power** – the power of some employees in negotiating terms of employment because of the rarity of their skills, level of seniority, relevant experience and qualifications. This suggests the need for richer benefits packages (not necessarily money).
- **Choice barriers** – the recruitment and pay policies set up by an employer to prevent people entering or leaving the firm. The goal of action here is to counter the bargaining power of some employee groups.

Although this example is specific to the 'employer brand', it illustrates nicely the use of segmentation principles in the internal market that are directly drawn from those used in the consumer market (Moroko and Uncles, 2009).

Internal marketing programmes

These specify which internal marketing programmes will be needed in each internal market segment to achieve the objectives we have set. In each area we need to collect our thoughts about the rational issues but also the human and cultural issues. To us the product may be a new marketing plan that we need to inform people about (internal marketing communications), through formal presentations (internal marketing distribution), adjusting commission and evaluation systems as need be (internal marketing price). To the internal customer, the same plan may be about disruption and threat (product), loss of initiative and status (price), imposed without consultation by management (communication) and rigorously 'policed' through coercion (distribution). If internal marketing is about anything, it is about confronting and coping with this conflict. It is this confrontation which will drive us away from thinking about internal marketing as simply writing customer care brochures and doing great plan presentations, towards coping with the human and organisational realities of what strategic change involves and costs. This is also the stage to take a look at the cost implications of what we now see to be necessary in our internal marketing: does the internal marketing cost mean that the external market strategy is no longer attractive? Do we have to account for internal marketing cost which is more than we expected, but bearable? Do we have to change the external strategy to reduce the internal marketing cost? Are there cheaper ways of achieving the critical internal marketing goals?

Internal marketing evaluation

What we can measure to see if we are getting there, ideally quantified and objective: reduced customer complaint rates or higher customer satisfaction scores. This may be ambitious and we should not abandon important objectives because they are difficult to evaluate – we may have to settle for a subjective or qualitative evaluation, which is better than nothing.

However, the possible problems to be anticipated in implementing internal marketing strategy programmes effectively should not be underestimated. For example, Don Schultz suggests that many, if not most, internal marketing approaches fail, for the following reasons:

- **Lack of financial measures of internal marketing success** – the goal should be to link measurable behavioural changes to financial returns for the business.
- **Weak management cohesion** – the organisational location of responsibility for internal marketing is confused and those responsible have no authority or responsibility for the people whose behaviours they are trying to change.
- **Lack of senior management support** – internal marketing is not perceived as a senior management issue, but the concern of middle managers with all the inherent problems of turf wars and organisational politics.
- **No connection between internal stakeholders and external customers** – the difficulty for employees in non-customer-facing roles to understand how internal marketing affects them, or how they affect the external customer.
- **Lack of a management calculus** – there are no clear ideas about the value or return of internal marketing and an effective internal marketing planning system.

For example, one initiative at Wells Fargo, the San Francisco bank, is the happy/grumpy ratio, to measure the proportion of cheery staff versus the less happy. They believe that happy employees are more likely to do the right thing than unhappy people, so they measure the proportions. They report that five years ago, the ratio of happy to grumpy was 3.8:1, but now it is 8:1, suggesting the effectiveness of current policies (Kellaway, 2015).

Schultz (2004) suggests that we should apply the lessons of integrated marketing communications in internal as well as external marketing. However, the issue of integration has yet further practical aspects, as we see in the next section of the chapter.

16.5   Cross-functional partnership as internal marketing

16.5.1 Rationale for cross-functional partnership

Perhaps the greatest contemporary challenge for internal marketing is the achievement of the effective cross-functional partnerships required to deliver superior customer value. Two things are increasingly apparent.

First, delivering value results from a complex set of processes and activities inside the organisation and possibly also in a network of organisations in a strategic alliance (see Chapter 15). Many of the processes of defining, creating and delivering value to customers are not 'owned' or directly managed by marketing or sales departments. The challenge may be looking at different units as a form of strategic alliance where benefits and costs should be carefully analysed (Campbell, 2006). Research suggests that organisations that collaborate well internally perform better in meeting customer needs, accommodating special customer requests and introducing new products, and as a result are perceived more favourably by customers (Wilding, 2006). *Second,* sophisticated customers will not accept anything less than seamless delivery of value in their terms – problems in the integration of processes in the seller's organisation are the seller's problem, not the buyer's (Hulbert *et al.,* 2002; Piercy and Lane, 2012).

The integration of the whole organisation around the drivers of customer value has become an imperative – all activities must work together, fit together, and be seen to appear together by the customer. Nonetheless, many organisations appear to struggle with this imperative. The model in Figure 16.5 provides a framework for analysing the challenges in identifying and integrating the complex of functional specialisms and internal and external resource centres that impact on the operation of the value processes of value identification, creation and delivery (however these processes are labelled in a particular company).

We consider briefly the nature of each of the interfaces between marketing and other functional groups, which may provide internal marketing targets for internal alliance-building.

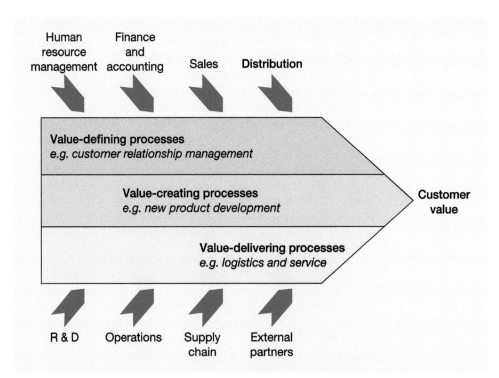

Figure 16.5
Cross-functional
contributions to
value processes

16.5.2 Marketing and human resource management

It is now a considerable time since Glassman and McAfee (1992) called for the full-scale integration of marketing and human resource management departments. Their logic was that the two functions were both focused on 'people issues' (the one on customers and the other on employees), yet seemed unable to integrate their activities effectively. However, HRM in many organisations has moved towards a 'strategic human resource management' approach, with a primary concern for aligning the skills and capabilities of employees and managers with the requirements of business strategy. The processes usually managed in HRM are extremely relevant to the goals of marketing strategy: recruitment and selection, evaluation and reward system, training and development, and other drivers of corporate culture. There is an opportunity for marketing to work with HRM in identifying the key elements of employee motivation, and the development of training and development programmes – but particularly in providing the research capabilities to evaluate the internal marketplace including employees, channel partners and customer service providers (Schultz, 2002).

Some companies are making large efforts to ensure that marketing and HRM work together to ensure that they communicate and deliver brand values to both internal and external audiences. The 'Everything is Possible' campaign at H-P Invest (formerly Hewlett-Packard) is aimed to be as inspirational for staff as it is for customers. Allied-Domecq sees its 'people brand' as one of its nine core brands. Some companies, such as Allied-Domecq and Sainsbury's, have appointed employer brand managers to bridge the gap between HR and marketing (Simms, 2003).

One view is that HR and marketing collaboration becomes critical when the priority is to maintain a coherent corporate brand and employer brand, and that the way forward is to: make internal brand management a strategic imperative; break down HR/marketing barriers; empower employees as brand ambassadors; establish and maintain aligned corporate and employer brands; and build internal brand management around brand-centred HR practices (Brown, 2014). Nonetheless, many company practices clearly fall short of this ideal.

An internal marketing agenda concerned with the contribution of HRM to value processes might include the following issues:

- The better alignment of employee and manager training and development processes with customer priorities.
- Tracking and comparing employee satisfaction and customer satisfaction to understand the relationship between them.
- Working on the links between customer satisfaction and retention issues, and employee training, reward and evaluation processes.
- Looking at the way in which internal communications approaches support external market strategies (Piercy, 2009a).

The importance of the marketing/HRM link is such that in many situations major customers are increasingly playing a direct role in participating in the operation of suppliers' internal HRM processes, such as recruitment into sales and service jobs.

Indeed, more operational views of the interface between marketing and HRM issues focus on the link between HRM and relationship marketing strategies (Perrien *et al.*, 1993; Perrien and Ricard, 1995), and the need to direct HRM policies to focus on customer service and customer value (Cripe, 1994; Gubman, 1995). Sheth and Mittal (1996) have even examined the use of HRM skills in the management of customer expectations. Nonetheless, research suggests that the marketing/HRM relationship is frequently associated with conflict and poor interdepartmental conflicts with a detrimental impact on strategy implementation (Chimhanzi, 2004).

16.5.3 Marketing and finance and accounting

The conflict between marketing and finance/accounting in the past has reflected the goal of accounting to cut costs and to increase reported short-term profit, compared to the objective of marketing to gain long-term investment in brands and market share. Conflicts have also centred on different views of pricing – the accounting model of cost-plus pricing produces very different outcomes to a marketing model of price based on customer value. However, these disputes have been rendered largely obsolete by two important factors. The first factor in the overwhelming pressure that marketing is under in a growing number of companies to 'prove' its added-value to the company and its shareholders (Ambler, 2003). Many of the metrics which marketing most needs to establish its shareholder value creation can only be achieved through collaboration with finance and accounting (Farris *et al.*, 2006). The second factor is the increasingly strategic view of business being taken by finance and accounting executives, which is likely to reduce the conflicts with marketing and sales. Moves towards internal alliances between marketing and finance/accounting are likely to be important in achieving the speed of change and market responsiveness required by modern customers.

16.5.4 Marketing and sales integration

In Chapter 14 we examined the growing role of the sales organisation in strategic customer management, and as a change agent inside the company. Nonetheless, for many companies the relationship between marketing and sales remains problematic. It has been noted: 'The relationship between sales and marketing functions has persisted as one of the major sources of organisational conflict' (Webster, 1997), and that 'The marketing-sales relationship, whilst strongly interdependent, is reported as neither collaborative nor harmonious' (Dewsnap and Jobber, 2000). For these reasons sales and marketing integration remains a high and very topical priority on the management agenda (Rouzies *et al.*, 2005). This question merits more detailed consideration, since it appears to be frequently one of the most critical obstacles to marketing strategy implementation.

The conventional literature often assumes that marketing departments and sales organisations are a single organisational unit, but they are frequently quite distinct functions in companies (Piercy and Lane, 2012). For example, in their 1998 study, Workman *et al.* suggest that 'it is highly significant that more than thirty years after the call to integrate sales and marketing activities under a CME [Chief Marketing Executive], we find no firms that had adopted this recommendation.' In fact, part of the reason is that marketing and sales should not be the same because the functions they perform are different (Shapiro, 2002). However, the new market conditions and strategic sales role we described in Chapter 14 place considerable importance on cross-functional collaboration and cooperation, which may align poorly with the traditional need for functional separation based on task specialisation.

What is far from well understood is what conflicts or elements of conflict actually have negative consequences for business performance and which do not (Deshpandé and Webster, 1989). While marketing and sales exist alongside each other as business functions, there are likely to be fundamental differences between them in perspective and priorities. However, in examining the coordination of these differentiated functions, Cespedes (1996) highlights an important dilemma: 'the solution is *not* to eliminate differences among these groups', but that 'paradoxically, there is virtue in *separating* and distinguishing functional roles in order to improve the cross-functional coordination needed' (Cespedes, 1995). The suggestion is that differences between marketing and sales may actually provide a much-needed breadth of perspective and richness of market understanding *because* of the differences between the functions. As collaboration and cooperation between marketing and sales grows in importance, this paradox provides an important insight – teamwork and joint-working has to accommodate differences in perspective and understanding, and to focus on enhanced business performance not simply smooth team operation or harmonious interrelationships.

The marketing/sales interface

To other functions in the business, the marketing and sales functions look alike – they are both focused on the customer and the market – but aligning sales and marketing has proved difficult in practice and is likely to be even more difficult in the future. The importance of the issue is quite simply that poor cooperation between marketing and sales will lead to inconsistent and weak strategy, coupled with flawed and inefficient implementation (Shapiro, 2002).

When the customer base was homogeneous, simple, and dominated by mid-sized accounts, marketing operated as a strategic function concentrating on product strategy, segmentation, and competitive positioning, while sales executed the strategy in the field, selling to end-users and distributors. The easy separation of sales and marketing has come to an end in markets dominated by very large accounts with sophisticated buying teams, and multi-channel strategies to reach medium and small accounts. With the largest accounts, marketing and sales need to make joint decisions to achieve an integrated offer that meets the standards required by purchasers who can dictate many terms to their suppliers. Marketing executives need to acquire new understanding of individual customers, key account needs, and the sales task – the reality is that 'As power shifted from the seller to the buyer, it also shifted from headquarters to the field' (Shapiro, 2002). With multi-channelling (e.g., a website, social media, online platforms like Amazon and Alibaba, telesales, direct marketing and personal selling working alongside each other), effectiveness and profitability also require shared sales and marketing decisions on channel strategy and execution (Shapiro, 2002).

While relatively little solid empirical evidence is available, executive opinion and anecdote suggest the relationship between marketing and sales remains problematic in many companies, with conflict surrounding such issues as the division of responsibilities and demarcation lines, ownership of customer information, competition for resources, control of price, and the short-term orientation of sales versus the long-term orientation of marketing. Differences in reward systems (volume-based in sales and margin-based in marketing), information needs (geographically- and customer-based in sales and product/brand-oriented in marketing), and competencies, underline the potential for conflict rather than collaboration between marketing and sales (Cespedes, 1993, 1994; Montgomery *et al.,* 1997; Dewsnap and Jobber, 2000).

Underpinning the potential for market/sales conflict is what has been described as the existence of different 'mindsets' in marketing and sales – different perspectives on issues and approaches for addressing problems – which have been described as:

- *Customer versus product* – focus and rewards for sales are based on customers and territories, while marketing champions products and brands.
- *Personal relationships versus analysis* – sales may be more 'people-oriented' and relationship-focused, while marketing emphasises aggregations of data and abstractions.
- *Continuous daily activity versus sporadic projects* – sales is driven by constant daily tasks, while marketing is organised around longer-term projects.
- *Field versus office* – sales is under immediate customer and budget pressures, while marketing may be removed from this environment.
- *Results versus process* – sales lives by fast, direct results from its selling efforts, while marketing activities are less easily linked to short-term results, so may emphasise process and intermediate outcomes.
- *Short-term orientation versus long-term orientation* – Sales emphasises month-to-month sales results, while marketing concentrates on long-term competitive position (Rouzies *et al., 2005).

Such differences in mindset provide the context in which marketing–sales collaboration must be achieved, but may provide important practical barriers.

The signs of poor marketing/sales integration

The pioneering study by Strahle *et al.* (1996) noted that sales managers frequently do not set sales objectives consistent with the strategy developed by marketing executives for a product, through poor communications and incompatibility between marketing and sales goals. They note also attempts by marketing executives to mislead sales managers about product performance in attempts to manipulate their behaviour. Unsurprisingly, the result is feelings of distrust and resentment towards marketing on the part of sales managers. Other research also suggests that changes in marketing strategy do not lead to consistent modification of sales operations (Colletti and Chonko, 1997).

A checklist of signals that marketing and sales are not well aligned is provided by the following statements, which may be assessed by marketing and sales executives in their own operations:

- Your marketing strategies fail to affect sales operations, impeding effective implementation.
- New marketing strategies ignore customer and competitor insights developed by the salesforce.
- Managers in other functions misunderstand what sales can and should achieve.
- Conflicts between sales and marketing managers frequently spill over into acrimony.
- You are experiencing serious salesperson retention problems and escalating replacement costs.
- There are serious mismatches between the tasks that salespeople must perform to implement marketing strategy and the ways in which they are organised, evaluated and rewarded.
- Career paths for salespeople take the best performers away from customers and place them in administration or management.
- Your salespeople struggle to cope with the ambiguous roles they now play.
- Your company offers little support for salespeople to make the transition from transaction to relationship selling.
- Your salespeople are hostile to your other routes to market, such as the Internet.
- Your customer relationships are getting weaker, not stronger (Hulbert *et al.*, 2002).

Careful assessment of these statements may be useful in identifying the beginning marketing/sales rifts which would otherwise remain hidden until becoming serious barriers to effective cross-functional working.

The internal marketing challenge

Shapiro (2002) notes that the prerequisites for effective marketing/sales relationships are a common understanding of the need for integration, and that both sales and marketing focus on the productive sharing of power, information and resources, but also warns: 'There are many approaches to improving integration. They work best when they themselves are well integrated (big surprise!) . . . the stress will be on "mixing and matching" the individual elements of coordination to get a robust, efficient program.' This need for understanding and alignment between marketing strategy and the sales organisation defines the internal marketing challenge. The challenge is to both marketing and sales, as we suggested when examining the underlying premises of the strategic sales organisation. Indeed, if organisations cannot do better in building partnership between marketing and sales, it does not bode well for marketing's ability to create alliances with other functional groups.

16.5.5 Marketing and operations functions: R&D, manufacturing and supply chain management

The relationship between marketing and R&D is most usually associated with effectiveness in areas like new product development. The synergy achieved by linking R&D spend to customer value is clear. However, the role of R&D may be significant to value defining and value delivering processes, as well as the classic function of value creation (new products). For example, companies like IBM and Xerox bring lead-customers into their R&D laboratories, to meet the challenge of translating technical advances into new business options and profitable products. On the other hand, in some high technology businesses R&D is a major component of relationship marketing – working with suppliers and customers on technology innovation is a key component of buyer–seller relationships (Tzokas *et al.*, 1997). Indeed, in industries associated with an accelerating rate of innovation, poor integration of marketing and R&D has been linked to reducing customer loyalty and long-term profits – innovations may be pushed into the marketplace without adequate commercialization and technology readiness, so while customers may buy the innovation, in the absence of superior quality and service, they are ready to migrate to the next 'big idea' as soon as it appears from a rival (Donath, 1997). The building of firmer links between R&D and marketing poses a greater challenge than simply providing new product pipelines.

In the other 'technical' functions, modern thinking is dominated by supply chain strategy – in particular the promise of the 'lean' supply chain to 'banish waste and create wealth' (Womack and Jones, 1996). The supply chain model of identifying value streams for products and organising around flow and the demand pull of products has been enormously influential, because of the potential it offers for reducing storage and waste costs to a minimum. Nonetheless, from a marketing perspective, the weakness of the lean supply chain lies in its rigid definition of customer value in purely technical terms, and the desirability of reducing product choices to reduce supply chain costs. However, the strategic link between supply chain and marketing strategy lies in the relationship between supply chain advantage and marketing/brand advantage. Applying internal marketing efforts to enhancing the understanding and collaboration between supply chain strategy and marketing strategy is a new mandate for marketing executives.

Certainly, at the supply chain operations level, there is evidence that internal marketing efforts to stimulate the impact of frontline logistics workers on customer value creation can lead to higher job satisfaction and performance in distribution centre employees, and increased interdepartmental customer orientation (Keller *et al.*, 2006).

16.5.6 Marketing and external partners

It will very frequently be the case that the successful implementation of marketing strategy will rely on the efforts of partnered organisations operating externally – distributors at home and abroad, outsourced manufacturers, third-party suppliers of customer services, network members delivering the product or service for the supplier. We examined in Chapter 15 the growing role of alliances and networks, and the way in which in some sectors like global air travel, competition is between networks rather than individual airlines. The challenge of achieving effective delivery of strategic goals through partnered organisations remains considerable in many situations. Networks are characterised by dependencies. These increasingly common situations define a new and possibly critical function for internal marketing: the positioning of strategic imperatives with partner organisations in the networks which have been formed to reach the marketplace.

16.5.7 A process-based role for internal marketing

The logic for this part of the chapter is based on the following premises: that increasingly the effective implementation of marketing strategies will rely on effectiveness in managing cross-functional relationships, and that the management of processes of collaboration and alliance-building in organisations (and extended alliance-based networks) extends the internal marketing agenda from simply planning implementation strategy to a process design and management role. The Figure 16.4 model provides a basis for addressing the nature of the main value processes in an organisation and then identifying the actual or potential contributions of diverse functional specialisms to the effectiveness of the value processes. Once identified, the cross-functional integration and collaboration needs define the internal marketing role.

16.6   Implementation and internal marketing*

The approach we have taken in this chapter to strategy implementation and internal marketing attempts to emphasise that strategy cannot usefully be examined in isolation from execution – developing strategic ideas around a company's markets achieves effectiveness only when placed in the context of implementation. However, when we focus on implementation, it is clear that we face both long-term and short-term issues. The short-term issues are what has mainly occupied us so far – gaining the execution of a given plan or strategy. The longer-term issues are more concerned with management decisions aimed at avoiding the implementation problems we have considered here.

This suggests that there is a need to consider both process management and execution skills in implementation. The difference is that managing the strategy process has the goal of integrating implementation and change issues with marketing strategy, with the goal of avoiding the emergence of implementation barriers. On the other hand, execution skills are concerned with how to manage a way though the change problems and barriers, which stand in the way of marketing strategy. While these are different approaches, they are not mutually exclusive, and in most practical situations attention will need to be paid to both.

The underlying rationale is summarised in Figure 16.6. The implementation scenarios suggested are four: **weak implementation** – where the management of process and execution skills are inappropriate to drive a marketing strategy; **management-driven implementation** – where the emphasis is on leadership and control by management to put a strategy into effect and to overcome problems or barriers which may exist; **implementation-driven strategy,** where the emphasis is on exploiting the capabilities of the existing organisation and adapting strategies to 'fit' with this reality; and **integrated strategy and implementation,** which achieves implementation by both managing key processes and applying management execution skills. In facing the implementation challenges in a given situation it can be useful to map positioning on this framework and to track the practical implications for an effective implementation strategy.

The weak implementation scenario is largely based on managers assuming that once plans and strategies are written, then people will go away and make them happen. Some managers make these assumptions implicitly in how they approach things, and fail to anticipate that the problems when their edicts and commands are not put into effect or are implemented half-heartedly or haphazardly. Any marketing strategy that matters to an organisation deserves to have implementation taken more seriously than this.

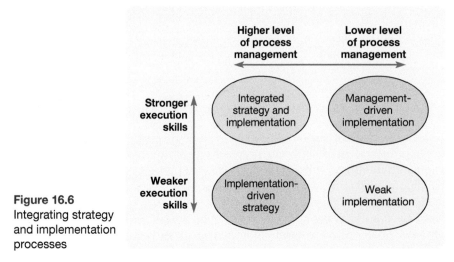

Figure 16.6
Integrating strategy
and implementation
processes

* This section draws on more detailed coverage of this issue in Piercy (2017).

The management-driven implementation scenario is probably closest to the traditional view of how things should be managed. The emphasis is on line management to take charge, to overcome obstacles, to lead, to coerce, and to make things happen – it relies on high-quality management execution skills to overcome implementation barriers. It is fast to put into practice and in the short term may achieve change, but the problem is it lacks longer-term effectiveness in sustaining change.

The implementation-driven strategy scenario is where the focus of market strategies is dominated by exploiting existing capabilities and skills in the organisation, mainly by adapting market strategies to 'fit' with the organisation's existing competencies. This is also fast to be put into effect, and will keep implementation costs low. It is weaker in achieving strategic change because the emphasis is on exploiting what we already have, not developing new capabilities – this is fine until the point when our capabilities do not provide what the market wants, i.e. our strategy becomes outdated by market change.

The integrated strategy and implementation scenario is the ideal to which we aspire. Implementation is not an issue because it is fully integrated with the market strategy, and we are not forced to cling to existing skills and processes, because part of developing strategy is developing the appropriate processes, structures, skills and capabilities to drive the strategy. It is slower to achieve and expensive, and in the short term not outstandingly effective. It is probably the only route to long-term sustained strategic change. It is also the scenario we understand least well, and find rarely in practice.

Understanding the reality of the implementation scenario faced and the implications of the approaches adopted by management provide insights into problems likely to be faced, and a foundation for planning a longer-term strategy to enhance implementation capabilities in a company.

Summary

The focus of this chapter is strategy implementation – the transition from plans to execution. Strategy implementation faces a variety of obstacles and poses several important challenges for marketing executives. Part of the challenge is to avoid the separation of strategy and implementation and to recognise their interdependence. We take the increasingly widespread view that part of thinking about implementing competitive marketing strategy should be concerned with managing the internal market (of employees, functional specialists, managers, and so on), because this may enhance a company's ability to deliver its strategies to customers in the external market. In part, this view is based on the recognition of the importance of relationship management with partners, achieving competition differentiation through the skills of the 'part-time marketers' in the organisation, and the role of internal branding to parallel external branding.

We saw that internal marketing may be traced back to early views about the synergy between the marketing concept and the 'human relations' concept, and to have developed operationally in a variety of ways. The scope of internal marketing was seen to encompass service quality enhancement, internal communications programmes, managing the adoption of innovations inside an organisation, cross-functional and cross-divisional supply of products and services, and a framework for marketing implementation. Our interest here is primarily, though not exclusively, in strategic internal marketing as a framework for managing implementation.

In this area we saw that internal marketing offers a framework for evaluating the costs of change and for managing change that utilises the same concepts, terminology and techniques as planning external marketing. This provides a pragmatic model for guiding implementation choices and actions.

The last part of the chapter gave attention to the more process-based view of internal marketing, which focuses on integration of company efforts around customer value creation, and the challenges of forming cross-functional partnerships to deliver marketing strategy to the marketplace. We examined the potentials for internal marketing efforts to build closer ties and collaboration between marketing, human resource management, finance and accounting, sales, operations functions, and external partners. We suggested that perhaps one of the most important roles of internal marketing goes beyond aligning employees' values and behaviours with strategies, and confronts the need to achieve superior customer value through seamlessness in strategy delivery. This role emphasises internal marketing to achieve cross-functional partnerships within the organisation, and crossing organisational boundaries to align external partners with the imperatives of marketing strategy.

The long-term approach to effective strategy implementation is likely to be one that balances process management and execution skills to produce an integrated strategy and implementation approach – one which enhances a company's implementation capabilities.

Case study   EasyJet blazes trail on customer service

At easyJet's training academy, a room of cabin crew are watching comedian Dawn French hurtle, screaming, towards a lake before launching herself in.

The video cuts to a drawing room of a stately home where a hushed circle of suspects is sternly informed by a detective of the crime – murder – but the weapon? Behaviour and poor treatment at the hands of sales assistants, which proved fatal.

EasyJet staff have gone back into the training room to be instructed on their ABC – attitude, behaviour and communication – and are being shown how unwitting actions make an impression on customers. There are disapproving tuts as they watch cabin crew actors on screen stow up trays with a weary sigh or a pouting stewardess flouncing towards a departure gate.

Customer service has become easyJet's own weapon, wielded against rivals in the highly competitive airline market. Under Carolyn McCall, chief executive, raising the customer satisfaction bar has been placed at the heart of what easyJet does, in its aim to seize more market share and reach its goal of becoming Europe's preferred short-haul airline.

The low-cost airline is pushing ahead with a programme to transform company culture and the results have been evident: its full year pre-tax profit increased 51 per cent to £478m and it will pay out a £175m dividend.

Furthermore, after two recent profit warnings Ryanair has acknowledged the success of its rival's efforts and done an abrupt U-turn, with chief executive Michael O'Leary admitting it needed to stop 'unnecessarily pissing people off'.

'As a low-cost airline it's where we can differentiate ourselves,' Angie Mullen, easyJet's cabin crew service and standards manager says of its drive.

As she walks through the academy she points out staff who have won awards and talks about the inter-airline competitions coming up. 'No pressure,' she says as she paces down the corridor, 'no pressure'.

Ms McCall has underscored the difference between it and the 'stuffy' and more formal competition. 'If you go on our planes, our crew will have a laugh with you,' she says. 'If it's appropriate, they'll have a joke – they're very easy.'

Getting that judgment right is down to experience, says crew member Jonathan Roberts. His colleague, Leslie Gamble adds: 'With businessmen often you get them a coffee, say '"anything else sir", get a '"no thanks" and you move on. But you get other passengers that want to share their life story.'

Meanwhile, the list of initiatives to raise standards and burnish the 'orange spirit' is lengthy and growing.

Out has gone the old uniform with the garish orange men's shirt, in instead are touches of orange and a 'fun' striped tie. A magazine-style book of style tips dispenses advice such as 'the tousled look has no place onboard' and instructing ladies to keep underwear to white or nude shades only.

There is a customer charter, made of promises from staff. There are scores of 'customer champions', employees with a brief to inform and inspire colleagues.

There is a pledge day, numerous internal awards and a Spirit Awards Portal, where staff log on to commend colleagues.

There are feel-good videos and next, behaviour pins, to be won by crew for displaying certain behaviours towards passengers.

The incentive is mainly company pride – winning your name on an aircraft, or becoming an ambassador for Unicef.

'We've been working really hard for two years on this cultural transformation around the customer,' says Lisa Burger, head of customer experience. Its homework includes studies such as What Does Friendly Look Like? Customer satisfaction is up, and the test now will be keeping the momentum to stay ahead.

'We're full of ideas,' says Peter Duffy, marketing and customer director. 'We have a raft of stuff coming, some small, some big, which is going to make us better and better.'

He is particularly proud of the work that has gone into repositioning the brand, into the website and app as well as on innovations such as allocated seating. Innovation is crucial, he says, flipping out his phone and scrolling through snaps that have inspired, from transport staff to Hare Krishnas on London pavements.

Rivals will not be able to catch up, he insists, because 'we've been hiring against the criteria of great service for years and that is very, very difficult to replicate'.

But Ryanair dismisses their argument. 'I don't buy that,' says Caroline Green, head of customer service. 'We've always had good service on board. Some of the policies being softened make it easier for excellent service to show through. They [easyJet] will have their work cut out because we're going to be up and on a par with them very, very quickly.'

It has followed in simplifying its website, is to introduce allocated seating in February and said last month it would take only three to six months to catch easyJet up.

Analysts point to the time needed to effect change. 'You can't put a time on how long it takes to strengthen your brand name, for the perception of the airline to improve among the general public,' says Gert Zonneveld, analyst at Panmure Gordon.

With many of the 30,000 staff being well educated and not direct employees, such as at airports, Ms Burger admits that other airlines may reap the advantages of their efforts. But she says: 'The industry is now challenging the industry to get better, that is only a benefit for everybody.'

Source: from 'EasyJet blazes trail on customer service', *Financial Times*, 23/12/13 (Wild, J.).

Discussion questions

1 What is the link between internal marketing and service quality in the airline industry?

2 What is the rationale for a cross-functional partnership in a company such as easyJet?

3 Is it sufficient for easyJet to have internal training programmes or should these be extended to external partners?

CHAPTER 17

CORPORATE SOCIAL RESPONSIBILITY AND ETHICS

All too often, large companies see corporate social responsibility as something entirely separate from their business goals. As high unemployment, rising poverty, and dismay over corporate greed breed contempt for the capitalist market system . . . Serving the intersecting needs of business and the community is the only path to winning back respect.

(Porter, 2010)

The concept of shared value – which focuses on the connections between societal and economic progress – has the power to unleash the next wave of global growth. An increasing number of companies known for their hard-nosed approach to business – such as Google, IBM, Intel, Johnson & Johnson, Nestlé, Unilever, and Wal-Mart – have begun to embark on important shared value initiatives. But our understanding of the potential of shared value is just beginning.

(Porter and Kramer, 2011)

Eco-friendly fabrics

Strong, light, warm to wear, and deliciously soft, cashmere is wonderfully luxurious but, with clothing production falling under increasing environmental scrutiny, questions are now being asked about cashmere production.

Woven from the soft hair of goats, cashmere is both natural and long-lasting but its production has raised concerns over desertification, caused by over-grazed grasslands, and the possible cruelty to goats kept in confined spaces. Such worries have prompted some cashmere manufacturers to investigate their supply chains more thoroughly.

'There is too little knowledge about the impact of cashmere production,' says Nick Falkingham, managing director of the British brand

Source: Alamy Images: Imagestate Media Partners Limited – Impact Photos.

Pure Collection, one of a growing group of companies working to raise awareness of the issues surrounding its production.

The Italian company Loro Piana, known for some of the world's finest luxury cashmere, has opened a subsidiary in Ulan Bator, Mongolia's capital, both to establish long-term relationships with nomadic herdsmen and to monitor quality control. Pier Luigi Loro Piana, joint chief executive, says: 'We believe it is vital to maintain optimal conditions for the animals to preserve the cashmere's quality. The flocks must live naturally.'

British retailer Marks & Spencer asks its cashmere suppliers to complete a questionnaire. Devised in 2008 after an M&S team visited suppliers in Inner Mongolia, it gathers information on animal husbandry and environmental issues. The company has also recently signed a deal to work with the Royal Society for the Prevention of Cruelty to Animals on all animal-derived materials, including cashmere.

John Lewis makes its suppliers commit to its code of practice on responsible sourcing. Stephen Cawley, the group's merchandise standards manager, says: 'There has to be trust but suppliers who understand our expectations on sourcing also understand that if that trust is broken, they risk their long-term trading relationship.'

Relaying the environmentally sound message to consumers, however, is another challenge. N Peal, a luxury cashmere brand, has yet to incorporate the standards applied to its supply chain into its marketing strategy, even though 'ethical' has become an increasingly valuable selling point. Managing director Adam Holdsworth says: 'For most manufacturers, the cashmere supply chain is so complicated that they have little chance to fully audit supply in order to make claims with assurance. But attitudes at the luxury end are slowly changing.'

As are attitudes beyond the fashion industry. China provides a government subsidy to farmers who can demonstrate good land management. Organisations such as Sustainable Agriculture Research and Education have funded projects to develop improved combing techniques. These techniques discourage the use of speedy shearing, a process that can leave goats with little or no coat for warmth. The United States Agency for International Development has launched a campaign to teach combing to some 170,000 Afghani goatherds, which will boost rural incomes from herds more typically farmed for meat, milk or leather. The aim is to make cashmere as long-lasting, and sustainable, as possible.

Source: from 'Eco-friendly fabrics', *Financial Times,* 16/04/10 (Sims, J.).

Discussion questions

1 What is the main issue raised here?
2 How are cashmere producers and marketers addressing it?

Introduction

Considering corporate social responsibility (CSR) as an element of, or at the very least a major influence on, marketing strategy, is now mandatory for executives in most organisations. This new imperative reflects the escalating importance of CSR in how companies manage their key processes and deliver customer value and the seriousness with which these issues are viewed by our stakeholders all the way from shareholders and employees through to suppliers, distributors and end-customers. Indeed, one writer talks of the pressure on business to act with a social conscience and uses the term the 'Conscience Economy' to designate this imperative (Overman, 2014).

Certainly, it appears that in a post-recession environment when trust in business and professional institutions is seen by some to be at an all-time low, the scrutiny and judgement of corporate behaviour has reached unprecedented levels. Nowhere in the business is this likely to be more significant than in the marketing and sales actions at the front-end of the operation where the company meets its markets.

In the past, it has been suggested that the marketing discipline has adopted a very partial perspective on CSR and companies need a far broader view of the concept in the value chain (Vaaland *et al.,* 2008). A starting point in developing that broader view is the Green Paper presented by the European Commission in 2001, which identifies corporate social responsibility as: 'a concept whereby companies integrate social and environmental concerns in their business operations and in their interaction with their stakeholders on a voluntary basis'. Moreover, the Green Paper identified four factors underpinning the growing attention by executives to issues of corporate social responsibility:

1 The new concerns and expectations of consumers, public authorities and investors in the context of globalisation and industrial change.
2 Social criteria increasingly influencing the investment decisions of individuals and institutions.
3 Increased concern about the damage caused by economic and business activity to the physical environment.
4 Transparency of business activities brought about by media and new information and communication technologies.

It is increasingly clear that business norms across the world have moved CSR into the mainstream of business practice. Non-governmental organisations like the World Resources Institute (WRI), AccountAbility, Global Reporting Initiative (GRI), International Standards Organisation (ISO 14000), and the United Nations, all have major initiatives aimed at improving the social involvement and performance of the world's business community (Godfrey and Hatch, 2007). Indeed, there is an increasingly widespread view that sustainability is now the key driver of innovation for companies (Nidumolu *et al.*, 2009). By 2014, more than 85 per cent of the companies in the FTSE 100 were reporting on social responsibility, and there was a clear expectation that companies should have a published strategy in place (Moore, 2014).

Indeed, Rosabeth Moss Kanter suggests that great companies think differently – they work to make money, but at the same time they think about building enduring institutions, and invest in the future while being aware of the need to build people and society. She claims that this social and institutional logic lies behind the practices of many widely-admired, high-performing and enduring companies (Kanter, 2011). The fundamental goal becomes one of focusing social initiatives onto alignment between a company's social and environmental activities and its business purpose and values (Rangan *et al.*, 2015).

CSR, ethics and corporate reputation

In a world that is media-intensive and Internet-literate, where the scrutiny of business occurs with an unprecedented frequency and intensity, one important link for executives to consider is that between a company's CSR and ethical positioning and its corporate reputation (Chun, 2005). Companies with strong positive reputations attract better staff; are perceived as providing better value, which allows a price premium; have more loyal customers; and have advantages in financial markets. In economies where 70 to 80 per cent of market value comes from intangible assets like brand equity and goodwill, companies are increasingly vulnerable to anything that damages their reputation (Eccles *et al.*, 2007).

For example, one analysis links corporate reputation – having a good name – directly to share values. They estimate that if Coca-Cola had the more responsible reputation of Pepsi, the company would be worth $4 billion more. Similarly, they suggest that if Wal-Mart had the superior corporate reputation for responsible behaviour of Target, then its market value would be $9.7 billion higher (Engardio and Arndt, 2007). Relatedly, brand leaders across the world are investing heavily to regain the trust among consumers that they lost in the economic downturn because of the impact on brand value (Kiley and Helm, 2009). It appears corporate reputation and particularly the impact of perceptions of social responsibility and ethical standards on reputation should be part of executive evaluation of strategic choices.

While many damaging corporate crises are concerned with issues like product defects (e.g., the repeated recall of defective vehicles by Toyota and GM because of safety issues) and failure to deliver the product or service promised (e.g., the mishandling by G4S of security arrangements for the 2012 London Olympics), yet more are concerned with events that lead to public disapproval of the behaviour of companies related to trust, legitimacy and impact on society. There is a perception that businesses generally fall short in their ethical standards (Smith, 2015). Examples of such corporate crises which seriously damage reputations include:

- The 'horsemeat' scandal of 2012–13 when mislabelled meat was found in ready-meals in the UK was probably less about the consumption of horsemeat and more about the perceptions of deception and unethical behaviour by a company like Tesco in selling cheap meat without revealing the fact it was horsemeat, causing a major glitch in Tesco's competitive recovery strategy.
- Allegations of price fixing in 2013 in the petrol business, with raids on the offices of Shell, BP and Statoil, and the public's perception, encouraged by politicians, that they had been deceived and cheated. The issue was more about the companies' behaviour than the actual price of petrol.
- The same period saw the emergence of a public attack on the tax avoidance ploys of multi-nationals like Amazon, Apple, Facebook and Starbucks, leading to them paying little or no tax in the UK. Anger and calls for boycotts emerged as the companies were seen to be cheating and behaving unethically (all such tax avoidance schemes are completely legal).
- The successful CEO of Abercrombie & Fitch, Mike Jeffries, committed what some have called brand suicide by his statements that his clothes were only for thin and attractive people, reflected in hiring only 'gorgeous' shop assistants and no clothes larger than size 10 to get 'cool, good-looking people' to wear the brand 'because they attract other cool kids'. He claimed once to have paid an unattractive customer not to wear his clothes. His statements were seen as offensive, discriminatory and arrogant. Celebrities in the US showed their anger by defiantly giving A&F clothes to homeless people. Mr Jeffries left the company in 2014 amid falling sales and profits and circling activist investors.
- Accusations of bribery and unethical marketing practices have plagued companies like GlaxoSmithKlein in the pharmaceuticals industry. GSK has been accused of bribing doctors and officials, paying rivals not to sell cheaper copies of its drugs to disadvantage customers like the NHS, and promoting medicines beyond their approved uses. It has paid fines in response to some of these charges. The problem is that the perceived ethical violation is likely to outlast the impact of financial penalties.
- The tragic clothing factory collapse disaster at Rana Plaza in Bangladesh in 2013 revealed the supply chain strategies of many clothing manufacturers and their reliance on low-wage workers operating in unsafe and foul conditions. Public judgements related both to the low-cost, low-price strategies of clothing retailers and also the level of integrity shown in their responses to the tragedy. The issue hinged on peoples' perceptions of right and wrong in employment conditions for workers in emerging countries.

Many of the most serious threats to corporate reputation come from perceptions of low ethical standards, poor executive behaviour, and social and environmental damage.

The cost of failing to examine issues of ethical behaviour, social responsibility and the impact on corporate reputation may be lost sales and profits, but longer-term loss of freedom of strategic flexibility – things you want to do and cannot because of reputational issues, and things you do not want to do, but have to.

What follows CSR?

It should be noted that while CSR and ethical mandates contribute a major topical issue in strategic decision making, and a very challenging one, executives should also be aware that thinking has not remained static, and there are emerging views of what follows CSR in changing corporate behaviours. They may have major impact in the future.

The last decade saw commentators identifying the 'new age of corporate responsibility' (Skapinker, 2005), and discussing what comes after the 'green corporation' (Engardio, 2007). However, an important article in 2011 by Porter and Kramer concerning the creation of shared value takes the vision much further. Porter and Kramer argue that the capitalist system itself is under siege and that paradoxically, the more business has begun to embrace corporate responsibility the more it has been blamed for society's failures, suggesting that companies must take the lead in bringing business and society back together. They expand on the concept of shared values as 'policies and operating practices that enhance the competitiveness of a company while simultaneously advancing the economic and social conditions in the communities in which it operates', so that economic and social progress are both addressed through value principles (benefits relative to costs). They see a blurring of the profit/non-profit boundary. In their view, companies can create economic value by creating societal value through reconceiving products and markets, redefining productivity in the value chain, and building supportive industry clusters at the company's locations. Shared value thus becomes an integral part of strategy.

While radical and visionary, it is likely that the shared value model will influence strategic thinking in many companies in the near future. By comparison, an even broader critique of the successes and failing of capitalism is provided by Philip Kotler in his book *Confronting Capitalism* (2015). Kotler identifies the underlying problems with capitalism varying from poverty, income inequality and unemployment to failing to bring social values and happiness into the market equation, and indicates possible solutions to address these interrelated issues. The similarity with Porter and Kramer and relevance to strategy decision makers is in requiring business and social problems to be addressed in combination, not separately, and for them to be addressed by company managers, not others. This represents a shift in thinking which goes beyond most current views of CSR, and is likely to be a recurring theme over the coming years.

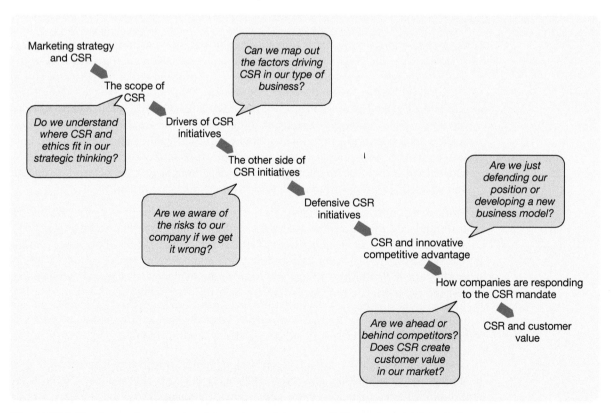

Figure 17.1 Key issues in assessing corporate social responsibility and marketing strategy

In fact, the twenty-first century is already seeing issues of social responsibility and the morality and ethics of company practices become a key element of managing customer relationships, and in how companies are perceived and understood by their customers, i.e., how companies and their products are positioned competitively. However, for some time it has been suggested that an integrated approach to CSR in marketing is largely missing both in theory and practice, and is overdue (Maignan *et al.*, 2005). Certainly, some attention has been given to the operational role of marketing in managing corporate social responsibility initiatives within companies, by expanding focus beyond consumers to include other stakeholders and integrating social responsibility initiatives (Maignan and Ferrell, 2004). These developments have been particularly associated with the development of social marketing, concerned with the contribution of marketing activities to socially desirable behaviours and goals (e.g., anti-smoking campaigns), and 'cause-related' marketing (e.g., the promotion of charitable donations to good causes). For example, some Australian companies are taking a stand against domestic violence, pioneering ways to tackle abuse at home and support victims at work (Batty, 2015).

While the impact of social marketing on the social role attached to the marketing discipline has considerable social importance, our focus here is somewhat broader, and is concerned with the impact of the corporate social responsibility stance of the firm on its marketing and business strategy and performance. Social initiatives and ethical standards have become part of how companies compete and create value. The structure we are adopting to evaluate these issues and the key questions to address are summarised in Figure 17.1.

17.1 Marketing strategy and corporate social responsibility

At one time the issue at stake was primarily as a matter of 'corporate philanthropy' (Porter and Kramer, 2002), such as making donations of financial or other support to good causes, or entirely a question of moral obligation or pure altruism – for example when MAC cosmetics decided to donate all earnings from its Viva Glam lipstick range to HIV-related causes (Jack, 2008). However, corporate social responsibility (CSR) is now increasingly recognised as a source of competitive advantage (or disadvantage if we are weaker than others in this area), and thus a corporate resource, as well as an important part of how competitive relationships operate. Certainly, good corporate citizenship is a marketing asset that can yield benefits in customer loyalty and employee commitment and business performance, but corporate social responsibility is now seen as a strategic resource. Strength in this resource, as in any other, may bring competitive advantages; weakness in this resource, as in any other, may bring vulnerability (Branco and Rodrigues, 2006). Consider, for example, the following situations.

In 2007, Microsoft dropped one of its UK suppliers because that supplier failed to meet Microsoft's standards on employee diversity. Microsoft in the UK is one of an as yet small but growing number of British companies which monitor suppliers to ensure that they employ a representative mix of women and ethnic minorities. The decision resulted from Microsoft's diversity audit at its 250 largest British suppliers (Taylor, 2007). In the US, many large companies, including Microsoft, already insist on good diversity practices from suppliers, and are reducing or terminating the business they do with suppliers who fail to heed requests to diversify their workforces. Suppliers unable or unwilling to meet the social responsibilities defined by major customers stand the considerable risk of losing those customers.

In 2014, Apple extended its supply chain clean-up beyond Chinese factories that produce its devices, to pressure all its suppliers to make their own sourcing more ethical. The goal was to cut the amount of conflict materials ending up in iPhones and iPads sourced from mines in Africa (conflict resources are materials extracted in a conflict zone and sold to perpetuate and support the fighting). The company wants to stop using materials from mines which are unacceptable from a human rights perspective (Bradshaw, 2014).

Further concern extends to questions of ethics in executive behaviour, to which we will return, where inappropriate behaviours in managing buyer/seller relationships can cause expensive losses. The accusations of corruption and bribery levelled against Volkswagen and Siemens executives in Germany – for example, the alleged Siemens 'slush fund' to pay bribes to win international contracts – have been extremely damaging to both companies (Woodhead, 2007). Appositely, it should be noted that many practices regarded in the past as wholly acceptable – for example, 'corporate hospitality' – may now be enough to undermine or destroy buyer/seller relationships, not to mention the careers of individual executives. The impact is magnified by growing transparency and information availability, so dubious practices are more difficult to hide. A review of the 'integrity land-mines' faced by companies concludes:

> The changes in laws, regulations, stakeholder expectations, and media scrutiny that have taken place in the past decade can now make a major lapse in integrity catastrophic. Fines, penalties and settlements are counted in the hundreds of millions (or billions) of dollars . . . And worse, in some cases (as Enron and Arthur Anderson demonstrated) – a company can actually implode.
> *(Heineman, 2007, pp. 100–101)*

The management of business-to-business buyer-seller relationships has to be placed into this more demanding ethical context.

Moreover, at the level of the brand, questions of social responsibility and the ethics and morality of corporate behaviour are increasingly significant, posing both risks and opportunities. In 2007, the ethically-minded coffee company Starbucks found itself in the midst of a damaging and intractable struggle over the legitimacy of coffee trademarking by the Ethiopian government. While the Ethiopian government – one of the world's poorest countries – wanted to trademark some of its most famous coffees, Starbucks objected to the trademarks as damaging to its own brand. The dispute was played out live on the video website YouTube. One commentator suggested that Starbucks was 'playing Russian roulette' with its brand (Rushe, 2007). Indeed, more recently, Starbucks' reputation has been further threatened by its tax avoidance policies – with the first-ever fall in UK sales after calls for a boycott from outraged consumers (Skapinker, 2014). Importantly, there may be an increasing number of trade-offs faced by companies between CSR and commercial goals.

There are important signs that consumers do indeed appear to be discriminating between brands and companies on issues of societal impact and ethical standards, although they may be less impressed by corporate posturing than some companies may believe. For example, consumers were less than amused to discover that Philips and Osram 'Eco' light bulbs were not actually 'green' and did not last longer – the makers claimed that 'Eco' stood for 'economy' not 'ecological' (Spencer, 2015a).

In fact, the real shift in attitudes towards consumption may be difficult to track – for example, while many consumers claim they would pay a 5–10 per cent premium for many ethical products, in practice such brands usually have tiny market shares (Grande, 2007b). Moreover, a five-country survey conducted by market research group GfK NOP suggested that consumers in five of the world's leading economies believe that business ethics have worsened in the past five years, and they are turning to 'ethical consumerism' to make companies more accountable (Grande, 2007a). Respondents believed that brands with 'ethical' claims – on environmental policies or treatment of staff or suppliers – would make business more answerable to the public, and that companies should 'promote ethical credentials more strongly' (Grande, 2007b).

Some commentators on branding have long suggested that ethical consumption is one of the most significant branding issues in modern markets, and underlies change in the automotive sector, food, retailing, technology, and health and beauty sectors. Its influence is behind the strong sales growth of hybrid cars, 'cruelty-free' beauty products, and dramatic growth in sales of organic food. The position appears to be that ethical and environmental questions are being posed by growing numbers of consumers, but they are not always favourably impressed by companies' responses. Nonetheless, the impact of 'ethical consumerism' is likely to be large and of escalating significance.

The growing frequency of issues of this kind suggests that questions relating to corporate social responsibility initiatives and the ethical standards evidenced by companies are increasingly relevant to the decisions about marketing strategy and positioning relative to competitors, because:

- they represent a new kind of corporate resource which has implications for building a sustainable and defensible competitive position
- the measurement and reporting of corporate social responsibility 'scores' (often computed with questionable methodologies) imposes new requirements for openness and transparency in company behaviour – the majority of the world's largest multi-nationals publish corporate social responsibility reports
- reflecting the norms of behaviour determined by buyer organisations is increasingly mandatory in sustaining buyer/seller relationships in business-to-business markets (and is made yet more complex where those relationships are global in nature and span different cultures)
- failure to conform to or exceed the standards of behaviour defined by a media-influenced and Internet-literate consumer may undermine conventional efforts to establish the credentials of a brand and to build a position in a market
- increasingly, employees and managers expect their companies to reflect emerging societal values as well as superior ethical standards, and the retention of critical talent in a company may be closely related to these perceptions and beliefs – indeed, companies like Azco, one of the world's biggest chemicals businesses, and TNT and DSM in the Netherlands, have already started to roll out executive bonus schemes linked directly to meeting sustainability targets (Goodman, 2010; Milne, 2010)
- most telling of all, increasingly corporate social responsibility is not being viewed as purely altruistic, but as an element of competitive advantage (Porter and Kramer, 2006) – companies are challenged to 'outbehave' their competitors in corporate virtue to achieve advantage (Murphy, 2010).

This chapter addresses the evolving question of the impact of corporate responsibility and ethical standards on marketing strategy and competitive positioning. First, we examine the scope of CSR, and the corporate drivers of CSR strategies. This is followed by a review of CSR as a defensive strategy, and then as a source of sustainable competitive advantage.

17.2   The scope of corporate social responsibility

The modern marketplace is increasingly characterised by a variety of anti-business sentiments and activism. Examples include the anti-globalisation movement, shareholder activism, and corporate governance reforms – indeed, some suggest that we are experiencing a climate of 'defiance' towards business (Maignan and Ferrell, 2004). Certainly, global business scandals, such as the accounting abuses uncovered at Enron and Andersons and the bribery accusations at VW and Siemens, cheating diesel emissions tests by VW, and economic downturn and recession, have done little to improve perceptions of business (Piercy et al., 2010a). Indeed, VW's position will not have been improved by the 2015 scandal regarding the 'defeat software' fitted to millions of its diesel vehicles, specifically to cheat emissions tests.

Even at a trivial level, businesses of various kinds are under media-orchestrated attacks for their normal ways of doing business. Recent examples of these pressures include: public campaigns to complain and demand repayment of bank charges; protests about '4×4' (SUV) vehicles, inspired by global warming fears; the conditions under which the tobacco and alcohol industries now operate; demands that airlines should reduce the number of flights they operate and that, like cigarette packs, holiday packages should carry 'health warnings' related to fears about carbon emissions; the anti-obesity campaign pressure on food retailers and restriction of the advertising of junk food products to children; and anti-salt and sugar campaigns to persuade food manufacturers to reduce sale and sugar content in processed foods. There is growing evidence that the way in which products are marketed in many sectors is changing because consumer groups and public authorities believe business practices to be irresponsible.

Accordingly, the belief that consumers are more likely to buy from companies they perceive as socially responsible, and would switch brands to favour products and stores that show concern about the community, has led to growing pressure on firms to behave as good 'corporate citizens'. In contrast to the traditional view that the only responsibility of the firm is to make a profit (Friedman, 1970), companies have been encouraged to undertake activities that provide benefits to various groups: supportive work–family policies, ethics compliance programmes, corporate volunteerism, green marketing. In this sense, 'corporate citizenship' has become a term that describes the activities and processes adopted by businesses to meet their social responsibilities.

One link between these various trends and issues is the effect of inhibiting the ability to companies to develop effective marketing strategy or to establish and defend their desired competitive positions, without making allowance for a societal dimension in their actions. Perhaps the most significant issue now in being a good 'corporate citizen' is not so much moral obligation, as a business case for initiatives which protect and provide new business opportunities.

The growth in corporate attention to CSR has not always been voluntary, instead reflecting surprise at public reaction to issues not previously thought to be their responsibility – Nike faced consumer boycotts after media reporting of abusive labour practices in its Indonesian suppliers' factories; fast-food and packaged food companies are being held responsible for obesity problems and poor nutrition; pharmaceutical companies are expected to respond to the AIDS pandemic in Africa, though it is far removed from their main product lines and markets (Porter and Kramer, 2006).

More positively, CSR may be associated with important and measurable benefits to companies. For example, cause-related projects may impact directly on income: if firms that create social gains realise cash value in terms of increased purchases by morally-conscious customers (or those customers are willing to pay higher prices), or in reduced costs. More broadly, CSR may have the impact of building long-term customer loyalty, legitimacy, trust or brand equity (Godfrey and Hatch, 2007). Indeed, some companies have made high-profile efforts to position themselves as socially responsible as a core part of their strategy, which may in part be a response to external critics, but also part of the underlying vision of what a business is about:

- Nike advertises its commitment to adopting 'responsible business practices that contribute to profitable and sustainable growth', having come through a decade or more of vocal condemnation of employment practices in its overseas supplier workshops.
- The Body Shop was positioned from its outset as actively involved in social improvement projects throughout the world and opposed to practices such as animal-testing of cosmetics and toiletry products, which is thought to be one of the resources of the business which made it an attractive acquisition for the more traditional cosmetics company, L'Oréal.
- Furniture retailer IKEA has a strategy of purchasing wind farms – already in France, Germany, Poland and the US, with other countries to follow – as part of efforts to reduce the carbon footprint of its furniture stores, and is pursuing a long-term goal of securing all its electricity needs from renewable sources.

Certainly, it has become increasingly important for strategic decision makers to understand the scope of corporate social responsibility (CSR) initiatives both in developing possible defences against attacks on their competitive position and ability to compete, but also as potential sources of new types of competitive strength.

Scoping CSR possibilities involves initially considering the specific dimensions of CSR. Attention has been given to initiatives such as the support of charitable causes, and the advent of 'cause-related marketing' (Barone *et al.*, 2000), as well as the protection of the natural environment as an influence on purchasing behaviour and marketing strategy.

In developing an integrative framework to examine CSR, Maignan and Ferrell (2004) provide a useful overview of how CSR has been understood, and how that understanding is changing. They distinguish between CSR as social obligation, as stakeholder obligation, as ethics-driven, and as managerial process. These distinctions are useful in understanding the case for CSR and providing a managerial framework for addressing the strategic implications of CSR.

- *CSR as social obligation.* Since the 1950s onwards there has been a strong link between CSR and the alignment of corporate actions with the objectives and values of society. This ethos is still found in contemporary marketing studies, particularly regarding the potential for both positive and negative consumer reactions to CSR initiatives of this type (Sen and Bhattacharya, 2001). Classically, Carroll (1979) distinguishes social obligations as: *economic obligations* – to be productive and economically viable; *legal and ethical obligations* – to follow the law and accepted values and norms; and *philanthropic obligations* – to actively give back to society.

- *CSR as stakeholder obligation.* The 1990s saw the emergence of the view that CSR as social obligation was too broad to allow the effective management of CSR (Clarkson, 1995), and the argument that businesses are not responsible to society as a whole, but only to those who directly or indirectly affect, or are affected by, the firm's activities – i.e., the firm's stakeholders (Donaldson and Preston, 1995). Accordingly, stakeholders can be grouped into: *organisational* – employees, customers, shareholders, suppliers; *community* – local residents, special interest groups; *regulatory* – local authorities, legal controls; and *media* stakeholders (Henriques and Sadorsky, 1999).

- *CSR as ethics-driven.* Viewing CSR as either a social or stakeholder suggests that CSR is motivated only by corporate self-interests, by enabling business to gain legitimacy with important external parties. It has been argued that such views fail to account for actions by companies which represent a positive commitment to society's interests that disregard self-interest and are genuinely altruistic (Swanson, 1995). Indeed, if CSR reflects only obligations, then it becomes difficult to evaluate whether business practices are or are not socially responsible, as opposed to simply reciprocal (Jones, 1995). An ethics-driven view of CSR is concerned with the rightness or wrongness of specific initiatives, independently of any social or stakeholder obligation. For example, justice-based ethics would lead a company to attempt to systematically favour decisions that stimulate equality and fairness for its partners and associates.

- *CSR as managerial process.* The three perspectives above attempt to identify the factors that persuade businesses to undertake CSR initiatives. An additional view concerns CSR in terms of organisational processes (sometimes called 'corporate social responsiveness') (Ackerman, 1975). One view advocates that 'issues management' and 'environmental assessment' constitute managerial processes relevant to working towards a proactive responsibility stance (Wood, 1991). Others suggest the type of sequential management process useful to systematic development of CSR initiatives (Ackerman, 1975): monitoring and assessing environmental conditions; attending to stakeholder demands, and designing plans and policies aimed at enhancing the firm's impacts. Carroll earlier described the managerial processes of response to social responsibility as involving: planning and social forecasting, organising for social response, controlling social activities, and developing corporate social policy (Carroll, 1979).

The importance of Maignan and Ferrell's integration of these disparate conceptualisations of CSR is that it provides us with an overview of the issues likely to be raised by CSR initiatives, and suggests the importance of developing appropriate organisational processes for managing CSR. Scoping the existing and likely future impacts of the diverse pressures towards CSR is becoming an important challenge for management. In this context, Porter and Kramer (2006) suggest that management attention should focus on:

- *Identifying the points of intersection between the company and society* – including the ways in which the business impacts on society in the normal course of business (e.g., transport emissions), but also the way in which social conditions impact on the business (e.g., regulatory standards). This involves both mapping the social impact of the value chain, and also the social influences on the company's competitiveness.
- *Choosing which social issues to address* – selecting issues which intersect with the business and which present an opportunity to create shared value, rather than trying to solve all society's problems.
- *Creating a corporate social agenda* – looking beyond external expectations to achieve both social and economic benefits.

Although the ways in which it can be addressed will differ greatly between company situations, the framework in this section provides an initial approach to making CSR issues explicit and integrating them into thinking about marketing strategy.

17.3 Drivers of corporate social responsibility initiatives

Notwithstanding the links between corporate social responsibility and marketing strategy, it would be wrong to suggest that altruistic, corporate philanthropy is disappearing or diminishing in importance. Indeed, while traditional philanthropy has been criticised as ineffective, the birth of the 'social enterprise' movement represents a new model addressing issues of social justice with approaches drawn from the business world. For example, Google.org is the philanthropic arm of the search engine company, established to invest in and support for-profit and not-for-profit groups that focus on energy, poverty and the environment. Certainly charitable gifts by UK companies have soared since 2007 (Smith, 2014). Achieving social goals through business means – social enterprise – represents a new type of business model, fuelled by individuals, like Microsoft's Bill Gates, who do not simply want to donate money to good causes, but to bring their own philosophy and skills to managing it to achieve social return. Social enterprise aims to break down traditional barriers between business, government and charity in ventures that aim to combine innovation, market orientation and an objective to generate a public benefit (Jack, 2007). It is speculated by some that there may even be a move away from shareholder capitalism to a radically different enterprise model, in which social purpose is placed above profit or profit is harnessed to social purpose (Smith and Ward, 2007).

However, while social enterprise is an important extension of traditional concepts of corporate philanthropy, and it may enhance the reputations of companies and leaders who devote resources to these ventures, our present interests are in the drivers of more conventional corporate social responsibility initiatives, and the links to business and marketing strategy in existing companies rather than new hybrid business models.

Porter and Kramer (2006), in their influential review of CSR, suggest that while CSR generally remains imbued with a strong moral imperative (as we saw in the last section of the chapter), modern supporters of the CSR movement rely on four arguments to justify attention and resources for these initiatives:

- *Moral obligation* – the duty for a company to be a good citizen and to do 'the right thing'. However, there are many dilemmas faced in such questions – Google's entry to the China market created a major conflict between Western dislike for censorship and the legal requirements imposed by the Chinese government.

- *Sustainability* – emphasis on the environmental and community impact of the business. To an extent this may reflect enlightened self-interest – changes to packaging at McDonald's have reduced its solid waste by 30 per cent.
- *Licence to operate* – the tacit or explicit permission a company needs from governments, communities and other stakeholders, to do business – this permission is being progressively withdrawn from the tobacco industry.
- *Reputation* – CSR initiatives to enhance a company's image, strengthen its brand, improve morale, or even raise share prices. Some organisations have a distinctive position based on an extraordinary long-term commitment to social responsibility, for example, Ben & Jerry's, The Body Shop.

Perhaps, to this list can be added the need to *respond to the CSR-based positioning of competitors* who are seeking advantage through an enhanced franchise with the customer, and to coping with explicit customer demands for the standards they expect in, for example, their suppliers. Interestingly, Porter and Kramer note that 'All four schools of thought share the same weakness: They focus on the tension between business and society rather than their interdependence' (2006, p. 83).

Thomas Stewart (2006) underlines this point. He notes the contradiction between the classic argument that a company's only responsibility to society is to make as much money as it legally can, compared to the modern reality that a company that shunned society would be ostracised in turn, to its cost. The opposite problem for executives may be the conflict between social initiatives and business goals – is there perhaps hypocrisy in the brewer urging consumers not to drink, or the oil company promoting fuel conservation? Stewart's point is that such views share a logical flaw: they assume that companies and society have opposing interests. Thus, it follows that starting from the premise that business and society are interdependent identifies CSR as a strategic opportunity which is far greater importance than moral duty alone.

Importantly, CSR may be associated with significant and measurable benefits for companies. Indeed, Peter Senge and colleagues argue that after years of scepticism, big companies are genuinely acting to cut waste, cut carbon emissions, find sources of renewable energy and develop sustainable business models (Senge *et al.*, 2008). There is an increasingly widespread view that there is a business case for social initiatives – behind the drive for sustainability lies a growing belief that environmental and social projects not only improve corporate reputations, but also foster innovation, cut costs and open up new markets (Skapinker, 2008b). Unilever's Pureit machine is illustrative – it cleans water to provide drinking water without boiling or the use of mains electricity, and purifies water more cheaply than boiling. Developed by Hindustan Unilever in India, the social and health benefits of lower costs for clean drinking water are evident, but also the potential market for the product in the rural areas of developing countries is huge.

Indeed, some companies have made high-profile efforts to position as socially responsible, as an explicit part of their strategy, which may in part be a response to external critics, but also part of the underlying vision of what a business is about. Some go even further in advocating the combination of business and social goals. Moss Kanter uses the term 'vanguard companies' to describe those which are 'ahead of the pack and potentially the wave of the future' because they aspire to be 'big but human, efficient but innovative, global but concerned about local communities [and] try to use their power and influence to develop solutions to problems the public cares about'. She concludes from her studies of companies like IBM, Procter and Gamble, Publicis, Cemex and Diageo that 'Humanistic values and attention to societal needs are a starting point for smart strategy in the global information age.' In particular, 'the leaders of a vanguard company espouse positive values and encourage their employees to embrace and act on them.' Social purpose creates strategic advantages, but only if those social commitments have an economic logic that attracts resources to the firm (Moss Kanter, 2009). The Moss Kanter concept of a 'vanguard company' reaches for a post-CSR setting of successful businesses sustained by moral purpose as well as economic achievement.

For example, in 2010 Paul Polman, Chief Executive of Unilever, outlined his company's 'sustainable living plan' to City investors. His commitment to sustainability and a new type of business led to the statement:

> Unilever has been around for 100-plus years. We want to be around for several hundred more years. So if you buy into this long-term value-creation model, which is equitable, which is shared, which is sustainable, then come and invest with us. If you don't buy into this, I respect you as a human being, but don't put your money in our company.
> *(Skapinker, 2010)*

This is a very strong statement for a chief executive to make to investors, which underlines his determination to combine commercial and social goals. Nonetheless, some investors are nervous that Mr Polman's focus on sustainability and climate and social issues may be a distraction from strategy and performance (Daneshkhu, 2015).

By way of further illustration, Table 17.1 lists *Fortune* magazine's top ten companies in 2015 that are changing the world, demonstrating the spread across different sectors of the concept of eco-friendly and socially responsible management helping company performance and profitability – but particularly, doing well by doing good.

Table 17.1 Companies changing the world – doing well by doing good

Rank	Company	
1	Vodafone and Safaricom	Connecting the unbanked masses to the global economy through M-Pesa the mobile-money platform that allows people who lack bank accounts to use their smartphones to save and transfer money, receive pensions and pay bills. Around 17 million people in East Africa, India, Romania and Albania use M-Pesa – a staggering 42% of Kenya's GDP is transacted through M-Pesa.
2	Google (Alphabet)	Knocking down more barriers to knowledge – not just search but the home of open science, while Google Translate closes cultural gaps in real time and Google Earth helps scientists track climate change.
3	Toyota	Building powerful weapons in the fight to lower vehicle emissions – the hybrid Prius accounts for 40% of the world's hybrid car market while 2015 saw the launch of the Toyota Mirai, the world's first mass-produced fuel-cell car powered by hydrogen and emitting nothing but drops of water.
4	Wal-Mart	Pushing an army of suppliers to cut waste – for ten years Wal-Mart has been working towards three goals: being 100% supplied by renewable energy, eliminating waste, and creating a more sustainable supply chain. Today Wal-Mart gets 26% of its electricity from renewable sources, operates with 9% less energy, and 1,300 of its suppliers now use its Sustainability Index. By the end of 2015, the company eliminated 20 million metric tonnes of greenhouse gas emissions from its supply chain.

Rank	Company	
5	Enel	Leading the way in cleaning up the power grid – Italy's power company generates 38% of its total power output from renewable sources, including wind, solar and geothermal energy. This figure will be 48% in 4 years' time, and the company aims to be carbon-neutral by 2050.
6	GSK	An innovative anti-malaria vaccine brings new hope – Mosquirix took 30 years to develop and is the first vaccine of its kind. Malaria strikes 200 million people a year and kills 600,000. In trials Mosquirix reduced malaria by 40% in children. It is priced 5% above cost of manufacture and the profit will be reinvested in tropical disease R&D.
7	Jain Irrigation Systems	Smarter water delivery becomes a cure for rural poverty – micro-irrigation systems that increase crop yield between 60 and 300%, improving the livelihoods of 5 million small farmers in India. Jain now does business with drip-irrigation systems in 116 countries.
8	Cisco Systems	Training a tech workforce to lift up the Middle East – pioneering an outsourcing collaboration between its Israel office and Palestinians with tech skills to help the West Bank's IT outsourcing sector grow by 64% in 4 years. Cisco has also staked $15 million in local incubators and youth training schemes. Cisco's Networking Academy has trained 5.5 million students around the world, providing IT skills but also giving Cisco a foothold in new markets.
9	Novartis	Bringing essential medicines to the poor – starting in India, Novartis brought basic remedies but also health education and doctors to raise awareness of the critical need for hygiene to prevent infection. In 3 years its Arogya Parivar (Hindi for 'healthy family') broke even. The programme is now being rolled out in Kenya, Indonesia and Vietnam.
10	Facebook	The app for philanthropy – the power of connectivity has had some bad outcomes (recruitment for ISIS), but generally good ones – the 2014 Ice Bucket Challenge raised $115 million for the ALS Association (ALS or amyotrophic lateral sclerosis is a progressive neurodegenerative disease that affects nerve cells in the brain and the spinal cord and research for a cure needs funding).

Source: adapted from: *Fortune* (2015), 'Change the World List', *Fortune*, September 1.

Nonetheless, there is wide recognition that firms face choices in their responsiveness to social responsibility (see section 17.7 below). This background provides the basis for examining the linkages between CSR and competitive advantage and strategic positioning in the marketplace, in ways which have not been fully recognised in earlier stages of the consideration of CSR initiatives. In particular, we distinguish between CSR as a *defence* against attacks that can undermine competitive position, and as a *strategy* which can provide new business opportunities. Prior to making that distinction, it is important to note that there are potential downsides to the innovation of CSR initiatives in companies.

<table>
<tr><td>**17.4**</td><td>**The other side of corporate social responsibility initiatives**</td></tr>
</table>

It is important that well-meant enthusiasm for combining social and commercial goals for the greater good of society and the business should not blind executives to the fact that there are vocal critics of CSR initiatives, and that not all CSR efforts have achieved their intended beneficial effects. There are risks to companies in CSR initiatives which misfire as summarised in Figure 17.2.

Some suggest, for example, that 'ethical shopping' is no more than a middle-class indulgence which offers very limited benefits to the good causes espoused (Hattersley, 2008). Indeed, one commentator suggests that the deadliest greenhouse gas is actually the 'hot air of CSR' – inclining to the view that the truly responsible thing is to run a business competently, not to be involved in social causes (Stern, 2009). Similarly, others suggest that organic food is 'a tax on the gullible' (Lawson, 2009). It is perhaps telling that with economic downturn, many government environmental policies were quietly dropped amid business opposition and signs that voter priorities were changing (Pickard and Harvey, 2008). Others believe that the more focused concept of sustainability (in the sense of meeting current needs without harming future generations) will replace that of CSR in management thinking.

17.4.1 Criticisms of CSR initiatives

The development of CSR initiatives by businesses is not universally welcomed. For example, some managers talk about the 'little green lies' – challenging the notion that making a company environmentally-friendly can be cost-effective and also profitable, accusing advocates of these initiatives of 'empty boasting' (Elgin, 2007).

Cynics also point to the collapse of markets like that for organic foods in the UK under the pressure of rising food prices and economic pressures on the consumer. Indeed, 2008 did see a 19 per cent fall in organic food sales, as consumers filled their shopping baskets with cheaper non-organic food. Some believe that organic farming is now in decline in

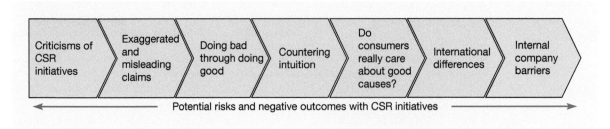

Figure 17.2 The other side of CSR

the UK (Daneshkhu, 2014). Certainly, there are strong signs that when times are difficult financially the shopper is prepared to sacrifice 'green' credentials in favour of cheaper food (Rigby, 2008).

Critics also suggest that the rush to 'carbon credit' projects yielded few if any environmental benefits – some organisations are paying for emissions reductions that do not take place; others are making large profits from carbon trading for clean-ups that would have been made anyway. The 'green gold rush' of carbon trading stimulated by environmental concerns appears seriously flawed (Harvey and Fidler, 2007).

Indeed, some opponents argue that though CSR can improve a company's reputation (perhaps rebuilding goodwill in the wake of corporate scandals and regulatory scrutiny) and attract talent (from employees who expect their companies to be active in social issues), it costs too much (possibly at the expense of other priorities like R&D), and is often misguided and ineffective (Grow *et al.*, 2005).

The tobacco industry provides an interesting illustration of the limitations of CSR. Notwithstanding vehement criticism by anti-smoking groups, and opponents like the World Health Organisation – which categorically questions the very possibility of social responsibility in the tobacco industry – recent years have seen tobacco companies starting to position themselves as good corporate citizens. These moves include corporate philanthropy – e.g., donations to universities for research and to environmental groups; CSR reporting – e.g., in annual reports and other publications; and self-regulation – e.g., BAT, Philip Morris and Japan Tobacco launching an international voluntary code of marketing. However, research suggests that these moves are likely to be ineffective or even counterproductive: some scientific journals refuse to publish research sponsored by the tobacco industry, many stakeholder groups will not risk their own reputations by engaging with tobacco companies, and CSR claims are regarded by many as window-dressing at best. While the tobacco industry can defend its position by showing integrity in its supply chain (e.g., improving the working conditions of plantation employees), it is unable to demonstrate a contribution to the well-being of society (because of the addictive and lethally dangerous nature of its products) (Palazzo and Richter, 2005). While defensive CSR may offer some advantages to tobacco companies, a proactive stance is unlikely to be effective.

17.4.2 Exaggerated and misleading claims for CSR

Indeed, some companies have been accused of unscrupulous marketing ploys which use green propaganda to attract customers, and the Advertising Standard Authority has already ruled against several spurious claims of 'greenery' (Hanlon, 2007). The ploy consists of aiming to sell more by making people feel guilty. For example, while British supermarkets compete aggressively to prove their green credentials (Goodman, 2006), groups like the National Consumer Council suggest that they fail to live up to their claims, when tested against objective criteria, such as making seasonal foods available; taking products from sustainable sources; stocking organic products; and cutting waste (Harvey and Rigby, 2006). Certainly, the fact that Tesco's 'local' chickens go on a 1,000 mile round-trip before being put on sale suggests a cynical use of the term 'local' (Allen, 2008). Supermarkets, including Tesco and Sainsbury's in the UK, stand accused of 'greenwash' – making false 'eco' claims about their products to deceive consumers seeking a 'green' lifestyle (Poulter, 2010). Certainly, a *Harvard Business Review* blog has suggested that increasingly CSR will be seen as a public relations sham (Skapinker, 2008a).

Similar controversy continues to surround the Fairtrade programme and brand. Although very successful – for example, from 2009 all Cadbury's chocolate carried the ethical logo, as well as all Tate & Lyle's retail sugar (Boyle, 2009; Beattie, 2008) – the Adam Smith Institute's report *Unfair Trade* (Adam Smith Institute, 2008) concludes that Fairtrade: (1) helps only a very small number of farmers, while leaving the majority worse off; (2) favours producers from better-off nations like Mexico rather than poorer African nations; (3) holds back economic development by rewarding the inefficient; (4) creates a situation where supermarkets profit more from the higher price of Fairtrade goods than do the farmers; and (5) that only a fifth of produce grown on Fairtrade-approved farms is actually purchased at its guaranteed fair price. For example, it was estimated in 2006 that of the £200 million spent on Fairtrade products in the UK, only £42 million went back to those in the developing world – supermarkets took 32p in every pound spent and the rest went to middleman and the licensing fees charged by the Fairtrade organisation (Ebrahami, 2006). The *Unfair Trade* report claims that 'At best, Fairtrade is a marketing device that does the poor little good. At worst, it may inadvertently be harming some of the planet's most vulnerable people.'

17.4.3 Doing bad through doing good

Others critics of CSR focus on the 'unintended consequences' of well-meaning social initiatives. For example, planting trees in Uganda to offset greenhouse gas emissions in Europe was an attractive idea, which became less appealing in the light of Ugandan farmers being evicted from their land at gunpoint to make room for a forest (Zizola, 2007). Similarly, fervent environmentalist support for biofuels has diminished somewhat as it has become clear that switching crops to biofuels has created food shortages in many emerging markets and contributed to rising food prices in the developed countries (Blas and Wiggins, 2007). More minor initiatives can also fail through their actual rather than intended consequences. In 2006, B&Q announced that it would cease selling environmentally-friendly roof top wind turbines, because they do not work in built-up areas and, worse, they create considerable noise pollution (Crooks, 2009).

A recent controversy surrounds diesel cars. For some 20 years manufacturers have been urged by the 'global warming' lobby and encouraged by governments through tax concessions to persuade motorists to switch to diesel-powered vehicles to protect the environment. Research now suggests that diesel emissions are actually more damaging to the environment and more health-threatening than those from petrol-powered vehicles. Around half the new cars sold in the UK are now diesels. One estimate is that diesel cars account for more than 5,000 premature deaths in the UK alone each year. The negative impact on the credibility of the green lobby and car manufacturers is considerable (Glover, 2015).

Similarly, while countries in the West have seen escalating sales of solar panels symbolising the drive for clean energy and greener lifestyle, the poisonous waste created in their production is blighting crops and water supplies. In China, the thriving renewable energy industry is accused of air, soil and water pollution, poor safety standards, and causing withered crops and poisoned rivers around solar panel factories at the heart of the renewable energy revolution (Sheridan and Jones, 2010). The overall effect currently appears negative, in spite of the best intentions of those who promote clean energy.

The well-meaning government incentives to persuade car drivers to adopt electric vehicles in Norway includes free access for electric cars to bus lanes. The result has been worse congestion as buses struggle to get around the additional extra electric cars in the restricted lanes, and a poorer service for those who leave their cars at home and take the bus (Jervell, 2014). This is not what was intended.

17.4.4 Countering intuition

Intuition (and some vocal opinion) would probably suggest that generally healthy food is 'good', traditional babies' nappies are 'good', dishwashers are 'bad', and plastic carrier bags are 'bad'.

While consumers who favour healthier eating are likely also to dislike animal testing, in 2007 it was reported that the trend towards healthier eating had led to an increase of more than 300 per cent in laboratory experiments on animals for food additives, sweeteners and health supplements. Animals appear to have become the victims of the fad for health foods (Woolf, 2007). In 2008, the British government tried to suppress an embarrassing report finding that old-fashioned reusable nappies damage the environment more than disposables – the findings are upsetting for proponents of real nappies, who have claimed that they can help save the planet (Woolf, 2008).

Reckitt Benckiser is understandably making much of the fact that calculations show that using a dishwasher (with Reckitt's detergent) is more environmentally-friendly than washing up by hand which uses more energy and water (Harvey, 2007). Even the much-vilified (and increasingly banned or for which payment is demanded) supermarket plastic bag turns out to be 'greener' than the paper equivalents, which consume more energy and water and produce more pollution (though more expensive reusable bags are better for the environment than any disposable bag) (Ball, 2009).

Sadly, it appears too that the electric car is not going to save the planet (or the automobile sector), because to achieve fuel efficiency they consume a disproportionate amount of scarce resource in production and use too much power in operation, and anyway buyers appear loath to pay the higher price for the electric vehicle (Reed, 2010). Indeed, in spite of the hype, it took Toyota a decade to sell the first million of its hybrid Prius (the 'Toyota Pious' to eco-cynics), while its sales of luxury limousines and gas guzzling pick-ups grew much faster. At the same time, the very poor financial performance of Tesla – the innovative electric car manufacturer – is under close scrutiny by investors (Wieczner, 2015).

17.4.5 Do consumers really care about good causes?

The answer to this question is probably that some do and some do not, suggesting that the issue for executives to examine is which consumers care and whether they make a coherent target for marketing strategies relating to CSR. Environmentalists were disappointed, for example, to see US sales of 4x4 gas guzzlers (SUVs) recover with low oil prices – as fuel prices dropped, consumer enthusiasm for eco-friendly cars appeared to decline also (Welch, 2008). Similarly, a recent survey in the UK by Pledge4Plastics revealed a high degree of consumer indifference to recycling initiatives (Hull, 2014). This may be why UK retailers gave out a billion more plastic bags in 2014 compared to 2010, in spite of the environmental pressures, and the number is only likely to drop with mandatory charging for plastic bags (Poulter, 2014).

The economic recession encouraged the view that a solid record in sustainability will not impress consumers unless there is a direct and easily identified benefit for them (Gary, 2013). While companies understand the value of green marketing and sustainability, there are signs that some consumers remain stubbornly indifferent or antagonistic about going green, suggesting the need for more efforts to promote sustainability-focused purchasing behaviours (Stafford and Hartman, 2013).

Certainly, a retail viewpoint suggests that consumers fall into four categories regarding ethics and social responsibility: (1) committed, cause-driven purchasers (8% of the total); (2) those who want to purchase ethically but are not sure how to, and are looking for help (30–35%); (3) those who feel the same but doubt their individual purchases can make much difference (30–35%); and, (4) those who are completely uninterested (the rest). Retailers have long commented on the 30:3 phenomenon (30 per cent of purchasers say that they thought about workers' rights, animal welfare and the planet when deciding what to buy, but sales figures show only 3 per cent of them act on those thoughts). However, the proportion of consumers buying ethically, or poised to do so, is now seen as much higher and growing (Skapinker 2007).

Interestingly, one recent US study concludes that companies that act in a socially responsible manner and advertise that fact may be able to charge more for their products. The researchers conclude that companies should segment their markets and make a particular effort to reach out to buyers with high ethical standards, because those are the customers who can deliver the biggest potential profit on ethically produced goods (Trudel and Cotte, 2008).

Nonetheless, while a company like Primark has been severely criticised for the labour abuses in its supply chain, Primark achieved record sales in the economic downturn and recovery because of the ultra-low prices on its fashion clothing imports – their customers appear to place a higher value on two T-shirts for £1 than ethical working conditions for those who make them. Similarly, ugly images of a 7-year-old boy working a 98-hour week in Delhi for 7p an hour to make Christmas decorations for British retailer Poundland seem to have had little negative impact on Poundland's sales (Smith, 2010).

17.4.6 International differences

For the international business, research by Globescan underlines the point that CSR is judged differently in different parts of the world because peoples' top priorities vary. So, for example, to Chinese consumers the hallmark of social responsibility is safe, high-quality products, while in South Africa what matters most is a contribution to social needs such as healthcare and education. In countries like the US, France, Italy and Switzerland, and much of South America, the highest priority is to treat employees fairly. In Australia, Canada, Indonesia and the UK, environmental protection is the highest priority. In Turkey, the most important indicator of corporate responsibility is charitable donation (Maitland, 2005).

There is an important need to balance global and local issues in examining the potential impact of CSR initiatives for the company operating across national and cultural boundaries. For example, it is clear that increasing global transparency is an unavoidable consequence of communications advances – so while Microsoft maintains a position of integrity and social awareness, as well as corporate philanthropy, in the developed world, paradoxically workers assembling its computer mice and webcams in China work 15-hour shifts in poor conditions for 34p an hour (Hull and Sorrell, 2010).

17.4.7 Internal company barriers

In 2014, the *Financial Times* (Moore, 2014) reported that the number of business leaders supporting CSR had fallen, amid suggestions that share prices did not reflect investments in social initiatives. In a post-recession context, the search for business performance has reduced the emphasis on the environment and sustainability for managers in some companies (Murray, 2014).

An Arthur D. Little report entitled *The Innovation Highground* suggests that while it is important for social and environmental concerns to receive explicit attention when setting strategy and designing products, relatively few companies display this as a capability (Arthur D Little, 2005). The report suggests that main barriers to CSR initiatives are: a lack of understanding among strategists of the significance of social and environmental trends; internal and external scepticism, often combined with a perception that these activities involve high risk and uncertainty; an absence of appropriate business models, particularly for emerging markets; a tendency to use available capital for 'more of the same' rather than new business models; and an unwillingness to finance new projects, particularly at the bottom of the business cycle. Interestingly, this research was conducted among major international companies including Sony, Dupont, HP and Vodafone.

Executives proposing strategic marketing programmes that rely on CSR-based positioning should be aware of the likely resistance and barriers from those who distrust CSR and do not understand it as a legitimate strategic tool. Moreover, the risks of damage to corporate reputation from unintended consequences and perceptions of insincerity should also be considered.

17.5   **Defensive corporate social responsibility initiatives**

Returning to the question of defensive versus strategic responses to CSR, if a firm is essentially defensive or accommodative in its stance to social responsiveness, then its primary concerns with CSR will be the protection of relationships, for example, with consumers, business-to-business customers, influential lobby or pressure groups, suppliers, employees and managers, and relative position against competitors. This array of pressures towards defensive CSR is summarised in Figure 17.3. Currently, the evidence is that most firms concentrate their communications regarding CSR with their consumers, employees and shareholders, showing some neglect of their competitors and alliance partners (Snider *et al.*, 2003).

For example, clothing company H&M along with other Scandinavian retailers suspended sales of items containing Angora wool in response to video footage distributed by animal rights activists showing the harvesting practices. The video was produced by the powerful People for the Ethical Treatment of Animals (PETA) lobby group and showed hair being torn or plucked from Angora rabbits, leaving the animals in agony. The retailer response was defensive to avoid damage by association with producer practices (Hansegard, 2013).

Porter and Kramer (2006) warn regarding defensive forms of CSR – particularly in terms of responding to the challenges of pressure groups – that companies seeing CSR only as a way to placate pressure groups often find that this approach turns into a series of short-term public relations actions, with minimal social benefit and no strategic benefit for the business. They suggest the most common corporate responses to CSR have not been strategic and are often little more than cosmetic. Nonetheless, the risks in remaining inactive when social demands become severe are considerable.

The changing policies at Coca-Cola are illustrative. Coke has attracted a barrage of negative publicity over recent years: the alleged mistreatment of workers in Columbia; the use of water in drought-stricken parts of India; delaying acceptance of responsibility for contaminated product in Belgium in 1999; violently ejecting shareholder activists from the AGM; and playing a major role in fuelling the childhood obesity epidemic sweeping the developed world. Coke has been actively boycotted on university campuses throughout North America, and in parts of Europe. The company was in danger of replacing Nike and McDonald's as the chief corporate villain for the anti-globalisation movement. The problem recognised by management was negative perceptions of the company progressively undermining the value of the brand. The new CEO of Coke mandated a proactive company approach to social issues, with a goal of making Coke the 'recognised global leader in corporate social responsibility'. The company has undertaken an audit of labour practices throughout its supply chain, launched several water conservation projects, embraced industry guidelines restricting the sale of sugary drinks in schools, and supported initiatives to encourage physical exercise among children. Nonetheless, critics still claim the company is pursuing these initiatives under pressure, not because they believe they are the right things to do (Ward, 2006). Certainly the company's recent attempt to present itself as an anti-obesity

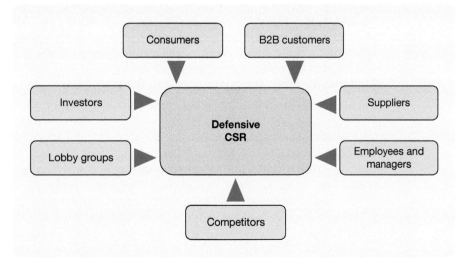

Figure 17.3
Pressures driving defensive CSR strategies

campaigner backfired badly, illustrating the difficult balancing act for food and drink companies in an increasingly health-conscious world (Rappeport, 2013).

The managerial goal in a defensive CSR mode should be to anticipate and develop appropriate responses to social demands from any source that threatens to undermine the value and credibility of brands, the attractiveness of the competitive position upon which the company's strategy depends, and the viability of the marketing strategy itself. However, it is important that social initiative responses to these pressures should be carefully evaluated for likely effects, rather than constitute an unthinking knee-jerk reaction by management.

Management attention can usefully be given to examining the links between CSR stance and the impacts on consumers, business-to-business customers, investors, lobby groups, suppliers, employees and managers, and competitors. The goal should be to carefully evaluate the possible positive and negative impacts of CSR efforts on each of these groups.

17.5.1 Consumers and CSR

The adoption of social causes by organisations has often been based on the assumption that consumers will reward this behaviour (Levy, 1999). It is, however, unlikely that consumers will blindly accept social initiatives as sincere, and so may or may not reward the firm with positive attitudes and purchases (Becker-Olsen *et al.*, 2006). Indeed, research suggests that consumers will 'punish' firms that are perceived as insincere or manipulative in their social involvement (Becker-Olsen *et al.*, 2006). Nonetheless, there have been some research findings suggesting that there is a link between a company's social initiatives and positive consumer responses in attitudes, beliefs and behaviours, and positive associations have been found between social initiatives and price, perceived quality, corporate attitudes and purchase intentions (Becker-Olsen *et al.*, 2006). In fact, one study underlines that: customers will pay a premium for ethically produced goods; conversely, they will punish companies not seen as ethical (by demanding a lower price); the punishment exacted is greater than the premium customers are willing to pay; and companies do not need to be 100 per cent ethical to be rewarded (Trudel and Cotte, 2009).

Certainly, there is a strong argument that to be effective, social initiatives must be consistent with a firm's operating objectives and values. Indeed, there is some evidence that when social initiatives are not aligned with corporate objectives and values, they may become a liability and diminish previously held beliefs about the firm. There is some priority for social initiatives and responses to be chosen carefully to reflect the firm's values and domain, so that consumers perceive initiatives as proactive and genuinely socially motivated (Becker-Olsen *et al.*, 2006).

Executives should be aware that the potential impact of ethical consumers may remain hidden for some time. One important concern is 'conflicted consumers' – they currently buy the product and on the face of things appear to have high satisfaction and display loyalty, but actually they would rather not buy from you and are poised to switch as soon as a viable alternative appears. They constitute a 'stealth segment' of apparently loyal customers who actually have major ethical concerns about your company (Fraser, 2007).

Business-to-business customers and CSR

The escalating demands of business-to-business customers for their suppliers to implement CSR policies and initiatives that are acceptable to the customer organisation have already been noted. For example, to reinforce its ethical credentials, jeans maker Levi Strauss & Co. now offers financial incentives to suppliers in Bangladesh and China to meet environmental, labour and safety standards, providing those suppliers with access to lower cost working capital – publicised as adding 'ethical cred to street cred' for Levi's (Donnan, 2014).

The 'vendor compliance' programme at Target Corporation is illustrative. Target Corporation is a successful US retailer with more than 1,500 Target stores and nearly 200 upmarket SuperTarget outlets. Target prides itself on its high ethical standards and business principles, emphasising the protection of human rights and extends these principles and standards to its suppliers. Target sources its purchases globally, through its Associated Merchandising Corporation subsidiary. Purchasing officers are required to uphold Target Corporation social responsibility standards wherever they buy in the world, even when these exceed the requirements of local laws – Target engineers do not just inspect suppliers' factories for product quality, but also for labour rights and employment conditions. Target operates a formal 'compliance organisation' for its purchasing, to enforce its vendor standards, focusing on vendor education and verification, with the following components:

- Implementation of a compliance audit programme, where audit staff conduct random visits to supplier manufacturing facilities, following which compliance violations are subject to administrative probation or severance of the relationship.
- Limitation of subcontractors used by suppliers to those approved by Target.
- Regular vendor evaluations as well as formal audits.

Target is not unusual in its attention to the ethical and social responsibility standards it demands of its suppliers throughout the world. The introduction of formal social responsibility dimensions to supplier relationships is becoming the norm rather than the exception with large customers. These social responsibility mandates impact on supplier selection, and on the continuation of relationships with existing suppliers.

Customer-oriented social strategies directly influence supply chain relationships. In dealing with suppliers, Home Depot (one of the biggest buyers of wood products in the US) demands that all its wood products come from suppliers who can provide evidence of sound forest management practices. These social responsibility mandates impact on supplier selection, and on the continuation of relationships with existing suppliers. Organisational customers' evolving social responsibility requirements mandate effective responses. The spread of vendor evaluation approaches which make CSR demands on suppliers requires continuous and systematic evaluation as the basis for an appropriate response.

Organisational customers' social responsibility mandates require effective responses. Certainly, one response may be that a customer's social responsibility demands reduce the attractiveness of that customer to the seller, and the business should be sacrificed. Nonetheless, the spread of vendor evaluation approaches which make CSR demands on suppliers requires continuous and systematic evaluation as the basis for an appropriate response.

Investors and CSR

Moreover, there are growing signs that many corporate boards of directors are under shareholder pressure to adopt more acceptable environmental policies and keep a closer watch on environmental issues, reflecting investor concerns about global warming and shortages of natural resources. We noted earlier a growing trend for linking executive remuneration to sustainability targets. In major companies it is now commonly the case that sustainability has become an important part of the activities of every board of directors (Lublin, 2008).

The attitude of investors towards CSR initiatives, however, may be positive or negative. For example, it may be from an investor perspective the case for sustainability is essentially a business case – initiatives are not about 'saving the planet', but about cutting waste, reducing costs and becoming more efficient. In 2006, Google launched a strategy to switch to renewable energy – while this reflects the personal beliefs of the founders of the business, it is also true that Google is a massive user of electricity and renewable energy provides a way to cut costs (Senge *et al.*, 2008). Nonetheless, when Google announced its renewable energy strategy, one leading New York stock analyst downgraded the company's shares, despite clear indications that the initiative would cut costs – his view was that the company was no longer focusing on its real priorities (Witzel, 2008).

On the institutional investment front, there are active pressures towards 'responsible investing' – both exclusion in removing certain companies or sectors from an investment fund based on environmental, social or government criteria, and integration by including environmental, social and government factors in the traditional analysis conducted by fund managers. The divestment campaign against fossil fuels and the Pope's eco-encyclical have brought social investing into the spotlight. Globally, more than 30 per cent of institutionally managed stocks have a social mandate, accounting for $21.4 trillion in assets (Authers, 2015). The ability of a company to raise capital, and its attractiveness to investors, will be influenced in part by its social and ethical initiatives.

Lobby groups and CSR

There is strong evidence that companies with poor CSR records risk serious negative consequences, such as large-scale consumer boycotts, weaker brand image, or reduced sales. Part of this effect may be accounted for by the growth of consumer groups who actively promote awareness of what they believe to be company wrongdoing, and actively promote consumer boycotts (Snider *et al.*, 2003).

Certainly it appears that activist organisations have become much more aggressive and effective in bringing public pressure to bear on companies. They may target the most visible companies, to draw attention to the issue, even if the company in question has little impact on the problem. Nestlé is the world's largest seller of bottled water, and has become a major target in the global dilemma about access to fresh water. In fact, Nestlé's impact on world water usage and availability is relatively trivial – but it is a very convenient target (Porter and Kramer, 2006).

In another example, in 2015, animal rights protesters opposing the UK badger cull pressured Caffè Nero to stop selling milk from badger cull areas by threatening to target them in an 'anti-austerity' march. Interestingly, Caffè Nero then found itself on the end of vocal public criticisms from farmers' groups for threatening their livelihoods by giving in to blackmail. The CEO somewhat publicly lost his cool when asked to apologise to farmers. This is the type of situation where it is difficult for a company to emerge unscathed. The same Stop the Cull protestors then moved on to Sainsbury's – sending pictures to the company's shareholders of bloody, wounded badgers shot to prevent the spread of bovine TB to cattle, and threatening to hijack Sainsbury's AGM. Unlike Caffè Nero, Sainsbury's chose to stand with the farmers, and take the consequences (Petre and Elliott, 2015).

In a continuing anti-sugar campaign in the UK, doctors via the British Medical Association are pressing for a 20 per cent tax on sugary drinks to fight the obesity crisis (Spencer, 2015b) – seeing a tax on sugary drinks announced by the government in the Spring budget of 2016 to the acclaim of anti-sugar campaigners and threats of legal action by the drinks companies. Yet, on the other hand, when Tesco decided to stop selling Ribena drinks cartons (the small cartons preferred for childrens' lunches and snacks) because of the sugar content, they faced a vocal consumer backlash of angry and Internet-literate customers who objected to being denied a favourite product (White, 2015). The long-term implications of sustained pressure on the food and drink industry are substantial and paradoxical.

One outcome of scoping CSR issues in the way we propose is to identify the issues which are likely to become high profile with different types of pressure groups. This provides some basis for responding effectively when they become live issues. Nonetheless, responses to external pressure groups have to be evaluated carefully for their potential 'unintended consequences' (Fry and Polonsky, 2004).

It is clear that lobby groups have the power to punish companies of which they disapprove. Pressured by PETA (People for the Ethical Treatment of Animals), 2008 saw companies from Timberland to H&M and Benetton banning Australian wool – PETA objects to the treatment of merino sheep in Australia, and as one European retailer noted: 'Who wants to be on PETA's radar screen?' (Capell, 2008). There is sound commercial logic that impels companies like Wal-Mart and Unilever to look to the Rainforest Alliance to help them certify the tea and coffee they sell (Skapinker, 2008b).

Lobby and pressure groups may or may not represent issues of widespread concern, and they may or may not be legitimate in their activities. Responses to pressures from unmandated groups of dubious standing are unlikely to have positive effects for a company, and may bring additional dilemmas. For example, in the sustained attacks on the animal testing company, Huntingdon Life Sciences, animal rights protestors targeted not only HLS for violent threats and protests, but also suppliers, including the company's banks. The dilemma facing the banks was whether to concede to the protestors' demands and cease trading with HLS, or to face violent actions against their own employees and premises. However, the first signs of concession to the protestors were criticisms from shareholders and the financial press that the banks had no right to cave in to the demands of animal rights protestors, and their dubious tactics.

More broadly, influential lobby groups may shape public (consumer) opinion and drive government actions to control business actions. Increasingly, governments use their power to mandate social responsibility or create new legislative demands. For example, in the UK the government is pressuring supermarkets to banish '2 for 1' deals on fresh food to reduce food waste – policy makers believe that 'bogoff' (buy one, get one free) offers are a main cause of the waste of a third of all food (Webster and Elliott, 2009). The same government is trying to prevent supermarkets from selling cheap alcohol, which is believed to encourage teenage drunkenness. When governments act on issues of social impact, the effect may be far more dramatic than would be voluntary compliance – the UK domestic appliance industry is looking at a bill of more than £500 million to meet government plans for recycling, which is more than their combined annual profits (Willman, 2006).

Responding to outside pressures, particularly where they are vocal and well organised, in order to defend a company's competitive position may be an appropriate management action. On the other hand, it may not – it may be impossible or undesirable to respond to some pressure groups' demands. In either case, the effects of such responses need to be carefully considered in the context of the entire value chain, and attempts made to control the 'unintended consequences' of such actions.

Suppliers and CSR

The issue of CSR and ethical standards in a company's supply base is the direct reflection of the questions raised above regarding the CSR-related demands made by major customers. Indeed, the ethical and social standards displayed by a seller's own suppliers may form part of a customer's CSR evaluation – as in the limitation of the use of subcontractors in the Target example above. Increasingly, our major customers may require that we adopt a proactive CSR stance towards the entire value chain. Currently, food and agriculture are at the forefront of efforts to make producers more accountable, and in areas like coffee, cocoa, palm oil and tea the market share of sustainable commodities has escalated rapidly (Terazono, 2015).

While the general trend is clear, managers still face choices. If CSR-related demands cannot or will not be met by suppliers, then the choice becomes whether or not to continue the relationship, accepting that then alternative suppliers will have to be located and new value chain arrangements made. Conversely, if suppliers are prepared to concede new standards in their behaviour, then there are likely to be implications for the prices they charge, and hence for the company's cost structure, and the prices it must ask of its own customers. This is likely to be a complex calculation. Careful evaluation is required.

Employees, managers and CSR

CSR is also seen as impacting on the perceptions of the employees and managers inside the company, and consequently on their motivation and commitment to the organisation. It is certainly apparent that many of the individuals now entering professional employment and providing the pool of talent from which future corporate leadership will be drawn, have important concerns about moral and ethical issues in business. The question is whether CSR initiatives will appeal to those concerns and generate the superior level of employee and manager commitment that should be associated with higher levels of job performance.

Research suggests two caveats to assuming that CSR will impact positively on employee beliefs and attitudes. First, employee attitudes and behaviours will be shaped in part by organisational culture and climate, and the impact of CSR will be influenced by whether initiatives are presented in terms of compliance or values, and whether such policies are integrated into business processes, or simply seen as 'window-dressing'. Secondly, the impact of CSR on employee motivation and commitment will be affected by the degree to which individuals can align their personal values with those of the organisation, by their perceptions of fairness and justice in the organisation, how CSR performance is rewarded, and by their perceptions of top management attitudes towards CSR and performance (Collier and Esteban, 2007).

Nonetheless, a research study by McKinsey suggests that as many as 70 per cent of company managers believe there is room for improvement in the way large companies anticipate social pressure and respond to it. Managers see risks for their businesses in some social challenges – such as climate change, data privacy and healthcare – but opportunities in other challenges – such as the growing demand for more ethical, healthier and safer products (Maitland, 2006). Further indications of the importance of ethical and social responsibility issues are shown in studies of the perceptions of business school students – who will provide the next generations of managers. Business students appear to believe that companies should work harder towards the betterment of society, and want to find socially responsible employment in their careers (Knight, 2006).

Competitors and CSR

We commented earlier on the pressure to meet, equal or exceed CSR moves by competitors. The 'environmental arms race' between UK supermarkets, with each company trying to outdo the others on their environmental protection strategies, is illustrative. Certainly, CSR initiatives provide one way in which competitors attempt to differentiate themselves, even if this is swiftly countered by rivals.

It should also be recognised that some social issues are shared by all members of an industry and joint or collaborative CSR initiatives may be to the benefit of all. For example, the Extractive Industries Transparency Initiative, initially based in London but now in Oslo, is a global collaboration including more than 90 major oil, gas, and mining companies, who have agreed to work against corruption by full public disclosure and verification of all company payments to governments in countries where they operate. The collective action by all the major companies makes it difficult for a government to undermine the social benefit of corruption-free trading by choosing not to deal with companies that disclose bribery payments.

There are clearly some risks for a company in adopting a wholly defensive approach to dealing with CSR issues. Failure to scope the CSR imperatives likely to be faced may be associated with ineffective short-term responses to social pressures. Nonetheless, in some cases a defensive stance may be all that is available, on some social issues. In such cases, initiatives should be carefully evaluated and implemented to avoid the risks of making the situation worse, being perceived as insincere and cynical, or undertaking actions with broader and undesirable consequences for the company or for society.

17.6 Corporate social responsibility and innovative competitive advantage

From the perspective of marketing strategy the important argument is that corporate social responsibility (CSR) provides a potential source of competitive advantage which is of increasing significance. For example, Michael Porter and Mark Kramer (2006) have made a compelling case for the position that businesses should not simply be taking corporate social responsibility seriously as an end in itself, but should be embedding it into their strategy to help build competitive advantage. They argue that conventional CSR approaches have often resulted in a mix of uncoordinated CSR initiatives and philanthropic activities that neither make meaningful social impact, nor strengthen the firm's long-term competitiveness. (We have earlier suggested the converse of this case: that companies neglecting issues of corporate social responsibility and ethical or moral standards, may find themselves wrong-footed by competitors who position themselves partly on the basis of these resources.) The Porter and Kramer model is highly influential in management thinking and it provides the underlying structure for this section of the chapter. Above all, Porter and Kramer link CSR directly to creating competitive advantage.

The logic linking corporate responsibility to competitive advantage follows these lines. Porter and Kramer (2006) argue that many prevailing approaches to CSR are fragmented and disconnected from business and strategy, while in fact the real challenge is for companies to analyse their social responsibility prospects using the same frameworks that guide their core business choices. The goal is to establish CSR not simply as corporate altruism, but as a source of opportunity, innovation and competitive advantage.

Porter and Kramer argue that companies should make choices about which social issues to address, from:

- *Generic social issues* – things that are not affected by the company's operations, not impacting on its long-term competitiveness.
- *Value chain social impacts* – social issues that are affected by the company's activities in the normal course of business.
- *Social dimensions of competitive context* – social issues in the external environment that significantly affect the underlying drivers of the company's competitiveness.

They suggest that a company should sort social issues into these three categories for each business unit and location, and then rank them in terms of potential impact. The category into which a given issue will fall will depend on the business and its location. For example, the AIDS pandemic in Africa might be a generic social issue for a retailer in the US or Europe, a value chain impact for a pharmaceutical company, and a competitive context issue for a mining company dependent on local labour in Africa for its operations.

The purpose of this ranking is to create an explicit corporate social agenda for a company, which 'looks beyond community expectations to achieve social and economic benefits simultaneously. It moves from mitigating harm to finding ways to reinforce corporate strategy by advancing social conditions' (2006, p. 85). Porter and Kramer reinforce the critically important distinction between responsive CSR and strategic CSR, suggesting it is through strategic CSR that a company can make the greatest social impact while also achieving the greatest competitive benefits. Their distinction is between two levels of CSR:

- *Responsive CSR* – involves acting as a good corporate citizen, reflecting the social concerns of stakeholders in the company, and also mitigating the existing or predicted adverse effects of business activities. The domain is generic social impacts and value chain social impacts. The limitation of many citizenship initiatives remains that however beneficial the social effects, such programmes tend to remain incidental to the company's business. The key to mitigating value chain social impacts is best practice, though competitive advantage through such endeavours is likely to be temporary.
- *Strategic CSR* – moves beyond good citizenship and value chain impacts to initiatives with large and distinctive effects. The goals are the transformation of value chain activities to benefit society while at the same time reinforcing the company's strategy, and strategic moves that leverage corporate capabilities to improve areas of competitive context. Strategic CSR may involve the introduction of radically different new products – the Toyota Prius hybrid car and now electric cars respond to consumer concerns about car emissions pollution, and provide both competitive advantage for Toyota and other

innovators like Tesla, and environmental benefits. However, the broader goal of strategic CSR is to invest in social aspects of the company's context to strengthen company competitiveness. This is achieved, in part, by adding a social dimension to the company's value proposition and ways of doing business. Only a small number of the social issues that could be addressed have this potential to make a real difference to society and build competitive advantage.

As a framework for examining these distinctions and differences, the Porter and Kramer logic is summarised in Figure 17.4.

Further, using the example of Whole Foods Market in the US, Porter and Kramer underline the competitive strength created by creating a social dimension to the value proposition. They suggest that the heart of strategy is a value proposition that rests on the set of needs that a company can uniquely meet for its chosen customers. The most strategic CSR adds a dimension to the value proposition, such that social impact is central to strategy. The value proposition at Whole Food Market is to sell natural, organic, healthy food products to consumers who are orientated to healthy eating and the environment. The company's stance on social issues is central to what makes them unique in food retailing and able to ask premium prices. For example: sourcing emphasises purchasing at store level from local farmers; buyers screen out ingredients considered unhealthy or environmentally damaging; the company offsets its electricity consumption; spoilt produce goes to regional centres for composting; vehicles are being converted to run on bio-fuels; cleaning products in stores are environmentally-friendly. The effect is that every aspect of the company's value chain reinforces the social dimensions of its value proposition, and provides strong differentiation from its competitors. (Nonetheless, the company is known as 'whole paycheck' in the US because of its high prices, and it is struggling to return to its roots as a health-food store rather than a source of 'foodie treats'! Whole Foods' UK operation has struggled to achieve profitability but the company is expanding in the US and now China [Smyth, 2009].)

Porter and Kramer conclude that while not every company can be a Whole Foods, adding a social dimension to the value proposition adds a new frontier for our thinking about competitive positioning. They also note that the number of industries and companies whose competitive advantage can involve social value propositions is rapidly growing. Their

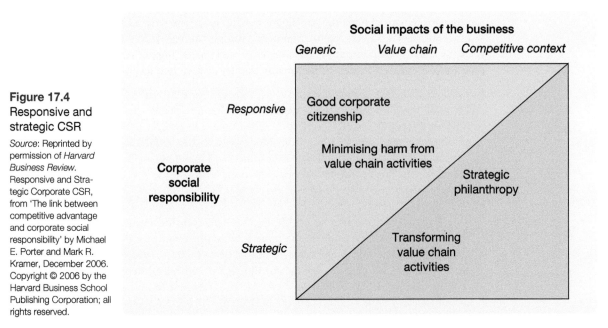

Figure 17.4 Responsive and strategic CSR

conclusion is important to how we consider the resource profile of an organisation and the ways in which it can leverage and strengthen that profile:

> Organisations that make the right choices and build focussed, proactive, and integrated social initiatives in concert with their core strategies will increasingly distance themselves from the pack . . . Perceiving social responsibility as building shared value rather than as damage control or as a PR campaign will require dramatically different thinking in business. We are convinced, however, that CSR will become increasingly important to competitive success.
> *(Porter and Kramer, 2006, pp. 91–112)*

A similar viewpoint is adopted by Andrew Savitz, who created the environmental practice at PwC and has worked on environmental issue with some of America's largest companies (Savitz and Weber, 2006). Savitz and Weber share the view that it makes financial sense for companies to anticipate and respond to society's emerging demands – anticipating reciprocal advantages in the longer term, i.e., the sustainable company will be more profitable as a result of its responsiveness. In their terms, sustainability is about conducting business in such a way that it benefits employees, customers, business partners, communities and shareholders at the same time – it is 'the art of doing business in an interdependent world' (Savitz and Weber, 2006). They suggest that the best-run companies have identified 'sustainability sweet spots' – areas where shareholders' long-term interests overlap with those of society. They point, for example, to Unilever's Project Shakti in India, where 70,000 female Shakti entrepreneurs have been employed and trained to distribute Unilever products to rural communities, providing economic income in a deprived area, but at the same time gaining market access and penetration in a difficult market.

Indeed, *Fortune* magazine lists the companies identified as the world's top 'eco-innovators' – the businesses doing the most to make the world smarter and more sustainable. The list includes: Tesla, in electric cars; Nest, with intelligent automation for the home; Solar-City, pioneering solar leasing programmes for the home; Environmental Initiatives at Apple, addressing electronic waste and recycling old Apple products for free; and Broad Group, with energy-efficient cooling systems for commercial buildings (Dumaine, 2014). There are close links between sustainability and exciting product and technology innovation (see Chapter 12).

Nonetheless, on occasion, there may be major questions surrounding the balance between business and social benefits in some CSR initiatives of this kind. For example, some companies are benefiting commercially by asking 'green' consumers to pay them for cleaning up their own pollution. Similarly, Blue Source, a US offsetting company, invites consumers to offset their carbon emissions by investing in enhanced oil recovery (pumping carbon dioxide into depleted oil wells to bring up the remaining oil). In fact, Blue Source admits that this process is often profitable in itself, and the 'carbon credit' represents additional revenue (Harvey and Fidler, 2007). It is likely that such schemes will fail to deliver more than short-term financial benefits rather than synergy between business and social benefits.

One example of the possibilities for large-scale competitive change around social benefit initiatives is provided by the MIT team who said in 2004 they were going to overcome the digital divide between the rich and poor by making a $100 laptop for the poor children of the world – the One Laptop Per Child (OLPC) project. While initially dismissed simply as a charitable project, the MIT team's vision has underlined to the commercial IT sector the market power of the poor – the fact that the majority of the world's population does not have a computer will be one of the main drivers of growth for the sector. The effects on hardware and software companies have been dramatic in driving the industry towards providing ultra-cheap laptops in various forms. The OLPC project underlines the social benefits and the commercial opportunities in a cheap laptop, which was relatively easy to make using newer technologies, open source software, and stripping our unneeded functions (Hille, 2007). The next socially-driven innovation in this area, this time from the UK, was the Raspberry Pi – a minicomputer to help children learn programming skills, priced at £22 (Palmer, 2012).

Relatedly in this sector, an interesting example of a company leveraging its distinctive competitive competences to further initiatives with both business and social benefits is provided by Dell Inc. Dell is using the strengths of its direct business model to generate collective efforts to reduce energy consumption and protect the environment. The initiative centres on improving the efficiency of IT products, reducing the harmful materials used in them, and cooperating with customers to dispose of old products. Michael Dell's environmental strategy focuses on three areas:

- Creating easy, low-cost ways for businesses to do better in protecting the environment – providing, for example, global recycling and product recovery programmes for customers, with participation requiring little effort on their part.
- Taking creative approaches to lessen the environmental impact of products from design to disposal – helping customers to take full advantage of new, energy-saving technology and processes, and advising on upgrades of legacy systems to reduce electricity usage.
- Looking to partnership with governments to promote environmental stewardship – for example, in Dell's 'Plant a Tree for Me' programme, offering customers the chance to offset emissions from the electricity their computers use, by making a contribution to buying a tree when they buy a PC.

As a company, Dell is also committing efforts to enhancing operational efficiencies and reducing its carbon footprint through the use of renewable energy (Dell, 2007). Importantly, Dell's initiative starts with the distinctive strengths of the company (the direct business-to-business model with corporate customers), applies these strengths to address an environmental issue (reduced pollution, lower energy use), but at the same time achieves business goals (reinforcing the company's leadership, strengthening customer relationships, faster take-up of newer, more efficient products and technologies). The link between this CSR initiative and the company's business model and value proposition is clear.

Similarly, Microsoft has partnered with governments in less developed countries to offer Microsoft Windows and Office software packages for a few dollars to governments that subsidise the cost of computers for schoolchildren. The potential business benefit for Microsoft is to double the number of PC users worldwide, and reinforce the company's market growth. The social benefit is the greater investment in technology in some of the poorest countries in the world, with the goal of improving living standards and reducing global inequality (*Financial Times,* 2007).

On the environmental front, General Electric – the largest company in the world – has its well-established Ecomagination initiative. Ecomagination has grown out of GE's long-term investment in cleaner technologies, and places these technologies under a single brand. To qualify for Ecomagination branding products must significantly and measurably improve customers' environmental and operating performance. However, the Ecomagination vision is driven by the principle that its green initiatives will have a positive impact on GE's competitive position and financial performance (Harvey, 2005; Hart, 2005).

CSR strategy at companies like Dell Inc., Microsoft and GE may provide a prototype of linking CSR to competitive advantage which will influence management thinking.

17.7 How companies are responding to the CSR mandate

The ways in which companies are developing responses to the imperatives to display more ethical and socially acceptable policies are not well codified. Certainly, there is wide recognition that firms face choices in their responsiveness to social responsibility. For example, corporate social responsiveness may reflect models or philosophies, ranging from 'do nothing' to 'do much' (Carroll, 1979). However, responsiveness alone may not be the same as good corporate citizenship. For example, a responsive organisation may address social pressures by moving to a less demanding environment – consider the growing emphasis by tobacco companies on the relatively unregulated developing countries, where tobacco consumption remains socially acceptable. The simple prescription of responsiveness oversimplifies the complexity of the situations that companies face. The issue is how a company responds, and what its responses represent to its stakeholders. There is also potential insight from benchmarking and making comparisons with competitors.

Certainly, there is a dilemma for some companies if their existing business model relies on resources and capabilities which become questionable in terms of social responsibilities and duty. We noted earlier that Primark is a very successful British fashion retailer. The Primark business model relies on sourcing fashion items from low-cost manufacturing areas and turning catwalk trends into products in as little as two weeks at extremely low prices. The result is that Primark buys from suppliers whose workers are paid as little as 9p an hour, working 90 hours a week in extremely poor conditions. Notwithstanding the company's 'charm offensive' in the ethics and social responsibility field – and the company's efforts to stop buying from suppliers using child labour (Urry, 2008) – the dilemma is that the low-price, lean supply chain business model relies on low-cost suppliers. This dilemma is shared by other low-price fashion retailers like Tesco and Asda.

The urgency of the issue is underlined by escalating transparency – for example, the growth in the use of new software packages that allow consumers and rivals to trace the provenance of products. Many companies have stopped using suppliers where there are suspicions of the use of forced or child labour or conflict materials are present, not least because of the ease with which these facts can be identified by consumers. For example, GoodGuide provides an online database of verified information regarding the health, environmental and social impact of more than 250,000 common products (Tyrell, 2010).

Figure 17.5 presents a framework for evaluating the ways in which companies are responding to pressures encouraging the adoption of corporate social responsibility initiatives in business and marketing strategy. This model suggests that responses vary in extent but also that the impact on customer value will depend in part on employee and manager

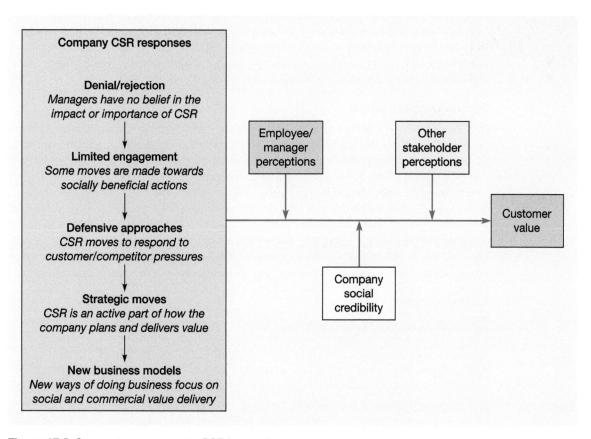

Figure 17.5 Corporate responses to CSR imperatives

Source: Adapted from Piercy and Lane (2009b).

perceptions of CSR, perceptions among other stakeholders like supply chain partners and investors, and the company's 'social credibility' – essentially whether its history and actions mean that its social intentions are interpreted positively by different stakeholders. The framework assists in identifying the linkages between CSR and customer value.

17.7.1 Company CSR responses

It is clear that companies differ substantially in their stance on corporate social responsibility and ethical behaviour initiatives (Pohle and Hittner, 2008). Variation includes both the extent and direction of response – how much they change their behaviour and in what ways.

Denial/rejection

There is little doubt that some executives remain unconvinced that corporate social responsibility represents anything other than charitable giving, and that such initiatives are unconnected, or at best only loosely related, to customer value. Underpinning such responses, and negative attitudes towards CSR, is probably the residual belief among some managers and investors that it is simply not the role of business to pursue social goals, but rather to create the economic wealth that underpins the pursuit of such objectives by public authorities and not-for-profit organisations. This is a legitimate and defensible position to take. CSR-related actions in this situation may amount to little more than meeting legal obligations and compliance with regulation in countries of production, operation and distribution, but the cost may be vulnerability to attack and missed opportunities.

Limited engagement

Philanthropy may involve some degree of alignment of charitable activities with social issues that support business objectives, although some charitable giving may be about 'doing good' rather than meeting business goals. However, even at the level of corporate giving to good causes, companies are increasingly choosing projects in which they can be actively involved and which encompass parts of their business model. This concept of 'strategic philanthropy' is gathering momentum alongside the idea of 'capitalist philanthropy' which suggests that charitable giving should be evaluated as an investment (Brewster, 2008).

Defensive approaches

If a firm is essentially defensive in its stance to social responsiveness, then its primary concerns with CSR will be the protection of relationships – for example, with consumers, business-to-business customers, influential lobby or pressure groups, suppliers, employees and managers, and relative position against competitors.

For example, when Greenpeace parodied Unilever advertisements, accusing the company of destroying Indonesian rainforests for palm oil (a key ingredient of the company's soaps and margarines), the company was quick to reverse its position and declare it would buy palm oil only from suppliers who can demonstrate they did not cut down forestry. As the world's largest seller of bottled water, Nestlé's response to environmental criticisms was more negative – they responded with a large advertising campaign linking soft drinks to obesity (Patrick, 2008).

Strategic moves

The underlying logic with more strategic approaches is that CSR provides a new growth platform potentially bringing access to new markets, new partnerships and new types of product/service innovation that generate value – this represents a shift from compliance and defensiveness to integrating CSR into strategy to achieve revenue growth and brand differentiation (Pohle and Hittner, 2008). Increasingly such strategic moves involve partnerships with non-government organisations (NGOs) to combine social and commercial activities. For example, Unilever has partnered with public health networks in Africa to promote its anti-bacterial Lifebuoy soap – the NGOs seek to promote handwashing to prevent the spread of disease, while Unilever aims to sell more soap (Jopson, 2007).

New business models

The compelling logic of the Porter and Kramer (2006) approach is that the real impact of corporate social responsibility imperatives is in encouraging the development of new business models that address both commercial and social needs at the same time. Porter and Kramer conclude that adding a social dimension to the value proposition adds a new frontier for our thinking about competitive positioning and competitive advantage in business and marketing strategy. They also note that the number of industries and companies whose competitive advantage can involve social value propositions is rapidly growing. We saw earlier that companies like Whole Food Market are illustrative.

For example, consider the emergence of 'eco-entrepreneurs' transforming traditional business models with new technologies. Fast-moving 'eco-upstarts' may be better positioned than established companies to pursue social goals with commercial benefits. For example, PlanetTran is a chauffeur and airport shuttle service that uses only hybrid cars and aims to save the planet 'one car journey at a time'. Successful with the eco-conscious business community in Boston and San Francisco, PlanetTran supplies corporate clients with quarterly reports measuring the environmental benefits of using PlanetTran compared to traditional transport arrangements (Knight, 2008).

Or, look at the impact of the 'sharing economy' on traditional car companies – BMW has extended its DriveNow, pay-as-you-go car sharing club to London after its start in Germany, Austria and the United States. One estimate is that one sharing vehicle removes the need for 32 personal car purchases (Sharman, 2014).

17.7.2 Employee/manager perceptions

The impact of CSR initiatives on customer value perceptions is also likely to be moderated by a company's employee and manager perceptions of the initiatives and the relevance and importance of them. On the face of things, companies can often anticipate positive and supportive employee/manager perceptions of CSR which will enhance the impact on customer value. Nonetheless, questions may still be raised about the degree to which CSR initiatives shape interactions between company personnel and customers in ways which impact positively on customer value. Giving approval to CSR concepts may differ from changing the way work is done to reflect actual CSR initiatives. For example, consider the degree to which salespeople buy in to CSR and the degree to which their selling efforts reflect CSR to enhance customer value – this appears often to be limited and a victim of salesperson cynicism (Piercy and Lane, 2011). Certainly, research suggests that high-performing companies fully engage their employees in their CSR objectives, rather than adopting a top-down approach (Pohle and Hittner, 2008).

17.7.3 Other stakeholder perceptions

Supply chain partners may be very significant to creating pressures towards more responsible behaviour. Wal-Mart has, for example, led the way in asking suppliers to measure and report their greenhouse gas emissions, with the goal of helping suppliers to 'get the costs of carbon out of the system' (Harvey and Birchall, 2007). (Recall we commented earlier on the impact of other stakeholders such as investors, the government and regulators, and other stakeholders in the value chain.)

17.7.4 Company social credibility

An additional complication is whether a company's corporate reputation supports CSR initiatives, in the sense that they are perceived externally as well-meaning and sincere (and likely to be reinforced and maintained), or alternatively as cynical and manipulative (and likely to be minimised or abandoned in favour of the next 'marketing gimmick').

The impact of social credibility (or the lack of it) may be profound. For example, US retailer Wal-Mart has long had a reputation for aggression and ruthlessness in dealing with suppliers, competitors and employees – branded the 'merchant of shame' by critics of its labour policies (Berner, 2005). Nonetheless, in recent years, Wal-Mart has focused considerable attention on employment diversity issues and environmental protection, and yet failed to convince its environmental critics of the company's sincerity. To champion Wal-Mart's social contributions, then-chief executive Lee Scott used his annual shareholder meeting to offer to partner with governments on issues from the environment to health-care reform. Yet many still doubt the sincerity of Wal-Mart's social change intentions (McWilliams and Zuckerman, 2008).

Similarly, as noted earlier, Coca-Cola continues to struggle to overcome the perception that its business model involves 'waste, pollution and questionable nutrition', and is working hard through water- and energy-saving projects to overcome criticisms, and collaborating with environmental campaign groups like Greenpeace (Wiggins, 2007). Establishing credibility as an ethical company may require overcoming perceptions of a company's history as well as initiating new CSR projects.

Indeed, company practices are not simply more visible as a result of aggressive questioning by customers, NGOs and advocacy groups, they face growing demands for transparency – taking the wraps off information once considered proprietary or confidential. Social credibility depends in part on developing information strategies which are relevant to customers' concerns, expectations and preferences – only the company that shares reliable information is likely to be perceived as a trustworthy 'partner in sustainability' by customers and other stakeholders (Pohle and Hittner, 2008).

The link between CSR efforts and customer value is likely to be moderated by the company's credibility as a social player, shaped by its history and corporate reputation. Low credibility may not be an absolute barrier to implementing useful CSR initiatives, but it may well reduce the impact of those initiatives on customer perceptions. When considering the impact of CSR on strategy and positioning choices, it is necessary to be realistic as well as visionary.

17.8 CSR and customer value

It follows from the last section, and is suggested in Figure 17.5, that from a strategic marketing perspective, the critical linkage is that between CSR initiatives and customer value. This is not deny the importance of CSR which simply does good in its own right, but emphasises value-creation through CSR which resonates with the development of new business models which combine social and business goals.

The central strategic marketing question is thus how CSR impacts on the customer value proposition. While widely used and loosely defined, the value proposition describes the unique offer made to the customer, with all its hard and soft dimensions, and is at the centre of how a company aims to differentiate itself from competitors in its target market segments. In fact, there are indications that many companies have a poor understanding of their customers' real concerns about social and environmental issues surrounding their businesses and few are asking them – leaving suppliers relying on assumptions about what CSR means to their customers. High-performing companies show a deeper understanding of their customers' CSR expectations (Pohle and Hittner, 2008). Businesses need new sources of operational, supply chain and customer information to gain the new levels of insight required to meet objectives in areas like sustainability (IBM, 2009).

In fact, in business-to-business marketing in particular, it is possible to identify three types of value proposition, providing an insightful framework for examining the link between CSR and the value proposition. Anderson *et al.* (2006) identify three kinds of value proposition: *all benefits* – when asked to construct a value proposition, managers list all the benefits they believe their offering might deliver to target customers, with the risk they claim advantage from features that actually provide no benefit or value to target customers; *favourable points of difference* – recognising that customers have alternatives, this identifies what differentiates the offering from the next best alternative, which risks assuming that all favourable comparisons create value for the customer; and *resonating focus* – concentrates on the one or two points of difference that deliver, and with improvement will continue to deliver, greatest value to target customers, though clearly this relies on deeper knowledge of what drives value for the customer. The researchers conclude that customer value propositions with a resonating focus should be the gold standard (Anderson *et al.*, 2006).

The Anderson *et al.* framework is used in Figure 17.6 to suggest the questions that should be asked regarding the relationship between a selling or supplying company's CSR, and customer value perceptions. Questioning moves progressively from investigating what specific customer benefits are linked to a supplier's CSR, in the all benefits value proposition, to seeking the ways in which CSR strategy achieves favourable points of difference compared to competitors, to examining how CSR initiatives align with customer priorities and thus drive value for the customer.

Consider the case of Philips environmentally-friendly Alto industrial lighting tubes. While containing less toxicity, the Alto product was more expensive than competing light tubes, and conventional suppliers sold on price and bulb life to purchasing officers. Telling buyers that the tube is more environmentally-friendly (as part of an all benefits approach) or that it is more environmentally-friendly than competitors' products (favourable points of difference) is unlikely to impress purchasing officers accustomed to evaluating alternatives on price and bulb life. However, appealing to, for example, shopping mall developers on the basis of reduced disposal costs (because the green product is less toxic) and environmental image (the cleaner lighting becomes part of their environmental appeal to consumers) was effective. Alto replaced more than 25 per cent of the US market for traditional fluorescent lamps (Kim and Mauborgne, 1999).

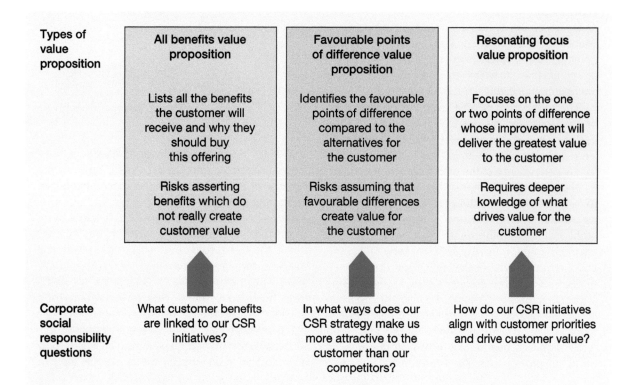

Figure 17.6 CSR and customer value propositions

Summary

This chapter sets out to establish the impact of corporate social responsibility on marketing strategy and customer value. Social responsibility and ethical standards are closely linked to corporate reputation and thus a company's freedom of strategic positioning. This is an area which is evolving rapidly, and one which is turning out to be highly significant to the ability of a company to maintain its chosen competitive position and to compete effectively. Nonetheless, it is an area where precise definitions and analytical methodologies do not yet exist. Our approach suggests that companies should devote efforts to understanding better the social pressures which are likely to affect their ability to compete through scoping or issue analysis. Company responses to social issues fall into several categories, ranging from altruistic company philanthropy and the concept of social enterprise, to defensive moves to protect competitive position, to strategic moves that aim to create competitive advantage through CSR initiatives. Our attention focuses on the latter areas: defensive CSR and creating competitive advantage through CSR. We place this into a strategic marketing context by examining the impact of CSR on customer value, and the varying ways in which companies appear to be responding to CSR imperatives.

Case study — How Skanska aims to become the world's greenest construction company

The built environment and the natural world have never been easy bedfellows, but Swedish construction group Skanska is trying to change that. Just ask the bees that live on the roof of its new headquarters in Stockholm.

The office, which opened in January and features Skanska's 'deep green' cooling system – provided by boreholes under the building – is the latest expression of a commitment to sustainable development, both as contractor and, in this case, developer.

'There we can let rip a bit,' says Noel Morrin, head of sustainability. 'We are the investor, we are the designer, we are the engineer, we have bought the land – so we can be held 100 per cent accountable for the performance of the product.'

Skanska has, for more than a decade, aimed to raise its environmental performance in its work as builder, refurbisher and project manager on high-profile developments and public-private partnerships – from the M25 motorway around London to the MetLife stadium in New York.

That is not always easy for a company with as big a global footprint as Skanska. For each of its 57,000 employees across three continents, it has between four and five subcontractors – making for a total workforce of about a quarter of a million people, working on 10,000 projects annually. It has 100,000 suppliers.

'We have a constant challenge to make sure those people understand and live our values,' says Morrin. 'Any one of those companies or subcontractors can destroy our ambition.'

Skanska is not short on ambition. It wants to be the greenest contractor in the world. It lives by what it calls the five zeros: zero accidents, zero ethical breaches, zero defects, zero lossmaking projects and zero environmental incidents. One former employee says: 'Every day there were conversations and reminders of the importance of this ethos.'

The Swedish group is not alone in its green mission. Sustainable construction is becoming an increasingly crowded field in an industry where margins are thin and competition for contracts is fierce. It is a sector with more to do than most. According to Action Sustainability, a consultancy, about half of global emissions come from buildings and half of all landfill comes from construction.

'The construction sector in general is starting to get the idea that there is a competitive advantage in sustainability,' says Shaun McCarthy, director of the consultancy.

That shift is not just coming from within building companies themselves. Investors, such as the large Canadian and German pension funds Skanska works with, want assets that will attract good tenants, produce high rental yield and offer a healthy return when they decide to sell.

Commercial tenants, too, have policies that mean they can 'only sit in properties that are good for the environment', says Albin Sandberg, analyst at Handelsbanken Capital Markets. 'That can win or lose you a contract.'

Regulation is increasing the pressure. New legislation in the UK could make less energy-efficient properties unlettable from 2017 – which is thought to affect about a fifth of Britain's commercial building stock, worth about £100bn.

Meanwhile, the EU's energy efficiency directive, which member states must implement by June, is expected to lead to a far-reaching revamp of Europe's building stock.

As the policy debate on green construction intensifies, Skanska is becoming increasingly active. In July, its US arm – which contributes almost one-third of the group's Skr136bn ($21bn) revenues – withdrew from the country's chamber of commerce in protest at its stance on green building codes.

Reforms of the US LEED (Leadership in Energy and Environmental Design) programme – a set of standards for sustainable buildings – were being opposed by chemicals groups backed by the chamber. 'It was very un-Swedish to stand out from the crowd in that way,' says Morrin. 'But this was a line that could not be crossed.'

Skanska's sustainability chief chairs a UN Environment Programme body looking at who is accountable for a building's emissions over its lifetime. Of total carbon emissions from a typical building over 50 years, about 80 per cent come from operating that building, he says.

'The construction industry provides the construction service. It is architects, engineers and investors who determine the carbon intensity of that product.'

'We are not saying Skanska or the construction industry is not responsible for part of the carbon emissions from the built environment. But our proportion is significantly less than the people who designed it, financed it, own it and operate it. At the moment there is a misunderstanding about how each of those pieces is allocated.'

Yet the construction process can reduce its impact in concrete ways, as Skanska showed in its work as main contractor on the redevelopment of two London hospitals, St Bartholomew's and The Royal London.

The company uses a 3D simulation technique, known as building information modelling, which allows it to identify exact quantities of materials required. Through its use of BIM, Skanska was able to halve waste plasterboard on the first phase of the Barts project, which is thought to have saved thousands of pounds in disposal costs and reduced truck deliveries.

It also worked with suppliers to come up with a system of collapsible, reusable plastic packaging for mechanical and electrical products. Along with eradicating waste to landfill, the measure eliminated breakages and reduced injuries from broken glass, for instance.

Skanska's focus on sustainability can be traced back to one project: in 1996, it was commissioned to blast and seal rock for a rail tunnel at Hallandsås Ridge, near Helsingborg, southwest Sweden.

The company used an industrial sealant that contaminated a nearby stream, harming fish and livestock. 'It was quite a scandal – locally at least,' says Sandberg at Handelsbanken. 'Since then, Skanska has worked quite hard to see it is not repeated.'

Skanska calls Hallandsås Ridge its 'environmental wake-up call'. It has worked to phase out hazardous substances and introduced a chemical database to control the use of chemicals.

It points to a number of milestones since the scandal. It was the first company to globally implement ISO 14000 standards on environmental management. It was the first company in Scandinavia to set up a global whistleblowing hotline, fully independent of the company. It has been a constituent of the FTSE-4Good index, the ethical investment benchmark, for more than a decade.

The Skanska-built Brent Civic Centre, which opened last year near Wembley Stadium in London, was the first public building in the UK to achieve an 'outstanding' environmental assessment rating from the Building Research Establishment. Its Väla Gård office, in Helsingborg, last year received the highest LEED rating for a new building in Europe.

Skanska has more to do. Critics argue its message has yet fully to permeate to all its subcontractors and suppliers, though tougher rules on procurement and initiatives such as the UK's Supply Chain Sustainability School – an online education resource operated in partnership with several rivals – have helped.

Morrin says Skanska's two biggest sustainability challenges are site safety, of employees and the public, and business ethics.

'Today we will open or close 40 or 50 contracts,' he says. 'Anywhere on one of those projects could be a bad apple. That is a worry, and we would be fools to think otherwise. We would be liars if we said otherwise.'

Innovation begins at home: Group puts its slant on sustainable housing

Skanska might be best known for its work on flagship commercial and institutional buildings, such as the UN headquarters in New York, but it is also putting its mark on residential developments.

In December, the company began to erect what will be the largest modular apartment block in the world – 32 storeys in Brooklyn made up of containers put together in a nearby hangar. The apartments will go up at a rate of up to five a week.

Off-site production means Skanska and its partner and client, Forest City Ratner, can cut by more than half the waste created on site. 'Anybody can build small stuff,' says Noel Morrin, Skanska's head of sustainability. 'But how do we scale this so there is a societal impact? That's what we're trying to do.'

The container project builds on Skanska's experience in making prefabricated – or 'flat-pack' – homes through BoKlok, its joint venture with Ikea, the furniture retailer. The schemes are intended to be low cost and high volume, with a block of four apartments able to be erected in an afternoon. The latest iteration of the design is almost 30 per cent more energy-efficient than standard Swedish housing requirements.

In 2010, Skanska even made a high-profile, if brief, entrance into UK housebuilding, as one of the first foreign entrants to break into the tight-knit industry.

In its Seven Acres development near Cambridge Skanska went beyond triple-glazing, hyperinsulation and solar panelling. 'One of its overarching ambitions from the outset was to build a community,' says Toby Greenhow, a director at Savills, the estate agent. That included lots of open space, allotments and benches in front of houses.

Skanska said recently it had no more plans for UK residential schemes, since other building projects were more profitable – much to the disappointment of 400 Cambridge residents who had inquired about the next Skanska village.

Source: 'How Skanska aims to become the world's greenest construction company', *Financial Times*, 23/03/14 (Sharman, A.).

Discussion questions

1 What is the key impact of CSR on marketing strategy?

2 How does Skanska express its sustainability ambitions?

3 What could be drivers of CSR initiatives for construction companies such as Skanska?

PART 6
CONCLUSIONS

Chapter 18 concludes *Marketing Strategy and Competitive Positioning* by looking ahead to marketing strategies for the next decade of the twenty-first century. Significant changes in the business environment are highlighted and a number of building blocks are suggested for developing adaptive strategies for a changing world. These include the need to develop learning organisations, capturing, internalising and utilising knowledge; the need for a clear market orientation and focus on creating superior value and greater levels of satisfaction for customers; the need to base positioning strategies firmly on marketing assets and competencies; the need to establish closer relationships with key customers; and finally, the need to rethink the role of marketing within the organisation. A number of dimensions are discussed that can provide keys to positioning in the future. Price, quality, innovation, service, benefit differentiation and customisation are compared as fundamental positioning dimensions and strategies, and the competencies and assets required for each explored.

The chapter, and indeed the text, concludes by predicting that marketing in the future will be seen more as a process for achieving a close fit between market requirements on the one hand and company competencies and assets on the other, than as a functional department within the firm. It is how this strategic, rather than operational or tactical, role for marketing is fulfilled in the future that holds much excitement for the discipline of marketing.

CHAPTER 18
TWENTY-FIRST CENTURY MARKETING

It is not the strongest of the species that survive, nor the most intelligent, but the ones most responsive to change.

Charles Darwin, *On the Origin of Species* (1853)

Hanwang sets its e-reader sights high

Liu Yingjian has grand plans. 'Before I retire, I'm going to make my company a member of the Fortune 500,' says the 57-year-old founder and chairman of Hanwang Technology.

Although China's leading e-reader maker has a long way to go to make Fortune magazine's elite list of the biggest companies, with only Rmb574m ($85m) in revenues last year, Mr Liu's optimism is understandable after Hanwang's initial public offering made him a millionaire. Mr Liu and his wife own 36.5 per cent of Hanwang, which last month raised Rmb1.1bn through its listing on the Shenzhen small business board. Its shares have since soared to Rmb155.50 from the initial public offering price of Rmb41.90.

Hanwang is one of the few technology companies in China with a strong intellectual property profile. It has long provided the technology for Chinese and other Asian language handwriting recognition on touch-screen handsets to Nokia, Samsung and others.

Mr Liu, a former researcher at China's leading pattern recognition laboratory at the Chinese Academy of Sciences, continues to drive an agenda of innovation at Hanwang. Each year, 10 per cent of the company's revenues are poured into research and development as well as into new solutions such as

Source: Associated Press: Imaginechina via AP Images.

stand-alone facial recognition devices. But Hanwang faces some severe challenges as it seeks to grow.

After surviving in technological niches for a decade, the company saw its revenues more than double and net profit more than triple to Rmb85m last year, but the explosive growth is driven only by e-readers, a product in which some analysts believe Chinese companies have no competitive advantage.

'The e-reader market in China is taking off, yes. But they have no unique strength in that field – they rely on Taiwanese manufacturers for the flat panels, on telecoms operators for the channel and on publishers for the content,' says Wei Yuhuai, an analyst at CCID, an industry researcher in Beijing. 'The other concern is what will become the mainstream among mobile Internet devices after the iPad, and will e-readers be marginalised?' he adds.

Mr Liu is unfazed. Hanwang's e-readers last year grabbed 43 per cent of the 620,000 units shipped in the fledgling Chinese market.

However, he admits that while Chinese banks or car makers can achieve international recognition just on the back of their huge home markets, that does not work for technology groups. 'All IT companies must be global,' he says.

Hanwang has found it challenging to meet foreign consumers' taste. The company is doing reasonably well in Russia and Spain but in Italy its distribution partner asked the company to redesign its casing and packaging.

For the time being, Mr Liu is staying away from the US market. 'We don't dare to boast about that. They have Apple.'

Source: from 'Hanwang sets its e-reader sights high', *Financial Times*, 26/04/10 (Hille, K.).

Discussion questions

1 What are the issues facing Hanwang?

2 What can the company do to address them?

Introduction

The emphasis throughout *Marketing Strategy and Competitive Positioning* has been on developing robust marketing strategies and competitive positioning to enable organisations to survive and prosper in the turbulent, competitive and frequently hostile markets they face. From the outset we have stressed the critical need to develop effective ways in which to cope with the change in customer markets and the ways in which companies go to market. This chapter reviews the major trends which are already apparent in the twenty-first century, and to suggest ways in which new competitive strategies can be fashioned to exploit the opportunities that are emerging. As Drucker (1997) has said:

> In human affairs – political, social, economic, or business – it is pointless to try and predict the future . . . But it is possible – and fruitful – to identify major events that have already happened, irrevocably, and that will have predictable effects in the next decade or two. It is possible, in other words, to identify and prepare for the future that has already happened.

18.1 The changing competitive arena

Chapter 3 reviewed some of the significant changes taking place in today's markets. Here we briefly summarise those changes.

18.1.1 Changes in the business environment

To claim that 'the only constant is change' is trite but true in today's business environment. The Royal Society for the Encouragement of Arts, Manufactures & Commerce (RSA) inquiry into Tomorrow's Company (1994) identified a number of major changes taking place in business markets.

- The pace of economic change is accelerating. During the Industrial Revolution it took 60 years for productivity per person to double. China and South Korea have done the same in 10 years.
- There is an explosion in innovation and new knowledge generation that is also accelerating. Every year as much new knowledge is generated through research and development as the total sum of all human knowledge up to the 1960s.
- Competitive pressures are intensifying. Computer manufacturers, for example, need to reduce costs and improve product performance by around 30 per cent per annum to remain competitive.
- Manufacturing can now take place almost anywhere. Companies are constantly seeking more efficient manufacturing options, and that typically means sourcing from wherever makes economic sense. For example, figures from the US Bureau of Labor Statistics indicate that in 2012, UK manufacturing labour costs were half those of Norway, but just over twice those of Portugal. From the same report, manufacturing labour costs in the Philippines were approximately a third of those in Mexico and a tenth of those in Israel; very clear illustrations of the significant differences that can occur across geographic boundaries. Early in 2002 Dyson switched manufacturing to Malaysia, where manufacturing costs were estimated to be around 30 per cent lower than the UK. While at the time this was a significant blow to the local economy, the move has benefited the organisation in the longer term. Indeed, it has subsequently allowed Dyson to reinvest many millions of pounds in the UK that may not have been available had the organisation chosen not to take advantage of favourable cost opportunities elsewhere.
- New organisational structures are emerging as firms seek to make themselves more competitive. Firms have reorganised, reduced overheads, de-layered, merged, created alliances and partnerships in attempts to create advantage in the marketplace.
- International trade is being liberalised through the World Trade Organization (WTO), but there are still massive regional trading blocs within which regional, national, ethnic and religious groupings seek to retain individual identity.
- Company actions are becoming increasingly visible, especially their effects on the environment. Customers are demanding more both economically and environmentally.

These trends have continued, indeed accelerated, in the 22 years since the report was published. The economic shocks of the 2008–10 global recession, coupled with increased concerns over climate change and sustainability, have served to drive companies to look increasingly at efficiency and how they can reduce costs.

At the macro-level changes can be grouped into economic, technological, social, legal and political issues. Just as water supply companies cannot change weather patterns, most macro-environmental factors are outside the control of individual firms. Few companies have the ability to influence political, economic, social and technological processes significantly. Most need to ensure they understand and predict the changes going on. Water companies need to predict both weather patterns (supply of water) and demand (water usage) so that they can then put strategies in place to meet that demand.

In a keynote address to the British Academy of Management (annual conference, Aston University 1996), David Cravens cited an example of a well-known firm that had failed to grasp the significance of technological change on its market (see Sammuels, 1994; Evans and Wurster, 1997). Encyclopaedia Britannica (EB) went from peak US profits in 1990 to severe difficulties in 1996 as it failed to anticipate the impact of computer technology, particularly the CD-ROM, on its business. In that period sales plummeted by more than 50 per cent. The business had been built through a highly motivated and successful salesforce selling encyclopaedias to middle-class families (often bought by parents for their children's education) at around $1,500 each.

Then along came home computers, with CD-ROM players and encyclopaedias such as Encarta at around $50. The new entrants may not have had the depth of coverage of EB but they were in a format the children enjoyed using, offered the opportunities for multimedia display (video and audio clips, animations), could be more easily updated and, perhaps most crucially, offered middle-class parents a justification for the purchase of often expensive home computer systems which in many cases were used primarily for games purposes!

With the advent of the 'information superhighway', the World Wide Web and Internet, the holding of large amounts of data on individual PCs is becoming a thing of the past, posing potential problems (and, of course, opportunities) for the marketers of CD-ROM-based encyclopaedias. In particular, the advent of open access, user-built encyclopaedias such as Wikipedia have significantly impacted on the CD-based products. Rapidly updated, and relying on users to submit, update and expand on the content, these are essentially free at the point of use (making their money out of advertising links), rapidly expanding in content and do not take up local storage space on hard disk or other media (see **www.wikipedia. com**). More recently EB has made its encyclopaedia available online to subscribers (**http:// www.britannica.com/**) recognising that a key advantage it has lies in the expert editorial staff – while Wikipedia relies on random contributors with minimal editorial control to check for accuracy, EB trades on its expert contributors and the constant updating available online.

Similarly, Hoover and Electrolux suffered greatly by the overnight success of the Dyson bagless vacuum cleaner; both losing a great deal of market share to the innovation (see below). However an often forgotten nuance of this story is that both were offered (prior to Dyson going to market with his own product) the rights to the new and innovative bagless technology. In essence the issue was not that Hoover and Electrolux did not see the innovation coming, indeed they knew about it in advance. Rather they both had a vested interest in preserving the *status quo*.

It is also easy to underestimate the practical realities of rapid accelerations in the speed and disruptive impact of change. For example, consider the unfolding impact of Internet telephony. While it took 50 years for the telephone to gain widespread diffusion, it took less than a decade for the mobile phone to do the same. It is expected that Internet telephony will reach critical mass in only a few years. Similarly, in the photography market, the disruptive and pervasive impact of digital technology demanded rapid transformation in business models by existing players like Kodak. The failure of Kodak to understand the speed of change and rapid decline in demand for traditional cameras and film has led to major financial losses, extensive lay-offs and plant closures.

No company can ever hope to predict every aspect of the macro-environment in which it operates, but organisations should aim to achieve profound understanding of their core markets. There will always be surprises and shocks as new technological breakthroughs emerge or political discontinuities occur. What is important, however, is to spot and act on more of the trends and changes than competitors. Shocks are less for companies prepared to think the 'unthinkable' and to challenge the *status quo* in their strategising. For example, the UK brewers and cigarette companies have been quite open in the past, admitting that they have contingency plans should cannabis be legalised.

Importantly, disruptive changes have the potential to make deep changes in the structure of a market, which may disadvantage existing competitors but offer important opportunities to others.

18.1.2 Changes in markets

A number of trends can be seen in modern markets that are likely to continue into the future (Figure 18.1).

First, customers are becoming increasingly demanding of the products and services they buy. Customers demand, and expect, reliable and durable products with quick, efficient service at reasonable prices. They also expect the products and services they buy to meet their needs. Different customers have different wants and needs, and hence companies have an opportunity to select segments where their offerings most closely align with those needs

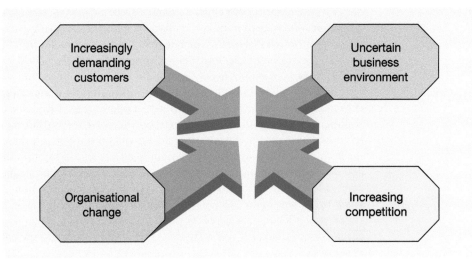

Figure 18.1
Pressures on
marketing

and where they can focus their activities to create a competitive advantage. What is more, there is little long-term stability in customer demands. Positions may be achieved through offering superior customer value, and yet the evidence is that without constant improvement 'value migration' will occur – buyers will migrate to an alternative value offering (Slywotzky, 1996).

For example, an executive in a computer company producing laptop computers complained in 1997:

> First they wanted the notebook with a colour screen – we gave it to them. Then, last year, it had to have a Pentium chip, so we gave them that. Now they tell us they still want all that, but the thing that really matters is that the computer has to have the weight of a feather . . .

A second major trend, one that particularly differentiates the early part of the twenty-first century, is that customers are less prepared to pay a substantial premium for products or services that do not offer demonstrably greater value. This has been exacerbated by the 2008–10 recession. While it is undeniable that well-developed and managed brands can command higher prices than unbranded products in many markets, the differentials commanded are now much less than they were and customers are increasingly questioning the extra value they get for the extra expense. New strategic thinking has to accommodate the fact that customers are becoming more sophisticated and more marketing-literate. Price comparison sites, such as Gocompare.com and Confused.com allow customers to rapidly compare not only competing product features, but also retail prices of the same product in different outlets. Phone apps are also now fuelling this issue, with the ability to scan barcodes in shops and to view instantly whether the same product is cheaper elsewhere online or locally; RedLaser is an example of such an app. The sophisticated customer is now much less likely to be attracted to cheap products with low quality, and yet neither can be won by image-based advertising. The implications are clear. Differentiation needs to be based on providing demonstrably superior value to customers (Figure 18.2).

A third major trend is in both the level and nature of competition. Competition is becoming more intense and more global in nature. As international trade becomes more liberalised

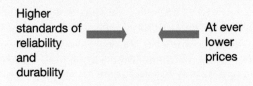

Figure 18.2
Increasing
customer demands

under the aegis of the WTO, so firms face tougher international competition at home and increased opportunities abroad. Time and distance are shrinking rapidly as communications become near instantaneous. Firms are increasingly thinking global in their strategies, especially as cross-national segments are beginning to emerge for products and services from fast foods through toys to computers and automobiles. The increasingly widespread use of the Internet for promoting and marketing both products and services now means that communications know no national borders. Not only are markets becoming more competitive through more players emerging in them, those firms that survive and thrive in these more competitive conditions are, by their very nature, tougher competitors. Weak firms are being shaken out of markets where they do not have clear positions and attendant capabilities. The implications of heightened, more aggressive competition, both domestic and international, are that firms will need to look even more closely at their scope of operations and targeting in the future.

And yet the executive must confront the central paradox in all this. As markets become harsher in their judgements and in the level of competitiveness faced, companies are under growing pressure to collaborate with and partner others. Increasingly, collaboration is taking place with suppliers, customers and even competitors. The clear demarcation lines of the past are blurring and executives have to deal with more ambiguous new roles. As we have seen, the demands of customers for suppliers to demonstrate their ethical credentials and to undertake social and environmental responsibility initiatives emerged at just the same time as those same customers demanded lower prices and higher quality. Not least among the unprecedented yet exciting challenges facing executives is to achieve economic efficiency at the same time as an environmentally and socially responsible organisation that creates competitive advantage from its integrity (see Carroll and Shabana, 2010).

18.1.3 Organisational change

While 'downsizing' is still very much a part of the commercial landscape, many firms have come to terms with the notion that there is only so much 'fat' that can be cut before you damage the muscle, and too aggressive slimming can lead to *anorexia industrialis* (the excessive desire to be leaner and fitter, leading to total emaciation and eventual death). The impact on organisational structures has been far broader, and this is manifest in two main directions. First, there is the impact within the firm. Second, there is the impact on inter-firm relations.

Within firms the boundaries between functional areas are becoming more blurred. Where firms were once organised with clear-cut divisions between marketing, finance and operations it is now recognised that 'functional silos' can result in myopic operations and suboptimal strategies. In leading firms the functional boundaries have long since been replaced by process teams that can view the operations of the organisation in holistic terms and will not be hampered by petty rivalries between functions.

At the same time, the role of marketing per se in the organisation has been challenged. Marketing departments can get in the way of serving customers for two main reasons. The first is territorial. They may see dealing with customers as their preserve and wish to retain the power and influence that goes with that. Secondly, however, they may encourage others in the organisation to offload responsibility for customer building to the marketing department. This creates the dangerous view that others do not need to concern themselves with customers; someone else will take care of it. Indeed, one view is that the days of conventional marketing have long since finished, and the challenge now is to design and implement better ways of managing the process of going to market. That process cuts across traditional functional boundaries as well as external boundaries with partners.

Between firms, the boundaries of where one finishes and the next starts are also increasingly blurred. Boundaries with suppliers, distributors and customers are changing as more businesses understand the need to manage the entire value chain from raw materials through to customers, and work more closely with partner firms to achieve added value through the chain.

Successful strategy initiatives may increasingly rely on finding ways around the lack of responsiveness and slow movement of traditional functional bureaucracies. Organisations that fail to address this important issue may not survive; a compelling need for change indeed!

In fact, the above changes taking place both in markets and organisations require businesses to reassess their strategy in general and marketing strategy in particular. The strategies that will be successful in the future will need to be responsive and adaptive rather than rigid and fixed. Key will be creating an organisational context in which learning can take place, market changes can be identified and capabilities can be fashioned to ensure a strategic fit between market and firm. In short, the development of dynamic capabilities will become more critical.

| **18.2** | **Fundamentals of strategy in a changing world** |

Figure 18.3 shows a number of factors that are increasingly essential in dealing with complex and changing circumstances.

18.2.1 The learning organisation

Central to developing a sustainable competitive advantage in rapidly, and often unpredictably, changing circumstances is the dynamic capability to learn and adapt (Sinkula, 1994; Kilmann, 1996; Evans and Wurster, 1997; Prokesch, 1997; Sinkula *et al.,* 1997; Morgan *et al.,* 1998). The competitive dynamics of markets with new entrants, substitute technologies and shifts in customer preferences can swiftly erode static advantages built on the 'generic' strategies of cost leadership or product differentiation (McKee and Varadarajan, 1995). Organisational learning, however, offers the potential both to respond to and act on opportunities in the markets of the firm. Indeed, Dickson (1992) suggests that the ability to learn faster than competitors may be the *only* real source of sustainable competitive advantage, echoing the quote from Charles Darwin at the start of this chapter.

Learning is manifest in the knowledge, experience and information held in an organisation (Mahoney, 1995). It resides in both people and technical systems. Learning involves the acquisition, processing, storing and retrieval (dissemination) of knowledge. A major

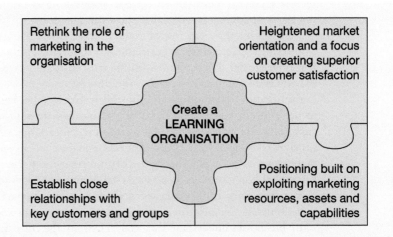

Figure 18.3
Fundamentals of strategy in a changing world

challenge for many organisations is to create the combination of culture and climate to maximise learning (Slater and Narver, 1995). At the human level managerial systems need to be established to create and control knowledge. At the technical level systems need to be established to facilitate the accumulation and storage of relevant information in a manner that makes it readily accessible to those who need to access it.

Much of an organisation's knowledge base typically resides in the heads of managers and workers. When personnel leave through retirement, 'downsizing' or recruitment by competitors, that knowledge may be lost or, more damagingly, gained by a competitor. Employment contracts of key personnel are increasingly including 'golden handcuffs' which prohibit critical managers from taking their knowledge to competitors. Organisations are also increasingly looking for ways of extracting the knowledge of their key people and transmitting it to others in the organisation through expert systems and training processes, so that the knowledge is more secure and embedded in the fabric of the organisation.

Of particular importance in the context of marketing strategy is the development of knowledge and skills in how to create superior customer value. Slater and Narver (1995) show that a primary focus of market orientation is to create superior customer value, and that in turn needs to be based on knowledge derived from customer and competitor analysis, together with knowledge gleaned from suppliers, businesses in different industries, government sources, universities, consultants and other potential sources. They conclude that learning organisations continually acquire, process and disseminate knowledge about markets, products, technologies and business processes based on experience, experimentation, information from customers, suppliers, competitors and other sources. This learning enables them to anticipate and act on opportunities in turbulent and fragmented markets.

And yet developing learning capabilities need not be complex and sophisticated. Superior learning capabilities may be as much about market sensing and understanding as it is about utilising technology. Indeed, research at the Marketing Science Institute has found that, of ten market-based capabilities, market sensing displayed the strongest impact on business process performance (Ramaswami *et al.*, 2004).

While the central requirement for competing in the future is learning, a number of other more specific building blocks can be suggested as important ingredients in fashioning competitive strategy.

18.2.2 Heightened market orientation and focus on creating superior customer value

In increasingly crowded and competitive markets there is no substitute for being market oriented. Put simply, a market orientation focuses the firm's activities on meeting the needs and requirements of customers better than competitors. This in turn requires finding out what will give customers value and ensuring that the firm's energies are directed towards providing that. Identifying ways of providing superior customer value is one of the central challenges of management for the twenty-first century.

A market orientation does not imply over-sophisticated marketing operation. Indeed, it has been argued by some that marketing departments can themselves get in the way of providing superior customer value (see above).

In the quest to provide superior customer value no firm can stand still. What offers better value than competitors today will be considered standard tomorrow. Innovation, the constant improving of the offering to customers, is essential for sustained competitive advantage.

The focus of activities in firms that are truly market-oriented and intent on creating superior value for their customers is on finding solutions to those customers' problems. Rather than a focus on selling the firm's own existing products it sets out first to identify current and future customer problems and then to find solutions to them. Solutions may involve creating new products and services, integrating the offerings of other providers (through alliances), and even in some instances accepting that customers cannot be well served and recommending alternative suppliers. After exhausting all other options a truly market-oriented firm can gain more customer goodwill (and ultimately more long-term business) by admitting that it cannot provide exactly what the customer wants rather than trying to persuade the customer to accept second best, or even pretending that the solution offered is appropriate.

18.2.3 Positioning built on marketing assets, capabilities and competencies

Much of the emphasis in the strategy literature today has focused on the 'resource-based theory' of the firm (see Chapter 6). This theory emphasises the need for strategies to be based on the resources and capabilities of the firm, rather than merely chasing customers irrespective of the ability of the firm to serve them. Resource-based theorists, however, are in danger of losing sight of the fact that resources are valuable only when they are translated into providing something that customers want. This is the essence of the 'resource-based marketing' approach espoused in this text.

Markets change, and so too must resources such as assets and competencies. They need to be constantly improved and developed if the firm is to thrive. An essential task for marketing management is to identify the competencies and assets that will be needed in the future, as well as those that are needed today, so that they can be built or acquired in advance.

As discussed in Chapter 6, marketing resources are any properties or processes that can be exploited in the marketplace to create or sustain a competitive advantage. They range from recognised brand names, through unique use of distribution channels, to information and quality control systems. These assets are the resource endowments the business has created or acquired over time and now has available to deploy in the market. Competencies are the skills that are used to deploy the assets to best effect in the market.

These definitions are in line with early resource-based theorists such as Barney (1991), who suggest that it is management that is the most important resource because they make use of the assets and other resources available to them based on their knowledge of the market acquired through their previous learning.

As we saw in Chapter 6, Day (1994) goes on to identify three main types of competencies: outside-in; inside-out; and spanning and integrating competencies. Outside-in competencies are those skills and abilities that enable a business to understand its customers and create closer linkages with them. Inside-out competencies are the internal capabilities of the firm and its employees that can be deployed in the marketplace to provide better products and services to customers. Spanning and integrating competencies bring together the inside-out and the outside-in to ensure delivery of appropriate products and services to customers.

More recently RBV theorists have emphasised the need for dynamic capabilities (Menguc and Auh, 2006; Helfat *et al.*, 2007). A dynamic capability is 'the capacity of an organisation to purposefully create, extend, or modify its resource base' (Helfat *et al.*, 2007, p. 4). Menguac and Auh (2006) show how dynamic capabilities can be built through capitalising on market orientation and innovativeness. They demonstrate empirically how the effect of market orientation on firm performance is enhanced when firms demonstrate a high degree of innovation.

Not all assets and capabilities may be vested in the focal firm. Increasingly, companies are creating alliances and networks with others that enable them to leverage further assets and competencies of partner firms (see Chapter 15). Alliances can offer four main sets of assets and competencies: access to new markets; access to managerial competence; access to technological competence; and economic benefits.

There are, however, problems in realising the advantages offered by alliances and networks of collaborating firms. Many of the alliances established in the late 1990s and early

2000s have failed. Understanding of the dynamics of alliances and the critical executive skills required by these new organisations are sadly limited (see Chapter 15).

Taken together, marketing assets and competencies/capabilities are the basis on which any competitive positioning is built. Ideally firms should seek to build their positions on the basis of assets and competencies which are superior to those of their competitors and difficult to duplicate. They should also seek to create or acquire assets and competencies that can be exploited in many other situations (e.g. extend their brand name into new markets, exploit their technology in new industries, use their networks in different ways). A critical issue for the future is how different assets and competencies can be combined to create new products and services (Hamel and Prahalad, 1994).

18.2.4 Establishing closer relationships with key customers

In Chapter 14 we discussed the ways in which firms can build closer relationships with their customers. Fundamental issues include which customers to build those relationships with and how to build them.

Relationship marketing (Payne and Frow, 2005) has been one of the most significant developments in marketing thought of recent years. While it has been recognised as important in some markets for some time and under different labels (e.g. the personal account managers in financial services), it is now generally agreed that customer retention, through superior service and relationship building, is applicable in far wider markets.

In consumer markets relationships can be built initially through branding and reputation creation. In the past, relationships in business markets have been stereotyped as between individuals – salesperson and purchasing officer. However, in modern business-to-business markets the pressure is for team-based selling and relationship building across the whole spectrum of internal departments. The challenge is to become the 'outsource of preference' by understanding the customer's business and adding value in excess of cost (Chally, 2006). Similarly, Simon (1996) stresses that the relationships which endure in business markets are those based on sound economic and business grounds rather than, perhaps ephemeral, personal/social bases. Relationships and reputations can be far harder for competitors to copy than possibly transitory product features, special offers or deals.

Not all customers, however, place great value on ever closer relationships with their suppliers. Similarly, the costs of creating closer relationships with some customers (in terms of time, effort and financial resource) may well outweigh the long-term commercial benefits. What will become increasingly important will be for firms to decide the optimum intensity of relationship with each customer or customer group and then find effective and efficient means of establishing that level. It is likely that any firm will be operating in a number of different marketing modes depending on the customers served. For some key accounts a heavy emphasis on one-to-one close relationship building to create 'partners' might be applicable, while at the same time other groups are marketed less intensively so as to create 'advocates' rather than partners. For yet other customers of the same firm a mass marketing approach might be applicable to secure their business in the first place. *Multi-mode marketing,* the adoption of different marketing approaches for different customers or customer groups, is likely to take the place of more uniform marketing to all customers.

18.2.5 Rethinking the role of marketing in the organisation

The above ideas lead to the inevitable conclusion that the role and function of marketing within the organisation (or within the 'virtual network') needs to be redefined and reasserted.

Basic to that rethinking is to escape from the notion that marketing is essentially a business function, a department on the organisation chart. Increasingly, marketing is being seen as a process within the value chain, a process responsible for ensuring the creation of value for customers in both the short and long term. Structures need to be created that facilitate rapid response and flexibility rather than hinder it. Indeed, it is interesting to note that many successful companies do not have specifically named 'marketing departments', yet few would dispute that they are close to their customers, and attentive and reactive to their needs.

Brown (1995) notes:

> There are now two types of corporation: those with a marketing department and those with a marketing soul. Even a cursory glance at the latest Fortune 500 shows that the latter are the top performing companies, while the former, steeped in the business traditions of the past, are fast disappearing.

Simon (1996) also notes that many of the firms in his sample of 'hidden champions' do not have marketing departments. They share, however, two main traits. First, they are extremely close to their customers and ensure that all employees recognise their role in serving them. Secondly, they focus on solving customers' problems through innovation to improve on their offerings to customers, continuously providing additional customer value. These two traits are the essence of a market orientation, but are achieved without the trappings of a marketing department.

It is important in defining the role of marketing for the future to recognise that marketing operates at two main levels: strategic and operational. At the operational level brand managers and marketing managers deal with day-to-day marketing tasks such as liaison with market research companies, advertising and public relations agencies and so on. In fast moving consumer goods (FMCG) companies they also spend much of their time organising trade and consumer promotions, special deals, competitions, etc.

At the strategic level, however, marketing is more concerned with decisions as to which markets to operate in and how to compete successfully in them. At this level marketing is not a functional activity, but requires input from across the organisation of alternative perspectives and skills. As noted earlier, the challenge is then to manage the process of going to market to build superior customer value, through a complex of resources, capabilities and relationships that make up the offering.

Marketing needs to become, and remain, flexible and responsive to change. That entails distinguishing the philosophy from the trappings. At a strategic level everyone in the organisation should place customers at the forefront of their minds. Xerox once summarised this in a mission statement – 'ultimately it is customers who will decide whether the firm survives and whether employees and managers have a job in the future'.

In the highly competitive markets envisaged for the foreseeable future, ability to assimilate and act on knowledge, to create strategies based on assets and competencies, to establish close, deep relationships with chosen market segments, and finally the ability to redefine the scope and role of marketing within the organisation will be the bases for creating competitive advantage.

18.3   Competitive positioning strategies

As has been argued above, competitive positioning is about making choices that ensure a fit between chosen market targets and the competencies and assets the firm can deploy to serve those chosen targets more effectively than competitors. While there are, in reality, an infinite number of different ways in which firms might position themselves in their markets, these can be summarised on the basis of the emphasis they give to six main dimensions of differentiation.

Figure 18.4 shows these six dimensions. Positioning could be based on: price; technical quality (or, more correctly, grade); service; customisation; benefit differentiation; or

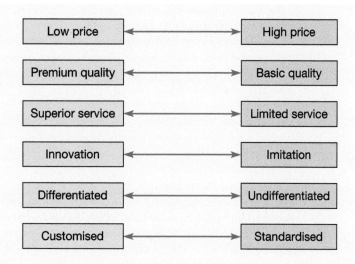

Figure 18.4
Basic positioning
options

innovation. While individual firms may choose to position on more than one dimension simultaneously they often find that they are contradictory. For example, offering a higher grade of product is generally incongruent with keeping costs, and hence prices, as low as possible. Indeed, charging low prices for a high-grade product may create confusion in the minds of customers. The key to creating sustainable positions is to ensure that they are built on the marketing assets and competencies of the firm.

18.3.1 Price positioning

Costs must be kept in check. By this we mean at least as low (or preferably lower) than competitors, in order for a low-price position to be achievable or sustainable. If there is no cost advantage, price wars may put the instigator at a financial disadvantage and the whole positioning strategy may not be sustainable. Positioning as the low-price supplier requires strong inside-out and spanning capabilities. Effective cost-control systems (through activity-based costing) are needed not only within the firm's own operations but also within suppliers' operations. Procurement of raw materials and other factor inputs is organised around keeping costs to a minimum. Distribution logistics are similarly managed for minimum cost (see Figure 18.5).

While the low-price position is a viable option for some firms there is a constant need to work at keeping costs down, especially when new competitors enter the market with new operating methods or unique assets that can be used to undercut the costs of incumbents.

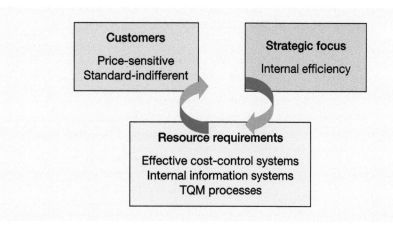

Figure 18.5
Low-price
positioning

For a price positioning strategy to be successful in the marketplace the existence of a viable, price-sensitive customer segment is also required. In most markets there are customers who will buy primarily on price. Also in most markets over the last 10 years, price-sensitive customers have been very much present, given the global economic conditions. Price positioning can be successful where there is a clearly defined, price-sensitive sector of the market and the firm has a cost advantage in serving that market.

Nonetheless, reliance purely on low price-based positioning can carry high risks as well. Executives are increasingly well aware of the effect of the 'China Price' threat. At the extreme, while a conventional competitor in the Triad countries – the US, EU and Japan – might undercut your price by 10 per cent to gain business, companies in countries like China and India are more likely to offer a price which is 10 per cent of your price.

Indeed, some firms position at the other end of the price spectrum. They deliberately price their products and services more highly than competitors to create exclusivity for their offerings. High-price positions are usually accompanied by higher quality, branded offerings requiring strong reputations and clearly superior images (e.g. Harrods department store in Knightsbridge). The competencies required for high-price (premium) positions to be effective are centred on the ability to create a superior, or exclusive, image that customers are willing to pay a premium to be associated with. Brand assets in particular need to be built through the use of creative promotional campaigns.

18.3.2 Quality positioning

Positioning as a high technical quality (grade) supplier also requires effective internal control systems, especially quality assessment and assurance. Beyond control, however, it also requires technical competence, particularly in engineering and manufacturing where physical products are produced. Most significantly, it requires a clear view of what constitutes 'quality' in the eyes of the customer. That entails the outside-in capabilities of market sensing and customer bonding (see Figure 18.6).

Also important in delivering high-quality products and services is supply-chain management, ensuring that the inputs are of the required quality, not simply the cheapest available. Marks & Spencer used to have a reputation for building long-term, demanding relationships with their suppliers to ensure that the products they put their labels on are of the required quality. M&S now sources more widely but still keeps a close eye on the quality of the fabrics used in its products.

There are four Betty's Tea Rooms in Yorkshire and one Taylor's. Together they sell 2 million cups of tea each year. They don't advertise, but people flock in their thousands and are prepared to queue for seats. The atmosphere is elegant, sophisticated. Waiters and waitresses are formally dressed in the style of Victorian servants. The tea is perfect and the

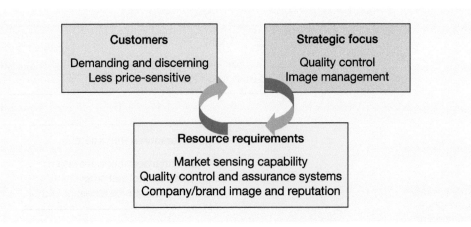

Figure 18.6
Premium-quality
positioning

cakes are delicious. The pastries range from exotic Amadeus Torte to local Yorkshire curd tarts. The company was started in Harrogate by a Swiss confectioner, Frederick Belmont, in 1919. The company's bakers and confectioners still train in Lucerne. The company has built on its brand asset by opening related gift shops on the premises, selling confectionery suited to the tourists who visit. They also sell their products by mail order. More recently they have marketed Yorkshire Tea, which has become a major brand in the beverages market (Kotler *et al.*, 1996).

Often critical to a quality positioning are the marketing assets of brand image and reputation (see above). Image and reputation can take years to create and, once established, need to be nurtured and, when necessary, defended vigorously.

To customers quality is manifest through better reliability, durability and aesthetic appearance. For quality positions to be viable customers must be prepared to pay for superior quality as there are usually, though not always, higher costs associated with offering a higher-quality product. In the automotive industry German manufacturers such as Mercedes, BMW and Audi have successfully positioned their offerings at the high-quality end of the spectrum through superior design, technical engineering skills ('Vorsprung durch Technik' – leading through technology) and attention to quality control through the manufacturing process.

We should bear in mind in all this, however, that quality and value are decided by customers in the marketplace, not by engineers in the factory, or advertising executives in the marketing department.

18.3.3 Innovation positioning

Where markets are changing rapidly, especially as a result of technological developments, there may be opportunities to position on the basis of innovativeness, or speed to market (see Figure 18.7). Hamel and Prahalad (1991) suggest that firms should encourage 'fast failure', that is, encourage the test launch of new products, in the recognition that many may fail but that some will succeed. Fast failure, they argue, is preferable to smothering new ideas at birth or delaying their launch through over-elaborate screening systems.

Similarly, the impressive success of Samsung Electronics in the 2000s is based in part on the CEO's deliberate culture of 'perpetual crisis', a powerful Value Innovation Programme, and a long-term strategic vision of controlling core technologies in an era of digital convergence. Samsung's goal of market leadership is being pursued through innovation in technology and design.

The key competencies required include excellent new product development skills together with technical and creative abilities. These are combinations of inside-out and spanning competencies. Once new product ideas are developed, it is important to test them

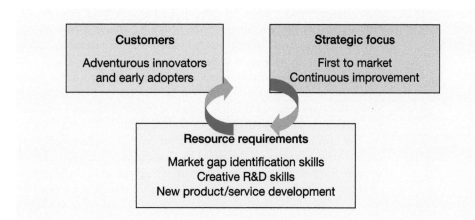

Figure 18.7
Innovation
positioning

out on customers (through fast failure or more conventional means) to avoid the launch of highly-innovative but essentially unwanted products. There are many high-profile examples of products that have failed throughout history. For example: the Ford Edsel (1950s), Sony Betamax (1970s), 'New' Coke (1980s), Microsoft Bob (1990s), Google Glass (although still in development, the original Google Glass launch has been viewed as a failure by many) and Burger King 'Satisfries' (2000s), along with many, many others!

Tellis and Golder (1996), in a study of first-to-market firms, concluded that for many firms a more successful strategy is to be a fast follower. Under this approach firms learn from the mistakes of the pioneers and capitalise on the growth phase of the market without incurring the costs of establishing the market in the first place. Moore (1991), in his study of innovation in high-technology markets, concludes that the critical aspect of new product success is bridging the 'chasm' between innovators (those who will be attracted to an innovation because of its innovative nature) and the early majority who represent the beginnings of the mass market. It is this chasm that, in Moore's opinion, accounts for the failure of many new products.

James Dyson is an inventor who has successfully positioned his firm as the provider of innovative solutions to everyday problems. In January 1997 he won the European Design Award for his innovative vacuum cleaner (see below). Dyson started inventing at the age of 28 when he recognised a design fault in conventional wheelbarrows. When full, the barrow, with a single, thin wheel at the front, was prone to tipping over. He replaced the wheel with a large red ball which solved the problem. When he set up in business the 'ball barrow' was an immediate success, selling over 60,000 per year. Following that success he designed a new garden roller which was light and manoeuvrable when not in use but heavy enough to roll lawns flat. His innovation was to use a hollow plastic roller that could be filled with water when in use but drained when not in use. The bagless vacuum cleaners followed, and Dyson have since launched hand dryers and an award-winning range of room fans and heaters. The success of the £100 million turnover company has been based on innovation, first to market with revolutionary designs of everyday products, offering superior value to customers.

18.3.4 Service positioning

Positioning on the basis of offering superior service, or rather service clearly tailored to the needs of the target market, is increasingly being used. Variations in the nature and level of service offered, coupled with differences in requirements across customer groups, mean that service positioning can be viable and attractive for more than one company in a market. Critical to providing superior service are market sensing skills which can identify what level/type of service is required; customer bonding skills that build closer relationships with key customers; service systems that assist the service providers in delivering service to customers, and monitoring skills that can regularly assess the customer satisfaction with the level and type of service provided. Most critical of all to providing superior service are the people, or staff, that actually provide the service. Selection, training, motivation and reward of service staff are areas that need high priority in firms seeking to establish a competitive edge through service provision (see Figure 18.8).

Firms seeking to create a service edge to position themselves as offering superior service to that of competitors need first to understand how their customers judge service, what dimensions are important to them and how they are manifest. They then need to put in place strategies and systems to ensure their staff can deliver superior service (see Chapter 13).

Otis Elevator recognised the importance of providing excellent service in the elevator business. Customers preferred to deal directly with Otis rather than go through an intermediary, and hence the company set up the OTISLINE through which customers can contact the firm's service centre 24 hours a day. The service has been used to market

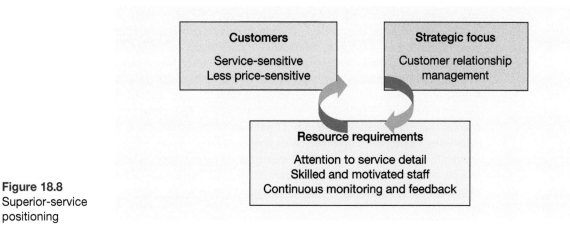

Figure 18.8
Superior-service
positioning

the firm's offerings and to give customers confidence in them. It also formed the basis for the company's making further improvements in information systems, including REM (remote elevator monitoring) identifying problems before lifts break down. The system improved response times through better call management, improved diagnostic capabilities and strengthened the service team by providing them with better communications. The result has been significant increases in customer satisfaction levels (Armistead and Clark, 1992).

18.3.5 Differentiated benefits positioning

Differentiated benefits positioning rests on clearly identifying alternative benefit segments within markets and then focusing on providing what they want (Yanklovich and Meer, 2006) (see Figure 18.9). As discussed in Chapter 9, segmenting markets on the basis of the benefits customers are seeking can often help identify new market opportunities and suggest ways in which marketing effort can be more effectively targeted.

Positioning on this basis is dependent on having well-developed outside-in competencies to identify the benefits customers are seeking in the first place and to segment the market creatively into meaningful but commercially viable sectors. It can also require effective new product/service development skills to ensure that the benefits sought are actually delivered to customers through building in the relevant features.

In the US mouthwash market for example, P&G successfully challenged the incumbent market leader Listerine with a better-tasting alternative (branded Scope); taking significant market share away very quickly. Surprisingly, mouthwashes were once advertised as being

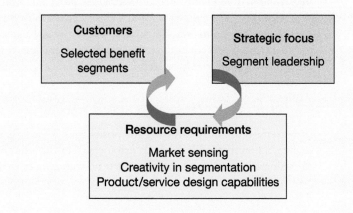

Figure 18.9
Differentiated
positioning

good because they tasted 'bad', connecting with a belief that mouthwashes had to taste bad in order to work effectively. Indeed in an early television commercial for Listerine, the closing phrase was: 'Listerine. The taste you hate twice a day.' Clearly a better-tasting alternative, that still promised the same benefits as the bad-testing incumbent, was particularly attractive to consumers. Fairy Liquid is a washing-up liquid that has been consistently positioned on the basis of the twin benefits it provides to users: clean dishes but smooth hands for the washer-up. The product was test launched in Birmingham, UK, in 1959 when the market was in its infancy, with only 17 per cent of consumers using washing-up liquid, the remainder relying on soap powders or household soap to wash their dishes. The national launch in 1960 involved a massive door-to-door programme, which delivered 15 million sample bottles to 85 per cent of houses in the UK. The launch platform stressed that the product was strong enough to remove dirt and grease from plates and dishes but was mild on hands.

By 1980, 1 billion bottles of Fairy Liquid had been sold. Product improvements in 1982 enabled the advertisements to demonstrate a 20 per cent improvement in the volume of dishes that could be washed with one bottle (a 20 per cent 'mileage' improvement) and the brand had reached 27 per cent market share. Further continuous product improvement followed with the launch of a lemon-scented variant in 1984–85 (share climbed to 32 per cent) and further increased mileage in 1988 (by 15 per cent) and 1992 (by a further 50 per cent and signalled by a change of name to Fairy Excel), taking market share above 50 per cent for the first time. In 1993 Fairy Excel Plus replaced Fairy Excel, offering yet a further 50 per cent mileage improvement but still retaining the mildness to hands. One manager was quoted as saying that 'the heritage of the brand is so linked with mildness it [putting anything less mild on the market] would be regarded as treachery by the consumer.'

Yamaha was world market leader in fine upright and grand pianos. Globally the company held 40 per cent of the market, but the market was in decline at around 10 per cent per annum. Market research showed that many pianos were seldom played, gathered dust and were out of tune. Using its competencies in digital music technology (the firm had pioneered electronic keyboards), the firm set about offering additional benefits in the pianos it sold. They developed the 'disklavier', which was a traditional piano (upright and grand) which could be played normally but also had an additional feature. Attached to the piano was an electronic device that enabled the owner to play pre-recorded music on their own piano. The device accepted a 3.5-inch disk, similar to a computer floppy disk, which contained the recorded music and played it on the piano. On its launch in Japan the product was an immediate success, rising to 20 per cent market share within three years. The firm also worked on the possibilities of retro-fitting existing pianos with the device to expand the market potential even further.

Interestingly, the concept was not completely new. In 1930s America, 'pianolas' (pianos that could play rolls of punched paper when pedalled) were very popular!

Positioning based on benefits sought by customers is conventionally associated with consumer markets. In fact, the same is true of the strategies of successful firms in business-to-business markets. In both cases, benefit segments provide a powerful basis on which to build positioning directly related to the requirements of customers.

18.3.6 Customised positioning (one-to-one marketing)

Perhaps the ultimate in targeting and positioning is the attempt to offer products customised to the requirements of individual customers. While this has been practised in many business-to-business markets for some time, it is now coming to others and consumer markets too (see Figure 18.10).

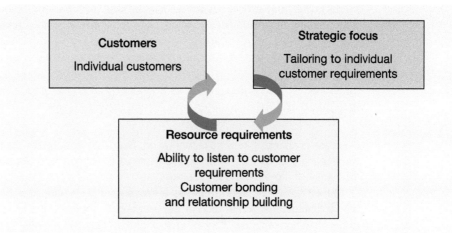

Figure 18.10
Customised
positioning

German car manufacturer Porsche produces around 150 cars a day from its assembly line in Stuttgart. Each car is customised so that customers have more than 1 billion combinations to choose from. They can choose interiors, seats, dashboards, engine types, body styles and colours. In fact, Porsche will paint the car any colour the customer desires, as will other leading quality manufacturers.

The important skills for customised positioning are a combination of outside-in com-petencies to enable the firm to identify what the customer wants, and to establish relationships with customers, with inside-out competencies of flexible production capability. Recent advances in manufacturing make it increasingly possible for firms to enjoy the cost and efficiency advantages of mass production while at the same time tailoring their offerings to individual customer requirements.

The clearest examples of customised positioning, however, are generally found in services, both consumer and business, where a customised service can be tailored to the requirements of individual customers. Financial consultants offer tailored analysis of investment needs, accountants offer tailored accounts, hairdressers offer tailored haircuts and architects can offer (if the customer can pay) individual house designs.

Customised positioning rests on understanding individual, rather than market segment, needs and having the flexibility to provide for them at a price the customer is willing to pay. While technology, such as the use of the Internet, can play an important role in enabling economically viable customisation, the process needs to be market-led rather than technology-driven. Increasingly, companies are looking to create synergies through the use of new technology to respond to customer demands.

Levi Strauss now offers customised blue jeans – tailored to the tight fit required by customers – by taking measurements in the shop which are sent electronically to the factory to produce a unique garment (and store the data for repeat purchases). The same type of customer offer is made by some shoe suppliers in the US, who respond to customer preferences for unique products by using technology to achieve this at a reasonable cost.

Amazon.com has millions of customers but manages to practise one-to-one marketing in a highly effective manner. The firm is very successful at tracking what customers do and, using that information, sends e-mails to them with information about new books and videos similar to those they have purchased, or by the same authors, or in the same genre. This customised information service has helped Amazon achieve good levels of customer retention and repeat purchase.

The above alternative approaches to positioning are not necessarily exclusive of each other. They do constitute, however, the main basic alternatives open to firms. The creative application of those alternatives offers an almost infinite variety of ways that firms might build competitive advantage for the new millennium. The task of marketing is to select among the alternatives, basing the choice firmly on the competencies and capabilities of the firm.

Summary

Business is changing and so is marketing. Successful strategies for the future will be based on creating a fit between the requirements of the chosen market and the resources of the firm, its ability to meet those requirements.

Marketing will be seen more as a process for achieving this type of matching, rather than a functional specialisation or department. To focus on the process of going to market, rather than conventional marketing structures, offers the chance to enhance the role of the customer as a driving force for the company and to finally achieve operationally the goal that 'marketing's future is not as a function of business but as the function of business' (Haeckel, 1997). The new processes of marketing will require us to learn new ways of doing business in unfamiliar organisations.

Neither resources nor markets are fixed. We may by now be well used to the notion of market requirements changing over time and the need to monitor those changes. We are perhaps less aware of the need, explicitly and constantly, to examine and develop our resources and capabilities over time. New dynamic capabilities must be built or otherwise acquired (e.g. through alliances, mergers or acquisitions) to enable the company to compete in the future. At the same time, the firm should examine how it can use its current set of capabilities and assets in different markets or combine its existing capabilities in innovative ways to create new opportunities (as Yamaha did with their digital pianos).

Fundamentally we can expect firms to be more selective and narrower in their choice of markets and customers to serve, but to concentrate their efforts on creating deeper relationships with those chosen to ensure long-term value creation through long-term relationships. There is, of course, an infinite number of ways in which firms can create relationships with their customers.

Marketers must also dare to think differently about their role and the strategies they pursue. Ideas that have been in the collective consciousness since the advent of formalised theories of marketing have to be challenged. Indeed, some of the notions and frameworks expressed in this text, while still very much relevant, may well be less so in the very near future. Sheth and Sisodia (2006) incorporate these ideas when they state:

> Forget all the old ideas about marketing warfare, customer conquest and capture, or aggressive marketing tactics of any kind. Indeed aggressive sentiments and mindsets have no place in marketing. Marketing must be about pursuing desirable ends (delighted customers, undamaged societal interests, fair returns to shareholders) through desirable means.

They then expand on this and list a number of virtues that they believe must be embedded in marketing practice, e.g. truth, integrity, authenticity, trust, respect, good manners and humility. Many of these words are not often associated with marketing or marketing strategy and, while this may be unfair, it is at the heart of the issue. The challenge for marketing and marketing practice in the twenty-first century is to achieve positive outcomes (that can be justified and demonstrated) not only for the organisations deploying the resource, but also for all associated stakeholders such as employees, customers, suppliers, society and government. In this way, issues of marketing strategy and competitive positioning can continue to be central to successful strategic decision making in modern, forward-thinking businesses.

Case study   Twitter builds on its character

Twitter has taken its fair share of criticism in the four years since its launch. Users complained it was unreliable; critics called tweets frivolous; analysts warned the micro-blogging website was not serious about making money.

In the past week, however, the San Francisco-based company has done much to answer its would-be detractors. It unveiled its revenue-making model, released impressive statistics about its size, and introduced a bevy of new products.

At Chirp, Twitter's first ever conference for software developers, which began in San Francisco on Tuesday, users and analysts said Twitter was growing up before their eyes, transforming from a 'start-up' to a 'big company'.

But at the same time, Twitter, which allows users to post short messages known as 'tweets', has provoked serious new questions about its direction, and raised tensions with both users and third-party developers who have been so crucial to its success.

Most in the Twitter community believe the service, which now boasts 106m registered users, is still in the early days of its growth. 'I think there's going to be more opportunity now than ever,' said Bijan Sabet, a partner at Spark Capital and an early investor. 'Getting to half a billion users, that's the next step.'

Twitter's most significant move this week was the unveiling of its revenue model – an advertising system similar to Google's highly profitable AdWords. Twitter will allow businesses to bid on keywords and have their 'promoted tweets' appear at the top of search results.

This is relatively unobtrusive as online advertising goes. Yet among Twitter's notoriously fickle community, some users have been rankled by the idea of the site bearing ads at all.

The business plan will also potentially hurt at least one developer. Just a day before Twitter unveiled promoted tweets, Bill Gross, a seasoned entrepreneur credited with inventing search advertising, disclosed his TweetUp service, which was relying on a near identical model.

This highlights a line in the sand that Twitter has drawn with its developers, who have built more than 100,000 applications that operate on the site and interact with tweets.

New direction: co-founder Evan Williams outlines his vision at Twitter's first conference for software developers
Source: Getty Images: Tony Avelar/Bloomberg.

Twitter, said co-founder Evan Williams, will focus on the 'core experiences' – keeping the platform up and running and implementing an advertising system. Developers should put their efforts into building specified products for niche audiences, such as applications that serve business customers, or harness the film and music communities.

But even this line between the host and the apps is blurring. One of the most fruitful areas of third-party development has been in apps that allow users to manage their tweets on a desktop or mobile phone. Indeed, 75 per cent of Twitter's traffic happens not on Twitter.com, but through the likes of the Tweetdeck, Seesmic and Echofon apps.

Last week, however, Twitter shocked the developer community, saying it had purchased the maker of Tweetie, the most popular iPhone client, and had developed its own app for BlackBerry smartphones.

This prompted an outcry from developers, who complained Twitter had pivoted from benevolent platform to aggressive competitor.

'The strength of the reaction is a testament to the naiveté of the community,' said Mike Hirschland, a partner at Polaris Venture Partners who has invested in Twitter developers. 'At some point the platform is going to get deadly serious about making money, and you better get out of the way.'

That time seems to have arrived. Mr Williams said Twitter was now focused on making money from its 55m daily tweets. 'It's a high priority for us.'

To developers nervous that the platform for which they are building software might compete with them, Mr Williams would give no reassurances. 'That's part of the game,' he said.

Source: from 'Twitter builds on its character', *Financial Times,* 15/04/10 (Gelles, D.).

Discussion questions

1 Why are developers reacting so negatively to Twitter's purchase of the maker of Tweety? What changes does this vignette illustrate?

2 Why is Twitter changing its business model?

3 What fundamentals of strategy can Twitter adopt to become more sustainable?

REFERENCES

Aaker, D.A. (1991), *Managing Brand Equity,* New York: The Free Press.

Aaker, D.A. (1995), *Strategic Market Management,* 4th edn, New York: Wiley.

Abell, D.F. (1978), 'Strategic windows', *Journal of Marketing,* 42(3), 21–6.

Aberdeen Group (2013), Sales and marketing alignment: The new power couple, aberdeen.com/Aberdeen-Library/7002/RA-sales-marketing-alignment.aspx, accessed 2013, March 3.

Achrol, R. (1991), 'Evolution of the marketing organisation: New forms for turbulent environments', *Journal of Marketing,* 55(October), 77–93.

Achrol, R. (1997), 'Changes in the theory of interorganisational relations in marketing: Toward a network paradigm', *Journal of the Academy of Marketing Science,* 25(1), 56–71.

Ackerman, R.W. (1975), *The Social Challenge in Business,* Cambridge, MA: Harvard University Press.

Act-On Software, Sales and Marketing Alignment (2015), www.act-on.com/whitepaper/introduction-to-sales-and-marketing-alignment/, accessed 2015, June 15.

Adam Smith Institute (2008), *Unfair Trade,* London: Adam Smith Institute.

Adamson, B., Dixon, M. and Toman, N. (2013), 'Dismantling the sales machine', *Harvard Business Review,* November, 102–9.

Agrawal, M., Kumaresh, T.V. and Mercer, G.A. (2001), 'The false promise of mass customisation', *McKinsey Quarterly,* 1, 31–43.

Ahuja, G. and Katila, R. (2004), 'Where do resources come from? The role of idiosyncratic situations', *Strategic Management Journal,* 25, 887–907.

Airline Industry Information (2007), 'Boeing and Lockheed Martin form strategic alliance', *Airline Industry Information,* January 23, 1.

Al Bawaba (2006), 'Dell/EMC extend multi-billion dollar strategic alliance until 2011', *Al Bawaba,* September 18, 1.

Alexander, L.D. (1991), 'Strategy implementation: Nature of the problem', in D. Hussey (ed.), *International Review of Strategic Management,* 2(1), 74.

Allen, V. (2008), '1,000-mile chicken', *Daily Mail,* 19 March, p. 35.

Allison, K. and Waters, R. (2007), 'Hewlett-Packard comes back fighting', *Financial Times,* 30 April, p. 27.

Allison, K. (2008), 'Apple unveils iPhone grand plan', *Financial Times,* 10 March, p. 23.

Almeida, P., Dokko, G. and Rosenkopf, L. (2003), 'Startup size and the mechanisms of external learning: Increasing opportunity and decreasing ability?', *Research Policy,* 32(2), 301–15.

Alsem, K.J., Leeflang, P.S.H. and Reuyl, J.C. (1989), 'The forecasting accuracy of market share models using predicted values of competitive marketing behavior', *International Journal of Research in Marketing,* 6(3), 183–98.

AMA (2008), http://www.marketingpower.com/AboutAMA/Documents/American%20Marketing%20Association%20Releases%20New%20Definition%20for%20Marketing.pdf.

Ambler, T. (2000), *Marketing and the Bottom Line: The New Metrics of Corporate Wealth,* Hemel Hempstead: Prentice Hall.

Ambler, T. (2003), *Marketing and the Bottom Line,* 2nd edn, Hemel Hempstead: Prentice Hall.

Ambrosini, V. and Bowman, C. (2009), 'What are dynamic capacities and are they a useful construct in strategic management?', *International Journal of Management Reviews,* 11(1), 29–49.

Ambrosini, V., Bowman, C. and Collier, N. (2009), 'Dynamic capabilities: An exploration of how firms renew their resource base', *British Journal of Management,* 20, S9–S24.

American Salesman (2002), 'Shift to value-added selling is biggest challenge in sales', *American Salesman,* November, 13.

Amit, R. and Shoemaker, P.J.H. (1993), 'Strategic assets and organisational rent', *Strategic Management Journal,* 14, 33–46.

Ancona, D. and Bresman, H. (2007), *X-Teams: How to Build Teams That Lead, Innovate and Succeed,* Boston, MA: Harvard Business School Press.

Anderlini, J., Jack, A. and Parker, G. (2014), 'China hits at GSK's "systemic" bribery"', *Financial Times,* 2014, May 15, p. 1.

Anderson, E.W. and Sullivan, M.W. (1993), 'The antecedents and consequences of customer satisfaction for firms', *Marketing Science,* 12(2), 125–43.

Anderson, E. and Trinkle, B. (2005), *Outsourcing the Sales Function: The Real Costs of Field Sales,* Mason, OH: Thomson.

Anderson, J.C., Narus, J.A. and van Rossum, W. (2006), 'Customer value propositions in business markets', *Harvard Business Review,* March, 91–9.

Anderson, L. (2008), 'Finding a true heart in business', *Financial Times,* April 21, p. 17.

Andrew, J. and Waldmeir, P. (2013), 'Bribery fears infect drug dealings in China', *Financial Times,* September 24, 19.

Ansoff, H.I. (1984), *Implanting Strategic Management,* London: Prentice Hall.

Anthony, S.C., Eyring, M. and Gibson, L. (2006), 'Mapping your innovation strategy', *Harvard Business Review,* 84(5), 104–13.

Armistead, C.G. and Clark, G. (1992), *Customer Service and Support,* London: Pitman Publishing.

Arndt, M. and Einhorn, B. (2010), 'The 50 most innovative companies', *Bloomberg BusinessWeek,* April 25, pp. 34–40.

Arnold, M. (2014), 'Banks failing to shed aggressive sales culture, report warns', *Financial Times,* November 26, p. 2.

Arrington, M. (2007), 'AT&T piles on Yahoo', www. TechCrunch.com, March 9.

Arruñada, B. and Vázquez, X.H. (2006), 'When your contract manufacturer becomes your competitor', *Harvard Business Review,* September, 135–44.

Arthur D. Little (2005), *The Innovation High Ground,* New York: Arthur D. Little.

Ashton, J. (2005), 'Marconi up for grabs', *Daily Mail,* May 4, p. 64.

Ashton, J. and Watts, R. (2008), 'Good payers face being axed by credit card firms', *Sunday Times,* February 3, p. S1, 7.

Aufreiter, N.A., Lawler, T.L. and Lun, C.D. (2000), 'A new way to market', *The McKinsey Quarterly,* (2), 52–61.

Authers, J. (2015), 'Vice versus nice', *Financial Times,* June 26, p. 11.

Baghai, M., Coley, S. and White, D. (2000), *The Alchemy of Growth: Practical Insights for Building the Enduring Enterprise,* New York: Perseus Books.

Baker, M.J. (1992), *Marketing Strategy and Management,* 2nd edn, London: Macmillan.

Baldauf, A., Cravens, D.W. and Piercy, N. (2001a), 'Examining business strategy, sales management, and sales-person antecedents of sales organisation effectiveness', *Journal of Personal Selling & Sales Management,* 21, 123–34.

Baldauf, A., Piercy, N. and Cravens, D.W. (2001b), 'Examining the consequences of sales management control strategies in European field sales organisations', *International Marketing Review,* 18, 474–508.

Baldauf, A., Cravens, D.W. and Piercy, N. (2005), 'Sales management control research – synthesis and an agenda for future research', *Journal of Personal Selling & Sales Management,* 25(1), 7–26.

Ball, J. (2009), 'The upside to a plastic bag', *Wall Street Journal,* June 16, p. 12.

Bamford, J., Ernst, D. and Fubini, D.G. (2004), 'Launching a world-class joint venture', *Harvard Business Review,* February, 90–100.

Barnes, S.J., Bauer, H.H., Neumann, M.M. and Huber, F. (2007), 'Segmenting cyberspace: A customer typology for the internet', *European Journal of Marketing,* 41(1/2), 71–93.

Barney, J.B. (1991), 'Firm resources and sustained competitive advantage', *Journal of Management,* 17(1), 99–120.

Barney, J.B. (1997), 'Looking inside for competitive advantage', in A. Campbell and K.S. Luchs (eds), *Core Competency-Based Strategy,* London: International Thomson Business Press.

Barone, M.J., Miyazaki, A.D. and Taylor, K.A. (2000), 'The influence of case-related marketing on consumer choice: Does one good turn deserve another?', *Journal of the Academy of Marketing Science,* 28(2), 248–62.

Barwise, P. and Meehan, S. (2004), *Simply Better: Winning and Keeping Customers by Delivering What Matters Most,* Boston MA: Harvard Business School Press.

Bass, F.M. (1969), 'A new product forecasting model for consumer durables', *Marketing Science,* 15(2), 215–27.

Batty, R. (2015), 'Taking a corporate stand against domestic violence', *Financial Times,* February 12, p. 14.

Baumwoll, J.P. (1974), 'Segmentation research: the Baker vs the Cookie Monster', in *Proceedings, American Marketing Association Conference,* 3–20.

Beattie, A. (2005), 'Unchained malady: Business is becoming ever more exposed to supplier problems', *Financial Times,* August 25, p. 13.

Beattie, A. (2008), 'Tate & Lyle sugar adopts Fairtrade label', *Financial Times,* February 23/24, p. 17.

Becker-Olsen, K.L., Cudmore, B.A. and Hill, R.P. (2006), 'The impact of perceived corporate social responsibility on consumer behavior', *Journal of Business Research,* 59, 46–53.

Bell, E. (1996), '"Bastards" are losing out to Mr Clean', *Observer,* June 30.

Bennett, J. and Ramsey, M. (2011), 'Ford, Toyota to team on hybrids', *Wall Street Journal,* August 23, p. 1.

Bensimon, S. (1999), 'Strategic alliances', *Executive Excellence,* 16(10), 9.

Berfield, S. (2013), 'Zara's fast-fashion edge', *Bloomberg Businessweek,* November 14, www.businessweek.com/articles/2013-11-14%2014-outlook-zaras-fashion-supply-chainedge; and information from the Inditex Press Dossier, www.inditex.com/en/press/information/press_kit, accessed 2014, September.

Berman, D. (2012), 'Google's challenge: a Motorola strategy'', *Wall Street Journal,* April 11, p. 21.

Berner, R. (2005), 'Can Walmart fit into a white hat?', *BusinessWeek,* October 23, pp. 73–5.

Bernhardt, D. (ed.) (1993), *Perfectly Legal Competitor Intelligence,* London: Pitman Publishing.

Bernoth, A. (1996), 'Companies show they care', *Sunday Times,* December 8.

Berry, L.L. and Parasuraman, A. (1991), *Marketing Services: Competing Through Quality,* New York: The Free Press.

Berstell, G. and Nitterhouse, D. (2005), 'Letting the customer make the case', *Strategy and Innovation,* March–April, 3–6.

Birchall, J. (2010), 'Open innovation powers growth', *Financial Times,* December 28, p. 10.

Birchall, J. (2010), 'P&G goes online to compete for sales', *Financial Times,* May 20, p. 20.

Black, H. (2015), 'Loyal customers leaving Barclays after being told they're too poor', *Daily Mail,* February 11, p. 41.

Blas, J. and Wiggins, J. (2007), 'Surge in biofuel production pushes up food prices', *Financial Times,* July 16, p. 7.

Bonoma, T.V. (1985), *The Marketing Edge: Making Strategies Work,* New York: Free Press.

Bonoma, T.V. (1990), 'Employees can free the hostages', *Marketing News,* March 19.

Booz, Allen and Hamilton (1982), *New Products Management for the 1980s,* New York: Booz, Allen and Hamilton Inc.

Borden, N. (1964), 'The concept of the marketing mix', *Journal of Advertising Research,* 4, 2–7.

Boston Consulting Group (1979), *Specialisation,* Boston, MA: BCG.

Bowen, D.E. and Lawler, E.E. (1992), 'The empowerment of service workers: What, why, how and when', *Sloan Management Review,* Spring, 31–9.

Bowman, C. and Ambrosini, V. (2003), 'How the resource-based and dynamic capabilities views of the firm inform corporate-level strategy', *British Journal of Management,* 14, 289–303.

Boyle, C. (2009), 'Fairtrade chocolate sales set to treble as Cadbury's Dairy Milk carries ethical logo', *Times,* July 22, p. 39.

Boyle, M. (2011), 'Who's really stocking your grocer's shelf', *Bloomberg BusinessWeek,* March 20–April 3, pp. 34–5.

Bradley, U. (1987), *Applied Marketing and Social Research,* 2nd edn, Chichester: John Wiley.

Brady, J. and Davis, I. (1993), 'Marketing's mid-life crisis', *The McKinsey Quarterly,* 2(2), 17–28.

Bradshaw, T. (2014), 'Apple in supply-chain purge at Africa mines', *Financial Times,* February 14, p. 20.

Branco, M.C. and Rodrigues, L.L. (2006), 'Corporate social responsibility and resource-based perspectives', *Journal of Business Ethics,* 69, 111–32.

Brewster, D. (2008), 'Smart solution for corporate philanthropists', *Financial Times,* October 1, p. 14.

Brittan, Sir L. (1990), 'A compelling reality', *Speaking of Japan,* February, 10(110), 18–24.

Broadbent, S. (ed.) (1983), *Advertising Works 2,* London: Holt, Reinhart and Winston.

Brown, A. (1995), 'The fall and rise of marketing', *Marketing Business,* February, 25–8.

Brown, S. (1995), *Postmodern Marketing,* London: Routledge.

Brown, T. (2104), 'Connecting brand promise and people', *The Marketer,* December, p. 15.

Brummer, A. (2005), 'Marconi crisis is a disaster for UK PLC', *Daily Mail,* May 11, p. 67.

Bruni, D.S. and Verona, G. (2009), 'Dynamic marketing capabilities in science-based firms: An exploratory investigation in the pharmaceutical industry', *British Journal of Management,* special issue, 20, S101–S17.

Bucklin, L.P. and Sengupta, S. (1993), 'Organising successful co-marketing alliances', *Journal of Marketing,* April, 32–46.

Buffington, B.I. and Frabelli, K.F. (1991), 'Acquisitions and alliances in the communications industry', in H.E. Glass (ed.), *Handbook of Business Strategy,* 3rd edn, New York: Warren Gorman and Lamont.

BusinessWeek (2009), 'The joys and perils of "reverse innovation"', *BusinessWeek,* October 5, p. 12.

Buzzell, R.D. and Gale, B.T. (1987), *The PIMS Principles,* New York: The Free Press.

Byron, E. (2008), 'A new odd couple: Google and P&G swap workers to spur innovation', *Wall Street Journal,* September 20, pp. 16–17.

Cable, D.M. (2007), *Change to Strange: Create A Great Organisation by Building A Strange Workforce,* Philadelphia, PA: Wharton School Publishing.

Calder, B.J. (1994), 'Qualitative marketing research', in Richard P. Bagozzi (ed.), *Principles of Marketing Research,* Boston, MA: Blackwell.

Campbell, A. (2006), 'Why in-house collaboration is so difficult', *Financial Times,* February 13, p. 14.

Cano, C.R., Rodriguez, Francois, A.C. and Jamarillio, F. (2004), 'A meta-analysis of the relationship between market orientation and business performance: evidence from five continents', *International Journal of Research in Marketing,* 21(2), 179–200.

Capell, K. (2008), 'The wool industry gets bloodied', *BusinessWeek,* July 14 and 21, p. 31.

Capizzi, M.T. and Ferguson, R. (2005), 'Loyalty trends for the twenty-first century', *Journal of Consumer Marketing,* 22(2), 72–80.

Capon, N. (2001), *Key Account Management and Planning,* New York: The Free Press, 2001.

Cardozo, R.N. (1979), *Product Policy,* Reading, MA: Addison-Wesley.

Carey, T. (1989), 'Strategy formulation in banks', *International Journal of Bank Marketing,* 7(3), 4–44.

Carroll, A. and Shabana, K.M. (2010), 'The business case for corporate social responsibility: A review of concepts, research and practice', *International Journal of Management Reviews,* 12(1), 85–105.

Carroll, A.B. (1979), 'A three-dimensional conceptual model of corporate performance', *Academy of Management Review,* October, 497–505.

Carroll, D.J., Green, P.E. and Schaffer, C.M. (1986), 'Inter-point distance comparisons in correspondence analysis', *Journal of Marketing Research,* 23, 271–80.

Carroll, D.J., Green, P.E. and Schaffer, C.M. (1987), 'Comparing interpoint distances in correspondence analysis: A clarification', *Journal of Marketing Research,* 24, 445–50.

Caruana, A., Ewing, M. and Ramaseshan, B. (2000), 'Assessment of the three-column format SERVQUAL', *Journal of Business Research,* 49, 57–65.

Cave, F. (2005), 'Surging costs put more pressure on manufacturers', *Financial Times,* July 12, p. 4.

Central Statistical Office (1995), *Annual Abstract of Statistics,* London: HMSO.

Cespedes, F.V. (1993), 'Coordinating sales and marketing in consumer goods firms', *Journal of Consumer Marketing,* 10(2), 37–55.

Cespedes, F.V. (1994), 'Industrial marketing: Managing new requirements', *Sloan Management Review,* Spring, 45–60.

Cespedes, F.V. (1995), *Concurrent Marketing: Integrating Product, Sales and Service,* Cambridge, MA: Harvard Business School Press.

Cespedes, F.V. (1996), 'Beyond teamwork: How the wise can synchronise', *Marketing Management,* 5(1), 25–37.

Cespedes, F.V. (2014), 'Putting sales at the centre of strategy', *Harvard Business Review,* October, 23–5.

Cespedes, F.V. and Piercy, N.F. (1996), 'Implementing marketing strategy', *Journal of Marketing Management,* 12, 135–60.

Chally Group, H.R. (1996), *The Customer Selected World Class Sales Excellence Report,* Dayton, OH: H.R. Chally Group.

Chally, H.R. (2006), *The Chally World Class Sales Excellence Research Report,* Dayton, OH: H.R. Chally Group.

Chandy, R.K. and Tellis, G.J. (1998a), *Organising for Radical Product Innovation,* Boston, MA: Marketing Science Institute, Report, 98–102.

Chandy, R.K. and Tellis, G.J. (1998b), 'Organising for radical product innovation: The overlooked role of willingness to cannibalise', *Journal of Marketing Research,* November, 474–87.

Chang, J.J. and Carroll, J.D. (1969), 'How to use MDPREF: A computer program for multidimensional analysis of preference data', unpublished paper, Murray Hill, NJ: Bell Laboratories.

Chang, J.J. and Carroll, J.D. (1972), 'How to use PREFMAP and PREFMAP 2 – programs which relate preference data to multidimensional scaling solutions', unpublished paper, Murray Hill, NJ: Bell Laboratories.

Chang, J. (2005), 'From the inside out', *Sales & Marketing Management,* August, 8.

Chao, L. (2012), 'Lenovo keeps production in-house as foes outsource', *Wall Street Journal,* July 10, pp. 14–15.

Chartered Institute of Marketing (2011), Marketing and Sales Fusion, CIMcomms/co.uk/AEM/Clients/CAM001/heather/MASF.pdf, accessed 2011, December.

Chattopadhyay, A., Nedungadi, P. and Chakravarti, D. (1985), 'Marketing strategy and differential advantage – a comment', *Journal of Marketing,* 49(2), 129–36.

Chesbrough, H.W. (2006), *Open Business Models: How to Thrive in the New Innovation Landscape,* Boston, MA: Harvard Business School Press.

Chimhanzi, J. (2004), 'The impact of marketing/HR interactions on marketing strategy implementation', *European Journal of Marketing,* 38(1/2), 73–98.

Christensen, C. and Bower, J. (1996), 'Customer power, strategic investment and the failure of leading firms', *Strategic Management Journal,* 17(3), 197–218.

Christensen, C.M. (1997), *The Innovator's Dilemma: When New Technologies Cause Great Firms to Fail,* Boston, MA: Harvard Business School Press.

Christensen, C.M., Anthony, S.D., Berstell, G. and Nitterhouse, D. (2007), 'Finding the right job for your product', *MIT Sloan Management Review,* 6(38), 2–11.

Christensen, C., Anthony, S.D. and Roth, E.A. (2004), *Seeing What's Next: Using the Theories of Innovation to Predict Industry Change,* Boston, MA: Harvard Business School Press.

Christensen, C.M., Kaufman, S.P. and Shih, W.C. (2008), 'Innovation killers', *Harvard Business Review,* January, 98–105.

Christensen, C.M. and Raynor, M.E. (2003), *The Innovator's Solution: Creating and Sustaining Successful Growth,* Boston, MA: Harvard Business School Press.

Chu, J. (2002), 'What top-performing retailers know about satisfying customers: Experience is key', IBM Institute for Business Value.

Chun, R. (2005), 'Corporate reputation: meaning and measurement', *International Journal of Management Reviews,* 7(2), 91–109.

Clark, P. (1986), 'The marketing of margarine', *European Journal of Marketing,* 20(5), 52–65.

Clarkson, M.B.E. (1995), 'A stakeholder framework for analyzing and evaluating corporate social performance', *Academy of Management Review*, 20(1), 92–117.

Clausewitz, C. von (1908), *On War,* London: Routledge & Kegan Paul.

Clavell, J. (ed.) (1981), *The Art of War by Sun Tzu,* London: Hodder and Stoughton.

Clegg, A. (2014), 'Maverick developers on the edge', *Financial Times,* January 7, p. 10.

Coad, T. (1989), 'Lifestyle analysis – opportunities for early entry into Europe with effective customer targeting', Institute of International Research Conference on Customer Segmentation and Lifestyle Marketing, London, December 11–12.

Collack, L. and Armstrong, R. (2014), 'Alibaba', *Financial Times,* September 10, p. 11.

Colletti, J.A. and Chonko, L.B. (1997), 'Change management initiatives: Moving sales organisations from obsolescence to high performance', *Journal of Personal Selling & Sales Management,* 17(Spring), 1–30.

Collier, J. and Esteban, R. (2007), 'Corporate social responsibility and employee commitment', *Business Ethics,* 16(1), 19–29.

Collis, D.J. and Montgomery, C.A. (1995), 'Competing on resources: strategy for the 1990s', *Harvard Business Review,* 73(4), 118–28.

Collis, D.J. and Montgomery, C.A. (1997), *Corporate Strategy: Resources and the Scope of the Firm,* Chicago, IL: McGraw-Hill.

Colvin, G. (2007), 'Power: A cooling trend', *Fortune,* December 10, pp. 37–51.

Colvin, G. (2006), 'The imagination economy', *Fortune,* July 10, p. 29.

Commission of the European Communities (2001), Green Paper: Promoting a European Framework for Corporate Social Responsibility, Strasbourg: COM, July.

Conlin, M. and Greene, J. (2007), 'How to make a micro-serf smile', *BusinessWeek,* September 10, pp. 57–9.

Cook, V.J. (1983), 'Marketing strategy and differential advantage', *Journal of Marketing,* 47(2), 68–75.

Cook, V.J. and Mindak, W.A. (1984), 'A search for constants: The heavy user revisited', *Journal of Consumer Research,* 1(4), 80.

Cookson, C. (2006), 'How Big Pharma is made to pay', *Financial Times,* November 8, p. 29.

Coy, P. (2015), 'What's in the innovation sandwich?', *BusinessWeek,* January 19–25, pp. 49–51.

Coye, R.W. (2004), 'Managing customer expectations in the service encounter', *International Journal of Service Industry Management,* 15(4), 54–71.

Coyles, S. and Gokey, T.C. (2005), 'Customer retention is not enough', *Journal of Consumer Marketing,* 22 (2), 101–5.

Cravens, D.W. (1995), 'The changing role of the sales force', *Marketing Management,* Fall, 17–32.

Cravens, D.W., Greenley, G., Piercy, N.F. and Slater, S. (1997), 'Integrating contemporary strategic management philosophy', *Long Range Planning,* 30(4), 493–506.

Cravens, D.W., Greenley, G., Piercy, N.F. and Slater, S. (1998), 'Mapping the path to market leadership', *Marketing Management,* Fall, 29–39.

Cravens, D.W. and Piercy, N.F. (2013), *Strategic Marketing,* 10th edn, New York: McGraw-Hill/Irwin.

Cravens, K., Piercy, N. and Cravens, D.W. (2000), 'Assessing the performance of strategic alliances: Matching metrics to strategies', *European Management Journal,* 18(5), 529–41.

Cravens, D.W., Piercy, N.F. and Low, G.S. (2002), 'The innovation challenges of proactive cannibalisation and discontinuous technology', *European Business Review,* 14(4), 257–67.

Cravens, D.W., Piercy, N.F. and Shipp, S.H. (1996), 'New organisational forms for competing in highly dynamic environments: The network paradigm', *British Journal of Management,* 7, 203–18.

Cravens, D.W., Shipp, S.H. and Cravens, K.S. (1993), 'Analysis of co-operative interorganisational relationships, strategic alliance formation, and strategic alliance effectiveness', *Journal of Strategic Marketing,* March, 55–70.

Crimp, M. (1990), *The Marketing Research Process,* 3rd edn, Hemel Hempstead: Prentice Hall.

Crimp, M. and Wright, L.T. (1995), *The Marketing Research Process,* 4th edn, Hemel Hempstead: Prentice Hall.

Cripe, E.J. (1994), 'Upgrading the service level of HR', *Human Resources Professional,* 7(3), 7–11.

Croft, M. (2007), 'Training and development: Brand ambassadors', *Marketing Week,* March 8, p. 39.

Crooks, E. (2009), 'B&Q halts sales of rooftop turbines', *Financial Times,* February 7–8, p. 2.

Crooks, E. (2015), 'Off the grid', *Financial Times,* January 14, p. 9.

Cross, J., Hartley, S.W., Rudelius, W. and Vassey, M.J. (2001), 'Sales force activities and marketing strategies in industrial firms: Relationships and implications', *Journal of Personal Selling & Sales Management,* 21(3), 199–206.

Crouch, S. and Housden, M. (1996), *Marketing Research for Managers,* 2nd edn, Oxford: Butterworth-Heinemann.

Crouch, S. and Housden, M. (2003), *Marketing Research for Managers,* 3rd edn, London: Butterworth-Heinemann.

Culliton, J. (1948), *The Management of Marketing Costs,* Boston, MA: Harvard University Graduate School of Business Administration, Research Division.

Cumbo, J. (2012), 'Private banks give marching orders to clients who are not rich enough', *Financial Times,* August 11–12, p. 1.

Czaplewski, A.J., Ferguson, J.M. and Milliman, J.F. (2001), 'Southwest Airlines: How internal marketing pilots success', *Marketing Management,* Sept/Oct, 14–17.

d'Astous, A. and Boujbel, L. (2007), 'Positioning countries on personality dimensions: Scale development and implications for country marketing', *Journal of Business Research,* 60, 231–9.

Dabholkar, P.A., Thorpe, D. and Rentz, J. (1996), 'A measure of service quality for retail stores: Scale development and validation', *Journal of the Academy of Marketing Science,* 24(1), 3–16.

Daily Telegraph (1997), 'Laura Ashley may defeat superman', 27 August.

Daneshkhu, S. (2014), 'Organic farming in decline despite rising sales', *Financial Times,* March 13, p. 2.

Daneshkhu, S. (2015), 'Unilever investors call for sale of Flora', *Financial Times,* March 2, p. 21.

Danneels, E. (1996), 'Market segmentation: Normative model versus business reality', *European Journal of Marketing,* 30(6), 36–51.

Dartnell Corporation (1999), *Dartnell's 30th Sales Force Compensation Survey: 1998–1999,* Chicago, IL: Dartnell Corporation.

Darwin, C. (1859), *On the Origin of Species,* London: John Murray.

Davidson, A. (2010), 'Guru who puts workers first, customers second', *Sunday Times,* May 9, pp. 3–6.

Davidson, H. (1983), 'Putting assets first', *Marketing,* November 17.

Davies, E., Eccles, L. and Groves, J. (2015), '6m cold calls from just one firm', *Daily Mail,* March 13, p. 8.

Day, G. (2000), 'Tying in an asset', in *Understanding CRM,* London: Financial Times.

Day, G.S. (1992), 'Marketing's contribution to the strategy dialogue', *Journal of the Academy of Marketing Science,* 20(4), 37–52.

Day, G.S. (1994), 'The capabilities of market-driven organisations', *Journal of Marketing,* 58(3), 37–52.

Day, G.S. (1997), 'Aligning the organisation to the market', in D.R. Lehmann and K.E. Jocz (eds), *Reflections on the Futures of Marketing,* Cambridge, MA: Marketing Science Institute.

Day, G.S. (1999), 'Misconceptions about market orientation', *Journal of Market Focused Management,* 4(1), 5–16.

Day, G.S. (2003), 'Feeding the growth strategy', *Marketing Management*, November–December, 15–21.

Day, G.S. (2007), 'Is it real? Can we win? Is it worth doing?', *Harvard Business Review,* December, 110–20.

Day, G.S., Shocker, A.D. and Srivastava, R.K. (1979), 'Customer-oriented approach to identifying product markets', *Journal of Marketing,* 43(4), 8–19.

De Boer, L., Labro, E. and Morlacci, O. (2001), 'A review of methods supporting supplier selection', *European Journal of Purchasing and Supply Management,* 7(2), 75–89.

de Chernatony, L. and MacDonald, M.H.B. (1992), *Creating Brands,* Oxford: Butterworth-Heinemann.

Deise, M.V., Nowokow, C., King, P. and Wright, A. (2000), *Executive's Guide to e-Business,* New York: John Wiley and Sons.

Delios, A., Inkpen, A.C. and Ross, J. (2004), 'Escalation in international strategic alliances', *Management International Review,* 44(4), 457–79.

Dell, M. (2007), 'Everyone has a choice', *Financial Times Digital Business – Special Report,* April 18, p. 1.

Deloitte Touche (2005), *Strategic Sales Compensation Survey,* New York: Deloitte Touche Development LLC.

Delves Broughton, P. (2012), 'Selling deserves a corner office', *Financial Times,* May 1, p. 14.

Deshpandé, R., Farley, J.U. and Webster, F.E. (1993), 'Corporate culture, customer orientation and innovativeness in Japanese firms: A quadrad analysis', *Journal of Marketing,* 57, 23–7.

Deshpandé, R. and Webster, F.E. (1989), 'Organisational culture and marketing: Defining the research agenda', *Journal of Marketing,* 53(January), 3–15.

Dewar, R. and Schultz, D. (1989), 'The product manager: An idea whose time has gone', *Marketing Communications,* May, 28–35.

Dewsnap, B. and Jobber, D. (2000), 'The sales–marketing interface in consumer packaged goods companies: A conceptual framework', *Journal of Personal Selling & Sales Management,* 2, 109–19.

Diamantopoulos, A. and Schlegelmilch, B.B. (1997), *Taking the Fear out of Data Analysis,* London: The Dryden Press.

Dibb, S. and Simkin, L. (1994), 'Implementation problems in industrial market segmentation', *Industrial Marketing Management,* 23, February, 55–63.

Dickson, P.R. (1992), 'Towards a general theory of competitive rationality', *Journal of Marketing,* 56, January, 69–83.

Dierickx, I. and Cool, K. (1989), 'Asset stock accumulation and sustainability of competitive advantage', *Management Science,* 35, 1504–51.

Divita, S. (1996), 'Colleagues are customers, market to them', *Marketing News,* October 21.

Dixon, M., Freeman, K. and Toman, N. (2010), 'STOP trying to delight your customers', *Harvard Business Review,* July–August, 116–22.

Dixon, N.F. (1976), *On the Psychology of Military Incompetence,* London: Futura.

Donaldson, T. and Preston, L.E. (1995), 'The stakeholder theory of the corporation: Concepts, evidence and implications', *Academy of Management Review,* 29(January), 65–91.

Donath, B. (1997), 'Marketers of technology make promises they can't keep', *Marketing News,* October 13, p. 5.

Donath, B. (2000), 'Big customers may cause bigger dilemmas', *Marketing News,* September 11, p. 16.

Done, K. (2003), 'Ryanair swoops to land buzz in £15 million deal', *Financial Times,* February 1/2, p. 1.

Donnan, S. (2014), 'Levi Strauss adds ethical cred to street cred by rewarding responsible suppliers', *Financial Times,* November 5, p. 17.

Dorsch, M.J., Swanson, S.R. and Kelley, S.W. (1998), 'The role of relationship quality in the stratification of vendors as perceived by customers', *Journal of the Academy of Marketing Science,* 26(2), 128–42.

Dowdy, C. (2001), 'Internal branding', *Financial Times,* November 6, p. 4.

Doyle, P. (1995), 'Marketing in the new millennium', *European Journal of Marketing,* 29(13), 23–41.

Doyle, P. (1997), 'Go for robust growth', *Marketing Business,* April, 53.

Doyle, P. (2000), *Value Based Marketing,* Chichester: John Wiley & Sons.

Doyle, P. (2008), *Value Based Marketing,* 2nd edn, London: John Wiley and Sons.

Doyle, P., Saunders, J.A. and Wong, V. (1986), 'A comparative study of Japanese and British marketing strategies in the UK market', *Journal of International Business Studies,* 17(1), 27–46.

Doyle, P. and Stern, P. (2006), *Marketing Management and Strategy,* 4th edn, Harlow: Pearson Education.

Drake, S.M., Galman, M.J. and Roberts, S.M. (2005), *Light Their Fire: Using Internal Marketing to Ignite Employee Performance and Wow Your Customers,* Wokingham: Kaplan Business.

Drucker, P. (1954), *The Practice of Management,* New York: Harper & Row.

Drucker, P. (1973), *Management: Tasks, Responsibilities and Practices,* New York: Harper & Row.

Drucker, P. (1997), 'The future that has already happened', *Harvard Business Review,* 75(5), 20–4.

Dumaine, B. (2014), 'The world's top 25 eco-innovators', *Fortune,* May 19, pp. 46–51.

Durman, P. and Box, D. (2005), 'Cut off', *Sunday Times,* 1 May, 3:5.

Dwek, R. (1997), 'Losing the race', *Marketing Business,* March.

Easterby-Smith, M., Lyles, M.A. and Peteraf, M.A. (2009), 'Dynamic capabilities: Current debates and future directions', *British Journal of Management,* special issue, 20, S1–S8.

Ebrahami, H. (2006), 'How supermarkets are squeezing fat profits from Fairtrade brands', *Financial Mail,* September 24, p. 3.

Eccles, R.G., Newquist, S.C. and Schatz, R. (2007), 'Reputation and its risks', *Harvard Business Review,* February, pp. 104–14.

Economist (1994), 'Death of the brand manager', April 9, 79–80.

Economist (2007), 'Globalisation's offspring', Economist. com, April 4.

Economist (2012), '*Economist* Fashion Forward; Inditex', March 24, pp. 63–4.

Edmunds, M. (2000), 'Your wish is on my database,' *Financial Times,* February 28, p. 16.

Eisenhardt, K.M. and Martin, J.A. (2000), 'Dynamic capabilities: What are they?', *Strategic Management Journal,* 21, 1105–21.

Eisenstat, R., Foote, N., Galbraith, J. and Miller, D. (2001), Beyond the business unit, *McKinsey Quarterly,* (1), 54–63.

Elgin, B. (2007), 'Little green lies', *BusinessWeek,* October 29, pp. 45–52.

Elkington, J. (1994), 'Towards the sustainable corporation: Win–win–win business strategies for sustainable development', *California Management Review,* 36(2), 90–100.

Engardio, P. (2004), 'Scouring the world for brainiacs', *BusinessWeek,* October 11, pp. 62–6.

Engardio, P. (2007), 'Beyond the green corporation', *BusinessWeek,* January 29, pp. 50–64.

Engardio, P. (2009), 'Why NCR said, "let's go back home"', *BusinessWeek,* August 24 and 31, p. 19.

Engardio, P. and Arndt, M. (2007), 'What price reputation?', *BusinessWeek,* July 9 and 16, 70–79.

English, J. (1989), 'Selecting and analyzing your customer/ market through efficient profile modeling and prospecting', Institute of International Research Conference on Customer Segmentation and Lifestyle Marketing, London, 11–12 December.

Ernst, D. and Bamford, J. (2005), 'Your alliances are too stable', *Harvard Business Review,* June, 133–41.

Evans, F.B. (1959), 'Psychological and objective factors in the prediction of brand choice', *Journal of Business,* 32, October, 340–69.

Evans, P.B. and Wurster, T.S. (1997), 'Strategy and the new economics of information', *Harvard Business Review,* 75 (5), 71–82.

Fahy, J. and Hooley, G.J. (2002), 'Sustainable competitive advantage in e-business: Towards a contingency perspective on the resource based view', *Journal of Strategic Marketing,* 10 (4), 1–13.

Fairtrade (2010), http://www.fairtrade.org.uk/press_office/ press_releases_and_statements/february_2010/pub- lic__leads_to_double_digit_growth_as_fairtrade_sales_ reach_800m.aspx.

Farley, J.U. (1997), 'Looking ahead at the marketplace: It's global and it's changing', in D.R. Lehmann and K.R. Jocz (eds), *Reflections on the Futures of Marketing,* Cambridge, MA: Marketing Science Institute.

Farris, P.W., Bendle, N.T. Pfeifer, P.E. and Reibstein, D.J. (2006), *Marketing Metrics: 50 Metrics Every Executive Should Master,* Upper Saddle River, NJ: Wharton School Publishing.

Feintzeig, R. (2014), 'When the boss says "make more friends"', *Wall Street Journal,* February 14–16, p. 25.

Felsted, A. (2010), 'Amazon to muscle in on Ocado's territory', *Financial Times,* July 8, p. 18.

Felsted, A. (2011), 'Alliance Boots extends Procter & Gamble tie-up', *Financial Times,* October 31, p. 20.

Felton, A.P. (1959), 'Making the marketing concept work', *Harvard Business Review,* 37(4), 55–65.

Ferrell, O.C. and Lucas, G.H. (1987), 'An evaluation of progress in the development of a definition of marketing', *Journal of the Academy of Marketing Science,* 15(3), 12–23.

Financial Times (2007), 'Footing the bill: Gates offers $3 software to poor', *Financial Times,* April 20, p. 1.

Financial Wire (2006), 'AT&T, Yahoo hit 5-year mark with broadband partnership', *Financial Wire,* November 22, p. 1.

Fink, R.C., Edelman, L.F. and Hatten, K.J. (2007), 'Supplier performance improvements in relational exchanges', *Journal of Business and Industrial Marketing,* 22(1), 29–40.

Fiol, C.M. and Lyles, M.A. (1985), 'Organisational learning', *Academy of Management Review,* 10, 803–13.

Fishburn, D. and Green, S. (eds) (2002), *The World in 2003,* London: Economist Newspapers Ltd.

Fitzgerald, D. (2012), 'Google to cut 20% of Motorola staff', *Wall Street Journal,* April 14, p. 19.

Fitzhugh, K.L.M. and Piercy, N.F. (2006), 'Integrating marketing intelligence sources: Reconsidering the role of the salesforce', *International Journal of Market Research,* 48, 699–716.

Fletcher, K. (1996), *Marketing Management and Information Technology,* 2nd edn, London: Prentice-Hall International.

Fogel, S., Hoffmeister, D., Rocco, R. and Trunk, D.P. (2012), 'Teaching sales', *Harvard Business Review,* July–August, pp. 94–100.

Foley, A. and Fahy, J. (2004), 'Towards a further understanding of the development of market orientation in the firm: A conceptual framework based on market-sensing capability', *Journal of Strategic Marketing,* 12, 219–30.

Forbis, J.L. and Mehta, N.T. (1981), 'Value-based strategies for industrial products', *Business Horizons,* 24(3), 32–42.

Fortune (2015), 'Change the world list', *Fortune,* September 1.

Foster, R.N. (1986a), *Innovation: The Attacker's Advantage,* London: Macmillan.

Foster, R.N. (1986b), 'Attacking through innovation', *The McKinsey Quarterly,* Summer, 2–12.

Frank, R.E., Massey, W.F. and Wind, Y. (1972), *Market Segmentation,* Englewood Cliffs, NJ: Prentice-Hall.

Fraser, K. (2007), 'Conflicted consumers', *Harvard Business Review,* February, 35–6.

Freedman, M. (2003), 'The genius is in the implementation', *Journal of Business Strategy,* March/April, 26–31.

Friedman, L.G. (2002), *Go To Market Strategy,* Woburn, MA: Butterworth-Heinemann Business Books.

Friedman, M. (1970), 'The social responsibility of business is to increase its profits', *New York Times Magazine,* 12 September, pp. 122–6.

Frosch, R. (1996), 'The customer for R&D is always wrong!', *Research-Technology Management,* Nov–Dec, 22–7.

Fry, M.-L. and Polonsky, M.J. (2004), 'Examining the unintended consequences of marketing', *Journal of Business Research,* 57, 1303–6.

Fulmer, W.E. and Goodwin, J. (1988), 'Differentiation: Begin with the customer', *Business Horizons,* 31(5), 55–63.

Galea, C. (2006), 'What customers really want', *Sales & Marketing Management,* May, 11.

Gallagher, L. (2015), 'Why employees love Marriott', *Fortune,* March 5, pp. 39–44.

Gapper, J. (2014), 'Mergers threaten golden age of television', *Financial Times*, July 24, p. 13.

Gapper, J. (2015), 'Software is steering the car industry', *Financial Times,* February 19, p. 11.

Gardner, N. (1997), 'Defining your class is as easy as ABC', *Sunday Times,* February 9, p. 7.

Gary, R. (2013), 'What's in it for me?', *The Marketer,* July/August, 33–6.

Giamanco, B. and Gregoire, K. (2012), 'Tweet me, friend me, make me buy', *Harvard Business Review,* July–August, pp. 88–94.

Gibbs, R. and Humphries, A. (2009), *Strategic Alliances & Marketing Partnerships: Gaining Competitive Advantage Through Collaboration and Partnering,* London: Kogan Page.

Giles, C. and Tricks, H. (2005), 'Suppliers' woes could provide limitation to retailer's ambitions', *Financial Times,* June 3, p. 24.

Gilly, M.C. and Wolfinbarger, M. (1996), *Advertising's Second Audience: Employee Reactions to Organisational Communications,* Cambridge, MA: Marketing Science Institute.

Glassman, M. and McAfee, B. (1992), 'Integrating the personnel and marketing functions: The challenge of the 1990s', *Business Horizons,* 35(3), 52–9.

Glover, S. (2015), 'It's an inconvenient truth, but the global warming zealots are to blame for the deadly diesel fiasco', *Daily Mail,* September 24, p. 14.

Gluck, F. (1986), 'Strategic planning in a new key', *McKinsey Quarterly,* Winter, 173–83.

Godfrey, P.C. and Hatch, N.W. (2007), 'Researching corporate responsibility: An agenda for the 21st century', *Journal of Business Ethics,* 70, 87–8.

Goodman, M. (2006), 'The green grocers', *Sunday Times,* September 24, p. 3.5.

Goodman, M. (2010), 'Azko's fresh basis for bonus', *Sunday Times,* 27 June, 3.9.

Gounaris, S.P. (2006), 'Internal-market orientation and its measurement', *Journal of Business Research,* 59(4), 432–48.

Govindarajan, V. and Trimble, C. (2012), *Reverse Innovation: Create Far from Home and Win Everywhere,* Cambridge MA: Harvard Business Review Press.

Gowers, A., de Jonquieres, G. and Fifield, A. (2005), 'When the cutting edge frightens the customers', *Financial Times,* October 14, p. 14.

Grande, C. (2005), 'Marconi's technology fails the price test', *Financial Times,* May 4, p. 23.

Grande, C. (2007a), 'Businesses behaving badly, say consumers', *Financial Times,* February 20, p. 24.

Grande, C. (2007b), 'Ethical consumption makes mark on branding', *Financial Times,* February 20, p. 24.

Grant, A.M. (2011), 'Customers can rally your troops', *Harvard Business Review,* July, 96–103.

Grant, J. (2005), 'Mr Daley's mission: To reach 6bn shoppers and make money', *Financial Times,* July 15, p. 32.

Grant, J. and Foster, L. (2005), 'McDonald's woos its "burger flippers"', *Financial Times,* April 15, p. 29.

Grant, R. (1996), 'Message from a bottle', *Financial Mail on Sunday,* December 15, p. 12.

Grant, R.M. (1995), *Contemporary Strategy Analysis,* 2nd edn, Cambridge, MA: Basil Blackwell.

Gratton, L. (2007), *Hot Spots: Why Some Companies Buzz With Innovation – And Others Don't,* Harlow: FT/Prentice Hall.

Green, J. (2013), 'The new Willy Loman survives by staying home', *Bloomberg BusinessWeek,* January 14–20, pp. 16–18.

Green, P., Carroll, J. and Goldberg, S. (1981), 'A general approach to product design optimisation via conjoint analysis', *Journal of Marketing,* 43, 17–35.

Green, P.E. and Wind, Y. (1975), 'New way to measure consumers' judgements', *Harvard Business Review,* 53(4), 107–17.

Green, P.E., Carmone, F.J. and Smith, S.M. (1989), *Multidimensional Scaling: Concepts and Applications,* Boston, MA: Allyn and Bacon.

Green, P.E., Tull, D.S. and Albaum, G. (1993), *Research for Marketing Decisions,* 6th edn, Englewood Cliffs, NJ: Prentice Hall International.

Greene, J., Carey, J., Arndt, M. and Port, O. (2003), 'Reventing corporate R&D', *BusinessWeek,* September 22, pp. 72–3.

Greenley, G.E. and Foxall, G.R. (1996), 'Consumer and nonconsumer stakeholder orientation in UK firms', *Journal of Business Research,* 35, 105–16.

Greenley, G.E. and Foxall, G.R. (1997), 'Multiple stakeholder orientation in UK companies and the implications for company performance', *Journal of Management Studies,* 34, 259–84.

Greyser, S.A. (1997), 'Janus and marketing: The past, present and prospective future of marketing', in D.R. Lehmann and K.R. Jocz (eds), *Reflections on the Futures of Marketing,* Cambridge, MA: Marketing Science Institute.

Griffiths, B. (2014), 'Glaxo fined £297m as bribery probes go on', *Daily Mail,* September 20, p. 107.

Griffiths, B. (2014), 'GSK hurt by sales collapse in China', *Daily Mail,* October 24, p. 85.

Grönroos, C. (1994), 'From marketing mix to relationship marketing: Towards a paradigm shift in marketing', *Management Decision,* 32(2), 4–32.

Grow, B., Hamm, S. and Lee, L. (2005), 'The debate over doing good', *BusinessWeek,* September 5/12, pp. 78–80.

Gubman, E.L. (1995), 'Aligning people strategies with customer value', *Compensation and Benefits Review,* 27(1), 15–22.

Gulati, R., Sytch, M. and Mehotra, P. (2007), 'Preparing for the exit: When forming a business alliance, don't ignore one of the most crucial ingredients: How to break up', *Wall Street Journal (Special Report),* March 3, R1.

Gummesson, E. (1987), 'The new marketing – developing long-term interactive relationships', *Long Range Planning,* 20(4), 10–20.

Gummesson, E. (1990), *The Part-Time Marketer,* University of Karlstad, Research Report, 90:3.

Gummesson, E. (1994), 'Service management: An evaluation and the future', *International Journal of Service Industry Management,* 5(1), 77–96.

Gummesson, E. (1999), *Total Relationship Marketing,* Oxford: Butterworth-Heinemann.

Gupta, A.K., Raj, S.P. and Wilemon, D. (1986), 'A model for studying R&D/Marketing interface in the product innovation process', *Journal of Marketing,* 50, 7–17.

Haeckel, S. (1997), 'Preface', in D.R. Lehmann and K.R. Jocz (eds), *Reflections on the Futures of Marketing,* Cambridge, MA: Marketing Science Institute.

Hagel, J. III and Seely-Brown, J. (2005), *The Only Sustainable Edge: Why Business Strategy Depends on Productive Friction and Dynamic Specialisation,* Boston, MA: Harvard Business School Press.

Hair, J.F., Anderson, R.E., Tatham, R.L. and Black, W.C. (1998), *Multivariate Data Analysis,* 5th edn, London: Prentice Hall International.

Haley, R.I. (1968), 'Benefit segmentation: A decision-oriented tool', *Journal of Marketing,* July, 30–5.

Haley, R.I. (1984), 'Benefit segmentation – 20 years on', *Journal of Consumer Marketing,* 5–13.

Hall, R. (1992), 'The strategic analysis of intangible resources', *Strategic Management Journal,* 13, 135–44.

Hall, R. (1993), 'A framework for linking intangible resources and capabilities to sustainable competitive advantage', *Strategic Management Journal,* 14, 607–18.

Hamel, G. (1996), 'Strategy as revolution', *Harvard Business Review,* 74 (4), 9 –82.

Hamel, G. (2000), *Leading the Revolution,* Boston, MA: Harvard Business School Press.

Hamel, G. and Prahalad, C.K. (1989), 'Strategic intent', *Harvard Business Review,* 67(3), 63–76.

Hamel, G. and Prahalad, C.K. (1991), 'Corporate imagination and expeditionary marketing', *Harvard Business Review,* 69(4), 81–92.

Hamel, G. and Prahalad, C.K. (1994), *Competing for the Future,* Boston, MA: Harvard Business School Press.

Hamel, G. and Välikangas, L. (2003), 'The quest for resilience', *Harvard Business Review,* September, 52–63.

Hamm, S. (2005), 'Beyond blue', *BusinessWeek,* April 18, pp. 36–42.

Hamm, S. (2006), 'Speed demons', *BusinessWeek,* March 27, pp. 67–76.

Hamm, S. (2008), 'Big blue goes for the big win', *BusinessWeek,* March 10, pp. 63–5.

Hammermesh, R.G., Anderson, M.J. and Harris, J.E. (1978), 'Strategies for low market share businesses', *Harvard Business Review,* 50(3), 95–102.

Han, J.K., Kim, N. and Srivastava, R.K. (1998), 'Market orientation and organisational performance: is innovation the missing link?', *Journal of Marketing,* 62, 30–45.

Hanlon, M. (2007), 'The great green con?', *Daily Mail,* July 23, pp. 30–31.

Hansegard, J. (2013), 'H&M suspends output of angora-wool items', *Wall Street Journal,* November 29–December 1, p. 18.

Hanssesns, D.M. and Kekimpe, M.G. (2012), in *Handbook of Marketing Strategy,* Shankar, V. and Carpenter, G.S. (eds), London: Edward Elgar Publishing Ltd, pp. 457–69.

Harris, L. and Goode, M. (2004), 'The four levels of loyalty and the pivotal role of trust', *Journal of Retailing,* 80, 139–58.

Harris, L.C. (1996), 'Cultural obstacles to market orientation', *Journal of Marketing Practice: Applied Marketing Science,* 4(2), 36–52.

Harris, L.C. (1998), 'Cultural domination: The key to a market-oriented culture', *European Journal of Marketing,* 32(3/4), 354–73.

Harrison, J.S. and St John, C.H. (1994), *Strategic Management of Organisations and Stakeholders,* St Paul, MN: West.

Harrison, M. (2007), To What Extent is the UK Market Research Industry a World Leader?, ESOMAR world research report, available at http://www.b2b international.com/library/whitepapers28php.

Hart, C.W.L., Heskett, J.L. and Sasser, W.E. (1990), 'The profitable art of service recovery', *Harvard Business Review,* 68(2), 148–56.

Hart, S. (2005), *Capitalism at the Crossroads: The Unlimited Business Opportunities in Solving the World's Most Difficult Problems,* Philadelphia, PA: Wharton School Publishing.

Harvey, F. (2007), 'Reckitt's plan to green-up its customers', *Financial Times,* November 1, p. 23.

Harvey, F. and Birchall, J. (2007), 'Walmart in greenhouse gas initiative', *Financial Times,* September 24, p. 25.

Harvey, F. and Fidler, S. (2007), 'Industry caught in "carbon credit" smokescreen', *Financial Times,* April 27, p. 1.

Harvey, F. (2005), 'GE looks out for a cleaner profit', *Financial Times,* July 1, p. 13.

Harvey, F. and Rigby, E. (2006), 'Supermarkets' green claims challenged', *Financial Times,* September 14, p. 6.

Hathi, S. (2007), 'Using blogs to involve', *Strategic Communication Management,* Feb/Mar, 8.

Hattersley, G. (2008), 'Does it really make any difference?', *Sunday Times,* April 2, p. 4.3.

He, H.W. and Balmer, J.M.T. (2006), 'Alliance brands: Building corporate brands through strategic alliances?', *Journal of Brand Management,* 13(4/5), 242–56.

Heineman Jnr, B.W. (2007), 'Avoiding integrity land mines', *Harvard Business Review,* April, 100–108.

Helfat, C.E., Finkelstein, S., Mitchell, W., Peteraf, M.A., Singh, H., Teece, D.J. and Winter, S.G. (2007), *Dynamic Capabilities: Understanding Change in Organisations,* Oxford: Blackwell Publishing.

Helm, B. (2008), 'How to sell luxury to penny-pinchers', *BusinessWeek,* November 10, p. 80.

Helm, B. and Arndt, M. (2007), 'It's not a McJob, it's a McCalling', *BusinessWeek,* June 4, p. 13.

Henriques, I. and Sadorsky, P. (1999), 'The relationship between environmental commitment and managerial perceptions of stakeholder importance', *Academy of Management Journal,* 42(1), 89–99.

Henry, D. (2006), 'Creativity pays: Here's how much', *BusinessWeek,* April 24, p. 76.

Heskett, J.L., Sasser, W.E., Jr and Schlesinger, L.A. (2003), *The Value Profit Chain: Treat Employees like Customers and Customers like Employees,* New York: The Free Press.

Hill, A. (2014), 'Corporate storytellers best left on the shelf', *Financial Times,* March 18, p. 12.

Hill, A. (2014), 'The serial adultery of the modern customer', *Financial Times,* February 4, p. 12.

Hill, R. (1979), 'Weak signals from the unknown', *International Management,* 34(10), 55–60.

Hille, K. (2007), 'The race for the $100 laptop', *Financial Times,* April 9, p. 8.

Hindle, T. and Thomas, M. (1994), *Pocket Marketing,* 2nd edn, Harmondsworth: The Economist Books.

Homburg, C. and Plesser, C. (2000), 'A multiple layer model of market-oriented organisational culture: measurement issues and performance outcomes', *Journal of Marketing Research,* 37, 449–62.

Homburg, C., Workman, J.P. and Jensen, O. (2000), 'Fundamental changes in marketing organisation: The movement toward a customer-focused organisational structure', *Journal of the Academy of Marketing Science,* 28(4), 459–78.

Homburg, C., Workman, J.P. and Jensen, O. (2002), 'A configurational perspective on key account management', *Journal of Marketing,* April, 38–60.

Hooley, G.J. (1980), 'Multidimensional scaling of consumer perceptions and preferences', *European Journal of Marketing,* 14 (7), 436–80.

Hooley, G.J. (1982), 'Directing advertising creativity through benefit segmentation', *Journal of Advertising,* 1, 375–85.

Hooley, G.J., Cox, A.J. and Adams, A. (1992), 'Our five year mission – to boldly go where no man has gone before', *Journal of Marketing Management,* 8(1), 35–48.

Hooley, G.J., Fahy, J., Cox, A.J., Beracs, J., Fonfara, K. and Snoj, B. (2000), 'Market orientation in the transition economies of central Europe', *Journal of Business Research,* 50(3), 273–85.

Hooley, G.J., Greenley, G., Cadogan, J.W. and Fahy J. (2005), 'The performance impact of marketing resources', *Journal of Business Research,* 58(1), 18–27.

Hooley, G.J. and Hussey, M.K. (eds) (1999), *Quantitative Methods in Marketing,* 2nd edn, London: Thomson Press.

Hooley, G.J., Möller, K. and Broderick, A.J. (1998), 'Competitive positioning and the resource-based view of the firm', *Journal of Strategic Marketing,* 6(2), 97–115.

Horobin, W. (2014), 'New French trains too wide for stations', *Wall Street Journal,* May 22, p. 3.

Hrebiniak, L.G. (2006), 'Obstacles to effective strategy implementation', *Organisational Dynamics,* 35(1), 12–31.

Huber, G.P. (1991), 'Organisational learning: The contributing processes and the literatures', *Organisational Science,* 2, 88–115.

Hughes, J. and Kirk, S. (2013), 'Li & Fung', *Financial Times,* January 24, p. 9.

Hughes, J. and Weiss, J. (2007), 'Simple rules for making alliances work', *Harvard Business Review,* November, pp. 122–31.

Hulbert, J.M., Capon, N. and Piercy, N.F. (2009), *Total Integrated Marketing: Breaking the Bounds of the Function,* New York: The Free Press.

Hulbert, J.M., Capon, N. and Piercy, N.F. (2002), *Total Integrated Marketing: Breaking the Bounds of the Function,* New York: The Free Press.

Hull, L. (2014), 'Recycling? 60% of Us Don't Care', *Daily Mail,* September 8, p. 27.

Hull, L. and Sorrell, L. (2010), 'Too tired to stay awake, Microsoft's Chinese workforce earning only 34p an hour', *Daily Mail,* April 17, p. 31.

Hussey, M.K. and Hooley, G.J. (1995), 'The diffusion of quantitative methods into marketing management', *Journal of Marketing Practice: Applied Marketing Science,* 1(4), 13–31.

IBM (2005), The Strategic Agenda for Customer Management in the Consumer Products Industry, New York: IBM Institute for Business Value Executive Brief.

IBM (2009), *Leading a Sustainable Enterprise,* Somers, NY: IBM Institute for Business Value.

Ihlwan, M. (2010), 'Sony and Samsung's strategic split', *BusinessWeek,* January 18, p. 52.

Imai, M. (1986), *KAIZEN: The key to Japan's competitive success,* Maidenhead: McGraw-Hill.

IMI plc (2010), *IMI plc – Key Themes,* www.imi.plc.uk/about.

Immelt, J.R., Govindarajan, V. and Trimble, C. (2009), 'How GE is disrupting itself', *Harvard Business Review,* October, 56–65.

Ingram, T.N., LaForge, R.W. and Leigh, T.W. (2002), 'Selling in the new millennium: A joint agenda', *Industrial Marketing Management,* 31, 559–67.

Jack, A. (2007), 'Beyond charity? A new generation enters the business of doing good', *Financial Times,* April 5, p. 13.

Jack, A. (2008), 'An unusual model for good causes', *Financial Times,* June 5, p. 16.

Jackson, S. (2007), 'Market share is not enough: Why strategic market positioning works', *The Journal of Business Strategy,* 28(1), 18–25.

Jackson, T. (1997), 'Dare to be different', *Financial Times,* June 19.

Jacobs, E. (2013), 'Old hands steered by the young', *Financial Times,* November 21, p. 16.

Jain, S.C. (1990), *Marketing Planning and Strategy,* 3rd edn, Cincinnati, OH: South Western.

James, B.J. (1984), *Business Wargames,* London: Abacus.

Janal, D. (2000), *Dan Janal's Guide to Marketing on the Internet,* New York: Wiley.

Janda, S. and Seshandri, S. (2001), 'The influence of purchasing strategies on performance', *Journal of Business and Industrial Marketing,* 16(4), 294–306.

Japan Corporate News Network (2006), 'Honda and Hong Kong Disneyland form strategic alliance', *Japan Corporate News Network,* July 12, 1.

Jaworski, B.J. and Kohli, A.K. (1993), 'Market orientation: Antecedents and consequences', *Journal of Marketing,* 57 (July), 53–70.

Jervell, E.E. (2014), 'In a Nordic power trip, bus drivers in Oslo mount an assault on batteries', *Wall Street Journal,* May 22, p. 31.

Jobs, S. (2008), quoted in *Fortune,* March 17.

Johnson, G. and Scholes, K. (1988), *Exploring Corporate Strategy,* 2nd edn, Hemel Hempstead: Prentice Hall International.

Johnson, G., Scholes, K. and Whittington, R. (2008), *Exploring Corporate Strategy: Text and Cases,* 8th edn, London: Financial Times/Prentice Hall.

Jones, E., Brown S.P., Zoltners, A.A. and Weitz, B.A. (2005), 'The changing environment of selling and sales management', *Journal of Personal Selling & Sales Management,* 25(2), 10–11.

Jones, R. (2000), *The Big Idea,* London: HarperCollins Business.

Jones, T.M. (1995), 'Instrumental stakeholder theory: A synthesis of ethics and economics', *Academy of Management Review,* 20(2), 404–37.

Jones, T.O. and Sasser, W.E. (1995), 'Why satisfied customers defect', *Harvard Business Review,* 73(6), 88–99.

Jopson, B. (2007), 'Unilever looks to clean up in Africa', *Financial Times,* November 15, p. 20.

Kale, P., Singh, H. and Perlmutter, H. (2000), 'Learning and protection of proprietary assets in strategic alliances: Building relational capital', *Strategic Management Journal,* 21, 217–37.

Kale, S. (2004), 'CRM failure and the seven deadly sins,' *Marketing Management,* 13(April), 42–6.

Kalligianis, K., Iatrou, K. and Mason, K. (2006), 'How do airlines perceive that strategic alliances affect their individual branding?', *Journal of Air Transportation,* 11(2), 3–21.

Kanner, B. (1996), 'In search of brand loyalty', *Sunday Business,* June 30, p. 11.

Kapelianis, D., Walker, B.A., Hutt, M.D. and Kumar, A. (2005), 'Those winning ways: The role of competitive crafting in complex sales', Working Paper, Arizona State University.

Kaplan, R.S. and Norton, D.P. (1996), *Translating Strategy into Action: The Balanced Scorecard,* Boston, MA: Harvard Business School Press.

Kavanagh, M. (2011), 'Premier Foods feels punch from retail woes', *Financial Times,* July 1, p. 18.

Kawasaki, G. (2012), *Enchantment: The Art of Changing Hearts, Minds and Actions – How to Woo, Influence and Persuade,* London: Portfolio/Penguin.

Kay, J. (1993), *Foundations of Corporate Success,* Oxford: Oxford University Press.

Kay, J. (2009), 'Innovation is not about wearing a white coat', *Financial Times,* December 16, p. 17.

Keegan, J. (1993), *A History of Warfare,* London: Hutchinson.

Keith, R.J. (1960), 'The marketing revolution', *Journal of Marketing,* 24(1), 35–8.

Kellaway, L. (2015), 'No need to "lean in" when laziness can be just as effective', *Financial Times,* February 23, p. 16.

Kellaway, L. (2015), 'Wells Fargo happy/grumpy ratio is no way to audit staff', *Financial Times,* February 9, p. 14.

Keller, S.B., Lynch, D.F., Ellinger, A.E., Ozment, J. and Calantone, R. (2006), 'The impact of internal marketing efforts in distribution service operations', *Journal of Business Logistics,* 27(1), 109–39.

Kerrigan, R., Roegner, E.V., Swinford, D.D. and Zawada, C.C. (2001), 'B2Basics', *McKinsey Quarterly,* (1), 45–53.

Khoo, P.C. (1992), *Sun Tzu and Management,* Petaling Jaya, Malaysia: Pelanduk.

Kiley, D. and Helm, B. (2009), '100 best global brands: The great trust offensive', *BusinessWeek,* September 28, pp. 38–60.

Kilmann, R.H. (1996), 'Management learning organisations: Enhancing business education for the 21st century', *Management Learning,* 27, 203–38.

Kim, W.C. and Mauborgne, R. (1997), 'Value innovation: The strategic logic of high growth', *Harvard Business Review,* January–February, 102–13.

Kim, W.C. and Mauborgne, R. (1998), 'Pioneers strike it rich', *Financial Times,* August 11, p. 11.

Kim, W.C. and Mauborgne, R. (1999), 'Creating new market space', *Harvard Business Review,* January–February, 83–93.

King, S. (1985), 'Has marketing failed or was it never really tried?', *Journal of Marketing Management,* 1(1), 1–19.

Kinnear, T.C., Taylor, J.R. and Ahmed, S.A. (1974), 'Ecologically concerned consumers: Who are they?', *Journal of Marketing,* 38(2), 20–4.

Klump, E. and Reed, S. (2010), 'How BP's spill tarred Anadarko', *BusinessWeek,* July 26–August 1, pp. 18–20.

Knight, R. (2006), 'Business students portrayed as ethically minded in study', *Financial Times,* October 25, p. 9.

Knight R. (2008), 'Green entrepreneurs with the drive to transform travel', *Financial Times,* September 26, p. 16.

Knox, S., Maklan, S., Payne, A., Peppard, J. and Ryals, L. (2003), *Customer Relationship Management: Perspectives from the Marketplace,* Oxford: Butterworth-Heinemann.

Koerner, L. (2005), 'Conducting an organisational assessment of your SAM programme', Presentation at Strategic Account Management Association Conference, Paris.

Kohli, A.K. and Jaworski, B.J. (1990), 'Market orientation: The construct, research propositions and managerial implications', *Journal of Marketing,* 54(2), 1–18.

Kotler, P. (2015), *Confronting Capitalism: Real Solutions for a Troubled Economic System,* New York: American Management Association.

Kotler, P. and Keller, K.L. (2007), *A Framework for Marketing Management,* 3rd edn, Pearson/Prentice Hall.

Kotler, P. and Keller, K. (2008), *Marketing Management,* 13th edn, Hemel Hempstead: Pearson/Prentice Hall.

Kotler, P. and Keller, K. (2012), *Marketing Management,* 14th edn, Hemel Hempstead: Pearson/Prentice Hall.

Kotler, P.C. (1997), *Marketing Management: Analysis, Planning, Implementation and Control,* 9th edn, Hemel Hempstead: Prentice Hall International.

Kotler, P.C., Armstrong, G., Saunders, J.A. and Wong, V. (1996), *Principles of Marketing: The European Edition,* Hemel Hempstead: Prentice Hall.

Kotler, P.C., Fahey, L. and Jatusritpitak, S. (1985), *The New Competition,* Hemel Hempstead: Prentice Hall.

Kotler, P.C. and Singh, R. (1981), 'Marketing warfare in the 1980s', *Journal of Business Strategy,* 1(3), 30–41.

Krohmer, H., Homburg, C. and Workman, J.P. (2002), 'Should marketing be cross-functional? Conceptual development and international empirical evidence', *Journal of Business Research,* 35, 451–65.

Kruskal, J.B., Young, F.W. and Seery, J.B. (1973), 'How to use KYST: A very flexible program to do multidimensional scaling', Multidimensional Scaling Program Package of Bell Laboratories, Murray Hill, NJ: Bell Laboratories.

Kumar, V., Jones, E., Venkatesan, R. and Leone, R.P. (2011), 'Is market orientation a source of sustainable competitive advantage or simply the cost of competing?', *Journal of Marketing,* 75(1), 16–30.

Lafferty, B.A. and Hult, G.T.M. (2001), 'A synthesis of contemporary market orientation perspectives', *European Journal of Marketing,* 35(1/2), 92–109.

Laing, H. (1991), *Brand Advertising Targeting System,* London: Laing Henry.

Lambert, D.M., Emmelhainz, M.A. and Gardner, J.T. (1996), 'So you think you want to be a partner?', *Marketing Management,* Summer, 25–41.

Lambert, D.M., Marmorstein, H. and Sharma, A. (1990), 'Industrial salespeople as a source of market information', *Industrial Marketing Management,* 17(May), 111–18.

Langerak, F. (2001), 'Effects of market orientation on the behaviours of salespersons and purchasers, channel relationships and the performance of manufacturers', *International Journal of Research in Marketing,* 18, 221–34.

Lashinsky, A. (2006), 'Chaos by design', *Fortune,* 2 October, pp. 34–42.

Lawson, D. (2009), 'Organic food is just a tax on the gullible', *Sunday Times,* August 9, p. 1.16.

Leadbeater, C. (2014), *The Frugal Innovator: Creating Change on a Shoestring Budget,* London: Palgrave Macmillan.

Leahy, J. (2007), 'Time for India's IT outsourcers to take a fresh look at the data', *Financial Times,* December 28, p. 20.

Leahy, J. (2009), 'Wipro begins to outsource its Indian workload', *Financial Times,* November 12, p. 25.

Leahy, J. (2010), 'Marriages of convenience', *Financial Times,* September 30, p. 15.

Lehmann, D.R. and Winer, R.S. (1991), *Analysis for Marketing Planning,* 2nd edn, Homewood, IL: Irwin.

Leigh, T.W., and Marshall, G.W. (2001), 'Research priorities in sales strategy and performance', *Journal of Personal Selling & Sales Management,* 21 (Spring), 83–94.

Leonard-Barton, D. (1992), 'Core capabilities and core rigidities: A paradox in managing new product development', *Strategic Management Journal,* 13(Summer Special Issue), 111–25.

Levitt, T. (1960), 'Marketing myopia', *Harvard Business Review,* 38(4), 45–56.

Levitt, T. (1986), *The Marketing Imagination,* New York: The Free Press.

Levy, R. (1999), *Give and Take,* Cambridge, MA: Harvard Business School Press.

Lilien, G.L. and Kotler, P.C. (1983), *Marketing Decision Making: A Model-building Approach,* London: Harper & Row.

Lilien, G.L., Kotler, P. and Moorthy, K.S. (1992), *Marketing Models,* Hemel Hempstead: Prentice Hall International.

Lings, I.N. and Greenley, G.E. (2005), 'Measuring internal market orientation', *Journal of Service Research,* 7(3), 290–305.

Lippman, S. and Rumelt, R.P. (1982), 'Uncertain inimitability: an analysis of inter-firm differences in efficiency under competition', *Bell Journal of Economics,* 13, 418–53.

Little, J.D.C. (1979), 'Decision support systems for marketing management', *Journal of Marketing,* 43(3), 9–26.

Lockett, A., Thompson, S. and Morgenstern, U. (2009), 'The development of the resource-based view of the firm: A critical appraisal', *International Journal of Management Reviews,* 11(1), 9–28.

Lombardi, L.J. (2005), 'Managing strategic customer relationships as assets', *LIMRA'S MarketFacts Quarterly,* 24(1), 23–5.

Loroz, P.S.and Helgeson, J.G. (2013), 'Boomers and their babies: An exploratory study comparing psychological profiles and advertising appeal effectiveness across two generations', *Journal of Marketing Theory & Practice,* Summer, 21(3), 289–306.

Lublin, J.S. (2008), 'Environmentally friendly corporate boards', *Wall Street Journal,* August 11, p. 30.

Lusch, R.F., Vargo, S.L. and Malter, A.J. (2006), 'Marketing as service exchange: Taking a leadership role in global marketing management', *Organisational Dynamics,* 35(3), 264–78.

Lynn, M. (2015), 'The dismal decline of W.H. Smith', *Management Today,* October 21, retrieved from http//www.managementtoday.co.uk.

MacArthur, K. (2005), 'McD's strategy hinges on "balance"', *Advertising Age,* 76(2), 6.

Mackintosh, J. and Simon, B. (2005), 'Ford to focus on business from "key suppliers"', *Financial Times,* September 30, p. 32.

Mackintosh, J. (2005), 'VW takes a hard line with parts suppliers', *Financial Times,* June 24, p. 30.

MacLeod, D. and Brady, C. (2007), *The Extra Mile: How to Engage Your People and Win,* Hemel Hempstead: FT Prentice Hall.

Macrae, F. (2015), 'So Mrs Slocombe was right all along', *Mail Online,* April 29, accessed 2015, October.

Mahoney, J.T. (1995), 'The management of resources and the resource of management', *Journal of Business Research,* 33(2), 91–101.

Mahoney, J.T. and Pandian, J.R. (1992), 'The resource based view of the firm within the conversation of strategic management', *Strategic Management Journal,* 13, 363–80.

Maier, J. and Saunders, J.A. (1990), 'The implementation of segmenttation in sales management', *The Journal of Personal Selling and Sales Management,* 10(1), 39–48.

Maignan, I. and Ferrell, O.C. (2004), 'Corporate social responsibility and marketing: An integrative framework', *Journal of the Academy of Marketing Science,* 32(1), 3–19.

Maignan, I., Ferrell, O.C. and Ferrell, L. (2005), 'A stakeholder model for implementing social responsibility in marketing', *European Journal of Marketing,* 39(9/10), 956–77.

Maitland, A. (2005), 'A responsible balancing act', *Financial Times,* June 1, p. 11.

Maitland, A. (2006), 'The frustrated will to act for public good', *Financial Times,* January 25, p. 15.

Mallaby, S. (2013), 'American industry is on the move', *Financial Times,* January 9, p. 13.

Mallett, V. and Crabtree, J. (2015), 'The American connection', *Financial Times,* May 25, p. 12.

Marketing Week (2003) 'Survey reveals "inadequate" state of internal marketing', *Marketing Week,* July 3, p. 8.

Marketing Week (2006), 'Marketing capability – blend for flexibility', *Brand Strategy,* July 17, p. 30.

Marsh, P. (2007), 'Back on a roll in the business of bearings', *Financial Times,* February 7, p. 10.

Marsh, P. (2009), 'Complexity is key to overcoming recession', *Financial Times,* July 28, p. 3.

Martin, R. (2011), 'The innovation catalysts', *Harvard Business Review,* June, 82–7.

Martin, R.L. (2010), 'The execution trap', *Harvard Business Review,* July–August, 64–71.

Matlack, C. (2013), 'Electrolux's holy trinity', *BusinessWeek,* November 4–10, 55–6.

Mattu, R. (2011), 'Expanded spheres of influence', *Financial Times,* November 29, p. 16.

Maunder, S., Harris, A., Bamford, J., Cook, L. and Cox, A. (2005), 'O2: It only works if it works – how troubled BT Cellnet was transformed into thriving O2', in A. Hoad (ed.), *Advertising Works 13: Proving the Effectiveness of Marketing Communications,* Henley-on-Thames, World Advertising Research Centre.

Mazur, L. (2000), 'The changing face of sales', *Marketing Business,* May, 31.

McGregor, J. (2007), 'Most innovative companies', *BusinessWeek,* 14 May, pp. 52–64. http://www.bloomberg.com/ss/08%04%0417_mostinnovative/index_01.htm, accessed 2015, June 12.

McKee, D. and Varadarajan, P.R. (1995), 'Introduction: Special issue on sustainable competitive advantage', *Journal of Business Research,* 33(2), 77–9.

McKitterick, J.B. (1957), 'What is the marketing management concept?', *Proceedings: AMA Teachers' Conference,* Philadelphia.

McWilliams, G. and Zuckerman, A. (2008), 'Walmart reached out', *Wall Street Journal,* June 9, p. 8.

Menguc, B. and Auh, S. (2006), 'Creating firm-level dynamic capability through capitalising on market orientation and innovativeness', *Journal of the Academy of Marketing Science,* 34(1), 63–73.

Menn, J. (2009), 'Schmidt's move is sign of the times', *Financial Times,* August 4, p. 17.

Miles, R.E. and Snow, C.C. (1984), 'Fit, failure, and the hall of fame', *California Management Review,* Spring, 10–28.

Miller, A.I. (1996), *Insight of Genius,* New York: Springer-Verlag.

Miller, D. (2002), 'Successful change leaders: What makes them? What do they do that is different?', *Journal of Change Management,* 2(4), 359–68.

Millman, T. and Wilson, K. (1989), 'Processual issues in key account management: Underpinning the customer- facing organisation', *Journal of Business & Industrial Marketing,* 14(4), 328–37.

Milne, R. (2008), 'Homesick producers lose taste for going overseas', *Financial Times,* June 5, p. 24.

Milne, R. (2010), 'Drive to link pay to sustainability begins', *Financial Times,* February 24, p. 22.

Mitchell, A. (1995), 'Changing channels', *Marketing Business,* February, 10–13.

Mitchell, A. (1997), 'Speeding up the process', *Marketing Business,* March.

Mitchell, A. (2008), 'If you want to be loved, just do it right', *Financial Times,* March 27, p. 16.

Mitchell, R.K., Agle, B.R. and Wood, D.J. (1997), 'Toward a theory of stakeholder identification and salience: defining the principle of who and what really counts', *Academy of Management Review,* 22, 853–86.

Mitchell, T. (2014), 'Carmakers "printing cash" in China', *Financial Times,* June 12, p. 21.

Mol, M.J. and Birkinshaw, J. (2007), *Giant Steps in Management: Innovations That Change the Way We Work,* Harlow: FT/Prentice Hall.

Montgomery, D.B. and Webster, F.E. (1997), 'Marketing's interfunctional interfaces: The MSI workshop on management of corporate fault zones', *Journal of Market-Focused Management,* 2, 7–26.

Moon, Y. (2005), 'Break free from the product life cycle', *Harvard Business Review,* May, 87–94.

Moore, E. (2014), 'Enthusiasm may wane as companies pursue growth', in *Responsible Business, Financial Times,* July 8, p. 2.

Moore, G.A. (1991), *Crossing the Chasm,* New York: HarperCollins.

Moore, G.A. (2004), 'Innovating within established enterprises', *Harvard Business Review,* July–August, 86–92.

Moore, G.A. (2006), *Dealing with Darwin: How Great Companies Innovate at Every Phase of their Evolution,* Chichester: Capstone.

Moorman, C. and Lehman, D.R. (2004), *Assessing Marketing Strategy Performance,* Boston, Cambridge, MA: Marketing Science Institute.

Morgan, R.E., Katsikeas, C.S. and Appiah-Adu, K. (1998), 'Market orientation and organisational learning', *Journal of Marketing Management,* 14, 353–81.

Morgan, R.M. and Hunt, S.D. (1994), 'The commitment–trust theory of relationship marketing', *Journal of Marketing,* 58 (3), 20–38.

Morgan, R.E. (2004), 'Business agility and internal marketing', *European Business Review,* 16(5), 464–72.

Moroko, L. and Uncles, M.D. (2009), 'Employer branding: Companies have long divided consumers into segments; They should do the same with potential – and current – workers', *Wall Street Journal,* March 23, R7.

Morrison, S. and Waters, R. (2005), 'Time comes to "think different"', *Financial Times,* June 7, p. 25.

Moss Kanter, R. (2009), *Supercorp: How Vanguard Companies Create Innovation, Profits, Growth and Social Good,* London: Profile Books.

Moss Kanter, R. (2011), 'How great companies think differently', *Harvard Business Review,* November, 66–79.

Moutinho, L. (1991), *Problems in Marketing,* London: Paul Chapman Publishing.

Murphy, J. (1991), *Brand Valuation,* 2nd edn, London: Business Books Ltd.

Murphy, P.E. and Staples, W.A. (1979), 'A modernized family life cycle', *Journal of Consumer Research,* June, 12–22.

Murphy, R.R. (2010), 'Why doing good is good for business', *Fortune,* February 8, pp. 59–62.

Murray, S. (2014), 'Search for growth hits progress on environment', *Sustainable Business, Financial Times,* May 22, p. 1.

Narayanda, D. (2005), 'Building loyalty in business markets', *Harvard Business Review,* September.

Narver, J.C. and Slater, S.F. (1990), 'The effect of a market orientation on business profitability', *Journal of Marketing,* 54(4), 20–35.

Nayar, V. (2010), *Employees First, Customers Second: Turning Conventional Management Upside Down,* Cambridge, MA: Harvard Business Press.

Nidumolu, R., Prahalad, C.K. and Rangaswami, M.R. (2009), 'Why sustainability is now the key driver of innovation', *Harvard Business Review,* September, 56–64.

Nussmaum, B. (2005), 'The evolution of the creative company', *BusinessWeek,* August 8/15, pp. 52–3.

O'Brien, N. and Ford, J. (1988), 'Can we at last say goodbye to social class?', *Journal of Market Research Society,* 16(2), 43–51.

O'Connell, D. (2003), 'Cassani throws a book at men who failed go', *Sunday Times,* October 26, pp. 3–11.

O'Connell, D. (2009), 'Rolls-Royce flies high despite airlines' nosedive', *Sunday Times,* August 2, p. 3.6.

O'Shaughnessy, J. (1995), *Competitive Marketing,* 3rd edn, London: Routledge.

Ogbuchi, A.O. and Sharma, V.M. (1999), 'Redefining industrial salesforce roles in a changing environment', *Journal of Marketing Theory and Practice,* 7(1), 64–71.

Ogden, S. and Watson, R. (1999), 'Corporate performance and stakeholder management: balancing shareholder and customer interests in the UK privatized water industry', *Academy of Management Journal,* 42, 526–38.

Ohmae, K. (1982), *The Mind of the Strategist,* Harmondsworth: Penguin Books.

Ohmae, K. (1990), *The Borderless World,* New York: Harper Business.

Olins, R. (1997a), 'Wilting', *The Sunday Times,* August 24, p. 3.

Olins, R. (1997b), 'W.H. Smith stalls on the road to nowhere', *Sunday Times,* August 31, p. 5.

Olson, E.M., Cravens, D.W. and Slater, S.F. (2001), 'Competitiveness and sales management: A marriage of strategies,' *Business Horizons,* March/April, 25–30.

Orme, B. (2005), *Getting Started with Conjoint Analysis,* Madison, WI: Research Publishers LLC.

Overell, S. (2005), 'Good ideas to generate more good ideas', *Financial Times,* June 28, p. 16.

Overman, S. (2014), *The Conscience Economy: How a Mass Movement for Good is Great,* Boston MA: Bibiomotion.

Oxx, C. (1972), 'Psychographics and life style', *Admap,* October, 303–5.

Ozretic-Dosen, D., Skare, V. and Krupka, Z. (2007), 'Assessments of country of origin and brand cues in evaluating a Croatian, western and eastern European food product', *Journal of Business Research,* 60(2), 130–6.

Palazzo, G. and Richter, U. (2005), 'CSR business as usual? The case of the tobacco industry', *Journal of Business Ethics,* 61, 387–401.

Palmer, M. (2012), 'Raspberry Pi Minicomputer sells out', *Financial Times,* March 1, p. 2.

Palmisano, S.J. (2007), 'The globally integrated enterprise', *Foreign Affairs,* 85(3), 127–38.

Pansiri, J. (2005), 'The influence of managers' characteristics and perceptions in strategic alliance practice', *Management Decision,* 43(9), 1097–13.

Parasuraman, A. and Colby, C.L. (2001), *Techno-Ready Marketing: How and Why Your Customers Adopt Technology,* New York: Free Press.

Parasuraman, A., Zeithaml, V.A. and Berry, L.L. (1985), 'A conceptual model of service quality and the implications for further research', *Journal of Marketing,* Fall, 41–50.

Parasuraman, A., Zeithaml, V.A. and Berry, L.L. (1988), 'SERVQUAL: A multiple-item scale for measuring customer perceptions of service quality', *Journal of Retailing,* 64(1), 12–40.

Parasuraman, A., Zeithaml, V.A. and Berry, L.L. (1994), 'Reassessment of expectations as a comparison standard in measuring service quality: implications for further research', *Journal of Marketing,* 58(1), 111–24.

Parasuraman, A., Zeithaml, V. and Malhotra, A. (2005), 'E-S-QUAL: A multiple item scale for assessing electronic service quality', *Journal of Service Research,* 7(3), 213–33.

Pardo, C. (1997), 'Key account management in the business to business field: The key account's point of view', *Journal of Personal Selling & Sales Management,* 17(4), 17–26.

Pascale, R., Millman, M. and Gioja, L. (1997), 'Changing the way we change', *Harvard Business Review,* November/December, 127–39.

Patrick, A.O. (2008), 'As water sales dry up, Nestlé pans soda', *Wall Street Journal,* November 13, p. 4.

Payne, A. (1993), *The Essence of Services Marketing,* London: Prentice Hall.

Payne, A. (ed.) (1995), *Advances in Relationship Marketing,* London: Kogan Page.

Payne, A. and Frow, P. (2005), 'A strategic framework for customer relationship management', *Journal of Marketing,* October, 167–76.

Payne, A., Christopher, M., Clark, M. and Peck, H. (1995), *Relationship Marketing for Competitive Advantage,* Oxford: Butterworth-Heinemann.

Penrose, E.T. (1959), *The Theory of the Growth of the Firm,* New York: Wiley.

Perrien, J., Filiatraut, P. and Line, R. (1993), 'The implementation of relationship marketing in commercial banking', *Industrial Marketing Management,* 22(2), 141–8.

Perrien, J. and Ricard, L. (1995), 'The meaning of a marketing relationship', *Industrial Marketing Management,* 24(1), 37– 43.

Peters, T. (1987), *Thriving on Chaos,* London: Macmillan.

Petre, J. and Elliott, V. (2015), 'Sainsbury's shareholders targeted by badger cull extremists', *Daily Mail,* June 7, p. 17.

Pfeifer, S. (2008), 'Rolls-Royce reaps the rewards of client care', *Financial Times,* June 2, p. 22.

Pickard, J. and Harvey, F. (2008), 'Wilting agenda', *Financial Times,* May 28, p. 12.

Piercy, N., Low, G.S. and Cravens, D.W. (2004a), 'Consequences of sales management's behavior- and compensation-based control strategies in developing countries', *Journal of International Marketing,* 12, 30–57.

Piercy, N., Low, G.S. and Cravens, D.W. (2004b), 'Examining the effectiveness of sales management control practices in developing countries', *Journal of World Business,* 39, 255–67.

Piercy, N.F. (1995), 'Customer satisfaction and the internal market: Marketing our customers to our employees', *Journal of Marketing Practice: Applied Marketing Science,* 1(1), 22–44.

Piercy, N.F. (1997), *Market-Led Strategic Change: Transforming the Process of Going to Market,* 2nd edn, Oxford: Butterworth-Heinemann.

Piercy, N.F. (1998), 'Marketing implementation: The implications of marketing paradigm weakness for the strategy execution process', *Journal of the Academy of Marketing Science,* 26(3), 222–36.

Piercy, N.F. (2002), *Market-Led Strategic Change: A Guide To Transforming the Process of Going to Market,* 3rd edn, Oxford: Butterworth-Heinemann.

Piercy, N.F. (2009a), *Market-Led Strategic Change: Transforming the Process of Going to Market,* 4th edn, Oxford: Butterworth-Heinemann.

Piercy, N.F. (2009b), 'Walmart's European adventure', in Nigel F. Piercy, *Market-Led Strategic Change: Transforming the Process of Going to Market,* 4th edn, Oxford: Butterworth-Heinemann, 2009, p. 39.

Piercy, N.F. (2009c), 'The clouds raining on the computer business', in N.F. Piercy, *Market-Led Strategic Change: Transforming the Process of Going to Market,* 4th edn, Oxford: Butterworth-Heinemann, pp. 162–7.

Piercy, N.F. (2009d), 'Ryanair: The master of non-service strategy', in N.F. Piercy, *Market-Led Strategic Change: Transforming the Process of Going to Market,* 4th edn, Oxford: Butterworth-Heinemann, pp. 46–48.

Piercy, N.F. (2016a), 'Privacy: The new product for the 21st century', in N.F. Piercy, *Market-Led Strategic Change: Transforming the Process of Going to Market,* 5th edn, London: Routledge.

Piercy, N.F. (2016b), 'Reinventing the healthcare business: An apple a day keeps the doctor away, but only if you throw it very hard indeed', in N.F. Piercy, *Market-Led Strategic Change: Transforming the Process of Going to Market,* 5th edn, London: Routledge.

Piercy, N.F. and Cravens, D.W. (1996), 'The network paradigm and the marketing organisation', *European Journal of Marketing,* 29(3), 7–34.

Piercy, N.F., Cravens, D.W. and Lane, N. (2010a), 'Marketing out of the recession: Recovery is coming, but things will never be the same again', *Marketing Review,* 10(1), 3–23.

Piercy, N.F., Cravens, D.W. and Lane, N. (2010b), 'Peek-a-boo: Finding and connecting with your customers', *Marketing Week,* Summer, pp. 18–24.

Piercy, N.F., Harris, L.C. and Lane, N. (2002), 'Market orientation and retail operatives' expectations', *Journal of Business Research,* 55(4), 261–73.

Piercy, N.F. and Lane, N. (1996), 'Marketing implementation: Building and sustaining a real market understanding', *Journal of Marketing Practice: Applied Marketing Science,* 2(3), 15–18.

Piercy, N.F. and Lane, N. (2006a), 'The underlying vulnerabilities in key account management strategies', *European Management Journal,* 24(2–3), 151–82.

Piercy, N.F. and Lane, N. (2006b), 'The hidden risks in strategic account management strategy', *Journal of Business Strategy,* 27(1), 18–26.

Piercy, N.F. and Lane, N. (2007), 'Ethical and moral dilemmas associated with strategic relationships between business-to-business buyers and sellers', *Journal of Business Ethics,* 72, 87–102.

Piercy, N.F. and Lane, N. (2009a), *Strategic Customer Management: Strategizing the Sales Organisation,* Oxford: Oxford University Press.

Piercy, N.F. and Lane, N. (2009b), 'Corporate social responsibility: Impacts on strategic marketing and customer value', *The Marketing Review,* 9(4), 335–60.

Piercy N.F. and Lane, N. (2011), 'Corporate social responsibility initiatives and strategic marketing imperatives', *Social Business,* 1(Winter), 325–345.

Piercy, N.F. and Lane, N. (2012), 'The evolution of the strategic sales organisation', in D.W. Cravens, K.L.M. Fitzhugh and N. Piercy (eds), *The Oxford Handbook of Selling and Sales Management,* Oxford: Oxford University Press, 19–50.

Piercy, N.F. and Morgan, N.A. (1993), 'Strategic and operational market segmentation: A managerial analysis', *Journal of Strategic Marketing,* 1, 123–40.

Pine, B.J. (1993), *Mass Customisation: The New Frontier in Business Competition,* Boston, MA: Harvard Business School Press.

Pink, D. (2006), *A Whole New Mind: Why Right-Brainers Will Rule in the Future,* London: Cyan Books.

Plank, R.E. (1985), 'A critical review of industrial market segmentation', *Industrial Marketing Management,* 14, 79–91.

Plimmer, G. (2015), 'Outsourcing rises sharply under the coalition', *Financial Times,* May 1, p. 4.

Pohle, G. and Hittner, J. (2008), *Attaining Sustainable Growth Through Corporate Social Responsibility,* IBM Institute for Business Value, February.

Popper, M. and Lipschitz, R. (1998), 'Organisational learning mechanisms: A structural and cultural approach to organisational learning', *Journal of Applied Behavioural Science,* 34, 161–79.

Porter, M.E. (1980), *Competitive Strategy,* New York: The Free Press.

Porter, M.E. (1985), *Competitive Advantage,* New York: The Free Press.

Porter, M.E. (1987), 'From competitive advantage to corporate strategy', *Harvard Business Review,* 65(3), 43–59.

Porter, M.E. (1996), 'What is strategy?', *Harvard Business Review,* 74(6), 61–78.

Porter, M.E. (2001), 'Strategy and the Internet', *Harvard Business Review,* 79, 63–78.

Porter, M.E. (2010), 'How big business can help itself by helping its neighbors', *BusinessWeek,* May 31–June 6, p. 56.

Porter, M.E. and Kramer, M.R. (2002), 'The competitive advantage of corporate philanthropy', *Harvard Business Review,* December, 57–68.

Porter, M.E. and Kramer, M.R. (2006), 'Strategy and society: The link between competitive advantage and corporate social responsibility', *Harvard Business Review,* December, 78–92.

Porter, M.E. and Kramer, M.R. (2011), 'Creating shared value', *Harvard Business Review,* January–February, 62–77.

Poulter, S. (2010), 'Greenwashed!', *Daily Mail,* April 29, p. 33.

Poulter, S. (2014a), 'Ghost town Britain', *Daily Mail,* October 9, p. 12.

Poulter, S. (2014b), 'Relentless march of the internet shopping army', *Daily Mail,* December 9, p. 11.

Poulter, S. (2014c), 'Shops give out 1bn more plastic bags than four years ago', *Daily Mail,* July 16, p. 29.

Pounsford, M. (1994), 'Nothing to lose: Is internal communications adding value in today's organisations?', *Internal Communication Focus,* September, 6–8.

Powell, W.W. (1990), 'Neither market nor hierarchy: Network forms of organisation', *Research in Organisational Behavior,* 12, 295–336.

Prahalad, C.K. and Hamel, G. (1990), 'The core competence of the corporation', *Harvard Business Review,* 68(3), 79–91.

Prahalad, C.K. and Krishnan, M.S. (2008), *The New Age of Innovation: Driving Co-Created Value Through Global Networks,* Maidenhead: McGraw-Hill Professional.

Price, B. and Jaffe, D. (2008), *The Best Service Is No Service: How to Liberate Your Customers From Customer Service, Keep them Happy and Control Costs,* San Francisco, CA: Jossey Bass.

Priem, R.L. and Butler, J.E. (2001), 'Is the resource-based theory a useful perspective for strategic management research?', *Academy of Management Review,* 26(1), 22–40.

Prokesch, S.E. (1997), 'Unleashing the power of learning: An interview with British Petroleum's John Browne', *Harvard Business Review,* 75(5), 146–68.

Punj, G. and Stewart, D.W. (1983), 'Cluster analysis in marketing research: Review and suggestions for applications', *Journal of Marketing Research,* 20(May), 135–48.

Quinn, J. (2005a), 'Suppliers turn the screw on Rover', *Daily Mail,* April 8, p. 89.

Quinn, J. (2005b), 'Gillette deal to put P&G ahead by a close shave', *Daily Mail,* January 29, p. 105.

Quinn, J.B. (1992), *Intelligent Enterprise,* New York: Free Press.

Radjou, N. and Prabhu, J. (2015), *Frugal Innovation: How to do More with Less,* London: Profile Books/The Economist.

Radjou, N., Prabhu, J. and Ahuja, S. (2012), *Jugaad Innovation: Think Frugal, Be Flexible, Generate Breakthrough Growth,* Chichester: Wiley.

Ramaswami, S., Bharghava, M. and Srivasta, R. (2004), *Market-based Assets and Capabilities, Business Processes, and Financial Performance,* Cambridge, MA: Report No. 04-102, Marketing Science Institute.

Rangan, V., Kasturi, L.C. and Karim, S. (2015), 'The truth about CSR', *Harvard Business Review,* January–February, pp. 40–49.

Rankine, K. (1996), 'Not a happy house', *The Daily Telegraph,* October 5, B2.

Rappeport, A. (2013), 'Out for the calorie count', *Financial Times,* January 26–27, p. 9.

Reed, J. (2008), 'Electric cars: How plug-in cars picked up speed and credibility,' *Financial Times,* January 8, p. 11.

Reed, J. (2010), 'Buyers loath to pay more for electric cars', *Financial Times,* September 20, p. 24.

Reed, J. (2012), 'Nissan and Daimler in engine tie-up', *Financial Times,* January 9, p. 17.

Reed, R. and DeFillippi, R.J. (1990), 'Causal ambiguity, barriers to imitation and sustainable competitive advantage', *Academy of Management Review,* 15, 88–102.

Reichheld, F. (1993), 'Loyalty-based management', *Harvard Business Review,* 71(2), 64–73.

Reichheld, F. and Sasser, W.E. (1990), 'Zero defections: Perfecting customer retention and recovery', *Harvard Business Review,* 68(5), 105–11.

Ries, A. and Trout, J. (1982), *Positioning: The Battle for Your Mind,* New York: McGraw-Hill.

Ries, A. and Trout, J. (1986), *Marketing Warfare,* New York: McGraw-Hill.

Rigby, D.K., Reichheld, F.F. and Schafter, P. (2002), 'Avoid the four perils of CRM,' *Harvard Business Review,* February, 101–9.

Rigby, E. (2008), 'Shoppers fill baskets with cheaper food', *Financial Times,* September 6/7, p. 4.

Rigby, E. and Felsted, A. (2010a), 'Alliance Boots and P&G sign deal on European skincare business', *Financial Times,* May 8–9, p. 17.

Rigby, E. and Felsted A. (2010b), 'Pessina to boost Alliance Boots skincare brands', *Financial Times,* April 27, p. 19.

Robertson, D.C. and Nicholson, N. (1996), 'Expressions of corporate social responsibility in UK firms', *Journal of Business Ethics,* 15(10), 1095–106.

Robinson, S.J.Q., Hichens, R.E. and Wade, D.P. (1978), 'The directional policy matrix – tool for strategic planning', *Long Range Planning,* 11(3), 8–15.

Rogers, E. (1962), *Diffusion of Innovations,* New York: The Free Press.

Rouzies, D., Anderson, E., Kohli, A.K., Michaels, R.E., Weitz, B.A. and Zoltners, A.A. (2005), 'Sales and marketing integration: A proposed framework', *Journal of Personal Selling & Sales Management,* 25(2), 113–22.

Rowe, A.J., Mason, R.D., Dickel, K.E. and Synder, N.H. (1989), *Strategic Management: A Methodological Approach,* 3rd edn, Wokingham: Prentice Hall.

Rowley, T.J. (1997), 'Moving beyond dyadic ties: A network theory of stakeholder influences', *Academy of Management Review,* 22, 887–910.

RSA (1994), *Tomorrow's Company: The Role of Business in a Changing World,* London: RSA (Royal Society for the Encouragement of Arts, Manufactures and Commerce).

Rushe, D. (2007), 'Starbucks stirs up a storm in a coffee cup', *Sunday Times,* March 2, 3.7.

Rust, R.T. and Zahorik, A.J. (1993), 'Customer satisfaction, customer retention and market share', *Journal of Retailing,* 69(2), 193–215.

Sales Educators, The (2006), *Strategic Sales Leadership: Breakthrough Thinking for Breakthrough Results,* Mason, OH: Thomson.

Salmon, A.-M. (1997), 'Transforming a brand with energy: Lucozade in sickness and in health', *British Brands,* 4(Summer), 3.

Sammuels, G. (1994), 'CD-ROM's first big victim', *Forbes,* February 28, pp. 42–4.

Saunders, J.A. (1990), 'Brands and valuations', *International Journal of Forecasting,* 8(2), 95–110.

Saunders, J.A. (1999), Cluster analysis, in G.J. Hooley and M.K. Hussey (eds), *Quantitative Methods in Marketing,* 2nd edn, London: International Thomson Business Press.

Saunders, J., Stern, P., Wensley, R. and Forrester, R. (2000), 'In search of the lemmus, lummus: An investigation into convergent competition', *British Journal of Management,* 11, S81–S94.

Savitz, A. and Weber, K. (2006), *The Triple Bottom Line: How Today's Best-Run Companies are Achieving Economic, Social and Environmental Success and How You Can Too,* San Francisco, CA: Pfeiffer Wiley.

Schmitt, B.H. (2007), *Big Think Strategy: How to Leverage Bold Ideas and Leave Small Thinking Behind,* Boston, MA: Harvard Business School Press.

Schultz, D.E. (2002), 'Study internal marketing for better impact', *Marketing News,* 14, 8.

Schultz, D.E. (2004), 'Building an internal marketing management calculus', *Interactive Marketing,* 6(2), 111–29.

Schultz, D.E. (2006), 'Definition of internal marketing remains elusive', *Marketing News,* January 15, p. 6.

Segnit, S. and Broadbent, S. (1973), 'Life-style research: A case history in two parts', *European Research,* January, 62–8.

Seidenschwartz, W. (2005), 'A model for customer enthusiasm: Connecting the customer with internal processes', *Strategic Account Management Association Conference,* February, Paris.

Selnes, F., Jaworski, B.J., Kohli, A.J. (1996), 'Market orientation in the United States and Scandinavian companies: a cross-cultural view', *Scandinavian Journal of Management,* 12(2), 139–57.

Sen, S. and Bhattacharya, C.B. (2001), 'Does doing good always lead to doing better? Consumer reactions to corporate social responsibility', *Journal of Marketing Research,* 38(May), 225–43.

Senge, P., Smith, B., Kruschwitz, N., Laur, J. and Schley, S. (2008), *The Necessary Revolution: How Individuals and Organisations Are Working Together to Create a Sustainable World,* London: Nicholas Brealey Publishing.

Sengupta, S. and Bucklin, L.P. (1994), *To Ally or Not to Ally,* Cambridge, MA: Marketing Science Institute.

Sevastopulo, D. (2014), 'Strategy to make the maths work', *Financial Times,* June 3, p. 14.

Shapiro, B.P. (2002), *Creating the Customer-Centric Team: Coordinating Sales & Marketing,* Harvard Business School, Note 9-999-006.

Shapiro, B.P. and Bonoma, T.V. (1990), 'How to segment industrial markets', in R.J. Dolan (ed.), *Strategic Marketing Management,* Cambridge, MA: Harvard Business School Press.

Shapiro, B.P., Slywotsky, A.J. and Doyle, S.X. (1998), *Strategic Sales Management: A Boardroom Issue,* Note 9-595-018, Cambridge, MA: Harvard Business School.

Sharman, A. (2014), 'BMW's Pay-As-You-Go Heads to London', *Financial Times,* December 1, p. 20.

Sheridan, M. and Jones, R. (2010), 'Toxic fallout of China's solar panel boom', *Sunday Times,* October 3, pp. 1–30.

Shermach, K. (1995), 'Portrait of the world', *Marketing News,* August 28, 20.

Shervani, T. and Zerrillo, P.C. (1997), 'The albatross of product innovation', *Business Horizons,* January–February, 57–62.

Sheth, J.N. (1994), 'Relationship marketing: A customer perspective', Keynote address, Relationship Marketing Conference, Emory University.

Sheth, J.N. and Mittal, B. (1996), 'A framework for managing customer expectations', *Journal of Market- Focused Management,* 1, 137–58.

Sheth, J.N. and Sisodia, R.S. (eds) (2006), 'The image of marketing', in *Does Marketing Need Reform? Fresh Perspectives on the Future,* New York: M.E. Sharpe Inc.

Shubber, K. (2015), 'Supermarkets battle to mop up excess space', FT.com, May 29, accessed 2015, October.

Siguaw, J.A., Brown, G. and Widing, R.E. (1994), 'The influence of the market orientation of the firm on sales force behavior and attitudes', *Journal of Marketing Research,* 31, 106–16.

Simms, J. (2003), 'HR or marketing: Who gets staff on side?', *Marketing,* July 24, p. 23.

Simon, B. (2005), 'Suppliers reorder priorities for survival', *Financial Times,* June 10, p. 28.

Simon, H. (1996), *Hidden Champions,* Boston, MA: Harvard Business School Press.

Simonian, H. (2010), 'Nestlé to target less well-off in Europe', *Financial Times,* October 7, p. 24.

Simons, R. (2014), 'Choosing the right customer', *Harvard Business Review,* March, pp. 48–55.

Simonson, I. and Rosen, E. (2014), *Absolute Value: What Really Influences Customers in the Age of (Nearly) Perfect Information,* London: HarperBusiness.

Sinkula, J.M. (1994), 'Market information processing and organisational learning', *Journal of Marketing,* 58(1), 35–45.

Sinkula, J.M., Baker, W.E. and Noorewier, T. (1997), 'A framework for market-based organisational learning: linking values, knowledge and behaviour', *Journal of the Academy of Marketing Science,* 25, 305–18.

Skapinker, M. (2003), 'Awkward customers', *Financial Times,* February 12, p. 12.

Skapinker, M. (2005), 'Nike ushers in a new age of corporate responsibility', *Financial Times,* April 20, p. 11.

Skapinker, M. (2007), 'There is a good trade in ethical retailing', *Financial Times,* September 11, p. 15.

Skapinker, M. (2008a), 'Corporate responsibility is not quite dead', *Financial Times,* February 12, p. 15.

Skapinker, M. (2008b), 'Why companies and campaigners collaborate', *Financial Times,* July 8, p. 15.

Skapinker, M. (2010), 'Long-term corporate plans may be lost in translation', *Financial Times,* November 23, p. 15.

Skapinker, M. (2014), 'Starbucks backlash was not just froth', *Financial Times,* May 15, p. 12.

Slater, S.F. (1997), 'Developing a customer value-based theory of the firm', *Journal of the Academy of Marketing Science,* 25(2), 162–7.

Slater, S.F. (1998), 'Customer-led and market-oriented: let's not confuse the two', *Strategic Management Journal,* 19, 1001–6.

Slater, S.F. and Narver, J.C. (1994), 'Does competitive environment moderate the market orientation-performance relationship?', *Journal of Marketing,* 58(1), 46–55.

Slater, S.F. and Narver, J.C. (1995), 'Market orientation and the learning organisation', *Journal of Marketing,* 59 (July), 63–74.

Slywotzky, A. (1996), *Value Migration,* Boston, MA: Harvard Business School Press.

Smith, A. (1997), 'Brand-builders perceive pattern', *Financial Times,* June 23, p.   14.

Smith, A. (2014), 'Companies' charitable gifts soar since 2007', *Financial Times,* August 14, p. 3.

Smith, A. (2015), 'Businesses fall short of the mark on ethics', *Financial Times,* January 19, p. 22.

Smith, D.J. (2003), 'Strategic alliances and competitive strategies in the aerospace industry: the case of BMW and Rolls-Royce GmbH,' *European Business Review,* 15(4), 262–76.

Smith, N. (2010), 'Lost and scared: The boy on 7p an hour', *Sunday Times,* July 11, p. 1.25.

Smith, N.C. and Ward, H. (2007), 'Corporate social responsibility at a crossroads?', *Business Strategy Review,* 18(1), 16–21.

Smith, S.M. (1990), *PC MDS Version 5.1: Multidimensional scaling package,* Provo, UT: Brigham Young University.

Smith, W.R. (1956), 'Product differentiation and market segmentation as alternative marketing strategies', *Journal of Marketing,* July, 3–8.

Smyth, C. (2009), 'We sell junk, says Whole Foods chief', *Times,* August 6, p. 18.

Snider, J., Hill, R.P. and Martin, D. (2003), 'Corporate social responsibility in the 21st century: A view from the world's most successful firms', *Journal of Business Ethics,* 48(2), 175–87.

Sorrell, J. (1989), 'Power tools', *Marketing,* November 16, 45.

Spencer, B. (2015a), '"Eco" bulbs that aren't green and only last weeks', *Daily Mail,* January 24, p. 46.

Spencer, B. (2015b) 'Slap 20% Tax on Sugary Drinks', *Daily Mail*, July 13, 1.

Spenner, P. and Freeman, K. (2012), 'To keep your customers, keep it simple', *Harvard Business Review,* May, pp. 108–14.

Spethman, B. (1992), 'Category management multiples', *Advertising Age,* May 11, 42.

Stafford, E.R. and Hartman, C.L. (2013), 'Promoting the value of sustainably minded purchase behaviours', *Marketing News,* January, 29–33.

Stalk, G. (1988), 'Time – the next source of competitive advantage', *Harvard Business Review,* 66(4), 41–51.

Stephens, H. (2003), The H.R. Chally Group, Presentation at the American Marketing Association summer Educators' Conference, August.

Stern, S. (2009), 'The deadliest greenhouse gas? The hot air of CSR', *Financial Times,* February 3, p. 14.

Stern, S. (2008), 'How to get staff to care about their work', *Financial Times,* January 31, p. 14.

Stewart, T.A. (2006), 'Corporate social responsibility: Getting the logic right', *Harvard Business Review,* December, 14.

Stewart, T.A. (2006), 'The top line', *Harvard Business Review,* July–August, 10.

Stock, K. (2014), 'Big blue apple', *Bloomberg BusinessWeek,* July 21–27, p. 23.

Strahle, W.M., Spiro, R.L. and Acito, F. (1996), 'Marketing and sales: Strategic alignment and functional implementation', *Journal of Personal Selling & Sales Management,* 16(Winter), 1–20.

Straub, D. and Klein, R. (2001), 'e-Competitive transformations', *Business Horizons,* 44(3), 3–12.

Strelsin, S.C. and Mlot, S. (1992), 'The art of strategic sales alignment', *Journal of Business Strategy,* 13(6), 41–7.

Sull, D. (2005), 'Strategy as active waiting', *Harvard Business Review,* September, 120–9.

Sull, D., Homkes, R. and Sull, C. (2015), 'Why strategy execution unravels – and what to do about it', *Harvard Business Review,* March, pp. 58–67.

Svendsen, A. (1997), 'Building relationships with micro-communities', *Marketing News,* June 9, 13.

Swain, C.D. (1993), 'Competitive benchmarking', in D. Bernhardt (ed.), *Perfectly Legal Competitor Intelligence,* London: Pitman Publishing.

Swanson, D.L. (1995), 'Addressing a theoretical problem by reorienting the corporate social performance model', *Academy of Management Review,* 20(1), 43–64.

Tallman, S. (2003), 'Dynamic capabilities', in D.O. Faulkner and A. Campbell (eds), *The Oxford Handbook of Strategy: Volume 1: A Strategy Overview and Competitive Advantage,* Oxford: Oxford University Press.

Talluri, S. and Narasimhan, R. (2004), 'A methodology for strategic sourcing', *European Journal of Operational Research,* 154(1), 236–50.

Tam, P.-W. (2006), 'System reboot – Hurd's big challenge at H-P', *Wall Street Journal,* April 3, A.1.

Tapscott, D. and Williams, A. (2007), *Wikinomics: How Mass Collaboration Changes Everything,* London: Atlantic Books.

Taylor, A. (2005), 'An operations perspective on strategic alliance success factors', *International Journal of Operations & Production Management,* 25(5), 469–90.

Taylor, A. (2007), 'Microsoft drops supplier over diversity policy', *Financial Times,* March 24/25, p. 5.

Taylor, P., Waters, R. and Palmer, M. (2007), 'Will Android be Google's transformer?', *Financial Times,* November 7, p. 20.

Taylor, W. and LaBarre, P. (2008), *Mavericks At Work: Why the Most Original Minds in Business Win,* London: Harper.

Teece, D.J., Pisano, G. and Shuen, A. (1997), 'Dynamic capabilities and strategic management', *Strategic Management Journal,* 18, 509–33.

Teinowitz, I. (1988), 'Brand managers: 90s dinosaurs?', *Advertising Age,* December 19, 19.

Tellis, G. and Golder, P. (1996), 'First to market, first to fail: Real causes of enduring market leadership', *Sloan Management Review,* 37(2).

Terazono, E. (2015), 'Sustainability creeps up the supply chain', *Financial Times,* April 21, p. 36.

Tett, G. (2015), 'How impatience hampers long-term growth', *Financial Times,* February 20, p. 11.

Thomas, N., Wells, P. and Wuild, J. (2015), 'Ryanair profits rise as caution prevails', *Financial Times,* May 27, p. 20.

Tighe, C. (1997), 'Lean sales machine', *Financial Times,* 25 June, p. 26.

Timmers, P. (1999), *Electronic Commerce,* Chichester: John Wiley and Sons.

Todeva, E. and Knoke, D. (2005), 'Strategic alliances and models of collaboration', *Management Decision,* 43(1), 1230–148.

Toffler, A. (1981), *The Third Wave,* William Collins/Pan Books.

Tovey, A. (2015), 'Fracturing airline alliances could signal wave of industry consolidation', www.telegraph.co.uk, accessed 2015, October.

Trai, C.C. (1991), *Chinese Military Classic: The Art of War,* Singapore: Asiapac Books.

Treacy, M. and Wiersema, F. (1995), *The Discipline of Market Leaders,* London: HarperCollins.

Trudel, R. and Cotte, J. (2008), 'Does being ethical pay?', *Wall Street Journal,* May 13, pp. R2 & R8.

Trudel, R. and Cotte, J. (2009), 'Does it pay to be good?', *Sloan Management Review,* Winter, 61–8.

Tull, D.S. (1967), 'The relationship of actual and predicted sales and profit in new product introductions', *Journal of Business,* 40(3), 233–50.

Tull, D.S. and Hawkins, D.I. (1993), *Marketing Research: Measurement and Method,* 6th edn, Englewood Cliffs, NJ: Prentice Hall.

Tyrell, P. (2010), 'Technology lets buyers unravel the ethics behind the brand', *Financial Times,* September 16, p. 16.

Tzokas, N., Saren, M. and Brownlie, D. (1997), 'Generating marketing resources by means of R&D activities in high technology firms', *Industrial Marketing Management,* 26, 331–40.

Ulrich, D. (1992), 'Strategic and human resource planning: Linking customers and employees', *Human Resource Planning,* 15(2), 47–62.

Urry, M. (2008), 'Primark takes action on child labour', *Financial Times,* June 17, p. 20.

US Bureau of Labor Statistics (2013), International Labor Comparisons Report, August, accessed through website: Unites States Department of Labor, International Labor Comparisons at http://www.bls.gov/fls/.

Vaaland, T.I., Heide, M. and Gronhaug, K. (2008), 'Corporate social responsibility: Investigating theory and research in the marketing context', *European Journal of Marketing,* 42(9/10), 927–53.

Van Alstyne, M.W., Parker, G.G. and Choudary, S.P. (2016), 'Pipelines, platforms, and the new rules of strategy', *Harvard Business Review,* April, 54–62.

Varadarajan, P.R. (1992), 'Marketing's contribution to the strategy dialogue: The view from a different looking glass', *Journal of the Academy of Marketing Science,* 20(4), 335–44.

Varadarajan, R. (2012), 'Strategic marketing and marketing strategy', in *Handbook of Marketing Strategy,* V. Shankar, and G.S. Carpenter (eds), UK: Edward Elgar Publishing, pp. 9–27.

Vargo, S.L. and Lusch, R.F. (2004), 'Evolving to a new dominant logic for marketing', *Journal of Marketing,* 68 (January), 1–17.

Vence, D.L. (2007), 'Just a variation on a theme', *Marketing News,* February 1, 18–20.

Wagstyl, S. (2011), 'Replicators no more', *Financial Times,* January 6, p. 11.

Wall Street Journal (2012), 'GM and Peugeot strike Europe car partnership', March 1, p. 1.

Walsh, J. and Godfrey, S. (2000), 'The Internet: A new era in customer service', *European Management Journal,* 18(1), 85–92.

Wang, C.L. and Ahmed, P.K. (2007), 'Dynamic capabilities: A review and research agenda', *International Journal of Management Reviews,* 9(1), 31–51.

Waples, J. (2008), 'Overhaul that put the beans back into Heinz', *Sunday Times,* September 7, pp. 3–9.

Ward, A. (2006), 'Coke joins the battle for the brand corporate responsibility', *Financial Times,* November 21, p. 10.

Ward, A. (2015), 'Rush to snap up assets in cancer drugs race', *Financial Times,* April 8, p. 17.

Ward, A. and Waldmeir, P. (2014), 'Big Pharma fights back from China scandal', *Financial Times,* April 3, p. 21.

Ward, J. (1963), 'Hierarchical grouping to optimize an objective function', *Journal of the American Statistical Association,* 58, 236–44.

Warner, W.L. (1960), *Social Class in America,* New York: Harper and Row.

Warrington, P. and Eastlick, M. (2003), 'Quality value perceptions and satisfaction in an e-shopping environment', *Academy of Marketing Science Conference Proceedings,* p. 75.

Waters, R. and Taylor, P. (2007), 'Google mobile strategy steals a march on rivals', *Financial Times,* November 6, p. 1.

Waters, R. (2006), 'Computer pack top dogs lose their bite', *Financial Times,* June 5, p. 19.

Waters, R. (2001), 'Never forget to nurture the next big idea', *Financial Times,* May 15.

Webster, B. and Elliott, V. (2009), '2 for 1 deals face axe', *Times,* August 11, p. 1.

Webster, F.E. (1992), 'The changing role of marketing in the corporation', *Journal of Marketing,* 56(4), 1–17.

Webster, F.E. (1994), *Market Driven Management,* London: Wiley.

Webster, F.E. (1997), 'The future role of marketing in the organisation', in D.R. Lehmann and K.E. Jocz (eds), *Reflections on the Futures of Marketing,* Cambridge, MA: Marketing Science Institute, pp. 39–66.

Weintraub, A. (2007), 'Will Pharma finally have to fess up?', *BusinessWeek,* October 8, p. 36.

Weintraub, A. (2008), 'Just say no to drug reps', *Business-Week,* February 4, p. 69.

Weitzman, H. (2011), 'Boeing's 787 ready for take-off after three year delay', *Financial Times,* July 19, p. 22.

Welch, D. (2008), 'The SUV is rising from the dead', *BusinessWeek,* December 8, p. 63.

Wells, K. (1994/5), 'The road ahead', *Marketing Business,* December–January, 18–20.

Wells, W.D. and Gubar, G. (1966), 'Life cycle concepts in marketing research', *Journal of Marketing Research,* 3(4), 355–63.

Wernerfelt, B. (1984), 'A resource-based view of the firm', *Strategic Management Journal,* 5(2), 171–80.

Wernerfelt, B. (1995), 'The resource-based view of the firm: Ten years after', *Strategic Management Journal,* 16, 171–80.

Weyer, M.V. (1997), 'The shop that time forgot', *Daily Telegraph,* August 30, p. 16.

Wheatcroft, P. (1997), 'Bright new look from Persil man', *Financial Mail on Sunday,* February 9, p. 9.

White, G.L. and Chazan, G. (2008), 'BP keeps TNK-BP stake but Russians gain clout', *Wall Street Journal,* September 5–7, p. 1.

White, J. (2015), 'A ban on Ribena? It's the last straw', *Daily Mail,* July 30, p. 31.

Wieczner, J. (2015), 'Tesla investors do the electric slide', *Fortune,* April 1, pp. 24–5.

Wierenga, B. (2010), 'Marketing and artificial intelligence: Great opportunities, reluctant partners', in J. Casillas and F.J. Martinez-Lopez (eds), *Marketing Intelligent Systems Using Soft Computing (Studies in Fuzziness and Soft Computing),* Berlin: Springer, Volume 258, pp. 1–8.

Wiggins, J. (2007), 'Coke develops a thirst for sustainability', *Financial Times,* July 2, p. 26.

Wiggins, J. (2009), 'Heinz develops appetite for fresh outlets', *Financial Times,* July 27, p. 19.

Wilding, R. (2006), 'Playing to the tune of shared success', *Financial Times Report: Understanding Collaboration,* November 10, pp. 2–3.

Willman, J. (2006), 'Business fears recycling will cost £500m', *Financial Times,* June 6, p. 2.

Wilmott, M. (1989), 'Whose lifestyle is it anyway?', Institute of International Research Conference on Customer Segmentation and Lifestyle Marketing, London, December, 11–12.

Wind, Y. (1978), 'Issues and advances in segmentation research', *Journal of Marketing Research,* 15(3), 317–37.

Wind, Y. and Mahajan, V. (1981), 'Designing product and business portfolios', *Harvard Business Review,* 59(1), 155–65.

Winter, S.G. (2003), 'Understanding dynamic capabilities', *Strategic Management Journal,* 24, 991–5.

Wissema, J.G., Van der Pol, H.W. and Messer, H.M. (1980), 'Strategic management archetypes', *Strategic Management Journal,* 1(1), 37–47.

Witzel, M. (2008), 'The business case for more sustainability', *Financial Times,* July 3, p. 16.

Witzel, M. (2005a), 'An alliance that can supply a competitive edge', *Financial Times,* June 13, p. 14.

Witzel, M. (2005b), 'Big spenders are a boon – but don't forget the little guy', *Financial Times,* August 8, p. 14.

Wolfinbarger, M. and Gilly, M. (2003), 'Etailq: Dimensionalizing, measuring and predicting etail quality', *Journal of Retailing,* 79, 183–98.

Womack, J.P. and Jones, D.T. (1996), *Lean Thinking: Banish Waste and Create Wealth in Your Corporation,* London: Simon and Schuster.

Womack J.P. and Jones, D.T. (2005), 'Lean consumption', *Harvard Business Review,* March, 58–68.

Wood, D.J. (1991), 'Corporate social performance revisited', *Academy of Management Review,* 16(4), 691–718.

Woodhead, M. (2007), 'Dirty rotten business', *Sunday Times,* January 28, p. 3.5.

Woodhead, M. (2007), 'German firms retreat from eastern front', *Sunday Times,* November 25, pp. 3–12.

Woolf, M. (2007), 'Health food fads spark huge rise in animal testing', *Sunday Times,* December 30, p. 1.1.

Woolf, M. (2008), 'Blow to the image of the "green" nappy', *Sunday Times,* October 19, p. 1.7.

Workman, J.P., Homburg, C. and Gruner, K. (1998), 'Marketing organisation: An integrative framework of dimensions and determinants', *Journal of Marketing,* 62(July), 21–41.

Workman, J.P., Homburg, C. and Jensen, O. (2003), 'Intraorganisational determinants of key account management effectiveness', *Journal of the Academy of Marketing Science,* 31(1), 3–21.

Wright, P., Kroll, M., Pray, B. and Lado, A. (1990), 'Strategic orientations, competitive advantage and business performance', *Journal of Business Research,* 33, 143–51.

Yanklovich, D. and Meer, D. (2006), 'Rediscovering market segmentation', *Harvard Business Review,* 84(2), 122–31.

Yeh, A. (2006), 'McDonald's seeks heavy traffic fast-food expansion', *Financial Times,* June 21, p. 12.

Yoon, E. and Deeken, L. (2013), 'Why it pays to be a category creator', *Harvard Business Review,* March, 21–3.

Young, D. (1996), 'The politics behind market segmentation', *Marketing News,* October 21, p. 17.

Young, S., Off, F. and Fegin, B. (1978), 'Some practical considerations in market segmentation', *Journal of Marketing Research,* 15, August, 405–12.

Zahra, S.A. and George, G. (2002), 'Absorptive capacity: A review, reconceptualisation and extension, *Academy of Management Review,* 27(2), 185–203.

Zander, I. and Zander, U. (2005), 'The inside track: On the important (but neglected) role of customers in the resource-based view of strategy and firm growth', *Journal of Management Studies,* 42(8), 1519–48.

Zielke, A. and Pohl, M. (1996), 'Virtual vertical integration: The key to success', *McKinsey Quarterly,* (3), 160–3.

Zizola, F. (2007), 'The other side of carbon trading', *Fortune,* September 3, pp. 67–74.

Zollo, M. and Winter, S.G. (2002), 'Deliberate learning and the evolution of dynamic capabilities', *Organisation Science,* 13(3), 339–51.

Zoltners, A.A., Sinha, P. and Lorimer, S.E. (2004), *Sales Force Design for Strategic Advantage,* New York: Palgrave Macmillan.

http://www.supplychainbrain.com/content/nc/sponsored-channels/kenco-logistic-services-third-party-logistics/single-article-page/article/top-25-third-party-logistics-providers-extend-their-global-reach/,

see www.luxottica.com/en/company/quick_view, accessed 2015, July.

INDEX